# THE
# WOMEN'S
# BIBLE
# COMMENTARY

Carol A. Newsom
*and*
Sharon H. Ringe
*Editors*

Westminster/John Knox Press
Louisville, Kentucky

First published in Great Britain in 1992 by SPCK, Holy Trinity Church, Marylebone Road, London NW1 4DU

First published in the United States in 1992 by Westminster/John Knox Press, 100 Witherspoon Street, Louisville, Kentucky 40202-1396

*Book design by* The HK Scriptorium, Inc.

This book is printed on acid-free paper that meets the American National Standards Institute Z39.48 standard. ∞

PRINTED IN THE UNITED STATES OF AMERICA
95 96 97 98 99 00 01 02 03 04 — 10 9 8 7 6 5 4 3 2

**British Cataloging-in-Publication Data**

A catalogue record for this book is available from the British Library.

ISBN 0-281-04581-X

**Library of Congress Cataloging-in-Publication Data**

The Women's Bible Commentary / Carol A. Newsom and Sharon H. Ringe, editors.
        p.    cm.
   Includes bibliographical references.
   ISBN 0-664-21922-5 (cloth)
   ISBN 0-664-25586-8 (paper)

   1. Bible—Commentaries. 2. Women—Middle East—History.
3. Women—Rome—History. I. Newsom, Carol A. (Carol Ann), 1950–
II. Ringe, Sharon H.
BS491.2.W66 1992       220.7'082—dc20       91-44831

# CONTENTS

# CONTENTS

# ABBREVIATIONS

## Books of the Bible (with Apocrypha)

**Hebrew Bible/Old Testament**

| | |
|---|---|
| Gen. | Genesis |
| Ex. | Exodus |
| Lev. | Leviticus |
| Num. | Numbers |
| Deut. | Deuteronomy |
| Josh. | Joshua |
| Judg. | Judges |
| Ruth | Ruth |
| 1 Sam. | 1 Samuel |
| 2 Sam. | 2 Samuel |
| 1 Kings | 1 Kings |
| 2 Kings | 2 Kings |
| 1 Chron. | 1 Chronicles |
| 2 Chron. | 2 Chronicles |
| Ezra | Ezra |
| Neh. | Nehemiah |
| Esth. | Esther |
| Job | Job |
| Ps. (Pss.) | Psalms |
| Prov. | Proverbs |
| Eccl. | Ecclesiastes |
| Song | Song of Songs |
| Isa. | Isaiah |
| Jer. | Jeremiah |
| Lam. | Lamentations |
| Ezek. | Ezekiel |
| Dan. | Daniel |
| Hos. | Hosea |
| Joel | Joel |
| Amos | Amos |
| Obad. | Obadiah |
| Jonah | Jonah |
| Micah | Micah |
| Nahum | Nahum |
| Hab. | Habakkuk |
| Zeph. | Zephaniah |
| Hag. | Haggai |
| Zech. | Zechariah |
| Mal. | Malachi |

**Apocrypha**

| | |
|---|---|
| 2 Esd. | 2 Esdras |
| Tobit | Tobit |
| Judith | Judith |
| Wisd. Sol. | Wisdom of Solomon |
| Sir. | Sirach |
| Bar. | Baruch |
| 1 Macc. | 1 Maccabees |
| 2 Macc. | 2 Maccabees |
| 4 Macc. | 4 Maccabees |

**New Testament**

| | |
|---|---|
| Matt. | Matthew |
| Mark | Mark |
| Luke | Luke |
| John | John |
| Acts | Acts of the Apostles |
| Rom. | Romans |
| 1 Cor. | 1 Corinthians |
| 2 Cor. | 2 Corinthians |
| Gal. | Galatians |
| Eph. | Ephesians |
| Phil. | Philippians |
| Col. | Colossians |
| 1 Thess. | 1 Thessalonians |

| | | | |
|---|---|---|---|
| 2 Thess. | 2 Thessalonians | 1 Peter | 1 Peter |
| 1 Tim. | 1 Timothy | 2 Peter | 2 Peter |
| 2 Tim. | 2 Timothy | 1 John | 1 John |
| Titus | Titus | 2 John | 2 John |
| Philemon | Philemon | 3 John | 3 John |
| Heb. | Hebrews | Jude | Jude |
| James | James | Rev. | Revelation |

## Other Abbreviations

| | | | |
|---|---|---|---|
| JB | Jerusalem Bible | B.C.E. | Before the Common Era (= B.C.) |
| NAB | New American Bible | C.E. | Common Era (= A.D.) |
| NEB | New English Bible | DH | Deuteronomistic History |
| NIV | New International Version | LXX | Septuagint |
| NRSV | New Revised Standard Version | par. | parallel(s) |
| RSV | Revised Standard Version | vol(s). | volume(s) |

# CONTRIBUTORS

Susan Ackerman, Ph.D.
Assistant Professor of Religion
Dartmouth College
Hanover, New Hampshire
*Isaiah*

Jouette M. Bassler, Ph.D.
Associate Professor of New Testament
Perkins School of Theology
Southern Methodist University
Dallas, Texas
*1 Corinthians; 2 Corinthians*

Claudia V. Camp, Ph.D.
Associate Professor of Religion
Texas Christian University
Fort Worth, Texas
*1 and 2 Kings*

Toni Craven, Ph.D.
Professor of Hebrew Bible
Brite Divinity School
Texas Christian University
Fort Worth, Texas
*Daniel and Its Additions*

Mary Rose D'Angelo, Ph.D.
Associate Professor of New Testament
Villanova University
Villanova, Pennsylvania
*Hebrews*

Katheryn Pfisterer Darr, Ph.D.
Assistant Professor of Hebrew Bible
Boston University School of Theology
Boston, Massachusetts
*Ezekiel*

Joanna Dewey, Ph.D.
Associate Professor of New Testament
  Studies
Episcopal Divinity School
Cambridge, Massachusetts
*1 Timothy; 2 Timothy; Titus*

Sharyn Dowd, Ph.D.
Associate Professor of New Testament
Lexington Theological Seminary
Lexington, Kentucky
*James; 1 Peter; 2 Peter; Jude*

Tamara Cohn Eskenazi, Ph.D.
Associate Professor of Bible
Hebrew Union College–Jewish Institute
  of Religion
Los Angeles, California
*Ezra–Nehemiah*

Kathleen A. Farmer, Ph.D.
Professor of Old Testament
United Theological Seminary
Dayton, Ohio
*Psalms*

Danna Nolan Fewell, Ph.D.
Associate Professor of Old Testament
Perkins School of Theology
Southern Methodist University
Dallas, Texas
*Joshua; Judges*

Carole R. Fontaine, Ph.D.
Professor of Old Testament
Andover Newton Theological School
Newton Centre, Massachusetts
*Proverbs; Ecclesiastes*

Tikva Frymer-Kensky, Ph.D.
Director of Biblical Studies
Reconstructionist Rabbinical College
Philadelphia, Pennsylvania
*Deuteronomy*

Susan R. Garrett, Ph.D.
Assistant Professor of New Testament
Yale Divinity School
New Haven, Connecticut
*Revelation*

Beverly Roberts Gaventa, Ph.D.
Professor of New Testament
Columbia Theological Seminary
Decatur, Georgia
*Romans*

Beth Glazier-McDonald, Ph.D.
Associate Professor of Religion
Centre College
Danville, Kentucky
*Joel; Obadiah; Haggai; Zechariah;
Malachi*

Deirdre J. Good, Th.D.
Associate Professor of New Testament
General Theological Seminary
New York, New York
*Early Extracanonical Writings*

Jo Ann Hackett, Ph.D.
Professor of Biblical Hebrew
Harvard University
Cambridge, Massachusetts
*1 and 2 Samuel*

E. Elizabeth Johnson, Ph.D.
Associate Professor of New Testament
New Brunswick Theological Seminary
New Brunswick, New Jersey
*Ephesians; Colossians; 2 Thessalonians*

Alice L. Laffey, S.S.D.
Associate Professor of Old Testament
College of the Holy Cross
Worcester, Massachusetts
*1 and 2 Chronicles*

Amy-Jill Levine, Ph.D.
Associate Professor of Religion
Swarthmore College
Swarthmore, Pennsylvania
*Ruth; Matthew*

Carol L. Meyers, Ph.D.
Professor of Biblical Studies and
   Archaeology
Duke University
Durham, North Carolina
*Everyday Life: Women in the Period
   of the Hebrew Bible*

Carol A. Newsom, Ph.D.
Associate Professor of Old Testament
Candler School of Theology
Emory University
Atlanta, Georgia
*Job*

Susan Niditch, Ph.D.
Professor of Religion
Amherst College
Amherst, Massachusetts
*Genesis*

Kathleen M. O'Connor, Ph.D.
Associate Professor of Biblical Studies
Maryknoll School of Theology
Maryknoll, New York
*Jeremiah; Lamentations*

Gail R. O'Day, Ph.D.
Associate Professor of Biblical Preaching
Candler School of Theology
Emory University
Atlanta, Georgia
*John; Acts; 1, 2, and 3 John*

Carolyn Osiek, Th.D.
Professor of New Testament
Catholic Theological Union
Chicago, Illinois
*Galatians*

Pheme Perkins, Ph.D.
Professor of New Testament
Boston College
Chestnut Hill, Massachusetts
*Philippians; 1 Thessalonians; Philemon*

Sharon H. Ringe, Ph.D.
Professor of New Testament
Wesley Theological Seminary
Washington, D.C.
*When Women Interpret the Bible*

Katharine Doob Sakenfeld, Ph.D.
Professor of Old Testament Literature
Princeton Theological Seminary
Princeton, New Jersey
*Numbers*

Judith E. Sanderson, Ph.D.
Assistant Professor of Hebrew Bible
Seattle University
Seattle, Washington
*Amos; Micah; Nahum; Habakkuk;*
  *Zephaniah*

Jane Schaberg, Ph.D.
Professor of Religious Studies
University of Detroit Mercy
Detroit, Michigan
*Luke*

Eileen M. Schuller, Ph.D.
Associate Professor of Religious Studies
McMaster University
Hamilton, Ontario, Canada
*The Apocrypha*

Drorah O'Donnell Setel, M.T.S.
Ph.D. candidate
Yale University
New Haven, Connecticut
*Exodus*

Mary Ann Tolbert, Ph.D.
Professor of New Testament and Early
  Christianity
Vanderbilt University Divinity School
Nashville, Tennessee
*Mark*

Renita J. Weems, Ph.D.
Assistant Professor of Old Testament
Vanderbilt University Divinity School
Nashville, Tennessee
*Song of Songs*

Judith Romney Wegner, Ph.D.
Visiting Associate Professor
The Department of Religion
University of Massachusetts
Amherst, Massachusetts
*Leviticus*

Marsha C. White, Th.M.
Ph.D. candidate
Harvard University
Cambridge, Massachusetts
*Jonah*

Sidnie Ann White, Ph.D.
Assistant Professor of Religion
Albright College
Reading, Pennsylvania
*Esther*

Amy L. Wordelman, M.Div.
Ph.D. candidate
Princeton University
Princeton, New Jersey
*Everyday Life: Women in the Period*
  *of the New Testament*

Gale A. Yee, Ph.D.
Associate Professor of Old Testament/
  Hebrew Bible
University of St. Thomas
St. Paul, Minnesota
*Hosea*

# INTRODUCTION

*Carol A. Newsom and Sharon H. Ringe*

Although women have read the Bible for countless generations, we have not always been self-conscious about reading *as* women. There are many reasons why it is important that women do so. Women have distinctive questions to raise about the Bible and distinctive insights into its texts: our experiences of self and family, our relationship to institutions, the nature of our work and daily lives, and our spirituality have been and continue to be different in important respects from those of men. But there is another reason, too. Because of its religious and cultural authority, the Bible has been one of the most important means by which woman's place in society has been defined. Throughout the centuries, of course, the Bible has been invoked to justify women's subordination to men. But it has also played a role, sometimes in surprising ways, in empowering women. Increasingly, it is difficult for a woman, whether she is a member of a religious community or not, to read the Bible without some sense of the role it has played in shaping the conditions of her life.

During the women's movement of the late nineteenth and early twentieth centuries there emerged a clear sense of the need for women to read the Bible self-consciously as women. Just over a hundred years ago Frances Willard, president of the Woman's Christian Temperance Union, made this appeal: "We need women commentators to bring out the women's side of the book; we need the stereoscopic view of truth in general, which can only be had when woman's eye and man's eye together shall discern the perspective of the Bible's full-orbed revelation" (Willard, p. 21). To that end she urged "young women of linguistic talent . . . to make a specialty of Hebrew and New Testament Greek in the interest of their sex" (Willard, p. 31). That was a problem. The interpretation of the Bible has always tended to be reserved to the "experts." In part this has been because of the specialized knowledge of ancient languages that is needed, but it is also a matter of institutional and cultural power. So long as women were excluded from both religious offices and educational opportunities, it was difficult for them to enter into the interpretation of the Bible in an authoritative way. Even as outsiders, however, some courageous women began to interpret the Bible and its bearing on women's lives.

In the 1890s Elizabeth Cady Stanton and a small group of collaborators produced *The Woman's Bible.* They excerpted and commented on those portions of the Bible in which women appear—or are conspicuously absent. In their comments the authors attacked both the male bias that had distorted the interpretation of the Bible and the misogyny of the text itself. Sharp and outspoken in its content, witty and pungent in its style, *The Woman's Bible* remains a fascinating work. Many of its observations, which seemed so daring at the time, have since come to be widely held, even treated as obvious. But *The Woman's Bible* was not, even by the standards of its day, a work of biblical scholarship. Although some women had begun to receive training in biblical languages and in the new forms of scholarship that were starting to make such an impact in biblical studies, they were reluctant to participate in Stanton's project. In her introduction she observes:

> Those who have undertaken the labor [of *The Woman's Bible*] are desirous to have some Hebrew and Greek scholars, versed in Biblical criticism, to gild our pages with their learning. Several distinguished women have been urged to do so, but they are afraid that their high reputation and scholarly attainments might be compromised by taking part in an enterprise that for a time may prove very unpopular. Hence we may not be able to get help from that class. (Stanton, 1:9)

What was the case in 1895 remained the case for almost three quarters of a century. Although a small but not insignificant number of women continued to be trained in biblical studies, women in the academy did not use their skills to read the Bible from a feminist perspective. It was not until 1964 that a female professor of biblical literature, Margaret Brackenbury Crook, published a study on the status of women in Judaism and Christianity entitled *Women and Religion* (see Gifford). Although insisting that hers was not a "feminist" project, Crook pointedly observed:

> [A] masculine monopoly in religion begins when Miriam raises her indignant question: "Does the Lord speak only through Moses?" Since then, in all three of the great religious groups stemming from the land and books of Israel—Judaism, Christianity, and Islam—men have formulated doctrine and established systems of worship offering only meager opportunity for expression of the religious genius of womankind. (Crook, p. 1)

The women's movement of the 1960s and 1970s and the increasing number of women attending seminaries renewed interest in what it might mean to read the Bible self-consciously as a woman. Books such as Letty Russell's *The Liberating Word* and Phyllis Trible's *God and the Rhetoric of Sexuality* introduced many women and men to the new possibilities opened up by feminism for reading and understanding the

Bible. With increasing self-confidence and sophistication, feminist study of the Bible has blossomed to become one of the most important new areas in contemporary biblical research. Over the last twenty-five years biblical scholarship by women has come into its maturity. Not only are women prominent in the discussions of traditional topics in biblical studies, but the new questions women have posed and the new ways of reading that women have pioneered have challenged the very way biblical studies are done.

There are many different directions that feminist study of the Bible has taken. Some commentators have attempted to reach "behind the text" to recover knowledge about the actual conditions of women's lives in the biblical period. Others have paid attention to what goes on in the telling of the stories and the singing of the songs, using literary approaches to shed new light on metaphors, images, and narratives about women. Still others have tried to discover the extent to which even the biblical writings that pertain to women are shaped by the concerns and perspectives of men and yet how it can still be possible at times to discover the presence of women and their own points of view between the lines. Many have struggled with the issues of how women in communities of faith can and should read the Bible in the light of what feminist inquiry has discovered. Contemporary feminist study of the Bible has not set out either to bring the Bible into judgment or to rescue it from its critics. But to read the Bible self-consciously as a woman is a complex experience, alternately painful and exhilarating. There is a great sense of empowerment, however, that comes from reading the Bible as a woman in the company of other women. That is an experience that this volume is intended to assist.

Although there has been a rapidly increasing number of books and articles on the Bible by women, *The Women's Bible Commentary* is the first comprehensive attempt to gather some of the fruits of feminist biblical scholarship on each book of the Bible in order to share it with the larger community of women who read the Bible. The title of this volume pays tribute to Elizabeth Cady Stanton's pioneering work almost a century ago. But whereas she entitled her work the "Woman's Bible," we have chosen the plural, "Women's Bible." The reason for this is our recognition of the diversity among women who read the Bible and study it. There is no single "woman's perspective" but a rich variety of insight that comes from the different ways in which women's experience is shaped by culture, class, ethnicity, religious community, and other aspects of social identity. Indeed, one of the insights of feminism has been the recognition of the extent to which knowledge is perspectival. People see things or are oblivious to them in part because of how they have been formed through their experiences. They ask certain kinds of questions and not others for the same reasons.

In choosing contributors for this volume we have tried to represent some of that diversity of perspectives shaped by different ways of being female in our pluralistic culture. Included in this volume are Jewish women, Roman Catholic women, Protestant women. Many are lay-women, but some are members of religious orders or ordained clergy. Our relationship to religious community differs, too. Many of us are actively involved with worshiping communities; some are in an uneasy relationship or can no longer make our spiritual homes within traditional religion; and a few have come to the study of the Bible from secular backgrounds.

As work on the volume was coming to an end, we invited the contributors to reflect on some of the factors that had both helped to form their interest in the Bible and shaped their way of interpreting it. For some, a sense of ethnic identity—as African American, Native American, Asian American—has been crucial. For others, too, an experience of crossing cultural boundaries was formative: growing up white in an urban black community in the South, being a European in America or an American in Europe. One contributor who grew up Jewish in a largely Christian neighborhood remarked on the way in which her experience of the sins of anti-Semitism and sexism not only formed her as a child but continues to inform her research. Several contributors indicated the strong connections between their feminist reading of the Bible and their involvement in issues of social justice. Jane Schaberg said eloquently of her work on Luke:

> This commentary is based on the conviction that feminism and social justice are inextricably linked, and that it is an urgent task to analyze this Gospel's thinking about women and the poor. The commentary is written in Detroit, which has been called the United States' first Third World city, where the inadequacies of capitalism and the evils of racism and anti-Semitism are daily experienced. It is also written from a position of anguished, stubborn membership in the Catholic church, whose official leaders currently uphold patriarchal values and resist egalitarian, democratic trends in contemporary society. Reading Luke in this context sharpens perceptions of its weaknesses and strengths.

Yet for all the variety of perspectives reflected in this volume, many voices are not represented or are underrepresented, even from among North American women. Readers might also pause and think how different a commentary on the Bible would be that was written by the women of Africa, Latin America, Asia, Europe, or the Levant.

One of the things that all the contributors to this volume have in common is a rather similar type of education. We are, in Frances Willard's words, "women of linguistic talent" who have decided "to make a specialty of Hebrew and New Testament Greek in the interest of their sex." To that end we have all spent many years in graduate study in American and

European universities. Our commitment to feminism has taught us not only to value expertise but also to be wary of the elitism that often goes with it. For our learning truly to be in the service of the larger community of women, it is vital that our work be shaped in dialogue with the laywomen, clergywomen, and students for whom this volume is intended. Many contributors have long been active in Bible study with women's groups, and all were encouraged to share their work in progress and receive comments from women in their communities. Claudia Camp, in particular, has stressed how important the women's Bible study group at South Hills Christian Church in Fort Worth, Texas, was in shaping the article she wrote on 1 and 2 Kings. Such an experience, Claudia says, helps to dispel the illusion of individual achievement and points toward new models of what authorship really means. If the women of South Hills had a direct role in shaping this volume, there are others whose influence was less direct but no less real. A number of the contributors named their mothers, grandmothers, and other women in their religious communities as the ones who in so many ways taught them how to read the Bible.

It may be helpful to say a few words about the contents and organization of the material that follows. One of the realities of the differences among religious communities is that when Jews, Catholics, and Protestants talk about the "Bible," we all refer to something different. The canon of scripture differs for each community, not only in the number and identity of books included but also in the order in which they appear. In some instances, even the chapter and verse references differ slightly between Jewish and Christian Bibles. As a project sponsored by a Protestant publisher, *The Women's Bible Commentary* follows the number and order of the biblical books in the Protestant canon, with one small exception: the deuterocanonical additions to Esther and Daniel, including the story of Susanna, have been grouped with the canonical books. The rest of the Apocrypha, included in the Old Testament by Catholics, is treated here in a separate article. We have designated the first section of the book with the dual title Hebrew Bible/Old Testament, in recognition of the fact that these scriptures have a different identity and role in Judaism and in Christianity. Similarly, we have identified dates with the designation B.C.E. (before the common era) and C.E. (common era). Unless otherwise noted, quotations and chapter and verse references are from the New Revised Standard Version of the Bible. There is one exception. The divine name, YHWH, is traditionally rendered by the title "Lord" in most translations. We have preferred to use either "YHWH" or "Yahweh."

*The Women's Bible Commentary* does not intend to be a general or complete commentary on the Bible. Each article on a biblical book does begin with an introduction that orients the reader to the contents of the book and provides an overview of the major issues raised by the book. Rather than asking the contributors to comment on each and every section of the biblical book, we have followed the model of Elizabeth Cady Stanton's *Woman's Bible* and asked contributors to select for comment those passages that they judged to be of particular relevance to women. What contributors have selected includes not only portions of the Bible that deal explicitly with female characters and symbols but also sections that bear on the condition of women more generally. Aspects of social life, marriage and family, the legal status of women, religious and economic institutions, the ways in which community boundaries were defined and maintained, and other such topics are all treated. In addition, there are discussions of certain symbolic ways of thinking, such as the notion of holiness or dualistic conceptions of the world, that are important for understanding the representation of women in the Bible and in the cultures from which it came. Finally, we have included several articles that go beyond the boundaries of the canon. Two articles consider the daily lives of women in the biblical period, drawing both on biblical and nonbiblical sources. One article explores the appearance of women in early Christian literature outside the canon. A final essay is devoted to feminist hermeneutics, that is, to the ways in which women in the modern world are engaged in interpreting and assessing the meaning of biblical texts from a self-consciously feminist perspective.

The reading of the Bible is a never-ending task, renewed and refreshed by each new community of readers who bring questions and perspectives nurtured by their own experiences. What we offer on the following pages is not intended as a definitive or final word but more as a model of some of the ways in which women reading *as* women can engage the biblical text.

* * * * *

In addition to the persons whose contributions appear explicitly in the book, there are several whose assistance in the development and preparation of this volume should be acknowledged. Above all, recognition should go to Cynthia Thompson of Westminster/John Knox Press, who first conceived of the project and persuaded us to undertake it. Cynthia's wise counsel and sense of perspective made the task of editing a much easier one than we could have imagined. Rex Matthews generously took the cacophony of divergent word-processing programs used by forty-one authors and translated the files into forms we could use. Colleen Grant and Dorcas Ford-Doward checked the manuscripts and prepared the final copy. To each of them we offer our thanks.

## BIBLIOGRAPHY

Crook, Margaret Brackenbury. *Women and Religion.* Boston: Beacon Press, 1964.

Gifford, Carolyn De Swarte. "American Women and the Bible: The Nature of Woman as a Hermeneutical Issue." In *Feminist Perspectives on Biblical Scholarship,* edited by Adela Yarbro Collins, pp. 11–33. Biblical Scholarship in North America 10. Chico, Calif.: Scholars Press, 1985.

Russell, Letty M., ed. *The Liberating Word: A Guide to Nonsexist Interpretation of the Bible.* Philadelphia: Westminster Press, 1976.

Stanton, Elizabeth Cady, ed. *The Woman's Bible.* 2 vols. New York: European Publishing Co., 1895–1898.

Trible, Phyllis. *God and the Rhetoric of Sexuality.* Overtures to Biblical Theology. Philadelphia: Fortress Press, 1978.

Willard, Frances E. *Woman in the Pulpit.* Chicago: Woman's Temperance Publishing Association, 1889.

# WHEN WOMEN
# INTERPRET THE BIBLE

*Sharon H. Ringe*

What on earth does the Bible mean? How can modern readers ever understand the assumptions and language taken for granted by ancient authors
and their communities? When the reader is a woman, how is the *process*
of reading the Bible, or the *result* of that process, different? How has the
Bible influenced the lives of women and men through history and in the
present? How ought it to shape the lives of women and men who look
to it as the norm for faith and practice? What does it mean to call the
Bible "the word of God"? What might compel one to say, "On this point,
the Bible is wrong"? At the heart of such questions is the process of
interpretation.

## Interpretation as Active Reading

Interpretation of the Bible begins with careful and active reading. Such
reading attempts to understand the time, place, and purpose for which
a particular biblical book was written, the principal concerns of the
author and of the communities that shaped the book, and the meanings
of particular terms found in the text. This part of the process is similar
to the effort to get to know a conversation partner in order better to
understand how she uses words, what life story has shaped him, what
prompts the conversation—in short, where he or she is coming from—so
as not to impose one's own agenda on the other and thus mute his or her
unique voice.

A conversation, however, requires two active partners, and even a
person carefully sensitive to where the other is coming from still filters
what is heard through his or her own experience. What is *perceived* is
thus not always exactly what was *intended*, and knowing who is reporting a conversation can be as important as knowing who is speaking! The
situation for a reader of an ancient text like the Bible is similar.
Although the careful reader attempts to distinguish between the voice

1

of the ancient author and his or her own concerns as a modern interpreter, this distinction is never absolute. The place in history, culture,
and society occupied by the reader inevitably influences what she or he
can perceive in any text and what questions seem important to ask about
the text and its context. Therefore, while commentaries, Bible dictio-
naries, and other scholarly tools can help in this reading process, each
of them represents the work of particular readers. Like the biblical
materials they seek to interpret, all such resources too reflect their
authors' contexts.

What sets *The Women's Bible Commentary* apart from others is its
authors' acknowledged commitment to read the biblical texts through
the varied lenses of women's experiences in ancient and modern religious and cultural contexts. The result is an attempt to understand and
even to ask questions of the biblical authors, through the legacy of their
work, concerning the situation of women in the communities from
which they come or which they envision as desirable.

## Biblical Authority and Interpretation

Clearly, women's perspectives or the consequences for women's lives
were not the primary concern of the biblical authors. In fact, it seems
evident that those authors rarely if ever raised such questions. But
women reading the Bible *do* want to know such things: they relate to our
foremothers' histories and to our own lives. An important question faced
by interpreters raising such questions is whether they are legitimate. If
they are not the agenda of the authors or even of their principal
audiences, should—or even *can*—they be pursued?

The question must be approached carefully. On the one hand, the
Bible does not address every issue of concern to women of this or any
other time, any more than it provides specific answers to modern questions in biomedical ethics. To read such answers or to pursue such
explicit agenda within the biblical text would not honor its—or the
reader's—historical context. On the other hand, the literary legacy of the
biblical authors does include female characters and introduce issues of
special concern to women's lives. To ask about those is to open up the
text itself and to make visible the invisible (and often unconscious)
values and assumptions of its author. Such a reading is part of the
process of "unmasking" the dominant culture and is the particular talent
of persons who live on its margins.

Women's questions about women of biblical times and about the
implications of the Bible for women's lives reflect the fact that, for good
or ill, the Bible is a book that has shaped and continues to shape human
lives, communities, and cultures in the West, as well as in those other
parts of the world under the hegemony or influence of Europe and North
America. The Bible is a collection of "classic" texts often referred to in

other literature, and the values of these texts (usually as they have been interpreted by dominant or powerful individuals and groups) have shaped both philosophies and legal systems. The Bible has become part of the air we breathe without our even being aware of its presence or power.

In addition to that common cultural or even "atmospheric" role, in both Christianity and Judaism the Bible as "scripture" or "canon" bears a variety of kinds of religious authority: guide for conduct, rule of faith, inerrant source of truth (factual and/or moral), or revelation of God. Within these communities, the authority of the Bible is explicit as well as implicit, but often ambiguous and finally ambivalent, especially for women.

## The Ambivalent Power of the Bible

The Bible *is* a powerful book. Because of that power, the question of interpretation goes beyond merely understanding the Bible, to ask also, Having understood it as best we can, what is its force in our lives and what are we to do with or about it? The question is not an easy one, especially for women. In the first place, the power of the Bible in women's lives has been at best ambivalent. It has functioned as a force for life, for hope, and for liberation. Women's lives have been enriched, sustained, and empowered in communities that affirm that within the Bible one encounters not only the divine will for human life and behavior, but the very presence of God. Women have found their own lives mirrored in the stories of quiet, valiant women who experience God's blessing on them. Poor women long accustomed to feeding their families with a handful of flour and a little oil (1 Kings 17) find confidence to carry on. For centuries, women have affirmed with Paul that "neither death, nor life, . . . nor anything else in all creation, will be able to separate us from the love of God" (Rom. 8:38–39).

At the same time, women reading the Bible have found themselves on alien and even hostile turf. Rarely if ever do women in the Bible get to speak for themselves. Rather, they are portrayed from the perspective of male authors and in the context of religious communities where authority finally came to be vested in men and where men's experience was the norm.

Women are thus absent from the Bible as persons working out their own religious journeys. It is clear that women have always undertaken such journeys, but within the Bible itself their legacy is not to be found. Rather, women appear—to use a metaphor from grammar—as direct and indirect "objects" and not as "subjects" of the verbs of religious experience and practice. Where aspects of their lives are described in stories or narratives, or where their behavior is prescribed (such as in the legal and moral codes of both Testaments), or where women's lives function as metaphors of religious realities (such as in Hosea or the book of

Revelation), women are often "flat" characters, perfectly good or villainously evil, or objects at someone's disposal.

Both the silence of women and their silencing—the contempt in which they are held and the violence with which they are treated—in the Bible mirror the realities of many women's lives. For them, the Bible is experienced as giving a divine stamp of approval to their suffering. Far from bringing healing of the hurt or empowerment toward freedom from oppression, the Bible seems to bless the harm and abuse with which women live and sometimes die.

## Approaches to the Task of Interpretation

The different ways women have experienced the power of the Bible individually and as members of different religious, social, and ethnic communities have led to a variety of approaches to the task of interpretation. Those approaches range along a continuum from affirmation that the entire Bible, as the word of God, positively informs faith and practice to, at the other extreme, outright rejection of the entire Bible as hopelessly and irredeemably misogynistic. Many women find themselves working in different ways with different parts of the Bible or in different contexts or occasions of interpretation. There is no single "correct" or "acceptable" way to work, but what should be kept in mind is that the various approaches yield different results or conclusions. Being aware of an interpreter's approach or stance toward the text is important to one's understanding or assessment of her work. Women who affirm the authoritative, even binding, role of the Bible as a positive force for women often distinguish sharply between the intent of the biblical authors and the results of interpretation and "application" of biblical teachings. Thus the biblical views of women are seen as affirming and supportive of women's dignity and worth, and where the Bible has been read as demeaning or even as warranting the abuse of women, the error is seen to lie in the interpretation.

Others—many African American and Latin American women, for example—recognize the important role played in past and present liberation struggles of their people by such parts of the Bible as the exodus narrative, the teachings of the prophets, and the teachings of Jesus found in the Synoptic Gospels. Those interpreters read these parts of the Bible as the heart of scripture, a "canon within the canon," which provides the key to interpreting all the rest. Under such a reading, any portion of scripture that might be detrimental to women is read through the lens of the liberating intent of its heart.

In a variation of that interpretive option, which focuses not on a generally "liberating" message but on texts specifically related to women, passages affirming women's role and value are posited as a countervoice to those "against" women. The former are then affirmed as representative of the heart of the biblical message, in their stance against the patriarchal assumptions of the surrounding society.

Still other women, recognizing the patriarchal values embedded in all of the biblical writings (despite the wide range of historical contexts out of which they arose and the varied purposes for which they were written), find in the negative views of women in the Bible a mirror of women's experience in any androcentric or male-centered and normed society. They read such texts in memory of the women whose lives are depicted in them and those who have suffered because of them. Such texts also become the raw material for critical reflection on the history, doctrine, and theology that have shaped contemporary communities of faith and practice. The power of such texts to reveal anything about God or about a community in faithful covenant with God is denied.

Finally, some readers experience the patriarchal values embedded in scripture as so overwhelming that they no longer read the Bible at all. According to this view, the authority of human experience, and especially of women's experience, to identify norms of justice and dignity stands in judgment over the human words of the biblical text: what *is* wrong in the treatment of women today always *was* wrong, and to continue to find any value in literature that perpetuates such wrong can only extend the harm done. For these readers, the interpretive task relative to the Bible is set aside, and the foundations of women's spirituality and women's religious experience are sought elsewhere.

## A Chorus of Voices: Contextual Readings

The variety of stances taken by women toward the biblical text and its authority is multiplied by other dimensions of difference as well. In each of these dimensions it is important to be aware of the specific factors shaping a particular reading and to incorporate a variety of voices into the project of interpretation.

### Variety Within the Text

The first dimension of diversity of which the interpreter must be aware is that of the biblical materials themselves. Written over more than a millennium and collected over even more years than that, and originating among people living in every size and shape of human society from small tribal communities to cosmopolitan cities, the biblical materials reflect widely different assumptions about social forms and values, theology, and religious practice. It is important to recognize the particular context and, as far as possible, the assumptions that context would convey in order not to misconstrue the particular voice of a text.

In addition to the variety of historical and social contexts of materials in the Bible there is also a variety of forms of literature—narratives, poetry, laws, letters, songs, and proverbs, just to name some general categories. These different forms reflect different purposes: one does not write a poem for the same reason that one organizes a code of laws! The different types of material not only reflect different purposes but also have different effects on a reader. The beginning "Once upon a time . . ." invites one to relax, settle back, and listen to a story, whereas the opening phrase "Thou shalt not . . ." evokes both tension and attention—or else! And different types of literature are read in different ways, questioned for different purposes, and assessed by different criteria. In a poem or psalm, for example, one might ask about meter or metaphor, while characterization or plot development would be the concern in a narrative. Even the meaning of "truth" is different in poetry from the meaning in a text that purports to be a historical chronicle.

## The "Context" of a Lectionary

The diversity within the Bible and the variety of contexts and purposes that gave rise to it are compounded when modern interpretation takes place in the context of public worship, as part of a "lectionary" or set of readings appointed to be read together. In the Christian church, those readings usually (but not always) include a psalm or other canticle, another reading from the Old Testament (Hebrew Bible or Apocrypha), a reading from an epistle, and one from a Gospel. Traditionally those readings have been grouped according to the season of the church year or according to the theme of the Gospel reading. Such a grouping provides a new context for interpretation, suggesting that the various readings be read not only for themselves but also as interpreting one another. The danger is that the specificity of each voice and its context will be muted. If one of the readings is focused on a female character or a teaching or other text of special concern to women, an added danger is that this focus will be lost in a more general thematic study.

## A History of Interpretation

It is important also to recognize that no modern interpreter comes to the Bible directly. Rather, she or he is influenced (often without being aware of it) by centuries of interpretation whose results become nearly indistinguishable from the text itself. If women are to be able to arrive at a fresh hearing of the biblical traditions as they relate to women, an important part of the task is to be aware of that history of interpretation.

Two aspects of that history of interpretation require special mention. One relates to passages such as the household codes of the New Testament (Eph. 5:21–6:9; Col. 3:18–4:1; 1 Peter 2:18–3:7), which have been read as mandating the submission and often subsequent abuse of women, children, and other marginalized people. Regardless of the original intent of such passages, the fact is that the history of their interpretation has included very hurtful readings, and even a short time listening to the stories of victims and survivors of domestic violence will make this clear. That history of (mis)interpretation and the damage it has caused must be taken into account. A second area where the history of interpretation is particularly relevant to women's reading relates to the picture that is presented of Judaism. In particular, that history has often confused later, even medieval, rabbinic teachings with Jewish values and practice at the time of Jesus. The result has been an inappropriate contrast between a "feminist" Jesus and a misogynistic Judaism. In fact, Palestinian Jewish life in Jesus' day is probably mirrored in the ambivalent picture of women's roles in the teachings stemming from the Jesus movement. In both cases women's roles were, by modern standards, circumscribed—but not to the degree that the popular caricature of the silent, veiled Jewish woman shut away in her kitchen would suggest. While it seems that women were active among the followers of Jesus, their roles in that context were probably similar to those of their other Jewish sisters in the religious life of *their* families and local congregations.

## Interpretation in a Global Context

In addition to being attentive to the consequences of the history of interpretation, women from the dominant culture, class, and ethnic group—especially in the United States—need to be careful not to generalize our experience as that of all women. Again, the role of social, historical, and economic context is crucial in shaping the questions one poses to the biblical material and in affecting what one can—and cannot—see in a text. Interpretation is therefore best done as a community project, where the voices of poor women and rich women, white women and women of color, single women and married women, women from one's own country and from other parts of the world, lesbians and heterosexual women can all be heard, if not in person, at least in their writings. With the involvement of many voices, the chorus of interpretation can begin to convey the rich texture of the biblical traditions themselves.

## Gender, Language, and Interpretation

A particular concern in women's interpretation is the problem of language and gender. The so-called generic use of words like "man," "brother," or "mankind" and of masculine pronouns in traditional translations of the Bible obscure or even negate the participation of women in the communities whose stories are conveyed in the Bible. The translators of the New Revised Standard Version (NRSV) worked strenuously and systematically to address these problems. Their translation, on which this commentary is principally based, uses words like "person," "human being," and "brothers and sisters" where the gender of a person is unspecified or where women as well as men are clearly being addressed.

A theological issue of great importance in feminist interpretation that was not addressed by the translators of the NRSV is the problem of gender and language about God. All pronouns referring to God in that translation are masculine singular. The explanation given is that these pronouns (or verb endings, as pronouns are often conveyed in Hebrew) are found in the original languages and that therefore the translation is accurate. In both Greek and Hebrew, however, all nouns have *grammatical* gender, which governs the gender of pronouns used to refer to the nouns. In that sense, those languages are like such modern languages as Spanish, where, for example, "table" (*la mesa*) is a feminine noun, requiring a feminine pronoun (*ella*, "she"). If one were translating from Spanish to English, however, where pronouns convey biological and not merely grammatical gender, the pronoun that refers to "table" would be translated with the neuter "it." The same freedom prevails in rendering pronouns from Greek or Hebrew. Thus, the decision about which pronouns to use for God is one that cannot be made on grammatical grounds. It is a theological decision, and one whose resolution affects the way one views God. An interpretive decision that many women make is not to use any pronouns to refer to God (simply to repeat the word "God"), thus conveying the theological affirmation that God is beyond human categories of gender.

A related but more complex problem is the use of pronouns and titles (such as "Lord") to refer to Christ. In the Christian confession that Jesus of Nazareth is the Christ, clearly the reference is to a human male. That fact itself presents problems for many feminist interpreters, for whom the idea that women are ultimately dependent on a male for their relationship to God is unacceptable. Whether or not one views Jesus' being a man as problematic for women, and whatever one might conclude about whether the Christ's being a male was a historical necessity in the religious tradition into which he came, theologically the accent is on the humanity, not the maleness, of the Christ—according to the creeds, fully human and fully divine. Again, the problem for the interpreter is how to convey that affirmation within the limits of the English language, or how to identify the problem when the structure of the language does not allow it to be resolved.

## Conclusion

One point that is clear, given the complexity of the task of interpretation, is that one cannot simply read a text and "apply" it to one's own context. For women in particular, the passage from ancient text to contemporary context is much more dynamic and multidimensional. It comes into focus finally in a decision by the interpreter concerning what to do about a particular text one has struggled to understand. Interpretation itself is thus an active project, undertaken in a particular context, in dialogue with many partners both ancient and modern, and with the pastoral and theological purpose of hearing and sustaining a word of healing and liberation in a hurting world.

## BIBLIOGRAPHY

Achtemeier, Paul J., ed. *The Bible, Theology, and Feminist Approaches. Interpretation* 42 (1988).

Bach, Alice, ed. *The Pleasure of Her Text: Feminist Readings of Biblical and Historical Texts.* Philadelphia: Trinity Press International, 1990.

Collins, Adela Yarbro, ed. *Feminist Perspectives on Biblical Scholarship.* Biblical Scholarship in North America 10. Chico, Calif.: Scholars Press, 1985.

Fabella, Virginia, and Mercy Amba Oduyoye, eds. *With Passion and Compassion: Third World Women Doing Theology.* Maryknoll, N.Y.: Orbis Books, 1988.

Fiorenza, Elisabeth Schüssler. *Bread Not Stone: The Challenge of Feminist Biblical Interpretation.* Boston: Beacon Press, 1984.

Pobee, John S., and Bärbel von Wartenberg-Potter, eds. *New Eyes for Reading: Biblical and Theological Reflections by Women from the Third World.* Bloomington, Ind.: Meyer-Stone Books, 1987.

Russell, Letty M., ed. *Feminist Interpretation of the Bible.* Philadelphia: Westminster Press, 1985.

———, ed. *The Liberating Word: A Guide to Nonsexist Interpretation of the Bible.* Philadelphia: Westminster Press, 1976.

Tolbert, Mary Ann, ed. *The Bible and Feminist Hermeneutics. Semeia* 28 (1983).

Trible, Phyllis. *God and the Rhetoric of Sexuality.* Overtures to Biblical Theology. Philadelphia: Fortress Press, 1978.

———. *Texts of Terror: Literary-Feminist Readings of Biblical Narratives.* Philadelphia: Fortress Press, 1984.

Weems, Renita. *Just a Sister Away: A Womanist Vision of Women's Relationships in the Bible.* San Diego, Calif.: LuraMedia, 1988.

# GENESIS

*Susan Niditch*

❦

## Introduction

### Contents, Composition, and Context

The group of narrative and genealogical traditions called the book of Genesis describes the origin of the cosmos and its first inhabitants and unfolds the life stories of the earliest ancestors of ancient Israel. In this way the creation of the people Israel is set within the context of the very creation of the universe itself.

To read Genesis is to immerse oneself in the worldview and values of a distant and foreign culture, of a people who believed in a deity, Yahweh God, imagined as parent, river spirit, traveling man, and warrior, communicating with the ancestors through dream visions and waking revelations. To read Genesis is to encounter a people who considered the land of Canaan an eternally promised possession, a people who regularly petitioned and appeased their God with the blood sacrifice of animals and who could imagine this God demanding as sacrificial offering a mother's only son (Genesis 22) and the father's submitting to the demand. Genesis portrays a people whose women do not appear to exercise power in the public realm but who hold considerable power in the private realm of household and children. Theirs is a different world and a different way of imagining and ordering reality from our own; yet they too love spouses and children, resent siblings, mourn the loss of kin, fear and face deprivation in the form of famine and infertility, attempt to take stock of the comprehensible and make sense of the incomprehensible features of their existence. All of these very human concerns and emotions emerge in the Israelite literature of Genesis; but in approaching this material with special interest in passages pertaining to women one must ask, Whose stories are these?

*Questions of history and historicity.* The culture of Israel was never monolithic. The history of Israel spans thousands of years and can be divided into three periods: the time before the monarchy (pre–1000 B.C.E.); the time when kings ruled (1000 B.C.E.–586 B.C.E.); and postmonarchic times (586 B.C.E. on). Given the major changes that took place in social structure over this long expanse of time, one must be careful not to generalize about "Israelite culture" or "the life of the Israelite woman" or "Israelite attitudes to women." Biblical texts reveal considerable variation in the ways Israelites lived and expressed their beliefs. Nevertheless, it is not easy to track changing Israelite attitudes via apparent differences in the texts of the Bible.

The Bible's own story provides a chronology that seems to match the historical periods sketched broadly above. In premonarchic times are the matriarchs (Sarah, Rebekah, Rachel, and Leah) and patriarchs (Abraham, Isaac, Jacob, Joseph), the exodus (the time of Moses, Aaron, and Miriam), and the age of the judges (including the warrior heroines Deborah and Jael); in monarchic times are Saul, David and Bathsheba, Solomon, the building of the great Temple in Jerusalem, the eventual establishment of the Northern and Southern kingdoms, the so-called Josianic reform of the seventh century, and the age of classical prophecy. This period ends with the Babylonian conquest and the destruction of the Temple. The postmonarchic period includes the rebuilding of the Temple, the last of the biblical prophets, and the work of Ezra and Nehemiah. Within the Bible's own chronology Genesis is clearly set in premonarchic times, but "real" history and biblical narration are not as neatly matched as they may seem at first reading. The stories now found in Genesis do not necessarily stem from premonarchic authors, nor do they necessarily contain information about the way of life of Israelites who lived before 1000 B.C.E.

### Questions about the genesis of Genesis.

Many of the stories in Genesis are very old, perhaps as old as storytelling itself. The essential pattern of world creation in Genesis 6–9, for example, is represented in the lore of many cultures and times: from a watery flood emerge or reemerge a world and its inhabitants. Long before the existence of the people Israel, ancient Near Eastern narrators preserved several versions of a tale about the great flood with its favored human survivor(s), very much like the biblical tale of Noah. The story of Noah was no doubt a popular tale in ancient Israel told by various tellers with their own nuances and variations long before it was first set down in writing. Nor did this writer have the last word, for the biblical tale has been transmitted, elaborated, and edited by subsequent writers until it reached the form in which we now read it. In exploring the text of Genesis one must be aware that the ancient stories were once told in a variety of ways, oral and written.

### Theories about the sources behind Genesis.

Over the last hundred years, biblical scholarship has spoken of separable "sources" or "documents" out of which the whole cloth of Genesis has been woven. The sources are called J (the Yahwist, or Jahwist, source), E (the Elohist source), and P (the Priestly source). J is characterized by the use of the name Yahweh for God, by a down-to-earth style, and by a theology that allows God a certain closeness to the human realm; for example, God walks in the garden (Gen. 3:8). The Elohist source calls God the more generic Elohim (Hebrew for "god"), supposedly reserving the special name Yahweh until the revelation to Moses in Exodus 3; in E, God communicates more indirectly through mediating dreams and angels. The P source employs the divine epithet El Shaddai (often translated "God Almighty") in Genesis; God emerges in this source as an even more transcendent being. The interests of P are genealogy, ritual matters, and laws of purity. J, E, and P sources are said to be layered throughout the first four books of the Bible. J is dated by scholars to the tenth or ninth century B.C.E. of the Southern or Judahite monarchy, E to the ninth or eighth century B.C.E. of the Northern or Israelite monarchy, and P to the sixth century

B.C.E., the exilic period. Thus Yahwist (J) tales in Genesis should be expected to reflect the worldview of a Davidic courtly writer, and so on.

This theory has been modified over the years and recently has been strongly criticized, though in some form it still reigns supreme among theories about the composition of Genesis. The often too neat, line-by-line assignments of verses and larger literary units of Genesis to J, E, and P are not convincing, though variations in style, content, literary form, and message do confirm that various authors, worldviews, and life settings lie behind Genesis. Some of these differences may point to sources of different date, while others may point to authors from different sectors of Israelite society: aristocratic versus popular authors, urban versus rural ones, or men versus women. To distinguish the various authors and origins of biblical texts is a complex matter, but one especially important for a feminist enterprise asking whether the Hebrew Bible reveals something about attitudes toward women in ancient Israel and/or about their actual lives.

### The patriarchal age.

Do the stories of the matriarchs and patriarchs actually tell us about life in pre–1000 B.C.E. Israel even if the final form of the tales are from a later date? The tales of Genesis portray specific marriage practices; customs of inheritance and the rights of the firstborn; work roles of men and women; and attitudes toward male and female children, toward family and sexual ethics, and toward widows, barren wives, and other marginal females such as prostitutes. Can one connect such information with the considerable extrabiblical information about life in the non-Israelite ancient Near East of the second millennium B.C.E. (e.g., from the ancient Mesopotamian cities of Mari or Nuzi), as does E. A. Speiser, in order to reconstruct a world of early Israelite women? Can one connect the view of the workaday roles of men and women implied in God's punishing words to man and woman in Genesis 3 with archaeological and ethnographic reconstructions of life in the pioneer highland culture of premonarchic Israel, as Carol Meyers attempts to do? Or should one assume that if the texts were written down and shaped during the tenth to sixth centuries B.C.E. they do not contain reliable information about the lives of women from an earlier, premonarchic period? Some scholars think that the evidence to reconstruct any history of Israel before 1250 B.C.E. is lacking and refuse to speak of this so-called patriarchal age. Others such as Claus Westermann remain confident that even though Genesis was written down in the first millennium B.C.E. it nevertheless does reflect the lives and attitudes of the second millennium B.C.E., of a people who lived by farming and herding, without kings or elaborate forms of government, whose lives and work centered on family and flocks.

Given these debates and difficulties, how should one read and understand the tales of the lives of the women of Genesis? Rather than beginning with assumptions about the historical reliability of a text and the date when it was written down, one should ask what sort of literature this is in terms of its style, structure, content, and messages. To what sort of audience would it have been meaningful? What are its author's apparent worldview and concerns, especially those pertaining to women's issues broadly defined? A range of authors and worldviews should emerge, providing a reflection of the richness and complexity of the tradition in its relationship to women.

## Traditional Literature, Genesis, and Women's Tales

Much of biblical literature is traditional literature. Recurring patterns in language, imagery, plot, and theme resonate in the ancient Israelite literary tradition. In the Hebrew Scriptures there are certain ways to describe God's victories, recurring reasons for a patriarch's initial lack of children, ways in which the long-awaited conceptions are announced, favorite plots about the success of the underdog or the escape from seemingly powerful enemies. There are ways to frame a genealogy, to compose a lament, to describe a receiving of divine revelation. When Israelite authors set about presenting a piece of the tradition, they were at home in these conventions and creatively adapted them in accordance with their own perception of aesthetics and their understanding of political and theological verity. Through time, from author to author and editor to editor various sorts of traditional patterns recur, giving the biblical tradition a certain unity even within its great variety. In exploring the women of Genesis, one must pay attention to the book's traditional style. Recurrences in language and literary form also imply recurrences in essential messages and meanings; changes in form may mark varying messages. Out of these patterns emerge symbolic maps in which woman is a key feature.

Paying attention to these similarities and differences gives rise to questions: Why does the creation myth of Genesis 1, which echoes the basic plot of creation found in the Mesopotamian myth *Enuma elish*, not depict the watery chaos as female, even though Isa. 51:9–11 does preserve this motif? Why are so many tales of women in Genesis tales about tricksters who employ deception to improve their marginal status? Why are wives regularly found by wells? Why are the important mothers barren? Finally, many of the tales in Genesis deal with matters of home, family, and children. These are issues typical of tales from other cultures considered by ethnographers to be women's stories. Is it possible that many of the Genesis tales were popularly told among women?

## Comment

### Creating and Ordering the World (chaps. 1–11)

Creation is not merely the initial coming into being of the universe and its life forms; it includes also the ordering and continuous unfolding of the world. All of Genesis 1–11 is about the creation of the cosmos, including the more obvious creation accounts in Genesis 1 and 2, the Eden narrative in chap. 3, the tale of fratricide in chap. 4, the flood story of chaps. 6–9, the story of the tower of Babel in chap. 11, and the genealogies in chaps. 5, 10, and 11, which help to weave together Genesis 1–11 and form the transition to the stories of the mothers and fathers of Israel in Genesis 12–50.

*The creation of woman in Genesis 1.* Woman first appears in the elegant creation account of Genesis 1. Repeating frame language neatly reveals the origins and ordering of the universe with its topography, its solar system, and its rich variety of plant and animal life. God creates by the word—"God said, 'Let there be'... and it was so"—building day by day— "there was evening and there was morning the xth day"—until the sixth and final day, on which God makes humankind, a mirror of the divine image itself. And of this creation "in the image of God," it is said "male and female he created them." Without establishing relative rank or worth of the genders, the spinner of this creation tale indicates that humankind is found

# GENESIS

in two varieties, the male and the female, and this humanity in its complementarity is a reflection of the deity. For feminist readers of scriptures, no more interesting and telegraphic comment exists on the nature of being human and on the nature of God. The male aspect and the female aspect implicitly are part of the first human and a reflection of the Creator.

Scholars often attribute Genesis 1 to a Priestly writer (P) because of its image of a transcendent, all-powerful deity, its almost genealogical style, and its explanation of the origin of the Sabbath. If so, *this* Priestly writer's views of men and women differ from the much more male-centered Priestly writers of Leviticus, for whom a woman's menstruation and childbearing are sources of pollution, separating her from the sacred realm. She regularly lacks the pure status necessary to participate fully in Israelite ritual life. In reading the Hebrew Scriptures as a narrative whole, including both Gen. 1:27 and Leviticus, one may receive the message that the genders were meant to be equal at the beginning.

In Genesis 1 the Hebrew term for "deep waters" (*tehom*) is related to the name of the mother goddess Tiamat in the Mesopotamian creation myth *Enuma elish*. Tiamat, the salt waters of chaos, is killed and split like a mussel by the young god Marduk, who builds the world out of her carcass. The Israelite author who has provided the opening chapter of the Bible wants none of the uncertainty of this battle motif. His account of creation by God's word is as solid and inevitable as his style. If his account lacks a matriarchal goddess, it also does not present the creation of the world as dependent on her death.

***The becoming of woman in Genesis 2–3.*** Written in an earthier style than Genesis 1, the tale of Genesis 2–3, with its less-than-complete outline of God's creations (2:4b–25), its homespun reflections on marriage (2:23–24), and its God who walks in the garden (3:8) and fears humans' potential divinity (3:22), has been more influential than Gen. 1:27 in shaping and justifying attitudes toward and the treatment of women in Western tradition.

This tale of creation has two parts: the emergence of the cosmos out of the mist of chaos and the emergence of "real life" from the ideal of paradise. Man is the first of God's creations in Genesis 2 (2:7). His formation is from the dust of the earth (*'adamah*). He is thus Adam/Earthling. The creation of other living beings (2:18) is motivated by God's concern that

"it is not good that the man should be alone." But none of the birds or beasts are deemed suitable counterparts for the man (2:20). So, out of man's own rib, God forms woman. The sayings in 2:23 and 2:24 comment positively on the closeness of the conjugal bond. Man and woman are parts of a whole, anticipating the genealogical patterning of Genesis. Men and women will unite and have children, the male children leaving to join wives and form new families. The conjugal couple is the foundation of social and cultural relationships for the writers of Genesis. Even when the world is temporarily subsumed by the renewed chaos of the flood in the tale of Noah (Genesis 6–9), social order remains afloat on the ark in the form of Noah and his wife, his sons and their wives (6:18). This generative, culture-affirming process, however, does not actually begin until Genesis 4:1, for 2:25 declares that man and woman are naked and not ashamed. That is, they are not aware of their sexual differences; their sexuality is yet to be discovered and expressed.

Jewish and Christian traditions postdating the Hebrew Bible and a long history of Western scholarship have viewed woman's creation in Genesis 2 as secondary and derivative—evidence of her lower status. The tale explaining the departure from Eden into a real world of work, birth, and death in Genesis 3 is taken to be an even stronger indictment of woman as the gullible, unworthy partner who let loose sin and death. Her biological function as conceiver and bearer of children is perceived as confirmation of her fall, a punishment shared by all women who come after her.

In fact, Genesis 3 has been misunderstood. Certainly, like Pandora in the comparable Greek cosmogonic tradition, the curious woman is a linchpin in the ongoing process of world ordering. She, like Lot's wife, dares to disobey a command not to use all her sensory capacities in a particular situation—to taste or to look—and perhaps this curiosity about forbidden fruit is often in Mediterranean tradition associated with the female. On the other hand, in the lore of all cultures interdictions such as Gen. 2:17 ("But of the tree . . .") exist to be disobeyed by the tales' protagonists. That is what makes the story. Eve, as she is named in 3:20, is the protagonist, not her husband. This is an important point, as is the realization that to be the curious one, the seeker of knowledge, the tester of limits is to be quintessentially human—to evidence traits of many of the culture-bringing heroes and heroines of Genesis.

*Reading Genesis 3.* Like Genesis 1 and Genesis 2, Genesis 3 is also about a movement from a fixed and unchanging world to a new nonstatic order. Genesis 1 and 2 describe the way in which a sterile world is replaced by one teeming with life. In Genesis 3 the change is from a well-provisioned, closely controlled world lacking discernment, social roles, and sexual status to a world in which man and woman relate to each other sexually and according to social roles, a world in which they work hard and know the difference between good and evil. The world after Eden is clearly one of birth and death, whereas the garden had been an in-between world, in which no human had eaten from the tree of life but in which no one had yet given birth. In a wonderful tale about a trickster snake, a woman who believes it, and a rather passive, even comical man, biblical writers comment on the inevitability of reality as they perceived it, wistfully presenting an image of an easier, smoother life. Woman, the one who will house life within her, helps to generate this new, active, challenging life beyond Eden.

All too often readers come to Genesis weighed down by Augustine's or Milton's interpretation of the story. What if one notices that the snake does not lie to the woman but speaks the truth when it says that the consequence of eating from the forbidden tree is gaining the capacity to distinguish good from evil, a godlike power which the divinity jealously guards (compare the snake's words at 3:5 with God's words at 3:22)? The snake, like the Greek giant Prometheus, who was said to have given fire to humankind, is a trickster, a character having the capacity to transform situations and overturn the status quo. The trickster has less power than the great gods but enough mischief and nerve to shake up the cosmos and alter it forever. The woman believes the snake, and in an important pun the narrator says that she sees the tree is good to look at/good for making one wise (3:6). She is no easy prey for a seducing demon, as later tradition represents her, but a conscious actor choosing knowledge. Together with the snake, she is a bringer of culture.

The man, on the other hand, is utterly passive. The woman gives him the fruit and he eats as if he were a baby (3:6). With the eating come the marks of social life and culture: knowledge of good versus evil, clothing that defines and conceals, and gender roles. The woman is to be the bearer of children, the Mother of all life. The husband is to work the ground, which will now only grudgingly yield its fruits. A clear hierarchy is established: woman and her offspring over the clever snake, who is now reduced to a mere dust-eating reptile, and man over woman. The status-establishing punishments meted out to man and woman and the social roles they are assigned do reflect the author's male-oriented worldview, but no weighty accusation of "original sin" brought about by woman is found in the text. That is a later interpretation from authors with different theologies and worldviews.

What the author of Genesis does reveal is that man and woman share responsibility for the alteration of their status. The man's self-defense, like his passive act of disobedience, portrays him in a childlike manner. When accused by God of defying his order, the man says comically, "The woman whom *you* gave to be with me, she gave me fruit from the tree, and I ate" (3:12). Whose fault is it? The woman's? God's? And yet the woman initiates the act. It is she who first dares to eat of God's tree, to consume the fruit of the divine, thereby becoming, as the rabbis say of human beings, like the angels in having the capacity to discriminate and like the animals who eat, fornicate, defecate, and die. The woman herself comes to have the most earthy and the most divine of roles, conceiving, containing, and nurturing new life. She is an especially appropriate link between life in God's garden and life in the thornier world to which all of us are consigned.

*"The daughters of men" (6:1–4).* Women—"the daughters of men"—are also involved in another, briefer creation tale in Gen. 6:1–4 that marks the passage from ideal to reality. Here the women themselves are the fruit attracting the divine "sons of God," members of God's entourage in ancient Israelite tradition. In this story, sexual intercourse rather than eating is the way that the border between God's realm and the realm of human beings is breached. Surely the two actions are symbolic equivalents in a pattern that leads to limits on the quality of human existence, in this case to the length of life allowed mortals (Gen. 6:3). In this brief mythological snippet, as in the fuller tale of Genesis 3, the female is integral to the passage to reality, to the onset of historical time and human culture, the days of the "heroes that were of old, warriors of renown" (6:4).

*Women in the genealogies.* One of the markers of time in the creation account of Genesis 1–11 is the genealogy. Women are absent from the lists of begetters and begotten in Gen. 4:17–26; 5:1–32; and 10:1–32, with one interesting exception. In 4:19, a descendant of Cain named Lamech takes two wives, Adah and Zillah. The women are each given credit for birthing sons who found groups responsible for one or another aspect of human civilization (e.g., dwelling in tents, raising cattle, playing music, forging instruments of bronze and iron). By giving birth, the women further the march of human culture. One daughter is also mentioned by name, Naamah (4:22). In 4:23 Lamech addresses to his wives what appears to be a war boast about his defeat of an enemy. Why does he address this enigmatic, taunting victory cry to his wives? Does he want to impress them with his prowess? Does he wish to encourage them to compose a woman's victory song of their own for him (see Judges 5; Ex. 15:20–21)?

Unnamed daughters are mentioned along with sons in the list of Gen. 11:10–32. Two women who are important in the genealogy of Israel's ancestors are mentioned by name. Sarai (=Sarah; see 17:15), the wife of Abram (=Abraham; see 17:5), is introduced in 11:29, along with the comment that she was barren. The genealogist of chap. 11 also mentions the name of Abram's brother's wife, Milcah. Her children, and notably her granddaughter Rebekah who will be Isaac's wife, are listed in Gen. 22:20–23.

## The Mothers and Fathers of Israel (chaps. 12–50)

Commentaries on Genesis 12–50 generally focus on Abraham, Isaac, Jacob, and Joseph, ancestral heroes of Israel. Their life stories are built from traditional elements such as the hero's unusual birth, his stormy relationship with his brothers, youthful adventures often including marriage, the constant presence of a divine helper, and the hero's aging and finally his death. Theologically, Genesis 12–50 is treated as the foundation story of the patriarchal religion of Israel. It includes important scenes of covenant making with God, altar building, divine promises of land and descendants, and tests of the patriarchs' faith.

Genesis 12–36 and 38 differ significantly from the Joseph tale in 37, 39–50 in style, setting, and orientation. The former's popular, down-to-earth style contrasts with the latter's more elaborate style. The context of the former is family, flocks, and sojourning in flight from famine. The characters are socially marginal and often confront authorities via trickery and deception. Joseph, on the other hand, sold into

slavery by his jealous, scheming brothers, leaves this pastoral world, eventually rising to become the leading bureaucrat of Egypt, a member of the establishment itself. He and his brothers, all sons of Israel, are later reunited in Egypt, setting the stage for the next book in the Bible, Exodus. Often ignored, the patterns of women's lives in Genesis are every bit as interesting and important as those of the men, for the women both reflect and help to create Israel.

*The matriarchs (chaps. 12–36; 38).* Introduction. Like the tales of Genesis 1–11, with their recurring patterns of world ordering, the tales of the matriarchs have recurring narrative patterns typical of traditional literature. In Genesis 12–36 and 38, certain motifs mark the life history of the women at the turning points of youth, marriage, and parenthood. The women often appear by wells or springs and are often soon to become wives (Rebekah, Rachel) or mothers (Hagar); they are often barren women soon to become mothers (Sarah, Rebekah, Rachel). If not barren, the women have other problems associated with sexuality (Dinah, Leah) or fertility (Tamar) that render them marginal unless or until the problem is solved. For those who are to have children, predictions about the birth and lives of their children are received in divinely sent annunciations. Finally, many of the women engage in acts of trickery or deception in order to further the careers of their sons or husbands (Sarah: 12:10–20; Rebekah: chap. 27; Rachel: 31:19, 33–35; Tamar: chap. 38). These recurring motifs or combinations of them tend to emphasize certain themes: (1) the role of the woman as wife and mother in the private rather than the public realm; (2) the frequent position of women intermediaries who link groups of men through marriage alliances; (3) the marginal status of women who are prevented from fulfilling the roles defined for women in Genesis 3 (e.g., the barren women, the raped Dinah, the abandoned Hagar, the childless widow Tamar, and the unloved Leah).

On one level, much of this defining appears to be done from men's perspectives. The tales of marriage, for example, really have to do with relationships between the men, be it Abraham and his kinfolk in Mesopotamia or Jacob and Rebekah's brother Laban, or Abraham and Pharaoh. So in Genesis 34, a tale of would-be marital relations gone awry, the central issue is less the victimization of Dinah, who had been the potential link between the sons of Hamor and the sons of Jacob, than the relationships between the men. These relationships have to do with face-saving, feuding, and vengeance, all causes of warfare in pre-state, decentralized societies. It is also a male point of view that regards woman with her potent sources of "uncleanness" (see Gen. 31:34–35) as a danger, and a male point of view that places her under man's control after eating from the tree in Genesis 3. It is logical to assume that men — male priests and a lengthy scribal tradition — are responsible for incorporating into law and custom notions of what the "proper" place of women is, namely, to be a young virgin in the father's home or a child-producing, sexually faithful wife in her husband's. Thus, all women who do not — or who do not appear to — fulfill these roles fall between the cracks of the social structure. They are either rehabilitated by other laws preserved by men or by the male God's intervention, or they fade away.

On the other hand, the God of Genesis, with whom the important value judgment lies, is partial to marginal people of both genders. On some level that god is the god of the tricksters who use deception to deal with the power establishment, whether the establishment is the elders of one's family or non-Israelites. Although their positions are circumscribed by the men around them, Sarah, Rebekah, Tamar, Rachel, and Leah exercise great power over husbands, father-in-law, and father in situations involving the family, children, and sexuality. It is, moreover, the women who are the critical ancestors for the proper continuation of the Israelites. Isaac must come from Sarah and no other woman. Abraham's seed is not enough to guarantee his status. Similarly, Joseph must be Rachel's son. The blessing and the inheritance go to Jacob, Rebekah's favorite son, not Esau, her husband's. The women's wishes and God's wishes are one in this respect. Finally, a number of the women are portrayed as active tricksters who, like Eve, alter the rules, men's rules. Would not women authors and audiences take special pleasure in Rebekah's fooling her dotty old husband or in Rachel's using men's attitudes to menstruation to deceive her father Laban, or in Tamar's more directly and daringly using her sexuality to obtain sons through Judah? Like Adam, the men in many of the women's stories of Genesis are bumbling, passive, and ineffectual.

*Wives at wells and water.* The associations in literature between fertility and water are ancient intuitive acknowledgments of our watery origins on earth and in mother, and of the source of life upon which we continue to depend. Four scenes involving water, women, and marriage or childbirth are found in Genesis: 16:7–14; 21:8–21 (Hagar); 24:10–27 (Rebekah); and 29:1–12 (Rachel). In the latter two scenes men from Abraham's kin come to Mesopotamia to seek a wife from among his kin. In Genesis 24, Abraham's senior servant is sent to seek a wife for Abraham's son Isaac. In Gen. 29:1–12, Jacob seeks a wife for himself from his mother's family (see 24:15) after fleeing from the brother whose birthright he has stolen (see below on Rebekah and Genesis 27). The man meets the wife-to-be at the watering hole, is welcomed by her family, and negotiates terms for the marriage. In each case wives are found by wells, but there are important differences. The appearance of Rebekah and her hospitable words are a sign requested of God by the emissary so that he might recognize the right wife for Abraham's son. God's control is certain and appears in the repetitious language of traditional literature. Rebekah herself is described as a beautiful, untouched young woman quick to serve and nurture and quick to agree to fulfilling her role in the divine plan (24:58). In a thematic echo of Gen. 2:24, Isaac loves her as soon as he sees her, for she is said to be an emotional replacement for his mother, Sarah, who had died (24:67). In Gen. 29:1–12, Jacob meets the woman, his cousin Rachel, at the well and shows his physical strength by rolling the heavy stone from the well and watering his uncle Laban's flock (compare Ex. 2:15–17). Jacob weeps when he greets Rachel, in ritualized behavior typical of kinship reunions in tribal cultures. The woman is acquired in exchange for seven years' work, but her elder and less attractive sister Leah is substituted on the wedding night by their father, Laban, himself a trickster. Jacob ends up with two wives, indentured to his father-in-law for seven more years. Jacob's tale of acquiring a wife is the more humorous of the two, as trickster confronts trickster. In both accounts, however, the emphasis on marriage within the kinship group is very strong. The central issue is relationships between male kin, mediated by the women, who are in effect items of exchange, extremely valuable commodities as precious as the water with which they are associated, but commodities nevertheless.

From a literary perspective, the themes of marriage within the group and of woman as mediator are emphasized, issues that were important to the stories' authors and audiences.

Can more be learned, however, from these scenes about real-life social behavior in ancient Israel? It has been suggested that Rebekah's interaction with her family in 24:57–58 indicates that the Israelite woman was asked her permission before marriage agreements were concluded. The story indicates, however, that Rebekah is merely agreeing to leave quickly rather than spend ten days with her family (24:55). No formal law involving the woman's permission appears to be involved here. The mention of a ten-day good-bye period is a reminder that the young woman's family and she might never see one another again. Provision of bride-price certainly seems customary in 24:53 and in 29:18, as it is in countless cultures. Was it customary, as Laban claims in his defense of the substitution of Leah for Rachel, to marry off the elder daughter before the younger, or is he as a trickster good at finding excuses for acts of deception? It has also been suggested that the tale of Jacob gives evidence of matrilocal customs among Israel's ancestors, that is, living with the wife's family. Jacob's living in Laban's household is, however, considered irregular by the tradition as we now have it. Things are put right only when he returns to Israel. What does seem clear from the accounts about Rebekah and Rachel is that marriage within the group is an important means of safeguarding group identity and that cross-cousin marriage, a means of maintaining in-group marriage relations in many traditional cultures, may well have been an actual custom in some period in ancient Israel.

*Hagar: Mothering a hero.* The story of Hagar leads to a wider discussion of the major themes of this study: the barrenness of the patriarch's wives, the annunciation scenes, and the wives' positions as mother of the patriarch of the next generation. Hagar's status is contingent on that of her mistress, Sarah, the wife of Abraham. Sarah bears no children and gives Hagar, her Egyptian maid, to Abraham as a wife (16:3), hoping she will become a surrogate mother for Sarah (16:2). The custom of having children through another woman (note the expression "that she may bear upon my knees," 30:3) is found also in the tale of barren Rachel. It is probably safe to assume that surrogate motherhood was an actual custom in the ancient Near East (see Speiser and Westermann for nonbiblical parallels) and would have been eminently possible in a world in which slavery was practiced and persons' sexual services could be donated by their masters or mistresses.

Surrogate motherhood allowed a barren woman to regularize her status in a world in which children were a woman's status and in which childlessness was regarded as a virtual sign of divine disfavor (see 16:2; 30:1–2; and below also on Genesis 38). Childless wives were humiliated and taunted by co-wives (Gen. 16:4). The tension in the scene between Jacob and Rachel in 30:1–2 is fraught with desperate realism, as she cries, "Give me children, or I shall die!" And he responds bitterly, "Am I in the place of God, who has withheld from you the fruit of the womb?" It is always the woman in this culture who is perceived as the cause of infertility—so Sarah, so Rebekah, so Rachel.

By the same token, virtually no hero worth his salt in Genesis is born under circumstances that are ordinary for his mother. It is the unusual and often initially infertile women who have special births. It is their sons who count in the ongoing tradition. These women mother nations and receive special communications about the child to be born. They often engineer the births, thereby showing considerable power in matters related to fertility and sexuality. Hagar is not a barren woman, but a victim sensing a new power on conceiving Abraham's child. She now finds her mistress "to be of less worth [literally, "lighter-weight"] in her eyes." Sarah knows she has lost status and complains to her husband, who tells her that the maid is hers to do with as she wishes, for this is a woman's world of competition concerning children. It is in this light that we understand the scene involving Jacob and Leah in 30:14–16. One of the sons of Leah, the fertile wife of trickery whom Jacob had never loved, finds some mandrakes, plants that were believed to have the capacity to produce fertility. Rachel, desperate for children, begs Leah for the plants, and she grudgingly agrees, in exchange for a night with their husband Jacob. Upon returning from the fields, Jacob is told by Leah that he is with her that night, having been "hired" with her son's mandrakes. Without a comment he goes to her. He obeys in this world of women, as Abraham defers to Sarah in the matter of Hagar.

Sarah afflicts Hagar, who flees to the wilderness. There by a spring of water God appears to her in the first of the annunciation scenes in Genesis. She is told about the son to be born and, like Abraham, is promised a multitude of descendants and declares that she has seen God. After the son Ishmael ("God will hear") is born, Abraham and Sarah are visited by three men, manifestations of God, who announce that a son will be born to them. Sarah has the nerve to laugh at the unlikely news (18:12), for she and her husband are old and past child-bearing. In these scenes the women see God and confront God; they demand and receive some answers. Similarly, when Rebekah, who finally becomes pregnant after her husband petitions God, feels the children moving around violently (literally, "crushing one another") within her, she inquires of God and is told about the feuding twins, Jacob and Esau. She is made the keeper of the information that the elder, Esau, will serve Jacob, the younger, and she actively sets out to fulfill God's prediction (25:21–23).

Hagar receives a second prediction from God about her son Ishmael in a setting of wilderness and water. Sarah sees Ishmael playing with Isaac (21:9) and demands that Abraham banish Hagar and her son. "The son of this slave woman shall not inherit along with my son Isaac" (21:10). Her words shiver with contempt for the upstarts, the upstarts that she herself had created. Abraham greatly disapproves, for his son Ishmael's sake, but again the voice of Sarah, the matriarch, and the voice of God are one. Abraham's wishes in the matter of inheritance are unimportant and misguided, as will be Isaac's once he has sons.

This passage is a difficult one in biblical ethics. Abraham cares not at all about the maid he has bedded, and Sarah is contemptuous of mother and child and would expose them to death. The author works hard to rationalize and justify the emotions and actions of Abraham and Sarah (21:12–13). Yet while reading this story one has the distinct feeling it is being told from Hagar and Ishmael's point of view. One is moved by the portrait of the mother who places the child apart because she cannot bear to watch him die: the weeping mother (21:16) and the divinely protected boy ultimately rescued by God and promised a great future; the blessed child and mother, for whom God opens a well of water in the wilderness so that they might drink and live.

The motif of the exposed, endangered, and delivered child is as common in the stories of great heroes as that of their mothers' unusual, difficult conceptions. Compare Moses' origins (Ex. 2:1–10). The motif occurs also in Greek narratives about Oedipus and about the Persian king Cyrus. Embedded in the Israelite tale of origins is thus another related people's story of its hero's youth, and on some level Abraham and Sarah are its necessary villains. God is the

god of those deserted in the wilderness, of those on the fringes, who are usually in the Hebrew Scriptures not Ishmaelites but Israelites, whose tales are those of the tricksters to follow.

*Tricksters, Israelites, and women.* One of the biblical authors' favorite narrative patterns is that of the trickster. Israelites tend to portray their ancestors and thereby to imagine themselves as underdogs, as people outside the establishment who achieve success in roundabout, irregular ways. One of the ways marginals confront those in power and achieve their goals is through deception or trickery. The improvement in their status may be only temporary, for to be a trickster is to be of unstable status, to be involved in transformation and change. In Genesis, tricksters are found among Israelites sojourning in foreign lands, among younger sons who would inherit, and among women.

*The wife/sister tales (12:10–20; 20:1–18; 26:1–17).* Three times in Genesis when the patriarch and his wife are "sojourning" — traveling as resident aliens — in a foreign land the ruler of that country is told that the wife is a sister of the patriarch. In two versions he takes her to be his own woman, and each time the couple is eventually found out. Despite their similarities, the three stories possess quite different nuances and voices. It is assumed in all three versions that a brother has more power to exchange his sister than a husband his wife. The patriarchs are portrayed as assuming that the foreigners would not hesitate to kill a husband in order to get a woman but that they would engage in normal marital exchanges with a brother. The story that makes the most sense in a crass, male-centered way is the version in 12:10–20, where it is clear that Abram has more to gain as the brother of an unattached, protected woman than as the husband of a "used" one.

In Gen. 12:10–20, Sarai and Abram are co-tricksters. Abram asks Sarai to participate with him in the deception that she is his sister, praising her beauty and using coaxing language (12:13 begins "Please say you are . . ."; author's translation). She is actually taken as wife by the dupe, Pharaoh, who showers wealth on the supposed brother-in-law. God, who has other plans, interrupts the trickery with a plague, and Pharaoh, now alerted, dismisses the con artists, who nevertheless leave with their newfound goods intact. This is no woman-affirming tale. Sarai is an exchange item to be traded for wealth. She is shown as accepting this role, as are all the women in Genesis. She and Abram play out their roles in a particular social structure, but do so as marginals. Facing famine in their own land, they flee to Egypt, where they have insecure status. There they use deception to improve their situation at the expense of those who have authority over them.

In Genesis 20 and 26 the gender roles are as clearly marked. These tales are again about underdogs but not necessarily about tricksters. In the version in chap. 20 the author apparently worries about the ethics of the situation. He reveals that Sarah *is* Abraham's half sister. As in some ancient Near Eastern dynasties, marriage between half siblings is not taboo. The deception is not really a deception after all. Authority is not duped but respected, for the ruler, Abimelech, never actually has relations with Sarah and is portrayed as morally outraged at the thought of taking another man's wife. Sarah's role is more sedate in this version, as perhaps befits a more aristocratic but still male-oriented tale. Finally, in Genesis 26, the role of the wife Rebekah is even more circumscribed. Isaac, out of fear that the ruler will take Rebekah and kill him, says without consulting her that Rebekah is his sister. But before anything happens Abimelech observes them "sporting" as man and wife and forgoes any interest in the woman. The three stories differ in their concern for piety and propriety. In Genesis 26, God tightly controls the action and protects the patriarch and his wife so that a good story never develops. Neither Isaac nor Rebekah plays an interesting role. In Genesis 20, a morally upright patriarch and equally blameless ruler relate on a somewhat more equal footing, the woman being a passive character. Only Genesis 12 reveals earthy tricksters who use the woman's sexuality as a resource to dupe a monarch. It belongs, in this way, to a fund of comparable male-centered folk literature.

*Rebekah the trickster (chap. 27).* In Genesis 27, the woman herself is the trickster who formulates the plan and succeeds, moving the men around her like chess pieces. Lest the reader think that here one finally encounters a more liberated woman, beware that again success is gained through the symbolic counterpart of sex—food. Moreover, the status in question is not that of the woman but of her son. Nevertheless, within the confines and assumptions of her male-dominated world, Rebekah is very good at what she does. Indeed, she determines and directs the course of the clan and in doing so is the one who knows and fulfills what God wants.

Genesis 27 begins with a father's intimate words to his eldest and favorite son. Isaac, now blind and elderly, tells Esau that he might die at any time. He asks Esau, the hunter, to catch game and make him the food he loves that he might bless him before his death. Someone has overheard the father's request and his promise. Rebekah, the wife and mother, who had received special information from God that her younger son Jacob, and not Esau, was meant to receive the eldest's rights and blessing, prepares to actualize that revelation. Is Jacob her favorite because of the annunciation received during her pregnancy, or does she love him because he is more like her, the smooth son who lives in tents in contrast to red, hairy Esau who is a man of the fields? What is interesting is that God loves Jacob too and prefers him to Esau. The theological message gains power from the inevitable pattern of the traditional tale. God's choice, like love itself, is often serendipitous and inscrutable. The youngest son in folktales inherits even though the patterns of custom and social structure would have it otherwise. But why in the case of Jacob and Rebekah is the younger and preferred son the more womanish one? And why, as in the case of Sarah and Isaac, is it the woman who knows he is the chosen one? And why are the husbands and fathers left out of the inner circle in the matter of their children? Why are they passive or blind—literally as well as figuratively?

One explanation is that children have to do with the private realm of home and hearth, woman's world. Rebekah's role as Jacob's mother is strongly emphasized by repetitions in language in 27:6, 8, 11, 13, 14. It is equally true, as in the creation literature, that women are sources of culture. Here they become the means by which a particular Israelite tradition is established and continued, not merely by giving birth but, in the case of Rebekah, by furthering the career of one of her sons, who does indeed become Israel. From a feminist perspective one might take pleasure in the fact that Rebekah is so important and in the realization that God's preference for underdogs here extends to women and to the man who is more his mother's son than his father's. One might also assume that Israelite women would have taken special pleasure in hearing the particular version of Rebekah and Jacob's story that is preserved in the Hebrew Scriptures, and one might ask if women were not also responsible for shaping such tellings.

Rebekah thoroughly controls the action in

Genesis 27. After overhearing her husband's words to Esau, she repeats them to Jacob and instructs him very much like the wisdom figure of Proverbs, "Now therefore, my son, obey my word as I command you" (27:8; cf. Prov. 8:32). She tells Jacob to bring her kids from the flock so she can prepare delicacies for Isaac. Jacob is to bring them to Isaac so he can eat and bless his son. The repetitious language of bringing, eating food, and blessing is economical in the traditional literary style. The repeated words or phrases are used to emphasize key themes. Through deception and disguise, Rebekah and Jacob will be Isaac's providers so that Jacob obtains from him the reciprocal blessing of fullness, fertility, and security (27:27–29).

Jacob hesitates, but not out of ethical compunction, for he is as good a trickster as his mother. Had he not earlier tricked Esau to sell his birthright for a bowl of red food (25:29–34)? He hesitates out of fear that he might be found out and receive a curse at Isaac's hands rather than a blessing. If the old man should touch him, Jacob's smoothness would give him away (27:11). Rebekah boldly offers to take the curse upon herself should things go awry, for curses are real as are blessings. They can be stolen or transferred. His mother prepares a disguise for Jacob, using Esau's clothes, which smell of the fields, and the woolly skin of the kids to cover his smooth hands and neck (27:15–16). The trickery works and Jacob receives his father's blessing. Finally Rebekah, again alert to the plans of all the men in her household, engineers Jacob's safe passage away from the vengeance of Esau (27:41–28:5).

Rebekah's wisdom is a wisdom of women that involves listening closely (recall Sarah in 18:10) and working behind the scenes to accomplish goals. It is a vicarious power that achieves success for oneself through the success of male children, a power symbolically grounded in the preparation and serving of food. It involves as well a willingness to sacrifice oneself ("Let your curse be on me," 27:13) if necessary for the sake of the son. Such is woman's power in a man's world, and it is not the sort of empowerment to which most modern women aspire. It is the power of those not in authority. The woman in ancient Israelite literature who would succeed almost must be a trickster, must follow the path typical of the marginalized. Yet so clever is this trickster, so strong and sure, so completely superior in wisdom to the men around her that she seems to be the creation of a woman storyteller, one who is part of a male-centered world

and is not in open rebellion against it, but who nevertheless subverts its rules indirectly by making Rebekah a trickster heroine, for this is also a woman's power in a man's world, a power of mockery, humor, and deception.

*Rachel: Stealing Laban's teraphim (31:19, 30–35).* In an interesting scene leading up to the departure of Jacob and his household from Laban's land (Gen. 31:4–16), Jacob speaks to the feuding wives/sisters. He reviews all that has happened to them, tells of a vision he had promising him much of Laban's flocks, and of God's message that the time had come to return to his own land. The women, Rachel and Leah, answer as one, making clear that their allegiance is to their husband and not to their father. They say they are thought of as "stranger women" by their father, who has "sold" them and proceeded to "eat up" all their money.

The language of 31:15 is very strong. Though men are said to acquire wives with the verb that often means "to buy," nowhere else in the Hebrew Scriptures is a proper marriage described as a father's selling (makar) his daughters. In the closely related languages of Aramaic and Syriac mekar means "to buy" and is used for "to marry." In rabbinic texts moker is a bride price, but in the Hebrew Scriptures one only sells humans into slavery (e.g., Gen. 37:27, 28, 36; 45:4, 5, about the selling of Joseph; Ex. 21:7–8, laws about selling one's daughter into slavery). Thus, bitterly and poignantly, the daughters of Laban describe themselves in their relationship to their father as exploited and dispossessed slaves, treated as foreign women unrelated to him. The author of this text assumes that women are economic objects, but implies that at least a man's own daughters should be treated as more than property. The sisters' complaint is a remarkably critical statement by women about their treatment and status. Although they do not directly condemn the whole system of which Laban is a part, they state that their rights have not been upheld even within the requirements of that exploitative system. Indirectly they call attention to a world in which people are bought and sold.

Playing the role of mother-wife whose voice is synonymous with the voice of God, the women encourage Jacob to go. It is only at this point that the wives have been fully exchanged from father to husband and that the sisters themselves set aside their own feud to unify with their husband and children as one family. It is at this point that they depart for the husband's homeland and at this point of transition that Rachel plays the trickster. She steals her father's teraphim while he is off shearing his sheep. Scholars have long debated what these objects were. NRSV translates "household gods," implying that they are minor, personal deities represented in statuettes that Rachel might easily carry and conceal. A recent article discusses the possibility that the teraphim are representations of ancestors, testifying to some sort of ancestor worship among the Israelites. In any event the role of these objects in the story provides some insight, however murky, into aspects of Israelite popular religion.

Laban chases after Jacob and his household, seeming more upset about the teraphim than anything else (31:30). The story receives added tension from Jacob's declaration that anyone with whom the gods are found shall not live (31:32). Jacob emerges as a full-fledged patriarch having the power of life and death over members of his household.

Laban searches in Jacob's tent, in Leah's, and in the two maidservants' but finds nothing. Finally he comes to Rachel's tent. Rachel has hidden the teraphim in the camel saddle and sits on them. She says to Laban, "Let not my Lord be angry that I cannot rise before you, for the way of women is upon me," that is, "I am in a menstruous condition" (31:35). Laban does not throw her off the saddle. Is this in gentlemanly deference? This interpretation seems inconsistent with the larger portrayal of Laban. He does not discover the teraphim. Is this because in such stories those being tricked have to be tricked—at least for a while? He does not pursue the matter more carefully. Is this because he fears the potent and visceral power issuing forth from the unclean woman, whose capacity to house life links her with the sacred, whose monthly bleeding sets her apart from what is ordinary and normal in a male world, that is, from what is physiologically male? (See Lev. 15:19–24.)

If uncleanness is the reason why Laban avoids examining the area close to Rachel, rather than respect for her feigned discomfort, then it provides an instance of a female trickster's employing woman's physical source of femininity, the dangerous and polluting power of menstruation, to deter her father from discovering her theft. Laban's paternal and therefore male authority—an authority related to his ownership of his own household gods—is undermined by his female offspring's clever exploitation of that which makes her most markedly female. Covert woman's power in this one brief scene dominates man's overt authority.

*Tamar: Trickster would-be mother (chap. 38).* Genesis 38 begins as a story of Judah, who is left in the land of Canaan during Joseph's ordeal in Egypt. In the Joseph narrative, Judah is one of the villain brothers. He does not actually want to kill the boy Joseph but suggests he be sold to a passing band of Ishmaelites (Gen. 37:26–27). Of course, being sold into slavery is not unlike a death sentence. At the very least, Judah is subjecting Joseph to social death, separating him from kin and culture and from his place as favorite of Jacob, son of the beloved Rachel, who would surely inherit. Judah wishes to keep his own hands free from blood, but is portrayed as guilty by proxy. Some scholars have suggested that the tale in Genesis 38 balances the misdeed to Joseph. As Joseph was taken in ambush, so Judah is taken by deception and forced to do his duty by Tamar. The larger stories of Jacob and Joseph are structured along such patterns of trickery and countertrickery, misdeed, and vengeance.

The opening section of Genesis 38 tells of Judah's marriage to Shua and of the birth of his three sons Er, Onan, and Shelah in the genealogical orientation typical of family foundation narratives. Then, as in tales of Abraham's sons and Isaac's sons, we are told of marriage arrangements made for the eldest son Er. In one verse (38:6) this brief account introduces Tamar, the heroine of the story.

The genealogical orientation continues in 38:7 but with a twist. Er is a wicked man and is slain by God, leaving no offspring. Judah tells his middle son Onan to go in to Tamar ("go in" being a biblical euphemism for sexual intercourse) to "perform the duty of a brother-in-law." As discussed in Deut. 25:5–10, the brother of a deceased man who has died without leaving children is to marry the widow. The children born from such a union are to be considered the dead brother's children and thereby "perpetuate his brother's name in Israel." On the one hand, this law might be interpreted as a male-preserving, male-protecting law, and Tamar's actions in 38:13–19 would be a wife's act of devotion to her dead spouse. The man's reproductive powers extend in this way even beyond the grave. In a symbol system like that of ancient Israel without belief in bodily resurrection, offspring are one's afterlife. In a world in which the souls of the dead are confined to a dismal place much like Hades, called Sheol, it is especially important to have one's name preserved among the living.

Within the confines of this male-centered world, however, the law of the levirate (brother-in-law) is also important to the widow herself. Under her father's protection and control as a virgin, she is, like Rebekah, transferred to the care and keeping of her husband and his family. Once married into her husband's family, she is to be a faithful and fruitful wife, providing children, especially sons. The barren wife is an anomaly, for she is no longer a virgin in her father's home, but she does not produce children in her husband's. Even more anomalous is the young childless widow who has no hope of becoming a fruitful member of her husband's clan once the husband is dead. Indeed, she has altogether lost her tie with that clan. Yet she, like the barren wife, no longer belongs in her father's household. The law of the levirate suits a male-centered symbol system in that it neatens up that which has become anomalous according to the categories of that system. But the law must have also saved young childless widows from economic deprivation and from a sort of social wilderness, no longer under father, but having no husband or son to secure her place in the patriarchal clan.

Onan takes Tamar as his wife, but instead of helping her to conceive Er's children, he practices a primitive form of birth control and spills his semen on the ground. Onan's refusal to help create another man's children, to become a surrogate father for the dead brother, can be explained in economic terms. Onan might prefer to divide his inheritance with the one remaining brother than to divide it among Er's descendants, his own, and Shelah's. God, whose voice and opinion are also the author's, condemns this selfishness and kills Onan. God's displeasure with Onan is not to be interpreted as an author's condemnation of birth control, but as a condemnation of Onan's refusal to raise up children in his brother's name and in the process to regularize Tamar's place in the social structure.

Judah's next step should have been to wed Tamar to his youngest son Shelah, but he hesitates, fearing that Shelah would die also (38:11). Perhaps Judah fears Tamar as a witch of sorts who kills her lovers or as the lover of a demon who will not share her with any human man (cf. the book of Tobit). He puts Tamar off, telling her to return to her father's home until Shelah grows up, but as 38:11 indicates, Judah has no intention of giving the woman to his only remaining son. Tamar returns to her father's house, neither a virgin nor a wife nor a mother. She is on the fringes of the Israelite social

structure, for nowhere does she properly belong. Tamar, the person of uncertain status, is thus the perfect candidate to become a trickster. Through deception she is able to confront those with the power to improve her status and to gain what she desires.

Tamar hears that Judah, whose wife has recently died, has gone to Timnah to shear his sheep (38:12–13). Tamar takes off her widow's clothing and assumes the disguise of a prostitute. Veiled, she waits for Judah at the entrance to Enaim. This trickster's disguise is an excellent symbolization of her status. As she is at a geographic border, so she is at a transition point in the course of her life. She is dressed as a prostitute, a woman whose sexual role is neither virgin nor wife. So is the real Tamar, though in a different way. Deception through sexual allure is a favorite motif in traditional trickster tales. As in Genesis 12, the attractive woman is not who she appears to be.

Judah sees her, thinks she is a prostitute, and asks her for sex (38:15–16). She demands to know what he will pay her, playing her role beautifully (38:16), and finally takes as a pledge his signet seal, the cord from which the seal hung, and his staff, which was probably marked with his seal. He promises to exchange a kid for them later as payment. As in the case of Laban's gods, Judah's possessions are a sign of his identity, his authority, and his self. Like a signet ring, the seal bore in relief the man's sign and would be used to make impressions on objects or documents to indicate ownership or origin. Only a man would carry a staff whether for support or defense. Tamar thus takes symbols of the very personhood of Judah.

He has intercourse with her and she conceives (38:18). She resumes her widow's garb, and when Judah sends his friend to exchange the kid for his things, the prostitute has disappeared. He tells his sidekick to let the matter drop "lest we become objects of contempt," having been fooled by the prostitute. Little does he realize how much the fool he has been.

When it is discovered that Tamar is pregnant, it is Judah, patriarch of the family into which she had married, not her own father, who is in charge of her fate. Again one sees law and custom enforced by the patriarch and not by some external group of elders or priests. The family headed by the patriarch is a self-contained microcosm of the larger community and its customs. Judah's decision is swift, unconsidered, and cruel. Tension in the story is heightened. "Bring her out and let her be burned"

(38:24). Is he happy finally to be rid of the woman he holds responsible for the death of his wicked sons? But Tamar, the trickster, sends to him the tokens of signet, cord, and staff with the message, "It was the owner of these who made me pregnant" (38:25). Judah recognizes his possessions—how could he deny his own seal? He acknowledges them and accepts responsibility, saying that Tamar is more righteous than he because he had not given her to Shelah.

Genesis 38:26 ends on an interesting note: Not again did he know her (sexually). Is this a later editorial comment by a writer anxious to minimize Judah's having sex with his daughter-in-law in light of the prohibition against incest in Lev. 18:15? The comment might also be read as a more integral part of the story. Judah, now more fearful than ever of the woman who survived two husbands and boldly bettered him, keeps his distance from her. Tamar, like Rebekah, gives birth to twin heroes, the mark of a special matriarch. From the younger, Perez, will be descended Boaz, the husband of Ruth, whose tale is very much like that of Tamar. Both women contribute to the genealogical line leading to Israel's greatest hero, David. Tamar's rise in status is to be understood within a particular symbol system. She is now under the protection of the patriarch and has produced sons for the line. The tale does not criticize the rules of the social structure overtly, but like the scene in Gen. 31:14–16 insists on a man's maintaining the status and rights allowed the woman within the system. Like the prelude to the story of the stolen teraphim (31:15–16), Genesis 38 provides an implicit critique, for one sees how easily even these rights can be abrogated.

*The female victim as bait: Trickery as vengeance (chap. 34).* Genesis 34 is another tale of trickery involving an aspect of female sexuality. In this case, however, the woman Dinah, daughter of Jacob, is not merely a victim of neglect as is Tamar. She is raped by Shechem, the son of Hamor. The question of status that is addressed through trickery is not her status but that of her brothers, whose rightful territory—that is, one of their women—has been breached by an outsider. The narrative not only is about women's status and rape but also deals with the relation between generations and with questions of marriage outside the kinship group.

Dinah goes out to visit the women of the land and is raped by Shechem. A strong impression is conveyed of insider versus outsider, us versus them. Within one's family is safety; among the people of the land lies danger. The Hebrew word for rape is from a root meaning "to be bowed down, afflicted." So the Israelites' oppression in Egypt is described. Yet the assumption in 34:3 is that such affliction is not incompatible with love. Verse 3 says that Shechem's soul is drawn to Dinah, that he loves her and speaks tenderly to her. He asks his father, Hamor, to obtain her for him as a wife.

One of the most striking aspects of the narrative is the degree to which Dinah is absent and present. She is, on the one hand, central to the action, the focus of Shechem's desire, the object of negotiations between Jacob and Hamor, the reason for her brothers' trickery, and the cause of tension between Jacob and his sons. On the other hand, she has no dialogue, no voice. How does she react to Shechem's speaking "tenderly" or to Jacob and Hamor's arrangements for her marriage to the rapist? What, for that matter, happens to her at the end of the story? She seems to fade out after her brothers retrieve her (34:26).

Does a thread in this tale, as in the story of the Benjaminites in Judges 21, condone wife stealing as one way in which new peoples are created? Jacob does not condemn the whole affair but "keeps silent" (34:5) and prepares to do business with Hamor. The brothers Simeon and Levi, however, consider Shechem's rape of Dinah a shocking outrage. How dare he take the daughter of Jacob without permission. And what of their feelings for Dinah or the narrator's? She is described as having been made unclean (34:5, 27). Like a prostitute, she has become a person of outsider status, unfit to be a bride. The brothers describe Shechem as having treated their sister like a harlot and condemn him and his kin to death. Once raped, however, Dinah is so consigned to the background of the story that the issue which emerges is less her status as a sufferer than the status of the men who control her sexuality. Shechem has raped Dinah but, in the point of view of the narrator, by doing so he shows lack of respect for the persons of Jacob and the brothers, lack of respect for the proper way of establishing kinship relations. Hamor attempts to mend matters after the fact with promises of trade (34:21) and proper marriage relations. Simeon and Levi reject his offer but not directly. They are, after all, sojourners in what is still the land of the Canaanites, God's promises for the future notwithstanding. Their position is a precarious one, as Jacob himself indicates (34:30), and so they take their vengeance through trickery.

In contrast to Gen. 31:30–35 and Genesis 38, the trickster is not the wronged woman. In contrast to Genesis 27, the point of view is clearly male. Genesis 34, not unlike the tale of Samson and the Timnites in Judges 14–15, is about a feud between two groups of men over ownership of one group's woman. Whereas Jacob is willing to make accommodation with the Canaanites for the sake of peace and to gain, in exchange for Dinah, permission to stay in the land and trade there, the brothers, more hotheaded and concerned for matters of face than the old man, prepare a deception using Dinah's sexuality as bait. They lie to Hamor, stating that if he and all males among his people will circumcise themselves, then they will let Shechem have Dinah and engage in further exchanges with them. Hamor agrees, and while his warriors are incapacitated, uncomfortable from the surgery, Jacob's sons attack. They kill all the men, "slaying them with the sword," taking all the enemies' possessions, their children, and their wives as booty. It is an act that evens the score but also serves as a reminder that wife stealing and rape were regularly associated with war in ancient Israel, even when the reason for war had nothing to do with ownership of the women.

Genesis 34 shares with the other trickster tales about women the pattern of a problem in status, deception to improve status, and success of the plan. The rape lowers Dinah's status but also that of her father and brothers, and it is their status that most occupies the author. Dinah herself does not engineer a deception that will restore her status, but instead she becomes a motif in the artful deception by her brothers. Their status is raised in turn by the success of their plan and the theft of other women, while Dinah's lowered status remains. Genesis 34 confirms that tales in which women are important to the action are most often about relations between men, at least in narratives as strongly marked by the male voice as this one. Men are the protagonists of the trickster pattern; the woman Dinah serves as an occasion for their contest, as the wives and daughters of Hamor mark its closure. The women are thus on the turning points and borders of narrative action in this tale echoing the patterns of actual women's economic and sociostructural roles in all traditional cultures, as those who go between the men of marrying groups and between generations of men within their own families.

*Women in the Joseph tales (chaps. 37; 39–50).* *The comparative absence of women in the Joseph tales.* The Joseph narrative has no heroes who are tricksters, and its women are only two: Asenath, daughter of Potiphera, priest of On, mentioned in one line (41:45) as part of the reward given to Joseph for successfully interpreting Pharaoh's dream, and Potiphar's wife, a stock character portrayed as one of the challenges in life faced by the wise hero. Whereas women find many places in the stories about marginals who enjoy temporary success but remain at odds with the establishment, they are virtually absent from the Joseph tales of Genesis, which are more confirming of authority and the status quo.

*Potiphar's wife (chap. 39).* The story of Potiphar's wife's attempted seduction of Joseph is often compared to the ancient Egyptian "Tale of Two Brothers." In each, the upright and trustworthy person who works for a superior (Potiphar in the case of Joseph and the elder brother in the Egyptian tale) is propositioned by the superior's wife. The younger man rejects her and remains loyal to his superior, whereupon the scorned woman accuses the young man of attempted rape. This plot is found in a wide range of traditional tales and in many popular works of modern fiction.

The tale of Potiphar's wife emphasizes themes found throughout the biography of Joseph. Recurring language indicates that everything touched by Joseph prospers because God is with him (see 39:2, 3, 5, 6, 8, 9). Seeming misfortunes in Joseph's life inevitably turn to Joseph's benefit and to that of Israel (45:7, 8). Thus the serious charge that Joseph attempted to cuckold his master does not lead to his death but to the royal prison. There Joseph interprets the dreams of fellow prisoners, one of whom later recommends Joseph to the Pharaoh as one who can interpret his troubling dreams of cows and sheaves. The incident of Potiphar's wife is one more link in a chain leading inevitably to Joseph's becoming vizier of all Egypt. Finally, the tale contributes to the portrayal of Joseph's character. This is the same, almost-too-honest Joseph who reports to his parents the dreams that predict that he will come to dominate them, the same Joseph who reports to his father about his brothers' indiscretions. The characterization of the almost-too-good-to-be-true Joseph is consistent throughout the narrative. He is a wisdom hero, a type represented in the biblical court narratives of Daniel and the book of Esther and in ancient Near Eastern works such as the story of Ahikar.

As has been noted, the wisdom hero lives by the sort of advice offered in wisdom collections such as the biblical book of Proverbs. One of the dominant themes in Proverbs is to keep one's distance from the loose woman, the adulteress (Prov. 2:16–19; 5:1–23; 7:6–27). Joseph exemplifies the wise man: hardworking, sober, God-fearing, and able to resist forbidden fruit. Potiphar's wife exemplifies the female personification of anti-wisdom: disloyal to her husband, quick to seek satisfaction in forbidden places, strongly sexual, and duplicitous. In vengeance she uses the garment she has ripped from Joseph to accuse him of her own misdeed. Her accusation to the servants (39:14–15), repeated to her husband (39:17), echoes the accurate description of what had happened in 39:12–13, but now recasts the information in a lie. Wisdom and anti-wisdom, truth and lies, are thus reverse images.

What sort of view of women is found in this tale and what sort of narrator's voice? The image of the vengeful and conniving woman scorned is an archetype more meaningful to men than to women, a means of asserting the male's desirability and innocence, projecting all sexual desire onto the woman who is a manifestation of the feminine frightening to men. She is aggressive, independent, and sexually demanding. Such women never prosper in the Hebrew Scriptures. In this scene Joseph is the marginal character, a foreign exile and a slave, while Potiphar's wife is his superior; and yet Joseph is no trickster. He is a different sort of hero, and his is a different sort of literature from that found in the tales of the matriarchs and patriarchs. Whereas the latter repeatedly describe the trickster's challenge to authority and include many women tricksters who make their way as marginals within a male-oriented system, the stories of Joseph suggest that if a man has God's favor and lives wisely, he can succeed in becoming a part of the ruling establishment itself.

## Conclusions

The women of Genesis are markers and creators of transition and transformation. In some sense their narrative roles parallel social positions of and attitudes toward women in male-dominated cultures in which women are marginal in terms of economic or political authority. Yet paradoxically their roles as the people "in between" can be powerful and critical for the development of the stories and for the progress of human civilization and Israelite culture as perceived by biblical writers. Without Eve, the present world would not exist. Without Rebekah, Jacob would not have fathered the people of Israel.

The women succeed in behind-the-scenes ways, through the medium of trickery, and their power is in the private rather than the public realm. They evoke sympathy as those whose rights are unstable and always at risk, for the line between successful tricksters such as Rebekah, Rachel, and Tamar and victims such as Dinah and Hagar is easily crossed. The tale of Potiphar's wife implies a culture in which powerful women are regarded with suspicion, as unnatural and evil. The voice that lies behind the tales of the matriarchs and patriarchs is markedly different from the voice underlying the tales of Joseph. Only the former are imbued with attitudes of those outside the establishment and speak with the voice of the feminine.

## BIBLIOGRAPHY

Jeansonne, Sharon Pace. The Women of Genesis: From Sarah to Potiphar's Wife. Minneapolis: Fortress Press, 1990.

Meyers, Carol. Discovering Eve: Ancient Israelite Women in Context. New York: Oxford University Press, 1988.

Niditch, Susan. Chaos to Cosmos: Studies in Biblical Patterns of Creation. Studies in the Humanities 6. Chico, Calif.: Scholars Press, 1985.

———. Underdogs and Tricksters: A Prelude to Biblical Folklore. New Voices in Biblical Studies. New York and San Francisco: Harper & Row, 1987.

Phipps, William E. Genesis and Gender: Biblical Myths of Sexuality and Their Cultural Impact. New York: Praeger Publishers, 1989.

Speiser, E. A. Genesis. Anchor Bible 1. Garden City, N.Y.: Doubleday & Co., 1964.

Trible, Phyllis. "A Love Story Gone Awry." In her God and the Rhetoric of Sexuality, pp. 72–143. Overtures to Biblical Theology. Philadelphia: Fortress Press, 1978.

Westermann, Claus. Genesis 1–11: A Commentary. Translated by John J. Scullion, S.J. 3 vols. Minneapolis: Augsburg Publishing House, 1984.

# EXODUS

## Drorah O'Donnell Setel

## Introduction

### Narrative Summary

Exodus, the second book of the Hebrew Bible, records the events surrounding the enslavement of the Israelites in Egypt, their redemption from bondage, and their journey in the wilderness, including the divine revelation at Sinai and the building of the tabernacle. It continues the narrative begun in the book of Genesis detailing the special relationship between the descendants of Abraham and Sarah and their deity. At the same time, Exodus represents a further stage in the history of the people, whose growing numbers necessitate the development of new forms of law and leadership. On various levels, both literal and metaphoric, the Exodus narrative relates the people's movement from powerlessness to self-determination as they are transformed from an extended family into a nation.

The content of Exodus can be viewed as consisting of two basic divisions: chaps. 1–18, which concern the redemption and flight from slavery, and chaps. 19–40, which recount the covenantal, cultic, and legal revelations at Sinai.

The opening chapters of Exodus (1–4) focus on the oppression of the Israelites and the selection of Moses as their divinely appointed leader. Moses and Aaron then represent the people before Pharaoh, demanding release for the Israelites (chap. 5). These encounters are presented as an opportunity for Yahweh, the deity of the Hebrews, to demonstrate superiority over the forces of Egypt, both political and divine, through a series of miraculous acts and afflictions (chaps. 6–12). Interspersed with passages concerning the establishment of the festival of Passover and the redemption of firstborn sons, the narrative proceeds to relate the divinely

guided escape of the Israelites from the Egyptians (chaps. 12–14). The climax of the section is the victorious Song at the Sea (chap. 15), attributed to both Moses (15:1) and Miriam (15:21). The following chapters provide both a literal and a thematic transition to the Israelite encampment at Sinai (15:22–18:27).

The Sinai section of Exodus (chaps. 19–40) begins with the dramatic covenantal revelations at the mountain, including the Decalogue (the Ten Commandments, 20:1–17). A long legal code follows, addressing both social and religious regulations (20:21–23:33). After overseeing the formalization of the covenant between the Israelites and Yahweh, Moses ascends the mountain and receives further divine instruction (chaps. 24–31). This revelation includes commandments concerning the construction of a wilderness sanctuary (the tabernacle, chaps. 25–27; 31); the vestments, consecration, and rites of the priesthood (chaps. 28–30); and the observance of the Sabbath (chap. 31). Moses' sojourn on the mountain is followed by the incident of the golden calf (chap. 32). Moses later returns to the mountain and is given additional divine teachings, which he brings back to the people (34:1–35:3). He then initiates and supervises the building of the tabernacle (35:4–39). The book of Exodus concludes with the consecration of the tabernacle and the entry of the divine presence into it (chap. 40).

### Historical Issues

**Date of text and authorship.** Contemporary scholars consider the current text of the first four books of the Hebrew Bible, including Exodus, to combine several original sources

26

that were probably edited during the sixth century B.C.E. Thus, Exodus reflects traditions dating from various periods. Included in the book is an example of some of the earliest Hebrew poetry (the Song at the Sea, chap. 15), narrative sections attributed to the time of the early monarchy, some legal codes that may have originated prior to the monarchy and others that are dated to priestly circles of the exilic or postexilic era.

***Representation of female traditions.*** Because the final editing of the text as we have it was in all probability the work of men with concerns specific to the priesthood, it is difficult to determine the extent to which the stories and traditions related to women reflect actual female experience. Given the sex-segregated culture of ancient Israel, it seems probable that distinct female traditions emerged simultaneously with the better-preserved male heritage. The inclusion of stories centered on independent women, such as the midwives (Shiphrah and Puah) and Pharaoh's unnamed daughter, may indicate the preservation of such traditions that, by virtue of their antiquity, were deemed inviolate by later editors. Such suggestions can, however, be merely speculative. They raise as many questions as they may answer: Should one assume that only women would tell stories focused on female characters and/or domestic issues such as childbirth? Or, conversely, should one exclude material concerning men from female authorship?

In the absence of clearer evidence regarding the origins of biblical material, feminist methodologies require that such issues remain open. For some, the possibility that biblical writings may reflect ancient women's traditions is an important source of empowerment and a sense of relationship to biblical traditions as a whole. Others are more concerned with developing a rigorous historical reconstruction of ancient Israelite culture and understanding, within that framework, whether and how women may have played a role in the development of specific biblical materials. The contents of the book of Exodus combine apparently female-centered texts, texts that explicitly exclude women, and a substantial amount of material open to varying interpretations regarding the significance of sex and gender.

***Historicity of the exodus story.*** The historical character of the events described in the book of Exodus is the subject of much debate.

Although the enslavement, liberation, and wilderness journey of the Israelites are of great importance within the context of the biblical writings, there are no extrabiblical sources to confirm their actual occurrence. Attempts to pinpoint a date for the exodus are similarly stymied by an absence of supporting resources. For the most part, scholarly reconstructions focus on the thirteenth century B.C.E.

Conflicting traditions regarding central events, such as the revelation at Sinai or Horeb, as well as distinctions between the northern (Leah) tribes and the southern (Rachel) tribes suggest that an exodus event may have been the experience of only a portion of the people who came to regard themselves as Israelites. Rather than trying to reconcile the apparent ethnic and historical diversity reflected in biblical traditions, some scholars now posit that a smaller "Moses group" was the source of the complex of traditions surrounding slavery, exodus, and Sinai. In joining with other West Semitic peoples, this group maintained leadership and hence the retention of their formative stories.

## General Themes

***Slavery and liberation.*** The English title of Exodus reflects the centrality of the transition from bondage to freedom in the concerns of the book; however, the materials concerned with the condition of the Israelites in slavery and their flight from Egypt constitute only half of the book. The Hebrew word for Egypt (*mitsrayim*) can also be understood as "place of constriction," a contrast to the open spaces of the wilderness and the promised abundance of the land of Israel. Thus it is possible to view these themes as metaphorically describing a process of spiritual as well as physical empowerment. It may be argued that within the biblical context, the wanderings in the desert, revelation at Sinai, and construction of the tabernacle are equally significant aspects of the process of liberation. From this perspective, freedom is not merely a flight from or a reaction to oppressive circumstances but also a positive movement toward a sacred objective. In addition, Exodus portrays liberation as a process entailing death as well as rebirth, sorrow as well as joy, and destruction as well as creation. The long-suffering of the slaves, the killing of their sons, the plagues, the death of all Egyptian firstborn males, and the drowning of Pharaoh's army are all part of the price paid for the Israelites' freedom.

**Divine sovereignty.** Throughout Exodus, the omnipotence and omnipresence of Yahweh, the Israelites' deity, are emphasized through acts of revelation (3:2–4:17; chaps. 19–20), the control of nature (7:20–11:10; 14:21), and the images of divine leadership (15:1–21). The allegiance of the Israelites to their divine sovereign is contrasted to the ultimately limited power of the human ruler, Pharaoh. Within the Israelite community, the authority of Moses is justified only by divine election.

**The life of Moses.** The central human figure in the Exodus narrative is Moses. From a literary perspective, his biography fits a legendary pattern that includes miraculous survival at birth (2:2–10); concealment and flight (2:15); divine calling (3:4); and victorious leadership (14:1–31). Within the context of Exodus, however, Moses is not merely a solitary exemplary figure but also a particular embodiment of the larger community he represents. For example, his individual birth and maturation parallel the origins and growth of the Israelites' movement toward liberation. Moses' initial hesitation at the responsibilities of leadership (4:10) is later echoed in the people's resistance to the demands of freedom (16:2–3). At the same time, there are clearly ways in which the biblical narrative sets Moses apart not only from his community but from all other human beings. Most significant in this regard is his relationship with the deity. Moses serves as Yahweh's representative and chosen communal leader, and he alone of all people encounters the deity "face to face" (33:11; see also Num. 12:6–8, where his unique status is reaffirmed).

**Covenant.** The nature of the relationship between Yahweh and the people of Israel is a central concern throughout the Hebrew Bible. In the book of Exodus it is given the characteristic of a covenant (berit). In contrast to the narratives in Genesis, which focus on agreements between individual patriarchs and the deity (e.g., Gen. 12:1–3), in Exodus it is the larger community that enters into the covenant (Ex. 24:3–8), although it is questionable whether women constituted a part of that covenantal body (see "Women and Covenant," below).

Scholars have related the language of biblical covenant to various forms of treaties found among other cultures adjacent to ancient Israel. What is unique to the biblical writings, however, is the application of this partnership agreement to theological understanding. The transference of the political institution of covenant to a seemingly religious context is a reminder that Israelite society did not distinguish between these spheres of life. The stipulations of the covenant made in the wilderness cover a wide array of ethical, juridical, familial, political, theological, and cultic concerns. For a modern reader, the notion of partnership implied by the term "covenant" may be misleading. In the Hebrew Bible, as well as in ancient Near Eastern sources generally, covenants are by no means agreements between equals. In the Exodus covenants it is Yahweh alone who sets the conditions, requires obedience to them, and establishes the penalties for transgression.

**Tabernacle.** The construction of the tabernacle occupies the final section of the Exodus text. It provides the only biblical example of active female participation in an activity related to the official cult (35:22, 25–26, 29). In contrast to even the revelation at Sinai, there is an explicit, albeit minor reference to women's inclusion among those who constitute "the people of Israel" (35:29). Details concerning the furnishings of the sanctuary hint at connections to earlier and contemporary worship of female deities (see "Women and Religion in Exodus," below).

## Women and Exodus

**Evidence concerning women's status.** Despite suggestive fragments in the Exodus text concerning female experience, the overall picture presented here, as in other biblical materials, is that of a society in which women were perceived as secondary and were excluded from positions of valued status and authority. Whether this is an accurate portrayal of the whole of Israelite society over time or whether it is merely a reflection of the attitudes of the final editors of the text is a matter of debate. It is possible to regard the stories of women found in Exodus, as elsewhere in the Bible, as records of those whose experience was exceptional rather than representative of the status of women in general. Conversely, such stories can be seen as the only surviving evidence of historical periods in which women's experience differed from later, more familiar patterns.

The evidence concerning women's status presented by Exodus is inconclusive. Women such as the midwives, Pharaoh's daughter, Jochebed, and Miriam are presented in a variety of roles involving autonomous action. No later comment on these activities is presented. This may indicate that these women were not considered unusual nor their status in need of explanation. Yet Exodus also contains numerous texts that record a much more limited concept of female status and capability, such as the passage in chap. 19 that instructs "all the people" to prepare themselves for the coming revelation by staying away from women for three days (19:15). Such an apposition between women and "all the people" argues strongly against any view of women as significant, let alone equal, members of the society.

These apparently contradictory positions may reflect not only diverse opinions but diverse contexts in which female (or male) status was evaluated. Within what appears to be an exclusively female sphere of birth and child-rearing, women act without male authority (1:17; 2:2–10). Inasmuch as she is portrayed as leading a celebration of women, the same may be true of Miriam's role as a prophet (15:20). From a perspective concerned with the political and religious spheres of men, however, women become subject to control and exclusion (e.g., 19:15; 21:7).

**Women and leadership.** The opening chapters of the book of Exodus introduce numerous women who play significant, although unelaborated, roles in the events described in the narrative. Their stories may be the remnants of a larger cycle that recorded women's as well as men's involvement in the leadership of the people. The texts we do have imply that to the extent women provided guidance they acted either in rebellion (1:17), without explicit authority (4:25), or within a separate female sphere (15:20–21).

One way in which the women of Exodus provide unauthorized leadership is through acts of intervention. The refusal of the midwives Shiphrah and Puah to carry out Pharaoh's order prevents the murder of Israelite boys (1:15–19). Decisive actions on the part of Pharaoh's daughter (2:5–6), the woman identified as Moses' sister (2:7), and Zipporah (4:25) are crucial to Moses' survival.

**Women and the priesthood.** The historical and cultural setting from which ancient Israel emerged was one in which women as well as men had official cultic roles. In seeking to explain why Israel alone excluded women from religious functions, biblical scholars have frequently assumed that female functionaries in neighboring societies served in a sexual capacity (e.g., as "sacred prostitutes") and viewed their exclusion as an Israelite rejection of such activity. An alternate perspective recognizes the possible diversity of women's religious roles in the ancient Near East (e.g., as cultic singers or oracular speakers) while noting their universal exclusion from activities related to blood sacrifice. The work of sociologist Nancy Jay points out a relationship between blood sacrifice and the institution of patrilineal descent (i.e., tracing descent through the male line). Thus, it may have been a developing association of the Israelite priesthood with blood sacrifice or a concern with establishing patrilineage, rather than a dissociation from ritualized sexuality that led to women's exclusion from the cult.

Exodus contains several indications that Israelite women originally may have had a religious status from which they were later barred. The lineage, actions, and title ("prophet") attributed to Miriam, as well as Zipporah's connections to a priestly household (2:16) and an apparently sacrificial act (4:25), point to a cultic status that was forgotten or repressed in the compilation of the text as it has been handed down.

**Birth imagery.** Stories and images of birth serve as metaphors of liberation in Exodus. While there is no acknowledgment of birth as an explicitly female expression of divine power, women are central to several of these stories. It is midwives, in fact, who initiate resistance to Pharaoh's oppression of the Israelites (1:17). The very emergence of the people from confinement in Egypt occurs through a dramatic image of birth: the parting of the waters of the sea. As if to underline this connection, the Hebrew word for Egypt (mitsrayim) is also associated with labor pains (see, e.g., Jer. 49:24).

A related image is that of water, conveying both the symbolism of amniotic fluid and the oceanic origins of life. Numerous women are associated with water in Exodus: Pharaoh's daughter, who bathes in the river from which she also draws out Moses (2:5); Miriam, who first appears at the banks of the river (2:7) and is last mentioned in Exodus at the shore of the sea (15:21); and Zipporah, who, like Rebekah and Rachel (Gen. 24:15–20; 29:9–10), is associated with the water of a well (Ex. 2:15–17).

## Exodus and Feminist Theology

*Immanence and transcendence.* Feminist perceptions concerning the oppressive nature of static hierarchies and dualistic modes of thought have led feminist theologians to develop concepts of the sacred based in values of diverse relationship and personal identification. Despite the dominant portrayals of Yahweh as king, warrior, and commander, Exodus also offers immanent images of the deity as present within the community. References to the divine glory (e.g., 24:16–17; 40:34–35) suggest a perceptible presence dwelling among the people. The smoke and fire by which the Israelites make their way through the wilderness (13:21) are images of divine guidance that do not rely on human metaphors. Yahweh is also referred to as a healer (15:26). In addition, Exodus emphasizes the connection between the name Yahweh and the verb "to be" (3:14), supporting an understanding of the deity as the source of being.

*Liberation theology.* The story of the exodus from Egypt has played a significant role in liberation theology. Within this framework, the unqualified advocacy for the oppressed and powerless evident in the biblical writings presents a clear model for liberation. In the United States the story of the exodus holds special significance for African Americans, who have identified their own experience of slavery with that of the Israelites. This emphasis on identification with and preference for the disempowered is an explicit and central aspect of many feminist theologies. Such a perspective has encouraged the development of a feminist approach to understanding biblical materials that evaluates the authority of texts on the basis of their affirmation of the full humanity of women. Liberation theology's understanding of the centrality of divine concern for the oppressed has also influenced feminist theologians who believe that the liberation of women is inextricably tied to the elimination of racism, classism, anti-Semitism, homophobia, and other forms of oppression.

## Comment

### Central Female Characters

*The midwives (1:15–22).* Resistance to Pharaoh's oppression of the Israelites begins with the refusal of the midwives Shiphrah and Puah to obey the royal order to kill all Hebrew boys at birth (1:15–16). Because of the ambiguous language of the text, in which they are called "Hebrew midwives" (1:15), it is unclear whether the two women are themselves Hebrews or midwives to the Hebrews. They are the only women in Exodus to act in an overtly political sphere, having direct contact with Pharaoh (1:15, 18–19). Such contact between the powerful ruler of an empire and two women who tend to the needs of slaves seems unlikely from a historical perspective. From a literary viewpoint, the brief appearance of Shiphrah and Puah within the larger exodus story is highly suggestive. As those who aid birth, they are the first to assist in the birth of the Israelite nation. Their work entails an understanding of the connection between transformation and risk, although the means by which they rebel against Pharaoh reiterates a biblical pattern of female deception (1:19; cf. Gen. 27:5–17; 31:34–35).

*Women and the childhood of Moses (2:1–10).* Numerous women make their appearance in the Exodus narrative in conjunction with the childhood of Moses. It is these women who make possible the survival and growth of the central character in the Exodus narrative; yet, in contrast to Shiphrah and Puah, they are not named. They are presented as mother, sister, daughter, or servant. Elsewhere the biblical text identifies Moses' mother as Jochebed (Ex. 6:20; Num. 26:59) and his sister as Miriam (Num. 26:59; 1 Chron. 6:3). Here they are of interest only in their relationship to the male protagonist.

Moses' adoptive mother is never named, although ironically, it is she who names him. She serves as a symmetrical counterpart of the woman who gives birth to the child and places him in the water, as she draws him up and raises him. The relationship between these two mothers is mediated through the sister. The concerns and activities of these women seem to take place in a distinct setting apart from male influence or authority.

*Zipporah (2:16–22; 4:21–26).* A Midianite of priestly lineage, Zipporah becomes Moses' wife during his flight into the wilderness (2:21). As the wife of the great prophet, leader, and in some traditions priest of Israel, it would not be surprising for such origins to be attributed to her. There are several indications, however, that

Zipporah herself may have been endowed with priestly status. Most suggestive is the passage relaying the events that take place during the journey that Zipporah and Moses make back to Egypt with their son (4:24–26).

The language of this "bridegroom of blood" episode is highly ambiguous and difficult to interpret. It begins by relating how "on the way, at a place where they spent the night, Yahweh met him and tried to kill him" (4:24). Is the deity trying to kill Moses or his son? Why? How does the specific action Zipporah takes, circumcising her son, prevent disaster? What is the significance of touching the foreskin to Moses' "feet," a common biblical euphemism for genitals? Is there any connection between this act and the sprinkling of blood in the anointing of the priesthood, as described in Ex. 29:20?

Although the specific meaning of Zipporah's action may remain a mystery, the elements of which it is composed clearly suggest ritual sacrificial significance. If that is so, this text is unique not only within a biblical framework but within the context of the ancient Near East as a whole, where there is no other evidence that women performed acts of blood sacrifice.

## Women and the Deliverance from Egypt

*Preparation (3:22; 12:1–51).* Little mention is made of women in conjunction with the preparations for the departure from Egypt. The one task specifically allotted to the Israelite women is that of taking the jewelry and clothing of the Egyptian women (3:22). From the language of the text it is unclear whether the females of the household partook of the Passover meal (12:3, 24). It is, however, possible to see a symbolic connection to women's experience in the act of smearing the Israelites' doorways with blood as a means of averting death (12:7, 22), an image suggestive of the birth passage. Although elsewhere women are depicted as the preparers of food (e.g., Gen. 18:6), the grammatical forms used to describe the preparation of the unleavened bread (12:34, 39) are masculine. In Hebrew this can mean that the subjects of the verb are both male and female or that they are exclusively male.

*Deliverance: The Song at the Sea (15:1–21).* The Song at the Sea is considered to be the oldest extant writing concerning the exodus from Egypt. In the received text the longer version of the ancient poem celebrating the divine victory over the Egyptians is attributed to Moses (15:1). Following that, however, is a shorter section that designates Miriam as the leader and presumably the author of the song (15:21). The phrase beginning "Sing to Yahweh" in v. 21 is understood as a title rather than a repetition of the poem. The fact that this citation has been preserved despite later perspectives that augment the significance of Moses while diminishing that of his sister has led scholars to conclude that the work was indeed originally preserved as her creation.

Miriam's association with the Song at the Sea challenges several stereotypes about women in ancient Israel. It conveys an image of women as singers of war songs, which is supported by other biblical texts (Judges 5; 1 Sam. 2:1–10). These militaristic hymns are among the oldest examples of Hebrew poetry. Although scholars have generally assumed that poetry, like other cultural creations, was exclusively the work of men, these examples raise the question of women's role in originating and developing poetic forms. Vocal and instrumental music, in addition to ritualized dance, may have recreated the sensations as well as the oral images of battle.

The thematic content of these biblical songs also demands consideration of the relationship between women and warfare. Within a larger cultural context, traditions surrounding the Canaanite deity Anat and the Babylonian Ishtar support an ancient Near Eastern familiarity with an image of female warriors. It is in fact Anat, rather than her divine counterpart, Baal, who may be the source of numerous militaristic qualities attributed to Yahweh. Although there is no material evidence to confirm women's actual participation in battle, modern cultural prejudices should not prevent the consideration of that possibility, especially in the early days of the settlement of Israel, when a low population may have created a demand for women's labor without discrimination. Other biblical passages mention women singing and dancing in celebration at the arrival home of victorious male warriors (Judg. 11:34; 1 Sam. 18:6–7).

Miriam's designation as a prophet and her unquestioned leadership of the victory celebration in Exodus 15 indicate that ancient Israelites were also familiar with forms of female authority that did not survive into later periods. The issue of Miriam's status is a complex one. Although she is called a prophet, her actions do not follow the patterns of oracular speech generally associated with Israelite prophecy. They do, however, suggest ritual, perhaps ecstatic, dance and song (15:20). This accords with some prophetic activity (1 Sam. 10:5) but can also be related to later traditions concerning the Levites, Miriam's tribe, as cultic musicians. Since there continued to be female prophets in Israel (e.g., Huldah, 2 Kings 22:14; Noadiah, Neh. 6:14), the title "prophet" applied to a woman would have been acceptable to later editors of the text in a way that the designation "priest" would not. Thus, it may have been that Miriam's title was changed at some point in the transmission of the traditions concerning her. In this light, it is possible to see the story of her seven-day exclusion from the camp in Num. 12:14–15 as the reverse of the priests' seven-day consecration (Ex. 29:35). Numbers 12 itself may be regarded as a legendary condensation of the story of women's exclusion from the lineage of the priesthood.

Miriam's genealogy is also complicated. In biblical references outside of Exodus (Num. 12:2; Micah 6:4), Miriam is grouped with Moses and Aaron in such a way as to suggest that the three of them formed a leadership triad. Her familial relationship with them, however, is not consistently documented. In Exodus she is identified solely as Aaron's sister (15:20). Although the narrative concerning Moses' childhood tells of a sister (2:7), she is never explicitly named as Miriam. The text states that she goes to call "the child's mother" (2:8), which seems strange if she is presumably her mother as well. In addition, Ex. 6:20 names Jochebed as the mother of Aaron and Moses but does not mention Miriam. References to Miriam as the sister of Moses as well as Aaron are found only in Num. 26:59 and 1 Chron. 6:3. Scholars view these depictions of the sibling relationship among all three Exodus leaders as deriving from later, Priestly sources rather than as original to the early narrative.

Even the meaning of Miriam's name is uncertain. No convincing arguments have been presented for its Hebrew origins. If it is, indeed, an Egyptian name, it is probably derived from a term for "love" (mer), perhaps with the implication of "beloved." Like Moses and Aaron, Miriam may be viewed as a legendary figure whose biblical biography provides insight into times and traditions now incompletely understood.

## Women and Religion in Exodus

*Representations of divinity: Names (3:13–15; 6:2–3).* The early chapters of Exodus provide two significant revelations of divine names. Moses elicits the first by asking how he should identify the one by whom he has been commanded to lead the Israelites (3:13). The answer is a simultaneously clear and ambiguous affirmation that is commonly translated "I Am Who I Am." The nature of Hebrew grammar, however, allows a range of meaning for this phrase, including, for example, "I am who I shall be" or "I shall become that which I am becoming." Furthermore, the response is a play on the Israelites' distinctive name for their deity, Yahweh, which is also a form of the verb "to be."

According to Exodus, the name Yahweh is established in contrast to the name El Shaddai (6:3). Both are uncertain in their meaning. Here El Shaddai is perceived as an earlier, patriarchal term for the deity. Although the element "El" is familiar both in Hebrew and other Canaanite languages as a name or title for deity indicating greatness or might, the origins of the term "Shaddai" are unclear. It has been traced to a term for mountain, and the name El Shaddai would thus mean "the mighty one of the mountain," more commonly, "God Almighty." However, a primary meaning of the same root word is "breast," raising the possibility that the early Israelites may have had an understanding of the deity as motherlike as well as fatherlike (see the poetic connection between the name El Shaddai and the word for breast made in Gen. 49:25).

Scholars have also been unable to trace conclusively the development of the name Yahweh. It does not specifically match known grammatical forms, although there is a consensus that it represents a masculine singular causal form of the verb "to be." The term could thus be translated "the one who causes to be," "the creator," or, less literally, "the Source of Being." Some understand "Yahweh" to be part of a longer phrase originating in a title of the Canaanite deity El as "the creator of the heavenly hosts." Later translations of "Yahweh" as "Lord" are inaccurate in a literal sense. They represent a historical substitution of the Hebrew term "Adonai," which does mean "lord," for the original "Yahweh," the pronunciation of which became forbidden and later forgotten.

*Representations of divinity: Images.* Despite a strong prohibition against depictions of the deity (20:4), Exodus presents numerous verbal portraits of divinity. In addition to the more familiar anthropomorphic depiction of Yahweh as "a warrior" (15:3), many of these images do not refer to human roles or forms. Fire appears throughout the book to represent the presence of the deity, beginning with the first revelation to Moses in Ex. 3:2. Yahweh's presence guides the Israelites on their journeying in the forms of smoke and fire (e.g., 13:21–22). Exodus 24:17 explicitly describes Yahweh's glory as "like a devouring fire on the top of the mountain in the sight of the people of Israel." At the close of the book of Exodus, the divine glory comes to rest in the tabernacle (40:34–38), which literally means "the place of the [divine] presence."

In another type of depiction, Yahweh is said to have carried the people to Sinai "on eagles' wings" (19:4). Winged images also appear in the tabernacle, where cherubim cover the ark (25:18–22). In addition to the cherubim, the presence in the wilderness sanctuary of a menorah indicates that the religion of the early Israelites maintained remnants of their Canaanite origins. While the cherubim may be seen as representations of lesser, perhaps attendant deities, the tree imagery of the menorah is associated with Asherah, who, evidence suggests, was held to be the consort of Yahweh in both popular and official belief well into the period of the monarchy.

### Women and covenant (chaps. 19; 20).
Nowhere is the secondary status of women and their exclusion from the central institutions of Israelite society more apparent than in Ex. 19:15, where those who are preparing to enter the covenant with Yahweh are exhorted "do not go near a woman." This distinction is especially striking, coming as it does after verses that describe "the people" and "all the people" as constituting the covenant-making body. It is unclear whether women can be considered part of the covenantal community that participates in the ritual described in Exodus 24. The prohibition in Ex. 19:15 can be interpreted as an injunction against sexual intercourse prior to the revelation, or it can be seen as a clear statement of the exclusion of women from the event altogether.

Presumably, the separation of women and men at this most significant moment is due to regulations concerning ritual purity and impurity. Although these concerns for ritual purity are commonly expressed in terms such as "clean" and "unclean," it is more accurate,

especially with regard to early biblical materials, to conceive of them as having to do with power rather than pollution. Activities or states that bring on ritual impurity, such as childbirth, menstruation, sexual activity, and care for the dead, all involve participation in the nexus of life and death, which is the very essence of divine power. They are the result of contact with the sacred. The ritual purification system can, therefore, be understood as making a distinction between the realm of human control and that of the divine. It is important, however, to keep in mind that within a biblical context this distinction is not the same as that between physical and spiritual. Ritual purity and impurity are states of both spiritual and physical significance. Originally, ritual purification may have been an act of renewal, acknowledging the beneficial nature of activities that continually rendered individuals ritually impure. Later, negative understandings of ritual impurity are due to a variety of factors. One was the reattribution of the life-giving female powers, present in birth and menstruation, to a male deity. This was done, in part, by using ritual purification as a demonstration of women's subservience to male authority, both divine and priestly.

The commandments in Ex. 20:1–17, considered to be at the very heart of both Jewish and Christian belief, state explicitly that it is a male community to whom they are addressed. In Hebrew, the pronoun "you" is in a masculine singular form. In translation, the subject is also clear in v. 17, which refers to "your neighbor's wife" (literally, "woman"). Like so many other biblical texts, however, this passage contains what appears to be a contradictory perspective when in v. 12 it instructs members of the community to honor mother as well as father. Likewise, in Ex. 21:15 and 17, a child may be put to death for abusive behavior toward both parents, not merely the father. These passages serve as reminders that patriarchy, as the rule of the father, is a system of domination based not only on sex and gender but also on age. Within patriarchy, therefore, women as parents have authority over children. Elsewhere it is evident that through this authority they can serve as agents, in addition to being victims, of oppression (see, e.g., Gen. 21:9–10; 1 Kings 3:23).

### Women and the cult.
Within Exodus (and the Hebrew Bible generally) women are given no authoritative role in the cult of Yahweh. It is men exclusively who serve as officiants and

men to whom the covenantal regulations are addressed. Presumably, as members of an Israelite household, women were obligated to obey regulations concerning the Sabbath, festivals, and other observances, but nowhere is this explicitly stated (see especially Ex. 20:10, where daughters and female slaves are explicitly included, but no mention is made of wives).

In the figures of Miriam and Zipporah, as well as the assembly of women at the sea (15:20), Exodus provides inconclusive glimpses of women as cultic actors. The evidence is open to numerous interpretations. One is that it represents a lost tradition of women as priests and participants in the early worship of Yahweh. Another possibility is that these texts are the only remaining testimony to the fact that women had their own community of worship, the traditions of which were not incorporated into the dominant male cult or writings. It may also be that the few references in Exodus do provide an accurate representation of women as marginal figures in the cult of Yahweh. The Hebrew Bible makes numerous associations between women and non-Yahwistic worship (e.g., 2 Kings 23:7; Jer. 44:15, 19). Perhaps as the Canaanite communities that evolved into the Israelites increasingly abandoned female representations of divinity and excluded women from the cult, the women of those communities maintained their earlier practices separately. Although women's marginalization in the cult of Yahweh may have given them special motivation to continue the old practices, there is some reason to believe that men as well as women may have continued to worship in these diverse ways at least until the Babylonian conquest and the exile in the sixth century B.C.E. The entire picture of what was and was not considered appropriate worship is very difficult to reconstruct, because the final version of the biblical text may represent an attempt to present later, more restrictive practices as normative throughout the history of Israel. In the narrative of the golden calf, Exodus 32 appears to preserve an example of a once-acceptable form of worship that was later suppressed. The calf can be related to the bull figures that served as both a symbol of and a throne for Yahweh in the northern shrines of Dan and Bethel (1 Kings 12:28–29).

***Women and the law.*** Legal codes, like other material in Exodus, reflect a mixed perspective on women. For the most part there is no consideration of female subjects. The text

is written from the perspective of male experience and is addressed to a male audience. Women enter this framework as exceptions to the (male) norm or as special cases.

Three such examples considered in Exodus are the cases of a daughter sold into slavery (21:7), violence resulting in miscarriage (21:22), and the rape of a virgin (22:16–17). All of these appear within a section termed the Covenant Code (20:22–23:33), considered to be one of the earliest of Israelite legal formulations because it reflects a rural, presumably premonarchic, society. The perspective on women offered by these examples is one in which they are understood solely as the property of fathers or husbands. In the instance of the daughter sold into slavery, it appears that the measures are intended as more protective than those extended to male slaves. Their effect, however, is to ensure that the captive woman may never leave male control. With regard to both the pregnant woman made to miscarry and the virgin who is raped, compensation is due the husband and father, respectively, indicating the extent to which women's bodies were not merely controlled but actually owned. Determining that a rapist must marry his victim (22:16) underscores the extent to which the text is devoid of female perspective.

In this context it should be noted that the Hebrew word generally translated "virgin" (*betulah*) probably indicates a young woman still within her father's household and is a term concerned with status rather than physical condition. Within this biblical framework virginity was an economic, not an ethical, concern. Furthermore, marriage in a modern sense was unknown in ancient Israel. There are, for instance, no words for "marriage," "wife," or "husband." The terms commonly translated as such mean "taking" in the sense of taking possession of something, "woman," and "master," respectively.

The same legal code, however, demands a high standard of social justice in other areas, particularly with regard to protecting vulnerable groups within the culture (e.g., 22:21–27). Throughout the Hebrew Bible, the Israelites' enslavement in Egypt is cited as the paradigmatic experience from which they are to learn compassion and to seek justice for the outsider. In some areas the Covenant Code itself provides an interesting and unusual example of gender inclusivity, where women as well as men are explicitly cited as the subjects of the law (21:17, 26–28, 31–32).

## Conclusion

For readers concerned with female experience, the book of Exodus offers an array of complex and controversial materials. Portraits of strong leaders are present along with restrictive laws; male images of the divine are interspersed with immanent forms taken from nature. These apparent contradictions are, in part, the result of differing perspectives from various historical periods represented in the final version of the text. The position of women, like all aspects of a culture, changes over time, and the materials that constitute the book of Exodus may extend over half a millennium.

Discrepancies in the text can be understood also as the inconsistencies present in any society. In ancient Israel the passion for freedom and social justice so frequently expressed in the Hebrew Bible coexists with the secondary status of women prevalent throughout the ancient Near East. In legal, economic, political, and social terms Israelite women had much in common with their Egyptian, Mesopotamian, and Canaanite counterparts, despite the existence in those cultures of normative cults devoted to female deities. These seemingly illogical complexities offer a reminder that ancient cultures should not be confused with simple ones, nor can the incomplete evidence remaining of those societies provide any definitive understanding of them.

For some feminists the stories of women such as Miriam and Zipporah provide sufficient basis for reconstructing a biblical society inclusive of the talents and traditions of women as well as men. Others view the lesser status of women as sufficient cause for rejecting the theological authority of the text while continuing to evaluate its historical significance. Yet another approach is to attempt an understanding of the relationships among disparate elements of the tradition as representing human inconsistencies present in our own societies as well as in the past. In this process of feminist exploration and debate, Exodus itself provides a clear expression of the fact that risk, loss, and great gifts are all present in movements toward liberation and transformation.

## BIBLIOGRAPHY

Burns, Rita. *Has the Lord Indeed Spoken Only Through Moses? A Study of the Biblical Portrait of Miriam*. Atlanta: Scholars Press, 1987.

Cross, Frank Moore. *Canaanite Myth and Hebrew Epic*. Cambridge, Mass.: Harvard University Press, 1973.

Jay, Nancy. *Throughout Your Generations Forever: A Sociology of Blood Sacrifice*. Chicago: University of Chicago Press (forthcoming).

Meyers, Carol. *Discovering Eve: Ancient Israelite Women in Context*. New York: Oxford University Press, 1988.

Olyan, Saul. *Asherah and the Cult of Yahweh in Israel*. Society of Biblical Literature Monograph Series 34. Atlanta: Scholars Press, 1988.

Reid, Stephen Breck. "Patriotism and Loyalty." In his *Experience and Tradition: A Primer in Black Biblical Hermeneutics*, pp. 53–83. Nashville: Abingdon Press, 1990.

Trible, Phyllis. "Bringing Miriam Out of the Shadows." *Bible Review* 5, no. 1 (February 1989), 13–25, 34.

# LEVITICUS

*Judith Romney Wegner*

## Introduction

Leviticus, the third of the Five Books of Moses that constitute the Pentateuch or Torah, forms the core of the biblical text that critical scholarship calls "P" (for Priestly source). Scholars have established that this core document, consisting of a body of rules known as the Priestly Code, begins at Ex. 24:15 and (excluding Ex. 32:1–34:28) extends beyond Leviticus through much of the book of Numbers. Unlike most other books of the Old Testament, Leviticus at first glance seems so dry and boring that readers may well think it can have little interest or relevance for the general Bible reader. Readers of *The Women's Bible Commentary* in particular could be forgiven for that assumption. After all, the book presents no portraits of individual women whose lives might repay study by women of today. Besides, what could seem less inspiring than a book that devotes its first ten chapters to the sacrificial rules of an esoteric temple cult? Why should any modern reader bother with the gory details of animal slaughter and the offering up of choice portions like the "fat covering the entrails," "the two kidneys," and "the appendage of the liver"—all so that a God called YHWH may smell the pleasing odor of the sacrifice! (Lev. 3:1–5).

However, this is not all there is to Leviticus; the book deals with many other topics. A paramount concern for the preservation of cosmic harmony in nature and society, as well as for the holiness and purity of individuals, led Israelite priests to make rules governing the day-to-day activities of priests and other Israelites, including women. The personal conduct of individual Israelites, as members of a chosen people in a covenantal relationship with God, was thought to have great cosmic significance and thus to require strict regulation in order to maintain holiness and purity. So Leviticus contains rules about various aspects of personal holiness as the priests understood this concept, including some of particular significance to women: sexual relations, childbirth, and menstruation. Exactly how *holiness* relates to these topics will be explained later.

Further, although animal sacrifice strikes the modern reader as a primitive practice, it in fact symbolizes a rather sophisticated idea found in most if not all religions of humankind. Anthropologists like Mircea Eliade have shown how religions developed out of the intellectual efforts of human beings to make sense of the cosmos. An innate craving for harmony and order prompted the view that the world was intended to be orderly rather than chaotic. When things went wrong, either in nature or in society, people perceived a breach of cosmic harmony, requiring symbolic action on their part to restore the shattered equilibrium by placating the powers that ruled the cosmos. A common response was to offer sacrifice to the tribal god or gods. Likewise, if a god had favored the group with an abundance of crops or herds, thereby tilting the balance in earth's favor, equilibrium could be restored by bringing a thank offering from those crops or herds. Or one could tilt the balance toward heaven by bringing an offering in advance, thus encouraging the god(s) to restore equilibrium by sending a good harvest in the following year. The goal of sacrifice was to maintain or restore order by neutralizing some accident or condition that had disturbed, or threatened to disturb, the balance of the cosmos.

Early rabbinic commentators called the Priestly Code the "Instruction for Priests" (*torat kohanim*). It was in fact a priests' manual for the practice of the Israelite cult in the Temple at Jerusalem. Whether this means the First (pre-exilic) Temple or the Second (postexilic) Temple or both depends on the date of composition of the book—a subject of ongoing scholarly debate. In either case the Temple is symbolized by a portable sanctuary reportedly built for God's worship during the forty years' wandering in the wilderness following the exodus.

The character of Leviticus as a priestly manual distinguishes it from all other books of the Old Testament. It is neither a myth of origins (like Genesis), nor a history (like Joshua through Kings), nor a work of poetry (like the Song of Songs), nor a philosophical treatise (like Ecclesiastes), nor a book of prophecy (like Isaiah or Jeremiah). Leviticus is primarily a lawbook. It narrates very few stories about individuals, male or female; indeed, apart from the Israelite leaders Moses and Aaron, few named individuals appear at all. The book speaks mostly to and about groups or classes of people, such as the sons of Aaron (who, so far as the Priestly Code is concerned, constitute the hereditary priesthood), or the Levite caste, or sometimes the common people, called simply "the children of Israel." Leviticus deals also with certain subgroups who were considered important in the context of cultic purity (discussed more fully below); these include sufferers from various skin diseases and genital discharges, menstruants, and men who infringe the laws governing sexual relations.

The priestly laws governing women must be viewed in the context of the entire Priestly Code. Topics covered include sacrificial rites (chaps. 1–10); dietary laws based on the fitness of particular animals for sacrifice (chap. 11); diagnosis and treatment of certain diseases (chaps. 13–14); rites of atonement for sin (chap. 16); and daily, Sabbath, and holy-day rituals throughout the year (chaps. 23–24). Into this cultic context the priests placed laws governing women's recovery from childbirth (chap. 12); regulations concerning cultic impurity generated by certain bodily emissions (chap. 15); and rules governing sexual relations and certain other matters (chaps. 17–26). It is no accident that the processes thought to generate the mysterious phenomenon of cultic impurity included such fundamental but poorly understood human experiences as childbirth (chap. 12), menstruation (chap. 15), and death (chap. 21).

The present discussion will focus mainly on the priestly rules governing sexual relations and menstruation and their relationship to holiness and purity—regulations that sociologically reflect and theologically define the place of women in ancient Israelite society. The priestly concern with sexuality affected the image and status of women as a class, through rules designed to preserve the holiness and purity of individual Israelites and of the community as a whole and thereby to maintain harmony in the cosmos. Leviticus thus sheds light on, among other things, women's perceived "place" in the private and public spheres of Israelite religious culture.

Here one must strike a note of caution: in studying Leviticus—as in Bible study generally—it is crucial to recall certain historical facts. The Israelite priests and scribes who transmitted and interpreted the biblical text during the Old Testament period worked within the framework of their national history and tradition. In the Israelite worldview, the Hebrew Bible (which Christians call the Old Testament) is more than simply "the word of God." For twenty-five centuries, Jews have treated the Hebrew Bible primarily as the *history* of their Israelite ancestors. That history was inseparable from "the word of God," understood as the direct communication between God and Israelites recorded at many points in scripture. Without remembering that the Old Testament comprises a political, literary, and cultural history of the people Israel, one cannot fully understand the book of Leviticus in the context of its time.

Above all, one must distinguish the ancient priestly cult from the rabbinic Judaism that began to develop shortly before the destruction of the Second Temple in the first century C.E. The later Old Testament books (Ezra, Nehemiah, Esther, Daniel) offer glimpses of early forms of Judaism, which grew out of the Israelite religion following the Babylonian exile in the sixth century B.C.E. But, contrary to a common misconception, the religion of the Old Testament differed considerably from Judaism as practiced in the past two thousand years. Rabbinic Judaism, though rooted in the laws of the Torah, dates only from around the turn of the era. It is technically incorrect to label the religion of the Hebrew Bible or of the Priestly Code as "Judaism." Rather, the Old Testament portrays the religion of Israel, which was destined in the first century C.E. to produce two offspring: rabbinic Judaism and Christianity.

# Comment

## Holiness and Purity: Dominant Themes of Leviticus

The paramount importance of holiness in Leviticus is most clearly expressed in the injunction "You shall be holy, for I YHWH your God am holy" (19:2; see also 11:44 and 20:26). But the meaning of holiness in the Torah in general and in Leviticus in particular is not readily apparent to the modern reader. This concept is inseparable from the companion concept of cultic purity. One must therefore know what the Israelite priests meant by holiness and purity in order to understand the purpose of priestly laws, especially those governing two topics involving the image and status of women: sexual relations in general and the phenomenon of menstruation in particular.

To the compilers of the Priestly Code, holiness meant something different from what it has come to mean to the modern mind. Today many people see holiness as the quality of a pious and probably rather ascetic individual—a saint, a priest, a pastor, a Mother Teresa. Historically speaking, the association of holiness with sexual abstinence is a distinctive development within Christianity, rooted in particular conditions of late antiquity. To grasp the meaning of holiness in Leviticus, one must set aside the specifically Christian concept and one's personal ideas about the meaning of "religion" and draw instead on the insights of the social sciences, especially anthropology, into the nature of ancient religions.

Holiness in the religion of biblical Israel resembled similar concepts found in other ancient religions, such as Hinduism. Holiness was not just a spiritual quality concerned with ethics, morality, or religious faith. These certainly played an important part, but holiness went far beyond such concerns. For the priestly caste in particular, it involved every aspect of human conduct, from rising in the morning to retiring at night. All acts of daily life were circumscribed by detailed prescriptions and proscriptions—a long list of "thou shalts" and "thou shalt nots." These included both cultic acts of divine worship (chaps. 1–10; 23–24; etc.) and ethical acts such as loving one's neighbor (Lev. 19:18, as quoted by Jesus in the three Synoptic Gospels). Also included were seemingly mundane physical acts, especially those basic to the survival of the individual and the group, such as eating (Leviticus 11) and sexual relations (Leviticus 18). Leviticus ordains that these acts be performed in a distinctive manner, subject to specified restrictions whose overall effect is to set apart or "sanctify" certain individuals and particular aspects of life.

Living in conformity with priestly regulations was designed to maintain holiness and its companion, cultic purity (designated in Rabbinic Hebrew as *qedushah* and *tohorah*). The concept of cultic purity is not readily accessible to the modern mind. Many ancient cultures believed that some bodily states or processes generated an invisible, intangible, yet somehow palpable state of impurity that impeded direct access of the human to the divine. In the priestly worldview, a man in a state of cultic impurity could not come "before YHWH" (15:14 and elsewhere) to bring an offering until he had taken prescribed steps to cleanse himself of the impurity in question. The case of a woman was different; except in one involuntary case (described in Numbers 5, and so outside the scope of this chapter), a woman never came directly "before YHWH." Acts of cultic worship belonged to the public domain of Israelite culture, from which women were rigidly excluded.

## The Place of Women in the Book of Leviticus

In the worldview of Leviticus, the holy and pure Israelite is one who lives his entire life from birth to death in accordance with the laws of the Torah. Those rules specify the conduct mandated by the chosen people's role in the divine drama of preserving and enhancing cosmic harmony, including the observance of laws of holiness and purity set down in the Priestly Code.

From this perspective, the largest and most important subgroup in Leviticus is *the entire class of women*. Women are perceived as a special class because of their role in protecting the holiness and purity of individual males with whom they have sexual contact, and thus of the community as a whole. Like other traditions preserved in the Bible, the rules governing women rest on the anthropological and sociological assumptions of the culture that produced this literature. Analysis of the priestly rules, therefore, reveals significant facts about women's image and status, both in the private sector of Israelite domestic culture and in the public arena of Israelite religious worship.

As in all patriarchal societies, the official institutions of Israelite culture and religion were androcentric (male-focused); they treated women largely as peripheral adjuncts to men's lives—an attitude succinctly expressed in God's creating for Adam a "helper fit for him" (Gen. 2:18, author's translation). Many traditional cultures (today as in times past) seek to confine women to the private sphere, emphasizing their social functions as sex partners, childbearers, and homemakers and their economic functions as cottage-industry workers who bake, cook, spin, or weave in the privacy of the home. Most ancient cultures excluded women, either by law or by custom, from the public domain of religious worship, which comprised a large part of the world of ideas and virtually defined the creative life of mind and spirit.

This view of women's place is reflected in the book of Leviticus; women are excluded from active participation in the priestly cult. The hereditary Israelite priesthood had two main functions: to perform cultic rites in a state of purity and to regulate objects or persons perceived to be a threat to the holiness of those who administered the cult. Viewing women as such a threat, the Priestly Code subjects them to special regulations designed to maintain the purity of the priesthood in particular and of Israelites in general.

## The Concept of Cultic Pollution in Leviticus

The converse of cultic purity is cultic impurity or pollution (tum'ah). This concept, found in the religions of many ancient cultures, is often associated, as in Leviticus, with vital bodily functions like eating or sexual intercourse. In addition, pollution was generated by physiological processes that people could not control, such as virulent skin diseases, genital discharges, nocturnal emissions, or menstrual flow. In Israelite religion priestly concepts of cultic purity and impurity (misleadingly rendered in most Bible translations as "clean" and "unclean") are quite distinct from popular understandings of "cleanliness" and "dirt." This crucial distinction was demonstrated in Mary Douglas's groundbreaking study of pollution and taboo, Purity and Danger. Her analysis showed that pollution "occurs" when bodily processes, insufficiently understood in primitive societies, are perceived as disturbing the harmony of the cosmos. In Leviticus these pollution-generating processes include the transition from life to death (21:1–4); the birth of new life (12:1–5); the onset of menstruation, which wastes the life-giving fluid that should ideally have nourished a fetus (15:19–24); and other uncontrollable discharges from the genitalia of males or females (15:2–12, 25–27).

While cultic pollution normally results from disruptions in the laws of nature, it may also, by analogy, result from human conduct that disrupts cosmic harmony by violating the laws of society. Anthropologists of religion believe that the notion that social misconduct actually throws the cosmos out of whack is the origin of the biblical concept of sin, meaning any violation of God's laws—ethical or cultic, individual or societal. As Baruch Levine points out, "Ancient man seldom distinguished between 'sin' and 'impurity.' In man's relation to God, all sinfulness produced impurity" (p. 74). Consequently, in the Priestly Code, any infraction of God's laws—cultic or ethical—is seen as a sin calling for appropriate expiation. The paramount pollution results from illicit sexual relations (18:6–23; 20:10–21), including adultery, incest, homosexuality, bestiality, and intercourse with menstruants. All cultic impurities must be symbolically "washed away" by a prescribed ritual of ablution followed by sacrifice to restore the shattered cosmic order. As historians of Christianity have pointed out, the purification laws of the Priestly Code form the basis of the Christian practice of baptism as a symbolic cleansing from sin. In both cases the pollution of sin is felt to exist even though it cannot be perceived by the senses; no one performing ritual ablution or baptism thinks the purpose is to remove actual physical uncleanness. Knowing that baptism evolved from the laws of Leviticus may help the Christian reader appreciate the symbolism underlying the ritual immersion still practiced by traditional Jews to this day—most notably by orthodox women every month, seven days after the end of the menstrual period.

## Women and Cultic Pollution

The Priestly Code's rules governing women are designed to maintain priestly standards of male holiness and purity. In relation to women, cultic pollution takes two main forms: (1) that generated by menstruation and (2) that caused by sexual contact with partners forbidden by the marriage laws. In the androcentric worldview of patriarchal Israel, both kinds of pollution are transmitted *by* the woman *to* the man having illicit relations with her.

### Menstruation and pollution (chaps. 12; 15).

The priestly regulation of menstruants in Leviticus 15 may be one of the most misconstrued passages in the entire Torah. Many people erroneously confuse the notion that menstruation causes "impurity" or "pollution" with the idea that the menstrual flow itself is physically unclean. That misperception probably stems from a misguided notion that everything connected with sexuality is "sinful" and hence "dirty." But biblical Israelite religion (like later rabbinic Judaism, which calls marriage *qiddushin*, "sanctification") sees sexual relations within marriage as among the highest, purest, and holiest human activities. God's first commandment was: "Be fruitful and multiply" (Gen. 1:28). Judaism has always assigned a high priority to procreation, even frowning on those who voluntarily chose celibacy over marriage, thus disobeying the divine command. Nothing connected with the divinely created sexual-reproductive function could be characterized as "dirty." Cultic purity and impurity have absolutely nothing to do with cleanliness or dirt in the popular sense of those words. The Hebrew terms *tame'* ("impure" or "cultically unclean") and *tahor* ("pure" or "cultically clean") have no linguistic or conceptual connection with the Hebrew words for "clean" (*naqi*) or "dirty" (*metunnap*). As Mary Douglas convincingly explained, notions of cultic purity and impurity generally result from lack of scientific knowledge about the causes of certain physical conditions. Menstrual taboos existed in many ancient cultures, including the early church, and persist in some Christian rites to this day; the Greek Orthodox Church still forbids women to go to the sacrament of confession during the menstrual period.

Leviticus (15:19–24) treats menstrual pollution like that caused by other genital discharges, whether occurring in males (15:2–12) or in females (15:25–27). Rules for symbolic purification by ritual immersion and for bringing an offering to expiate the pollution are prescribed for men and women alike—with one significant difference to be discussed in a later section. Leviticus 12 spells out for a woman who has just given birth a set of rules similar to those governing menstruation, concerning the period of impurity following the birth and the offering to be brought thereafter. Curiously, while the specified offering of a lamb and a pigeon is the same for either a newborn son or a newborn daughter, the period of cultic impurity incurred for a baby girl (a total of eighty days) is twice that incurred for a baby boy (forty days). No satisfactory explanation of this discrepancy has yet been found.

### Illicit sexual relations and pollution (chaps. 18; 20).

The Holiness Code (a scholarly designation for chaps. 17 through 26) sees illicit sexual relations as sources of cultic pollution that defile both those who engage in them and also the Holy Land itself. If Israelites commit these "abominations," the land will "vomit" them out as it spewed out earlier inhabitants for committing these affronts to divine will and cosmic order (18:24–30). The sexual regulations begin significantly with an admonition not to imitate the practices either of Egypt, whence God had delivered them, or of Canaan, the promised land to which God would bring them. The ensuing list of forbidden unions covers various degrees of incest, including brother–sister marriage (historically practiced by Egyptian royalty) and male homosexuality (apparently practiced by Canaanites; see Genesis 19). The point of the warning is that Israelites must set themselves apart from the surrounding nations, in their sexual practices as well as their dietary laws, which likewise distinguish between the cultically clean and unclean (11:46–47). The literal meaning of the Hebrew word *qadosh* (normally translated "holy") is actually to "set apart" (someone or something), to consecrate it to a particular use—most often, to the service of God. The Israelites, as a "priestly kingdom and a holy nation" (Ex. 19:6) are required to set themselves apart in imitation of God—"You shall be holy, for I YHWH your God am holy" (Lev. 19:2)—by observing strict rules of cultic purity in the two aspects of life most crucial to personal and national survival: food (11:44) and sex (19:2; 20:26).

The regulation of sexual conduct is as much an anthropological as a theological matter. All societies make rules restricting sexual unions in some way; even today's permissive American culture still retains the incest laws of Leviticus, though it has virtually dropped the biblical prohibition against homosexuality and has ceased to prosecute adultery as a crime. These recent legislative amendments underscore the cultural relativity of such laws.

The sexual strictures of chap. 18 are diverse. Beyond the prohibitions against adultery (v. 20); male homosexuality (v. 22; cf. Paul's condemnation of male and female homosexuality in Rom. 1:26–27); bestiality (v. 23); relations with a menstruant (v. 19); and marriage with two sisters or with a mother and daughter (vv. 17–18), the chapter mainly presents a detailed list of women standing in specified blood or marriage relationships to the Israelite male addressed by the text. Biblical scholars have traditionally viewed these incest prohibitions as expressions of sexual morality in a religious sense. But this is not their primary purpose; if it were, the prohibitions would surely include a man's daughter—yet she is conspicuously missing from a detailed list that specifies his mother (v. 7), his sister (v. 9), and his granddaughter (v. 10). This omission bothered later interpreters; rabbinic Judaism explicitly prohibits sexual intercourse with the daughter on pain of death (*Mishnah Sanhedrin* 9:1). Unable to comprehend the biblical lacuna, commentators either passed over it in silence or claimed that the daughter was somehow "included" in the mention of the granddaughter—not a very compelling argument. But if one views from a strictly legal standpoint the omission of the daughter from the list, a logical explanation does present itself—one, moreover, that sheds interesting light on the status of women in patriarchal Israelite culture.

What is primarily at stake here is the question of legal ownership by certain males of the sexual and reproductive function of certain females (see further Wegner, *Chattel or Person?*). Disregarding the special cases of the menstruant and the closely related pairs of women mentioned above, most of those with whom sexual relations are forbidden by Leviticus 18 are women whose sexual and reproductive function is the legal property of some other man related by blood or marriage to the man addressed by the text. That category includes, for instance, the man's mother (married to his father); his father's other wives, if any; his minor sister (whose sexual-reproductive function is the legal property of her father until he transfers her at puberty to a selected husband in exchange for the bride-price of virgins, Ex. 22:16–17); or his granddaughters (whose biological function belongs to their fathers in the same way). The notion that an unmarried girl's biological function belongs legally to her father can readily account for the omission of the daughter from her logical spot between the man's sister (v. 9) and his granddaughter (v. 10).

This does not mean that Israelite fathers actually practiced incest with their daughters;

the Bible offers not a shred of evidence for that. Indeed, the story of Lot (not an Israelite) and his daughters reflects moral repugnance at such an act (Gen. 19:30–38). The Priestly Code's omission of the daughter probably resulted from the preservation and transmission of a list dating from prebiblical times (when some cultures permitted fathers to use their daughters as they pleased). But the Torah certainly expects a father to protect his daughter's chastity until she reaches puberty and is married off, at which point the financial benefit of his ownership of the daughter's virginity accrues to the father in the form of bride-price (Ex. 22:16–17; see also Deut. 22:13–21).

The assumption that the prohibitions and penalties of Leviticus 18 and 20 reflect a divine imposition of sexual mores as such ignores the sociological context of biblical Israel. Most of these prohibitions reflect the fact that their violation amounted to stealing another man's property. In ancient times, helping oneself to the neighbor's wife or daughter was somewhat analogous to stealing his cow (see the Tenth Commandment, Ex. 20:14). At the same time, the Bible clearly distinguishes marriage (acquisition of a woman's sexual-reproductive function) from slavery (acquisition of the entire woman). The Israelite wife had many legal rights (spelled out in Ex. 21:10–11; Num. 30:1–16; and elsewhere) that clearly distinguish her status from that of a slave (see Wegner, *Chattel or Person?*).

### Marriage restrictions on the priestly caste (21:7–8, 13–15).

Israelite priests were charged with the sacred trust of performing various cultic rites within the precincts of the sanctuary. It was crucial that priests preserve a higher level of sanctity than Israelites in general. So Leviticus places additional restrictions on the classes of women with whom a priest might enter into marriage. Thus, Lev. 21:7–8 forbids a priest to marry a harlot or even a divorced woman, because he may not consort with any woman of dubious morality.

The prohibition against marrying a harlot testifies to Israelite culture's moral disapproval of prostitution. Yet this was not completely outlawed, provided the harlot was not legally dependent on any man. Israelite society recognized three classes of women whose sexual function did not belong to any man and hence could be used as these women pleased: widows, divorced women, and adult single women. This distinction between law and morality became conflated in modern legal systems, most of which have criminalized prostitution. Yet most ancient cultures saw nothing illegal in freely entered sexual relations between an unmarried man and an unmarried woman. Furthermore, polygynous cultures like that of the Bible applied a double standard, confining the definition of adultery to cases where the female partner was a married woman. A married man who had relations with an unmarried woman was not guilty of adultery, so there was no reason to treat prostitution as a sin or a crime. The priestly ban on marriage with a harlot was designed mainly to ensure certainty of paternity, which was essential to a hereditary priesthood.

The prohibition against marrying a divorced woman is more problematic. In Semitic systems like biblical law, a husband could divorce his wife at will, for any reason at all (still the rule in Islamic law), so being divorced did not automatically imply sexual misconduct. But an assumption that divorce somehow suggested impropriety barred divorced women from marrying priests. Moreover, the high priest, whose offspring must avoid even the slightest confusion of paternity (21:15), must marry a virgin (21:13–14). Even a widow was forbidden, lest a birth soon after remarriage raise doubts.

These rules highlight the relationship between sexuality and the biblical concept of holiness. Unlike religions that elevate celibacy above marriage, Israelite religion insisted that even its highest religious functionary take a wife and beget children. Sexuality was an integral part of human life, and marriage and paternity were indispensable aspects of "complete" manhood. Priestly sanctity is further underscored in Lev. 21:9, where the death penalty is imposed on a priest's daughter who commits harlotry (though prostitution usually invoked no penalty if the harlot was of full age and unmarried). The priest's daughter incurs the penalty not because she degrades herself but because "she profanes her father." Her flouting of priestly sanctity disgraces her family—a shame that only her death can expunge.

## Cultic Purity and the Status of Women in the Public Domain (15:13–15, 28–30)

In the private domain of Israelite culture, a woman's status depended on the existence or nonexistence of a man who legally owned her sexual-reproductive function. Normally this was the property of her husband or her father. But widows, divorced women, and the rare adult daughter not married off at puberty were legally independent (as clearly emerges from Num. 30:1–16; but see Deut. 25:5–10 for the special case of a widow whose husband died childless). These distinctions in the legal rights and powers of dependent and autonomous women are not discussed in Leviticus, where they have no relevance. The Priestly Code is primarily concerned with the temple cult, a religious activity in the public domain of Israelite culture, in which no woman—dependent or autonomous—could take part.

The rigid exclusion of women from the public religious enterprise is implicit in repeated references to "Aaron's *sons*, the priests" (chaps. 1–3). Aaron's female descendants play no role, though priests' daughters may partake of special food designated as priestly rations (10:14; 22:12–13).

The Priestly Code offers another, more subtle clue to the exclusion of women from public religious worship. This is found in chap. 15 in the purification rites for menstruants and for men or women who suffer discharges of fluid (semen, blood, or pus) from the genitalia. While the rules laid down for men and women look virtually identical (cf. vv. 13–15 with vv. 28–30), there is a significant difference. Upon recovery, both male and female sufferers must bring an identical offering to the priest at the sanctuary: two turtledoves or pigeons to expiate the impurity. But while the man is instructed to "take two turtledoves or two pigeons and come before YHWH to the entrance of the tent of meeting and give them to the priest" (v. 14), the corresponding provision for the woman is: "Take two turtledoves or two pigeons and bring them to the priest to the entrance of the tent of meeting" (v. 29). The crucial phrase "before YHWH" is missing in the woman's case. This discrepancy is no accident; it makes an important statement about the priestly perception of the differing relationship of men and women to the public domain of Israelite religious practice. There is no difference in the offering itself, nor (apparently) in the physical location to which it is brought; yet only the man is described as coming directly "before YHWH." The Israelite woman approaches God only indirectly. That the omission is intended is clear from the fact that, of the two recovered patients, only the man is required to "wash his clothes and bathe his body in fresh water" (v. 13) before approaching the sanctuary. This symbolic cleansing will restore his state of cultic purity so that he may come before YHWH. For the woman, the text does not specify purification, because she will not be coming directly before YHWH.

After the destruction of the Temple in 70 C.E., it was no longer possible for anyone, male or female, to "come before YHWH" in the technical sense. Unlike a church, a synagogue is not literally a "house of God" but rather a "house of assembly" for prayer and study (the designation "house of YHWH" being reserved for the Temple at Jerusalem). Despite the loss of the Temple, the Jewish woman's state of cultic purity remained crucial in the context of menstruation and conjugal relations. Leviticus specifically forbade contact with a menstruant (18:19; 20:18), so this rule did not lapse with other cultic pollution laws of Leviticus 15. Husband and wife must abstain during menstruation and for seven days thereafter (15:28). Following rabbinic law based on Leviticus 15, the wife must then visit the *miqveh* (ritual immersion pool) for symbolic purification prior to resumption of conjugal relations. The other purity rules became obsolete when the Temple was no more. Yet the traditional Jewish wife continues to pay monthly visits to the *miqveh*. (This is done primarily for the husband's benefit; unmarried girls who menstruate but who presumably do not engage in sexual relations are not required to immerse themselves.)

The modern mind tends to regard the *miqveh* as an outmoded relic of a primitive idea. Yet what matters is not the physical immersion but its symbolic value. Just as with Christian baptism—a symbolic cleansing from the intangible impurity of sin—so with the *miqveh*, the significance lies not in the physical act but in its spiritual symbolism. While feminists may deplore the one-sidedness of the system, observant Jewish wives and husbands perceive the monthly purification rite as a constant reaffirmation of the sanctity of marriage.

## Relative Valuations of Women and Men (27:3–7)

Leviticus 27 (an appendix to the book's epilogue) specifies monetary valuations for Israelite males and females in various age groups. These sums establish the monetary value of pledging the valuation of oneself or one's child as a donation to the sanctuary. Though the basis of these "equivalents" is not stated, Carol Meyers has suggested that they accurately assess the relative economic productivity of males and females at different stages of life. Notable is the consistently lower value assigned to females as compared with males in the same age group (27:3–7). At the most productive stage (20 to 60 years), men are assessed at fifty shekels, women at thirty. No matter how the priestly writer arrived at these figures, they reflect a discrepancy in the perceived capacity of men and women to contribute "economically" to society. Women occupied with childbearing and nurturing would have less time to devote to their "economic" labor at spindle or loom. Then, as now, the facts of life produced a differential in the biblical equivalent of male and female wages!

## Conclusion

The image and status of women in Leviticus must be viewed in the context of an ancient patriarchal system. Failure to place ancient texts in their historical and cultural setting risks the fallacy of comparing apples with oranges.

Biblical law displays three different approaches to the status of women. For the most part, the Torah treats women as persons, though—as in all patriarchal cultures—the level of female personhood (defined as the sum total of an individual's rights, duties, and powers) never equals that of men. Whenever some man legally owns a woman's sexual-reproductive function, that function—not the woman herself—is treated as the property of that man (father, husband, or, for childless widows, the deceased husband's brother). In all other cases (normal widows, divorced women, and unmarried adult women) a woman's personal status in the domain of private law was surprisingly close to that of a man. In this connection, it is noteworthy that Lev. 19:3, "Every one of you shall revere his mother and his father" (author's translation), places the mother first, a fact interpreted in rabbinic Judaism to mean that one should revere one's mother equally with one's father. Only in the capacity of parenthood does Leviticus grant women equality. But the Priestly Code's main significance for women lies in its rulings governing the public domain of Israelite religious culture. In that context, an overriding concern with holiness and cultic purity viewed women's mysterious bodily functions as a potential source of cultic pollution, which barred them from participation in the public religious enterprise.

Meaningful value judgments about Israelite society demand comparison with the status of women in surrounding cultures. Space precludes discussion here, but current scholarship by Sarah Pomeroy and others indicates that the overall position of Israelite women at the time of the composition of the Priestly Code, and in subsequent centuries, was no less favorable (and in some ways more favorable) than that of women in surrounding cultures.

## BIBLIOGRAPHY

Douglas, Mary. *Purity and Danger: An Analysis of the Concepts of Pollution and Taboo.* London: Routledge & Kegan Paul, 1966.

Eliade, Mircea. *The Sacred and the Profane.* New York: Harcourt, Brace & Co., 1959.

Levine, Baruch. *Leviticus: The Traditional Hebrew Text with the New JPS Translation.* Philadelphia: Jewish Publication Society, 1989.

Meyers, Carol. *Discovering Eve: Ancient Israelite Women in Context.* New York: Oxford University Press, 1988.

Milgrom, Jacob. "Leviticus." *Encyclopaedia Judaica,* 11:138–147. Jerusalem: Encyclopaedia Judaica; New York: Macmillan Co., 1971.

Pomeroy, Sarah B. *Goddesses, Whores, Wives, and Slaves: Women in Classical Antiquity.* New York: Schocken Books, 1975.

Wegner, Judith Romney. *Chattel or Person? The Status of Women in the Mishnah.* New York: Oxford University Press, 1988.

# NUMBERS

*Katharine Doob Sakenfeld*

## Introduction

### Place of Numbers in Pentateuch and Canon

The book of Numbers is the fourth of five books that make up the Pentateuch or Torah. These books appear first in the Bible partly because they belong there chronologically; they tell the story of God's dealing with the world and with ancient Israel from the creation onward until the Israelites are poised to cross the Jordan River into the land promised to their ancestor Abraham. But the Pentateuch appears first in the Bible also because its content is theologically foundational to understanding the rest of the Old Testament. Thus, the book of Numbers, even though it is not well known today by comparison to Genesis or Exodus, helped to provide basic religious guidance for the ancient Israelite community.

### Authorship

Biblical scholarship of the last 250 years has reached a broad consensus that the Pentateuch is a composite of materials put together over many centuries in the life of ancient Israel and attributed to Moses only very late in its history. Although there is disagreement about details, it seems likely that the first four books of the Pentateuch received their present shape during the period called the Babylonian exile (587–538 B.C.E.). It is hypothesized that this work was done by a group of Jerusalemite priests who had been exiled to the city of Babylon in Mesopotamia after its king, Nebuchadrezzar, and his army had destroyed Jerusalem. These priests drew on ancient traditions from their own religious heritage and are thus responsible for a great deal of our knowledge of Israel's priestly and sacrificial system. They also incorporated

significant portions of an earlier tradition that scholars call the Old Epic, probably written as early as the time of kings David and Solomon (about 1000–922 B.C.E.) and updated periodically in the intervening centuries.

### Literary Forms

The basic framework of Numbers is a prose narrative about Israel's forty years "In the Wilderness" (the Hebrew name for this book). Into this narrative are incorporated all sorts of other literary forms, most notably instruction for religious practice (e.g., chaps. 2; 4; 19), elaborate examples of "case law" (e.g., 5:11–31), poetry, and lists. The poetry includes a blessing (6:24–26), several songs (e.g., 10:35–36; 21:27–30), and a series of oracles in chaps. 23–24. The lists include a travel itinerary (chap. 33) and two census summaries (chaps. 1, 26). It is from these "numberings" of the people that the book received the name "Arithmoi" in the ancient Greek version and its English name "Numbers."

### Contents

Numbers is among the most disjointed books of the Bible. Although it contains a narrative sequence, many of the pieces of religious instruction and civil legislation seem to be introduced randomly, so much so that explanations of their location in the book seem artificial or arbitrary.

Scholars have attempted to outline the book in various ways. The approach of Dennis Olson in *The Death of the Old and the Birth of the New* is now gaining increasing acceptance. Olson focuses on the two censuses of the "whole congregation of the Israelites" in chaps. 1 and 26 as markers of two major divisions of Numbers. Chapters 1–25 present a picture of the original generation of Israelites, those who fled from Pharaoh's oppression in Egypt, as a sinful generation disobedient to God. By the end of chap. 25, all of this generation has died in the wilderness; chap. 26 then provides an enumeration of the second generation, born in the wilderness. This new generation, by contrast, is presented as living fully obediently and is meant to serve as a positive example to future generations. Beyond these two major divisions, it is difficult to identify a coherent outline; here only the broad contours of the sequence of material can be traced.

After the initial census of the adult males (except for the Levites), Moses is given instruction for the arrangement of the Israelite camp during the wilderness march, along with elaborate instruction for the special duties of the Levites. A census of male Levites is followed by a miscellany of laws relating to uncleanness, restitution of damages, suspicion of adultery, and nazirite vows. After the famous Aaronic benediction (end of chap. 6), the dedication of the altar and consecration of the Levites are reported. Then the people move out from the area of Mount Sinai (10:11). Complaints about food lead to the establishment of a body of elders (all male) to assist Moses (chap. 11). Aaron and Miriam complain against Moses and are rebuked (chap. 12). In an important climax of the narrative, the people refuse to obey God's command to go up into the land (chaps. 13–14). As a result of their disobedience, this first generation is condemned to die in the wilderness.

The events recorded for the remaining thirty-eight years of that generation include a rebellion against Moses (chap. 16), confirmation of Aaron's leadership (chap. 17), Moses' and Aaron's failure to "show God's holiness" (chap. 20), and the well-known story of Balaam and his talking donkey (chaps. 22–24). Again regulations of special interest to priestly groups are interspersed in the narrative.

After the second census (chap. 26), the capture of the east side of the Jordan is reported (chap. 32), and the book concludes with the people poised near the Jordan River opposite Jericho. For the most part, chaps. 27–36 give the impression of miscellaneous appendixes, including topics such as regulations for land apportionment (chaps. 27; 36), women's vows (chap. 30), and cities of refuge (chap. 35).

## Themes and Central Concerns

*Communal faithfulness.* In both explicit and very subtle ways, the narrative of Numbers deals with the meaning of living faithfully before God and with how God deals with unfaithfulness. The people's failure to enter the land (chaps. 13–14) is the central example, but their various other rebellions are also part of this theme. Throughout, women remain "invisible" within a community counted as adult males, except for the appearance of Moabite/Midianite women as the villains leading Israelite men astray (chap. 25).

*Inheritance and land distribution.* The censuses function to show that the size of the Israelite community remained constant through the wilderness period. The basis for land distribution in the promised land will be the ancestral houses identified in the second census. In this context women and their concerns play a key role, as the daughters of Zelophehad ask whether women may receive land if there are no male heirs.

*Leadership of the community.* Moses' complaint about his inability to lead single-handedly results in a cadre of divinely designated assistants (chap. 11). Challenges to leadership are made by Moses' immediate relatives (chap. 12), by the people as a whole (chap. 14), and by the Korahites (chap. 16). Moses and Aaron are rebuked for failing as leaders (chap. 20). With the significant exception of Miriam's challenge to Moses, women play no role in these leadership questions.

*Worship.* Likewise, women have at best a peripheral role in the material concerning correct worship. The duties of priests and Levites as worship leaders are specified, but these roles were reserved for men in Israelite practice. The various texts concerning offerings, sacrifices, and festivals do not make clear what other role, if any, women could play on these occasions. It seems to be assumed that among the laity the male heads of households, clans, or tribes had primary responsibility for carrying out the commanded religious rites.

*Purity.* Numbers incorporates a variety of rules concerning spiritual and bodily purity, most of which explain how to reestablish a "clean" state of being after some defilement. Defilement may come through the committing of an unintentional sin (15:22–31) or through contact with a dead body or a person with a skin disease (5:1–4; 19:1–22). In these cases the rituals appear to be applicable equally to men and women, as the inclusive phrasing of the NRSV indicates. The laws concerning nazirite vows (6:1–21) may be regarded as a special case of ritual purity, especially since the prohibition concerning contact with dead bodies is so stringent for the Nazirite (vv. 6–8). Here the law is specifically applied to women as well as to men (v. 2).

**Family relationships.** Scattered legal material provides guidance for the Israelite community in matters of family life. Most notable are the regulations concerning women who make sacred vows and concerning wives whose husbands suspect them of adultery.

# Comment

Numbers refers to women sporadically and in uneven ways. In large sections of the book they are noticeable by their absence, most deliberately with respect to priestly and levitical leadership in worship but also as they are absorbed invisibly into a community in which male spies are chosen to represent each tribe (13:2), unfaithful males use worry about their wives as an excuse for rebellion (14:3), or only males of military age are counted in each census (chaps. 1; 26). Nonetheless, women have some significant part in no fewer than nine of the thirty-six chapters of this book.

## Incidental Yet Essential

*Women as seducers (chap. 25).* In this complicated narrative, both Moabite women generally and a specific Midianite woman named Cozbi (v. 15) are portrayed in a classical biblical role of the foreign woman who leads Israel (at least the males) astray from the true God. The theme reappears, for example, in the criticism of Solomon's foreign wives (1 Kings 11) and in the requirement of divorcing foreign wives (Ezra 10 and Nehemiah 13). Here the narrator explains God's selection of the descendants of the priest Phinehas for special privilege; this honor is gained because Phinehas killed Cozbi and her lover and thus averted a threat to Israel's faith. Elsewhere in the canon the book of Ruth presents a powerful challenge to this negative perspective on foreign women.

*War captives (chap. 31).* After a military victory over the Midianites, the Israelite soldiers kill all the males but keep all the women, children, and animals as booty. An angry Moses reminds the officers that these Midianite women were responsible for the apostasy of Israel recorded in chap. 25 (the stories disagree about which women were involved) and commands that all except the virgin women be killed (vv. 17–18). The number of virgin women reported (32,000, v. 35) is surely an exaggeration, but it leaves the reader appalled at the number of others who must have been slaughtered. What became of those allowed to live was not of interest to the narrator, but Deut. 21:10–14 gives some indication of the procedures involved if an Israelite man chose to marry a war captive.

*Civilians left at home (chap. 32).* After the capture of land east of the Jordan, Moses rebukes the tribes of Reuben and Gad for asking to settle there before the rest of the land has been taken. After extended discussion Reuben and Gad are given the land on condition that they cross the river to fight alongside the other tribes. For their part, they decide to leave their children, wives, and animals settled east of the Jordan for the duration of the military action (v. 26). The story highlights the full obedience of the generation born in the wilderness, but it shows the thoughtful reader that it is solidarity among the males of Israel that is the focal point of obedience for the narrator. Reflection on the place of the women and children in this story also points to the Bible's glaring silence concerning the role of the women and children of the other tribes in the battle narratives of the book of Joshua.

## Leadership Disputes: Miriam

*Miriam's challenge to Moses (chap. 12).* Together Miriam and Aaron, Moses' sister and brother, complain about Moses' Cushite (Ethiopian) wife and go on to ask whether God has not spoken through them as well as through Moses. In the narrative, the matter of Moses' Cushite wife is quickly dropped in favor of a focus on God's pronouncement that Moses' relationship to God is indeed unique. But the Cushite wife must not be overlooked; she was presumably black, and this text has therefore played significantly in religious debates over interracial marriage. Because of their questioning, whether about Moses' wife or about his special authority, Miriam and Aaron are rebuked by God (vv. 5, 8c).

In the course of emphasizing Moses' unique position, the narrator uses Miriam as a foil. This is the same Miriam who led Israel in song after the deliverance at the Reed Sea (Ex. 15:20–21) and presumably is the sister who watched Pharaoh's daughter find the baby Moses (Ex. 2:4–8, although there she is not named). The prophet Micah remembered her as a leader together with Aaron and Moses (Micah 6:4). And yet here Miriam is severely punished for speaking against Moses, while Aaron receives no punishment at all. God's anger is kindled against both, but only Miriam becomes "leprous" (i.e., having some skin disease, probably not modern Hansen's disease, which did not occur in the Middle East until later times).

Why is only Miriam punished? One may speculate that the answer is related to the role of Aaron as priest and the rules about ritual cleanness of the priests that are known from Leviticus 21–22. The regulations of Leviticus emphasize that the Aaronic priesthood must be physically unblemished and that those priests who find themselves ritually unclean at any time must absent themselves from priestly duties and special priestly food until they are purified. Skin diseases such as that infecting Miriam are explicitly listed as a source of such uncleanness (Lev. 22:4). Since Aaron was the paradigmatic priestly figure, the one from whom all priestly lineage was descended, it probably was not conceivable to the narrator that Aaron could be presented as contracting such a skin disease. This "narrative impossibility" was further compounded by the great care exercised by the Priestly writers throughout Exodus and Numbers to achieve a delicate balance between the power and authority of Moses and Aaron. This balance would clearly be upset if Aaron were pictured as unclean and outside the camp. Our modern question of "unfairness" to Miriam does not appear to have worried the ancient storytellers; at least they did not express any explicit concern for the difference in treatment of Aaron and Miriam.

If the reason for Aaron's escape is difficult to fathom, it is equally difficult to interpret God's response to the intercession of Aaron to Moses and Moses to God in Miriam's behalf. Their request for her healing is met with the command that she "be shut out of the camp for seven days, and after that she may be brought in again" (v. 14). Numbers 19 prescribes seven days outside the camp with certain attendant rituals in cases of impurity. According to Numbers 5, those with skin disease, male and female, are to be put outside the camp. Perhaps Aaron's and Moses' intercession is effective and Miriam, unlike other persons with skin disease, is made well at once, but with a seven-day period of ritual purification still required. Yet the unfairness of Miriam's punishment is still not erased, even on this generous interpretation of God's response.

The lineage of Miriam is a lineage of generations of women who have been rejected or humiliated for doing exactly the same thing as their male counterparts. But the larger biblical tradition presents us with another face of God, beyond the face of the One who puts Miriam out. That other is the face of God who stands close to and defends those on the "outside," a God who has likewise been rejected, put outside, by people who thought they knew best. The starkness of Numbers 12 must not be undercut, but Miriam outside the camp may point us not only to the painful arbitrariness of her situation but also, however indirectly and allusively, to the suffering of God.

**Miriam's death (20:1).** In contrast to the fuller reports of the deaths of Aaron (20:22–29) and of Moses (Deut. 34:1–8), the one-sentence statement concerning the death and burial of Miriam is uninformative. Its very brevity, with absence of detail and no reference to a period of mourning, indicates her lesser status in the tradition in comparison with her two brothers. On the other hand, that her death is reported at all suggests her importance, and the location of her death geographically and narratively functions to raise her status closer to that of her brothers.

Miriam dies in the same location (Kadesh) where the immediately following story concerning Moses and Aaron takes place. In 20:2–13 her two brothers fail to respond properly when the people cry out for water. What exactly they did wrong is debated, but clearly they violated their responsibilities as God's designated leaders. God therefore says to Miriam's two brothers, "You shall not bring this assembly into the land" (v. 12), and by the end of this chapter Aaron's death is also reported. Moses, of course, continues on to lead the people to the edge of the Jordan, but here in Kadesh where

Miriam dies, Moses' death outside the land is announced as well. Thus the narrator heightens the significance of Miriam's death by reporting it immediately before the announcement of the fate of her brothers.

## Two Laws of Family Life

*Suspicion of marital infidelity (5:11–31).* This legislation specifies the procedures that a husband is to follow if he suspects his wife of having intercourse with another man but has no proof that she has done so. (Various cases susceptible to proof are covered in Deuteronomy 22.) The text begins in a style typical of ancient Near Eastern case law: "if thus and such circumstances happen . . ." (v. 12b), with a variety of subclauses (vv. 13–14), followed finally by a "then . . ." clause (v. 15) specifying what the husband shall do. According to this law, the husband may bring his wife before the priest whether he has genuine suspicions or whether he is simply overcome by a "spirit of jealousy." The wording of the law generally presumes that the woman is guilty; it is only in the last phrase of v. 14 that the possibility of her innocence is finally mentioned.

Verses 16–28 describe the procedure to be undertaken by the priest to determine the woman's guilt or innocence. The key to understanding the procedure is the requirement that the woman say "Amen, Amen" (v. 22), thus accepting the potential results of the curse to be laid upon her if she is guilty. The effect of drinking the potion not only shows her guilt or innocence but also constitutes the punishment if she is guilty. The meaning of the Hebrew describing the results in a guilty case ("her womb shall discharge, her uterus drop," v. 27) is obscure, so it is not possible to associate the phrase with a specific medical condition. The social consequences of being regarded as "an execration among her people" are not spelled out but may well have involved severe social ostracism.

The concluding paragraph of the law (vv. 29–31) provides a topical recapitulation typical of such legislation. It then goes on, however, to note that "the man shall be free from iniquity." Since the law presupposes that the woman's partner (if she is guilty at all) is not legally identifiable, the man referred to here is apparently the husband, who is absolved of any guilt for making a false accusation. Not only may he invoke this procedure on mere suspicion; he is not to be held accountable for his suspicions, even if his wife is vindicated.

Even though this law seems outrageous to modern Western sensibilities, and even though the possibility that the potion (apparently only dirt and water) might have a real effect on a woman seems remote by modern Western standards, one should not conclude that the practice was never carried out or that that curse-bringing water could not produce an effect in the context of a culture that accepted the possibility of such powers. The law invites readers to reflect upon the many ways in which diverse cultures have sought to control women's sexual behavior, as well as upon the terror reigning among women wherever such customs prevail.

*Women's vows (chap. 30).* This law is concerned to specify the conditions under which vows made by women are and are not binding. It treats vows made by women living within their fathers' households (vv. 3–5) or within their husbands' households (vv. 10–15), covers divorced women and widows (v. 9), and gives special attention to changes in jurisdiction when a woman marries (vv. 6–8). There is very little evidence concerning the typical subject matter of women's vows, though it seems likely that they were often concerned with fertility and the possibility of children (see 1 Sam. 1:9–11; Prov. 31:2). Whatever was typical, there is no evidence for restriction on the goals women could hope to gain through their vows.

With regard to what women vowed to do or to offer if their requests were granted by God, again the evidence is slim. Three main possibilities have been suggested: fasting, sexual abstinence, and some economic payment. What might a male authority figure gain, practically speaking, by being able to nullify such vows? With regard to sexual abstinence, a father might want the right (for economic reasons) to ensure that his daughter remain marriageable, while of course a husband would want control of his conjugal rights. If the goal of a vow was to bear a child, of course, it seems unlikely that sexual abstinence would be what the woman would offer. But with regard to sexual abstinence as well as to fasting, interpretation is hampered by lack of information about special women's rituals that may have existed alongside the more official male world of religious practice attested in the Bible. Was there "another world" of religious practice over which men hoped to have at least some rudimentary control? Might it have provided a means for women to "evade" or "get an intermission from" an oppressive family situation? The absence of evidence must be noted, but the possibility of such women's rituals cannot be discounted.

Finally, it seems obvious that men would have sought to maintain economic control within their households. Vows often involved payment of animals, property, or even persons to the sanctuary. If a woman in her desire for a child followed the example of Hannah, the mother of Samuel (1 Samuel 1), that child would either be lost to the economic future of the family or perhaps have to be redeemed for a payment according to the categories laid out in Lev. 27:1–8. A vow involving animal sacrifice might likewise affect the economic status of a family rather substantially. However the law is read, its ancient purpose seems to have been the promotion of family stability within a culture of male-dominated households.

## Family Inheritance: The Daughters of Zelophehad

*Challenge to authority (27:1–11).* This chapter presents the first of a two-part story about five daughters whose father had died without sons. The story occurs just at the end of the forty years in the wilderness, immediately following the second census of the people and instructions to Moses about how the promised land is to be allotted among the families of the second generation. The five daughters of Zelophehad present to Moses their special situation, pointing out that according to the rules (of 26:52–56) their father's name will be lost because no one from his family will receive an inheritance in the land. Moses seeks God's guidance and God announces the specific decision concerning their petition (v. 7), followed by a more general and extended law of inheritance (vv. 8–11). Only v. 8 of this extended law is directly related to the petition of the five women.

How incredibly daring are Mahlah, Noah, Milcah, Hoglah, and Tirzah in coming forward to speak personally and publicly (v. 2) to the great Moses! Moreover, their question involves not just Moses' opinion but a suggestion that a direct decree of the deity is inadequate and should be revised. The narrative is dramatic and suspenseful. What will Moses' response be in this extraordinary situation? Once he turns to the deity, what will be God's response? The rustle in the crowd is almost palpable as the women approach, as everyone waits, as the word

is announced: "The daughters of Zelophehad are right."

But why was this story preserved in the canon? The drama of the story and the courage of the sisters are not sufficient explanation. It seems probable that the story survived because the basic point at issue was the preservation of the *father's name* (v. 4). The storyteller presumes an intricate connection between possession of land and preservation of family name. The women themselves are pictured as taking action for the sake of their father's name, not for the sake of their own opportunity to possess land. This story could be heard even in ancient Israel as a story of comfort for women who would not be left destitute, but it was preserved primarily as a story of comfort for men who had the misfortune not to bear any male heirs—their names would not be cut off from their clans.

*Repercussions (36:1–12).* After the capture of Transjordan, the male relatives of the tribe to which Zelophehad belonged suddenly wake up to what from their point of view is a major omission in the ruling announced back in chap. 27. Numbers 36 is concerned with their appeal. The heads of the other families of the Joseph tribe to which Zelophehad belonged come before Moses and state their concern: If these five women marry men from other Israelite tribes, then "their inheritance will be taken from the inheritance of our ancestors and added to the inheritance of the tribe into which they marry . . ." (v. 3). Moses announces the divine decision that the daughters of Zelophehad must marry within their own tribe so as to avoid any possibility of transfer of property from one tribe to another, and again the law is generalized beyond the specific case. The story concludes with an account of the women's compliance with this regulation, so that the entire book ends with an illustration of the narrator's overarching theme of the perfect faithfulness of the second generation (see "Introduction").

Although chaps. 27 and 36 exhibit a superficial similarity of pattern, there are significant differences between them. In the second story the place of meeting is not specified and the only audience is the (male) heads of ancestral houses. The specifically religious elements (tent of meeting, priest, and congregation) are missing from the proceedings in chap. 36, as indeed are the five women themselves. Furthermore, in the second story Moses proceeds directly to the announcement of God's decision, without consultation with the deity. Thus the narrator here reports Moses' speech to the Israelites, rather than God's speech of command to Moses, as is recorded in chap. 27. The women themselves are completely invisible, and the deity is present only by indirection. In fact, the pronouncement that "the descendants of the tribe of Joseph are right" (v. 5) appears quite abruptly, since the petitioners, unlike the daughters in chap. 27, have not proposed any solution to their problem.

Information concerning Israelite marriage customs and regulations is so scanty that it is difficult to project the effect of this law. If the story implies that women without fathers or brothers could choose their own husbands (v. 6), then the law would simply restrict their choice of mates. It is equally likely, however, that other males in the extended family were responsible for the choice of husbands for such women. If so, then the law would restrict the greed of such men (who might otherwise maneuver to get the best price for that rare woman who brought to marriage a parcel of arable land, the ideal dowry in an agrarian society).

In this sequel to the basic story, the focus has shifted; suddenly land and rights to it, rather than the father's name, are the center of attention. It becomes evident that the daughters' landholding is only temporary, until their marriage, at which time the property will pass to their husbands; a battle among males for male property rights takes shape. The women do not end up where they began, with no place or space of their own within Israel's inheritance and property structure, and yet the limits of their freedom are made very clear by the end of the story.

## Conclusion: Numbers and Women's Experience

In many ways the presentation of women in the book of Numbers illustrates the typical existence of women in many cultures throughout many historical periods. The book, written by males from an elite group, proceeds generally as if there were no real difference between women and men. Thus, stories about the "congregation" or the "people" are told as if everyone were involved in the same way. But from time to time unintended clues remind attentive readers that women are not really in the narrator's mind, as when the dissidents against Moses worry about

their wives (chap. 14) or when the laws governing unintentional taking of human life (35:22–28) seem highly unlikely to be enforceable for female perpetrators. The absence of women from public religious leadership is completely taken for granted, and their role as congregational participants is left unspecified.

When questions concerning women come explicitly to the fore, they are focused primarily in the domestic realm, the realm in which most women of that culture functioned and the realm which the male writers regarded as in need of special regulation with regard to women's place. Marriage, divorce, sexual relations, passing on of the family name, control of land, and family economic condition are all singled out for special attention in this book.

The notable exception to this domestic focus is, of course, Miriam. She serves as a reminder that even in cultures that emphasize domestic roles for women, some women do achieve public leadership. Miriam's story here typifies much of such leadership: it is exceptional, it is not regarded as fully comparable to that of the men, and it is much more easily challenged, compromised, and undercut.

As people attuned to the modern debate about the place of women in contemporary cultures read this ancient book, they may well be first aware of the great gulf between that ancient culture and their own. But it is important that this sense of distance not deceive the reader, for the correspondences to the situation of modern women and men continue to be very great indeed.

## BIBLIOGRAPHY

Burns, Rita. *Has the Lord Indeed Spoken Only Through Moses? A Study of the Biblical Portrait of Miriam.* Atlanta: Scholars Press, 1987.

Frymer-Kensky, Tikva. "The Strange Case of the Suspected Sotah (Numbers V 11–31)." *Vetus Testamentum* 34 (1984), 11–26.

Olson, Dennis T. *The Death of the Old and the Birth of the New: The Framework of the Book of Numbers and the Pentateuch* (Brown Judaic Studies 71). Decatur, Ga.: Scholars Press, 1985.

Sakenfeld, Katharine Doob. "In the Wilderness, Awaiting the Land: The Daughters of Zelophehad and Feminist Interpretation." *Theology Today* 46 (1989), 154–168.

# DEUTERONOMY

*Tikva Frymer-Kensky*

## Introduction

### Context and Central Concerns

Deuteronomy is the fifth book of the Torah (Pentateuch), cast in the form of the final teachings of Moses to the people of Israel before he died. Contemporary scholarship identifies it with the Book of the Law found during the rebuilding of the Temple in the days of King Josiah. However, one should not dismiss the book as a pious fraud, because many of the passages were written earlier than the seventh century B.C.E. and represent ancient Israelite traditions. The traditions of Deuteronomy may have originated in the Northern Kingdom of Israel and been brought south at the time of the destruction of the Northern Kingdom by Assyria. Deuteronomy clearly involves a learned reflection on these traditions and on other ancient elements of Israel's culture.

Deuteronomy is marked by its own characteristic phraseology, style, and tone. It uses the vocabulary of knowing and memory and is a "preachy" book, full of repetitions, reminders of history, and moral lessons. This tradition probably has its roots in the ambience of ancient scholars and teachers of Israel who considered and taught Israel's ancient traditions. To them learning and knowledge brought one to live the godly way.

Deuteronomy's central lesson is the close relationship between Israel and God, and the human responsibility for fidelity and social justice that it entails. This relationship is conceived of as a "covenant," a contractual relationship between God and Israel. The outline of the book closely parallels the form and outline of international treaties in the ancient Near East, particularly those between a superior overlord and his subject vassals. Like them, it contains (among other things) a historical prologue, the obligations of Israel, and blessings and curses. Deuteronomy's core demand is "you shall love your God with all your heart." The use of the term "love" is significant. Love may be a term that originally referred to family relations, but it is also used as a political term in the ancient treaty documents. Love is more than an emotion of affection. It is a demand for absolute faithfulness to the overlord—and to no other lord. Moreover, it is a demand that one act out of this love in deeds, by concern and obedience. The people of Israel must know the rules of God and must observe them, thus living the way of Torah.

The heart of the covenant—and of the book of Deuteronomy—is the Decalogue, the Ten Commandments, which set out the basic obligations of Israel. The arrangement of the laws that follow the Decalogue may be influenced by the order of these commandments, but they were not written as an expansion or a reflection of them. Deuteronomy's laws are part of the long ancient Near Eastern tradition of law collections. Like other collections, the laws of Deuteronomy are a work of jurisprudence—learned scholarly reflection on received legal tradition, a product of the study of law by trained experts who examined their received traditions in the light of their principles of equity and justice.

Deuteronomy shows a strong sense of social morality and a humane concern for society's underprivileged. It often explains its laws with "motive clauses" that tell why people should observe them. Sometimes the motivation is a reward ("living long on the land") or a punishment. Most often it is a reminder that the people of Israel owe it to God to consider other parties as much as themselves because God redeemed them from Egypt. Having been oppressed, they need to guard against oppressing others. Just as important in Deuteronomy, since God did such a great deed for them, they *owe* God obedience and need to conform to God's wishes even when the law demands that they do something against their own economic self-interest. Deuteronomy sees history and memory as calls to action and believes that the failure to know and remember the deeds that

God did for Israel can lead to apostasy. The book is therefore eager to *teach* and concentrates on the essential lessons: knowledge of the sacred history, the fact of God's might and uniqueness, and the laws. The wise are to teach and impart these things, and everyone who hears them should then inform others that God is one, that Israel must love God, and that Israel must live according to the laws.

# Comment

## Jealousy: The Background of a Religious Metaphor

The laws of Deuteronomy begin with the Ten Commandments, which start with a demand for the worship of only one God and elaborate this demand with a statement that "I YHWH your God am a jealous God" (5:9). The term "jealousy" (qin'ah) is specialized language and cannot be used loosely. Unlike love, jealousy is not a term found in the ancient political treaties. The concept of jealousy comes from the realm of marriage, and the word appears in the trial of the suspected adulteress in Num. 5:11–31. There the whole problem begins when a "spirit of jealousy" comes over the husband and he suspects that his wife has been unfaithful. Deuteronomy often uses metaphors drawn from family life to express Israel's relationship with God, but "jealousy" is even more specific. It is marriage language, and it expresses the attitude of the one whose prerogatives have been undermined: the husband, whose wife owes him exclusive loyalty; and God, whose people owe God the same exclusive fidelity. The other side of jealousy is inconstancy, unfaithfulness, or "whoring" (zanah). This term, used for a wife who does not remain faithful to her husband, can also be used as a term for apostasy from God (Deut. 31:16; Num. 15:39). The use of these terms probably indicates that the authors (and their hearers) were familiar with the marital metaphor of Israel as the wife of God, which the prophet Hosea uses extensively and powerfully and which is picked up by Jeremiah and Ezekiel.

## The Unity of God and the 'Asherah Symbol

The central creed of Israel, that God is One, shows an absolute monotheism in which YHWH, who by gender is male, stands to Israel as a husband to a wife. This command of unity

includes the prohibition of any other, lesser gods, such as the heavenly host. It also eliminates the possibility of 'asherim (Deuteronomy 12), the cultic tree images or actual trees that helped define the local altars as sacred. In fact, Deuteronomy takes the unity of God to demand a unification of cult. Only one sanctuary is to be permitted, "the place where God chooses to set his name," and this sanctuary is identified by those who read Deuteronomy with the Temple in Jerusalem. Deuteronomy views all the local altars, long part of Israel's tradition, as "Canaanite" and therefore deserving of destruction. The stone monoliths and altars and the sacred tree and its image, the 'asherah, are to be wiped out, and worship is to be limited to one central altar. The cultic 'asherah that stood in Samaria was removed in the eighth century; the one in the Jerusalem Temple was removed several times, most recently during the reign of Josiah in the seventh century. Deuteronomy is part of this anti-'asherah tendency. It may be that some people in Israel had considered the 'asherah to be the representation of a goddess-consort of YHWH. The 'asherah might also have been a symbol of the immanence of God in nature and fertility, and the little figurines found throughout Israel with tree trunks and breasts may be household manifestations of this desire for God's fertile presence. In any case, Deuteronomy will have none of this: God is One, and God is totally transcendent. Even the one main sanctuary does not house God, but only God's *name.*

## Are Women Addressed by the Laws?

The Ten Commandments instruct the people in the proper worship of God. To whom are they addressed? It is not solely to the king, as divine instruction in the ancient Near East often was, nor to the people as a whole, but to each individual. This is indicated by the use of the second person singular imperative. But the form is grammatically masculine, and the question arises whether the women are invisible but present in this masculine "you," or whether the Ten Commandments are addressed only to the men of Israel. The last commandment, "Neither shall you covet your neighbor's wife . . ." (5:21), addresses the men and treats the wife as an object to be desired, like the neighbor's house, field, slave, ox or ass, all of which one may not covet. But the commandment to observe the Sabbath day clearly includes women in the "you." The commandment reads "you shall not do any work—you, or your son or your daughter, or your male or female slave, or your ox or your donkey, or any of your livestock, or the resident alien in your towns" (5:14). The inclusion of the daughter and the female slave shows that women are to stop working on the Sabbath. Is the wife not mentioned because "a woman's work is never done" and the wife still has to work? But if the wife worked, so would the daughter and the maidservant. Quite the contrary, the omission of a phrase "and your wife" shows that the "you" that the law addresses includes both women and men, each treated as a separate moral agent.

The other commandments also include women, for they were certainly not allowed to make wrongful use of the name of YHWH or to steal or to commit adultery (which means an extramarital sexual relationship of or with a married woman) or to murder. It is only when the text considers sexual lust that it stops being inclusive and looks at the wife as the object rather than the subject of the law. In other realms of behavior, the Decalogue and the laws of Deuteronomy treat women as autonomous beings and often protect their rights.

## Women as Subject and Object of the Laws

The fact that the Ten Commandments and other laws in Deuteronomy address women does not mean that women's rights were comparable to those of men. Like all ancient law, Deuteronomy assumes a social system in which women are clearly disadvantaged: the very command to take care of widows and orphans (10:18; cf. 24:17–22; 26:13) rests on the unexamined presupposition of patriarchy. If women had equal access to property and privilege, then the law would not have to worry about widows. Nevertheless, women are not totally objectified in these laws.

*The law of Hebrew slaves (15:12–18).* This pattern of seesawing between woman as subject and woman as object, between woman as member of the people and woman as subordinate, is also found in the legal provisions of Deuteronomy, one group of which obliquely considers when women are separated from the community and when not. The law of the Hebrew slave reexamines and modifies the traditional law of Hebrew slaves that is expressed in Ex. 21:2–11, part of the Covenant Code (Ex. 20:22–23:33), and in Lev. 25:39–44, part of the Holiness Code of Leviticus (chaps. 17–26). The law in Exodus forbids acquiring a Hebrew slave forever and mandates that slaves be set free after seven years unless they voluntarily choose to become permanently attached to the master. Leviticus decrees that people are manumitted at the jubilee. Deuteronomy retains the sabbatical manumission but makes a characteristic change in the law: mindful of the fact that persons usually sell themselves into slavery because of extreme poverty, it recognizes the futility of setting slaves free without providing for their economic well-being and demands that the owner make sure that the poor slave has enough provisions to operate as a freed person (15:13–15). Deuteronomy makes another important change. Exodus does not apply the law to maidservants, who may be acquired as permanent slaves. Deuteronomy, on the other hand, quite deliberately demands that maidservants also be set free in the seventh year: no Hebrew woman can be made into a slave (including a slave-wife) in the same way that no Hebrew man can be permanently made into a slave without his consent (15:17b).

*Additional laws specifically including women (17:1–5; 18:10; 22:5).* There are other occasions in which Deuteronomic law explicitly includes women. Deuteronomy commands the Israelites to stone anyone, man or woman, who worships other gods or the hosts of heaven (17:1–5), and prohibits passing both sons and daughters through fire (18:10). These rules reflect the religious situation of the Assyrian period, which witnessed both the sacrifice of children by fire to the god Molech and the forbidding of the worship of the hosts of heaven. The conscious and explicit inclusion of women may also be a product of that time. Similarly, the conscious distinction between men and women implied in the prohibition of wearing the clothes of the other gender (22:5) may also be a part of the religious conflicts of the Assyrian period, for the cult of the goddess Inanna/Ishtar in Mesopotamia involved cross-dressing.

### Women as objects in the laws: The context of war (20:5–7; 21:10–14).

The laws of Deuteronomy begin to see women as objects when they consider marital or sexual relations. The rules of battle focus on the *acquisition* of women. A man who is betrothed but has not yet married his wife is exempt from army service, "lest he die in the battle and another man take her" (20:7, RSV). In the same way, the person who has planted a vineyard and has not yet eaten from it, or built a new house and not yet lived in it, is exempt from fighting so that he can complete his acquisition (20:5–6).

Women can also be acquired *during* war, for the women and little children of Canaan are the spoils of the war in which the men are killed (20:14). If a man does acquire a beautiful woman in war and takes her home, he can take her as his wife after she shaves her head, pares her nails, takes off her captive's clothes, and mourns her parents for a month. If he does not want her at this point, he must set her free: he cannot sell her, for he has dishonored her (21:10–14). The word used for "dishonor" (*'innah*) is a significant word in the Bible. Often translated "rape," the word means to treat abusively, without regard to proper behavior. By not asking her father's permission, Shechem abused Dinah (Gen. 34:2). In completely nonsexual ways, Sarah mistreated (*'innah*) Hagar by treating her without the proper respect due a concubine-mother (Gen. 16:6). Egypt abused Israel (*'innah*) with heavy forced labor (Ex. 1:11). In this law of the captive bride the man has put his captive in a position in which she expected to become a wife, and then he has not carried through. Does this law apply only if he has sexual intercourse with her and then does not want to keep her as his wife? Taking her home and letting her go through this ritual of separation may mislead her even if he lets her go after the month without having intercourse with her. He cannot be allowed to gain by such behavior and instead must emancipate her.

## Deuteronomy's Limitations on the Rights of the Head of Household

### The law of the firstborn (21:15–17).

At first glance the law of the captive bride seems to limit the power of the man in a strange way. After all, he has acted as the head of his own household. He has acquired a slave through war, the most common way of acquiring slaves. He should be able to sell her for profit if he so wishes. Instead, because he allowed her to mourn her past life (and thereby to expect to become a wife), he must suffer the loss of her price. This seems to be a drastic curtailment of the right of a man to control the members of his own household and to determine freely his behavior toward them. In fact, this limitation of the rights of the head of household is one of the characteristics of Deuteronomy. It is evident also in the law of the firstborn (21:15–17), which immediately follows the law of the captive bride.

Near Eastern texts, particularly the family law documents from the city of Nuzi, show that the term "firstborn" was a legal designation. The firstborn son was definitely advantaged: he inherited twice as much as any of his brothers and may also have had control of the family's cultic objects. But birth order did not determine the "firstborn." A man could stipulate who his firstborn was to be without regard to when the child was born. Contracts of adoption sometimes state quite clearly who is to be considered the firstborn, and even after such stipulation, at least one Nuzi document shows that a man on his deathbed could choose someone else as his firstborn heir.

The ancestor stories of Genesis show the same legal understanding of firstborn. Esau sold his "firstborn right" to Jacob (Gen. 25:29–34); Jacob tricked Isaac into giving him the final blessing (Genesis 27). Jacob's own sons did not know who would be the chief heir. He had two wives, Leah and Rachel, and two concubines, Bilhah and Zilpah. Rachel's firstborn son Joseph had ten older brothers. Nevertheless, the young Joseph had dreams that his brothers would bow down to him, dreams that frightened his brothers precisely because it was possible that they would come true and that Jacob would appoint his beloved Joseph the firstborn heir (Gen. 37:5–11). In effect, after many adventures and tribulations, something like this did happen when Jacob proclaimed Joseph's two sons, Ephraim and Manasseh, equal to their uncles in inheritance, thus giving Joseph the double portion after all. Jacob even arbitrarily reversed the birth order of Ephraim and Manasseh (Gen. 48:8–22). Deuteronomy denies the father this power to declare the son of his favorite wife to be his firstborn. Instead, he must accept the son born first (to either wife) as the firstborn. The head of household cannot freely exercise patriarchal power to designate the order of inheritance.

### The law of the rebellious son (21:18–21).
The next law, that of the rebellious son, also deals with parental rights. This law depicts a situation in which the parents have lost control over their rebellious son, perhaps a juvenile delinquent or possibly a grown son who is terrorizing elderly parents. The parents can no longer control their son, who does not "obey his father and mother" and pays no attention to their attempts to discipline him. They can bring him to the elders of the city and declare that they cannot control him; he will then be stoned by the men of the city. At first sight, readers may react with horror at the thought of a parent sending a child to death and can only imagine what horrendous behavior would impel a parent to do this. Obviously, such an event could not have been commonplace. As one looks deeper into this law, one sees the hierarchical order that this law sets up. A child must obey father *and mother.* In many societies sons control the mother; but not in Deuteronomy. Moreover, this law presents the nadir that parental *power* can reach, as the prerogatives of the father are whittled away, but acts to buttress parental *authority* under threat of death. Death is by stoning, a special penalty reserved in the Bible for offenses that are seen to threaten the stability of the whole universe by upsetting the hierarchical arrangements of the cosmos. If a beast can kill a human, if a child can disobey a parent, society cannot long survive. The entire community feels itself threatened and endangered. The father cannot kill his son: he must bring the case before the elders of the town, and they try the recalcitrant son. This council of elders has other functions in Deuteronomy: they investigate the question of a bride's virginity (22:13–21); they oversee the release of a *levir* (Latin, "husband's brother"; 25:7); and they perform the decapitated heifer ceremony (21:1–9). They constitute a public segment of society that supersedes the rights of fathers and oversees relationships within families as well as between them. But this is not a centralized national government. In Deuteronomy, the "patriarchal state" that intervenes in family matters is the local unit, the council of elders. The entire local community then serves as executioner.

## The Control of Sexuality: Fathers, Daughters, and Wives (22:13–30)

Deuteronomy contains several laws that consider the integral place of sexuality in the social order and raise the issue of its control. To a large extent this means control over female sexuality; the laws delineate who has the right to mate with which females and how this should be done. Men and women were equally bound by the laws, but the laws revolve around the sexual activity of women. As always in the Bible, sexuality is bonded to family. For a man to have sexual intercourse with a woman who belonged to some other household threatened the very definition of "household" and "family"; but a married man having intercourse with an unattached woman is not mentioned as an item of concern.

### The slandered bride (22:13–21).
The Deuteronomic laws of sexual control begin with the questions of sexual intercourse with a young woman still living in her father's house. Unmarried girls were expected to be chaste, and sexual intercourse with them was a wrongful act. The series of laws begins with the case of a slandered bride. Her new husband, who does not care for her, publicly defames her, declaring that he did not find her to be a virgin. The father and mother then bring before the elders in the gate "the daughter's virginity," that is, the blood-stained sheet from the consummation of the marriage. The father declares that he gave the daughter in marriage and that the husband has slandered her, and he spreads the cloth bearing his daughter's virginity. As a result the elders beat the man and fine him one hundred shekels of silver for defaming a virgin of Israel; they give the money to the father. The man is further punished by never being allowed to divorce his wife. If, however, the accusation was true and marks of virginity were not found, then she is to be stoned by the men of the city because "she did a grossly improper thing in Israel, being unfaithful to her paternal home" (22:21, author's translation).

The punishment of the slandering husband seems odd to our modern sensibility, for maintaining the marriage seems a punishment as much of the wife as of the husband. In the context of ancient Israel there was concern for the financial support of a wife. Still, the law ignores the woman's wishes or her prospects for a more congenial marriage in its concern to ensure that men not be permitted to rid themselves of unwanted wives in this way.

This reading of the law seems clear and is supported by the abundant examples of the custom of proving the wife's virginity by displaying the bloody sheet of consummation. There is one major philological problem. Normally the Hebrew term *betulah* refers to a young adolescent girl; it does not necessarily connote virginity. When sexual virginity is meant, a phrase such as "who has not known a man" is sometimes added (e.g., Gen. 24:16). Indeed, the prophet Joel speaks of a *betulah* lamenting the husband of her youth (Joel 1:8). If the term *betulim* here does not refer to virginity, the marks on the cloth would be the blood of menstruation rather than first intercourse. Absence of blood, then, would suggest marriage before puberty. However, there is no reason to suspect that the Bible considered marriage before puberty such a disgrace that an accusation of prepubescent marriage would constitute slander and that, if true, it would incur the death penalty for the girl. It seems much more probable that *betulim* means "marks of virginity" despite the fact that *betulah* simply means an adolescent girl. A similar problem of interpretation arises with the case of Jephthah's daughter, who goes out to the mountains "to bewail my virginity" (*betulay*, Judg. 11:37–40). She, and the women of Israel after her, may have mourned the end of their virginity, the passing of their youth. However, they may also have been mourning the fact that she would be sacrificed as a virgin. *Betulim* also seems to mean virginity in the rules of the priest's marriage, for he is to take a "woman in her *betulim*," a woman who is also called a *betulah* (Lev. 21:13–14). In Lev. 21:13–14 the word *betulah* probably means a pubescent girl, and *betulim* are the marks of such pubescence, which is menstruation, even though in Deut. 22:13–21 it refers to the evidence of first intercourse. The law in Deuteronomy itself indicates the reason for this overlap in meaning, for a not-yet-married pubescent girl living at home was expected to be chaste. If it is proved that the young woman is not a virgin, she is said to have "prostituted herself (*zanah*) in her father's house" and is punished by stoning. The secretly nonvirginal bride has seriously disrupted the community's expectations of daughterly obligations and threatened society's control over female sexuality. Convicted by the elders of the community, she is put to death by the entire community.

But do the elders and the community really determine her conviction? Upon close analysis, the procedures prescribed by this law seem rather bizarre. The bridegroom wants out of the marriage because "he dislikes her." If he were simply to divorce her (assuming that this would be permitted), he would lose the bride-price he

had given to her father. He therefore makes the affair a matter of public gossip, thus impugning the young woman's father's honor, since he allegedly could not control the behavior of his daughter. If the father can prove her virginity, the man must pay one hundred shekels, which may be double indemnity for the virgin's brideprice. The parents have a lot at stake. If they prove virginity, they gain one hundred shekels; if they do not prove it, they will be shamed publicly and will lose status in the community, which would jeopardize their chances of marrying off the rest of their children favorably. Nevertheless, it is they (rather than the bridegroom's family) who are entrusted with showing the cloth to the elders, and they do so not at the consummation of the marriage but after the public accusation. It is quite easy to imagine a scenario in which the parents, finding a blank cloth and either believing their daughter's protestations of virginity or having a vested interest in "believing" them, simply falsify the blood on the cloth. The parents would allow the young woman to be proved a nonvirgin (and stoned to death) only if they were enraged at her to such an extent that they were willing to bring dishonor upon themselves and to cause her death. In the final analysis the fate of the young woman rests with her parents.

But if this is so, why force the father to go through this subterfuge? Why does Deuteronomy not give the father the right to decide openly that his daughter has shamed him and should die, as Judah declared when he heard that his daughter-in-law Tamar was pregnant (Genesis 38)? Once again, one sees in Deuteronomy the transfer of authority from the family and its patriarch to the "public" sphere of the community of elders. The case of the slandered bride has much in common with the case of the rebellious son. In both, the well-being and status of the father and mother are at stake; in both, the parents have the actual power to determine whether their child dies: in the son's case by accusing him before the elders, in the daughter's by bringing out an unbloodied sheet. Nevertheless, in both cases the elders hold the legal authority to decide, and the public has the power to execute. The public, through this council of elders, has placed itself in the position of maintaining the family structures of the society and has taken the authority to punish erring members.

***The law against adultery (22:22).*** The rule of the slandered bride is followed immediately by the law against adultery, which decrees death for both the married woman and the man who has sexual relations with her. This is not new: all the biblical law collections prescribe death for adultery. By means of such law, the ancient Near Eastern states (including Israel), safeguarded the "nuclear family." Deuteronomy characteristically goes even further by addressing the collective: "You shall purge the evil from Israel." In Assyrian law it is the husband, as the prime injured party, who decides how to punish his wife, and the law declares that whatever the husband does to his wife should be done also to the adulterer. In Israel the husband has no such power: the public community declares itself the injured party, and the people must act to rid Israel of this evil.

Biblical law, like other ancient law, defines adultery as the act of extramarital sexual intercourse of or with a married woman. The wife is the adulteress; the adulterer is the man who has sexual relations with her. A husband who has extramarital sexual relations with an unmarried woman is not considered an adulterer: the very existence of prostitution implicitly tolerates nonexclusive sexual behavior by men. A man's sexuality is his to control, though he must be careful not to impinge on the rights of other men. A woman's sexuality is not hers to control, for only her father and husband have "rights" to her. These "rights" are themselves highly circumscribed: the father may give her to another; the husband enjoys her but may not give her to another.

### The betrothed woman (22:23–27).

Israel had a system of formal betrothal before marriage, in which agreement was made for marriage and possibly goods were exchanged. If a betrothed woman has sexual relations with a man other than the one to whom she is betrothed, has she committed adultery? Is she married or not? Deuteronomy 22:23–27 declares unequivocally that she is to be considered married. The laws consider two possibilities: that a man finds a betrothed woman in the city and has intercourse with her; and that he takes her by force in the fields. In this latter case, there is a presumption of rape; the woman may have cried for help, and there was no one around to save her. The man is to be put to death—but only the man. Deuteronomy is emphatic that "you shall do nothing to the young woman; the young woman has not committed an offense punishable by death" (22:26). It explicitly recognizes that rape is a crime of violence and the young woman is absolutely not culpable, "because this case is like that of someone who attacks and murders a neighbor" (22:26). But if the sexual intercourse took place in the city, the law presumes that the intercourse was not forced, for if the woman had cried out she could have been heard. In this case, they are both culpable and are stoned. The man "has violated his neighbor's wife" (22:24). (The verb used is 'innah, usually translated "rape," the same verb that Deut 21:14 uses to describe the actions of a man who does not marry his captive bride.) The young woman is betrothed, that is, "a wife"; even if she consented, she had no right to consent. Having intercourse with her is improper treatment, what we might call statutory rape. Moreover, it is adultery, and both are deserving of death. Finally, it offends against a very important prerogative of the father (to negotiate a marriage for his daughter), and the couple is therefore stoned, like the nonvirgin bride and the rebellious son. There is a clear hierarchy of offenses here, with the state acting to buttress the father's position.

### The nonbetrothed virgin (22:28–29).

When the young woman is not betrothed, sexual intercourse with her is still improper. The verb 'innah is used, for the young woman does not have the right to give her consent. Whether forcible or consensual, the sexual act is still wrongful intercourse. The same verb is used in Genesis 34 to describe this very situation: Shechem had intercourse with Dinah without obtaining her father's consent, and the verb used is 'innah (Gen. 34:2). In this case, says Deuteronomy, the man must pay the virgin's bride-price and marry her without right of divorce. It is irrelevant to Deuteronomy whether the young woman was actually raped: the issue is not crime and punishment, but wrong and compensation. Deuteronomy does not consider this act a crime against the public. Even if it involves forcing the young woman, the polity is neither endangered nor aggrieved. Instead, this act is treated as a civil matter between the man and the young woman's parents. This may seem shocking, but it has its positive aspects. On the one hand, the rapist is not a criminal, even if he forced her. On the other hand, the young woman is also not a criminal, even if she agreed.

Sexual intercourse with a single woman is not a criminal act; nevertheless, it is contrary to Israel's mores. The special term for this type of act is *nebalah*, sometimes translated "folly." This is the term that Dinah's brothers use to describe Shechem's action (Gen. 34:7); it is the word that Deuteronomy uses for the sexual activity of the nonvirgin bride before marriage (22:21), and the same word that Tamar, daughter of David, uses to try to dissuade Amnon from raping her (2 Sam. 13:12). Sexual activity with an unmarried woman, though not a legally punishable crime, is a gross impropriety, and even though the fathers of Dinah and Tamar do not seek legal redress, their brothers take bloody revenge for the shame inflicted on them.

Deuteronomy's laws strongly deter such sexual activity. Even if the act is not discovered, a nonvirgin woman can later be accused by her husband, and if her parents are sufficiently angry at her not to falsify the sheet, she can be stoned. The man faces the prospect that if the act is discovered, he has assumed a permanent economic responsibility for the woman and must, in addition, pay the full bride-price of a virgin so that he does not profit from his wrongful act in any way (and so that the family of the young woman does not suffer loss). Despite these repercussions, one can imagine a scenario in which a young man and a young woman are eager to marry, and the young man has not yet acquired the necessary capital; in this case they could have premarital sex. If discovered, they have found a way of effecting a betrothal, for by this sexual act the young woman is automatically betrothed to the youth and becomes his wife. He must still pay the bride-price, but possibly at some future time when he might acquire it.

Exodus 22:16 also has a law about intercourse with an unbetrothed young woman. Here the act is clearly consensual: he has talked her into it. The law provides that he must pay the bride-price and marry her. By having intercourse with her, he has contracted to marry her. However, the father may refuse to give her to him, in which case he must still pay the virgin's bride-price. In Exodus, the marriage is at the discretion of the father; in Deuteronomy, it is obligatory. The reason for this difference *may* be that in Exodus the act is consensual whereas the act in Deuteronomy could be considered forcible. More likely this is not the issue, and Deuteronomy is once again limiting the authority of the father to determine his children's fate. Just as the father can no longer decide which of his children will be the prime heir, so too he cannot decide to accept the bride-price and still keep his daughter.

***The prohibition of the father's wife (22:30).*** The rules of illicit sexual relations conclude with a note about another forbidden relationship that illustrates once again the intersection between sexual attraction and obligations to one's parents. At issue is the desire of a man for his father's wife. He may not marry her, for he may not, as it is idiomatically stated, "uncover his father's skirt" (22:30). Clearly the woman is not the man's mother, since that would be incest. Similarly, she is not currently married to the man's father, for that would be adultery. The law deals with the father's widow or divorced wife. She is a free woman, and one might assume that there was no impediment to another man's marrying her. However, the fact that she was once his father's wife makes her forever off limits to the son. Once again, Deuteronomy buttresses paternal privilege at the same time as it limits parental authority.

## The *Qedeshah* and the *Zonah* (23:17–18)

Two women stand completely outside the family structure — the *qedeshah* and the *zonah*. The *zonah* is a prostitute, someone who has sex for a price. The *qedeshah* was probably *not* a sacred prostitute, that is, someone who has sex as part of her duties to the temple (contra the translation of the NRSV, "temple prostitute"). Recent research has shown that there is no basis for this interpretation. The male *qadesh* was a type of Canaanite priest; the female *qedeshah* was probably the same. Deuteronomy forbids Israelites to be such priests, and King Josiah threw the *qedeshot* out of the Temple (where they were weaving garments for '*asherah*, 2 Kings 23:6–7). Deuteronomy forbids the ancient forms of worship (with steles, local altars, and '*asherah*s) with which the *qadesh* and the *qedeshah* may have been associated and therefore prohibits Israelites from being *qedeshah* or *qadesh* (Deut. 23:17). The text immediately follows this rule with a prohibition against using the wages of a prostitute (*zonah*, 23:18). Despite the fact that the *qedeshah* was not a prostitute, they had one characteristic in common. Both were women outside the family, and they could therefore make their own decisions about their sexual activity. This contributed to the unsavory reputation of the *qedeshot*: they were able to have sex without being married, and this "promiscuity" resulted in their being considered "whores" and being grouped with them by the lawgiver.

Deuteronomy does not outlaw prostitution. It does, however, radically dissociate it from the temple cult, even to the extent of not allowing the wages of a prostitute to be used in payment of a vow. One might suspect that a place of assembly and pilgrimage like the Temple would be a place around which prostitutes would congregate in order to find customers, and Deuteronomy may have been trying to distance them from any participation in temple ritual. In addition, one of the characteristics of biblical religion is the radical separation of the sexual from the sacred. Not only is there no role for sexual behavior in the cult itself, but sexual activity renders persons unfit for cultic activity for the day and unable to approach the sancta, or holy things, for three days. Deuteronomy understands this to mean that money or goods involved in prostitution cannot also be involved in sacrificial activity.

## The Law and Marriage (24:1–5)

*Limitations on remarriage.* Deuteronomy 24:1–4 considers a complicated case. A man has married a woman; he is displeased because he has found something wrong with her; he writes her a bill of divorce and sends her away. She remarries and her second husband dislikes her and gives her a bill of divorce, or else her second husband leaves her a widow. Her first husband cannot come back and remarry her.

This puzzling law reveals several important facts about Israelite marriage. First, divorce was permissible. It is not mentioned in Exodus or Leviticus, but is found in other ancient Near Eastern laws and seems to be part of the common ancient legal tradition. Deuteronomy provides for a bill of divorce, so that the woman can prove that she is no longer married and can be free to remarry. There are some restrictions on divorce. A man who has had sexual intercourse with a young woman before marriage and has paid double the virgin's price to her father cannot later divorce her, nor can a man who has slandered his new bride. Since he can simply divorce a wife that he does not like, a man would slander a new bride only if he had something to gain. A comparison with ancient laws reveals what that could be. If a man divorces his wife without reason, because he "hates" her, she is entitled to compensation: certainly her dowry, whatever gifts her husband had given her during or in anticipation of marriage, and probably whatever portion of the bride-price the father had given to the couple. She takes these and leaves. If, however, the husband finds cause to divorce her (such as declaring her a nonvirgin or naming other

misdeeds), then she goes out without compensation and the husband profits economically from the divorce. The Deuteronomic law deals with just such a case, where a husband has divorced his wife for cause. She remarries and later becomes free through no fault of hers, by the death or displeasure of her second husband. One can assume that she has some property from her second marriage, either divorced woman's or widow's compensation. Having once declared her an unfit wife, the husband cannot remarry her and profit from her once more.

There may also be another factor at stake here. In Israel, sexual morality was considered one of the pillars of the world's existence. The well-being of the earth depended on avoiding murder, sexual abomination, and idolatry: all of these polluted the earth. Here the admonition not to "bring guilt on the land" (Deut. 24:4) may be an allusion to this whole complex of ideas in which improper sexual relations can bring disaster upon the land. By using this phrase, the law invokes thoughts of the pollution that results from intercourse with a former wife who has in the meantime had sex with another.

*The newly married woman (24:5).* These laws of sexuality and marriage end with a decree that a newly married man should not leave his wife for business or war for a year, so that he can make his wife happy. The law positively values sexuality within marriage, not simply for consummation or offspring but for pleasure. One should note the assumption of this law that women are the ones who desire sexual pleasure: the husband is not exempt so that he will be happy but so that he will make his wife happy. A man, after all (the law implicitly reasons) finds joy in his business trips or his warfare as well as in his sex life; a woman's joys are dependent on her marital satisfaction.

## Levirate Marriage (25:5–10)

Two more laws remain to be considered. One is the law of the *levir* (25:5–10); the other is the case of a woman who grabs a man's genitals (25:11–12). These are not as unrelated as they might seem. The levirate concerns the situation of a man who dies without having begotten children. He has no remnant in Israel, a fate literally worse than death and reserved to those who have grievously trespassed God's prerogatives. In order to ensure that this will not happen to a guiltless man, his widow is to "marry" one of his brothers. The brother, the *levir*, is to impregnate his dead brother's wife. The child that will be born from this union is counted as his dead brother's son for purposes of inheritance (and, one may assume, funerary obligations toward his "father"). The dead man has his remnant; the woman has been reattached—she remains in her marital family as the mother of her dead husband's son. But the *levir* has undergone a great financial sacrifice. Without the levirate there would be one less person to divide the patrimony: If there were originally three sons, each of the surviving two would now get one half. With the levirate, the dead man is replaced, and each surviving son will now get less. Moreover, if the dead man were the firstborn, then the *levir* would get much less, for the double portion would go to the biological son that he engendered for his dead brother. Again, if there were originally three sons, and the eldest died, then with the levirate the newborn son would get one half of the estate when it was divided, and each of his uncles would get only one fourth. The story of Judah and Tamar (Genesis 38) illustrates the seriousness of this financial loss and the reluctance toward the levirate that resulted. Onan did not want to impregnate his dead brother's widow precisely because it represented such an economic sacrifice. God punished Onan. Then, when Judah was afraid to give his third son as *levir*, Tamar had to trick Judah himself into performing the levirate.

Deuteronomy provides another method for a woman to take care of herself in this situation: she can perform a ceremony of removing the reluctant *levir's* shoe and spitting in his face, and his house will thereupon be known as "the house with the shoe removed" (25:10, author's translation). This is public defamation, and one can assume that it served to shame men into performing the levirate. As the house became known as one that did not provide for its widows, it would be more difficult for the men of the household to contract marriages for their children. Even when the threat of this shoe ceremony was not enough to bring the brother to perform the levirate, the ceremony at least ensured that the woman would be free to go and would not, like Tamar, be bound as a widow. The woman could acquire her freedom as a result of this action, and could go marry someone else. Ultimately, as the economic system became less dependent on multigenerational holdings, and as women could find more of a livelihood in an urban setting, this ceremony was preferred to the levirate and became standard practice.

## The Woman Who Grabs a Man's Genitals (25:11–12)

The Deuteronomic laws show a diminution of the control of the father. The family was subordinated to the public realm, and the men of the family had to follow public rules in the disposition of internal family matters. This was a decidedly mixed blessing for women. On the one hand, there was far less vulnerability for the disadvantaged, particularly for the children, for the father could not arbitrarily decide to advantage one son over another or to deny a daughter to a lover who wanted to marry her. The head of household could not treat a captive woman as a potential wife and then sell her as a slave, nor could he punish his wayward children as he wished. Moreover, a woman who was wronged had some protection and redress: the woman divorced for cause was protected from coming under the sway of the man who injured her; the nonimpregnated widow could take the initiative and make herself free with the ceremony of the loosened shoe.

But there was a flip side to this picture: as the woman became less subject to the absolute control of her particular head of household, she came more directly under the authority of the public realm: the elders and the nondiscretionary law. This had two negative consequences. First, although some women suffered terribly under the sovereign authority of a dictatorial head of household, most fathers/husbands were not absolute tyrants. They *needed* the women of the household for economic performance, companionship, love, and sexual satisfaction. Most women, even though they had no open authority, could actually exercise considerable informal power by persuading and manipulating the men who were interdependent with them. Once authority moved away from the family to the public tribunal and law, women actually had less influence on those under whose authority they came than they did in the household. Moreover, since the public hierarchy of ancient Israel was composed of men, the shift of authority over the woman moved from the concentrated authority of *one* man to the diffuse authority of many.

The consequences of this shift can be seen in Deuteronomy's final law concerning women, the case of the woman who grabs a man's genitals (25:11–12). The scene is similar to that in Ex. 21:22–25. Both are introduced by the phrase "if men get into a fight with one another . . . ," and both end with the possibility of mutilation (the only two such penalties in the Bible). Exodus deals with the case of a pregnant woman who gets in the way and is injured in the brawl: the issue is unintentional injury that can arise when social disorder erupts. Deuteronomy deals with a case in which a woman intervenes in the fight. She acts in faithfulness to her marital bond and enters the fray for the noblest of reasons: to save her husband from the man who is striking him. To do so, she grabs her husband's opponent by the genitals. The text does not stop to indicate whether the man is maimed or just temporarily pained. That is an irrelevant consideration to the law, which is setting up an important legal principle: even though the woman acts to defend her husband, she has done something horrendous enough to deserve mutilation in response (most probably severing the hand, but also possibly injuring the hollow of the thigh). A man's genitals—any man's genitals—are now sacrosanct. Women must not only follow the authority of their head of household: all men are now a privileged caste protected by the state, and their genitals, the emblem and essence of their manhood, are now sacrosanct. Concern for and allegiance to the males of one's family, even to one's husband, cannot be allowed to cause disrespect for maleness. Even the primary husband–wife bond, so protected by biblical law (including that of Deuteronomy), must bow to this diffused authority of "maleness," which literally embodies the public realm.

## Concluding Observations

Deuteronomy is a fascinating book. It is the product of continuing biblical reflection on Israelite history and laws. The laws sometimes comment on, extend, and modify laws in the other biblical legal collections. They also frequently reflect on the sacred family history of Israel found in the ancestor stories of Genesis, stories that seem like object lessons of what can go wrong when the rights of the head of household are uncurtailed. The rivalry of Isaac and Ishmael, Jacob and Esau, and Joseph and his brothers could only exist because the father had the right to choose his chief heir. Deuteronomy eliminates that right. Judah could order Tamar killed for getting pregnant while she was still bound to the son he had not given her. Even the binding of Isaac shows the disaster that *almost* occurred when a father could put his son to death. Deuteronomy places the council of elders between a father and his children's death. Dinah shows the tragedies that result when

a woman is not properly married to her lover. Deuteronomy requires that she be married to him. Tamar shows the problems of a widow bound to her dead husband's family. Deuteronomy provides for her release. At the same time, the father's prerogatives cannot be totally abrogated, and Deuteronomy prevents a story like that of Reuben, who slept with his father's concubine. Are the stories of Genesis written to illustrate the dangers of totally family centered law? Or are the laws of Deuteronomy written in response to the social messages of these stories? Given what is known of the development of biblical traditions, the two probably developed into their final form in constant relationship with each other, each genre reacting to and helping shape the other.

The stories in Genesis, and their even more gruesome counterparts in the historical books, witness the same development as the laws of Deuteronomy: from self-contained extended family to national polity. They both lead to the development of government as it exists today, the "patriarchal" state that interferes in family life. It protects women (and sometimes men) from domestic violence, and it claims the right to interfere in the parent–child relationship by punishing the abuser, by taking away the children, and by trying to regulate abortion in the interests of fetal rights. In the modern world there exists a continuing debate over the right of the state to protect its disadvantaged members versus the autonomy of the family. Analogous issues can be seen in the complex balance struck between public and paternal authority in Deuteronomy.

## BIBLIOGRAPHY

Frymer-Kensky, Tikva. *In the Wake of the Goddesses*. New York: Free Press, 1992.

Miller, Patrick D. *Deuteronomy*. Interpretation. Louisville, Ky.: John Knox Press, 1990.

Tigay, Jeffrey. *The JPS Torah Commentary: Deuteronomy*. Philadelphia: Jewish Publication Society (forthcoming).

Weinfeld, Moshe. *Deuteronomy*. Anchor Bible 5. New York: Doubleday & Co., 1991.

———. *Deuteronomy and the Deuteronomic School*. Oxford: Clarendon Press, 1972.

Westbrook, Raymond. "The Prohibition on Restoration of Marriage in Deuteronomy 24:1–4." In *Studies in Bible*, edited by Sara Japhet, Scripta Hierosolymitana 31. Jerusalem: Magnes Press, 1986.

# JOSHUA

*Danna Nolan Fewell*

## Introduction

The journey from Egypt through the wilderness completed, Israel begins a new chapter in its story: the people invade the land promised by Yahweh. The narrator of Joshua, combining various genres (stories, lists, exhortations, etc.) and literary and theological traditions from the Pentateuch (espionage, waters parting, circumcision, Passover), recounts Israel's attempt to dispossess the Canaanites and to establish their own community in the land.

The book falls into three parts, suggesting, on the surface, that the land is taken (chaps. 1–12), the community is established (chaps. 13–22), and the future holds naught but the challenge of fidelity to Yahweh (chaps. 23–24). A closer reading, however, reveals a more complex picture of the events and ideologies inscribed in this text.

Joshua 1–12, in lengthy narratives (1:1–10:27), short summaries (10:28–11:23), and lists (12:1–24), describes the early conquests and attempts to reaffirm Israel's identity as Yahweh's people. Interspersed with the victories over Jericho (chaps. 2, 6), Ai (chaps. 7–8), and elsewhere (chaps. 10–12) are events reminding the people who they are and from where they have come. The Jordan River parts for the Israelites to enter Canaan (chaps. 3–4), just as did the Reed Sea when the people came out of Egypt, thus closing the frame on the liminal wilderness experience and symbolizing the people's transformation from wanderers to settlers. The circumcision ceremony, too, ties past to future. Just as the generation leaving Egypt were circumcised, so are those now entering the land. This circumcision, however, represents a new phase in the nation's identity: "Today," says Yahweh, "I have rolled away from you the disgrace of Egypt" (5:9). The covenant is renewed; the law is again written on stones and read in the hearing of all the people (8:30–35).

The concern to define identity controls the logic of holy war in Joshua. All native inhabitants must be destroyed because they threaten Israel's identity. Goaded by divinely ordained intolerance, Israelites are pitted against Canaanites in a struggle for differentiation.

While this predominant logic polarizes insiders (Israelites) and outsiders (Canaanites), making nationality a defining factor, there is yet a subversive descant fostering ambiguity about identity. Joshua 5:13–15 is a paradigm case. A man with sword drawn appears before Joshua. Joshua interrogates him: "Are you one of us, or one of our adversaries?" The man responds, "Neither; but as commander of Yahweh's army I have now come." The messenger of Yahweh is neither insider nor outsider. He represents neither Israel nor Canaan, but holiness itself. His command is that holiness be recognized. It is the recognition of holiness, not one's nationality, suggests this story, that identifies one with God's people.

Other stories support this notion. Rahab (chaps. 2, 6) and the Gibeonites (chap. 9) are outsiders who become insiders because they recognize Yahweh's power. Their counterparts are Achan and his family (chap. 7): by not recognizing Yahweh's holiness, these are insiders who become outsiders. Fluid identity boundaries render nationalistic categories ambivalent and call into question the obsession with annihilating outsiders.

Joshua 13–22, mostly descriptions of geographical boundaries (13:1–15:12; 16:1–19:51) and city lists (15:20–63; 20:1–21:42), represents the administrative ordering of the nation. Here the reader discovers that insiders are not homogenous: "the people" dissipate into a mélange of individual tribes and families. Here the land allotments, and even the few narratives, illustrate that eradicating outsiders is not the only problem: dealing with the diversity of insiders presents yet another challenge. In Joshua 22, for example, the nation readies itself for civil war when the transjordanian tribes act independently by building an altar on the banks of the Jordan. Discrepant points of view are apparent. What the majority deems to be apostasy, the minority considers imperative for constructing identity. In the stories of Achsah (15:13–19) and the daughters of Zelophehad (17:3–6) we find that diversity exists within tribes, even families, and exceptions must be made. Marginal women, unentitled to property, aggressively seek and secure a more central place in the Israelite social system.

Chapters 23–24 close the book: all Israel gathers to hear exhortations by Joshua and Yahweh. As Joshua leaves Israel with a challenge and a choice, the predominant logic of exclusion pervades the rhetoric. The challenge is codified behavior for all Israel: "Be very steadfast to observe and do all that is written in the book of the law of Moses . . . that you may not be mixed with these nations left here among you, or make mention of the names of their gods, or swear by them, or serve them, or bow yourselves down to them, but hold fast to Yahweh your God, as you have done to this day" (23:6–8). The unsavory alternative is to become an outsider: "If you are unwilling to serve Yahweh, choose this day whom you will serve, whether the gods your ancestors served in the region beyond the River or the gods of the Amorites in whose land you are living; but as for me and my household, we will serve Yahweh" (24:15). Israel renews its commitment to the covenant, to singularity of purpose and identity.

But even here the descant lingers. "All Israel" (23:2) is, in fact, people with individual inheritances (24:28)—and there are those invisible ones who are without inheritance at all.

## Comment

### Invisible Women

Were one to reconstruct a picture of ancient Israelite society on the basis of Joshua, one might easily conclude that Israel was composed almost exclusively of men. Even the women who appear—Rahab (chaps. 2 and 6), Achsah (15:13–19), and the daughters of Zelophehad (17:3–6)—are visible only because they represent some kind of exception. Where are all the other women in Joshua? Deftly tucked, one might answer, between the lines.

*Women and (holy) war.* Joshua could be construed as a book about holy war—holy war fought by men. Joshua tells the transjordanian tribes, "Your wives, your little ones, and your livestock shall remain in the land that Moses gave you beyond the Jordan. But all the warriors among you shall cross over armed before your kindred and shall help them" (1:14). (Notice here that though Joshua is said to speak to the tribes, he clearly addresses only the men.) The warriors are also carefully distinguished from "all the people" in the battle of Jericho (6:3, 7, 9). On the seventh day the people shout loudly and assist in the city's capture, but it is doubtful that the phrase "all the people" includes women and children. Rather, as in the circumcision ceremony (see 5:5, 8), it most likely refers here to all the men.

Men may fight the battles, but women certainly share in the victimization. The Israelites make no distinction between warriors and civilians among the Canaanites. Every living thing is to be obliterated. Consequently, it is not difficult to understand Rahab's persistent negotiation with the spies (2:8–14).

One cannot assume, however, that because the women did not fight they were pacifists. The stakes of winning and losing were too high. More likely, these women, knowing the fate of the defeated and the rewards of victory, would have been as bellicose as their men.

*Women and corporate punishment.* That the fates of women are tied to their men is no more apparent than in the story of Achan (chap. 7). He takes for himself booty that was to be destroyed, according to the practice of holy war. When discovered, he and all his household are stoned to death. He is the direct opposite of Rahab. Whereas Rahab, a Canaanite woman, saves her whole family, Achan, an Israelite man, is instrumental in destroying his.

Several ideas underlie corporate punishment here. First, women, children, and servants are thought to be extensions of the father rather than independent individuals. They are considered accomplices, whether willing or unwilling. Consequently, they are given no separate hearing; the father speaks for all. Second, sin is thought to have a contagious quality; it can be passed from person to person. The whole household is likely to be contaminated and so must be destroyed if the evil is to be rooted out.

***Women and tribal organization.*** If in the book of Joshua women have little voice in the family, they certainly seem to have no place in the administration of Israel. The "elders, heads, judges, and officers" summoned by Joshua (23:2; 24:1) are all male. Only men can become priests and only men represent their tribes (4:1–3). Land ownership and inheritance are also rights belonging to men, passing patrilineally from generation to generation. Achsah and the daughters of Zelophehad are exceptions to the rule.

***Women and Israel's allegiance to the covenant.*** Like the inheritance of property, the religious traditions of Israel were also, according to the book of Joshua, passed down patrilineally. It was the fathers' duty to educate their sons concerning Yahweh's saving acts:

And [Joshua] said to the sons of Israel, "When your sons ask their fathers hereafter, 'What are these stones?' then you shall inform your sons, 'Israel crossed over the Jordan here on dry ground.' For Yahweh your God dried up the waters of the Jordan for you until you crossed over . . . so that all the peoples of the earth [or, "land"] may know that the hand of Yahweh is mighty, and so that you may fear Yahweh your God forever." (4:21–24, author's translation)

The terms "sons" and "fathers" might, of course, be inclusive, meaning "children" and "parents" (cf. NRSV). Much more likely is that such inclusiveness was not in the purview of ancient Israelite society. Modern readers might easily translate the text as an exhortation to general parental responsibility, but in all probability the narrator of Joshua never expected such curiosity on the part of daughters nor entertained the importance of the equal education of women.

Women are marginal to this educational process because women are marginal to the covenant between Yahweh and Israel. Circumcision, the symbol of the covenant, is performed on Israelite males, who ironically are referred to as "all the people" (5:5) and "all the nation" (5:8). Women, who cannot be identified physically with the covenant, are not likely to be considered central participants.

Similarly, the reading of the law (8:30–35), another symbol of covenant fidelity, also marginalizes women as well as children and resident aliens. Although the narrator reports that the law is read in the hearing of "all the assembly of Israel" (8:35) which to some extent includes women, children, and resident aliens, the narrator's language, through distinction, moves these parties to the fringes. Here gender, age, and ethnicity define the degree to which one can be central in the community of "all Israel."

If women are not integral to "all Israel," then it is hardly surprising to find that "Israel" often deems them expendable. Despite exhortations against exogamy (23:11–13), the exchange of women becomes commonplace in Israelite society (Judg. 3:6). "Israel" can trade its women because women are peripheral. The Israelites turn their women into outsiders, bring in foreign women as their own, and then conveniently blame these women for the nation's apostasy. Women bear the brunt of male religious anxiety but none of the identifying marks and few of the privileges of covenantal status.

***Women and men's history.*** As can be seen from the book of Joshua itself, women are marginal to Israelite history. Even historical retellings within the book reveal that, as far as the narrator of Joshua is concerned, histories are told by men to men (4:6–7, 21–24) about men (24:2–13). Fortunately, there is a larger story of Israel that also acknowledges the importance of the family unit as well as the administrative structures of the nation and, at least from time to time, highlights the participation of women. While Joshua may only focus on Abraham, Isaac, Jacob, Esau, Moses, Aaron, and the "fathers" liberated from Egypt (24:2–13), the larger story reveals that the "fathers" were squarely matched by the "mothers" — Sarah, Hagar, Rebekah, Rachel, Leah, Miriam, and the midwives. Histories are told, whether consciously or unconsciously, from particular perspectives with particular political agendas. The primary perspective of Joshua is clear: Yahweh has chosen men to bring this nation into being.

## Visible Women

Subverting the primary perspective of Joshua, however, are the stories of Rahab (chaps. 2; 6), Achsah (15:13–19), and the daughters of Zelophehad (17:3–6).

Israel's problem with foreigners has a decidedly sexual dimension. Foreign *women* are targeted as the problem, easily seducing Israelite men into worshiping other gods. The lure of such women manifests itself in the story of the spies at Jericho (chap. 2). The spies are sent forth from Shittim—where Israelite men, to their detriment, first get involved with foreign women (Numbers 25). From this inauspicious starting place, the spies go directly to a brothel and "they lay there." The verb "lie" is loaded with sexual overtones, and the context suggests that the spies are not above mixing business with pleasure. The common argument that a brothel would have been the best place to secure information about the city only accents the fact that the spies neither ask questions nor eavesdrop on any conversations.

From Israel's perspective Madame Rahab is the epitome of the outsider. She is a woman, a prostitute, and a foreigner. As a prostitute she is marginal even in her own culture, and her marginality is symbolized by her dwelling in the city wall, in the very boundary between the inside and the outside. Yet it is Rahab who understands best the nature of Yahweh. "Yahweh your God is indeed God in heaven above and on earth below" (2:11b). And it is Rahab who saves the lives of the feeble Israelite spies, who willingly cavort with foreigners, indeed with a woman whom they would have eventually slaughtered in combat.

Rahab's faith and kindness raise serious questions about the obsession with holy war in the book of Joshua. How many Rahabs are killed in the attempt to conquer the land? How many people with vision and loyalty surpassing that of the Israelites are destroyed in the attempt to establish a pure and unadulterated nation?

If the story of Rahab subverts Israel's vision of outsiders, the stories of Achsah and the daughters of Zelophehad undermine Israel's vision of itself as a monolithic, male-centered institution. Men, the daughters of Zelophehad remind the elders, are not the only alternative. Life can go on, identity can be sustained, even when there are no men to perpetuate the family name and inheritance. Achsah issues a reminder as well. Male vision of what is necessary for survival and prosperity is severely limited. The woman knows the requirements for life. Dry land must have water. Dry land without water, men without women, equal sterility and death.

## BIBLIOGRAPHY

Gunn, David M. "Joshua and Judges." In *The Literary Guide to the Bible*, edited by Robert Alter and Frank Kermode, pp. 102–121. Cambridge, Mass.: Harvard University Press, 1987.

Hawk, L. Daniel. *Every Promise Fulfilled: Contesting Plots in the Book of Joshua.* Literary Currents in Biblical Interpretation. Louisville, Ky.: Westminster/John Knox Press, 1991.

Polzin, Robert. *Moses and the Deuteronomist: A Literary Study of the Deuteronomic History.* New York: Seabury Press, 1980.

Rowlett, Lori. "'All Israel' as Literary Trope: Inclusion, Exclusion and Marginality in the Book of Joshua." Paper presented at Southwestern regional meeting of the Society of Biblical Literature, March 1991.

Zakovitch, Yair. "Humor and Theology or the Successful Failure of Israelite Intelligence: A Literary-Folkloric Approach to Joshua 2." In *Text and Tradition: The Hebrew Bible and Folklore*, edited by Susan Niditch, pp. 75–98. Atlanta: Scholars Press, 1990.

# JUDGES

*Danna Nolan Fewell*

## Introduction

Judges, along with Joshua, marks a pivotal point in the story extending from Genesis to 2 Kings. This larger story, completed during Israel's captivity in Babylon, tells of Yahweh's promise and gift of the land of Canaan and Israel's subsequent loss of it. Here at the center the promise is being fulfilled; the Israelites take possession of the gift only to reveal themselves to be no better caretakers of the land and their community within it than the Canaanites before them.

Introducing the book, Judg. 1:1–3:6 recounts the final stages of settlement. The Israelites, however, have been less successful at dispossessing the Canaanites (1:27–36) than the book of Joshua would have us believe. The theological ramifications of this failure are grave, for Israel's tolerance of the Canaanites threatens its identity and relationship with Yahweh (2:11–19).

In the main body of the book, 3:7–16:31, Israel's destiny unfolds through extended accounts and brief notices of judges who judge Israel or who deliver the people from oppression. The rhetorical framework introduced in 2:11–19 (cf. 3:7, 12; 4:1; 6:1; 10:6; 13:1) forms a common pattern for each story: Israel does evil in Yahweh's sight; Yahweh gives the people into the hand of oppressors; Israel cries to Yahweh; Yahweh raises up a deliverer; the deliverer defeats the oppressor; the people are faithful while the deliverer is alive and the land has rest.

In actuality this formula is inconsistent and its variations telling. The "deliverer" in the Deborah and Barak story is not explicitly identified. The people do not remain faithful to Yahweh during Gideon's lifetime; rather, Gideon's own construction of a golden ephod becomes a snare both to him and to them. By the time of Jephthah, the list of Israel's

apostasies is considerably expanded (10:6), and when the people first cry out in repentance, Yahweh refuses to deliver them. Neither the Jephthah story nor the Samson story depicts the land as regaining "rest," nor do the people of Samson's time bother to cry to Yahweh. Furthermore, Samson himself dies in captivity to the oppressor. Thus, the formula deteriorates and so ominously foreshadows Israel's future.

The stories themselves also illustrate a downward spiral for Israel and its leaders. The first judge, Othniel, is an ideal hero of notable lineage (a nephew of Caleb, the only one of the wilderness generation besides Joshua allowed to enter the promised land) who delivers Israel, with Yahweh's explicit help, from an ideal villain: Cushan-rishathaim, "Cushan, double evil."

After Othniel, Yahweh uses more unlikely deliverers. Ehud, the left-handed Benjaminite, kills Eglon ("Fat Calf") and frees his people from Moabite bondage. The woman Deborah rallies Israel to fight against the Canaanites, and the woman Jael, who is not even an Israelite, kills the Canaanite commander herself.

Gideon, too, is an unlikely candidate ("How can I deliver Israel? Behold, my clan is the weakest in Manasseh, and I am the least in my family" [6:15]; all translations are the author's), but he regresses to the category of the unfit. Not only does he insist on one divine sign after another before he is willing to fight the Midianites, but he wreaks vengeance on the Israelite cities who do not support his campaign. Persuaded reluctantly to become Israel's ruler, he immediately sets up an idol that leads his people into apostasy.

Not only is the lineage of Jephthah the Gileadite in question, but so are his motives for leading Israel's army. He fights the Ammonites not out of zeal for Yahweh or concern for Israel's oppression but out of a need to show himself superior to the community that ostracized him in his youth. So obsessed is he with personal victory and political authority that he seeks to secure God's power with a vow that costs his daughter her life.

Samson's story (chaps. 13–16) begins with promise, as a divine annunciation affirms his special birth. His confrontation with the Philistines, however, is not unlike Jephthah's bout with the Ammonites. Conflict does not arise from theological conviction or regard for his people. Rather, it is jealousy and vengeance ensuing from his infatuation with Philistine women that induce most of his violence. He lives his life in violation of Yahweh's covenant, and it is soon clear that whatever liberation Samson effects for Israel is done in spite of himself and not because of any special merit on his own part.

Israel's leadership sinks a long way from Moses to Samson. The people too show their

decline. Quickly forgetting their commitment to the covenant, they call on Yahweh only when in dire straits or wanting to take vengeance on others. Even then Yahweh is often a last resort. In several cases, eighteen, twenty, even forty years of oppression go by before the people turn to God. By the time of Philistine oppression, the people would rather live in subservience than petition Yahweh for help.

The concluding chapters, 17–21, are often viewed as merely a supplement; however, they bring appropriate completion to the story of Israel's decline. As the people conduct their own worship (chaps. 17–18), plan their own wars (chaps. 18; 20–21), abuse their own citizens, even their very family members (chaps. 19–21), no longer is the "sight of Yahweh" the standard of behavior. The old rhetorical formula gives way to a new one: "In those days there was no king in Israel; all the people did what was right in their own eyes" (17:6; 21:25; cf. 18:1; 19:1). As the book closes, the people recognize no leadership, either human or divine, and their community has degenerated into chaos.

## Comment

### Relating Women

How, precisely, do the women of Judges fit into this overall picture of decline? The construction and destruction of female characters and their relationships form a pattern that mirrors the deterioration of Israel's relation to Yahweh.

*Father and daughter: The gift of life (1:11–15).* The first woman appearing in Judges is one who has been encountered before (Joshua 15). As Israel enters the land, Caleb, rallying a war effort, offers his daughter Achsah as the prize for military heroism. Though hardly suiting modern tastes for equality, this is the stuff traditional fairy tales are made of, a plot motif certainly acceptable in ancient culture. Achsah's hand in marriage is offered to an ideal hero, Othniel, who of all the deliverers in Judges is of impeccable lineage and unquestionable integrity. When Achsah joins her new husband, she persuades him (some translations emend to read "he persuaded her") to ask her father for land. The text implies that the field is granted, because Achsah returns in the next scene to confront her father with an additional request. "Give me a blessing," she insists. "Since you have given me desert land, you should give me springs of water." Caleb complies by giving her

the upper and lower springs. Achsah is a woman who understands the importance of the land and its life-giving water. She recognizes that the land is a gift, and she takes the initiative to secure the water that will sustain life in the land.

Against this positive paradigm of a daughter being given to an ideal hero is juxtaposed the notice of Israel's apostasy of intermarriage with the inhabitants of the land (3:6). Rather than being allowed to marry within the tribe, the daughters of Israel are given to foreigners. For these daughters, the gift of the land will never be theirs. They are in essence dispossessed, and their fate foreshadows not only the plight of other women in Judges but the later dispossession of the people from the land in the Assyrian and Babylonian exiles.

*Voices of authority and victims of violence (chaps. 4–5).* In the second story involving women, there is a call for battle as in the days of Achsah and Caleb, but the situation differs greatly. The war now is defensive rather than offensive. The Israelites, having done evil in Yahweh's sight, have been oppressed by the Canaanites for twenty years.

Deborah is introduced as the wife of

Lappidoth. It is not, however, Deborah's relationship to her husband that will prove significant, but her relationship to Israel and to her appointed commander. Linguistically, the phrase "wife of Lappidoth" could also be translated "woman of fire," a designation that says more about Deborah's character than any familial relationship implies.

Deborah is a prophet and a judge, who settles disputes for Israel beneath a palm in the hills of Ephraim. Her relationship to Israel has public dimensions, both religious and judicial, but it is not without its familial dimensions as well. Later she will be called a "mother in Israel" (5:7) and in the context of this story one might well envision a Spartan mother who goads her children to fight. Allusion too may say something of Deborah's relationship to Israel. The only other Deborah in the Hebrew Scriptures, Rebekah's nurse, is also associated with a tree in this same territory (Gen. 35:8). Hence one is invited to see Deborah the judge as nursemaid to a politically incapacitated Israel.

Deborah summons Barak, the son of Abinoam, and instructs him, on the word of Yahweh, to raise a large army from the tribes of Naphtali and Zebulun and to fight the Canaanite army of Sisera at the Wadi Kishon. Barak responds cautiously, "If you will go with me, I will go; but if you will not go with me, I will not go" (4:8). It is unclear whether Barak's response indicates cowardice, lack of self-confidence (the Greek text adds here "for I do not know the day that the messenger of Yahweh will grant me success"), or distrust of Deborah's authority. The response is, however, in keeping with the changed times. In Caleb's day all the people heard God's command to conquer the land, and Israel was assured of victory (1:2). One can imagine, on the other hand, that Deborah's authority, though well recognized, is hardly a match for the commanding voices of Moses, Joshua, and Caleb. Neither Barak nor any of the people has heard Yahweh speak. He has only this woman's word for it, a word that has come out of the blue after twenty years of persecution, a word backed by no military experience, a word that is strategically naïve, that hardly takes into account the Canaanites' nine hundred iron chariots. Barak may well be testing Deborah. If she will stake her own life on this message from God, then so will he.

Deborah mocks his hesitance: "I will indeed go with you, but the path you take will not lead to your glory, for Yahweh will sell Sisera into the hand of a woman" (4:9). How far this is from the story of Caleb, Achsah, and Othniel! A woman rather than a man raises the rallying cry; a hesitant hero replaces an eager one; and a woman, not a man, will win the glory.

In the meantime, Sisera, the commander of the Canaanite army, hears of Barak's forces gathering at Mount Tabor. One might well visualize Sisera, in his haste and arrogance, leading his chariots down the dry riverbed to his destination. Barak's troops swarm down the steep banks, trapping the chariots where they cannot maneuver. Sisera's only means of escape is to abandon his chariot and flee on foot (4:12–16).

While his army is being slaughtered, Sisera flees to the tent of Jael, the wife of Heber the Kenite ("Joiner the Smith"). In an earlier aside (4:11), the narrator noted that Heber had moved away from the other Kenites and had camped near the Canaanites. The latter, with their iron chariotry, no doubt provided the smith ample trade. An alliance with the smith ("peace between King Jabin of Hazor and the clan of Heber the Kenite" [4:17]) assures Sisera that he can find asylum with Heber's wife, Jael.

Jael, however, has more pressing matters to consider than an obsolete political and economic alliance between her husband and this defeated commander. Though her thoughts are never revealed, she is clearly a woman caught in the middle. The Israelites have obviously won. They cannot be far behind Sisera, and they are unlikely to take kindly to a family that has allied itself with the enemy—especially if found to be hiding the Canaanite commander. Jael does what she has to do. She offers Sisera a seductive welcome, treats him with maternal care, and when he falls asleep assured of his safety, drives a tent peg through his mouth (raqaq = "parted lips," often translated misleadingly as "temple"), severing his spinal column, leaving him to die a convulsive death.

Intercepting the approaching Israelite forces, Jael leads them to their quarry. The sight of the dead man placates the victorious army and guarantees her that she faces no peril from the men of Israel. Jael wins not only her security, but in the song of Deborah and Barak, she wins Israel's praise as well (5:24–27). In their description of her feat, her violent act becomes larger than life. No seduction and deceit here. No ambush of a sleeping giant. In the song, Jael does combat with a standing Sisera. The killing and the dying take place in slow motion with Sisera falling between her legs, ravaged.

As the song continues, the graphically violent and rapacious imagery colors Sisera's downfall with poetic justice. Deborah and Barak move from Jael and Sisera to imagine Sisera's mother standing at her window awaiting her son. As soon as the listener is captured by the poignancy of the scene, the singers wrench sympathy away by attributing to the mother words that make the blood run cold: "Are they not finding and splitting the spoil? — A womb, two wombs, per head, per hero . . . ?" (5:30a).

On the one hand, the speech makes explicit what has been implicit in the story, that is, the threat to women during war. Women on the losing side can expect to be captured and raped if not killed. Hence the poetic justice with which the Israelite singers depict Sisera's death: the one who would threaten their women, and perhaps has threatened them in the past, is himself ravaged by a woman. On the other hand, by attributing to Sisera's mother such a casual approval of rape, they show her to be deserving of violation herself. The hoofbeats for which she listens will not be those of her son but those of the Israelite army. Whatever violence the Israelites use, it is justified in the rhetoric of the song. They will do to the Canaanites what the Canaanites would have done to them.

As Deborah and Barak contend that Sisera and his mother get what they deserve, the reader might surmise that in the end the difference between Israel and Canaan is not so vast after all. Israel, though now identified as Yahweh's friend (5:31), has been and will be again Yahweh's enemy. In forty years' time they will again do evil in the sight of Yahweh, and the cycle will begin again. And though she stands outside the window, Deborah, Israelite mother, envisions a Canaanite mother not unlike herself. Deborah is a bellicose mother who pushes her "children" to victory; hence, she easily invents the callous Canaanite mother eagerly awaiting the spoils of war. One mother reduces her enemy to a "womb"; the other reduces hers to a caricature of moral insensitivity. Each mother has justified the violence of her "children" by dehumanizing their victims.

And what of Jael, the woman who mothers Sisera to death? Some might call her a hero; others have labeled her sinister. More likely she is simply a survivor, a victim of her husband's politics who acts as she must in order to save herself and the remnant of her family.

The relationships depicted in this story may also reflect the evolving relationship between Yahweh and Israel. Yahweh's authority, like that of Deborah, is questioned (4:1: "The Israelites again did evil in the sight of Yahweh"; 5:8: "new gods were chosen"). When people find themselves in dire straits, they appeal to Yahweh, just as Jael appeals to violence. And like Jael, perhaps Yahweh too does what must be done in order to save the family of Israel and is lauded, like Jael, not for who he is but for what he has done to benefit Israel.

*Father and daughter: The sentence of death (chap. 11).* Judges 11 presents another father who gives his daughter as a reward for military victory. This story, however, falls far short of the ideal enacted by Caleb and Achsah. Their world is, no doubt, guided by patriarchal values, but it is not without respect for human worth. Jephthah and his daughter live in no such world. Jephthah's story begins with the hypocrisy of patriarchy. Blurring the person Gilead with the town, the narrator suggests that Jephthah's father might be any man in the town of Gilead. The town sires him by a prostitute and then kicks him out because he is a prostitute's son. The child becomes a man; he lives the life of an outlaw gathering about himself a raiding party of other "empty men" (11:1–3).

When the Ammonites threaten Gilead, the elders cast about for someone to fight for them. Jephthah emerges as a likely candidate. He is a proven warrior and, no doubt in their view, expendable to the community should he fall in battle. The elders petition him to become their general, but Jephthah holds out for a more permanent political position (11:9–11). He then tries his negotiating skills on the king of Ammon, but to little avail. When his speech fails, Jephthah prepares for war.

As Jephthah returns to his hometown of Mizpah to rally his troops, Yahweh's spirit, a sure sign of divine favor, comes upon him. Perhaps not recognizing the spirit's presence, perhaps not satisfied with its power, perhaps driven by it, Jephthah proceeds to bargain with God. For assured victory he trades the life of whoever (or whatever) comes first to meet him when he returns home (11:29–31). It is not clear whether his vow is made in public or in private or whether he has someone in mind, but once the battle is won, Jephthah returns home to be greeted by his daughter, his only child, coming out to meet him. He appears to respond with genuine surprise and sorrow. Since most interpreters have understood her to have stumbled unwittingly into her father's vow, his remark to her is often seen as a classic case of blaming the victim: "Alas, my daughter, *you* have brought me down. *You* are among my troublers. I have opened my mouth to Yahweh and I cannot recant" (11:35).

As an unwitting victim the daughter, though courageous and tragic, embodies the ultimate patriarchal value, that of women being submissive unto death. This act of self-sacrifice has received no little praise from male commentators. As one turn-of-the-century interpreter wrote concerning the young women who yearly mourned Jephthah's daughter:

[They] came back to be far better daughters than they went out. They came back softened, and purified, and sobered at heart. They came back ready to die for their fathers, and for their brothers, and for their husbands, and for their God. (Alexander Whyte, cited in Beal and Gunn)

An unknowing character who had no option but obedience is not, however, the only possible reading. Jephthah's vow was most likely made at Mizpah and not necessarily in secret. The daughter could very well have known the substance of her father's bargain. Indeed, when she responds to her father, she seems quite aware of what his vow entails. Rather than reading her answer as innocent submission, one might hear a tone of ironic judgment: "My father, you have opened your mouth to Yahweh. Do to me that which has gone forth from your mouth. After all, Yahweh has given you vengeance over your enemies, the Ammonites" (11:36).

Perhaps Jephthah had intended that his daughter hear the vow, to warn her against coming out first. Perhaps he had in mind forfeiting a servant or a bodyguard left behind to protect his home. In that case the daughter intends her greeting. She *is* one of Jephthah's troublers because, as she steps forth, she takes the place of someone whom he has considered expendable. She thereby passes judgment on her father's willingness to bargain for glory with the life of another. Her action condemns his priorities, and perhaps those of all Israel. In this sense she is not unlike Achsah confronting her father with the shortsightedness of his promise of dry land.

Some interpreters may have difficulty seeing such powerful initiative in this young woman, but it is in character with her subsequent speech and action. She, not her father, takes control of the situation. A reprieve of two months is requested and granted; she and her female companions retreat to the mountains to mourn her young womanhood. She chooses to take upon herself his vow, but she does not choose his company. She spends her remaining days with other young women who know her, who know what it is like to be a young woman in the midst of a violent society, and who, in the end, will not forget what she has done. After she returns to her father to be burned, she becomes a tradition in Israel. For four days every year, the women of Israel, young and old, would go forth to recount the story of the daughter of Jephthah (11:40). The song of Deborah had "recounted" the triumphs of Yahweh (5:11, the only other occurrence of this verb), but the songs of these women retell a sadder story, a story that is, no doubt, more in keeping with the state of Israel's affairs.

The male-oriented narrator, who has all along neglected to reveal the young woman's name, is now concerned to tell us that she had never known a man (11:39), as if this somehow makes her end more tragic. A woman reader might reply that she had known men, at least one all too well, and that is the heart of her tragedy.

And what of Jephthah, the abused child who grew up to murder his own daughter? He continues, for a while, to be a man of violence, victory, and verbal manipulation, but after only six years he dies and is buried in the same obscurity in which he was born. Just as (all of) Gilead is his father (11:1), he is buried (somewhere) in the towns of Gilead (12:7), high price for such short-lived glory.

A reader who recalls God's last-minute deliverance of Isaac in Genesis 22 might legitimately ask, Where is God in this story? Or one who remembers Saul's willingness to keep his vow and execute his son Jonathan (1 Samuel 14) might question, Where are the people who, as in Saul's case, might stay a violent father's hand? Do these parallels suggest that sons are valued more highly than daughters, by both God and society? Perhaps that is the prejudice of the communities that told these stories. Perhaps, too, the death of the daughter, the silence of God, and the absence of the people are but signs of something rotten with the state of Israel. God has been abandoned so many times by Israel and remembered again only when the people are under major threat that, by the time of Jephthah, God has grown impatient with the troubling of Israel (10:16; an alternative translation to NRSV "he could no longer bear to see Israel suffer"). Yahweh, like Jephthah, has been cast out and is only recalled when there is fighting to be done. Yahweh is merely another party to be bargained with and, once the victory is granted, to be dispensed with, like the daughter.

### Women among men: Promises, threats, and bribes (chaps. 13–16).
In Judges 13 the narrative turns from father and daughter to a mother and her son. An angel of Yahweh appears to the barren and unnamed wife of Manoah the Danite and announces that she will bear a son. He instructs her to abstain from strong drink and unclean food. Once the boy is born, the angel charges, no razor is to touch his head. The child is to be a nazirite "from the womb" and will begin to deliver Israel from the oppressive Philistines.

The woman tells her husband Manoah about the visit from the strange "man of God," who had revealed neither his name nor his origin. She repeats his promise of a nazirite son and the instructions concerning food and drink. She mentions neither the razor nor the boy's destiny. She seems to understand that her son's heroism will be incomplete, for when she reports that he will be a nazirite "from the womb," she ominously, and perhaps prophetically, adds "to the day of his death" (13:7; cf. 13:5).

Though the woman has received a message from God, the husband, like Barak before him, questions the woman's authority. Disregarding the instructions already received by the woman, Manoah prays to Yahweh, asking that the man of God might return "to teach us what we are to do concerning the boy who will be born" (13:8). The angel, eluding Manoah, reappears to the woman as she sits alone. She fetches her husband and, though she identifies the man as the previous visitor, Manoah must ask that question for himself. Once the man has confirmed who he is, Manoah makes his superfluous inquiry, "What guideline will there be for the boy? What is he to do?" (13:12). The angel, much to Manoah's frustration and perhaps intentionally so, reveals less to Manoah than earlier to the woman, merely repeating the dietary instructions and adding with an air of mystery, "Let the woman heed all that I told her."

Manoah, not perceiving the true identity of his wife's guest and not willing to let the man go, insists that he stay for a meal. The angel instructs him to offer the food as a burnt offering to Yahweh instead. Manoah, still unenlightened, asks the man's name, but the angel declines to answer, saying, "It is too extraordinary." It is not until the angel ascends in the flame of the offering that Manoah realizes who the stranger is. "We shall surely die," he says to his wife, "for we have seen God." The wife, clearly the wiser of the two, points out the absurdity of this assumption: "If Yahweh had meant to kill us, he would not have accepted [our] offering . . . or revealed to us all these things, or now proclaimed such things as these" (13:23). In the course of time the woman bears a son and names him Samson.

When Samson grows up he becomes quite taken with a Philistine woman from the vineyard country of Timnah. On one of his trips to court her, he is attacked by a lion which he kills bare-handed. On a later excursion he comes upon the lion's carcass and finds its cavity filled with bees and honey. He eats some of the honey and shares the rest with his parents (14:1–9).

Loving a Philistine woman, spending his time in wine country, handling dead carcasses and eating unclean food all hardly bode well for a nazirite who is to be Israel's champion against the Philistines (cf. Num. 6:1–8). Just as Samson "breaks the rules," so this story breaks many of the plot patterns established thus far in Judges. Samson is not to be a military hero, for Israel is not keen to take up arms against the oppressor. Israel seems, in fact, to want no deliverer at all, whether divine or human. The people do not cry to Yahweh for help; they even chide Samson for stirring up trouble: "Do you not know that the Philistines are lords over us? What then have you done to us?" (15:11). Indeed, Israel seems quite satisfied with its lot.

So God has a problem: How does one deliver people who do not want to be delivered? Here the answer seems to come in the form of the unexpected—a nazirite who breaks the rules, an Israelite who loves the enemy, a mighty fighter who is no leader, a deliverer who, in fact, does not seem to know that he is meant to deliver.

It is Samson's propensity to "break rules" that allows the plot to develop. At his wedding feast he poses a wager and riddle to his thirty Philistine companions. Thirty garments he will give for the answer to the riddle: "Out of the eater came something to eat; out of the strong came something sweet" (14:14). Despite the many feasible answers that would have reflected the sexually laden atmosphere of a wedding feast, the "right" answer comes, of course, from

Samson's experience with the lion and the honey. In this sense, not only has he broken the rules of the nazirite by handling a dead carcass and eating unclean food, but he has broken verbal rules as well. Riddles are supposed to be unlocked through association and word play, general connections that anyone can make. Samson's riddle, however, is tied to his particular experience, and no amount of cleverness is going to reveal what only he himself knows.

The riddle's answer, like the outcome of Jephthah's vow, is unknowable, and like Jephthah's vow, the riddle endangers a woman who is innocent of the interchange. Samson's companions, desperate to win the wager, threaten Samson's bride and her family with death by fire. The bride, caught between a foreigner and thirty kinsmen, between the wrath of one and the wrath of thirty, succumbs to the threat of thirty. She wheedles the answer from Samson and tells the companions. His riddle made known, Samson responds with violence. He takes the lives and garments of thirty strangers in order to pay off the wager and then returns to his father's house. The young woman's father, assuming that his daughter has been abandoned, gives her to Samson's best man.

When, after a time, Samson returns to visit his wife, he is denied conjugal rights. His wife, he is told, has been given to someone else. Another burst of rage drives him to burn the fields, the vineyards, and the groves of the Philistines. When the Philistines discover who has done this and why it has been done, they retaliate, not by pursuing Samson but by burning his wife and her father. In a world of male competition and violence, the woman cannot win. She is but a pawn in a larger conflict. The burning of the woman by her own people recalls again the story of Jephthah and his daughter. The reader might well wonder, Is there, in the end, much difference between the Israelites and the Philistines?

The woman's murder further ignites Samson's revenge. Violence escalates as, occasion after occasion, Samson slaughters the Philistines. The relationship between marriage and the martial has turned upside down. Instead of successful military exploit leading to marriage, land, and life, as in the case of Achsah and Othniel, here, unsuccessful marriage leads to murder and unending vengeance.

The next major female character to appear is the notorious Delilah (16:4). Usually considered by interpreters to be the *femme fatale par excellence*, Delilah is rarely examined in her own right. Because Samson is often labeled a hero, Delilah is cast in the role of the villain who brings about the downfall of God's chosen. Delilah, however, is more than an (un?)supporting actress. In this part of the story, the spotlight is hers. Of all the women in Samson's story, she alone is named. Once introduced, she initiates the action. It is her desire that drives the plot; Samson is merely a respondent. The woman is the focus of the reader's attention.

Delilah's identity is not bound to any man. Introduced simply by name, she is a woman who takes care of herself. She conducts her love affair with Samson and her business affairs with the lords of the Philistines without any father, brother, or husband acting as mediator. The narrator says that Samson loves Delilah. How Delilah feels about him is not revealed. Some degree of ambivalence is probable since she readily agrees to the Philistine proposal that she seduce Samson and discover the source of his strength. Eleven hundred pieces of silver from each Philistine nobleman are promised in exchange for information on how Samson might be subdued. Doubtless, as a woman alone, Delilah finds that the love of a wanted man is no match for the security of wealth.

Delilah sets out to discover Samson's secret. She does not, however, as many commentators are eager to assert, deceive him. She asks him directly what she wants to know. Samson is the one who deceives her. Three times he lies to her concerning the source of his strength and how he might be bound. She tests him, each time binding him according to his instructions. Though interpreters often assume that each time she binds him while he sleeps, on the first and second trials there is no mention of his being asleep. He submits to her willingly, as if it were some kind of game. Neither is he surprised when, upon the third occasion, he awakes from sleep to find that she has woven his hair as he had told her. Each time when she cries out a warning, he breaks his bonds as if they were nothing.

He is indeed playing games with her, and she repeatedly accuses him of such, but to no avail. When she questions his love for her, however, pressing him day after day (cf. 14:16–17), he grows impatient and succumbs. The secret of his strength lies in the fact that a razor has never touched his hair. He has been a nazirite, he tells her, from his mother's womb.

The mention of the mother's womb is telling, for he is to become a child again. He transfers his allegiance from his real mother to his substitute lover-mother. Not only does he reveal the secret known only to himself and his mother, but he entrusts himself to Delilah as a child might trust his mother (cf. Sisera's trust of Jael). As he sleeps upon Delilah's lap (some texts read, "between her knees"), he loses his manly hair and his manly strength. Samson, overpowered by a woman, is captured by the Philistines. Delilah disappears from the story, financially secure for life.

Sandwiched between the story of Samson's bride and his lover Delilah is Samson's encounter with a Philistine prostitute (16:1-3). About this woman's character nothing is revealed apart from her profession. It is her profession, however, that is key to understanding the behavior of the other two women with whom Samson has been involved. The analogy here is not moral but sociological. A prostitute is a businesswoman, a woman who uses her sexuality as a means of feeding and clothing herself. She does what she does in order to ensure her survival. The bride and Delilah behave in like manner. They do what they do in order to survive. The bride attempts (unsuccessfully) to protect herself and her family from the threat of death. Delilah, a woman without father, brother, or husband to support her, secures for herself financial stability.

In this light, these women are not unlike Jael, or Rahab in the book of Joshua. Self-interest is a strong motivator. The difference is that we, as readers, experience a shift in point of view. While Jael and Rahab, despite their personal motivations, are celebrated for their allegiance to Israel, the women in Samson's life ally themselves with their own people, the Philistines. If this had been Philistine literature, they would have doubtless been remembered as heroes.

Samson's fascination with foreign women recalls the beginning of Judges and the juxtaposition of the ideal, internal tribal union of Achsah and Othniel and the narrator's indictment of Israelite men for taking foreign wives and giving their daughters to foreign men (3:6). The last deliverer of Israel does what is most symptomatic of apostasy. While these women do not lead him to follow other gods, they do divert his attention away from Yahweh so that Yahweh's work gets done as it suits Samson's personal vendettas.

**Women betrayed (chaps. 17–21).** The theme of self-interest continues to play through the remainder of Judges. As one moves from Samson, the last deliverer, who does and takes what he pleases (see 14:3, 7) and the women in his story, who, by the nature of their status in society, must do what is best for themselves, one comes to the concluding episodes of Judges, which depict a society in which "all the people do what is right in their own eyes" (17:6; 21:25).

Another mother and son introduce this final portion of the book. The son, Micah, has betrayed his mother. The reader is not allowed to witness the betrayal but is permitted to overhear his confession. Micah, fearing his mother's curse, admits that he has stolen from her eleven hundred pieces of silver (17:2; cf. 16:5). The mother replies not with a curse but with a blessing upon her son. When he returns the money, the mother announces that she is consecrating the silver to Yahweh for her son and (according to the Hebrew text) promises to return the silver to her son. She has a smith cast two hundred pieces of the silver into an idol which finds its home in the house of Micah. What becomes of the remainder of the money is not disclosed, but in the end, one might assume that she keeps it for herself.

Micah builds a shrine for the idol. He contributes other sacred objects and installs one of his sons as priest. This is one step beyond Samson's story. While Samson had little concept of covenantal religion, he did acknowledge Yahweh as a source of his strength. In this religious family, however, there is no reliance on Yahweh. The divine name gets bandied around, but the deity is never addressed. Yahweh's identity is lost upon tangible objects. Private shrines, idols, and unordained priests have splintered the community of Israel into individuals making up their own rules, much as Samson had done, and seeking religious security in the privacy of their homes.

And what of this mother and son? What kind of son steals from his own mother? And what kind of mother leads her son into idolatry? She is not like the mother of Samson, carefully keeping religious tradition for the sake of her son, nor a "mother in Israel" making judicious decisions and leading her people in liberation. Micah and his mother are looking for the secret to security—Samson's hair or the promise of an angel or the bribe of a Philistine lord. Security finally comes, so they think (17:13), in the form of a Levite whom Micah hires as his personal priest. Security, however, is short-lived, as his possession soon becomes the possession of an entire tribe (18:1-31). The security of priesthood goes to the highest bidder.

The final story in Judges also involves a Levite. By focusing on Levites in the concluding episodes, the narrator communicates the extent of Israel's moral decline. The corruption that has infected the people and their deliverers has even spread to those who are entrusted with keeping Yahwistic tradition.

The Levite in question, a resident of Ephraim, takes for himself a wife. "Concubine" is an unsatisfactory translation of the woman's status. She is neither simply a mistress nor a servant, since the man is called "her husband" (19:3) and her father is identified as the man's "father-in-law" (19:4).

Things do not go well in the Levite's household. The young woman "resists" him (reading *zanach* instead of *zanah*), "gets away from him," and returns to her father's house in Bethlehem. The nature of the domestic problem is not disclosed, but judging from the Levite's later behavior, one might easily imagine a scenario of abuse. Four months pass before the Levite decides to go after his wife and woo her back.

The "wooing" is never described and, for all the reader knows, never takes place. A scene of excessive male bonding replaces any attempt at romantic persuasion. The young woman's father, pleased to see his son-in-law, makes an elaborate show of hospitality, encouraging the Levite to stay three, then four, then five days. When, on the evening of the fifth day, the Levite insists on leaving with his wife, still nothing has been said as to the wishes of the young woman. We do not know if she wanted to return with her husband or if her father had persuaded her or had, more likely, simply arranged for her to return.

They begin their journey in the late afternoon and, rather than spending the night in Jebusite Jerusalem, they push on to Benjaminite Gibeah. In Gibeah they find no one to take them in except an old man, himself a native of Ephraim.

While they are relaxing in the old man's house, the men of the city, a worthless lot, surround the house insisting that the Levite be brought out that they might "know" him. Hardly a welcoming committee, their intent is torture and humiliation, "sport" at the expense of the Levite. The old man protests, offering them his daughter and the Levite's wife instead. The men, however, are adamant, and the Levite, in desperation, seizes his wife and throws her out to the mob. The mob, satisfied with this diversion, leaves the Levite alone and proceeds to gang rape the woman all night long. In the dawn they let her go, and she stumbles back to the old man's house and collapses at the door. Abandoned by her father, betrayed by her husband, raped and tortured by a mob, the woman is trapped in a world of men. She has nowhere to go but back to the husband who threw her out, only to find that the door of hospitality and safety is still closed against her.

The Levite arises to go on his way as if nothing has happened. Opening the door, he finds his wife lying with her hands on the threshold. "Get up, let's go," he says. But there is no answer.

Putting her battered body upon his donkey, he takes her home. When he enters the house he takes *the* knife (the definite article in the Hebrew text indicates premeditation, cf. Gen. 22:10), seizes his wife (cf. 19:25), and cuts her body into twelve pieces, as if she were some sort of sacrificial animal. At what point the woman dies we are not told. He sends her piece by piece throughout the tribes of Israel in an effort to summon an assembly.

Throughout the story the woman has been allowed no speech. Now it is her broken body that speaks to all Israel. What her body says, what the Levite intends for it to say, and what Israel hears, however, are hardly congruent. Just as her body became every man's that night in Gibeah, now her body is given to all Israel. Her message is that she has been abandoned and betrayed by all the men with whom she has come in contact. The Levite's message is that his honor has been insulted, his life threatened, and his property damaged. Even his version of the story (20:4–7) removes him from culpability. What Israel hears is a message of outrage and an excuse for war.

As Israel rallies against Benjamin, they are careful to inquire of Yahweh. They are not careful, however, to ask the right question, which is whether or not they should fight at all. Having already decided to fight, they arrogantly ask, "Who shall go up first?" Yahweh, allowing them to do as they please, responds, just as he had at the beginning of the settlement of the land (1:1–2), but this time with what might be interpreted as ironic indifference: "Judah shall go up first" (20:18).

The ending is filled with echoes of the beginning—Judah leading the fight (1:1–2), a story of dismemberment (1:5–7), a woman on a donkey (1:11–15)—all images that have been skewed in the course of time. Judah goes up first, not against a foreign enemy but against fellow Israelites. The dismemberment is not that of an enemy king, but that of an innocent and unprotected Israelite woman. The woman on a donkey rides not erect and determined to secure life for herself and her family, but limp and immobile, a victim of violence, the embodiment of betrayal and death.

The war against Benjamin is bloody and the tribe is left all but extinct. Six hundred men remain, but the Israelites have slaughtered all the women and children. The Israelites, stained with the blood of other Israelite men, women, and children, cry again to Yahweh with ironic gall: "O Yahweh, God of Israel, why has it come to pass that today there should be one tribe missing from Israel?" (21:3). Like the Levite, they accept no responsibility and use violence to beget violence. They slaughter yet another town, Jabesh-Gilead, to secure virgins for the remaining Benjaminite men. These four hundred women are not enough, and the Israelites, further relieving themselves of blame, seek to repair the damage that *Yahweh* has done: "The people had compassion on Benjamin because Yahweh had made a breach in the tribes of Israel" (21:15). They conspire against the young women of Shiloh, permitting the men of Benjamin to abduct them while engaged in their festal dances. Two hundred more young women are seized to satisfy the needs of Benjamin.

Despite the people's eagerness to blame Yahweh for this devastation, the narrator is quick to remind us that "in those days there was no king in Israel"—not even Yahweh was sovereign—"and all the people did what was right in their own eyes." As the book has progressed, the motivations toward violence have become increasingly personal. From the progress of the nation (1:1–26), to the defense of the nation (4:1–5:31), to the concern for personal glory and acceptance (11:1–12:7), to personal vengeance (14:1–16:31), to the wounded honor of the dishonorable (19:1–20:7), violence has turned from a tool for the common good to the weapon of anarchy.

## Speaking of Women

In addition to the pattern of violence, the characterization of women in Judges maps the moral and theological deterioration of Israel in this text. The control that these women have over their lives, their pasts and their futures, is reflected in their speech. This, in turn, measures Israel's own development through time.

Achsah's speech to her father is respectfully confrontational. She has a vision of the future,

and the future rests with the land. Her request for water is her move to secure her future. Deborah, also, has a vision of the future. She calls the Israelites to break out of their victimization and embrace that new future. In fact, so strong is her vision of Israel's future that she, in her song, can reshape the past. She can ambiguate Israel's evil, she can exaggerate Israel's courage, all in the interests of restoring the friendship between Israel and Yahweh (5:31).

Like Achsah's speech, the speech of Jephthah's daughter to her father is also respectfully confrontational. She, like Achsah, has been promised to another. Her lover, however, is not a husband but a silent deity of death. She can request only the briefest of a future, because she has sacrificed her own future and that of her father in the attempt to save someone else and to deliver Jephthah from his misplaced obsession with glory. The women who retell her story realize that their future and the future of Israel are dependent on a recounting of the past. Unlike Deborah, they are unable to reshape or uninterested in reshaping the past. For them it is truthful tragedy, not whitewashed victory, that can bring about change in the future.

Samson's mother, like Deborah a mother in Israel, is also privy to the future, and her speech, like Deborah's, is questioned. Samson's mother, however, has a more somber vision. The future is not open-ended and full of possibility. She sees the beginning (womb) and the ending (the day of [his] death), and she knows that the future is conditional (upon obedience to nazirite law) and limited (Samson will only *begin* to deliver Israel from the Philistine oppression).

For the next three women we encounter— Samson's bride, Delilah, and Micah's mother— the future is immediate and elusive. Their speeches reflect their attempts to take care of themselves, to protect themselves from physical harm, as in the case of Samson's bride, or to shield themselves from economic destitution. To some extent, their speeches are not their own because they are manipulated by the threats, bribes, betrayals, and confessions of the men in their lives. For these women the future is mere survival and not much more. Indeed, this is where Israel is—unable to see beyond the immediate situation, content to live with foreign oppression, and eager not to upset the status quo (15:11–13).

Neither the Levite's wife nor the women who are subsequently murdered or abducted and raped are allowed speech. The world of

Israel has become a place where women have neither voice nor choice. Their future is decided for them, and they have no place in the land. The Levite's wife may attempt to flee to the past (her father's house) to avoid a future with her husband, but her father will merely make sure that she returns. The woman, in the end, is caught between her father's house and her husband's. No other house offers refuge to her. Trapped on the threshold, unable to move, she is torn apart and displaced by the men of Israel.

Recounted in the Babylonian exile, this tale was but one attempt to explain what had become of Israel at this particular juncture in its history. The Israelites, like the Canaanites before them, had lost sight of the gift of the land, of the commitment to family and community, and of the leadership of Yahweh. They, like the Canaanites before them and, ironically, like the young women of Shiloh and Jabesh-Gilead, were, by the end of 2 Kings, all dispossessed. No amount of retelling could change that part of Israel's story; the "future" had become the past.

Knowing the end of this story does not, however, preclude the possibility of new beginnings. The Israelite narrator perhaps knew that the call to change, to transformation, is inherent in every text, whether it be the deepening of knowledge, the altering of a worldview, or simple self-recognition. Like the women who remembered Jephthah's daughter, this narrator knew the power of retelling the troubling stories, of "writing the wrongs," of one's own society, knew that self-critique is hope that a happier story can be told.

## BIBLIOGRAPHY

Bal, Mieke. *Death and Dissymmetry: The Politics of Coherence in the Book of Judges.* Chicago: University of Chicago Press, 1988.

——. *Lethal Love: Feminist Literary Readings of Biblical Love Stories.* Bloomington, Ind.: Indiana University Press, 1987.

Beal, Timothy K., and David M. Gunn. "The Book of Judges." In *Dictionary of Biblical Interpretation*, edited by John Hayes. Nashville: Abingdon Press (forthcoming).

Exum, J. Cheryl. "Promise and Fulfillment: Narrative Art in Judges 13." *Journal of Biblical Literature* 99 (1980), 34–59.

Fewell, Danna Nolan, and David M. Gunn. "Controlling Perspectives: Women, Men, and the Authority of Violence in Judges 4 and 5." *Journal of the American Academy of Religion* 58 (1990), 101–123.

Gunn, David M. "Joshua and Judges." In *The Literary Guide to the Bible*, edited by Robert Alter and Frank Kermode, pp. 102–121. Cambridge, Mass.: Harvard University Press, 1987.

Hamlin, E. John. *At Risk in the Promised Land: A Commentary on the Book of Judges.* Grand Rapids: Wm. B. Eerdmans Publishing Co., 1990.

Polzin, Robert. *Moses and the Deuteronomist: A Literary Study of the Deuteronomic History.* New York: Seabury Press, 1980.

Trible, Phyllis. *Texts of Terror: Literary-Feminist Readings of Biblical Narratives.* Philadelphia: Fortress Press, 1984.

# RUTH

*Amy-Jill Levine*

## Introduction

In this deceptively simple narrative a poor, widowed foreigner becomes the wife of a respected man from Bethlehem and the great-grandmother of King David. Ruth is depicted as the ideal daughter-in-law, wife, and Gentile. For Naomi, she offers the loyalty and support associated less with daughters-in-law than with husbands, and her worth is proclaimed by the women of Bethlehem as being greater than that of seven sons. In motivating Boaz to action and in bearing his child, Ruth proves herself a worthy wife. Finally, Ruth testifies to the contributions Gentiles can make to the covenant community. Through her loyalty, fortitude, and cleverness, she secures the future for herself, for her mother-in-law, and for the Davidic line. Yet underlying these idealistic representations are complex social issues, gender relations, and personal motivations. The narrative's focus on such matters as the lot of single women in rural Palestine and the problem of interethnic (i.e., mixed) marriages makes the book of Ruth substantially more than an unambiguous, pious idyll. Complicating the narrative even more is the depiction of Ruth: her reactions to Bethlehem, to Boaz, to her marriage and child, her odd reports to Naomi, even her reasons for leaving Moab remain unexplained.

Set during the time of the Judges, the book of Ruth does not concentrate on international relations or community apostasy, war or death. Rather, it speaks of food, plenitude, and "loving-kindness and loyalty" (*chesed*) shown not by the deity but by a Moabite woman (1:8; 2:20; 3:10). Beginning with a famine, departure from Judah, childless marriages, and the deaths of three men,

the text moves from the emptiness of Moab to the renewed fertility of Bethlehem: a good harvest, marriage and security, and the birth of a son.

Through dialogue and action, Ruth also attempts to move Naomi from emptiness to fullness. Although the text's only mention of "love" concerns that of Ruth for her mother-in-law (4:15), Naomi continues to believe that a woman's happiness and fulfillment require men, that is, a husband and sons. The biblical tradition elsewhere speaks of Gentile daughters-in-law who make life difficult for their husband's mother (e.g., Esau's Hittite wives and Rebekah, Gen. 27:46), but the book of Ruth offers the opposite perspective: Naomi, set in her ways, must learn Ruth's value. Ruth also provides a corrective to Boaz's initial passivity. She arranges their meeting, motivates his willingness to serve as a redeemer, and provides him with a rationale to make his relationship with the Gentile widow socially acceptable. Her various actions, which contravene social expectations, justifiably locate Ruth not only among David's ancestors but also among the other unconventional women—Tamar, Rahab, and Bathsheba—who appear in the genealogy of Jesus (Matt. 1:5).

But Ruth's actions offer no means for improving the social system of Bethlehem. The book of Ruth offers no prescriptions for changing the circumstances in which women, either native or foreign, find themselves impoverished and unprotected. Women have a voice in the community, but that is all. Their fates are determined by men: their husbands and sons and the town elders. Moreover, Ruth's Gentile background remains a stigma: her Moabite ancestry associates her with an aggressive form of seduction and with the taint of idolatry. For her loyalty she is commended, but her Gentile associations prevent her from being fully incorporated into the covenant community. Ruth remains "Ruth the Moabite."

Ruth's Gentile origins may also explain her general lack of reference to God. Naomi, Boaz, and the women of Bethlehem, much more so than Ruth, express belief in divine intervention. Ruth, although she expresses fidelity to Naomi's deity (1:16), locates her confidence primarily in herself. Whether this attribute is a strength or a flaw remains debated.

With all the language of piety, God appears actively only once in the book—in allowing Ruth to conceive (4:13). With this divine intervention the depiction of Ruth shifts from that of active agent to one in the power of God. Her limited role in the final chapter is consistent with the text's ambivalent attitude toward Gentiles: the Israelite woman Naomi, not the Moabite Ruth, becomes the acclaimed mother of Obed (4:17).

Given this denouement, and considering the difficulties faced by women like Ruth and Naomi, the tale might be seen less as a celebration of Ruth's abilities and *chesed* than as a pernicious, exploitative tract. The book praises Ruth, but it may also preach that women's principal worth is in producing sons and that Gentile women, sexually manipulative and therefore dangerous, should not be fully incorporated into Israel. Perhaps

Ruth's unconventional actions are acceptable in this book only because she is a Moabite; perhaps her model is not to be appropriated by Israelite women. It is the reader's task to determine whether this book affirms Ruth or ultimately erases her, whether she serves as a moral exemplar or as a warning against sexually forward Gentile women.

In the Greek translation of the Hebrew Bible (the Septuagint) and consequently in most Christian Bibles, the book of Ruth is placed between Judges and 1 Samuel. There, it breaks the narrative flow from the description of anarchy that ends Judges to the explanation for the monarchy that begins 1 Samuel. In the Jewish canon, Ruth is included among the *Ketubim*, or "Writings," and is traditionally read on *Shebu'ot* (the feast of "Weeks"), the spring harvest festival. The actual date of composition is debated. Some linguistic analysis suggests a period as early as the Solomonic empire (ca. 950 B.C.E.). This date would explain the emphasis on the genealogy and the interest in Bethlehem; having an ancestor like the loyal Ruth would serve both to glorify David's house and to excuse the various international marriages of his son Solomon. However, the presence of Aramaisms and the generally positive treatment accorded the relationship between Ruth and Boaz suggest a response to the postexilic laws against intermarriage (Ezra 9–10; Neh. 10:30; 13:23–29). If this later date is accepted, then the text may be a reaction against enforced divorce even as it reflects the society's suspicion of foreign wives.

## Comment

### The Journey (chap. 1)

During a famine not mentioned in Judges, Elimelech moves his family from Bethlehem (literally, the "house of bread") to Moab. Although reminiscent of Israel's settling in Egypt (Genesis 46), this move is problematic: Moab is associated with hostility (Numbers 22–24; Judg. 3:12–30; but cf. 1 Sam. 22:3–4) and with sexual perversity (Gen. 19:30–38). Its food is used not for supplying hungry Israelites but for feasting before local gods (Num. 25:1–5). Deuteronomy 23:3–6 (cf. Neh. 13:1) excludes both Moabites and Ammonites from the "assembly of God," and the context of this legislation reinforces the association of Moab with improper sexuality. Elimelech consequently

may be seen as disloyal to his land and his God. Thereby he offers an initial contrast to Ruth, who leaves her own land out of loyalty to Naomi.

Elimelech then dies and so leaves his wife Naomi and two sons, Mahlon and Chilion, in Moab. Whether Elimelech's death is associated with the move is unexplained. The sons next marry local women. Not only are Orpah and Ruth Moabites and so members of an already stigmatized nation, their marriages are childless when the sons die ten years later. Supposedly a land of plenty, Moab proves to be the site of sterility and death.

Bereft of sons and husband and hearing that there was food in Judah, Naomi resolves to return. Her daughters-in-law accompany her, but she urges each to return to her "mother's house." The more prevalent term is "father's house" (cf. Gen. 38:11; Lev. 22:13; Num. 30:16; Deut. 22:21; Judg. 19:2–3), and various ancient translations of the Hebrew replace "mother's house" with the more common, male-defined expression. But "mother's house" is found also in Gen. 24:28; Song 3:4; 8:2, and elsewhere, where it appears in contexts of sexuality, marriage, and women who determine both their own destiny and that of others. In the book of Ruth, the expression indicates in particular Naomi's wish that her daughters-in-law would find new husbands. For Naomi, marriage and sons are the only sources of a woman's security and value.

Not recognizing that the Moabite women might want to remain with her because of love or loyalty, Naomi describes her own worth as reproductive only. Since she has no more children, she cannot offer these women sons. Her comments do not reflect the custom of levirate marriage: that institution would pertain only to sons of Elimelech (Deut. 25:5–10). Rather, Naomi is expressing her own emptiness. She defines herself literally as "too old to have a husband" (1:12) or, more colloquially, to have sexual intercourse (cf. Hos. 3:3). Lacking men in her family, she sees herself as cursed by the "hand of YHWH" (1:13).

Orpah kisses Naomi good-bye, but Ruth, assuming the closest physical position a woman takes to another in the scriptures, "clung" to her (*dabaq*, 1:14) and refused to "leave" her (*'azab*, 1:16). The terms echo the ideal marital relationship expressed in Gen. 2:24 (cf. Prov. 18:24). The text's further uses of *dabaq* continue to focus on relationships between women. Boaz and Naomi both urge Ruth to "cling to" the women in the fields (2:8, 21; NRSV: "stay close," "keep close"). It is in the company of women that Ruth, like Naomi, will find safety.

Naomi then appeals to Ruth's theological loyalties: like Orpah, she should return not only to her people but also to her gods. But Ruth insists that Naomi's people will become her people and that their God will become hers. Sounding more like a spouse than a daughter-in-law (cf. 3:13), Ruth even vows to lodge with and be buried with Naomi. She concludes with the statement that the deity should strike her were anything but death to part them. Like Abraham, she is willing to leave her home for Israel, but unlike the patriarch she is motivated by

loyalty toward her mother-in-law, not by divine command. Nor does she have the promise of land and children; her future at best is one of economic uncertainty. Yet Naomi never acknowledges her daughter-in-law's fidelity. Following Ruth's speech, she is silent.

Naomi's view of her misfortune and her lack of appreciation of Ruth accompany her to Bethlehem. While the "whole town" stirs at both travelers, the women ask, "Is this Naomi?" Only after Ruth has a son do these women explicitly acknowledge her existence. Naomi rejects not only their greeting but also her name, which means "Pleasant"; she insists that she be called Mara, or "Bitterness," because she has returned from Moab empty. Naomi defines "full" and "empty" only in relation to offspring; but the terms, and so women's worth, have wider applications. "Full" reappears in 2:12, where the full reward Boaz wishes for Ruth goes beyond children to include security, marriage, and—given the immediate context—food. "Empty" is repeated in 3:17, in the context of grain.

Naomi had not left Bethlehem "full" as she claims (1:21), since she left for Moab during a famine. Nor has she returned empty, even though all the verbs and pronouns she uses are in the singular. Ruth is by her side. Silently Ruth provides the ironic commentary and the corrective to Naomi's homecoming.

## Introductions (chap. 2)

Contradicting Naomi's claims of emptiness, the second chapter opens with the mention of Boaz, a "prominent, rich" relative of Elimelech. The scene immediately shifts to Ruth, who suggests that she should glean and perhaps find favor in someone's sight. Supporting her plan, Naomi addresses Ruth as "my daughter," but she says nothing more. Naomi's failure to mention Boaz is never explained. Ruth, however, fortuitously finds herself on Boaz's property. Only when she returns home with grain and mentions Boaz does Naomi engage in conversation with her.

The narrator's complimentary introduction of Boaz is confirmed by his entrance: he blesses the reapers and receives their blessing in return. Next, he notices Ruth and asks, "To whom does this young woman belong?" Although his query implies that Ruth belongs to another, it is taken by the overseer to refer to her lineage; hence the response, "She is the Moabite who came back with Naomi." Ruth is no one's wife, betrothed, or servant. Nor is she a member of the community; thus she is identified by race rather than, as Naomi is, by name. The overseer adds that Ruth requested to "glean and gather among the sheaves behind the reapers" (2:7). As a widow and a resident alien, Ruth was legally entitled to glean wherever she chose (Lev. 19:9–10; 23:22; Deut. 24:19–22); however, perhaps because she sought to glean among the sheaves themselves, or perhaps because she was a foreigner, she requested Boaz's permission. Thus Ruth engineers her introduction to Boaz, and the two meet in this fecund setting.

Boaz paternally addresses Ruth as "my daughter," but he is more loquacious than Naomi. He warns her to keep close to his women workers and informs her that his men have been ordered not to bother her or prevent her from drinking the water they have drawn. This scene offers a reverse of the typical meeting, found elsewhere in the Bible, between men and women who will eventually marry (cf. Genesis 24; 29; Ex. 2:15–22), with Ruth in the man's role: she is the one who leaves home, seeks her fortune, encounters hardships, and has water drawn for her. Complementing the literary convention is Boaz's explanation for his kindness to Ruth. He has been told what she has done for Naomi and the price she has paid in so doing: "how you left your father and mother and your native land and came to a people that you did not know before" (2:11). Although the women of Bethlehem will recognize Ruth's value in the context of the child she bears, Boaz sees the full extent of her *chesed*. His more accurate evaluation of her worth provides both his own motivation for marrying her and a corrective to Naomi's narrow perspective.

In an exaggerated expression of thanks that prolongs their conversation, Ruth prostrates herself and asks why Boaz would take note of a "foreigner" (2:10). This is the first of several terms in their dialogue that have multiple associations. The term *nokriyah* (cf. Gen. 31:15; Ps. 69:8; Job 19:15) does not simply mean "foreigner" but may refer to one who should be recognized as a family member but is not. Observing that he has spoken "kindly to" (literally, "to the heart of") his maidservant (2:13), Ruth does more than acknowledge Boaz's generosity. The expression connotes wooing (cf. Gen. 34:3; Judg. 19:3; Hos. 2:14). Her statement that she is not his servant (2:13) is not only a truthful claim; it foreshadows her future role not as servant but as wife.

Boaz's language is also charged with multiple meanings: he expresses concerns about Ruth's being molested (2:9; cf. 1 Sam. 21:5); he

warns the young men not to "reproach" her (2:15; the term might be better translated "abuse" or "shame"); and he commends her for not "going after" young men (3:10; Prov. 7:21–22; Jer. 2:23–25). Boaz does not want the Moabite woman to be sexually harassed, but his language could suggest that he himself is attracted to the woman. His comments in 2:11 recapitulate Ruth's promises to Naomi in 1:16–17; no mere object to him, Ruth is a woman of worth. Boaz then prays that her full reward will come from the deity "under whose wings (*kanap*) you have come for refuge" (2:12). That Ruth has in fact done this is not clear. The metaphor returns when Ruth seeks not heavenly protection but refuge under Boaz's "cloak" (*kanap*, 3:9). Since *kanap* can also connote "genitals" (cf. Deut. 22:30; 27:20), the sexual subtext is reinforced.

That Boaz takes an interest in Ruth is evident also during the meal, when he invites her to dip her morsel in the wine and when he hands her roasted grain. By granting her a place among his reapers, Boaz in effect incorporates Ruth into his household. By handing her the morsel, he plays the role of spouse; offering food is what Ruth does for Naomi. Filled, Ruth has food left over, which she saves for Naomi. This notice foreshadows her future; she obtains a new family but retains her loyalty to Naomi and secures a place for her, too.

Boaz then arranges that his reapers provide Ruth with extra grain; his command grants her earlier request (2:7) and more. She returns with an ephah of barley (somewhere between thirty and fifty pounds, enough to satisfy a number of men; cf. 1 Sam. 17:17), as well as with her leftovers (2:18). Naomi is astounded by Ruth's good fortune and offers a blessing to "him who took notice of you" (2:19; the NRSV's "the man" is not explicit in the Hebrew text). The prayer is more easily interpreted as having a heavenly referent, but Ruth provides a corrective: the one who occasioned her good fortune was Boaz. Naomi ignores the correction and continues to focus on God (2:20).

Suddenly, Naomi remembers that Boaz might function as "our" redeemer (*go'el*, 2:20). Literally, "one with the right to redeem," a *go'el* is a male relative who ensures that the family property remain held by family members and who prevents a relative from entering into slavery (Lev. 25:25–55). Consequently, it may be translated "kinsman." But the term may also designate one who saves from sin, slavery, exile, and death, and so sometimes describes God's activity (Gen. 48:16; Ex. 6:6; 15:13; Isa. 41:14;

43:1; 52:3; Hos. 13:14). Naomi thus conflates the roles of the deity and kinsman; for her, men function as the representatives of heaven on earth.

Ruth does not acknowledge this remark; she comments instead that Boaz protected her in the fields. But her statement is curious. She speaks of his command to "stay close" (dabaq) to his young men (the NRSV "servants" [2:21]) obscures the gender distinction in Hebrew), when in fact he had said that she should stay close to his "young women." This comment motivates Naomi to advise that Ruth glean among the women. Thus it forces her to take specific notice of Ruth. Whether Naomi is concerned primarily about Ruth's personal safety or whether she would prefer her daughter-in-law cling to Boaz rather than to one of the men in the fields is not explained.

## Seduction (chap. 3)

At the end of the harvest, Naomi devises a plan. She advises Ruth to wash, put on perfume and her best dress, and go down to the threshing floor. Marking where Boaz lies down after eating and drinking, Ruth is to join him and to uncover his "feet" (a euphemism for genitals). Naomi adds: "He will tell you what to do" (3:4). Both this plan and Ruth's lack of questioning are problematic. First, they are reminiscent of the trickery depicted in Gen. 29:21–30, with Naomi playing the role of Laban, Ruth that of Leah (see 4:11), and Boaz that of Jacob. Second, the threshing floor is associated with extramarital sexual activity (see Hos. 9:1). Finally, Boaz's condition ("When Boaz had eaten and drunk, and he was in a contented mood," 3:7) recalls the incestuous relationship between the drunken Lot and his daughters (Gen. 19:30–38). Ruth the Moabite, the descendant of this union, is typecast.

At midnight, at the edge of the grain pile, and so perhaps in some privacy, Boaz awakes with fear, notices a woman next to him, and twists away. But Ruth, repeating his earlier words (2:12), asks him to "spread [his] cloak" (kanap) over her and redeem her (3:9). Contrary to Naomi's instruction, Ruth tells Boaz "what to do." And whereas Boaz had asked God to bless Ruth, Ruth seeks the blessing directly from Boaz.

Boaz's response mirrors Ruth's requests. First, he blesses his "daughter" (cf. 2:8) and her latter deed as more worthy than the first. The lesser deed may be Ruth's accompanying

Naomi and the greater her interest in having Boaz act as redeemer. Or the greater may be her attempt to find a go'el for both herself and Naomi and the lesser her attempt to obtain a husband. By serving as go'el, Boaz will be primarily protecting the future of Naomi, not that of Ruth (cf. 4:3–4, 15). It is Naomi's property he will protect.

His notice that Ruth had not "gone after young men, whether poor or rich" is unclear. The point of 3:10 may be that Ruth has paid an old man a compliment by approaching him rather than someone younger. In this case, her greater deed may be her attempt to establish a relationship with Boaz. However, nowhere does the text state that Boaz is old; nor need the verse suggest that Boaz might have expected Ruth to chase after all men in order to find a husband. Rather, the term "young man" may be read as referring to one who could serve as go'el for Naomi. Jack Sasson translates the verse: "There will henceforth be no need to seek men whether poor or rich." This future-oriented reading implies that Boaz will secure Ruth's future, most likely through marriage. In referring to her as "worthy" (chayil, 3:11), Boaz equates Ruth with himself; the narrative introduces Boaz with the same term (2:1; NRSV: "prominent [and] rich"). Finally, he agrees to serve as "redeemer" if the closer relative refuses his responsibility. His focus is, however, on Ruth; he never mentions Naomi.

Concern for reputation is evident both in Boaz's comments regarding Ruth's status and in his exhortation that she "remain this night" (lyn, 3:13; cf. 1:16). Whether or not they engaged in intercourse or whether Boaz thought they had is unrecorded. Before dawn, he discreetly sends "the woman" off with a large quantity of barley (3:14). No longer perceived as a "foreigner," a "servant," a "handmaid," or a "daughter," she is suitable for the role of Boaz's wife. Perhaps by sending her away before the light permitted recognition, Boaz wished to preserve her reputation. Or perhaps he wished their relationship to be unknown to the next of kin, wanting his motives to be seen as dispassionate and pious, rather than as personal and sexual.

Ruth's reunion with Naomi repeats the pattern of 2:18b–23. Again Naomi poses a question, Ruth summarizes what had just transpired in an adapted manner, and Naomi offers advice. Her initial question, "Who are you?" (3:16; NRSV: "How did things go with you?"), parallels Boaz's fearful query (3:9). Is she still

Ruth the widow, or has she become Ruth the (future) wife? Yet Naomi also calls her "my daughter"; regardless of Ruth's change in status, their relationship remains constant. Ruth responds by pointing to the gift of barley and adds that Boaz did not want her to return "empty-handed" to her mother-in-law. He had said no such thing, but Ruth adapts his words to include Naomi. Ruth's comment may be a double entendre. She symbolically carries what Naomi most wants: Boaz's seed. By handing Naomi the grain, Ruth anticipates the handing of the child Obed to her mother-in-law. Through Ruth's efforts, Naomi will no longer be "empty-handed."

With her final words, invented to include the older woman, Ruth the active, vocal character vanishes from the text. Ruth's future is now in the hands of the next of kin and the elders at the gate. Having left her home, risked attack in the fields, placed both herself and Boaz in a compromising position, and twice lied to Naomi, she has done all a woman could do. The text may be implying that only through separation, deception, and trickery can women obtain redemption. Even so, one should not necessarily assume that the story condemns Ruth for employing these means. The figure of the trickster has a respected place in the biblical tradition (see the commentary on Genesis).

## Marriage (chap. 4)

Boaz next encounters the unnamed relation and convenes a formal court of ten elders. Noting that Naomi plans to sell Elimelech's field (4:3 may indicate that women could inherit and sell property; see 2 Kings 8:1–6 but contrast Num. 27:8–11), he asks if the relative will redeem it to keep it within the family (see Lev. 25:25; Jer. 32:6–12).

The first *go'el* agrees; likely he cannot imagine any circumstances in which Naomi will produce an heir to the family property who might reclaim the land from him, so his redemption of the land entails no economic loss. What Boaz then states (4:5) varies with the translation adopted. The Hebrew text has Boaz state that "I am acquiring" Ruth for a wife. Most English translations, as well as many ancient ones, however, read with a scribal emendation: "You are acquiring" (i.e., Ruth and the land are a package deal). The first reading is to be preferred. The relative could not afford to have Boaz marry Ruth and produce a child who would inherit the dead man's estate.

Since Ruth was free to marry whomever she chose, why Boaz had to deal with these questions in public rather than simply marry Ruth remains debated. Perhaps by obtaining the community's sanction for the marriage, Boaz justifies his otherwise problematic relationship with a Moabite. If so, then Ruth has provided him with this justification by naming him *go'el*. Boaz then frames his plan in the conventional terms of levirate marriage (see Deut. 25:5–10).

Practicing an otherwise unattested form of release from responsibilities, levirate or otherwise (see Deut. 25:9), the relative hands his sandal to Boaz. Boaz has now acquired "all that belonged to Elimelech" (4:9) as well as Ruth. The previously active Ruth is now described as an object to be acquired. Because Boaz's plan does not match the specifications of levirate marriage, he makes explicit the connection between the land and the lady, and he asserts that the first child Ruth bears with him will be Mahlon's heir (4:5, 10). Such social and economic concerns reinforce Naomi's notion of women's worth. In the presence of the elders Boaz proclaims his marriage to be based on Ruth's ability to "maintain the dead man's name on his inheritance" (4:10), not on his love or respect for her.

The townspeople first bless not Boaz but Ruth; they wish for her fertility that she may build up Boaz's house as Rachel and Leah had done for Jacob. Here the one Moabite, Ruth, will fulfill the roles it took two matriarchs to accomplish. They also pray that Boaz's house be like that of Perez, "whom Tamar bore to Judah" (4:11–12). Since the widowed Tamar (Genesis 38) posed as a prostitute and seduced her father-in-law when he failed to fulfill levirate custom and marry her to his remaining son, the narrative might imply that the townsfolk knew about the earlier relationship between Boaz and Ruth.

Parallels and contrasts between the book of Ruth and Genesis 38 are suggested also by the shared motifs of a move to foreign soil, marriages to foreign women, and the deaths of two sons and a spouse. They both also share a striking treatment of their heroines. While Ruth and Tamar both refuse to remain in their parents' house after being widowed, and while both produce children who continue the threatened family line, their fates and even their motivations are unrecorded. Judah at least eventually recognized the righteousness of his daughter-in-law, but Naomi never explicitly comes to this realization: she offers no final words either to or about Ruth. Nevertheless, just as the book of Ruth reclaims Tamar (4:12, 18), so the towns-women reclaim Ruth from Naomi's silence (4:15).

The marriage occurs, and the conception soon after (4:13). At this point, Boaz too drops out of the story, and the focus returns to Naomi, now no longer empty. The women bless the deity who provided Naomi a redeemer (but is this Boaz or the child Obed?), and they bless the child as one to comfort Naomi. Finally, they remark that the child is of particular value because Ruth gave birth to him, and Ruth is worth more to Naomi than "seven sons." Yet it is only in the context of childbirth that these women acknowledge Ruth's value or even her existence.

In the final ironic moment, Ruth—whose language and actions sought to incorporate Naomi into her new family—is erased from the text. Her mother-in-law nurses the child, the local women name him, and they even pro-claim, "A son has been born to Naomi" (4:17). This erasure removes the child from any Moabite stigma. Confirming this pure pedigree is the genealogy with which the book concludes. Beginning with Perez, the genealogy continues through Obed to Jesse and then to David. Although Boaz had vowed to "maintain the dead man's name," Mahlon, the husband who died in Moab, is absent from the list. And Ruth, the ostensible heroine of the story, is left an enigma; her continuing relationship to Naomi, her feelings for her son and husband, and her sense of belonging in Israel are never addressed.

## BIBLIOGRAPHY

Beattie, D. R. G. *Jewish Exegesis of the Book of Ruth.* Journal for the Study of the Old Testament Supplement Series 2. Sheffield: JSOT Press, 1977.

Bos, Johanna W. H. *Ruth, Esther, Jonah.* Knox Preaching Guides. Atlanta: John Knox Press, 1986.

Campbell, Edward F., Jr. *Ruth.* Anchor Bible 7. Garden City, N.Y.: Doubleday & Co., 1975.

Fewell, Danna Nolan, and David Miller Gunn. *Compromising Redemption: Relating Characters in the Book of Ruth.* Literary Currents in Biblical Interpretation. Louis-ville, Ky.: Westminster/John Knox Press, 1990.

LaCocque, André. "Ruth." In his *The Feminine Unconventional: Four Subversive Figures in Israel's Tradition,* pp. 84–116. Overtures to Biblical Theology. Minneapolis: Fortress Press, 1990.

Sasson, Jack M. *Ruth: A New Translation with a Philological Commentary and a Formalist-Folklorist Interpretation.* Balti-more: Johns Hopkins University Press, 1979.

Trible, Phyllis. "A Human Comedy." In her *God and the Rhetoric of Sexuality,* pp. 166–199. Overtures to Biblical Theology. Phila-delphia: Fortress Press, 1978.

# 1 AND 2 SAMUEL

*Jo Ann Hackett*

## Introduction

### Composition and Literary Structure

The books of 1 and 2 Samuel are a gold mine for readers interested in women in ancient Israel. Many of the narratives concern women, more or less centrally. There are stories about royal women involved in events that had major political repercussions throughout Israel, but there are also narratives in which nonroyal women play a significant role: Hannah, the medium at Endor, and the two "wise women" from Israel's villages. There is also a surprising amount of incidental information about women's lives, so much that there is simply no room here for every interesting detail.

First and Second Samuel are part of a larger work known as the Deuteronomistic History (DH) that traces the history of Israel from the conquest to the exile in the books of Joshua, Judges, 1 and 2 Samuel, and 1 and 2 Kings. The editors of the Deuteronomistic History used already-existing narratives, adding interpretive material at various points. The extent of Deuteronomistic revising and editing is not consistent in the various books. In Samuel there is very little of the sometimes heavy-handed interpretive comment that one finds in the book of Judges with its system of divine rewards and punishments and in 1 and 2 Kings with their judgments on the reigns of each king. In Samuel the narratives are for the most part allowed to speak for themselves, and editorial activity is most conspicuous in the simple arrangement of originally separate stories into several cycles (e.g., the stories of Saul's reign, the narratives of David's rise, and so forth).

### Summary of Contents

The books of Samuel are organized around the careers of Samuel, Saul, and David. They begin with the story of Hannah and her giving birth to Samuel and Samuel's early life at the Shiloh sanctuary (1 Samuel 1–3). Then come narratives about the ark, the portable chest that was said to contain the tablets of the law and that represents the invisible presence of Yahweh within the community (chaps. 4–6). Chapter 7 reports Samuel's activities as judge in the context of the ever-present conflicts with the Philistines.

Israel's desire for a king is the topic of chaps. 8–12 and the occasion for the introduction of their first king, Saul. The story of Saul's struggle with the Philistines and his loss of his dynasty continues through chap. 15. David is introduced in chap. 16, and in 17 is reintroduced in the famous Goliath story. At first Saul is pleased to have David as part of his court. The focus of the narrative quickly shifts, however, to the rivalry between the two for the affections of Saul's family and of Israel as a whole; to Saul's attempts to kill David; and to David's flight from Saul, which takes him ultimately into the company of the Philistine enemy (chaps. 18–27; 29–30).

In chap. 28, when Saul has lost all contact with Yahweh but desires to know the outcome of his upcoming battle with the Philistines, he has a medium call up the spirit of Samuel, whose death was reported in chap. 25. As Samuel predicts, Saul loses the battle, in which he and three of his sons die. The book of 1 Samuel ends with a major character's death, as do Genesis, Deuteronomy, and Joshua (the deaths of Joseph, Moses, and Joshua).

The book of 2 Samuel begins with David's reaction to the deaths, particularly Saul's and Jonathan's (chap. 1). It moves on to David's gradual acquisition of the thrones of both Judah and Israel, and of Jerusalem as his capital city (chaps. 2–5). In chap. 6 David brings the ark to his new capital, and in chap. 7 he is promised an eternal dynasty. Chapters 8–10; 21; and 23:8–39 recount David's military administration and accomplishments.

David's affaire with Bathsheba (chaps. 11–12), the wife of one of his soldiers, is a watershed, marking the beginning of a downward spiral for David and his family. Chapter 13 is the story of the rape of David's daughter Tamar by one of his sons, Amnon, and the consequent killing of Amnon by another son, Absalom. Absalom flees and is brought back on the advice of a "wise woman" (chap. 14) and immediately begins his attempt to take over the throne from David (chaps. 15–19), an attempt that ends in Absalom's death. Chapter 20 reports another revolt against David's throne and the intervention of another wise woman.

The books of Samuel end with an assortment of pieces. Second Samuel 22 (=Psalm 18) is thought to be a very old poem of thanksgiving, here attributed to David; the beginning of chap. 23 is another lovely poem about the relationship between Yahweh and Israel's rulers, generally known as "the last words of David." Chapter 24 begins with the story of David's census of Israel and Judah, presumably for military draft and taxation purposes, and the plague that resulted because of Yahweh's anger with the census. The final verses in Samuel record David's purchase of the threshing floor of Araunah, where he erects an altar, at the place that will later be the site of the Temple of Solomon.

## Comment

### Roles of Women in 1 and 2 Samuel

Despite the apparent abundance of information about women in 1 and 2 Samuel, the reader needs to be careful not to assume that the narratives are simply straightforward historical accounts. It is extremely difficult to judge the extent to which the narratives give information about the historical Bathsheba, for instance. Part of the problem is that the persons involved in the narratives are never mentioned in contemporary writings outside the Bible. Further, some of the stories in 1 and 2 Samuel are shaped according to traditional storytelling patterns, making it difficult to separate historical facts from the storyteller's art. In sum, it would be hazardous to use these narratives to try to reconstruct a historical biography of Michal or Abigail. But the stories do show how Israel's early narratives remembered and represented women and their involvement in this formative period of Israel's history.

Even if one must be cautious in moving from the stories about women to historical knowledge of their individual lives, that is not to say that 1 and 2 Samuel can tell nothing about how women actually lived. The biblical narratives are full of information about women's lives. The authors did not specifically intend, so far as we know, to record for posterity the details of women's lives; rather they seem to have included these details quite incidentally, with little attempt to make them fit a particular religious or political agenda. Ironically, it is precisely because these details are mentioned just "in passing" that they might be historically reliable. As valuable as this incidental information is, the fragmentary nature of it and the difficulty of confirming it from other sources mean that one should remain cautious in estimating how much one can know about women's lives in early Israel.

With these cautions in mind, one can collect important information about women's roles scattered throughout the books of Samuel. The following list is not exhaustive but includes the most important of those scattered notices.

The intersection between domestic events and public affairs is reflected in the brief account of how a woman who is not named, the wife of Phinehas, gives birth to a child during a battle in which the Philistines defeat Israel's armies (1 Sam. 4:19–22). As was undoubtedly typical, women attend at her childbirth. Their words to her, "Do not be afraid, for you have borne a son," suggest that bearing a son is more important than bearing a daughter. The woman herself names the child, and the name she chooses, Ichabod (explained in the text as "the glory has departed"), reflects her concern for public, national events. "She said, 'The glory has departed from Israel, for the ark of God has been captured'" (1 Sam. 4:22).

There are also many scattered mentions of women as victims of war, both Israelite women and Amalekite women: women killed in holy war (1 Sam. 15:3); women bereaved by war (1 Sam. 15:33); women and children killed alongside men in a revenge attack (1 Sam. 22:19); women killed as part of a general annihilation to leave no witnesses (1 Sam. 27:9, 11); women as captives recovered and restored (1 Samuel 30). As in most societies, the warriors in Israel all seem to have been male. First Samuel 21:4–5 observes that in order to be eligible to eat holy bread, soldiers are required to have kept themselves from women.

First and Second Samuel disclose only a little information about the religious roles of women. According to 1 Sam. 2:22 (cf. Ex. 38:8), there were "women who served at the entrance to the tent of meeting," the major religious shrine of Israel before the building of the Temple. It is not certain what the exact service of these women was. There is no evidence for the suggestion sometimes made that they were cultic prostitutes (see the commentary on Hosea). Although their service was somehow involved in cultic matters, it was apparently not priestly. Probably, like that of the Levites, it was more concerned with physical, day-to-day maintenance of the tent and its apparatus than with blood sacrifice itself, something women are almost never involved with throughout the world (see the discussion in Jay). In the story of Hannah, for instance, all blood sacrifice involves Hannah's husband, Elkanah, and the priests. Even in 1 Sam. 1:24–25, where Hannah brings the sacrificial animals to Shiloh, the verbs switch to the plural when the actual sacrifice is made (v. 25), presumably to signify that the priests, or Elkanah and the priests, perform the ritual. The sacrifice, of course, is part of the fulfillment of the vow that Hannah had previously made when she asked Yahweh to give her a son. That women made religious vows and incurred obligations is also recognized in the law of Num. 30:3–16. In that passage the conditions under which a father or husband may and may not annul the vow are stipulated. The involvement of women in religious activities outside the official cult will be discussed below in connection with the medium of Endor.

The reader gets other glimpses of women's world and work. There are references to young women who come out to draw water (1 Sam. 9:11–13); to a nurse who saves Jonathan's son Mephibosheth when Saul and Jonathan die (2 Sam. 4:4); to women as mourners, when the Israelite women are encouraged to mourn Saul (2 Sam. 1:24); and to women as singers of victory songs, when the Israelite women sing of Saul and David (1 Sam. 18:7; 21:11; 29:5) and when the daughters of the Philistines are imagined as rejoicing over the death of Saul and Jonathan (2 Sam. 1:20). That a man who holds a spindle is a sign of a curse suggests that spinning wool was a woman's occupation and improper for a male (2 Sam. 3:29). Other occupations filled by women include those of perfumer, cook, and baker (1 Sam. 8:13). These details, as precious as they are, also serve as a measure of how little is known about the lives of women in early Israel.

## Sources of Women's Power

No discussion of the sources of women's power in 1 and 2 Samuel can be undertaken without an attempt to describe some of the features of the society the narrative assumes. The books of Samuel describe Israel as a society where power was becoming centralized, inherited, and hierarchical, that is, the kind of society where males tend to dominate positions of public power. Such a society is different from the one described in the book of Judges, where there are only the beginnings of centralized inherited power. In Judges there is in general a decentralized society more open to "charismatic" leadership. Decentralized charismatic power can lead to a society that is more chaotic and less stable than one with an inherited monarchy, but it is also the kind of society in which women may hold positions of public power more easily or more commonly. It is then not surprising that there is no Deborah in the books of Samuel and no Jael.

Royal women can be an exception to this general rule, sometimes wielding a great deal of power: when no male of the appropriate bloodline is available to rule, a royal woman can fill the position. But in the books of Samuel even the royal women are not rulers, whatever else they may be. All women in a patriarchal society derive much of their power from their family position, and in a royal family in particular this can mean a great deal of jockeying for power: it is desirable to be the chief wife of a king, or the wife who bears the heir (a wife who, if she outlives her husband, will be the queen mother). This kind of lobbying is not obvious in the books of Samuel, but will be immediately afterward in the story of Bathsheba's involvement in Solomon's rise to the throne in 1 Kings 1–2.

In the social organization represented by 1 and 2 Samuel, the primary forms of authority are passed down from father to son, regardless of the moral qualities of the son. The priesthood, the role of judge, and the monarchy are all represented as hereditary. Eli's two sons become priests even though they are described in derogatory terms (1 Sam. 2:12–17, 22–25, 27–36; 3:10–14). Samuel's sons seem to inherit his office as judge, in spite of their poor qualifications (1 Sam. 8:1–3). Saul's loss of the kingship is really a loss of dynasty, in which his son would become king after him, since he personally remains king until he dies (1 Sam. 13:8–15a; chap. 15). The royal theology expressed in 2 Samuel 7 declares that a son of David will rule after him (vv. 12–14a).

In most societies, the more hierarchically organized and centralized public power is, the less likely it is that women will hold positions of public power. This analysis holds true within the institutional forms of power depicted in the books of Samuel. Given such a situation, it is not surprising that three stories about women wielding public power in the books of Samuel concern women who are depicted as operating in areas somewhat removed from, and so perhaps less dependent on, the central monarchical government. Saul appeals to a medium at Endor and assumes her ability to help him when his usual means of contacting Yahweh fail (1 Samuel 28). The two stories of "wise women" in Tekoa and Abel of Beth-maacah (2 Samuel 14 and 20) assume the status and authority of these two women.

In 1 Samuel 28 Saul's kingship and life are at risk in a battle with the Philistines. The story is set up with two notes in v. 3: that Samuel has died and that Saul has expelled the mediums and wizards from the land. It is a sign of Saul's desperation that, in spite of this attempt at expulsion, he asks his servants to find for him a woman who is a medium. He has been consulting Yahweh to attempt to determine the battle's outcome, as was customary (see, e.g., 23:1–5), but the usual methods were not eliciting a response (28:6). When told that there was a woman at Endor who was a medium, he disguises himself to visit her. Since Saul had expelled the mediums previously, she could hardly be expected to cooperate with him if she recognized him or his apparel. When Saul swears that she will not be punished, she does as he asks and brings up the spirit of Samuel, whom she describes as a god coming up out of the ground (v. 13).

What is of interest in this passage is the fact that the medium is female. In nearly all religious systems, there are both central institutions and practices and those that operate on the periphery. In ancient Israel, with its all-male priesthood, the only professional contact women could have had with the central religious hierarchy would have been as temple servants of various kinds, presumably performing the kinds of domestic tasks that would be necessary there as everywhere (see Bird). Women could have performed priestly or quasi-priestly duties only in the set of practices Saul had recently banned in 1 Samuel 28, divination and consultation of spirits (cf. Lev. 20:27 and Ezek. 13:17–23).

After Saul's seance with Samuel, in which his defeat and death are predicted, Saul is distraught and falls to the ground. He has not eaten, probably in preparation for this seance. The woman and his servants urge him to eat, and he finally agrees. The text says that the medium slaughtered the fatted calf she had and baked cakes and served Saul and his servants. The Hebrew verb used of her action in slaughtering usually, though not always, means "to slaughter as a sacrifice." There is, then, some ambiguity about her actions. Although she may simply be preparing an ordinary meal, it is also possible to understand that Saul and his servants participated in a sacrificial meal prepared by this female medium as part of her quasi-priestly function in a peripheral, and banned, religious subsystem.

The second example of a woman exercising public power in a village setting comes in the first "wise woman" story in 2 Samuel 14. Joab calls upon a wise woman from Tekoa to speak to David in such a way that he will make a decision that will apply to bringing Absalom back to Jerusalem without realizing that he has done so. (Compare the strategy of the prophet Nathan's story of the "poor man's ewe lamb" in chap. 12.) The text says that Joab put the appropriate words into her mouth, but even so, she was presumably a good actor, or a clever speaker, or someone David would listen to because of her position at Tekoa—or all three (see Camp).

The second story about a wise woman (2 Samuel 20) is more instructive. When Joab is besieging the town of Abel of Beth-maacah and attacking it in order to drive out a rebel who had taken refuge there, a wise woman from within the city calls out to him to speak with her. He does so, perhaps an indication that she holds a position of authority that Joab would have recognized. She uses clever language, as did the wise woman in chap. 14, and negotiates for the lives of the people in Abel by agreeing to turn over the rebel (or, rather, his head) to Joab. The narrator does not hesitate to paint her as the representative of the people of Abel and as a person they will listen to in matters of war and politics. They agree to her plan, and the attack is called off. Both the woman from Tekoa and the woman from Abel lived in places that may not have been much affected by the institutional structures of the monarchy and where older patterns of authority persisted. In any event, their authority is recognized both by their people (2 Samuel 20) and by national figures (in both stories). They seem to be quick thinkers and good talkers—hence, one assumes, their designation as "wise."

In sum, the books of Samuel do not describe a great deal of public power for women, although on a local level there is perhaps a hint of power that operates outside the centralized government and religious establishments. Most of the women mentioned are royal women who derive their power not from ruling but from their relationships to ruling men. The centralization of the government and the beginning of centralization of worship in Jerusalem brought with them traditions of inherited male power that meant fewer public positions for women.

## Status, Power, and Children: The Story of Hannah (1 Samuel 1–2)

The books of Samuel begin with the story of the birth of a son to a woman previously childless. According to the narrative, Hannah, the favored wife of Elkanah, has no children because Yahweh has "closed her womb." Hannah is not Elkanah's only wife. His other wife, Peninnah, had several sons and daughters and tormented Hannah because of the differences in their families.

This motif occurs elsewhere in biblical narrative: a similar story is told about the sisters Rachel and Leah, both wives of Jacob, in Genesis 29–30. One of the implications of both of these narratives is that children were seen as a solace or even compensation to a woman whose relationship with her husband was not good enough to fill her emotional needs. First Samuel 1 goes further, however, and actually suggests that, from a man's point of view, a woman with a happy marriage need not be distraught about not having any children. Hannah's situation made *her* very unhappy, especially at the time of the annual sacrifice, when she would cry and would not eat.

Elkanah's reaction to Hannah's unhappiness is worth noting: "Hannah, why do you weep? Why do you not eat? Why is your heart sad? Am I not more to you than ten sons?" (1:8). This is hardly the response of a patriarch who can see value in women only as childbearers and implies the possibility of a relationship in which love was more important than childbearing. It should be noted, however, that Elkanah was not himself childless. His society gave him the opportunity, and he was apparently able to afford, to have both a wife to love and a wife to make children. Since he had already filled his need for a family to remember and honor him (the only kind of "immortality" known to these narratives), his lack of understanding for Hannah's unhappiness begins to look less sentimental and more naïve or even insensitive.

Hannah, for her part, while she may have loved her husband, still needed children, and not only for her personal emotional fulfillment. In her society a woman's prestige was based at least partly on her demonstrated ability to produce offspring. It was in such a situation that Peninnah could torment her. The same situation is behind v. 5, where the extent of Hannah's participation in the celebration of the sacrifice was determined by the number of her children. Such an attitude is reflected even in the narrator's choice of words: it was Yahweh who closed Hannah's womb. To the narrator, and presumably his audience, childlessness was not understood as a physical phenomenon, but as a decision of God—and, indeed, in some instances as a punishment from God (see Genesis 20).

Hannah seems to agree with this understanding and takes her case directly to Yahweh. If it is Yahweh who "closed her womb," only Yahweh can give her children. She goes to the temple and vows that if Yahweh will give her a son, she will, in effect, give him back to Yahweh as a temple servant. This vow is in itself telling: far from wanting a child for emotional comfort, she is offering to forgo the pleasure of having him with her while he is growing up. She seems simply to want to *give birth to* a son. At that point her societal position will be secure, even though she would still live without children.

It is possible to take another view of Hannah's vow, however, that is perhaps more nuanced. In Israel one gave the firstfruits of animals and of the harvest to Yahweh, probably in hopes of receiving in return the blessing of continued fertility. (See, e.g., Ex. 13:2, 12–15; 23:16, 19a; 34:19–20, 22, 26a; while continued fertility is nowhere explicitly named as a motive, the covenant blessings and curses in Leviticus 26 and Deuteronomy 28 supply broader fertility motives for Israel's ritual system.) If Hannah's offer to dedicate her firstborn to Yahweh can be seen in this light, her motives are more complex. She does not simply desire the societal status and relief from rival-wife torment that bearing a son would bring but also "offers up" her firstborn to Yahweh in hopes of receiving more children in return. The priest Eli operates within the same frame of reference, and after Samuel's birth and dedication to his temple, habitually blesses Elkanah this way: "May Yahweh repay you with children by this woman [Hannah] for the gift [Samuel] that she made to Yahweh" (1 Sam. 2:20). And this is what happens: Hannah bears three sons and two daughters (v. 21). Meanwhile Samuel grew up literally "in the presence of Yahweh."

Following the story of Samuel's being taken to Shiloh to live with Eli comes the Song of Hannah (1 Sam. 2:1–10). Most scholars suggest that the insertion of this song into the narrative is secondary, since there seems to be little detailed connection between the song and the narrative that surrounds it. Further, it mentions a king, although in the surrounding narrative Israel does not yet have a king. The song does, however, include themes appropriate to Hannah's story. It is, after all, a hymn of praise for good fortune that is attributed to Yahweh. The theme of reversal is particularly appropriate for Hannah's story as told in the surrounding narrative. Verses 4, 5a, and 8a describe general reversals of fortune with no obvious application in Hannah's story, but v. 5b reports the overturning of the status quo between a previously childless woman and a woman who had many children ("the barren has borne seven, but she who has many children is forlorn"). Even if this phrase was originally used in the poem as a general illustration, in the poem's secondary setting in Hannah's narrative the phrase obviously takes on significance as a reference to Hannah and Peninnah's relationship.

Some of the expressions of praise included in this song may seem odd to us in a poem that purports to be written by a woman: for instance, the use of martial language in v. 1 ("my mouth derides my enemies"), v. 4 ("the bows of the mighty are broken"), vv. 9–10 ("for not by might does one prevail. Yahweh! His adversaries shall be shattered"). But women in ancient Israel are often credited with singing battle songs: com-

pare Ex. 15:20–21; Judges 5; 11:34; 1 Sam. 18:7; 21:11; 29:5; 2 Sam. 1:20.

There is significance to incorporating into a narrative of childbirth a poem that includes language and themes appropriate to a wide range of Israel's religious life: thanksgiving and praise of holiness, defeat of enemies, wisdom, battle, creation and power over life and death, storm god imagery, Yahweh's relationship to chosen leaders. This juxtaposition has the effect of recognizing, without fanfare, fertility in childbirth as an issue equal in importance to the others and worthy of the attention of Yahweh and of Israel's singers. Fertility and childbirth are mainstream religious issues in this literature and are not treated separately from other pressing matters.

### The Politics of Marriage: David's Wives

In the societies of the ancient Near East, a woman's sexuality was generally under the control of a man in her family. A father controlled his daughter's sexuality, and a husband his wife's. The marriage of a young woman was a matter of negotiation and financial arrangements between the groom or a male member of his family and the father or leading male of the bride's family (see, e.g., Genesis 24; 29; 34). Among royal families, not only financial but also political matters had to be negotiated. For a king of Israel or Judah to marry a princess from a neighboring country implied that the Israelite king and the king of the neighboring country had concluded negotiations that would include not simply the usual dowry arrangements and marriage contract but also, presumably, agreements about friendship between the two countries, nonaggression pacts, and so forth. See, for example, the marriage of Solomon to a daughter of Pharaoh (1 Kings 9:16–17) and to many foreign women (1 Kings 11:1–8). Ahab's marriage to Jezebel, a Phoenician princess, is perhaps the most famous biblical example of a political marriage (1 Kings 16:31). Since the narratives in 1 and 2 Samuel cover the emergence of the Israelite monarchy, the story of David's marriages casts important light on the role of women in securing political power—and also in losing it.

David's marriages offer an intriguing narrative of gender relations and power on a number of levels. When King Saul becomes jealous of David's success and the love of his people for David, he offers David his elder daughter, Merab, in marriage (1 Sam. 18:17–19).

From David's point of view, marriage to the king's daughter would bring him close to the center of power. Saul in return negotiates David's services in his battles against the Philistines, but Saul's motives are more complex. What he hopes is that David will be killed in the fighting. When David offers a humble disclaimer to be worthy of the alliance, Saul does not withdraw the offer but does impetuously marry Merab to another man. Merab herself has no role in the dealings. The proposed and the actual marriages are negotiated between the men.

Next Saul offers a younger daughter, Michal, to David in exchange for the foreskins of one hundred Philistines (1 Sam. 18:20–29). Saul again hopes that David's quest for Michal will result in his death at the hands of the Philistines; but David delivers the payment. In this case, it is at least said that Michal loves David, but as before, the real negotiations over her are out of her hands. Saul sets the price and David pays.

The story of Michal's relationship with David is a puzzling one. When she first appears in the story she loves David, is won at a dangerous price, and is married to him. Soon afterward, with her father still obsessed with getting rid of David, Michal helps David to escape her father and lies to her father's messengers about David's whereabouts. When she is discovered, she lies again, this time to her father, telling him that David had threatened to kill her if she did not help him escape (1 Sam. 19:17). (One assumes that her story is a cover; no such conversation between David and Michal is reported.) Nothing more is heard of Michal until 1 Sam. 25:44, during a report of David's next two marriages, when it is said that Saul had, at some time in the past, given Michal to another man. (Note that the narrator still calls her "David's wife" in that passage.)

After Saul's death, his son Ishbosheth inherits the throne of Israel, while David is king only in Judah (2 Sam. 2:4, 8–11). Ishbosheth so alienates his commander, Abner, that Abner offers to bring all Israel into covenant with David. David's response is not what one expects: he agrees to make a deal with Abner, but only if Abner will bring Michal, here called "Saul's daughter," back to David (3:13). According to 2 Sam. 3:14–16 David actually recovers Michal through King Ishbosheth, Saul's son and Michal's brother, although it is apparently Abner who supervises the return, since it is he who chases off Michal's upset second husband.

What are David's motives? The most obvious explanation for David's insistence on the return of Michal before he will enter into negotiations with Abner is that Michal was or could easily become a hostage. The story makes it clear that she was under Ishbosheth's power, since he is the one who actually takes her from her second husband and sends her back to David. If David still cared for Michal, he might have been afraid that Michal would become a victim of his overt attempt to capture the throne of Israel. If this is indeed what the narrative means, then one notices that either Ishbosheth is somewhat stupid or else Abner has him completely cowed (see 3:11). It is also possible that Michal, as Saul's daughter, in some way legitimates David's claim to Saul's throne, so that it was not necessarily affection that prompted him to worry about her welfare before he accepted Abner's offer.

Michal's last major scene is certainly not one of affection between her and David. David's bringing the ark of the covenant to Jerusalem and housing it there with great ceremony (2 Samuel 6) is usually interpreted as an attempt on his part to help legitimate his rule (and his choice of Jerusalem as capital) by tying himself to the traditions of Israel's past. It is perhaps this attempt at legitimation that is behind Michal's anger with David over his performance. David has been dancing clad only in a linen ephod, a garment usually worn by priests. Michal says that her indignation is over his shameless display of his body before even the lowliest women in Israel (v. 20), but when she complains, she pointedly calls him "king of Israel." His response to her is equally telling: he justifies taking her father's throne, as if that were the issue, saying that it was Yahweh who made him king instead of her father and, in fact, instead of all her father's house. There is an odd mixture of royal conflict and sexual conflict here. The result of Michal's outburst (which is either about David's abundant sensuality or about his occupying a throne that should have remained in her family) is that she remains childless until the day of her death.

It is not said whether Michal is unable to have children, an affliction generally believed to be from Yahweh, or whether David simply refuses to impregnate her. But whichever is meant, the punishment resembles the outburst in that it is for Michal both a sexual tragedy and a family tragedy, since it means that no children will be born to one of the few surviving offspring of Saul's house.

David's second wife, Abigail, is introduced as the wife of Nabal (1 Sam. 25:3). While she is described as "having good sense," his very name means "fool" (surely an epithet and a joke within the story; who would name a child Fool?). Unlike Nabal, she understands the gravity of the threat that David and his men represent to their property and their lives and rushes to counteract the bad impression her husband has made on David. The narrator takes care to mention that she goes to meet David secretly, without her husband's knowledge. When she does tell Nabal what she has done, he is so stricken by this information that he is paralyzed and eventually (and conveniently) dies. Abigail is not only sensible but beautiful, and now a wealthy widow, whose land and assets David and his people could surely use (in fact, have been using, hence the problem in the first place).

The third of David's marriages, to Ahinoam of Jezreel, is mentioned in a single verse immediately after the Nabal-Abigail story and immediately before the notice that "Saul had given his daughter Michal, David's wife, to Palti son of Laish" (1 Sam. 25:44). Nothing is known with certainty about Ahinoam's identity, but it is tantalizing that the only other Ahinoam mentioned in the Hebrew Bible is Saul's wife (1 Sam. 14:50). The text does not say that the woman David married was Saul's wife (or, if so, how he managed to obtain her). In a later episode, however, the prophet Nathan delivers an oracle from Yahweh to David that includes the following statement: "I anointed you king over Israel, and I rescued you from the hand of Saul; I gave you your master's house, and your master's wives into your bosom, and gave you the house of Israel and of Judah" (2 Sam. 12:7–8). If David had managed to obtain one of Saul's wives, his action could have signaled his desire to displace Saul as king as well. Because the text does not identify Ahinoam more explicitly, these possibilities must remain speculations, however tantalizing.

David's most famous wife was Bathsheba, also the wife of another man when her story begins (2 Samuel 11). It seems the narrator is portraying David, albeit subtly, as a consummate usurper—of kingdoms and of wives. At the beginning of 2 Samuel 11 it is said that David noticed Bathsheba bathing and that she was purifying herself (probably from her menstrual period). The import of this information is that when David and Bathsheba have intercourse, she has just menstruated and so is clearly not pregnant with her absent husband's child but that she is within the part of her monthly cycle that would allow her to become pregnant. Bathsheba is pictured as almost entirely passive in this episode; except for her first-person message to David ("I am pregnant"), she is always spoken of in the third person. The only hint that she might have cooperated willingly in her predicament is her initial act of bathing in a place where she could be observed by the king out walking on his roof (not an uncommon place to stroll in the Middle East for the cool evening breeze). Still, the text offers no judgment on her for that. Bathsheba is rarely even called by name here. In the books of Samuel her name occurs only in 2 Sam. 11:3 and 12:24 (where she is also called David's wife); otherwise she is called Uriah's wife (11:3, 11, 26; 12:9, 10, 15), the woman (11:5), or just "she," "her." The narrative does not seem to hold her responsible for her actions with David, and the punishment that is meted out, that their child should die, is aimed by Yahweh and Nathan at David, not Bathsheba. Her feelings are not ignored completely: it is said that David comforted her in her grief (though it is David's grief and not Bathsheba's that the narrator describes at length). Further, she and David have another son, Solomon, to replace the dead child. This rather passive picture of Bathsheba as royal wife will be replaced in 1 Kings 1–2 with a portrait of her as a strong and active favorite wife and queen mother.

In addition to Michal, Abigail, Ahinoam, and Bathsheba, 2 Sam. 5:13 notes that David "took more concubines and wives" (see also 3:2–5). The purpose of these marriages will have been largely political, to forge relationships with neighboring kingdoms (as with Maacah, the daughter of the king of Geshur and mother of Absalom) or with prominent families in Israel and Judah.

Perhaps because a king's wives and concubines were such a symbol of his political connections and authority, a usurper often manifested his displacing of a reigning king by sleeping with members of the king's harem. To claim a king's harem was tantamount to claiming his throne. The clearest examples of this practice occur in the stories of David's sons, vying for the throne both before and after his death. Second Samuel 15–19 tells the story of Absalom's revolt against David and of his temporary success at taking the throne in Jerusalem. David is forced to flee Jerusalem and cross to the eastern side of the Jordan (15:13–16:14; 17:21–22), leaving ten concubines behind "to look after the house." When Absalom and his men then move in to Jerusalem, Absalom is declared king by Hushai. The first thing Absalom is advised to do as the new king is to "go in to [his] father's concubines" whom David had left behind; and Absalom does so, before all Israel. The explanation offered in the text for this act is that Absalom will demonstrate to all Israel that he is "odious" to his father, but it is suggestive that this is his first royal act. Note the anticipation of this situation in Nathan's oracle in 2 Sam. 12:11; compare 1 Kings 2:13–18, 22–23, where a comparable dynamic is involved.

A similar conflict arose between Ishbosheth, the son of Saul and ruler of Israel who was David's rival for the throne of a combined Judah and Israel, and Abner, Ishbosheth's army commander (2 Sam. 3:16–10). The text reports first that Saul had had a concubine named Rizpah, who presumably became Ishbosheth's concubine or was at least under his protection after Saul's death. Ishbosheth angrily accuses Abner of having sexual intercourse with her. Abner's response is instructive: he interprets Ishbosheth's accusation (whether true or not) as a challenge to his loyalty to Ishbosheth and the house of Saul. Why would having intercourse with Saul's concubine be disloyal to the house of Saul? Apparently because it threatens to attempt to establish a house of Abner as the successor to Saul.

## Rape, Revenge, and Revolt:
## The Story of Tamar (2 Samuel 13)

The story of the rape of Tamar by her half brother Amnon and the revenge taken against Amnon by Tamar's full brother Absalom cannot be read apart from some of the details of the palace and family politics that the narrative takes for granted. According to 2 Sam. 3:2, Amnon was David's first son (by Ahinoam). We know of David's second son (by Abigail) only that he was called Chileab in 2 Sam. 3:3 and Daniel in 1 Chron. 3:1; he figures in no narrative. Absalom is David's third son. His mother Maacah is royal, the daughter of a transjordanian king (Talmai, king of Geshur; 2 Sam. 3:3); Tamar is his full sister (2 Sam. 13:1). Jonadab, Amnon's adviser in the affair, is himself a member of the family—a nephew of David and so first cousin to the other three (13:3). Whatever justification Absalom might have claimed for killing Amnon, such as

Amnon's rape of Tamar, Absalom's own royal ambitions are not hurt by having Amnon out of the way. Indeed, as soon as Absalom is admitted back into the royal household following his murder of Amnon and subsequent flight to his maternal grandfather, he begins to plot his own rule, even while David is still alive and well (2 Sam. 15:1–12).

It has often been pointed out that this narrative is sprinkled liberally with relational words. Absalom is called David's son in 13:1, and Tamar is Absalom's sister. Amnon is also called David's son (v. 1), and Tamar Amnon's sister (v. 2). Jonadab's relation to them all is clearly spelled out in v. 3, and he addresses Amnon as "son of the king" in v. 4. In the same verse Amnon refers to Tamar as "my brother Absalom's sister." And so it goes, as the narrator emphasizes the intertwining relationships in this polygynous family.

It is Jonadab who puts the idea into Amnon's head that there is a way to be alone with Tamar with David's blessing, by pretending to be ill. The narrative report of Jonadab's advice stops short of suggesting rape, but if his recommendation were in any way innocent there would be no need for the deception.

David apparently goes along with the plot without suspecting anything. Amnon is his eldest son and presumed heir; one would expect David to be anxious for Amnon's health and well-being. What Amnon has asked Tamar to do, and what she does, is to make heart-shaped dumplings. The very words are, perhaps, meant to be suggestive. The noun for heart (*lebab*) and a related verb (*labab*) are used five times here: twice in v. 6, twice in v. 8, and once in v. 10. In vv. 6 and 8 the word is used both as a noun, "heart-shaped dumplings," and as a verb that describes their making. That the word has erotic overtones is suggested by the use of the verb in Song 4:9.

Verse 12 is a crux for understanding what is at stake in the situation. Tamar says, "No, my brother, do not force me; for such a thing is not done in Israel; do not do anything so vile!" Just exactly what is Tamar protesting against? Amnon has just called her "sister" when he grabs her and urges her to have sex with him willingly. When she begs him not to rape her and says that such a thing is not done in Israel, is it rape she is referring to or incest? What precisely is it that is "vile"? In v. 13 she goes on to say that he need only speak to "the king," for he would not withhold Tamar from Amnon. But how is one to read even this declaration?

Several possible answers have been suggested. Perhaps the narrative operates as if there were no laws in effect at the time of Amnon and Tamar to prevent brother–sister marriages or, more specifically, to prevent marriages between two persons with the same father (cf. Abraham and Sarah, Gen. 20:12). This interpretation assumes that the narrative does not know, or ignores for this setting, the laws in Lev. 18:9, 11; 20:17; and Deut. 27:22, which prohibit such unions. Dating the legal material in the Bible is notoriously difficult, and it is certainly possible to make such an argument about this narrative. Another possibility is that such laws were known and were followed as custom for most people but that the royal family lived by its own rules, although no loophole for the royalty is included in Leviticus or Deuteronomy. The nuances are important, because one would like to know whether Amnon would have been considered guilty of incest as well as of rape. If marriage between brother and sister was forbidden, then Tamar is saying in v. 13 that David would be willing to override even this and allow them to be legally married. If, however, there is no incest implied in the narrative, then Tamar is making a much simpler argument: Why rape me when you can marry me simply by asking our father? A royal daughter, especially a beautiful one, could be a great asset to David in forging alliances with wealthy or royal potential fathers-in-law, but he would not say no to Amnon even if it meant giving up such a resource.

Whatever the precise meaning of Tamar's outcry, it is futile. Amnon rapes her and then immediately hates his victim. Amnon's response is generally described as realistic. In fact, there is good evidence that people who force their dominance on others (rapists and sadists, for example) are fighting what they perceive as weakness in themselves and that their victims' defeat only reminds them of their own weakness and consequently enrages them.

Amnon becomes so enraged that he has Tamar removed from his presence. What does she mean when she says that sending her away is worse than raping her? Presumably she understands that according to Israelite law he now *must* marry her (see Ex. 22:16; and especially Deut. 22:28–29; if the narrative assumes similar laws to be in force, he *cannot* send her away). The reproach that she had said she could not bear ("Where could I carry my shame?") is now hers. She tears the robe she wears, puts

ashes on her head, and cries out, as signs of her grief.

Absalom has a suspiciously easy time determining the source of Tamar's grief, but tells her not to dwell on the episode. Surprisingly, the reason he gives is that Amnon is her brother, as if that removes the horror of it. Or perhaps one is to understand that the close relationship makes impossible the kind of blood revenge that Dinah's brothers exacted from Shechem and all the men of his city in Genesis 34; or perhaps the point is that since Tamar's brother is the firstborn and heir apparent, care must be taken before her rape can be avenged.

The last that is heard of Tamar, whom Absalom has just called "my sister," is that she remained "a desolate woman" in her brother Absalom's house (2 Sam. 13:20). Relational language dominates to the end of this story. David does not punish Amnon (because he was his firstborn son, according to several versions), and Absalom hates Amnon because he raped his sister. Finally, after two years, Amnon goes to a feast at Absalom's sheepshearing, apparently not suspecting that Absalom harbors such intense feelings still. Absalom has his servants kill Amnon, and then Absalom flees across the Jordan River to his maternal grandfather. He is later allowed to return, and the text reports (14:27, but cf. 18:18) that Absalom had three sons and one daughter, a beautiful woman whose name was Tamar.

## Conclusion

In the summary of the contents of the books of Samuel in the introduction, it was said that the books are organized around the careers of three men: Samuel, Saul, and David. Yet that is a somewhat misleading summation, as the subsequent discussion has made clear. Women play a larger role in the books of Samuel than in most of the rest of the Bible, and they appear in these narratives in the domestic sphere (Hannah, for instance), in the public sphere (the medium of Endor and the two wise women), and in the gray area that is the domestic sphere of a ruling family, where private decisions have public consequences. It has, in fact, been suggested that one of the major themes in the stories of David and his family is precisely the unavoidable link between public and private life within a ruling family. When David stops ruling himself and his family, the succession to the throne is threatened, and in this way all Israel suffers. The same could be said for Saul: he loses control of himself, and his use of the women in his family to control David backfires. Even the women who sing battle songs are more impressed with David than with their king.

Some of the more fascinating narratives about women in Samuel are all the more tantalizing because the text offers so little information to help in understanding them. The women who serve at the tent of meeting and the medium of Endor are clearly religious professionals, but in systems that can no longer be fully described. What kind of local power did the "wise women" have and what was the relationship between the system that supported them and the central government? Hannah offers her long-awaited son to a kind of religious order and then receives more children. Does the text imply a connection? Was it common among childless women to offer to "repay" the deity if the requested child was granted?

It is clearly easier to understand the roles of the men in these stories than those of the women. The men's stories seem straightforward and typical; the women are not so accessible. As a general rule less is known about women's lives in the ancient world than about men's, and so it is more difficult to fill in whatever gaps may appear. But ironically this situation makes the women's stories more intriguing and all the more inviting to the interpreter.

## BIBLIOGRAPHY

Ackerman, James S. "Knowing Good and Evil: A Literary Analysis of the Court History in 2 Samuel 9–20 and 1 Kings 1–2." *Journal of Biblical Literature* 109 (1990), 41–60.

Bird, Phyllis. "The Place of Women in the Israelite Cultus." In *Ancient Israelite Religion: Essays in Honor of Frank Moore Cross*, edited by Patrick D. Miller, Jr., Paul D. Hanson, and S. Dean McBride, pp. 397–419. Philadelphia: Fortress Press, 1987.

Camp, Claudia. "The Wise Women of 2 Samuel: A Role Model for Women in Early Israel?" *Catholic Biblical Quarterly* 43 (1981), 14–29.

Gunn, David M. *The Fate of King Saul: An Interpretation of a Biblical Story.* Sheffield: University of Sheffield Press, 1980.

———. *The Story of King David: Genre and Interpretation.* Sheffield: University of Sheffield Press, 1978.

Hackett, Jo Ann. "In the Days of Jael: Reclaiming the History of Women in Ancient Israel." In *Immaculate and Powerful: The Female in Sacred Image and Social Reality,* edited by Clarissa W. Atkinson, Constance H. Buchanan, and Margaret R. Miles, pp. 15–38. Harvard Women's Studies in Religion Series. Boston: Beacon Press, 1985.

Jay, Nancy. "Sacrifice as Remedy for Having Been Born of Woman." In *Immaculate and Powerful: The Female in Sacred Image and Social Reality,* edited by Clarissa W. Atkinson, Constance H. Buchanan, and Margaret R. Miles, pp. 283–309. Harvard Women's Studies in Religion Series. Boston: Beacon Press, 1985.

Levenson, Jon D., and Baruch Halpern. "The Political Import of David's Marriages." *Journal of Biblical Literature* 99 (1980), 507–518.

McCarter, P. Kyle, Jr. *I Samuel.* Anchor Bible 8. Garden City, N.Y.: Doubleday & Co., 1980.

———. *II Samuel.* Anchor Bible 9. Garden City, N.Y.: Doubleday & Co., 1984.

# 1 AND 2 KINGS

*Claudia V. Camp*

## Introduction

### Summary of Contents

First and Second Kings narrate the "history" of the Israelite kingdoms from 962 B.C.E., the death of David, through 560, the release of Judean king Jehoiachin from Babylonian prison in the middle of the exile. First Kings 1–11 reviews Solomon's achievements and the prophet Ahijah's foretelling of his kingdom's future division after he succumbs to the idolatry of his foreign wives. Chapters 12–14 describe the secession of the northern tribes under Jeroboam at the beginning of the reign of Rehoboam, Solomon's son, and Jeroboam's building of the golden "calves," a sin that would haunt the Northern Kingdom (now called "Israel," the Davidic South being called "Judah"). Plagued by tension with neighboring Aram, Israel experiences rapid dynastic turnover until the dynasty of Omri (876–842) (1 Kings 15–16). The struggles of Omri's son Ahab and his Phoenician wife, Jezebel, with the prophets Elijah and Micaiah are detailed in 1 Kings 17–22. Second Kings 1–2 relates Elijah's "ascension" and his succession by Elisha. Several miracle stories involving Elisha are recorded (2 Kings 2–8), as well as his involvement in both Aram's and Israel's political and military situations, including the anointing of Jehu, who would unseat the Omride dynasty (2 Kings 9–10). Jehu slaughters the Israelite ruling family, including the queen mother Jezebel and the visiting Judean king, Ahaziah. Athaliah (Jezebel and Ahab's daughter, and, by virtue of a political marriage, the murdered Ahaziah's mother) takes control of Judah by coup. Athaliah is eventually assassinated by the high priest, who restores the male Davidic heir (2 Kings 11).

Chapters 12–16 relate the chronologies of the northern and southern kings, with notes on their wars and repeated theological commentary on their failure to keep faith with Yahweh. Second Kings 17 describes, with an elaborated theological justification, the fall of the North to Assyria in 721. Chapters 18–25 continue the tale of Judah. "The book of the covenant" is discovered during King Josiah's reform (640–609) and is ratified by the prophet Huldah, but Jerusalem still falls to the Babylonians (587).

### Authorship and Date

The books of Kings are part of the Deuteronomistic History (DH), which takes its definitive theological theme, "military punishment for religious faithlessness," from Deuteronomy and applies it to Israel's history from the time of the conquest (Joshua) through the end of the monarchy. In Kings, the leaders are held particularly responsible for sin. Yet a second, seemingly contradictory, promonarchic theme appears, that of the faithfulness of David and Josiah. Does thematic tension point to the work of more than one author? If so, who were they and when did they work? The conclusion of DH with Jehoiachin's release means that its final form must be dated between 560 and 550, though an earlier edition, produced during the reign of Josiah, is also possible. Whether there were one or two editions, the authors involved would have been of the same status and role, members of the educated elite of the king's court (or former court) who also took seriously the prophets' criticism of monarchy. Since this group was both invested in the monarchy and capable of attending to the prophetic message, the combination of pro- and antimonarchic themes may be less surprising.

## First and Second Kings as (Women's) "History"

Even a one-edition theory of DH's composition must take account of the fact that this editor used earlier sources, possibly both written and oral, as the basis for the work. Assessment of the historical accuracy of its reports must consider their temporal distance from the events reported; the variety of their literary forms, some of which are more purely historiographical (e.g., the explicitly mentioned "chronicles of the kings of Israel and Judah") and some more storylike; and their varied theological perspectives. With respect to women, the following questions must be raised. Do the narratives depict "actual" events that happened to "real" women? Even if the answer is no, do they provide insight into the kinds of lives women led, given the environmental and institutional factors of the time? On a literary level, what functions do female characters serve as images in a theological work produced by male authors and editors? The discussion of particular passages below will focus on this last question, but some further observations on sociohistorical setting and genre (=literary form) are first in order.

## The Social and Religious Background and the Literary Forms in Narratives About Women

*Women of the farms and villages.* Although full gender equality is never found in agricultural societies, one can conjecture that during the period of the tribal confederacy women in Israel were accorded a relatively high status (Meyers). The intense labor of the pioneer period, coupled with the need for a high level of fertility, demanded the participation of all persons, while the decentralized political system allowed for a variety of formal and informal leadership roles. A woman was never "just a mother," though she was (biology willing) unavoidably that. As manager of an extended family household, she was largely responsible for its economic viability. As the wife of an influential citizen and the mother of wisely trained children, she had at least an indirect voice in village affairs. As a wise woman (2 Samuel 14; 20) or a prophet (Judges 4-5), her authority was openly acknowledged.

In many respects the monarchy changed little in the daily lives of these village women.

Under the surface, however, the monarchy's centralization of both political and economic decision making eroded the base of female authority in the village kinship structures, while robbing that culture of its autonomy and self-sufficiency. This disempowerment of Israel's peasantry likely provided the impetus for stories about the prophets' miracles.

*"Prophet meets woman" and the miracle story genre.* There are eight miracle stories in 1 and 2 Kings. Five of these involve the direct interaction of Elijah or Elisha and a woman: Elijah's famine-long provision of oil and meal for the Sidonian widow and her son (1 Kings 17:8-16) and the subsequent revivification of the boy when he dies (1 Kings 17:17-24); Elisha's supplying of oil to pay the debts of the widow of one of the prophetic guild, thus saving her children from slavery (2 Kings 4:1-7); his prophecy of a son for the wealthy Shunammite woman (2 Kings 4:8-17) and that child's revivification (2 Kings 4:18-37). These female characters are best understood as generic rather than historical; that is, they represent groups within the population (either peasants, as in the case of the two widows, or the faithful among the ruling elite, as the Shunammite) who were struggling for survival amid the political strife and agricultural hardships of mid-ninth-century Israel (see Rentería). The miracle story functions as a genre of empowerment, shared among such persons to encourage their own initiative in the face of despair.

*Worship of the goddess.* In contrast to these orthodox stories of faith, references occur throughout Kings to Asherah and *'asherim*, polemical vestiges of the worship of a Canaanite goddess and her symbol, a pole or stylized tree. Although most scholars have accepted DH's assertions that worship of Asherah represents a pagan invasion of pure Yahweh worship, there is increasing weight given to the possibility that Asherah was regarded as Yahweh's consort and a legitimate part of the normative Yahweh cult, at least until the time of DH, which put unprecedented emphasis on worshiping one god (see Olyan). Inscriptions from two sites, Kuntillat Ajrud and Khirbet el-Qom, that refer to "Yahweh and his *'asherah*," suggest the role of the goddess in popular piety. Two objects in the Jerusalem Temple may place her in the official cult as well: the "pillar," a symbol related to the *'asherah* pole; and Nehushtan, the Mosaic snake image that is also associated with Asherah. Most telling of all, however, are DH's full-scale attacks on Asherah worship, hardly necessary unless confronting a pervasive practice. Regrettably, establishing the likelihood of goddess worship in Israel still tells little about women who may have been involved. The Bible clearly attests, however, that more than one queen or queen mother staked her power on Asherah (see below).

**The women of the palaces.** Although the peasantry and its women lost power under the monarchy, the palace corridors occasionally gave issue to royal women exercising their own strategies of power. In fifteen out of eighteen cases, the succession notice of a Judean king includes the name of his mother, for example, "Josiah was eight years old when he began to reign; he reigned thirty-one years in Jerusalem. His mother's name was Jedidah daughter of Adaiah of Bozkath" (2 Kings 22:1). These "queen mother formulas" attest to the power of this position. Contrast, for example, the body language that signals power when Bathsheba

comes as queen mother before her son, King Solomon (he rises to meet her, bows, and seats her on a throne at his right hand [1 Kings 2:19]) as opposed to her earlier visit to her husband David, when she "bows and does obeisance" (1:16). The queen mother served as both representative of and counselor to the king in political affairs and could represent the people before the king (Andreasen). Her authority may at some points have been drawn from her role in the Asherah cult. Maacah is removed from being queen mother by her son Asa because she "made an abominable image for Asherah" (1 Kings 15:13), and Jehoiachin's mother, Nehushta, shares a name with the Temple's snake image (2 Kings 24:8). Jezebel—regarded by Judeans as a queen mother, whether or not the Northern Kingdom formally recognized such a position (2 Kings 10:13)—is an outspoken proponent of Baal and Asherah. Her daughter Athaliah presumed but was ultimately denied the authority of "standing by the pillar" in the Jerusalem Temple (2 Kings 11:14), and the priest of Baal was deposed with her.

## Comment

### The Solomon Narrative (1 Kings 1–11) and Biblical Wisdom Literature

The wise Solomon was later regarded as the patron and ideal of the biblical "wisdom tradition." It is not surprising that the story of his reign is laced with themes and images from wisdom literature, especially Proverbs. Of particular importance is Proverbs' use of female images to personify two central ideas—wisdom and strangeness, or folly. The Solomon narrative draws on these symbolic portrayals of Woman Wisdom (love of whom leads to life) and Woman Stranger/Folly (whose embrace brings death) to construct its female characters.

*Abishag and Bathsheba (1 Kings 1:1–2:25).* Surrounding and mediating the transition from the reign of David to that of Solomon are two female characters, one passive and one active. Abishag the Shunammite is "a beautiful maiden" sought "throughout all the territory of Israel" to lie in the aging David's bosom and be his nurse. If this fairy-tale-like characterization implied that Abishag was expected to work a revitalizing miracle, those who sought her were disappointed, for "the king did not know her sexually" (1:4). This report of the final failure of David's sexual energy leads immediately to the

claim of coregency by Adonijah, David's eldest son by his wife Haggith.

Although joined by David's general, Joab, Adonijah did not have the support of the prophet Nathan. Nathan counsels Bathsheba to "save [her] own life and the life of [her] son Solomon" (1:12) by challenging the apparently beclouded David to resist Adonijah's power play and remember his oath that Solomon would succeed him. The reader is left curiously (purposefully?) in the dark, however, as to whether David had ever made such an oath. Bowed to the floor, using both Nathan's words and harsher ones of her own, Bathsheba presents the alternatives to David: either designate Solomon king or ensure both his and her deaths. As she speaks, Nathan enters with a similar message. David then recalls Bathsheba to his presence (another textual oddity: When had she left?). As she stands before him, he affirms Solomon's reign.

Although King Solomon initially shows mercy to his opponents, his approach changes after David's death. Indeed, his father's final words (2:1–9) counsel a deadly "wisdom" (vv. 6, 9), the executions of general Joab and one Shimei of Benjamin. Though Solomon finds ways to rationalize these killings (2:28–46), they bear the mark of political assassination, as does the murder of Adonijah after another curious episode involving Abishag and Bathsheba (2:13–25). Adonijah approaches Bathsheba with the request that she speak to Solomon in his behalf, asking that Abishag become his wife and expressing confidence that Solomon will heed his mother. Solomon greets Bathsheba with honor and agrees to grant her "small request." He reacts violently, however, to the message from Adonijah, equating his request for Abishag with a request for the kingdom itself. Immediately, he orders Adonijah executed.

This story of the "establishment" (2:12; 2:46; cf. 2 Sam. 7:12–13) of Solomon's kingdom raises many questions concerning its female characters. The identity of Abishag as a historical person is shadowy. Her home of Shunem, in northern Israel, is noteworthy only—though perhaps not inconsequentially—as the home of a wealthy woman who later will aid the prophet Elisha (2 Kings 4:8) and for being in the vicinity of the medium of Endor (cf. 1 Sam. 28:4). It may seem easy to classify Abishag as an almost stereotypical case of the beautiful sex object who is seen but never heard. This evaluation comes almost *too* easily, however, for other questions must be noted.

First, what was expected of this woman when she was brought to David? Although many commentators seem to suppose an effort to sexually "jump start" the aged king, a sexual *test* may be more to the point. The narrative's abrupt shift from David's impotence to Adonijah's self-elevation to the throne may suggest that Adonijah's supporters had devised a symbolic test of potency, in which the sexual equals the kingly. Repetition of key words supports this reading: in 1:4, the narrator reports that David "did not know" Abishag; in 1:11, Nathan informs Bathsheba that David "does not know" of Adonijah's presumption. The king's sexual impotence is mirrored in his political blindness. If this interpretation is accurate, it is still hard to say whether such practices occurred in the early Israelite monarchy or whether, on the other hand, such a symbolic test was part of the story genre (see Long) that shapes this narrative. In either case, a woman functions (or malfunctions) as a mediator or channel of power from male to male.

Bathsheba is also a mediator. She, however, is positioned to act more powerfully and effectively than Abishag. Though the initiative for her action appears to come from Nathan, she possesses her own power, skills, and motives for her role. At stake for her is the position of supreme female power in the land, that of queen mother. In this, she implicitly battles Haggith, as well as Haggith's son. She stands to lose not only power but life, for Adonijah would suffer his opponents to live no more than did Solomon. Moreover, with Abishag in place as David's companion, if not his sexual partner, Bathsheba would face another potential rival. The narrator explicitly includes Abishag in the scene when Bathsheba confronts David, suggesting the underlying reality of this woman-versus-woman conflict. This is no sex object to sex object competition, however, for Bathsheba hardly speaks so as to curry favor. Despite her humble obeisance, her words are direct and demanding, repeating to David's face that he "does not know" what is going on (1:18). Nathan then enters to provide backup, but it is for Bathsheba that David calls when he renders his decision.

At this moment (1:28), there is an apparent gap in the story's unfolding. Having heard Nathan's words, David calls for Bathsheba's presence, though there had been no indication of her prior withdrawal. While one might suspect an editorial glitch, the textual gap may rather be a means for emphasizing a point, namely, the significance of Bathsheba's name. Her name actually bears at least two somewhat conflicting meanings. Pejoratively it could be understood as "daughter (*bat*) of seven (*sheba'*)," a reference to uncertain parentage. Here, however, the root *shb'* clearly takes its alternate meaning of "oath." In an unusually emphatic phrasing, David says, "Call for me to Bathsheba." When she arrives, the king swears (*yishshaba'*) his oath. The call to Bathsheba, when one expects her to be already at the king's side, focuses attention on her name. This woman is identified as "daughter of an oath" at the moment the oath is taken. Whether this is its first or second swearing (see 1:17) will remain forever a mystery, but Bathsheba's formative role in the oath is clear.

The complementary mediation of Abishag and Bathsheba continues in the narrative following David's death, as more questions emerge. Given that it led so inexorably to his death, why did Adonijah approach Bathsheba for Abishag's hand in marriage? Why did Bathsheba agree to intercede with Solomon? From the standpoint of social roles, the approach to Bathsheba can be understood. As queen mother, she would be a powerful adviser to her son and, if cross-cultural parallels hold, may have been in charge of the king's harem (see Andreasen). Solomon obviously interprets

Adonijah's request as a claim on his father's harem and thus as a symbolic claim on the throne (cf. 2 Sam. 16:20–22), recalling once again the association of sexual and political power. Does Adonijah make a stupid mistake, with Bathsheba as his witless accomplice? Or is the narrator providing a justification for Solomon's execution of Adonijah with this story of his rival's arrogance?

Although a mistake it certainly was, neither Adonijah nor Bathsheba need be seen as stupid. Rather than staking a claim to the throne, Adonijah may have been seeking a negotiated settlement: the release of Abishag from a situation of possible reprisal in return for his acquiescence to Solomon's rule. Given that Abishag's relationship with David had not been consummated, he may have reasoned that Solomon would not regard her as part of the harem and that Bathsheba would prefer her rival out of the palace. Although Bathsheba may have been responding to the latter appeal, other motives may be imagined. Perhaps she agreed to intercede on Adonijah's behalf in the interest of gaining the support of the losing party (see Andreasen). Alternatively, she may have been as eager as her son to be rid of Adonijah and, predicting or even encouraging Solomon's outraged response, found this the perfect excuse for action. One way or another, Adonijah's attempted use of a woman as a channel to power once again fails, for the queen mother serves no interests but her son's.

***The two prostitutes and the test of wisdom (1 Kings 3).*** The bloodshed ended, the first two verses of this chapter point to two crucial themes in the Solomon narrative, his foreign marriages and the building of the Temple. The tale then turns to a third theme, that of wisdom. In language redolent of Proverbs, 1 Kings 3:3–15 relates Solomon's choice for wisdom and Yahweh's promise of riches and honor as well. This wisdom is immediately tested (3:16–28) with the dilemma posed by two prostitutes. One woman speaks, describing a situation in which each of the two, who share a house (a brothel?), had borne a child within the space of three days. She claims that the other woman had lain on her son, killing him, and then traded the dead child for the living one in her own bosom. The second woman, however, claims that the living child is hers. Solomon proposes dividing the living child with a sword in order to apportion him equitably, an order resisted by, and thus marking, the child's true mother.

This episode reveals both the social reality and the literary manipulation of the role of prostitute. The prostitute is the tolerated outsider to patriarchal urban culture, both despised by society and enjoyed by the men who run it. As a woman whose sexuality is uncontrolled by either father or husband, she represents a threat to the very fabric of society. This "liminal" (at-the-margins) position generates the social expectation that all one would hear from such a woman would be lies (see Bird). As Phyllis Bird suggests, however, this stereotype is confronted with another one, namely, the mother who loves her child so much as to surrender him rather than have him harmed. Solomon's wisdom is manifest in his ability to uncover one stereotype hidden beneath another. The story continues to move modern readers, however, because at least certain aspects of these "stereotypes" reflect emotional realities with which women can still identify, especially the protectiveness of the living child's mother. But why would one woman agree to the deadly division of the remaining child? Is there another emotion at work? Stuart Lasine suggests that an envy born of bereavement motivates this inhumane response.

Considered from the perspective of wisdom thought, these female characters yield another reading as well. In Proverbs, the task of the sage is to discern one female figure—Woman Wisdom, who brings social order—from another who is portrayed in often similar terms, Woman Stranger or Folly, the promiscuous purveyor of social chaos. Significantly, these "women" are known by their speech: Wisdom's "mouth will utter truth" (Prov. 8:7), while the seductive Stranger's lips "drip honey and her speech is smoother than oil" (Prov. 5:3). Female sexuality that exists outside of male control functions as a metaphor for deceitful speech, and the character of the "harlot" thus poses the ultimate test of kingly wisdom. Solomon demonstrates his ability to bring social order by dividing from the chaos of female sexuality before him the "true speech" of the mother, the woman whose sexuality is controlled and thus acceptable.

Chapter 3 is crucial to the larger narrative not only thematically but also structurally. Vocabulary, theme, and structure link 1 Kings 3, the authorization of Solomon's rule, to 2 Samuel 11–12, the affaire of Bathsheba and David that culminated in Solomon's birth (see Fontaine). Whereas David made a choice definitive of folly, the choice for adultery (cf. Prov. 6:24–35), Solomon chooses wisdom. David's choice led to deceit, trickery, and the ultimate murder of Uriah, while Solomon's choice brings riches, honor, and long life. The foolish father was brought to judgment with the death of Bathsheba's first child and the pronouncing of a curse upon his house, while the outcome of the wise son's judgment is a living child restored to its mother. By discriminating between these sexually defined women, Solomon resolves the thematic tension and seems to absolve the lineage of David's sexual folly: the foolish father is redeemed in the wise son. Neither resolution nor absolution, however, will last the generation.

***Women, wisdom, and folly in Solomon's reign (1 Kings 3–11).*** First Kings 3 not only looks backward to 2 Samuel; it also turns forward to the ensuing chapters of the Solomon narrative, where the themes from 3:1–2 of foreign (=strange) women and house building play key roles, along with the theme of wisdom from 3:3–28.

In 4:1–19, having divided the women with the threat to divide the child, Solomon turns to dividing the kingdom into twelve districts, not conforming to old tribal boundaries, and assigning them (along with two of his daughters) to his officers. Each administrative district is charged with supplying food for the king and his household for one month out of the year. For the peasant women and men of Israel, the combination of divide-and-control districting with the centralization of planning and taxes to support the king must have had deleterious effects, in spite of DH's saccharine comment that "Judah and Israel . . . ate and drank and were happy" (4:20). In typical wisdom thinking, however, the establishment of social control and the abundance it brings to the king (4:22–28) are narratively linked to Solomon's God-given wisdom and understanding (cf. Prov. 8:15–21), which also produces wisdom speech (3,000 proverbs and 1,005 songs) and an international reputation (4:29–34).

First Kings 5–9 details Solomon's building of the house of Yahweh (5:1–6:38), his own house (7:1–12), and the bronze and other metalwork for the Temple (7:13–51), followed by the ceremony of consecration (8:1–66) and Yahweh's response (9:1–9). Although this recitation of measurement and design may seem dry to the modern reader, for the ancient writers it may represent a loving attention to detail comparable to the lovers' physical descriptions of each other in the erotic poetry of the Song of Songs. If so, then it is not so surprising to find laced through this material references to Solomon's

other competing loves: the daughter of Pharaoh, for whom he builds a house like his own (3:1; 7:8; 9:16, 24), and the wisdom of God, which he will forsake at his own peril (4:29–34; 5:12; 9:1–9).

Overlapping these allusions to women and wisdom are also references to Solomon's international relations, reflecting the ambivalence Israel will feel toward foreigners. Solomon's widespread reputation for wisdom (4:29–34) and his avuncular relationship with King Hiram of Tyre, who supplies Solomon with both encouragement and timber for the Temple (5:1–11), are noted with apparent approval: Solomon's wisdom is manifest in his treaty with Hiram (5:12). The same passage, however, records without comment the enormous cost of this treaty to Israel in food (5:11) and forced labor (5:13–17). The metalwork for the Temple is done by an artisan of Tyre, also named Hiram, of whom two notable things are said (7:13–14). First, he is "filled with wisdom, understanding and knowledge" (NRSV: "skill, intelligence, and knowledge") to do any work in bronze. Although "wisdom" often refers to a person's intellectual and moral capacity, it appears here in its most concrete sense, as the consummate skill of a craftsperson worthy to do the Temple's work. Second, Hiram is the son of an Israelite widow and a man of Tyre. This characterization of mixed ancestry may suggest the writer's perspective on the Temple itself: it is the product of Solomon's treaty with the foreign king and will bear the burden of foreign worship within it. A further moment of tension connecting the themes of women, foreignness, and the Temple occurs in 1 Kings 8:41–43 and 9:24. The first passage appears in the midst of Solomon's dedicatory prayer, where he asks Yahweh, quite remarkably, to hear the prayer of foreigners who will come and "pray toward this house." The second (ironically?) notes that the quintessential foreigner, Pharaoh's daughter, "went up from the city of David *to her own house,*" a movement that, in contrast to Solomon's prayer, foreshadows the turning of *his* heart away from Yahweh's house by the "strange women" in chap. 11.

Before that bleak moment, however, chap. 10 sounds one last chord harmonizing Solomon's wisdom and the foreignness embodied in a woman. Although the story of a distant queen with fabulous wealth coming to test a king with hard questions (literally, "riddles") is no doubt legendary, there are elements in it that can be broadly grounded in history. Inscriptions locate Sheba in either southwest or northwest Arabia. One of these inscriptions, from the Assyrian king Tiglath-pileser IV, records tribute from a queen who ruled in Arabia, although this event (732–731 B.C.E.) was later than the time of Solomon. The framing and interrupting of the queen of Sheba story with (however exaggerated) information on Solomon's international trade (9:26–28; 10:11–12, 14–29) correlates with our knowledge of the southwest Arabian Sheba as a center of trade and suggests that at the core of this tale may have been the memory of a female-led trade delegation.

As it is told, however, the queen of Sheba episode is very much a legend, and therefore its place in the literary machinery of the Solomon narrative must be examined. Chapter 10 provides the concluding framework to the tale of the Solomonic golden age begun in chap. 3. In the opening frame, Solomon chose wisdom (implicitly, though not here explicitly, construed as a female personification) over riches and honor, though God then promised the latter as well. The following scene confirmed the king's wisdom by his ability to order with justice the chaos represented by the two prostitutes, "strange women" within their own society. In the final frame, the queen of Sheba comes to test Solomon with riddles, a form of speech that is crucial to the wisdom tradition (Prov. 1:6). The queen, therefore, is Woman Wisdom, cast in narrative form. True to her role, she fulfills Yahweh's earlier promise by bringing the riches and honor that should accompany Solomon's choice for wisdom. She is also, paradoxically, a strange or foreign woman, so it is narratively important that Solomon should best her by answering her riddles and, after all due ceremony, see her on her way.

As is typical in wisdom thought, however, this tale of verbal sparring only partly conceals an erotic subtext. The contest between Solomon and the queen is framed as a language game: a riddle match that Solomon wins, as he had solved the prostitutes' dilemma, by discerning the truth in the midst of trickery. While the narrative speaks of Solomon's victory of wits, however, later tradition will elaborate on its unspoken possibility of sexual relationship between the wise king and the foreign queen. In the foreground is the power of wisdom; in the background, a seductive strangeness that can be suppressed but not eliminated.

This penultimate triumph of (male) wisdom over woman is thus finally undone

by the power of foreign women. The final verses of chap. 10 anticipate the outcome of chap. 11 while at the same time signaling the hand of the Deuteronomistic editor. Deuteronomy 17:16–17 requires that an Israelite king refrain from the acquisition of three things: horses from Egypt, many wives, and silver and gold. First Kings 10:14–29 records Solomon's massive accumulation of Egyptian horses and wealth; 1 Kings 11 makes the unity of his kingdom hinge on many wives. Interpreters have debated whether the sin of Solomon lay primarily in the *number* of his wives and concubines, and thus implicitly in an excess of sexuality, or in their status as foreigners, which led to foreign worship. The interweaving of the themes of strangeness and sexuality in wisdom thought recommends a both-and rather than an either-or interpretation. In many other biblical contexts as well, improper sexual behavior is a metaphor for foreign worship. Thus, although Deut. 17:17 states simply that "many women" will "turn away" a king's heart, 1 Kings 11:1 specifies the problem as one of "many *foreign* women." Having "clung to these in love" and built temples for their deities, in his old age Solomon's heart is finally "turned away" by them to follow after these deities. The story of David and Solomon has come full circle: while the sexual folly of David's youth was mediated by the youthful wisdom of his son, this same son replicates that folly in his own dotage.

Women appear in the unraveling of Solomon's kingdom, even as they had in its formation. For "Yahweh raised up an adversary against Solomon, Hadad the Edomite" (11:14), who, having fled from David to Egypt, was given in marriage the sister of Pharaoh's queen Tahpenes. In contrast to the fruitless union of Solomon to Pharaoh's daughter, Hadad's Egyptian liaison produces a son, and Hadad himself returns to try to wrest his country from Solomon.

Solomon's ultimate adversary, however, is one Jeroboam, a former functionary of the king, who receives the prophetic appointment to take ten of the twelve Israelite tribes away from the hand of Rehoboam, Solomon's son. Like most of the future Judean kings, Jeroboam is identified by the name of his mother, the widow Zeruah, a sign perhaps of the fatherless — and thus perpetually chaotic — Northern Kingdom.

## Jezebel and Athaliah

In Ezek. 16:44, the prophet uses the proverb "Like mother, like daughter" to castigate the abominations of Judah, which are like those of her foreign "mother," the Hittites. Had he lived two centuries earlier, he might have said the same about the famous Jezebel and her less well known but nonetheless important daughter, Athaliah.

***Jezebel (1 Kings 16–21; 2 Kings 9).*** Ezekiel perfects the art of describing religious faithlessness in sexual, indeed almost pornographic, terms, a metaphor by which later ages have condemned Jezebel. Sexuality, however, is not the heart of DH's antagonism toward this queen from Sidon of Phoenicia. Here, as in the Solomon narrative, sexuality is a thread in a larger thematic tapestry of gender, power, foreignness, and idolatry.

Jezebel first appears in 1 Kings 16:31, where the note on her marriage to Ahab, king of Israel, is included in an introductory summary of that king's evil ways. Walking in the ways of Jeroboam, he not only took a foreign wife but also built a house and an altar for Baal and made an 'asherah. Moreover, during his reign, the city of Jericho was rebuilt, at the cost of the lives of two of the sons of Hiel the builder. While the text does not say directly that Ahab was responsible for these sacrifices, such is the implication. Other texts emphasize Jezebel's royal initiative. First Kings 18:4, 13 contain parenthetical reference to her efforts to "cut off the prophets of Yahweh." This action is elaborated in 19:1–3, where, following Elijah's slaughter of the prophets of Baal at Mount Carmel, Ahab tells Jezebel of the event and *she* sends a message to Elijah, swearing to kill him.

Again in chap. 21 Ahab seems the passive partner to Jezebel's wanton use of royal power. The childish king turns "resentful and sullen" because Naboth refuses to sell him his vineyard, claiming it as the "inheritance of my fathers." Learning the cause of Ahab's unwillingness to eat, Jezebel devises a plan. Writing a letter to the "elders and nobles" of Naboth's city, she instructs them to proclaim a fast during which "two base fellows" will accuse him of cursing God and king, which will result in his execution by stoning. When word is brought to Jezebel of Naboth's death, she sends Ahab out to take possession of the vineyard. At the vineyard, however, Ahab encounters Elijah, who has been sent by Yahweh to curse the king and his house, a curse extended to include Jezebel as well. Ironically, Ahab's "dejected" attitude after hearing these words is regarded by Yahweh as appropriate humbleness; thus, as was the case with Solomon, the curse is delayed until the time of his son's reign.

The religious tendencies of Jezebel are given a characteristic metaphorical twist in 2 Kings 9:22. After Ahab's death, when his son King Jehoram sues for peace with the divinely appointed usurper Jehu, Jehu asks, "What peace can there be, so long as the many whoredoms and sorceries of your mother Jezebel continue?" He then kills Jehoram and proceeds to Samaria, where Jezebel herself, eyes painted and head adorned, confronts him from an upper window with a masterful bit of political name-calling. She addresses him as "Zimri," an earlier usurper famous for his assassinations. Her own eunuchs, however, take Jehu's side and cast her down to her death, where she is trampled by horses and her corpse eaten by dogs, in accord with the earlier words of Elijah.

It is no doubt these last two passages, Jehu's words to Jehoram and Jezebel's face painting, that led later tradition to define the character of her sin in sexual terms. A fuller understanding of this powerful queen must, however, take further account of both her own social setting and the Bible's theological polemic.

As a Phoenician princess, Jezebel would naturally have worshiped Baal and Asherah (or Astarte, "the goddess of the Sidonians," 1 Kings 11:33). It is unlikely that her polytheistic religion would have motivated her to eliminate the prophets of Yahweh unless these presented a political threat. If anything, the reverse would have been the case: the exclusivistic nature of prophetic Yahwism might have induced some of its adherents to adopt a crusade mentality against worshipers of other deities. Given the activity of prophets of Yahweh in the political arena—anointing kings and promoting coups—Jezebel's concerns were probably not first and foremost religious. As a Phoenician princess, moreover, she was accustomed to royal prerogative and unused to the democratic impulse in Israelite culture that regarded land as a gift given to each Israelite family by Yahweh, rather than at the behest of the king. Thus her brutal response to Naboth's refusal to sell his vineyard may be understood from her point of view as an appropriate royal response to insubordination, in contrast to Ahab's unconscionable weakness as a leader.

An appreciation for Jezebel's remarkable strengths as a leader can also explain her final appearance at the window, painted and be-decked. If she is to have any hope at all of rallying people behind her, she must appear in all the glory of her queenship. Indeed, a modern reader would not think twice to read of a man in her position putting on his most regal robes and crown. Even a queen about to meet her death does so with pride and defiance, as marked in her spiteful words to Jehu and, indeed, in his own later command—too late!—to bury her, "for she is a king's daughter."

It would be a mistake, however, to imagine that the text reflects directly the concerns of the ninth century, in which Jezebel actually lived. The account in its present form is no earlier than the late seventh century, and the Naboth story may be even later. Alexander Rofé compares the version of this story in 1 Kings 21, where Jezebel is given most of the criminal credit, with allusions to the incident in 2 Kings 9, where she is not even mentioned but rather Ahab is indicted. This possibility that Jezebel was not the real culprit is reinforced at the end of 1 Kings 21 as well, where her inclusion in the judgment oracle of Elijah against Ahab appears to be a secondary addition. In a typical DH accusation against a king, Ahab is held accountable for making "all Israel to sin," but then Jezebel is blamed for inciting Ahab! Rofé concludes that the whole tale of Jezebel's treachery against Naboth is the work of a postexilic author-editor, whose shifting of the blame to the foreign woman forms part of that era's polemic on the dangers of intermarriage (see the commentary on Ezra-Nehemiah). Jehu's attack on Jezebel's "whoredoms," when confronting her son Jehoram, may be explicable in the same way. From one perspective no more than a nasty bit of "mother swearing," by the postexilic period there was a strong tendency metaphorically to identify anything apart from exclusive worship of Yahweh with sexual promiscuity, as the allegory in Ezekiel 16 so graphically represents. What was initially a metaphor, however, came to be understood with increasing literalness. Thus Jezebel is often interpreted today not as the woman of political power that she was, but as a seductress.

***Athaliah (2 Kings 8:16–19; 11:1–21).*** This daughter of Jezebel and Ahab is painted by the editor with the same broad brush used for her parents' portraits. Married to King Jehoram of Judah (not to be confused with his northern counterpart of the same name), no doubt for the purpose of sealing a treaty between the two nations, she is assigned blame for the sin of both her husband and her son: Jehoram "walked in the way of the kings of Israel, as the house of Ahab had done, for the daughter of Ahab was his wife" (2 Kings 8:18). Ahaziah, Athaliah's son, did the same because of his relationship to "the house of Ahab" (8:27). Ahaziah succeeded his father on the Judean throne, but it was his misfortune to be accompanying the northern Jehoram at the time of Jehu's coup and to be slain. The bloodbath that resulted in Israel, killing seventy princes, was replicated in Judah at the hand of the queen mother Athaliah, who attempted to destroy the rest of the Judean royal family. One of Ahaziah's young sons, Joash, escaped her grasp, however. His aunt, Jehosheba, stole him away from the others who were about to be killed. He then "remained with her six years, hidden in the house of Yahweh, while Athaliah reigned over the land" (2 Kings 11:3). At that time, Jehoiada the priest (according to 2 Chron. 22:11, the husband of Jehosheba) engineered the proclamation of Joash as king in the Temple and the assassination of both Athaliah and Mattan, the priest of Baal.

Although Athaliah's ruthlessness is shocking, her political position must be considered. Her power and position derived from two sources, her royal family in Israel and her status as queen mother in Judah. With the death of Jezebel and the rest of her blood kin, as well as that of her ruling son, she was suddenly cut off not only from her power bases but also from any means of retreat or escape. Like her mother, she responded with power rather than surrender. The complexity of the political situation is worth noting. On the one hand, Athaliah considered herself greatly threatened; on the other, she could not have then ruled for six years without support. Backing for the new female ruler would have come from the Jerusalem-based politicians who had promoted the Judean-Israelite alliance symbolized by Athaliah's marriage to Jehoram. The threat probably came from the so-called "people of the land." These were Judean nationalists, opposed to the alliance with the North. They were also adherents of exclusive Yahweh worship, appalled at Athaliah's religious practices, and thus later at Jehoiada's disposal.

The narrator has a vested interest in delegitimizing Athaliah and also in distinguishing her overthrow by Jehoiada from that of Jezebel by Jehu (see Nelson). The first mention of her, as the wife who led Jehoram astray, is accompanied by the note that in spite of Jehoram's evil, Yahweh did not destroy Judah "for the sake of his servant David" (2 Kings 8:19). Athaliah's own rule—a rule by a woman and an alien—is thus set against the legitimate succession of Davidic males, even those whose faithlessness would presumably deserve punishment. Similarly, though her grandson Joash would ultimately prove no better than his forebears, the moment of his restoration is presented as popularly supported by the people of the land, legitimated by the priestly authorities, and carried out with proper protocol, as opposed to the murder and mayhem of Jehu's coup.

This story also provides a glimpse of the politics of women in the royal house. The queen mother's position was a powerful one but, as Athaliah's story shows, also fraught with danger, sometimes from rivalry of other women. Jehosheba is described as "King J(eh)oram's daughter, Ahaziah's sister" (2 Kings 11:2). Presumably, however, she was born to a wife other than Athaliah. Here, then, the inherent rivalry of co-wives is ignited between one wife and another's daughter. This rivalry may have had larger political ramifications as well. The people of the land seem to have supported queen mothers from the provinces rather than those from Jerusalem (see Andreasen). It is not insignificant, then, that when Jehosheba chose one royal son to save, she chose one whose mother was Zibiah of Beer-sheba, a city over forty miles from the capital.

What about Jehosheba herself? The question of her status, beyond that of royal daughter, is intriguing. She obviously had a position in the Temple that made her presence there unremarkable to the new ruling faction. Although Chronicles describes her as the wife of a priest, DH does not. Is this because DH assumes readers will know of her husband, or is the Chronicler supplying "information" to explain what seems strange in his own day, the presence of an unattached woman in the Temple? Whatever Jehosheba's marital status, the story of Huldah, a prophet in her own right (see below), raises the possibility that Jehosheba was an independent temple functionary of some sort.

## Women and Male Prophets

As noted above, in five of the eight miracle stories involving the prophets Elijah and Elisha, a woman is the recipient: the Sidonian widow benefits from two miracles, as does the wealthy woman of Shunem; and the widow of a member of the prophetic guild benefits from one. There

is another, apparently related episode that portrays a queen's interaction with a prophet. Because these prophetic narratives portray women from a wide variety of backgrounds, but always with a focus on their motherhood, they seem to constitute a literary pattern. A final story, in which two mothers converse with a king, may function as a countertype to these others.

***Ahijah and the wife of Jeroboam (1 Kings 14:1–18).*** Jeroboam was the first king of Israel, appointed by Ahijah after Solomon's sin. Jeroboam, however, disappointed the prophet's hope for a king faithful to Yahweh. Interestingly, the prophetic judgment against this builder of Israel's golden calves is made through his unnamed wife.

When their son Abijah becomes sick, Jeroboam sends his wife in disguise to the nearly blind Ahijah for word on the child's fate. Forewarned by Yahweh of the woman's identity, Ahijah confronts her with a message for Jeroboam that every male of his household will perish, their bodies eaten by dogs or birds. Only his son, in whom is found "something pleasing to Yahweh," will escape this destiny, dying in time to be mourned and buried. The bitter irony of this "reprieve" is excruciatingly sharpened for the boy's mother: she is told that he will die "when [her] feet enter the city" (14:12). The mother is transformed into the secondhand agent of death; it is not, finally, until "she came to the threshold of the house" that the child dies (14:17).

What may have been an old legend has been shaped by the hand of DH, as is evident in anachronistic allusions in vv. 9 and 15–16. The focus on a child pleasing to Yahweh, who was spared not death but at least ignominious death, may be an allusion to the later king Josiah of Judah (see below), who tried unsuccessfully to steer his nation from their wicked ways and died before their ultimate defeat. In Josiah's case too a prophet announces both the national disaster and the individual exception.

***Elijah and the Sidonian widow (1 Kings 17:8–24).*** Chapter 17 contains three episodes that introduce the prophet Elijah. His first act is to announce to Ahab a drought in the land. While his proclamation is sworn in Yahweh's name, there is no indication that it comes at Yahweh's behest. Instructed by God to go to a wadi east of Jordan, Elijah is fed by ravens, acting on God's command, until the wadi runs dry (17:3–7). In the second episode,

God sends him to Zarephath in Sidon (Jezebel's homeland!), where the agent of feeding is to be a widow. The widow, however, is both less willing and less able than the ravens to fulfill the divine command to fill another mouth: her supplies almost at an end, she turns aside Elijah's request for water, swearing, as he himself had done, "as Yahweh lives," that she is about to prepare a last meal for herself and her son and die. Elijah now speaks directly as God's messenger, proclaiming that her oil and meal shall not fail until the day of rain. Whereas human words—whether the prophet's oath of power or the widow's oath of resignation—have signified death, the divine word effects life.

This narrative is concerned with prophetic recognition and authorization as well as with prophetic power. Thus, the introduction of Elijah closes with a conversion scene (17:17–24). "After this the son of the woman, the mistress of the house, became ill. . . ." This third episode was likely originally independent of the one preceding, for its female character is more well-to-do than the widow (she is called "mistress"; her house has two stories). The present narrative sequence, however, identifies the two and presents her assessment of Elijah as evolving. Earlier she had resisted him at first meeting, then obeyed him without comment, without even a response to the miracle of oil and meal. Now she addresses Elijah as "man of God," perhaps an indirect acknowledgment of that feat; but her accusation of him as responsible for her son's illness indicates her ambivalence. Her complaint that "you have come to me to bring my sin to remembrance" does not presume any particular offense; rather, in accordance with the ancient perspective on retribution, she assumes that her son's mortal illness must have its source in some generalized guilt of hers. Elijah's miraculous restoration of the boy allows her to move beyond the mere title "man of God" to its real meaning: "Now I know that you are a man of God, and that the word of Yahweh in your mouth is truth" (17:24).

Elijah is then prepared to go public, confronting the prophets of Baal at Mount Carmel and, on a grand scale, inducing in the people of Israel a "conversion" replicating that of the woman: "Yahweh indeed is God; Yahweh indeed is God" (18:39), an acclamation that accompanies the life-giving rain. Elijah's victory is short-lived, however, for Jezebel swears to kill him and he must flee to the wilderness of Mount Horeb. Communicating with Yahweh in "a sound of sheer silence" (19:12), he is sent back

to Israel to select his successor, Elisha, representative of the "seven thousand in Israel" whose knees have not bowed to Baal.

The prophet's interaction with the Sidonian widow looks both forward and backward in the narrative. On the one hand, her inability to feed Elijah recalls by contrast the gift of food offered by Jeroboam's wife to Ahijah. In both cases, too, the life of a single child becomes a sign of the fate of the larger body of Israel. The Sidonian woman's conversion, moreover, marks the beginning of a pattern of such life-changing commitments—next of Israel and then of Elisha—that ensure the continuity of Yahweh worship in Israel and the authority of Yahweh's prophets (see Nelson). Here, a foreign woman is a sign of and to God's people!

### The prophet's widow and Elisha (2 Kings 4:1–7).

This episode and those involving the wealthy woman of Shunem that follow it have much in common with the sequence on Elijah and the Sidonian woman. Here, however, the distinction between the poor widow and a second, well-to-do woman is clear. The tales are varied in other ways as well. The prophet's widow's problem is not starvation but debt. Thus the threat to her offspring is not death but slavery. Selling a child was one of the few antidotes to debt available to a peasant. The responding miracle, therefore, involves only the proliferation of oil, which can be sold, without reference to the subsistence item of grain.

The focus of this variant on the miraculous act itself, rather than on the emerging relationship of the woman and the prophet, points to its origin among ancient folktales used to impress upon listeners the power of the prophet. The concerns addressed, however, are real-life concerns of struggling peasants whose lot was made all the worse by unprincipled creditors and landholders. The miracle story thus also communicates the values of the just society promoted by the prophets of Yahweh (see Rentería).

### Elisha and the wealthy woman of Shunem (2 Kings 4:8–37; 8:1–6).

The portrayal of this unnamed woman is one of the most remarkable in the Bible. Both independent and maternal, powerful and pious, she brings to mind a number of other female characters, yet surpasses them all. She is observant in both practical and spiritual ways: she notices not only Elisha's regular passing through Shunem but also the aura that marks him as a "man of

God." As Abigail had perceived, in spite of her husband's thickheadedness, that alliance with David was in her household's interest (1 Samuel 25), so the Shunammite takes an initiative that might have been her husband's. She has an upper room built and furnished for Elisha's use (compare Elijah's lodging with the Sidonian woman).

In response, the prophet offers her a boon—perhaps a good word put in with the king or army commander?—which she refuses. Elisha's offer is notable for two reasons. First, though it is refused, it foreshadows later events in the relationship of this woman and the prophet. Second, it is suggestive of the particular life setting of such a woman and her family. As one of the landed gentry, she does not suffer the privation of the peasants. Her life is hardly secure, however, for her property and possessions are to some degree subject to the demands of the king and his army, with whom members of her class have at best an uneasy alliance. The Shunammite's response, then, refers to the source of whatever political power she might claim: "I live among my own people" (4:13b).

In the face of this self-reliance, Elisha makes a move typical of wonder-workers in folktales, promising the barren woman a child. This motif is a common one in the Bible, but it takes some unexpected turns in this instance. Most childless women in the Bible are defined by that status from the outset, and the stories about them revolve around their desire for a child and the social lack they experience without one. The Shunammite woman, on the other hand, is presented as having a self-sufficiency and an authority independent of motherhood and is defined by her relationship to the prophet. Indeed, it comes as a surprise to the reader to learn at this point that she has no child, a surprise marked by and reflected in the prophet's own unawareness of the fact! Elisha has to be informed by his otherwise ineffective sidekick Gehazi. Even after receiving Elisha's promise of pregnancy, the woman responds not with joy but with wary caution. Pious she is, but hardly awash with an easy faith in miracles. In her response, though, one also gets a glimpse of the tender desire beneath her competent exterior. Her plea not to be deceived by his words moves the action to the next scene, where heartache rears its head.

Her son falls ill while working in the fields with his father. The father, as paternally insensitive to the boy as he had been spiritually insensitive to the presence of the prophet, orders him carried to his mother. He falls dead in her lap. Again one can trace this woman's character from competence to compassion. As if she knows how a prophet does his work, she takes the child to Elisha's upper room and lays him on Elisha's bed (compare the actions of Elijah and the dead child in 1 Kings 17). Again recalling the relationship of Abigail and her foolish husband, she brushes off her husband's objections and has a donkey saddled to take her to the man of power, some twenty-five miles distant at Mount Carmel. Elisha sees her coming and sends Gehazi running to meet her. She brushes off the servant with the same irrelevance as she had her husband: "It is all right." When she finally reaches Elisha, however, her facade melts away as she grasps his feet and shows her distress. Still far from obsequious, however, she confronts him with her earlier plea not to deceive her with false promises.

The woman's ride to Mount Carmel and her encounter with the prophet hark back to the earlier journey of Jeroboam's wife to Ahijah in the name of her dying son, though with differences. The royal woman had gone at the command of her husband; the Shunammite goes in spite of hers. Jeroboam's wife had taken the proper sort of gifts; the landowner's wife does not even wait until the proper time of new moon or Sabbath. Jeroboam's wife had gone in disguise to a blind prophet, who had, nonetheless, divine knowledge of both her identity and her mission. The Shunammite comes assertively to a prophet who can see at a distance but who admits that Yahweh has hidden her plight from him.

Elisha's first reaction is to send Gehazi, carrying the prophet's staff, to lay "on the face of the child." Once again the woman knows more than the prophet: Gehazi will not succeed; Elisha himself must come. Verbally skilled, even in her distress, she swears the same oath sworn by Elijah to cause a drought and by the Sidonian woman to announce her and her son's death, and even intensifies it: "As Yahweh lives, and as you yourself live, I will not leave without you" (4:30). The eventual miracle of resurrection proceeds in the same magical terms as that of the Sidonian woman's son. Although the Shunammite makes no verbal response, it may be possible imaginatively to fill in one similar to the Sidonian's. Twice she has cautioned Elisha against deceit. Could she not now say, "I know that the word of Yahweh in your mouth is truth"?

Given this genre-typical "happy ending" to

the mother's distress, it is almost surprising that this woman appears again a few chapters later (8:1–6). Here she is instructed by Elisha to take her household away from their lands, to "settle wherever you can," to avoid a seven-year famine sent by Yahweh (see 4:38). Once again the reader is impressed with her competence and independent authority. The prophet counsels her rather than her husband. He tells her to go "wherever"; she chooses the land of the Philistines. On her return, she goes to the king to petition for return of *her* house and *her* land. As with other of the "prophet-meets-woman" stories, this one too combines elements of legend with insight into real social pressures faced by Israelites in this period. The woman's loss of her land may have resulted from encroachment by her neighbors or from imposition of the monarchic ideology that the land belongs to the king by right and is his to assign to his subjects. In either case, the appeal to the king for economic justice was standard procedure. As is typical of the prophetic narratives in the books of Kings, however, the king proves ineffective without the help of a prophet (cf. 2 Kings 5:1–8; 6:24–7:2). This episode is particularly interesting because the "miracle" involved is not of the magical sort we find elsewhere in this material (see Nelson). Rather, the restoration of the woman's property comes about because of the effectiveness of the prophetic legends themselves! The king is so impressed by the story of resurrection told by Gehazi and the woman that he is motivated to do as a king should, restoring to the woman her family estate. He thus implicitly recognizes that, in Israel, the land is *not* the king's to control but rather God's. The reader here experiences the effectiveness of the oral tradition that authorized the prophets and led eventually to the creation of the canon.

### Countertype: The king and the two mothers of Samaria (2 Kings 6:24–31).

The immediate literary context of the episode of the cannibal mothers is very disjunctive. In chap. 5, Elisha heals the leprosy of the Aramean commander Naaman, who actually converts to Yahwism. By 6:8, however, the Aramean army is attacking Israel with particular designs on the prophet whose extrasensory perception has been hurting them in battle. In 6:21–23, Elisha and the unnamed king of Israel seem to have a good relationship; in this episode, however, the king swears to kill the prophet for causing famine in Samaria because of the Aramean siege (compare Jezebel's almost identical oath against Elijah in 1 Kings 19).

This disjunction in the immediate context is somewhat relieved by the "fit" of this episode into a larger pattern of narratives dealing with women and Yahweh's appointed leaders. The appeal of the two mothers to the king's justice reminds the reader of the prostitutes' trial before Solomon and also foreshadows the Shunammite mother's appeal for the return of her land in chap. 8. Moreover, the motif of the mother's concern for a child's life places this episode as the last in a sequence of such tales in Kings. The similarities between this tale and the others make the differences all the more notable. In contrast to Solomon, who is wise enough to make judgments even in an impossible case, and to the prophets, who are powerful enough to restore dead children to life, this king is ineffective. At first he resists even hearing the woman's complaint ("Let Yahweh help you"); then, the only response he can make is to swear against Elisha.

The story presents greater perplexities, however, than mere portrayal of a weak king set against a powerful prophet. Unlike Jeroboam and his wife, who lose their son because of enormous sin, this king actually expresses belief in Yahweh and, when he tears his clothes in distress at the woman's story, reveals the sackcloth next to his skin, an act of proper contrition. Thus the narrator builds sympathy for the ruler's inability to help his people. For the woman, however, in spite of the magnitude of her loss, we feel nothing but horror. Eat her child so she could survive! How could she! Our expectations of self-sacrificing motherhood, which so win us to the real mother in Solomon's case, turn us against the cannibal mother here. Stuart Lasine, citing the motif of a "world upside down," argues that it is not merely the cannibalism that offends. It is rather the woman's blindness to her heinous crime and her presumption in suing for the "justice" of another child's death! Indeed, the story suddenly reveals itself as "too much." Though evidence exists for the reality of cannibalism in besieged and starving cities, the narrator does not here ask one to imagine a real situation. Rather, the woman's incongruous appeal for justice embodies a grotesque humor whose purpose is to point to deeper issues of social disruption, distrust, and greed. A mother whose "predictable" maternal instinct has failed symbolizes a world in chaos as surely as Solomon's reliance on it marked his capacity to bring order. The cannibal mothers are only one sign, however, of the deep disarray in this upside-down world. Perhaps the only thing worse than not being able to count on "maternal instinct" is the inability of a faithful king to count on the good will of Yahweh and Yahweh's prophet.

## Woman as Prophet: Huldah (2 Kings 22)

The story of the divided kingdom begins and ends with words of women, words of prophets, words about a single life saved, words about a nation doomed. In 1 Kings 14, the wife of Israel's first king—Jeroboam, whose name would come to define a nation's sin—went to a prophet for a word about her child. The message she received about him sounded hopeful only in comparison to the fate of Israel. In 2 Kings 22, set in the year 621, messengers from Judah's last good king, Josiah, go to a woman prophet with a newfound scroll—"the book of the law"—for a word on the fate of that nation. Jeroboam's words at his wife's departure signaled hope by recalling that Ahijah had, after all, named him king of Israel. The hope was dashed, and one wonders if it were ever there, knowing this king's sinful ways. Josiah, however, is already at work on reform. Surely there is hope here, in spite of the scroll's gloomy message, which prompts words from Josiah as apprehensive as Jeroboam's were optimistic. Surely Huldah will reverse his expectation, as Ahijah had Jeroboam's. But no, her oracle virtually repeats that of the earlier prophet: the nation is irrevocably doomed; only one man, Josiah, will go to his grave in peace. Within thirty-five years, her prophecy is fulfilled.

While the story of Huldah thus provides a fitting conclusion to the story of Yahweh's kingdoms, it is still remarkable to the modern reader unaccustomed to imagining women in positions of authority in ancient Israel. It appears, however, that prophecy was one religious vocation open to women on an equal basis with men. Certainly the narrator of Kings takes no notice whatsoever of Huldah's gender. Some scholars have suggested that the tri-generational lineage of her husband spelled out in 22:14 places authority with him rather than her, but there is no basis for this assumption. As a married woman, her identity is tied up with his; but this says no more or no less about her capabilities than does the use today by a married woman of her husband's name. Huldah speaks in Yahweh's name with the authority of any other biblical prophet.

Huldah is different from other prophets in one respect, though, for her words of judgment are centered on a written document as no others have been before her. The scroll "found" by the priest Hilkiah (where it had been is undisclosed) now forms part of Deuteronomy, which ends with a series of curses on an unfaithful nation. While the king recognizes the book's authenticity (22:13), it takes a prophet to actualize its words in history, to set its truth in motion. This woman thus not only interprets but also authorizes the first document that will become the core of scripture for Judaism and Christianity.

## BIBLIOGRAPHY

Andreasen, Niels-Erik. "The Role of the Queen-Mother in Israelite Society." *Catholic Biblical Quarterly* 45 (1983), 179–194.

Bird, Phyllis. "The Harlot as Heroine: Narrative Art and Social Presupposition in Three Old Testament Texts." *Semeia* 46 (1989), 119–140.

Fontaine, Carole. "The Bearing of Wisdom on the Shape of 2 Samuel 11–12 and 1 Kings 3." *Journal for the Study of the Old Testament* 34 (1986), 61–77.

Lasine, Stuart. *Justice and Human Nature.* Semeia Studies. Atlanta: Scholars Press (forthcoming).

Long, Burke. *1 Kings: With an Introduction to Historical Literature.* The Forms of the Old Testament Literature 9. Grand Rapids: Wm. B. Eerdmans Publishing Co., 1984.

Meyers, Carol. *Discovering Eve: Ancient Israelite Women in Context.* New York: Oxford University Press, 1988.

Nelson, Richard. *First and Second Kings.* Interpretation. Atlanta: John Knox Press, 1987.

Olyan, Saul. *Asherah and the Cult of Yahweh in Israel.* Society of Biblical Literature Monograph Series 34. Atlanta: Scholars Press, 1988.

Rentería, Tamis. "The Elijah/Elisha Miracle Stories: A Socio-Cultural Investigation of Prophets and People in Ninth-Century Israel." In *Elijah and Elisha in Socio-literary Perspective,* edited by R. Coote. Semeia Studies. Atlanta: Scholars Press (forthcoming).

Rofé, Alexander. "The Vineyard of Naboth: The Origin and Message of the Story." *Vetus Testamentum* 38 (1988), 89–104.

# 1 AND 2 CHRONICLES

*Alice L. Laffey*

## Introduction

### Contents and Authorship

The books of 1 and 2 Chronicles contain the history of the people of Israel from Adam through the Babylonian exile. First Chron. 1:1–9:34 contains a genealogy that traces the ancestry: (a) Adam to Abraham (1:1–24); (b) Abraham to Jacob (1:25–2:53); (c) the families of the children of Israel, including Judah (2:1–4:23); Simeon (4:24–43); Reuben (5:1–10); Gad (5:11–22); Manasseh (5:23–26; 7:14–19); Levi (5:27–6:66); Issachar (7:1–5); Benjamin (7:6–11; 8:1–40); Dan and Naphtali (7:12–13); Ephraim (7:20–29); Asher (7:30–40); and (d) those returning to Jerusalem after the exile (9:1–34). The remainder of 1 Chronicles is devoted to the reign of King David (1 Chron. 9:35–29:29).

Second Chronicles begins with a history of the reign of King Solomon (1:1–9:31) and then proceeds to trace Judah's history before King Hezekiah (10:1–27:9), to detail his and Josiah's reforms (28:1–36:1), and to conclude with the final days of the kingdom and its demise (36:2–23).

Because the author of this material is unknown, he has been designated "the Chronicler." Though there is always the possibility that the unknown "he" could have been an unknown "she," most scholars believe that 1 and 2 Chronicles originated in priestly circles and consequently they presume male authorship. The date of the composition of this history also is unknown, but it is usually believed, based primarily on the books' contents, to have been produced in Judah after the exile, that is, after 538 B.C.E.

### Major Themes of the Chronicler's History

Although 1 Samuel to 2 Kings (part of the Deuteronomistic History) also contains an account of the monarchy, certain narratives contained in that account are entirely absent from the Chronicler's history. On the other hand, the Chronicler seems to emphasize certain aspects of the history that do not appear to be of major significance to the Deuteronomistic historian, aspects that would, however, be of keen interest to priests. For example, in the Chronicler's account not only does David bring the ark to Jerusalem; he appoints Levites to minister before it (1 Chronicles 16). David establishes in great detail most of the future Temple's personnel — levitical and priestly classes, singers, gatekeepers, treasurers (1 Chronicles 23–26). He also furnishes most of the precious materials to be used for the Temple's decoration — gold, silver, bronze, and so on (1 Chronicles 29). Moreover, the Chronicler emphasizes King Asa's reform of the cult (2 Chronicles 15); Hezekiah's restoration of the Temple, his celebration of the Passover, and his many liturgical reforms (2 Chronicles 29–31); and Josiah's celebration of the Passover (2 Chronicles 35).

During the Babylonian exile the people of Judah had no land of their own, no king, no capital, no political autonomy. It was not a time of royal or even prophetic leadership. Furthermore, they had no Temple at which to worship Yahweh. Their very identity, which during the monarchy had come to be understood in terms of land, political autonomy, economic prosperity, and Temple had now collapsed. Consequently, during the exile the Jews began to develop a new sense of who they were, one less dependent on land and king. This changing sense of identity the Jews brought back with them from Babylonia and developed further. Since they had no king but only a governor appointed by the Persian king, they now looked to their priests for leadership. They built a new Temple and concentrated their new identity around it. Second Temple Judaism is the term often used to describe Jewish self-understanding, belief, and practice after the exile.

The Chronicler, then, reconstructs Israel's history from a postexilic priestly perspective. King David is in the foreground. He came to be remembered as fully faithful to Yahweh, for which reason his reign abounded in Yahweh's abundant blessings: victory over the Philistines and the Ammonites, a secure and relatively peaceful rule, economic prosperity, and unbroken dynastic succession. Perhaps even more significant than those accomplishments was his desire to build Yahweh a fit dwelling place. Though Yahweh prevented him from actually building it (1 Chronicles 17), David did everything but the actual construction of the Temple. In accordance with the oracle of the prophet Nathan to David, David's son Solomon built it (2 Chronicles 3–4). For the Chronicler, the greatest time in Israel's past was the reign of King David, and the greatest event was the building of and worship at Jerusalem's Temple.

These two moments in Israel's history function not only as the glory of the past but also as the inspiration for the present, as a model for reconstructing Israel's identity after the exile. Though not explicitly expressed in 1 and 2 Chronicles, in the absence of David's royal leadership the priests "should" and in fact had assumed leadership of the postexilic community. The First Temple, which David had prepared and Solomon had built, had now been replaced by a new Temple, which served to manifest Israel's faithfulness to Yahweh and Israel's identity as a worshiping community.

The Deuteronomistic History, that is, the books of Joshua through 2 Kings, is unified by a specific theological perspective: covenant faithfulness issues in blessings, while disobedience to the covenant leads to curses. The Deuteronomistic editors framed narratives with judgments consistent with this theology (e.g., the bad king Jeroboam does not have a lasting dynasty; the good king Josiah does not live to see the fall of Judah). Nevertheless, there are certain inconsistencies in the pattern which, one presumes, reflect the editors' proximity to actual historical events. For example, King Hezekiah of Judah is judged to be faithful to the covenant, yet his reign suffers from Assyrian threat, and he even cooperates with Judah's eventual conqueror, Babylonia. (One would expect such political and military opposition to accompany the reign of an evil king.) Similarly, King Manasseh, though judged an evil king of Judah, reigned for fifty-five years. (One would expect an evil king to have a short reign.)

The Chronicler conforms to Deuteronomistic theology with greater precision than the Deuteronomist. Hezekiah and his people may have been subject to Assyrian aggression, but the Chronicler adds much detail to convince his audience of Hezekiah's staunch covenant fidelity in *responding* to the situation. Yahweh eventually sends an angel who destroys the entire Assyrian camp (2 Chron. 32:1–23). The Babylonian emissaries are relegated to one verse in the Chronicler's account (32:31). Likewise, since King Manasseh did in fact reign for fifty-five years, he must not have been as bad as the Deuteronomist portrayed him. The Chronicler recounts an eventual conversion back to covenant faithfulness. When in great distress, Manasseh called on Yahweh, who heard his plea and delivered him (2 Chron. 34:12–13).

Both 1 and 2 Chronicles and Ezra-Nehemiah attempt to articulate a postexilic identity for the Jews that is consistent with their history but appropriate to their radically changed historical situation. Most biblical scholars have assumed that the Chronicler also produced the Ezra-Nehemiah materials; however, that is not necessarily the case. (See the commentary on Ezra-Nehemiah.)

Although it is appropriate to distinguish between the Deuteronomistic History and 1 and 2 Chronicles in perspective and emphasis, there is not much to distinguish the two accounts with respect to their approaches to women. First and Second Chronicles contain not one additional narrative in which a woman's story is recorded. In fact, several women referred to in the Deuteronomistic History are missing from the Chronicler's account: for example, Michal's saving David from Saul (1 Samuel 19), Abigail's saving David from shedding Nabal's innocent blood (1 Samuel 25), David's taking of Bathsheba (2 Samuel 11), Amnon's rape of Tamar (2 Samuel 13), Absalom's rape of David's concubines (2 Sam 16:22), Abishag's presence at David's death (1 Kings 1), Solomon's decision between the two prostitutes (1 Kings 3:16–28).

A careful examination of these omissions indicates that all of the narratives threaten the Chronicler's portrait of David as Israel's foremost hero. Should the nation's hero need to be delivered by women? Would he seduce another man's wife? Would he allow the rape of his daughter and the rape of his concubines to go unpunished? The Chronicler omits these narratives lest they compromise David, in the same way that he discreetly suppresses David's sexual impotence and his son's extraordinary wisdom.

## Comment

### Women: Daughters, Wives, and Mothers

The importance of women's identity in ancient Israel as daughters, wives, and mothers has a great deal to do with survival in the ancient Near East generally during the second and first millennia B.C.E. (see the article "Everyday Life: Women in the Period of the Hebrew Bible"). The people's social organization derived from their perceived needs. Polygamy made possible large families that were needed to herd cattle, to farm crops, and to defend against hostile aggressors. Because many women died during childbirth and many infants and children died before reaching adulthood, the begetting of many offspring was essential to guarantee a family's and, by extension, the people's survival. Hence women came to understand bearing children as their primary task in life, though this did not rule out their participation in other work needed for the survival of the family. Daughters prepared to become wives; wives longed to become mothers; mothers rejoiced in their children, especially their sons, and derived high self-esteem from having borne them. It is necessary to understand this background to appreciate the few women who are named in the Chronicler's genealogy and the naming of Judah's queen mothers.

*Genealogy.* The genealogy in 1 Chron. 1:1–9:34 refers to the following women: Keturah, Abraham's concubine (1 Chron. 1:32; cf. Gen. 25:1–6), who bore six sons; Timna, Lotan's sister (1:39; cf. Gen. 36:12, 22); Mehetabel, Hadad's wife, and Matred, Me-zahab's daughter (1:50; cf. Gen. 36:39); Bath-shua, the Canaanite wife of Judah (2:3; cf. Gen. 38:1–5); Tamar, Judah's daughter-in-law who bore him two sons (2:4; cf. Gen. 38:6–30); Zeruiah and Abigail, daughters of Jesse (2:16); Azubah, Caleb's wife; Jerioth, who bore Caleb three sons (2:18); Ephrath, Caleb's wife who bore him Hur (2:19; cf. 2:50; 4:4); Ephrathah, Hezron's wife who bore him Segub and who later bore Ashhur to Caleb (2:21, 24); Atarah, Jerahmeel's wife who bore Onam (2:26); Abihail, Abishur's wife who bore him two children (2:29); Sheshan's unnamed daughter who married his Egyptian slave Jarha, to whom she bore Attai (2:34–35); Ephah, Caleb's concubine who bore him three children (2:46); Maacah, another of Caleb's concubines, who bore him four children (2:48–49); Achsah, Caleb's daughter, named last in the list of Caleb's children (2:49; cf. Judg. 1:12–15).

Ahinoam, the Jezreelite wife of David who bore Amnon; and Abigail, the Carmelite wife of David who bore Daniel (3:1; cf. 1 Samuel 25); Maacah, who bore Absalom to David; and Haggith, who bore Adonijah to him (3:2; cf. 2 Sam. 3:3–4); Abital, who bore Shephatiah to David; and Eglah, who bore Ithream to David (3:3); Bath-shua (=Bathsheba), who bore four children to David, including Solomon (3:5; cf. 2 Sam. 11:1–12:25); Tamar, here referred to as David's sons' sister, named last in the list of David's children and identified not by her father but by her brothers (3:9; cf. 2 Sam. 13:1–22); Shelomith, Zerubbabel's sons' sister (3:19); Hazzelelponi, Etam's sons' sister (4:3); Helah and Naarah, the two wives of Ashhur, who each bore him children (4:5–7); Jabez's unnamed mother (4:9); Bithiah, the Egyptian wife of Mered who bore three children, including Miriam (4:17); the unnamed Judean wife of Mered, who also bore him three children (4:18); Hodiah's unnamed wife, who was also Naham's sister and who bore Hodiah two sons (4:19); and Shimei, who bore six unnamed daughters (4:27).

Miriam, listed among the children of Amram in addition to Moses and Aaron (6:3); Issachar's "many wives and sons" (7:4); Bilhah, who bore Naphtali four children (7:13; cf. Gen. 30:7–8, where Bilhah is identified as the mother of Naphtali); Manasseh's unnamed Aramean concubine, who bore him two children (7:14); the unnamed wives of Huppim and Shuppim; Maacah, Machir's sister; and Zelophehad's daughters (7:15; cf. Num. 27:1–11; 36:1–12); Maacah, Machir's wife, who bore him one child (7:16; cf. v. 15); Hammolecheth, Gilead's sister who bore three children (7:18); Ephraim's unnamed wife who bore Beriah (7:23); Ephraim's daughter Sheerah, "who built both Lower and Upper Beth-horon, and Uzzen-sheerah" (7:24; note that Solomon is also said to have built Upper and Lower Beth-horon in 2 Chron. 8:5; cf. 1 Kings 9:17); Serah, Asher's sons' sister (7:30); and Shua, Heber's sons' sister (7:32).

Hushim and Baara, Shaharaim's wives (8:8); Hodesh, Shaharaim's wife who bore him seven sons (8:9-10); Hushim, Shaharaim's wife who bore him two sons (8:11); and finally Maacah, Jeiel's wife (8:29; 9:35).

A total of forty-two named women are listed in the genealogy, several of whom are sufficiently significant to be mentioned elsewhere in the Bible (e.g., Keturah, Tamar, Miriam, Bathshua, and Tamar). Thirteen of the references are to women named only here. When one asks why they were included in the Chronicler's account, one can only surmise that they and their children add to the prestige of their husbands. If the Chronicler wished to assert the faithfulness of the man before God, one way to do it was to attribute to him more wives and children. Ephah and Maacah are each identified as Caleb's concubines. Caleb's goodness is emphasized by his numerous wives and their fertility (1 Chron. 2:46, 48-49).

The Chronicler lists three additional families, descendants of the family of Judah, who are not mentioned elsewhere in the Bible: Etam and his four children, including Hazzelelponi (1 Chron. 4:3); Ashhur, his wives Helah and Naarah, and their several children (4:5-7), and Mered and his Egyptian wife Bithiah (4:17). It is not surprising that the family of Judah—the family of David, Solomon, and the other kings of Judah—receives emphasis in the Chronicler's genealogy.

The families of the half-tribes of Joseph, Manasseh and Ephraim, also receive the Chronicler's emphasis. Though Machir is named elsewhere in the Hebrew Bible, his wife Maacah appears only here (1 Chron. 7:13); though Gilead and one of his sons are named elsewhere, two others of his sons and his sister Hammolecheth are named only here (7:17-18); they are from the family of Manasseh. Ephraim's daughter, Sheerah, who built Lower and Upper Beth-horon and Uzzen-sheerah, is named only here (7:24). It is not surprising that the family of Joseph—the family through whom the Hebrews came to Egypt—receives emphasis in the Chronicler's genealogy.

The Chronicler adds persons not mentioned elsewhere to two other Israelite families: Asher and Benjamin. Though the Asherite Heber is mentioned elsewhere in the Bible, his three named sons and their sister Shua are mentioned only here (1 Chron. 7:32). Neither Shaharaim, nor his wives Hushim and Baara, nor his sons are mentioned elsewhere. Though Jeiel is named elsewhere in the Bible, neither his wife Maacah nor their sons are. These latter two families are descendants of the family of Benjamin. Why the Chronicler emphasizes the family of Asher is not totally clear. The importance of Benjamin to Israel's history (e.g., as the tribe of Saul) and postexilic present (e.g., proximity to Jerusalem) makes the Chronicler's emphasis obvious.

***Queen mothers of the Davidic dynasty.*** Women's prestige in ancient Israelite society was directly related to the men to whom they were attached: the father, the husband, and the sons whom they bore. The wife of a prominent male in the society derived prestige from his place of prominence. The wife of a prominent male who had borne him many sons would indeed be regarded highly by the society.

When one applies this perspective to 1 and 2 Chronicles, one discovers that the Chronicler usually names the mother of Judah's reigning king. For Judah's twenty kings, eleven queen mothers are named. The mothers of Judah's last seven kings are not named. The Chronicler identifies the women thus: Bath-shua (=Bathsheba in the books of Samuel and Kings), the mother of King Solomon (1 Chron. 3:5); the Ammonite Naamah, the mother of King Rehoboam (2 Chron. 12:13; cf. 1 Kings 14:21); Micaiah, the daughter of Uriel of Gibeah and mother of King Abijah (13:2; Maacah in 2 Chron. 11:21-22; cf. 1 Kings 15:2); Maacah, the mother of King Asa (2 Chron. 15:16; notably, she is said to have been removed by Asa from being queen mother because she made an image for Asherah; cf. 1 Kings 15:13); Azubah, the daughter of Shilhi and mother of King Jehoshaphat (20:31; cf. 1 Kings 22:42); Athaliah, the granddaughter of Omri and mother of King Ahaziah (22:2; cf. 2 Kings 11); Zibiah of Beersheba, the mother of King Joash (24:1; cf. 2 Kings 12:1); Jehoaddan of Jerusalem (Jehoaddin in 2 Kings 14:2), the mother of King Amaziah (25:1); Jecoliah of Jerusalem, the mother of King Uzziah (26:3; cf. 2 Kings 15:2); Jerushah, the daughter of Zadok and mother of King Jotham (27:1; cf. 2 Kings 15:33); and Abijah

(Abi in 2 Kings 18:2), the daughter of Zechariah and mother of King Hezekiah (29:1).

These names are recorded partly because these women were attached to prominent husbands, former kings. Several are identified as daughters of a particular father, so one might surmise that their fathers also were prominent. All became mothers of sons who were prominent. One may conclude also that the kings had many women—wives and concubines—and that it was important to distinguish which among the women had borne the new king.

When one compares the listing of queen mothers in 1 and 2 Chronicles with the listing recorded in 1 and 2 Kings, one finds several differences. Three of the women's names appear differently in the two histories (i.e., Bathshua/Bathsheba, Solomon's mother; Jehoaddan/ Jehoaddin, Amaziah's mother; and Abijah/Abi, Hezekiah's mother). King Rehoboam's wives are given more attention by the Chronicler than they are by the Deuteronomistic historian (2 Chron. 11:18–21). It is said of Abijah that he took fourteen wives and had sixteen daughters (13:21). That Athaliah was Jehoram's wife is implicit in 2 Chronicles and explicit in 1 Kings (22:2). The wives of the last seven kings of Judah are named in 2 Kings but not in 2 Chronicles.

## The Chronicler's Women: Additions to and Omissions from 2 Samuel to 2 Kings

*First Chronicles.* The Chronicler's genealogy does not appear in the Deuteronomistic History. For this reason the names provided by the Chronicler are all one knows of many of these women. There are some women, however, who have only a fleeting reference in Chronicles but who appear more extensively in the Deuteronomistic History. For example, Bathshua, wife of David and mother of Solomon, and Abigail, wife of David and mother of Daniel, appear in narratives in 2 Samuel 11–12 and 1 Kings 1–2 (Bathsheba) and 1 Samuel 25 (Abigail). One can only conclude that the Chronicler condenses their existence and their role in David's history to conform to his emphasis, namely, that David was Israel's ideal king whose central focus was Yahweh worship at the soon-to-be-built Temple.

Outside the genealogy, 1 Chronicles contains a few other references to women who are absent from the Deuteronomistic History. There is a reference to Eleazar's daughters (1 Chron. 23:22) and one to Heman's daughters

(25:5). In fact, references to Eleazar and to Heman are considerably fewer in the Deuteronomistic History than in Chronicles. The likely reason for the Chronicler's emphasis is their identification—Eleazar as priest and Heman as chanter. That 1 Chronicles enlarges on their role in the story is not surprising since the narratives derive from a priestly perspective.

*Second Chronicles.* In 2 Chronicles also there are women who appear in the Deuteronomistic History but who are absent from 2 Chronicles; women who appear in both the Deuteronomistic and the Chronicler's histories but with different emphases in each account; and women who do not appear in the Deuteronomistic History but who do appear in 2 Chronicles.

Second Chronicles omits at least one woman who figures prominently in the Deuteronomistic History: Jezebel. The omission does not tell anything about the Chronicler's views of women or of Jezebel herself; it is just that the Chronicler does not include a history of the Northern Kingdom of Israel at all. He names only those Israelite kings who affect Judah's history (e.g., Jeroboam, Baasha, Ahab). The reasons for this omission seem obvious. The Chronicler produced his history long after the Northern Kingdom had ceased to exist. Moreover, from its beginning as an independent kingdom, the North had separated itself from the Jerusalem Temple.

In narratives that parallel the Deuteronomistic History, the Chronicler makes some additional comments about women. Most of these are very brief and reinforce the Chronicler's priestly emphasis. For example, in 2 Chron. 8:11, Solomon says of his Egptian wife: "My wife shall not live in the house of King David of Israel, for the places to which the ark of Yahweh has come are holy." The Chronicler adds a list of Rehoboam's wives, including two—Mahalath and Abihail—not mentioned in 1 Kings (2 Chron. 11:18–23). The Chronicler's portrayal of Rehoboam is somewhat similar to the Deuteronomistic portrayal of Solomon, a king who is faithful at the beginning, has many wives, and then becomes unfaithful, though Rehoboam's wives are not explicitly connected to his infidelity. The same may be said of Joash. The Chronicler adds to the account of 2 Kings that Jehoiada got for him two wives, "and he became the father of sons and daughters" (24:3). Joash is portrayed as faithful until after the death of Jehoiada; still, the Chronicler does not explicitly connect his wives with his later infidelity. On the other hand, the Chronicler spares Solomon the wives and the infidelity! There is no parallel to 1 Kings 11:1–13.

Although Athaliah is identified in the Deuteronomistic History as the mother of Ahaziah, the Chronicler makes plain that at least one reason for the evil Ahaziah perpetrated was that "his mother was his counselor in doing wickedly" (22:3). The Chronicler's account of Athaliah's seizure of power after Ahaziah's death (2 Chron. 22:10–23:15) is similar to that of 2 Kings 11. Shimeath, an Ammonite, and Shimrith, a Moabite (Shomer in 2 Kings 12:21), are named as the mothers of the two men who killed King Joash (24:15–27), although the report in 2 Kings 12:21 identifies Shimeath and Shomer with no indication that they are women and no indication that they are foreigners. This shift may be accounted for by the postexilic effort to rid Judah of foreign women (cf. Ezra-Nehemiah). Their nationalities recall Israel's ancient enemies (cf. Deut. 23:4).

In all of the above citations, the additional details provided by the Chronicler do not enhance the women. At best they are indifferent. What they do is to explain further why the men have been unfaithful, though this is in some cases only implied. One exception to this is the addition in 2 Chron. 22:11 that identifies Jehoshabeath (Jehosheba in 2 Kings 11:2) as the wife of the priest Jehoiada. It is she who saves the young king Joash from Athaliah. Jehoshabeath has done a courageous deed. Should one be surprised that the Chronicler adds that she is the wife of a priest?

An examination of 2 Chronicles reveals seven texts that contain references to women omitted from the Deuteronomistic History. The Chronicler paints a portrait of the faithfulness of King Jehoshaphat and consequently mentions a marriage alliance with King Ahab of Israel in connection with the Judah–Israel alliance against Syria (18:1–2). This carries no negative connotation but is omitted from

1 Kings 22. The Chronicler condemns the unfaithfulness of King Jehoram and adds to the account of 2 Kings 8 that Elijah sent Jehoram a letter that promised that Yahweh would strike Jehoram's people, his children, his wives, and all that was his with "a great plague" (21:12–15).

Second Chronicles contains two references to "women captives" omitted from the Deuteronomistic History. Both refer to Judean women. The first is to their being taken by Israel during the Syro-Ephraimite war (28:6–15) when Israel attacked Judah. The second is to the good king Hezekiah's effort to restore them (29:3–36).

The Chronicler adds two other comments not found in the Deuteronomistic History. One is a reference to the Levites' wives and daughters (31:2–21), an addition that should not surprise. The second and more interesting comment is about "singing men and women" who lament the death of Josiah (35:25). When viewed against the backdrop of such texts as Ex. 15:21; Judg. 5:1; 1 Sam. 18:7 (cf. 21:12; 29:5); and Ps. 78:64, this allusion may suggest that women played a more significant role in temple activities than the narratives would lead one to believe. The verse may even suggest a long tradition of women's participation in the celebration of Israel's sacred moments.

## BIBLIOGRAPHY

Brenner, Athalya. *The Israelite Woman: Social Role and Literary Type in Biblical Narrative.* Sheffield: JSOT Press, 1985.

Laffey, Alice L. *First Chronicles, Second Chronicles.* Collegeville, Minn.: The Liturgical Press, 1985.

Myers, J. M. *1 Chronicles.* Anchor Bible 12. Garden City, N.Y.: Doubleday & Co., 1965.

———. *2 Chronicles.* Anchor Bible 13. Garden City, N.Y.: Doubleday & Co., 1965.

Williamson, H. G. M. *1 and 2 Chronicles.* New Century Bible Commentary. London: Marshall, Morgan & Scott, 1982.

# EZRA–NEHEMIAH

*Tamara Cohn Eskenazi*

## Introduction

### The Book and Its Context

To the remnant of Israel in exile, the conquest of Babylon by King Cyrus of Persia in 539 B.C.E. signaled the dawn of a new era and the rebirth of the nation; Ezra-Nehemiah recounts the story of this rebirth. Only fifty years earlier the Babylonians had destroyed Jerusalem (587/586 B.C.E.) and exiled its inhabitants. Israel suffered a devastating shock that irreversibly altered its religion and culture. Suddenly all the secure structures were demolished: the land that had been so essential to the religion and politics of the nation was now controlled by strangers; the Temple had been razed; Jerusalem was in ruins; and many people (including the leaders) were taken captive to a foreign land. When Cyrus defeated the Babylonians and permitted the exiles to go home, the survivors of what had been ancient Israel faced an overwhelming challenge, having to rebuild not merely their homeland but their very identity as a people and a religion.

Ezra-Nehemiah is the only biblical book that attempts to give a history of the crucial yet obscure postexilic era. The book itself is complex and often difficult to interpret. Most English translations of the Bible separate it into two books: Ezra and Nehemiah, even though Ezra-Nehemiah constitutes a single book in the most ancient manuscripts and is best interpreted as such. It had been common to attribute Ezra-Nehemiah and the books of Chronicles to the same author, but most modern scholars recognize that Ezra-Nehemiah is a distinct work with its own literary and theological coherence.

The book begins with Cyrus's edict, exhorting the people of God to go up to Jerusalem and build the house of God. It concludes about one hundred years later, after Jerusalem's Temple had been rebuilt (516/515 B.C.E.) and the walls of the city restored and rededicated (445/444 B.C.E.). Ezra-Nehemiah focuses its account on three stages of response to the edict, each with its own distinct contribution. The first, in which Zerubbabel and Jeshua were prominent, restored proper worship and rebuilt the Temple (Ezra 1–6). The second, in which Ezra was prominent, implemented the teachings of the Torah and reshaped the community by excluding foreign wives from its midst (Ezra 7–10). The third, under Nehemiah, rebuilt the walls of Jerusalem, thereby enclosing the community with a solid and secure boundary—both physically and metaphorically (Nehemiah 1–7). Once rebuilding was complete, the community celebrated its renewal in grand ceremonies climaxed with a public reading of the book of the Torah (Nehemiah 8–13).

In recounting these events, Ezra-Nehemiah weaves a specific ideology into the very fabric of the story it tells. Through an effective use of sources and literary techniques such as repetition and shifts in perspective, the book articulates three themes: first, that the community as a whole, not simply its leaders, was responsible for postexilic reconstruction; second, that the house of God was no longer confined to the Temple but encompassed the whole city of Jerusalem; and, third, that the written text became the authoritative vehicle for divine communication and the source for insights and guidance. These themes express a shift away from hierarchy toward greater democratization of society and therefore imply greater opportunities for women. To what extent these opportunities were realized in the lives of actual women remains unclear. In the book itself women remain silent. Their voices are not heard in the text even when decisions directly involve them.

Some easily overlooked details in Ezra-Nehemiah, however, offer intriguing glimpses into women's lives and at least acknowledge their presence in each important event. In addition, certain extrabiblical sources help round out these glimpses into a fuller view by providing information about several Jewish women from the Persian period.

A crucial issue for the postexilic community was self-definition and identity. What had been ancient Israel was suddenly reduced to a small province, known as Judah, under the rule of the Persian empire. It became, in the words of one scholar, a colonially subject people. Notable portions of its population continued to be dispersed in other lands such as Babylonia, Persia, and Egypt. The term *yehudim,* "Judahites" or "Jews," gained currency alongside "Israelites," because the dominant portion of the population considered itself heir to the Southern Kingdom and the tribe of Judah, even when living for generations outside the land.

During this era the land of Israel was populated by diverse ethnic groups (including Ammonites, Moabites, and others); diversity also characterized the Jewish community. There was tension between Jews whose families had gone into exile (and were transformed by the experience) and those who had not. Tension arose also between Jews who permitted exogamous marriages (marriages outside the clan) and those who did not. It is difficult to determine to what extent these groups overlapped (i.e., to what extent exogamy was directly related to the specific background of the population). The composition of these groups and their historical controversies remain subject to speculation because the evidence is limited and tendentious.

According to the perspective of Ezra-Nehemiah, the decisive Judahite community was constituted by the returnees from Babylon. These returnees distinguished themselves from another group called "people of the land," who, according to Ezra-Nehemiah (e.g., Ezra 4:4), were people of foreign origins who now dwelt in the land. Earlier scholars had identified the people of the land with the Samaritans, but they may actually have been Judahites who had not gone into exile and who did not, therefore, share the traditions of the transformed returnees. The conflict between the returnees and the "people of the land" thus could have been an inner-Judahite one rather than one between different ethnic groups.

Two particular issues in this period prove especially pertinent for understanding women's lives: the consequences for women of ethnic and religious crises of identity and the effect of pioneer life on the place of women in a society.

*Ethnic and religious crises of identity.* Sociological studies of both ancient and modern societies reveal some common survival patterns in the face of the radical experience of exile and return. Typically, boundaries against the outside world become more rigid in an attempt to protect a fragile sense of communal identity. Internally, flux and reorganization follow the disruption of stable patterns and hierarchies: new groups rise to leadership, and gender roles become more fluid under the pressure of ad hoc adaptation to rapid change. Ezra-Nehemiah clearly reflects similar patterns. It advocates ethnic purity and prohibits intermarriage in order to sustain group identity. Such strategies, however, were not universally accepted. Apparently, some of Judah's best families either did not have the same concern or defined the community in more inclusive terms. They considered "foreign" women as acceptable marriage partners even for priests (Ezra 9–10; Neh. 13:28).

Several scholars connect opposition to exogamy explicitly with the need to protect land rights. Religious membership and land ownership, they claim, were closely intertwined. Lacking a native king, the community was organized around the Temple with all members bearing responsibility for its upkeep. The land owned by members of the Temple community constituted, in fact, the Jewish province. Intermarriage, however defined, endangered the physical as well as the spiritual boundaries of the community. A non-Jewish partner who had legal control over property could, once the Jewish spouse had died, rejoin the ethnic community of origin and remove the land from Jewish jurisdiction. Children of such marriages could do likewise, reducing the actual land belonging to the Jewish community and hence the province of Judah. As a result, foreign partners became a particular threat, because through them territory might be lost to the community as a whole. According to this scholarly view, Ezra-Nehemiah seeks to prevent such losses by prohibiting marriage with outsiders.

***Women and pioneer life.*** In *Discovering Eve* Carol Meyers points out that women gain power during times of pioneer conditions in rural societies, when families constitute a central socioeconomic and political unit. She argues on the basis of sociological and archaeological data that women in premonarchic Israel, living in pioneer societies, must have possessed more power and greater equality than readers have recognized. Although Meyers herself does not analyze the postexilic era, her findings, if correct, suggest that women in the postexilic era would have benefited from a similar redistribution of power because, in some important ways, they lived in similar circumstances. As in the premonarchic period, the family became central. Ezra-Nehemiah underscores the fact through the frequent use of the term *'abot* (literally, "fathers") to designate the family as the dominant force in the community.

These two factors—the evolving communal boundaries in the face of radical change and the greater importance of families—combine to suggest that women in the postexilic community possessed more power than the fleeting references to them in the canonical literature indicate at first glance. Extrabiblical sources corroborate this conclusion.

## Extrabiblical Sources: Elephantine, Egypt

Persian-period contracts and letters in which women figure quite prominently give evidence concerning the diversity of Jewish women's roles and powers. The Elephantine documents unambiguously show that Jewish women in the postexilic era had more power and privileges than biblical texts and later traditions suggest. These documents come from the Jewish colony in Elephantine, Egypt, and can be precisely dated (sixth to fourth centuries B.C.E.). They contain original contracts and letters, many belonging to Jewish women. From this storehouse of information about actual postexilic practices among one group of Jews, one can reconstruct social and economic realities of women's lives.

Various contracts from Elephantine show that these Jewish women were able to initiate divorce, buy and sell property, and inherit property even when there were male siblings. The Elephantine documents also illustrate how women were able to climb the social and economic ladder. An interesting example is the case of an Egyptian slave named Tamut (or Tapmut) and her daughter. Tamut married a Jewish temple official and eventually gained some kind of position in the temple (the precise nature of her title is unclear). Her daughter (born during slavery as a child of either the master or the mother's future husband) became wealthy and important in the community. Tamut's daughter, not only her son, was a designated heir to the parents' property, belying the notion that women could inherit only when there were no male descendants (cf. Numbers 27).

Marriage contracts from Elephantine are particularly fascinating. They list what each woman brought into the marriage and state that she retained control over such possessions. In cases of divorce, her belongings remained hers. The marriage contracts also indicate that either partner could initiate divorce. Some even specify procedures and financial responsibilities in cases of abuse. Tamut's marriage contract, for example, includes the following:

> If tomorrow or another day Hanani rises on account of her [?] and says, "I divorce Tamut my wife," the divorce money is on her head. He shall give to Tamut in silver 7 shekels, 2 R and all that she brought in. . . . If tomorrow or another day, Tamut rises up and says, "I divorce my husband Anani," a like sum shall be on her head. She shall give to Anani in silver 7 Shekels, 2 R, and all which she brought in her hand she shall take out. . . . (Kraeling, 2:7–10)

Upon the death of the husband, the property was to go to the wife—not to a male relative, not even his son.

Several documents concern another woman, the thrice-married Mibtahiah, who was a wealthy property owner and also her husband's business partner. Mibtahiah's third husband appears to have been an Egyptian who eventually took a Hebrew name and presumably joined her Jewish community. Their children bore Hebrew names and were clearly influential members of the community.

These documents greatly augment the understanding of the lives of women in the Persian period and help to shed light on the more shadowy references in the biblical texts themselves. Although there is no parallel evidence from Judah concerning women's legal status in that society, it may be reasonable to assume that the practices in one Jewish community (Egypt) were consistent with those of another (Judah) during the postexilic period

when both were under the same Persian authority.

## Comment

### Cyrus's Edict to Build the House of God in Jerusalem (Ezra 1:1–4)

Cyrus's edict opens Ezra-Nehemiah with an exhortation to the people of God to go up to Jerusalem and Judah to build the house of God. Although this edict is not preserved outside the Bible, it is consistent with what is known about Cyrus and conforms to other ancient decrees. If historical, this declaration would have been proclaimed in 538 B.C.E.

### God's People Build the House of God in Jerusalem (Ezra 1:5–Neh. 7:73)

A brief introduction sums up the events to follow: "Then rose up the heads of the families of Judah and Benjamin, and the priests and the Levites, and everyone whose spirit God had stirred, to go up and build the house of God in Jerusalem" (Ezra 1:5, author's translation). Ezra-Nehemiah describes three stages of return and reconstruction. Each begins in exile and ends in Jerusalem, highlighting the book's main themes: the centrality of community, a broadened notion of the house of God as city, and the authoritative role of the written text. The book recounts these stages by focusing primarily on the roles and deeds of men, but includes some intriguing references to women at each important event.

*First movement: Returnees build the altar and Temple (Ezra 1:5–6:22).* The first section describes the return from Babylon of a large contingent of exiled Judahites (or Jews). Upon their arrival, the Judahites built an altar and resumed proper worship. They also began to rebuild the Temple in accordance with Cyrus's decree. Their leaders included Zerubbabel, a descendant of David, and Jeshua, a priest. But the real focus of the story is on the larger participating community. The people of the land, whose earlier background, according to Ezra 4, was non-Judahite (but see the introduction above), volunteered to help rebuild the Temple but were rejected. After difficulties and delays, the returnees finished building the Temple (probably in 516/515 B.C.E.) and celebrated the event (Ezra 6:14).

One of the most striking aspects of this first part of the book is the list (repeated in Nehemiah 7) that enumerates the returnees as descendants of specific ancestors or people of a particular place.

The names of household heads are typically male. However, according to Ezra 2, the returnees included the descendants of *hassoperet* (Ezra 2:55). The word *hassoperet* literally means "the female scribe" (see also Neh. 7:57). The most obvious reference of this term is to a group (perhaps a guild) whose members traced their descent to a female scribe. Unfortunately, this meaning is usually lost in translation. Translators typically treat the word as a personal name, and most commentators confine themselves to noting a guild without mentioning the possibility that a female stood at its head. The rationale for ignoring the possible reference to a woman is based on Eccl. 1:1, where a similar grammatically feminine noun refers to an apparently masculine subject (*qohelet*, "one who gathers an assembly"). This argument overlooks the numerous other occurrences of such grammatically feminine nouns that are recognized as references to women (for example, the feminine herald in Isa. 40:9). It is noteworthy, however, that one medieval Jewish commentator (Ibn Ezra) supposed that *hassoperet* in Ezra-Nehemiah referred to a female scribe. There were female scribes in the ancient Near East in preexilic times, although there is no clear information about them for the postexilic period.

Another intriguing reference in the list of returnees mentions "the descendants of . . . Barzillai (who had married one of the daughters of Barzillai the Gileadite, and was called by their name)" (Ezra 2:61//Neh. 7:63). Although families generally did not trace their descent through the mother's line, this reference shows that men did sometimes relinquish their own family name for that of their wife (and presumably also for the wife's family inheritance).

The list of returnees in Ezra 2 and Nehemiah 7 claims that approximately forty-two thousand people returned. In addition, there were male and female servants and singers (Ezra 2:65//Neh. 7:67). It is tempting to link these female singers with the temple cult, but their place in the list (between servants and animals) suggests rather that they were entertainers of relatively low status. Temple singers appear earlier in the list without specific references to women.

### Second movement: Ezra and the exiles build the community according to Torah (Ezra 7–10).

The second stage of the return featured Ezra as an outstanding figure, commissioned by the Persian king Artaxerxes to implement divine teachings in Judah. According to the biblical account, Ezra arrived in Judah in 458 B.C.E. Ezra is presented as a priest and scribe of the Torah, entrusted with virtually unlimited powers to bring the Jewish province into conformity with the law of God and the law of the king (Ezra 7:26). It is generally assumed that Ezra's Torah is some form of the Pentateuch or portions thereof. Recent studies link Ezra's seemingly religious mission with the political agenda of the Persian empire in the face of military unrest in the Mediterranean region.

Among the new arrivals with Ezra appeared the descendants of Shelomith (Ezra 8:10). In the Bible the name Shelomith can refer to either a man or a woman. The Greek versions of Ezra add a name in a way that precludes reading Shelomith as a woman's name ("of the descendants of Bani, Shelomith son of Josiphiah"). Such a translation could either reflect later discomfort with the implication of a feminine name or represent a genuine alternate tradition. Many English translations follow this reading. The Hebrew text, however, leaves the gender unspecified. Given the pattern in the other names in the list, the sentence should be translated: "From the descendants of Shelomith: the son of Josiphiah, and with him 160 men." According to 1 Chron. 3:19, Shelomith was a daughter of Zerubbabel, the last known descendant of David to possess any political power (see his role in the return in Ezra 1–6). A postexilic seal referring to Shelomith and to Elnathan the governor has been discovered. If this is the seal of Shelomith the daughter of Zerubbabel, it might indicate that Elnathan, a governor of Judah (approximately 510–490 B.C.E.), attached himself to the Davidic line by marrying Shelomith. It is conceivable that Ezra 8:10 also refers to relatives of the famed princess.

According to Ezra 9:1–4, shortly after his return to Jerusalem, Ezra learned that some of Judah's leading citizens had married so-called foreign women from the peoples of the land. This crisis led Ezra to mourn publicly and to convene an assembly. The offending men were pressed to divorce their foreign wives, and many of them did (Ezra 10). The actual background of these women is unclear. They could have been really foreign or simply from Judahite families whom the author of Ezra-Nehemiah refuses to recognize as members of the people of Israel. Both possibilities can be supported by the available evidence.

The reasons given for divorce in the text are what one might call religious. Economic and political factors, however, would have been important, possibly *the* important considerations (the distinction between such categories is itself modern and does not adequately represent ancient societies). The urgent need to redefine identity probably combined with practical and economic concerns to establish specific boundaries from which certain groups were excluded. Ezra-Nehemiah does not record any protest from the women, nor does it report what specific arrangements were involved. The documents from Elephantine lead one to suppose that economic compensations had to be made (which may account for the length of time it took to effect the separation), but the book shows no interest in these details. It is noteworthy that although the prohibition against marrying outsiders applies to both men and women, Ezra 9 does not mention any Jewish women marrying foreigners.

Modern readers react in different ways to the exclusion of the foreign wives. Unsympathetic readings focus on the harshness of the expulsion and on the exclusivism it reveals. In particular, the silence about the reaction of the women is striking; they appear to have no choice and no voice. Sympathetic readings stress the plight of the new Judahite community struggling for spiritual, economic, and ethnic survival when it found itself a minority society in a sea of diverse cultures. Recent studies of the postexilic Judahite community link religious concerns with socioeconomic ones. Opposition to mixed marriages is placed in a larger context in which the issue is not simply one of ethnic or religious purity, but rather is tied to the impact of marriage on communal land ownership: marriage with outsiders spells loss of land to the Jewish province.

In addition to political concerns, sympathetic readings point out the need to secure partners and families for the women of the new Judahite community in the face of competing possibilities (see the emphasis on remaining faithful to the wife of one's youth in the contemporary writing of Mal. 2:14). The pressures on new immigrants to marry up and out is well documented in ancient and modern situations. An opposition to foreign women is thus understood not as a misogynist restriction but rather a defense of the rights of women in the community against outside competition and therefore a matter of maintaining communal cohesiveness and continuity.

Whatever the attitude of the reader, Ezra-Nehemiah's preoccupation with separation of foreign wives implies that women and their status were important in reshaping religious and social life. This preoccupation also implies that women's rights to property in Judah were similar to those in Elephantine. It is when women can inherit land from their husbands or fathers that foreign women pose an economic threat; without such rights they would not represent a loss of land to the community.

***Third movement: Nehemiah and the Judah-
ites build Jerusalem's wall (Nehemiah 1–7).***
The third stage is presented through the eyes and words of Nehemiah in a first-person recollection often labeled "memoirs" (which many scholars attribute to Nehemiah himself). These chapters relate how Nehemiah, at first a favored cupbearer to King Artaxerxes, was overcome by concern for the welfare of his people. Leaving the comforts of the royal court, he hastened to Jerusalem as its newly appointed governor in order to rebuild the city's walls (445 B.C.E.). Nehemiah spurred the Judahites to rebuild despite threats from neighbors. Under his leadership the walls were quickly restored and Jerusalem repopulated.

Nehemiah 3 lists the names of the actual builders, emphasizing communal involvement. That list of builders includes the daughters of Shallum (Neh. 3:12). Although the reference to daughters is unquestionably clear in the Hebrew text and in all ancient manuscripts, some translators have obscured their presence. One translation even replaces the word "daughters" with "sons," presumably under the assumption that daughters would not have been mentioned. Writing earlier in this century, L. W. Batten stated:

"Daughter" is a regular term for the hamlets which grow up about a city and which are dependent upon it, 11:25–31. Ryle prefers a literal interpretation that Shallum's daughters aided him in the work. But as women in the East were quite sure to have a large share

in such work as this, their special mention here is unnecessary. Against the other view it may be urged that a solitary mention of hamlets is inexplicable. Berth. [Bertholet] says it would be easiest to reject the words but that such a course is arbitrary. *The meaning is really unknown. (A Critical and Exegetical Commentary on the Books of Ezra and Nehemiah,* International Critical Commentary [New York: Charles Scribner's Sons, 1913], pp. 213–214, emphasis added).

It is intriguing to read that the meaning of "he and his daughters" is unknown. The confusion of commentators in the face of such a clear statement appears to be bred solely by a refusal to recognize the role of women in building the city walls. Fortunately, modern commentators fare better, both as translators and interpreters. They usually preserve the reference to women. Some, like H. G. M. Williamson, conclude on the basis of Num. 36:8 that, if Shallum had no sons, "it would be natural for the daughters to help on an occasion like this, since they would inherit his name and property" (Williamson, p. 207). From the Elephantine documents one learns that daughters may inherit even when there are sons.

Nehemiah's "memoirs" describe his confrontations with opponents whose opposition he viewed as interference with the cause of God. After one confrontation with the prophet Shemaiah, Nehemiah called upon God to punish his opponents: "Remember Tobiah and Sanballat, O my God, according to these things that they did, and also the prophetess Noadiah and the rest of the prophets who wanted to make me afraid" (Neh. 6:14). Nehemiah's words ignore Shemaiah and complain instead about two of Nehemiah's best-known opponents and about an otherwise unknown prophet. Tobiah was an Ammonite official who hampered Nehemiah all along; Sanballat was the governor of Samaria. The mention of this mysterious prophet together with such highly placed officials suggests that her status was comparable to theirs and that she, like them, was a prominent person. The importance of this reference to Noadiah the prophet is highlighted when one realizes that the Hebrew Bible names only four women as prophets. The other three are preexilic (Miriam, Deborah, and Huldah). With Noadiah there is evidence that the prophetic office was open to women in the postexilic period. The basis of her disagreement with Nehemiah remains unknown.

## God's People Celebrate and Dedicate the House of God (Nehemiah 8–13)

Ezra-Nehemiah reaches its climax with the public reading of the book of the Torah, after the walls of Jerusalem were restored. As the celebration began, all the people gathered in the plaza before the Water Gate. Ezra read from the Torah to an attentive communal assembly. The reading was followed by a celebration of the holy day of Sukkot and by several days of festivities and rededication ceremonies.

Perhaps the most significant reference to women in Ezra-Nehemiah comes on this momentous occasion. Later Judaism compares this time of rededication to the giving of the law at Sinai. But although there have been doubts about the role and presence of women at Sinai, since the message "do not go near a woman" (Ex. 19:15) implies that only men were addressed, no such doubts occur in this receiving of the Torah. Ezra-Nehemiah is explicit:

> And Ezra the priest brought the Torah before the assembly, both *men and women* and all who could hear with understanding, on the first day of the seventh month. And he read from it facing the square before the Water Gate from early morning until midday, in the presence of *the men and the women* and those who could understand; and the ears of all the people were attentive to the book of the Torah. (Neh. 8:2–3, author's translation, emphasis added)

The Hebrew term *qahal* used here for the assembly does not refer to a mere aggregate of people but to a religiously constituted community. The fact that this assembly includes men and women implies religious egalitarianism at least on this level of participation. Men and women gathered; men and women heard and heeded; men and women celebrated. The teaching of God belonged to the entire community. Women, however, were not named (as far as one can discern) among the citizens who later help Ezra read aloud and interpret the teachings to the community.

Women are mentioned in the festive events that follow, though their roles are not specified (Neh. 12:43). It is particularly important to observe that the communal pledge that delineates communal responsibilities for the Temple, for keeping Sabbath, prohibiting foreign marriages, and other obligations (Nehemiah 10) explicitly includes women as signatories, even though no individual woman is named (Neh. 10:28).

As the book concludes, the danger of foreign wives looms once more. Having erected the wall as a physical boundary, Nehemiah engaged in securing other communal boundaries. He mounted an attack on a wide array of religious violations, including the marriage of Judahite men with outsiders (this time described as women of Ashdod, Ammon, and Moab). Enraged, Nehemiah railed against foreign partners: "You shall not give your daughters to their sons, or take their daughters for your sons or yourselves. Did not King Solomon of Israel sin on account of such women?" (Neh. 13:25b–26a). Nehemiah did not allege that woman was dangerous by virtue of being a woman. Nevertheless, his association of sin with foreign women helped pave the way to views that too easily link women in general with sin.

## Conclusion

A careful reading of Ezra-Nehemiah discloses a little more than one expects concerning women but not as much as one would like: one knows of an important prophet Noadiah but not about her concerns; one knows that Shallum's daughters helped build the wall but no longer knows their names; one knows that women were expelled but does not know their story; one knows that women celebrated with men but not to what extent. These and other tantalizing references offer glimpses into a world that the literature largely ignores. They acknowledge the participation of women in each important task: return, rebuilding, and reading of the Torah. Combined with the evidence from Elephantine, such glimpses lead to a more precise reconstruction of the postexilic era. Although the women still remain silent, their presence and growing visibility help to fill in the empty spaces in the text and in Israel's pivotal age of return and rebirth.

## BIBLIOGRAPHY

Clines, David J. A. *Ezra, Nehemiah, Esther.* New Century Bible Commentary. Grand Rapids: Wm. B. Eerdmans Publishing Co., 1984.

Eskenazi, Tamara Cohn. *Ezra-Nehemiah.* Anchor Bible. New York: Doubleday (forthcoming).

———. *In an Age of Prose: A Literary Approach to Ezra-Nehemiah.* Society of Biblical Literature Monograph Series 36. Atlanta: Scholars Press, 1988.

———. "Out from the Shadows: Biblical Women in the Postexilic Era (Sixth to Fourth Century BCE)." *Journal for the Study of the Old Testament* (forthcoming).

Kraeling, Emil G. H. *The Brooklyn Museum Aramaic Papyri: New Documents of the Fifth Century B.C. from the Jewish Colony at Elephantine.* New Haven, Conn.: Yale University Press, 1953.

Meyers, Carol. *Discovering Eve: Ancient Israelite Women in Context.* New York: Oxford University Press, 1988.

Meyers, Eric M. "The Shelomith Seal and Aspects of the Judean Restoration: Some Additional Reconsiderations." *Eretz Israel* 17 (1985), 33–38.

Porten, Bezalel. *Archives from Elephantine: A Life of an Ancient Jewish Military Colony.* Berkeley, Calif.: University of California Press, 1968.

Williamson, H. G. M. *Ezra, Nehemiah.* Word Biblical Commentary 16. Waco, Tex.: Word Books, 1985.

# ESTHER

*Sidnie Ann White*

## Introduction

The book of Esther is part of the section of the Hebrew Bible (Christian Old Testament) known as the Writings. Esther is an account of the events that led to the inauguration of the Jewish festival of Purim. Its plot is fast-paced and exciting, the story well told, and all ends happily. The book, however, has been the subject of much controversy in both Jewish and Christian circles, not least because of the actions and character of its heroine, the Jewish woman Esther.

### The Story

The book of Esther begins at a banquet held by the Persian king Ahasuerus for all the inhabitants of his capital, Susa. After a drinking bout, the king summons his queen, Vashti, to appear before the court so that they may admire her great beauty. Vashti refuses, and the king, angry, banishes her. After a time, the king regrets losing his queen, and his nobles suggest that he hold an empire-wide search for a new queen. Ahasuerus agrees, and all the eligible virgins in the kingdom are gathered into his harem. At this point the narrative introduces the heroine, Esther, and her guardian, Mordecai. Esther enters the harem of the king and wins the regard of all who know her. When her turn with the king arrives, Esther also gains the admiration of Ahasuerus, who makes her his queen. After this, Mordecai discovers a plot to assassinate the king and reports it to Esther, saving the king's life.

Some time later, the king promotes Haman the Agagite to the position of vizier. Haman demands that all the people bow down to him. Mordecai, however, refuses. Angered, Haman plots revenge on Mordecai by slaughtering all the Jews in the Persian empire. Mordecai learns of the plot, and turns to Esther to intercede with the king. At the climax of the story, Esther, in peril of her life, appears unsummoned before the king in an attempt to save her people. She gains Ahasuerus's favor and then in a series of skillful maneuvers uncovers Haman's plot and foils his scheme. Haman is put to death, the enemies of the Jews are destroyed, and Mordecai is elevated to the position of vizier. The book ends with Esther and Mordecai instituting the festival of Purim to commemorate these great events.

### Provenance, Date, Genre

Esther was composed in the eastern Jewish Diaspora of the Persian empire. The strongest arguments in favor of this location are the story's setting in Susa, its knowledge of the Persian court and its surroundings, and the book's total lack of interest in Judah and in particular its cultic institutions. The audience the book addresses appears to be Jews who live in close proximity to foreign rulers and must learn to make their own way in a society in which they are a minority and in which there is always danger of persecution and oppression.

The book of Esther gives no firm indication of date, and therefore a range of dates, from the fourth century to the second century B.C.E., has been proposed for it. The earliest possible date depends on the identification of King Ahasuerus. Ahasuerus is normally identified as Xerxes I, who reigned from 486 B.C.E. to 465 B.C.E. The latest possible date is less solid, but can be posited on the lack of Hellenistic elements in the book. In the Persian period the Jews, for the most part, were willing servants of their Gentile rulers (witness Nehemiah). However, the Hellenistic period witnessed a change in that attitude, brought about by the increasingly harsh policy of the Seleucid rulers toward their Jewish subjects (see 1 and 2 Maccabees). Esther reflects a more sympathetic attitude toward the Persian king and toward Gentiles in general than would be expected in a work from the Hellenistic period. Therefore, the most likely date for the composition of the book lies between the late fifth century and the late fourth century. Since the book's portrayal of the events of the reign of Xerxes is not historically accurate (e.g., Amestris was Xerxes' queen, not Vashti), a certain distance from that reign is probable. Thus, a date in the early fourth century B.C.E. is preferable.

The genre of the book of Esther is most easily described as an early Jewish novella. A novella is a fictional piece of writing in prose that is not designed to meet any tests of historical accuracy. It is written by a single author and meant to be read, not recited. Its plot moves from the establishment of a tension through complications to its resolution, depicting only one chain of events over a limited time frame, and concentrating on the development of characters and situations. In its final form, the book of Esther fits the description of a novella; however, as with most biblical books, the author seems to have used preexisting material in the composition of the book. There are two, or possibly three, separate tales behind the final form of the book, one story focusing on Esther and depicting a problem between the Jews and the Gentiles in the provinces around the time of the New Year, and the other centered on Mordecai and the court intrigues that threatened to result in a persecution of the Jews in Susa. The latter has the form of a royal courtier tale; see also Daniel 1–6. The presence of the "royal courtier tale" form in Esther explains the existence in the book of many elements found in wisdom literature, such as the court setting, the struggle between two royal courtiers, the relationship of Esther to Mordecai as the adopted child of the wise courtier, and the portrayal of Ahasuerus as the type of the foolish king. The third story may be an apocryphal harem story concerning Vashti. It is likely that these stories did exist prior to the composition of the book of Esther and that the author drew on them during the creation of his or her work.

Some have also argued that the connection of the story of Esther and Mordecai to the festival of Purim is very doubtful. The only link between the story and the festival is the word *pur*, or "lot," which Haman casts to determine the most propitious day for the slaughter of the Jews. The addition of the Purim material to the story appears as an afterthought, an association made after the composition of the original work, to legitimate a festival already celebrated by diaspora Jews. Others have claimed that the book should be considered a coherent whole, since the book contains themes and structures that span all ten chapters. The question remains unresolved, although the festival of Purim was the original impetus for the inclusion of Esther in the Hebrew canon.

## Reception and Interpretation

Esther did not achieve undisputed canonical status in Judaism until after the third century C.E. The Western church accepted the book as canonical in the fourth century C.E., while the Eastern church did not accept it until the eighth century. The reason for the difficulty that the book had in achieving canonical status is its perceived lack of religiosity. Most glaring is the complete absence of any mention of God. In addition, the concepts of law and covenant are absent, and there are no prayers. In fact, Esther, the heroine of the tale, is married to a non-Jew, does not uphold the dietary laws, and lives in a completely Gentile environment. These facts indicate that for the audience of the book of Esther, being a Jew was more an ethnic designation than a religious one. To compensate for this lack of religiosity, the Septuagint Additions to Esther (see below) and rabbinic traditions attempt to add religious elements to the book (e.g., Rabbi Johanan states that Esther, like Daniel, ate only vegetables). Nevertheless, the book remains one of the most secular in the Hebrew Bible. A religious element is not entirely absent, however. Esther calls for a fast before going to confront the king. Fasting is a religious practice in Judaism (e.g., the fast of Yom Kippur, the Day of Atonement). More important, God's control of events and the Jews' status as God's chosen people seem to be assumed by the book. In 4:14 Mordecai tells Esther, "For if you keep silence at such a time as this, relief and deliverance will rise for the Jews from another quarter, but you and your father's family will perish." The word "quarter" seems to be a veiled reference to God, and the action of God in the events taking place seems to be assumed by the verse.

The probable reason for Esther's final inclusion in the Hebrew canon is its connection with the festival of Purim, an extremely popular festival which began to be celebrated in the Diaspora and later was accepted in Judah. During the celebration, the merrymaker is told to get so drunk that he can no longer distinguish between "Blessed be Mordecai!" and "Cursed be Haman!" The festival continues in popularity today. The inclusion of the book of Esther in the Jewish canon was probably the result of popular pressure.

Esther's interpretive problems did not cease upon its acceptance into the canon. The book's indifference to religious practices, its dubious sexual ethics, and its female heroine continued to baffle commentators, particularly male Protestant commentators, who wished to make the book conform to the expectations of a Western Christian audience. The tendency among scholars was to exalt Mordecai as the true hero of the tale and to downplay or even villify the role of Esther. As late as 1971 Carey Moore states, "Between Mordecai and Esther the greater hero in the Hebrew is Mordecai, who supplied the brains while Esther simply followed his directions" (Moore, p. lii). Esther's sexual ethics in particular are called into question. "Esther, for the chance of winning wealth and power, takes her place in the herd of maidens who became concubines of the king" (Paton, p. 96). This attitude indicates a failure to accept the book on its own terms. Modern women are also made uncomfortable by the actions of Esther—her entry into the king's harem and her lack of challenge to the status quo. However, in order for the character Esther to be fully appreciated as the heroine of the story that bears her name, the book must be accepted in the cultural milieu that produced it.

In the world portrayed by the book of Esther, Esther has no choice but to obey the king's command. Disobedience would mean death for her and for her guardian Mordecai. Once made queen, Esther skillfully manipulates the power structure of the Persian court in order to attain her goal, the salvation of her people. This goal takes precedence over any personal considerations, including her fear for her own life. In fact, Esther, precisely because she was a woman and therefore basically powerless within Persian society, was the paradigm of the diaspora Jew, who was also powerless in Persian society. Because she was successful in attaining power within the structure of society, she served as a role model for diaspora Jews seeking to attain a comfortable and successful life in a foreign society.

## The Additions to the Book of Esther

The Septuagint version of Esther, produced in the late second or early first century B.C.E., contains six passages not found in the Hebrew text of the book of Esther. When the Christian scholar Jerome revised the Old Latin translation of the Bible, he collected them and placed them at the end of the canonical book. In English translations, Protestant Bibles will place the Additions in the Apocrypha (either alone or integrated with Hebrew Esther), while recent Roman Catholic Bibles (JB, NAB) translate Hebrew Esther but include the Greek Additions in the appropriate places.

Tradition assigns the additions the letters A–F.

| Hebrew Bible | Septuagint Additions |
|---|---|
| 1:1–3:13 | |
| | A. Mordecai's dream; the conspiracy against the king. |
| 3:14–4:17 | |
| | B. The royal edict of Haman. |
| | C. The prayers of Mordecai and Esther. |
| 5:1–2 (omitted in Septuagint) | D. Expansion of the account of Esther's audience with the king. |
| 5:3–8:12 | |
| | E. The royal edict of Mordecai. |
| 8:13–10:3 | |
| | F. Explanation of Mordecai's dream; conclusion and colophon. |

The purpose of the Additions was to add a specifically religious element, to heighten the dramatic interest, and to lend a note of authenticity to the events of the book. God is mentioned over fifty times, as well as prayer, the Temple, its cult, and the practice of the dietary laws. The role and importance of Mordecai are heightened, while Esther becomes more "Jewish" by claiming to have followed the dietary laws and, in particular, by declaring her loathing for her heathen environment. The festival of Purim is deemphasized, and a more strongly anti-Gentile attitude is espoused. The Additions, by turning what was originally a court intrigue into a cosmic conflict between Jew and Gentile, make God, the champion of the chosen people, into the real hero of the book. In this way the demand for a more religious tone is satisfied.

The colophon (Addition F) attributes the

translation of the book to one Lysimachus, who translated it in Jerusalem, "in the fourth year of the reign of Ptolemy and Cleopatra" (either in 114 B.C.E. or 77 B.C.E.). Additions A and F, Mordecai's dream and its interpretation, were composed together, probably originally in Hebrew or Aramaic. The original language of Additions C and D is not clear, but they were composed expressly for the book of Esther for the purpose of adding an explicit religious element and for heightening the dramatic interest. The atmosphere of the book is made more romantic by the change in the character of Esther in Additions C and D. In Addition C, Esther turns to God for aid and throws herself entirely upon God's mercy. When she appears before Ahasuerus in Addition D, her beauty and her fear are emphasized. At the climactic moment, when the king sees her in the court, she faints! Ahasuerus's response to her is motivated by pity for her weakness and fear; Esther becomes a negative stereotype of a weak, helpless woman. Additions B and E, originally written in Greek and completely spurious, endeavor to add a note of authenticity to the proceedings. It must finally be said, however, that the additions add nothing to the dramatic quality of the book and, in fact, lessen the impact of the heroine Esther. The comments below address the original Hebrew version.

## Comment

### The Story of Vashti (1:1–22)

The first female character the book of Esther introduces is Vashti the queen, the wife of Ahasuerus. Ahasuerus summons her to appear before his court in the midst of a wild drinking party, in order that he may show off her beauty. She refuses, and Ahasuerus, on the advice of his nobles, who fear that her example may cause other wives to rebel against their husbands, banishes her from court. The author here introduces a touch of the burlesque; Vashti's refusal to comply with the king's demand is perceived by the men as a grave threat to the dominance of every husband in the kingdom. Ahasuerus and his courtiers appear as hapless buffoons before the calm strength of Vashti and, by implication, of all their wives! The motive for her refusal is not given in the text, which has led to much speculation in the commentaries. For instance, the Targum (the Aramaic translation of the Hebrew Bible) informs the reader that the king wished Vashti to appear naked before the company and that out of modesty she refused. Vashti serves mainly as a foil for Esther, although her character is in some ways more congenial to the modern woman. She is a strong female character who loses her position as a result of her refusal to acquiesce to the greater society's demands upon her. It is ironic that her punishment gives her exactly what she wanted: she is no longer to appear before the king!

### Esther Becomes Queen (2:1–23)

This chapter introduces the reader to the main characters, Esther and Mordecai. Esther, the cousin and ward of Mordecai, is described as very beautiful, but no hint concerning her character is given. In v. 8 Esther is taken, with all the other virginal women in Susa, into the king's harem. The text gives no judgment on the matter and seems to take her obedience to the king's command for granted. To disobey would be suicidal. Verse 9 begins to portray Esther as more than merely beautiful. She earns the regard of Hegai, the king's eunuch, who gives Esther the best of everything in the harem. Esther, in other words, has taken steps to place herself in the best possible position within her situation.

Mordecai, the guardian of Esther, is described as "sitting at the king's gate" (v. 19), that is, as a royal courtier. He is portrayed as very concerned for Esther's welfare. Among other things, Mordecai charges her not to reveal her Jewish identity. The motive for this advice is not given (it serves as a plot device to heighten tension later in the story). Esther sensibly follows the advice of her more seasoned guardian and mentor.

When Esther's turn with the king arrives (again, it must be emphasized that the text does not give a negative judgment on this process), she wins the love of Ahasuerus and becomes the queen. She wisely follows the advice of Hegai, and by working within the power structure of her environment (the Persian harem system), she moves from a completely powerless position into the relatively more powerful one of queen. Her last act before the main events of chap. 4 is to inform the king of the plot of the eunuchs which Mordecai had uncovered. She is attempting to use her position to enhance the status of her relatives, the action of a wise courtier.

## The Downfall of Haman and the Triumph of Esther (3:1–8:2)

The central section of the book chronicles the rise and fall of the royal favorite, Haman the Agagite, and the actions of Esther that bring about his downfall and save the Jews of the Persian empire. Haman is identified as a descendant of Agag, the king of the Amalekites, the ancient and bitter enemies of Israel (Ex. 17:14–16). Therefore the struggle between Mordecai and Haman is not merely personal but has national implications. Because of this, it is important to investigate the behavior of Esther and Mordecai during the crisis precipitated by Haman and to question the interpretation that casts Mordecai in the role of the wise courtier.

Chapter 3 outlines the struggle between Haman and Mordecai. Haman, having been made the king's vizier, desires that everyone in the kingdom should bow down to him. Mordecai refuses, and an angry Haman plots the destruction of all the Jews in the Persian empire. The reason for Mordecai's refusal to bow down to Haman is not given in the text. Commentators, beginning with the rabbis, have sought to supply the reason. *Midrash Rabbah* suggests, for example, that Haman had an idol pinned to his breast. Among modern commentators, L. B. Paton sees in Mordecai's action a "spirit of independence." The text itself, however, is silent. With no reason for it given, Mordecai's action appears foolish in the extreme, placing his life and the life of his people in jeopardy. In 3:4 the other servants wait to see who will prove stronger, Mordecai the Jew or Haman the Agagite (Amalekite). At this point in the story, Haman seems to be winning.

Mordecai's reaction to Haman's plot is less than helpful to his own cause. He appears to go into a panic, putting on sackcloth and wailing in the king's gate (4:1). Mordecai's sole response to the crisis that he set in motion is to bring the problem to the attention of Esther. Esther now reappears in the story, responding to the report of Mordecai's behavior by sending messengers to discover the cause of his actions. Mordecai responds by sending word to Esther of the disaster and charging her to go to the king. This is the turning point of the story. Esther ceases to be the protégée of the male characters surrounding her and instead becomes the chief actor and controller of events.

In 4:11 Esther speaks directly for the first time in the narrative.

All the king's servants and the people of the king's provinces know that if any man or woman goes to the king inside the inner court without being called, there is but one law—all alike are to be put to death. Only if the king holds out the golden scepter to someone, may that person live. I myself have not been called to come in to the king for thirty days.

Esther's reaction to Mordecai's demand is not cowardice but a statement of fact. If she goes to the king unsummoned, the chances are good that she will die. In addition, what influence would she have with the king if he has not wished to see her in thirty days? Mordecai responds, however, by prodding her to act, emphasizing the importance of human action in accomplishing God's purpose (4:13; a major underlying theme in Esther) and reminding her that as queen she does have power (4:14). Thus prodded, Esther springs into action; the reactor becomes the actor.

Esther orders a fast and then prepares to go to the king. In her decision to confront the king, Esther continues on the same wise course she has taken until now. As a subordinate member of the court, she does not risk direct confrontation without first taking every possible precaution to safeguard herself and to obtain her desire. She uses her knowledge of the king's character in order to attain her goal by appealing to his emotions. The author has already demonstrated that Ahasuerus reacts emotionally rather than rationally (e.g., his banishment of Vashti). Esther's best way to appeal to this king is clearly through his emotions.

After her fast, Esther appears unsummoned before the king. She has put on her royal robes in order to appear as attractive and queenly as possible. Her strategy works, for she wins his favor (5:2). Ahasuerus offers to grant any request of hers up to half of his kingdom. This might seem like the right time to ask the king to save the Jews; however, that would not neutralize Haman, as Esther appears to realize. Rather than making her request and leaving the results to the discretion of this mercurial king, she sets out to lull Haman into a false sense of complacency and to place the king in a position where a strong emotional response from him is guaranteed. She invites the king and Haman to a private dinner party. This places the king in her territory, the women's quarters, where she can more easily control the situation. It also puts Haman off his guard (your enemies don't invite you to dinner!). Her strategy is again successful: the king is further inclined to do Esther's will, and "Haman went out that day happy and in good spirits" (5:9).

Chapter 6 contains a short interlude in which Ahasuerus unwittingly humiliates Haman. Haman, brought down by his own arrogance, is forced to give Mordecai (for saving the king's life in chap. 3) the reward that he constructed for himself, namely, to parade Mordecai through the streets on the king's horse, loudly proclaiming that Mordecai is favored by the king.

The king's attendance at the second banquet to which Esther invites him is the affirmation that he means to grant Esther's request. It should be noted that although the reader has the benefit of chap. 6 and knows of Haman's humiliation before Mordecai, there is no indication in the text that Esther knows anything about it. She views Haman as just as dangerous as before. So when she makes her request, she must convince the king of the rightness of her position. She appeals to Ahasuerus's emotions by the raw urgency of her plea: "Let my life be given me—that is my petition—and the lives of my people—that is my request" (7:3). She then argues, against Haman, that the destruction of the Jews would be a great (financial) loss to the king. Later in the scene, when Haman pleads for his life, the fact that she does not try to save him may appear unattractive. However, Esther must act on her primary loyalty to her community, which has motivated her throughout this scene. Haman left alive would still constitute a threat to the Jewish community. Esther acknowledges by her silence that Haman must die for the Jews to be safe.

By 8:2 Esther has won a complete victory. She has received Haman's property from Ahasuerus and persuaded the king to make Mordecai his vizier in place of Haman. Esther now controls wealth, court appointments, and access to the king.

### The Festival of Purim (8:3–10:3)

The last section of the book describes how Esther and Mordecai overturned the edict of Haman, the subsequent victory of the Jews, and the inauguration of the festival of Purim. Esther and Mordecai act together in the king's name, assuring the complete triumph of the Jews over their enemies. In fact, so complete is this victory that many Gentiles "profess to be Jews" (8:17). The oppressed and endangered minority has become the most powerful group in society. This reversal has been accomplished by human action motivated by ethnic solidarity and an underlying faith in the providence of God, specifically by the action of the woman Esther, a powerless member of a powerless group. She serves as the role model for all diaspora Jews who find themselves in a minority status. This, then, is the original purpose of the book: to acquaint the Jews in the Eastern Diaspora with a mode of conduct that will enable them to attain security and to lead happy and productive lives. Esther the queen, by her deeds and in her character, typifies this mode of life.

## BIBLIOGRAPHY

Berg, Sandra Beth. *The Book of Esther: Motifs, Themes, and Structure.* Society of Biblical Literature Dissertation Series 44. Missoula, Mont.: Scholars Press, 1979.

Clines, David J. A. *The Esther Scroll: The Story of the Story.* Journal for the Study of the Old Testament Supplement Series 30. Sheffield: JSOT Press, 1984.

Fox, Michael V. *Character and Ideology in the Book of Esther.* Studies in Biblical Personalities. Columbia, S.C.: University of South Carolina Press, 1991.

LaCocque, André. *The Feminine Unconventional: Four Subversive Figures in Israel's Tradition.* Overtures to Biblical Theology. Minneapolis: Fortress Press, 1990.

Moore, Carey A. *Daniel, Esther and Jeremiah: The Additions.* Anchor Bible 44. Garden City, N.Y.: Doubleday & Co., 1977.

———. *Esther.* Anchor Bible 7B. Garden City, N.Y.: Doubleday & Co., 1971.

Paton, L. B. *A Critical and Exegetical Commentary on the Book of Esther.* International Critical Commentary. Edinburgh: T. & T. Clark, 1908.

White, Sidnie Ann. "Esther: A Feminine Model for Jewish Diaspora." In *Gender and Difference in Ancient Israel,* edited by Peggy L. Day, pp. 161–177. Philadelphia: Fortress Press, 1989.

# JOB

*Carol A. Newsom*

## Introduction

A woman reading the Bible for the first time might wonder whether the book of Job would be worth her while. It appears to be another of those books in which men do all the talking. In fact, the only time a woman ventures to make a comment, she is silenced with the criticism that she talks like a fool. It would be a great mistake, however, for women to ignore the book of Job. When one reads it closely, some surprising things appear. What Job and his friends are debating turns out to include some important issues that feminist theology has been raising in recent years: the significance of personal experience as a source of religious insight, the importance and difficulty of solidarity among those who are oppressed, a critique of traditional models of God, and the relationship between human existence and the whole of creation.

### Composition and Structure

Dates for the composition of Job have ranged from the tenth century B.C.E. to the second century B.C.E., although most scholars assume that the book was written during the early postexilic period, perhaps during the fifth century. As elusive as the date is the question of what kind of literature Job is. While it is usually associated with the wisdom books of Proverbs, Ecclesiastes, and Sirach, Job is unique within biblical literature.

The book of Job has a curious structure. The first two chapters, which introduce the characters and set up the plot, are written in a "once upon a time" style, almost like that of a fairy tale. In these chapters Job appears as the traditional character of patient endurance, bearing his misfortunes with complete acceptance. In chap. 3, however, both the style and the character of Job change dramatically. The simple prose is replaced with beautiful but highly demanding poetry, and Job, no longer patient, begins to speak bitter, almost blasphemous words. From chap. 4 through chap. 27 Job and his three friends, Eliphaz, Bildad, and Zophar, argue with one another about the meaning of Job's misfortunes and what light they shed on the character of Job and of God. A poem on the inaccessibility of wisdom (chap. 28) provides an interlude before Job takes up his speech again to challenge God directly (chaps. 29–31). Although one expects God's response to follow immediately, instead there occurs the long speech of a fourth friend, Elihu, who has not previously been mentioned (chaps. 32–37). In all probability these chapters are a later addition to the book, provided by someone who thought he could do a better job of answering Job than the three friends. In the opinion of most subsequent readers, he does not. The climax of the book occurs in the speeches of God from the whirlwind and Job's response to them (chaps. 38:1–42:6). What is initially puzzling about the divine speeches is that they do not address Job's questions directly but are mostly concerned with an elaborate description of the created world. At the end of the speeches, however, Job retracts his accusations against God. The ending of the book (42:7–17) returns to the simple prose of the first chapters as it describes Job's restoration.

### Religious Issues in Job

In the opening chapters Job's perfect character becomes the occasion for a disagreement between God and the *satan*. Not to be confused with the later Jewish and Christian figure of the devil, the *satan* in Job is a member of God's heavenly court whose functions are rather like those of a prosecuting attorney. The *satan* raises questions about the motivation of Job's piety, suggesting that Job is pious because God has blessed his life abundantly and that if all his blessings were suddenly destroyed, he would curse God. To determine the motivation of Job's piety, God permits two sets of disasters to befall Job: the loss of his possessions and his children, and the loss of his health. The notion of a wager in heaven at Job's expense is, of course, quite outrageous, but to dismiss the book as unworthy would be to miss an important experience. The book of Job is rather like a parable in that it tells its frankly outrageous tale for the purpose of disorienting and reorienting the perspectives of its readers.

The initial question of the book is whether truly disinterested piety exists. Job's behavior and responses in chaps. 1–2 seem to affirm that his piety is offered without expectation of reward. But once the friends arrive and Job breaks the sympathetic silence of their presence with his harrowing curse on the day of his birth (chap. 3), the issues quickly become more complicated. Though all of them are ignorant of the events in heaven, Job and his three friends assume that his misfortunes come from God. The friends essentially understand Job's sufferings as either a punishment from God or a disciplinary warning. In either case they urge him to adopt a penitent and humble attitude, and they assure him that God will restore him if he turns to God in trust. But Job, who knows that he has not been guilty of any conduct that would warrant such punishment, cannot accept their advice. To do so would be to destroy his own integrity. Because he suffers without being guilty, Job can only conclude that either some enormous mistake has been made about him or, more disturbingly, that God is not a just god but rather a monstrous tyrant. The book had begun as an inquiry into the motives of human piety. Through the compelling speeches of Job it becomes an examination of the character of God. But God's response to Job once again reframes the issues, challenging the whole set of assumptions that Job and his friends had made the basis of their argument and offering a radically different model of God, creation, and human existence.

## Comment

### Women Characters in the Book of Job

Although they have only "bit parts," Job's daughters and his wife have long intrigued readers and commentators. Job's daughters seem to have a status within the family that is more prominent than what is typically assumed about the position of daughters in ancient Israel. Perhaps it is the author's way of underscoring the exceptional nature of everything that has to do with Job. In describing the cycle of banquets held by the seven sons of Job, the narrator specifically mentions that the sons would invite their three sisters to join the festivities (1:5). More intriguing is the note about the three daughters born to Job after his misfortunes. The narrator gives the names of each: Jemimah ("Dove"), Keziah ("Cinnamon"), and Keren-happuch ("Box of eye shadow"). Not only are they said to be exceptionally beautiful; Job gives them an inheritance among their brothers (42:14–15). That their inheritance is mentioned suggests that it was not a customary practice. Later interpreters were fascinated by the mention of the daughters' inheritance. The *Testament of Job*, a Jewish writing from the first century B.C.E., speculates that Job gave his daughters golden sashes with mystical properties that allowed them to understand and speak the language of the angels.

It is Job's wife, however, who is of most interest as a female character. Her words to Job are radical and provocative: "Do you still persist in your integrity? Curse God, and die" (2:9). What she says echoes God's assessment of Job as one who persists in integrity (2:3b), but the course of action she urges would end the wager on the *satan*'s terms (2:5). There is an ambiguity in her words, however, that is seldom recognized, one that revolves around the thematically crucial word "integrity." The term "integrity" (*tummah*) denotes a person whose conduct is in complete accord with moral and religious norms and whose character is one of utter honesty, without guile. Job's wife's disturbing question hints at a tension between these two aspects of the word. Her question could be understood in two different senses. She could be heard as saying: "Do you still persist in your integrity (=righteousness)? Look where it has gotten you. Give it up, as God has given you up. Curse God, and then die." Or she could be understood as saying: "Do you still persist in your integrity (=honesty)? If so, stand by it and say what is truly in your heart. Curse God before you die." However Job has understood her words, his reply, criticizing her in the strongest terms ("you speak as any foolish woman would speak," 2:10) has generally set the tone for her evaluation by commentators from ancient times to the present.

There have occasionally been more sympathetic interpretations of her motives both among ancient and modern writers. The Septuagint gives her a longer speech in which she talks movingly of Job's sufferings and of her own. In the *Testament of Job* she is clearly a figure of pathos, whose sufferings and humiliations as she tries to provide for her ailing husband are vividly described. Even in these treatments, however, she remains a foil for the morally superior Job, who corrects her understanding. By making Job's wife a more sympathetic character, both the ancient writers and the modern commentators who follow their lead patronize her. Her words become "excusable," and consequently it is not necessary to take them seriously. What gets overlooked in this approach is that Job's wife is the one who recognizes, long before Job himself does, what is at stake theologically in innocent suffering: the conflict between innocence and integrity, on the one hand, and an affirmation of the goodness of God, on the other. It is the issue with which Job will struggle in the following chapters.

The honesty and religious radicalism of Job's wife have not been entirely overlooked, at least in modern literary rewritings of the story of Job. Robert Frost ("A Masque of Reason") portrays her as a sharp but rather shrewish protofeminist. He hints at her "heretical" stance by naming her Thyatira, the city from which John's opponent, "Jezebel," came (see Rev. 2:20–25). In Archibald MacLeish's well-known play *J.B.*, it is Sarah, J.B.'s wife, who first understands and then expresses the humanistic, postreligious vision of the play.

> *Sarah:* You wanted justice and there was none—Only love.
> *J.B.:* [God] does not love. He Is.
> *Sarah:* But we do. That's the wonder.*

Both in the original Hebrew book of Job and in many of the retellings of the story, Job's wife is the prototypical woman on the margin, whose iconoclastic words provoke defensive condemnation but whose insight serves as an irritant that undermines old complacencies.

## Experience and the Critique of Tradition

It is interesting that Job's outburst against his wife is the last thing he says for some time. Apparently not acknowledging the presence of the three friends who come to comfort him, Job sits in silence for seven days. When he finally speaks in chap. 3, his words sound distinctly like those of his wife. Though he does not exactly curse God, he curses the day of his birth. Though he does not die, he speaks longingly of death. In the chapters that follow, his persistence in his integrity—both his moral righteousness and his honesty—motivates his angry, iconoclastic words. His wife's troubling questions have become his own.

In an ironic reversal Job's disturbing words provoke a defensive reaction from his friends, just as he had rebuked his wife. They attempt to recall him to reason, that is, to the received traditions that are accepted as common sense within their community. The friends' response to Job takes a variety of forms but is largely a variation on a few themes. Their fundamental conviction is that God acts in accordance with justice, treating persons as they deserve. At first they urge Job to steadfastness. Since he is basically a good man, he can rest assured that his misfortunes are but temporary, for God always protects the righteous from utter destruction (4:6–7; 5:19–22). Indeed, Job should even rejoice at his misfortunes, because they are the reproof and discipline of God (5:17), designed to alert him to hidden faults before they become fatal (33:15–18). In any event Job should not be astonished if God seems to treat him as unrighteous and impure; all creatures, even the angels, are so before God (4:17–21). Of course, as Job persists in what they perceive as his obstinacy, his friends gradually become convinced that Job is in fact a wicked man. Since only a sinner could talk as he does (15:4–6), they are warranted in charging him with serious moral offenses (22:2–11).

What is of interest to a feminist reading of Job is to notice the sources of authority upon which the friends ground their confident assurance that they know what is true. They appeal to common sense, what "everybody" knows ("Think now, who that was innocent ever

---

perished?" 4:7), confident that their perceptions are the same as Job's ("See, we have searched this out; it is true. Hear, and know it for yourself," 5:27). Sometimes they cite anecdotal evidence ("I have seen . . . ," 4:8; 5:3). Or they may argue deductively from what they assume are universally agreed principles ("Far be it from God that he should do wickedness. . . . For according to their deeds he will repay them. . . . Of a truth, God will not do wickedly . . . ," 34:10–12). The friends buttress their own arguments with the weight of tradition ("For inquire now of bygone generations . . . for we are but of yesterday, and we know nothing. . . . Will they not teach you and tell you . . . ?" 8:8–10). Even the transcendent authority of revelation is invoked ("When deep sleep falls on mortals . . . a spirit glided past my face. . . . There was silence, then I heard a voice . . . ," 4:13–16).

The friends' sources of authority are powerful ones, not to be discounted lightly. Where, then, does Job find the basis to contest their construction of reality? Although his arguments are sophisticated and varied, Job holds his ground for a single fundamental reason. He knows that his friends' common sense and their traditions, their rationality and their revelations are inconsistent with his own experience. For Job, to hold fast to his integrity means to insist on the validity and authority of his own experience, even when it seems to be contradicted by what all the world knows to be true.

What is at stake between Job and his friends should sound familiar to women. The sense of what is normative in a society—its highest values, its ideal of human nature, its notions of God—has been constructed largely on the basis of male experience. Women who have found that their experience is inconsistent with or not adequately described by these norms have often tended to discount their own experience. Where women's lives do not fit the patterns of male experience, women are frequently judged to be defective or inferior. It has been one of the tasks of feminist thought to encourage women to hold fast to the integrity of their own experience.

To be sure, Job and his friends are not engaged in a debate about men's and women's experience. But what is important for feminist thought is that the issue of different sources of authority is explicitly raised in this book in such a way as to authenticate the crucial role of personal experience in the critique of received tradition. Although Job's own perceptions are incomplete and in need of correction, it is the friends and not Job who are rebuked for failing to speak truly (42:7).

## The Moral World of Biblical Patriarchy and the Problem of Solidarity

For the author's purposes it was necessary that the hero of the book be a character at the top of the social order. The hero must be one who quite literally has everything to lose. It is scarcely surprising, then, that Job is depicted as a patriarch rather like Abraham, the wealthy and respected head of a large household with many dependents.

Readers are accustomed to thinking of Job as a universal character, at least as "everyman" if not "everywoman." Although it is certainly possible to gain insight into the human condition in general from the book, it is important to remember that Job experiences his suffering precisely *as* a patriarch. Without his really being aware of it, his sense of identity, his expectations about the world and his place in it, and even his image of God had all been shaped by his status in a particular social and moral order. When his world is shaken by the suffering he undergoes, it becomes possible to see something of the dimensions and the limitations of that world.

The term "patriarchy" is a problematic one, because it has been used in so many different contexts and for so many different purposes. It is not only a matter of male–female relationships but a whole set of social and moral arrangements in which authority resides primarily with older males. In Israel the basic social unit was the household, within which the senior male had considerable authority over its members. The social values of biblical patriarchy were what one could call paternalistic. Within the village or larger social area, wealthier men also had responsibilities for those who could not provide for themselves and were subject to exploitation: traveling strangers, the poor of both sexes, but especially women and children who had no male to provide for them. In return for this patronage the patriarch received their loyalty and respect. Even more important, the patriarch received honor from his peers.

Maintaining the social order was also part of the responsibility of the senior males. Not only were they responsible for justice within their own households, but when issues of a broader community nature arose, the senior males would meet at the city gate to take counsel together and to adjudicate disputes (see, e.g., Ruth 4; Jeremiah 26). The prosperity and the dignity of these men were generally seen as divine approval for the proper fulfillment of their social responsibilities. Indeed, to a significant extent the biblical image of God is drawn from the model of the patriarch.

When Job's three friends come to comfort him, they form a group of society's most privileged members who are trying to make sense out of a disturbing disruption in their world. As they grope for an explanation, the three friends attempt to account for the way in which prosperity and loss, good and bad fortune, are distributed. It is not surprising that the three friends are convinced that people essentially get what they deserve and deserve what they get. Apparent discrepancies, such as Job's misfortunes, are merely temporary. Although they are not aware of it, their complacency about the order of their society is rooted in large measure in their own privileged position. They simply cannot see injustice in the world.

Job, however, has been shocked out of his own previous complacency by the wholly undeserved suffering he has experienced. Gradually he begins to see things from a different perspective, from the perspective of others who suffer. In a powerful speech in 24:1–17 Job describes the desperate condition of the very poor who are without food, shelter, or adequate clothing, exploited by those who hire them or lend to them and subject to repeated violence. Job draws particular attention to the plight of the widow and the orphan, for, then as now, women and children make up a disproportionate number of the poorest of the poor. Here Job stands in solidarity with all the wretched of the earth.

Readers who find Job's speech in 24:1–17 so moving are often disconcerted by his next speech in chaps. 29–31. As he sums up his experiences and challenges God to confront him, Job no longer orients himself according to the suffering of the poor. Instead, as he speaks, he is very much the proud patriarch. It is a valuable speech, however, for anyone who wishes to understand the moral world of Israelite patriarchy. In chap. 29 Job recalls the days when all was well with him, contrasting them in chap. 30 with the misery of his present existence. In chap. 31 he challenges God through a series of oaths in which he vows to accept terrible curses upon himself if he has committed any of the sins he enumerates.

What Job remembers most fondly is the honor and deference he received from his peers. When he went to the city gate, not only would the young men withdraw before him; the elders would rise and stand, as everyone waited silently for Job to speak (29:7–10, 21–25). The reason Job commanded such respect did not have to do with wealth and power as such, but with the fact that he exercised his authority in order to bring relief to the weak: "I delivered the poor who cried, and the orphan who had no helper. . . . I caused the widow's heart to sing for joy. . . . I was eyes to the blind, and feet to the lame. I was a father to the needy . . ." (29:12–16). Even in the nobility of Job's words, however, it becomes evident why true solidarity with the oppressed is an impossibility for Job. The moral world of ancient patriarchy was an essentially paternalistic and hierarchical one. It placed a high value on alleviating the distress of the poor and weak, but for the most part it could not conceive of the fundamental changes in the organization of society that would prevent the powerlessness and destitution that so often struck the widow and the orphan. This is not to accuse Job individually of moral failure; rather, it is to recognize the limitations of the very moral world that formed him.

An even less attractive face of patriarchy's moral world appears in the following chapter. The paternalism expressed in chap. 29 is an apparently benevolent form of hierarchical social relations. But social resentment lurks in even benevolent hierarchies, to be unleashed, as Job discovers, when a previously high-ranking member of the social order falls on hard times. "But now they make sport of me, men who are younger than I, whose fathers I would have disdained to set with the dogs of my flock . . ." (30:1, 9, RSV). Job's scathing contempt for these lower-class people takes the form of mocking their poverty: "Through want and hard hunger they gnaw the dry and desolate ground. . . . They are driven out from society; people shout after them as after a thief. In the gullies of wadis they must live, in holes in the ground, and in the rocks" (30:3, 5–6). Job's former solidarity with the poor seems to have evaporated before his perception that his honor—the most precious possession a man could have in his moral world—has been trampled by those without honor.

Similarly, Job's great oath in chap. 31 is a virtual catalogue of the values of ancient Israel's patriarchal society. Job swears that he has never engaged in deceit for the sake of greed (31:5–8) nor overvalued wealth (31:24–25). He has respected the daughters and wives of other men (31:1–4, 9–12). Within his own household he has upheld justice (31:13–15), and never has he taken legal advantage of the powerless (31:21–23). He has been generous to the poor (31:16–20), hospitable to the stranger (31:32), responsible to his land (31:38–40). He has not engaged in idolatry (31:26–28), nor exulted over his enemies' misfortune (31:29–31), nor hidden his own transgressions (31:33–34). But for all the genuine nobility of this inventory of moral values, a modern woman cannot but feel aghast at the oath Job takes in defense of his sexual integrity: "If my loins were seduced by a woman and I loitered at my neighbor's door—let any man take my wife and grind in between her thighs!" (31:9–10, trans. Mitchell, p. 73). Job's words are in keeping with the patriarchal perspective that saw a woman's sexuality as the property of her husband and an abuse of it as an injury to the husband rather than to the woman herself (see the commentary on Leviticus).

Although modern readers are critical of the proprietary view of women in Job 29–31 and of the way concern for honor tends to translate into social resentment and contempt, there is little indication that an ancient audience would have so reacted. For them, chaps. 29–31 would have presented Job in the noblest possible terms—a model patriarch. He is, as God has described him, a man who "fears God and turns from evil" (1:8).

## Models of God

There is one important respect in which Job's patriarchal assumptions are put in question by the book. Job's mounting frustration with God comes from his expectation that God should behave toward him as Job behaves toward his own dependents. Job had envisioned God in his own image, as a sort of divine patriarch. It is a model of God drawn from the highest and best that ancient Near Eastern culture could imagine. Job had expected God to be benevolent and paternal, but above all Job had expected God to be just, intervening directly to vindicate righteous conduct and punish wickedness. Repeatedly, Job's language has turned to legal metaphors as he imagines coming before God (chaps. 9–10; 13; 16; 19; 23). Job knows how he has conducted himself in the seat of judgment (29:12–17) and when he heard complaints within his own household (31:13–15). Despite his own recent inexplicable experiences, he

clings to the belief that God will yet vindicate him, if he can summon God to judgment.

The radicalness of the book of Job lies in this: the rejection of Job's model of God as inadequate. The God who meets Job in chaps. 38–41 is not the great patriarch Job had anticipated. That the book remains a difficult challenge to modern readers is an indication of the extent to which the model of God as patriarch still prevails.

Whereas Job's speeches were oriented to themes of rights and injustices in the human realm and to a God who should see that justice is always done, God speaks of the ordering of creation: the foundation of the earth; the birthing of the sea; the ordering of day and night; and the mysteries of water in its myriad forms of snow, hail, rain, frost, and dew. Already in this section there is a hint of the strategy by which God attempts to reorient Job. Although tradition spoke of the giving and withholding of rain as a response to human conduct (e.g., Amos 4:7–8), here God speaks of the rain that falls in the desert where no human lives (38:25–27).

Job's categories had been too narrow, his conception of God hopelessly anthropocentric. That is to say, both Job and his friends had assumed that God primarily *reacts* to human conduct, a view of the world that puts the individual human being at its center. God's education of Job continues as God turns to speak of the animals for whom God has provided (38:39–39:30). These are not domestic animals but wild ones—the lion, the raven, the mountain goat, the wild ox, the ostrich, and so on. God quite evidently delights in their very wildness and their freedom from human use— another implicit criticism of Job's exclusively anthropocentric views. Images of birth, nurture, and vitality abound. This is, however, an unsentimental view of the natural world in which food for the lion's cubs and the eagle's nestlings means the shedding of blood.

Job's categories of rights and wrongs and his conception of God as a larger version of himself are simply inadequate to encompass the vision God shows him. The egocentricity of Job's view is underscored in the concluding speeches as God describes the wondrous legendary creatures Behemoth and Leviathan (chaps. 40–41), reminding Job that Behemoth is one of God's creatures as well as Job and that Leviathan too is a creature proud, fearless, and magnificent (much as Job had presented himself in chap. 31).

For all the beauty of the divine speeches, many readers are disturbed by the fact that

God's reply does not directly address Job's questions. Truly, God does not tell Job how to think through the issues of suffering and oppression—that remains a human task. What God has done by ignoring Job's way of posing the question is to illumine the inadequacy of Job's starting point, his legal model of rights and faults and his image of God as the great patriarch. From Job's perspective, innocent suffering had to imply the injustice of God. The divine speeches hint at a different perspective. Moral and theological thinking after Job 38–41 has to begin with a new image of God and a new image of the world that can be glimpsed in these speeches. This new image is one of God as a power for life, balancing the needs of all creatures, not just humans, cherishing freedom, full of fierce love and delight for each thing without regard for its utility, acknowledging the deep interconnectedness of death and life, restraining and nurturing each element in the ecology of all creation. It is a description of God and the world that has strong points of contact with contemporary feminist thought.

Job's verbal response to the divine speeches, though somewhat enigmatic, is certainly a retraction of his earlier accusations and an embrace of this new vision of God (42:1–6). His trust in a new understanding of reality is given concrete expression as this previously isolated and alienated sufferer reestablishes relationships. Not only is he reconciled with God; he also prays to God for his friends, receives his brothers and sisters, and becomes a father to ten more children (42:7–17). Women may regret that nothing is explicitly said about Job's wife, but her own outspoken integrity, as much as her husband's, remains a model for those who seek truth.

## BIBLIOGRAPHY

Alter, Robert. "Truth and Poetry in the Book of Job." In his *The Art of Biblical Poetry*, pp. 85–110. New York: Basic Books, 1985.

Good, Edwin M. *In Turns of Tempest: A Reading of Job*. Stanford, Calif.: Stanford University Press, 1990.

Gutiérrez, Gustavo. *On Job: God-Talk and the Suffering of the Innocent*. Maryknoll, N.Y.: Orbis Books, 1987.

Habel, Norman. *The Book of Job, A Commentary*. Old Testament Library. Philadelphia: Westminster Press, 1985.

MacLeish, Archibald. *J.B.* Boston: Houghton Mifflin Co., 1958.

Mitchell, Stephen. *The Book of Job*. Translated with an introduction by Stephen Mitchell. Rev. ed. San Francisco: North Point Press, 1987.

Reid, Stephen Breck. "Suffering and Critical Awareness: The Foundation of a Quest for Witnesses." In *Experience and Tradition: A Primer in Black Biblical Hermeneutics*, pp. 85–138. Nashville: Abingdon Press, 1990.

# PSALMS

*Kathleen A. Farmer*

## Introduction

The book of Psalms is an anthology of songs, poems, and prayers that have been sung, spoken, and prayed by individuals and by communities in a wide variety of social and historical settings. These religious lyrics are clearly confessional in character. They are expressed mostly in the first person (using I, we, me, us, and so on) and represent the full range of human emotions in conversation with God. In all but a few cases these deeply human utterances are addressed directly to God. The English name for the book comes from the Greek word *psalmos*, which seems to have been an attempt to translate the Hebrew word *mizmor*, meaning a "song" of faith (particularly one sung with instrumental accompaniment).

### The Headings

The original authors or composers of these religious lyrics cannot be identified with any degree of certainty; the evidence available is not sufficient. Although many of the psalms have titles or headings that contain references to a person or persons (such as David, Asaph, the sons of Korah, or an unnamed leader or "choir director"), the titles themselves seem to have been added many centuries after the psalms were composed. Most scholars think that these headings are interpretations, referring to the ways in which the psalms were understood and used rather than to the persons who composed them. Thus, the traditional rendering of the Davidic titles by the English phrase "psalm of David" may be misleading. In Hebrew the phrase can also mean "belonging to David," "dedicated to David," or "for David's use" (which

may have implied "for the use of David's descendants" as well). Whereas the heading of Psalm 7, for instance, indicates that later interpreters believed David had sung this song on a particular occasion, the heading of Psalm 3 may merely indicate that interpreters thought that this psalm would have been an appropriate one for David to use "when he fled from Absalom his son."

Some headings also refer to specific historical settings, but the origins of the psalms themselves cannot be directly tied to known periods or events in the history of the people of Israel. Psalm 137, which mentions the dislocation of the inhabitants of Jerusalem during the Babylonian exile, is a notable exception to this rule. Speakers in the Psalms often allude to the experiences of Israel in history, but they refer to them as traditions of the past. They rehearse the details of various traditions (such as the exodus or the wilderness wanderings) in order to remind themselves of God's faithfulness (or their own lack of faith) in the past. They speak graphically and vividly of their joys and their sorrows, crying out in triumph and defeat, radiating doubt as well as faith, hope as well as despair. But they avoid mentioning their current circumstances in historically specific ways. Instead, most psalmists speak of typically human situations: those experiences, desires, and needs that arise whenever and wherever human beings live together.

It is partly the confessional way in which the speakers address themselves directly to God and partly their degree of detachment from specific times and events that enable succeeding generations of worshipers to pray the psalms as their own prayer.

## Women and the Psalms

Since first-person pronouns (I, we, and so on) and first-person verb forms are not divided according to gender in Hebrew, it is quite possible that some of the speakers who addressed God in the psalms were women (see the commentary on Psalm 131, below). In other biblical traditions (outside the book of Psalms) prominent women are portrayed as singers of hymns in Israel's worship (Miriam in Ex. 15:20–21 and Deborah in Judges 5). In Ps. 148:12–13 women are commanded to praise Yahweh, along with the rest of creation, and in Ps. 68:25, girls are pictured as playing musical instruments in a liturgical procession of praise.

From biblical times to the present age, the psalms have nourished and enriched the prayer lives of women in public and in private worship. Jewish and Christian women alike have found their thoughts, their needs, and their life experiences reflected in the texts of the psalms. Hannah (the mother of Samuel), Judith (the heroine who saved her city from destruction in the deuterocanonical book of Judith), and Mary (the mother of Jesus) are all said to have used psalmic traditions to respond to highly significant situations in their own lives (1 Sam. 2:1–10; Judith 16:1–17; Luke 1:47–55). Since the times of Paula and Melania, who established monasteries for women in Bethlehem and Jerusalem in the fourth century C.E., women living in Christian ascetic communities have organized their daily lives around the praying of psalms.

One way in which succeeding generations of women have been able to claim the psalms as their own can be illustrated by a closer look at Psalm 46. Most translators think that the heading or the title of this psalm contains directions to the "leader" or choir director concerning how the song should be sung. In another context the Hebrew term 'alamot (which RSV and NRSV leave untranslated in the heading) would probably have been understood to mean "young women." Untranslated, it appears to be the title of a tune or a metrical notation. However, some scholars think that 'alamot is a technical term referring to women's voices and that the heading indicates that the psalm should be sung by women. If so, then women in the community of faith that preserved this psalm are being encouraged to claim that "God is our refuge and strength, a very present help in trouble. . . . Yahweh of hosts is with us; the God

of Jacob is our refuge" (46:1, 7, 11). The fact that the tradition handed down to them refers to the God of Jacob rather than to the God of Rachel and Leah does not prevent women from claiming the God of that tradition as their own. When the psalms are sung by women's voices, when women claim the traditions as their own, then the God whom our ancestors called "the God of Jacob" becomes the refuge and the strength of women.

Women have also claimed the psalms as their own by singing "new songs." Just as Judith, giving praise to God for having foiled the enemy "by the hand of a woman," raises a "new psalm" to God (Judith 16:1, 13), using traditional forms and language, so might others choose to sing new songs based on the old forms, reflecting ever-new circumstances in the lives of those who sing. See Pss. 33:3; 40:3; 96:1; 98:1; 144:9; 149:1.

## Recurring Patterns in the Psalms

Modern critical scholarship has tended to look for recurring literary patterns in the psalms. Since there is good evidence that recurring needs in the life of any human community will give rise to recognizable conventions or patterns of speech, scholars commonly assume that literary patterns contain clues either to the purposes for which various psalms were written or to the ways in which the psalms were used. Most scholars conclude that the psalms were composed for liturgical uses in worship settings. Recently, Walter Brueggemann has suggested that the predominant patterns of thought and speech in the psalms also correspond to the characteristic flow of human life, from "satisfied seasons of well-being," through "anguished seasons of hurt, alienation, suffering and death," to "turns of surprise when we are overwhelmed with the new gifts of God" (Brueggemann, p. 19). The mood of the book of Psalms moves back and forth from assurance to doubt, from contentment to pain, from joy to despair and back again. But those who speak from peaceful, secure, and prosperous settings in life often have different things to say to God and different ways to say them than do those who are in the midst of crisis, trouble, pain, or struggle. As people address God from the midst of varying personal circumstances, their patterns of thought, speech, and imagery change in characteristic ways.

# Comment

## The Psalms Women Sing

In the biblical texts five women (Miriam, Deborah, Hannah, Judith, and Mary) are said to have responded to significant circumstances in their lives with psalmlike songs and prayers. Each woman reflects on a recent experience of "reversal" in her life, and each uses the form of a psalm to give thanks and praise to God for turning the unhappy circumstances of her life upside down. Miriam, Deborah, and Judith rejoice over communal reversals in which the people of Israel are freed from various oppressors. Hannah exults in a reversal of a very personal sort (from barrenness to motherhood) and Mary celebrates the surprisingly glorious role she (a woman of humble origins) has been chosen to play in God's plans. The new situations in life for which Hannah and Mary give thanks are specific personal situations, but the psalms they pray refer to typical rather than specific experiences of reversal. Both women see that God's actions in their lives are part of a larger pattern. "Yahweh makes poor and makes rich; he brings low, he also exalts," prays Hannah in 1 Sam. 2:7. "He has brought down the powerful from their thrones, and lifted up the lowly; he has filled the hungry with good things, and sent the rich away empty," Mary says in Luke 1:52–53. Both women recognize that their own particular reversals in fortune are merely instances of the way God characteristically acts in human lives (cf. Ps. 113:7–9).

## Psalms of Reversal by and for Survivors

A significant portion of the book of Psalms consists of songs of reversal similar to those sung by women in the biblical texts. These might be called psalms of thanksgiving, sung by survivors who attribute their present well-being to God's intervention in their lives. As they rejoice over the reversal of their previously intolerable circumstances, the faithful sing a "new song" (Ps. 40:3) acknowledging that their survival is a gift of grace from the hand of God. In Psalm 124 the community of faith confesses that "if it had not been Yahweh who was on our side, when our enemies attacked us, then they would have swallowed us up alive" (124:2–3a); in Psalm 30 the individual admits that it is God alone who has brought about healing and the restoration of life to the afflicted (30:2–3); and in Psalm 118 the figurative statement of reversal, "The

stone that the builders rejected has become the chief cornerstone," is followed by the affirmation that "This is Yahweh's doing" (118:22–23). The speaker in Ps. 34:4 says, "I sought Yahweh, and he answered me, and delivered me from all my fears"; and the survivor in Ps. 116:6 recalls that "when I was brought low, [Yahweh] saved me."

*Psalm 30.* In this prayer of thanksgiving, recovery from a near-death experience is figuratively described as being "drawn up" from Sheol (like a bucket of water from a well). The terms "Sheol" and "Pit" (vv. 3 and 9) refer to the state of being dead, rather than to a place where rewards or punishments might be given after death. Ancient Israelite concepts concerning what happens to humans after they die were never formulated into a coherent doctrine, but Sheol appears in most Old Testament passages as an underworld where all the dead go (regardless of whether their lives had been lived in good or evil ways). In the Psalms, Sheol (or the Pit) is used as a poetic equivalent for the concept of death or for the grave. It seems to be thought of as a place of silence, where the dead neither remember nor praise God (Pss. 6:5; 30:9; 115:17).

The psalmist looks back on two different kinds of reversal. At one time, the speaker confesses to God, "I said in my prosperity, 'I shall never be moved'" (30:6). I thought I had found security in your favor, says the psalmist, but "you hid your face" and "I was dismayed" (30:7). The first reversal (from prosperity and security to a precarious perch on the edge of death) is interpreted by the psalmist as a mark of God's anger, but the psalmist's second experience of reversal (recovery from a nearly fatal ailment) leads to the theological conclusion that God's "anger is but for a moment" compared to God's "favor," which lasts a lifetime (30:5).

There is no doubt in the psalmist's mind about who has been in control in either reversal. Survival clearly has come through the mercy of God. "You have turned my mourning into dancing," declares the psalmist to God, "you have taken off my sackcloth and clothed me with joy" (30:11). It is clear, however, that the psalmist had not merely waited passively in the midst of pain and distress for God to act. The one who has survived through the mercy of God also bears witness to the efficacy of crying out to God for help when all other hope is gone (30:2, 8, 10).

## The Cry for Help in the Psalms

In the book of Psalms, songs of thanksgiving consistently refer to "cries for help" which seem to have called God's attention to those in distress (e.g., 30:2, 8, 10; 34:6, 17; 40:1; 118:5; 107:6, 13, 19–28; 116:4). As the refrain in Psalm 107 recalls, those who are now rejoicing in their deliverance once "cried to Yahweh in their trouble," before God "delivered them from their distress." In two of the very rare instances in which divine speech is quoted in the Psalms, God says, "Call on me in the day of trouble; I will deliver you, and you shall glorify me" (50:15) and "When they call to me, I will answer them; I will be with them in trouble, I will rescue them and honor them" (91:15).

Going back to the contexts in which the psalms sung by women are found in biblical texts, one sees that the act of crying to God for help also plays a part in four out of five of the women's stories. When the Israelites were slaves in Egypt "their cry for help rose up to God" and "God heard their groaning" (Ex. 2:23, 24). Miriam's psalm celebrated God's role in their deliverance from bondage (Ex. 15:21). In Deborah's time, God is said to have responded to the Israelites who "cried out to Yahweh for help" (Judg. 4:3) by selling Sisera, the commander of Jabin's army "into the hand of a woman" (Judg. 4:9), the reversal that Deborah celebrates in her song. Judith also cries out to God for help in her endeavors (Judith 9:1–14). But it is the narrative in 1 Sam. 1:1–28 that gives the clearest picture of the role that crying out to God for help plays in the movement from distress to relief. In the first part of the chapter we are told that Hannah was childless (in a society that placed a very high value on bearing children) and that her grief over her barrenness was made even worse by the taunts of her husband's second wife (1 Sam. 1:6). So Hannah "was deeply distressed and prayed to Yahweh, and wept bitterly" (1 Sam. 1:10) as she asked God to give her a child. When the priest at the sanctuary accused her of being drunk, Hannah replied, "I am a woman deeply troubled.... I have been pouring out my soul before Yahweh.... I have been speaking out of my great anxiety and vexation..." (1 Sam. 1:15–16). It was only after God had responded to Hannah's prayers, after Samuel was born, weaned, and dedicated to the service of God, that Hannah "prayed" the psalm of thanksgiving preserved in 1 Sam. 2:1–9, which praises the one who continually reverses the fortunes of both the proud and the humble, the rich and the poor,

the mighty and the feeble, the barren and the mother of many.

The text of Hannah's cry for help is not recorded in the narrative, but we are told enough about it to see resemblances between it and a number of prayers now found in the book of Psalms. Over a third of the book of Psalms consists of formalized cries for help in which the faithful put their doubts, fears, pain, grief, remorse, and rage into words addressed directly to God. Psalms of this type are often called "laments," although that term in English does not communicate the degree to which urgent petitions or requests for relief also play a part in these prayers. Like Hannah, grieving over her barrenness, the speakers in the psalms of lament share their feelings of fear, resentment, despair, and rage with God. They do not wait passively for God to notice their pain and come to their aid. Rather, they cry out as an act of faith in the steadfast love of the one they confidently trust will not reject them for what they feel or say.

## Psalms of Anger, Alienation, and Pain

The psalms of lament articulate the innermost feelings and desires of human beings caught up in situations of crisis. The troubles with which the faithful are plagued seem to run the gamut of human experience, from poverty and powerlessness to life-threatening ailments, from slander and oppression by enemies to betrayal by friends. It might be possible to divide these psalms into subgroups based on the type of distress that seems to give rise to the complaint, but any attempt to pinpoint the life circumstances of the psalmists must proceed with caution. Distressful situations are often multifaceted. Persons suffering from sickness and depression may also feel that they have been abandoned by their friends (as seems to be the case in Psalm 38), and persons who feel persecuted may also suffer from loneliness and isolation (as in Psalm 42). The psalmists tend to use either conventional expressions (e.g., "evildoers" or "the wicked") or highly figurative language (e.g., bulls, lions, roaring beasts) to describe their "enemies" and the evil these enemies do (seek my life, mock me, lay snares, and so on). When an entire community speaks of its "enemies," one is inclined to picture military opponents (as in Psalm 44) or natural disasters (such as drought or famine). But the enemies confronted by various individuals are more difficult to identify. In Psalm 41 the "enemy" might be identified as death (v. 11) or as those who are eagerly waiting for the psalmist to die (v. 5). Sometimes it is difficult to say whether the speakers are suffering more from physical or from spiritual pains. The bruises of body, mind, and spirit are often intertwined.

## Vindictive Petitions

Psalms of lament occasionally contain vicious petitions, requesting God to do terrible things to the "enemies" of those who pray. One psalmist, angry that the wicked seem to escape punishment for their sins, asks God to "break the teeth [of the wicked] in their mouths" (58:6). Another hopes that they will be "blotted out of the book of the living" (69:28). The exiles who have witnessed the destruction of Jerusalem and who have been taken as captives to a foreign land wish their captors might experience the same suffering they have inflicted: "O daughter Babylon, you devastator! Happy shall they be who pay you back what you have done to us! Happy shall they be who take your little ones and dash them against the rock!" (137:8–9). Women who attempt to make the language and the imagery of the psalms their own may find such viciousness offensive, but those who read or pray the psalms are not asked to admire or to respect the speakers' desire for revenge. The words of the psalmists are descriptive rather than prescriptive: they describe human reality (the psalmists actually did have such thoughts and desires) but they do not suggest that others should imitate or encourage the attitudes described. While the psalmists feel free to present such wishes to God without fear of condemnation, they also know that God is not bound to act in human-guided ways.

## From Complaint to Assurance

As a category, the psalms of lament are remarkable for their use of abrasive, impetuous language. The psalmists refuse to mince words or to couch their demands in polite, euphemistic terms. Thus, for instance, the speakers in Psalms 35 and 44 bluntly tell God to wake up, pay attention, and get busy helping them before it is too late for them to be saved. The psalmists remind God that human beings have too limited a life span to wait for justice to come at God's own convenience (Psalm 90). The psalmists also use remarkably vivid, picturesque, and exaggerated language to describe the unbearable situations in which they find themselves. Most

remarkable of all is the consistency with which the psalmists seem to find themselves empowered by their prayers to move from their situations of grief and despair into situations of hope and confidence in the trustworthiness of God. This typical movement from complaint to assurance, expressed within the body of the lament psalm, can be illustrated by a brief look at Psalm 13.

**Psalm 13.** The first two verses contain the psalmist's complaint, addressed to God (i.e., I have pain in my soul and sorrow in my heart all day long, but you seem to have forgotten me). The phrase "How long," which occurs four times in vv. 1–2, is an impatient protest against God's apparent inactivity rather than a polite request for information (cf. Hab. 1:2; Job 18:2; 19:2). The third verse contains an urgent petition, asking God for a specific response (consider and answer me), and v. 4 gives a rationale or reason why the speaker thinks this request is justified (otherwise I will die and my enemies will triumph over me). Then suddenly in vv. 5–6 there is a change of attitude, and the speaker now expresses the utmost confidence in God's response. This abrupt change of mood, from complaint and petition to trust and assurance, is a consistent characteristic found in almost all psalms of lament.

In Psalm 13 the speaker's assurance is based on the understanding that God "has dealt" (and will continue to deal) "bountifully with me." Assurance does not come only to those who wait passively for their pain to be noticed or for their needs to be filled. The psalm shows that a renewal of faith can come through the articulation of rather than through the denial or repression of innermost thoughts, no matter how far those thoughts seem to go beyond the "accepted norms" of society or of organized religions.

## The Ebb and Flow of Assurance

In the book of Psalms the flow of human life and faith is seen to be more like an ocean wave than like a river current. Assurance and doubt can wash back and forth over the faithful. Comfort and anguish can intermingle within the same psalm as within the same speaker. The transition from anxiety to assurance in the psalms, as in human life, is not always neatly or permanently made. Psalm 40, for instance, begins with a statement of thanksgiving and praise. Having been rescued by God in the past (40:2), the psalmist is thoroughly acquainted with God's "steadfast love" and "faithfulness"

(40:10). Yet the second half of the psalm turns back into a cry for help: "Do not, O Yahweh, withhold your mercy from me. . . . O Yahweh, make haste to help me" (40:11a, 13b). In the first half of Psalm 22, cries of despair ("My God, my God, why have you forsaken me?" v. 1) and pleas for help ("Do not be far from me," v. 11) alternate with affirmations of trust and assurance ("In you our ancestors trusted; they trusted, and you delivered them," v. 4; "since my mother bore me you have been my God," v. 10; etc.).

The speaker in Psalm 88 recalls that God has worked wonders in the past (vv. 10, 12) and that God is renowned for "steadfast love" and "faithfulness" as well as for "saving help" (vv. 11, 12). But within the context of the psalm itself, the speaker's depression "unto death" is not banished by these memories. The psalm ends in darkness, in what the mystics call the "dark night of the soul."

## The Foundations of Trust and Assurance

How do the faithful, overwhelmed by danger, pain, or depression, recognize that God is a trustworthy presence in their midst, "a very present help in trouble" (46:1)? How do survivors, looking back on narrow escapes from threats to their physical, mental, or spiritual health, recognize that their survival "is Yahweh's doing" (118:23)? In the book of Psalms, past experience (both the speakers' own experience and that of their ancestors) provides the faithful with a key for recognizing and relying on God's presence in current occasions. The speaker in Psalm 77, who is extremely anxious about the present (vv. 7-9), characteristically turns to the witness of the past for reassurance: "I will call to mind the [past] deeds of Yahweh" (v. 11). The psalms that traditionally are called "hymns" or "songs of praise" and those that are called "psalms of confidence" present the community of faith with the bases from which succeeding generations of worshipers learn to recognize and to trust in the present involvement of God in their lives. The hymns or psalms of praise typically invite the faithful to remember with gratitude what they have been told about the nature of God, about the structures of the universe created by God, and about the saving actions of God in the lives of their predecessors. The psalms of confidence invite readers to recall their own previous experience of God's steadfast love in their lives.

Two foundational psalms of particular interest to women are discussed briefly below.

Psalm 8 is a hymn in praise of the created order which provides women with a basis for claiming their authority as active agents within God's plans. Psalm 131 is a psalm of confidence that illustrates the way in which one woman of faith has experienced and testified to the presence of God in her life.

*Psalm 8.* This song of praise celebrates the special position God has given to human beings within the created order. All of the phrases that allude to humankind in vv. 4-6 are generic terms (i.e., in Hebrew they are masculine in grammatical form but inclusive of both masculine and feminine human beings in meaning). Verses 3-4 emphasize the fragility and the limited life span of the human species, compared to such works of God as the moon and the stars, while vv. 5-6 acknowledge that both privilege and responsibility accompany this special placement below God but above all other creatures. Though mortal, we receive "glory and honor" from God. Though fallible, we are given "dominion over" the rest of God's creatures. The phraseology in vv. 6-8 reminds one of Gen. 1:26-28, in which "dominion" over the rest of creation is clearly given to both male and female human beings. Two different words are used to express the idea of "having dominion" in Gen 1:28 and in Psalm 8. Although human beings have often been tempted to misunderstand the nature of this assigned task, both words for "having dominion" imply supervision for the good of the creation rather than exploitation of creation for the benefit of humankind.

To a certain extent, psalms that praise the created order may be said to glorify the status quo. Those who sing or pray them seem to find satisfaction in the way things are. At the same time, however, such psalms of "well-being" may also recognize that God's orderly universe makes some demands upon those who seem to have a secure place in it. Thus Psalm 8 invites women both to enjoy the favored position they occupy in God's created order *and* to accept the responsibility that comes with this advantageous placement.

*Psalm 131.* The term "ascents" in the title of this psalm is usually understood as a reference to a liturgical ceremony of some sort. Scholars suggest that it might have been recited by a pilgrim going up the mountain road to the city of Jerusalem or by a worshiper going up the stairs into the Temple precincts. If the Hebrew in v. 2 is taken in its most literal and natural sense, the speaker appears to be a woman carrying a small child. As she approaches the place of worship she asserts that she is properly prepared to come into the presence of God. "I have calmed and quieted my soul," she says. "My soul is like the contented child I carry" (author's translation). The term *gamul*, which is translated "a weaned child" in NRSV and NIV, comes from a root that is used in other Old Testament texts to refer to the time when a child ceases to be breast-fed (as in Isa. 28:9). However, the root itself means "to deal fully or adequately with" or "to deal bountifully with" and connotes contentment rather than incompleteness as far as the child is concerned. The play on words implies that the weaned child has not been forced against its will to give up nursing. Rather, the child has been "dealt with" so bountifully that it no longer feels the need to suckle.

The word translated "soul" refers to the person's essential self or innermost being, inseparable in Hebrew thought from the whole person. The psalmist asserts that she is quietly content, even in her innermost thoughts and feelings, knowing that God has dealt so bountifully with her that she has no need yet to be filled. She urges all Israel to "wait for" (or "hope in") God with a similar degree of quiet trust.

## Theology and Piety in the Psalms

It is clear that the traditions of Israel, from which the psalmists draw information and illustrations, speak of God as both merciful *and* just. Justice is a concept that expects God to respond "appropriately" to human behavior, with rewards and punishments given in response to right or wrong actions. In contrast, the concept of mercy acknowledges that in fact God does *not* always "deal with us according to our sins, nor repay us according to our iniquities" (Ps. 103:10; cf. 130:3).

Some psalmists lean heavily on the traditions of retributive justice. Psalms of lament frequently call upon God to reward the virtuous and to punish evildoers. The psalmists seem to assume that God's justice will be carried out in observable ways, here on earth, during the lifetime of the one who sins or avoids sin (Ps. 58:11). Thus, human suffering and human prosperity are sometimes (but not always) seen as marks of God's disfavor or favor. "By this I know that you are pleased with me; because my

enemy has not triumphed over me" (Ps. 41:11). At the same time, however, many of the psalmists believe that "no one living" is completely innocent of sin (Ps. 143:2). They appeal to God's mercy and compassion, arguing that on the basis of a strict accounting they could not survive (Ps. 130:3–4). While Psalm 8 celebrates the dominion humans have been given over creation, in spite of our fragile mortality, Psalm 90 complains that we are held more strictly accountable for our sins than our mortality warrants.

When things go wrong in their lives, the psalmists can respond in a variety of different ways. Some psalmists are penitent and humble. They acknowledge, repent of, and ask forgiveness for the sins they assume are the cause of their suffering (Psalms 6; 32; 38; 51; 102; 130; 143). However, other psalmists are indignant and protest their innocence (Psalms 17; 26). The problem, as many of the protesters see it, is not their behavior but the disruption of their expectations. They complain that the ordered structures of life on which they had depended are not functioning properly (Psalm 26). They may even conclude that God has fallen down on the job and needs to be roused or reminded that all is not right in their part of the created world (Psalm 44).

While those who cry out to God in the psalms look in various directions for the origins or the sources of their problems, they look only to God for a solution. Whether they appeal to God's justice or to God's mercy, they all recognize that their salvation lies in God's hands. Even Psalm 88, which ends on a note of deep negativity, is addressed to the "God of my salvation" (88:1).

The most frequently made theological statement in the Psalms is that God's "trustworthy love" is perpetual. As Psalm 136 affirms, everything God does, has done, or will do demonstrates "trustworthy love." Whether the psalmists think of what happens to them under the heading of justice or of mercy, they know they can with confidence put themselves and their fate in God's trustworthy hands (Psalm 73).

Religious tradition has sometimes encouraged believers to define faith as nonresistance to whatever is perceived to be the will of God. The passive, acquiescent child pictured in Psalm 131, contentedly trusting in the care-giving God, is sometimes seen as the only possible model for the true believer to follow. However, this is not the only nor even the most prevalent model of faith presented in the biblical texts. In the book of Psalms the faithful are not always prosperous, healthy, or secure. They are not always content and do not always celebrate the status quo. Those who speak with complete candor in the presence of God, those who articulate their doubts and their pain as well as their trust in God are all included among the faithful in the Psalms. Women who have been taught (like children) to be "seen and not heard" in relation to faith and religion should notice that the very act of putting anger, impatience, and frustration into words often enables the speakers in the Psalms to come to a renewed sense of assurance in God's continuing care. The confessional stance of the psalmists (their willingness to articulate feelings of anger and pain as well as joy in the presence of God, their refusal to submit passively to oppressive circumstances, and their confidence in God's concern for their needs) has had and continues to have a significant influence in shaping the theology, the piety, and the lives of many women.

## BIBLIOGRAPHY

Allen, Leslie C. *Psalms 101–150.* Word Biblical Commentary 21. Waco, Tex.: Word Books, 1983.

Brueggemann, Walter. *The Message of the Psalms: A Theological Commentary.* Augsburg Old Testament Studies. Minneapolis: Augsburg Publishing House, 1984.

Craigie, Peter C. *Psalms 1–50.* Word Biblical Commentary 19. Waco, Tex.: Word Books, 1983.

Hopkins, Denise Dombkowski. *Journey Through the Psalms: A Path to Wholeness.* Kaleidoscope Series. New York: United Church Press, 1990.

Miller, Patrick D., Jr. *Interpreting the Psalms.* Philadelphia: Fortress Press, 1986.

Schreck, Nancy, and Maureen Leach. *Psalms Anew.* Winona, Minn.: Saint Mary's Press, 1986.

Tate, Marvin E. *Psalms 51–100.* Word Biblical Commentary 20. Waco, Tex.: Word Books, 1990.

# PROVERBS

*Carole R. Fontaine*

## Introduction

### Date and Setting

The book of Proverbs is not a unified work, as the various titles for different collections in the text make clear (10:1a; 22:17a; 24:23a; 25:1; 30:1a; 31:1). Although its authorship has been ascribed to Solomon, which would point to an early date, the book in fact seems to have received its final editing in the early postexilic period (last part of the sixth century B.C.E.). Thus, it reflects both the wisdom teachings of the earlier monarchies and the instructional needs of the later Jewish community.

Proverbs is the oldest of the Israelite works that are considered "wisdom literature." It shares a special theological perspective and literary and social setting with Job and Ecclesiastes. Its authors were the bureaucrats or "sages" of their society, working in court circles as counselors and educators, though the book probably also includes elements from folk wisdom that did not originate with its elite editors. These men used literary forms and theological concepts borrowed and modified from wisdom traditions of the surrounding nations, since it is probable that as diplomats they were in closer contact with their counterparts in other countries than would be the average member of society.

### Literary Form and Content

Many of the literary forms found in the work are known from the literature of other peoples. The "Instruction," a sustained poem addressed by a father to a son (or teacher to student, Prov. 1:1–9:18), comes from the Egyptian court. Proverbs 22:17–24:22, for example, mirrors the *Instruction of Amenemope*, from which it was adapted by Israelite sages. "Numerical sayings"

(see Proverbs 30) are attested in Ugaritic literature and are a favorite of the sages. Poems about the virtues of wisdom are frequent, as in the acrostic poem of Prov. 31:10–31. The sages also use commands and prohibitions to make their educational points. The two-line, artistic wisdom saying or proverb dominates the book as the sages' favorite form. These proverbs are written in "parallelism," with the second line of the verse restating, contrasting, or amplifying the thought in the first line. The sages rely most heavily on antithetic parallelism, where the two lines present a contrast. This practice is in harmony with the agenda of the wise men, which is to present recommended behavior in such a way that young men choose the "right path." Such a presentation of life's bewildering variety of choices tends to perpetuate dualism (a thing is either "good" or "bad" in this thinking) and is less helpful when events appear ambiguous—a problem that will later be addressed by Job and Ecclesiastes.

The content of Proverbs is wide-ranging and, like all wisdom literature, distinctive, because of its somewhat foreign flavor. Unlike the Torah and the Prophets, which view God primarily in terms of covenant and national history, for the wisdom tradition God is primarily Creator. God used Wisdom to create the world and placed Wisdom within creation, where people could observe its harmonies and live in right relation to it (Prov. 3:13–20; cf. Job 28). One does not need a special covenant relationship to know God's rules or to be assured of the Creator's blessing—simple common sense and responsible living will ensure that.

Unlike the content of the Prophets, which is often critical of abuses in society, most of the wisdom traditions of Proverbs are associated with the preservation of the status quo of the male elite. One of the ways this may be observed is through the sages' belief in the act–consequence relationship that undergirds much of the thinking in the book. For the wise men, every deed contains within it a corresponding outcome, so that good acts produce good consequences and vice versa. Sin and sloth produce poverty, illness, and social evil. Though the sages know that the poor may be at the mercy of the ruthless whims of the rich, the act–consequence concept makes it easy to blame victims for having caused their own misfortunes, as is the case in the book of Job. With this kind of worldview, the struggle for social justice lacks the energy and zeal observed elsewhere in the Hebrew Bible.

Proverbs 1–9, consisting mostly of instructions and wisdom poems, details the sages' program for education and celebrates the excellence of Wisdom, amazingly personified as a woman. These poems also warn against the perils of Woman Wisdom's "evil twin," Woman Stranger, whose temptations lead to death. These longer compositions act as a theological and literary prologue to the proverb collections that follow. Though most scholars consider this section postexilic, some prefer to date it in the Solomonic period of the tenth century because of the strong Egyptian parallels.

Proverbs 10:1–15:33 is the first collection introduced as "The Proverbs of Solomon." It contains mostly antithetic parallelism and restates many of the themes of the prologue. Proverbs about Yahweh in chap. 15 serve as a link to the next collection. Proverbs 16:1–22:16 is another royal collection of proverbs, covering a wide variety of familiar topics. "The Words of the Wise" in Prov. 22:17– 24:22 is based on the Egyptian *Instruction of Amenemope*, with some parallels to the Aramaic *Words of Ahiqar* as well. It may have served as an educational piece for young men about to enter service in the royal court. Proverbs 25:1–29:27 is a collection "that the officials of King Hezekiah of Judah copied" (25:1); this section may be subdivided further into chaps. 25–27, about nature and economics, and chaps. 28–29, concerning the poor, the king, and justice.

"The Words of Agur Son of Jakeh" in Prov. 30:1–14 returns in part to the instruction style and covers familiar wisdom topics. Proverbs 30:15–33 contains mostly numerical sayings and favors the natural world as a source of knowledge about human society. Proverbs 31:1–9 is highly unusual in presenting an instruction given by the mother of Lemuel rather than the typical father-to-son form. It deals with the duties of rulership along with warnings against women and strong drink, both intoxicants a king should avoid. The book concludes with Prov. 31:10–31, an acrostic poem praising the "Woman of Worth," a human parallel to the remarkable Woman Wisdom of the Prologue.

## The Significance of Proverbs for Women

The significance of this book for women goes far beyond the positive and (mostly) negative comments about women encapsulated in the various proverbs. The figure of Woman Wisdom may be a survival of goddess worship within the monotheistic structure of Israelite theology, since the wisdom traditions of Mesopotamia and Egypt were sanctioned by tutelary goddesses. At the very least, Woman Wisdom represents a synopsis of all the positive roles played by wives and mothers in Israelite society, even as Woman Stranger combines all male fears of female temptation into one figure. Female imagery, positive and negative, begins and ends the book, acting as a lens that focuses men's attention on the meaning of the "good life." As such, it offers a guide to understanding the implications of individual proverbs in chaps. 10–30.

The book also stresses the importance of family life and gives tantalizing glimpses into the important roles of mother and wife. Good wives—providers of obedient, unpaid, silent labor—are so highly prized that they are considered a gift from God. The mother's role in the education of the young is also highlighted by the approving sages, and the household management skills of the hardworking wife are the subject of much praise in Prov. 31:10–31. As always in male-centered scripture, the positive and negative roles of women are viewed primarily from the perspective of what they provide for the men involved. Nowhere does one hear the sages condemn a society that forces some women into prostitution; one hears only warnings about the havoc such women can wreak on a young man's promising career. This is not unique to Israelite wisdom but is typical of the international traditions as well.

Despite the male-centered perspective of the actual text of Proverbs, the intellectual processes that undergird wisdom thinking may also provide resources for women readers. Wisdom values personal experience as the starting place for doing theology and constructing a model of how the world works. Insights drawn from the natural world reveal a high value placed on the deity's revelations encoded within creation. For those who have been mostly excluded from participation in the great traditions of covenant and prophecy, the wisdom tradition's emphasis on the world of daily life offers a basis for valuing women's experience as an authentic, revelatory way of knowing and being.

## Comment

### Wisdom and Folly Personified (chaps. 1–9)

*Proverbs 1.* After a general introduction setting forth what may be learned by heeding the sages' teachings (vv. 2–6), the important concept of "fear of the Lord" is introduced in v. 7. This term refers not simply to the weak's fear of the strong but to the right relationship to God recommended by Israelite religion. The wise men state that such a proper alignment to the Holy One is the prerequisite for wisdom. In 1:8–19 the instruction form appears as the parent/teacher extolls the blessings of wisdom's teachings to the child/pupil. It is important to note that "your mother's teaching" appears in synonymous parallelism with "your father's instruction" in v. 8, signaling the importance of the mother's role in educating the young.

In 1:20–33 the remarkable figure of Woman Wisdom is encountered addressing men from all the busiest parts of the ancient city (vv. 20–21). Who is this female who speaks where judges or prophets customarily issue their condemnations of wrongdoing and prostitutes call out to potential customers? Normally this kind of speech, with its emphasis on divine offer and human rejection (vv. 24–30), is associated only with God or an authorized intermediary such as a prophet. Yet the sages endow this august woman with such power that to disregard her teaching is to court death in the scheme of the act–consequence relationship (vv. 31–33). Scholars speculate that the Israelite figure of Woman Wisdom may reflect international wisdom's association with tutelary goddesses: Sumerian Nisaba, Egyptian Ma'at, or perhaps a Canaanite fertility goddess developed from the Sumerian Inanna or Semitic Ishtar. Others view this figure as an amalgam of the highly valued roles of wife, mother, wise woman, and princess-counselor, which operate as literary paradigms in other portions of scripture. Still others see this figure as a simple literary personification—like modern Mother Nature or Mother Church—but this position does not account adequately for the striking amount of power attributed to a female figure within a male-dominated society.

*Proverbs 2–3.* Instructions resume with the theme of the search for wisdom, which may be understood here as still referring to the personified figure. According to 2:6 wisdom is a gift from God that may guard its possessor from the perils of those who pervert language (2:12). In 2:16 the first encounter with Wisdom's evil twin, the Strange Woman, occurs. Here she is identified with the adulteress who commits treason against the man to whom she belongs (2:17). Like the fertility goddesses who descended to the underworld in ancient myth, her paths lead down to death (2:18–19), though the Israelite sages omit the conclusion of the goddesses' triumphant return to life. The praise of Woman Wisdom takes on a decidedly Egyptian flavor in 3:13–18, where she is portrayed much like the scribal goddess of justice, Ma'at, who holds the symbol for long life, the *ankh*, in one hand and a symbol of power (=riches and honor, 3:16) in the other. Woman Wisdom is likened to a tree of life in 3:18, a symbol familiar from Genesis and with strong ancient Near Eastern roots in the portrayal of vegetation goddesses. In 3:19–20 the first of several important associations of Woman Wisdom with God's activity in creation occurs (see the commentary on chap. 8, below).

*Proverbs 4–7.* The father's voice is heard again in these chapters as Woman Wisdom is recommended to the young in the sort of language that recalls the joy of finding a true mate (4:8–9; 7:4). Warnings against Woman Stranger in chap. 5 (NRSV: "loose woman," 5:3) image her as the negative counterpart of Wisdom. This contrast leads to the inescapable conclusion that the gender of those addressed in these instructions is male. That the adjective chosen to refer to her is "strange, foreign" is an indication of the ambivalent attitudes obtaining among the covenant community at this period (probably postexilic), when ethnic purity was perceived as a serious issue of survival. Most notably, her language, one of the sages' major preoccupations, is seductive and inviting (5:3; 6:24; 7:5, 21) but in the end leads to death and disaster. The literary imagery combines several features: she is viewed as an adulteress who breaks Israelite laws (5:20; 6:24b, 29, 32–35); as a prostitute (5:7–14; 6:26a; 7:10); she is spoken of in language typical of goddesses (5:5; 7:18, 27) and as one who devalues the meaning of cultic religious observances (7:14). Any wrongdoing that may result from an encounter with her is attributed to her powers of persuasion and seductive bearing; the man's complicity and cooperation—other than stupidity—go unnoted. The sages recommend instead that men's sexual thirst be assuaged with their legitimate partners (5:15–20), whose attributes may be equally intoxicating.

**Proverbs 8.** This passage concerning Woman Wisdom's speech of self-praise (vv. 4–21) and role in creation (vv. 22–36) contains two of the most hotly debated compositions in the entire book. As in 1:20–21, Woman Wisdom addresses her audience in public spaces where power is exercised. As she lauds herself in a style reminiscent of Hellenistic praise of the goddess Isis, she makes clear her relationship to the political power: by means of her, kings and princes get and keep their high positions (8:15–16). This may be another place where Egyptian influence occurs, for Ma'at, the goddess of justice, is the literal underpinning of Pharaoh's throne and the language of 8:17a is familiar from various Egyptian texts. These verses may also carry the nuance of Mesopotamian goddess traditions where sexual union with the goddess of fertility confers on the king his right to rule. In the Israelite tradition, one is reminded of 1 Kings 3, where Solomon, who was not the son expected to succeed David, is given the gift of wisdom by God in order to legitimate his reign.

There is disagreement about the correct translation of the first half of 8:22. The verb translated as "created me" in the NRSV is more normally understood as "begot me" (so in the Targum and in Greek and Syriac versions; see Gen. 4:1). It might be better translated "conceived me," because the clause "I was brought forth" in 8:24–25 refers to the activity of the female, not the male, in giving birth. An equally valid reading supported by literalistic ancient translations would be "Yahweh acquired me as the beginning of his way." The problem for monotheistic editors and translators both in antiquity and in modern times has been to avoid the notion that Woman Wisdom is either a sexually conceived child of God or a preexistent entity whom Yahweh acquires in order

to begin creation. Both versions can be supported by Egyptian parallels, where Ma'at is both the child of the creator god and the master plan he uses in his work. Both nuances occur in 8:30, where Woman Wisdom claims that she was daily beside God during creation as a "master worker" (NRSV) or "darling child." The Hebrew term can reasonably be translated either way, and parallels to Ma'at attest to both meanings. Given Wisdom's statement that she was rejoicing in the created order and delighting in humanity, the reading favored here is "darling child."

In 8:32 Wisdom instructs humanity. Her words are more striking than ever, for in v. 35 she states that whoever finds her finds life. This is the sort of thing that only a salvific deity says, so it is no surprise that wisdom creation theology becomes an important source for the theology of the Word (logos) found in the Prologue to the Gospel of John. Other important parallels for this theology of Wisdom occur in Job 28; portions of Job 38–42; Sir. 1:1–10; 4:11–19; 14:20–15:10; 24:1–19; and Wisd. Sol. 7:22–8:1. In the New Testament, see also Matt. 11:19; 23:34–36; Luke 11:49; 1 Cor. 10:4; and Col. 1:15–16.

**Proverbs 9.** The theological introduction to Proverbs ends with the contrast between the invitations of Woman Wisdom and Woman Folly. Wisdom's banquet is set in a house she has built of seven pillars. This is perhaps an allusion to her role in creation, since it was believed in antiquity that the world stood on seven pillars. Woman Wisdom sends out her maids to bring men to her, even as the devotees of the fertility goddesses solicited men to worship their lady. Verses 7–12 sum up a variety of themes from the preceding instructions and act here as the substance of the conversation at Wisdom's table. Oddly, the chapter ends not with Wisdom but with her wicked sister, who directly parodies Wisdom's earlier call to the untutored (9:16; cf. v. 4). The sages end on a dire note: acceptance of her invitation leads to death (9:18). Woman Folly brings together here the selective misogyny of the sages as she symbolizes competing religious traditions, foreignness, frightening female "otherness" as well as pragmatic warnings to young male professionals against such fatal attractions.

## The Proverb Collections (chaps. 10–30)

In contrast to the unified poems of chaps. 1–9, the bulk of the book is composed of collections of individual proverbs. Some may have derived from folk or tribal traditions, especially those that are simply observational rather than hortatory (compare 14:4 with 10:17). Most of the proverbs, however, show signs of high literary artistry and the sages' worldview, where righteousness and wisdom are necessarily rewarded and wickedness, laziness, and folly bring their own punishments. Some scholars view the pragmatic proverbs as representing an earlier stage in wisdom thinking, with subsequent theological compositions added as a later corrective to the somewhat amoral observations of an earlier era. However, if Proverbs 1–9, which is highly theological in tone, is dated to the Solomonic period, then it is not necessarily the case that all the religious and moral proverbs in the collections should be seen as late developments.

***Proverbs 10:1–15:33.*** This collection consists of mostly antithetic (contrasting) proverbs that give concrete examples of themes treated generally in chaps. 1–9. Typical phrases associated with Wisdom in the theological introduction occur, such as "fear of the Lord" (10:27; 14:27; etc.), "fountain of life" (13:14; 14:27), and "tree of life" (11:30; 15:4). The overall tone of this collection is one that affirms the blessings of righteousness, wisdom, and self-control and favorably recommends discipline (12:1; 13:1, 18, 24; 15:10, 12). Psychological insights into human behavior are also a preoccupation here (12:25; 13:12, 19; 14:10, 30; 15:1, 13, 30), as is the usual interest in the power of language (13:3; etc.).

Women who were mentioned earlier in chaps. 1–9 now crop up in individual proverbs. The mother who instructs her child is disappointed by foolishness in her offspring (10:1; 15:20). The fact that the unpleasant outcome of upbringing is mentioned each time in connection with the mother should not be overinterpreted; "mother" is simply the second half of the word pair father/mother in forming the negative contrast of the proverb's parallelism. The gracious woman (11:16) and good wife (12:4) are likewise compared to their negative counterparts, who wreck a man's homelife. Beauty is worthless without knowledge of one's place in patriarchal society, according to 11:22, and women possessing wisdom build up the household (14:1) even as Woman Wisdom built her house in 9:1. Yahweh, who is frequently mentioned in these chapters, shows special concern for the care of widows (15:25).

It is of interest that the sages, despite their adherence to act–consequence principles, do acknowledge the ambiguities of life. Things are not always as they seem on the surface, and the wise would do well to take note: giving can bring riches, while hoarding produces want (11:24); pretense of wealth can hide poverty (13:7); things that appear correct can be disastrous (14:12). In the final analysis, it is better to have little and be happy than to have wealth with continual bitterness (15:17). Such proverbs can be particularly useful to women as they reflect upon their lot in a male-dominated society: What good is material wealth if it is accompanied by abuse? The traditional goals recommended to women may look satisfying at first glance but may be very different in practice.

***Proverbs 16:1–22:16.*** Often understood as a royal collection because of its preoccupation with kingship, this group of proverbs departs from the heavy reliance on antithetic forms. Considerations of the way divine and human perceptions vary is a major theme (16:1, 2, 9, 33; 19:21; 21:2, 30, 31). Humans may plan and plot, but in the end God's way prevails. Psychological observations are made in 16:18; 17:22; 18:14, and ambiguities are again noted in 16:8, 19, 25; 17:1, 28. The excellence of Wisdom appears in familiar terms in 16:16, 22; 18:4; and 19:8. Ma'at, the Egyptian goddess of wisdom against whom the heart of the dead is weighed in the underworld, may provide imagery for Yahweh's judgments in 16:2 and 17:3.

Parent-child relationships also constitute a major theme for this collection. A wise slave is preferred to a shameful child (17:2), but grandchildren are fondly extolled as the "crown of the aged" (17:6). In 17:25 one finally meets a foolish child who is a grief to both mother *and* father. The sages suggest strong discipline to avert such calamities (19:18; 22:15). The act–consequence relationship operates even among the young, so children can be known by their acts (20:11). If children are trained when they are young, there is hope (22:6). The sages recognize that childrearing can go astray, producing offspring who do violence or abandon their parents (19:26), and they try to guard against this with an exhortation (20:20). Unfortunately, the sages were unaware of the modern psychological insights into the cycle of domestic violence, for their approval of child beating in 22:15 is likely to produce only another generation of abusers. It is important to note that the sages come from a society that valued its children as precious gifts from God and probably did not treat them simply as disposable commodities or available victims on whom parents could freely vent their frustrations. The kind of corporal punishment of which they approve was probably not considered excessive or violent in their day, but it is still doubtful whether their ideas on this topic should be implemented today without serious consideration.

Female imagery occurs in 17:12, where a she-bear robbed of her cubs is considered safer than a fool (she-bears were noted for their protective nature toward offspring and were considered especially violent). Lady Tongue, the personification of "Language" appears in 18:21. Good and bad wives are the subject in 18:22; 19:13, 14; 21:9, 19; the good wife is considered a blessing from Yahweh, but the quarrelsome wife makes a desert seem like paradise. A warning against Woman Stranger ends this collection in 22:14, just as Woman Folly ended the theological prologue in 9:13–18.

***Proverbs 22:17–30:33.*** Proverbs 22:17–24:22, based on the Egyptian *Instruction of Amenemope,* follows the instruction form as it discusses traditional themes. The word pair father/mother occurs in 23:22; the prostitute is again associated with the Pit in 23:27–28. Wisdom, praised throughout, builds up a household in 24:3. In 24:23 another short collection begins, perhaps an addendum to the previous group, and is followed in 25:1–29:27 by a group of proverbs collected by the sages of King Hezekiah of Judah (25:1). Within this group, proverbs about the "contentious wife" appear to be a traditional favorite (25:24; 27:15–16). Children who delight or disappoint their parents are considered (28:7, 24; 29:3, 15). Discipline of children and slaves is advised (29:17, 19). Though the sages are quick to condemn violent behavior in others as a sign of lack of self-control, they are quite willing to recommend it to men for controlling their own households (cf. 13:24; 19:18). Since the collectors of these proverbs are the same ones who advise a person counseling the king in 25:15 to use patience and a soft tongue, it can only be assumed that a double standard is in operation here. Against those who cannot defend themselves—wives, children, slaves—violence is permissible; with those of higher status, gentler means must suffice.

***Proverbs 30.*** Typical wisdom themes surface again in this collection of oracles attributed to "Agur son of Jakeh." His name may be translated symbolically as referring to Israel as the "Sojourner" (*ger*) who is the figurative son of Yahweh. Rhetorical questions, prohibitions, proverbs, and numerical sayings are used. Concerns about those who dishonor their parents occur in 30:11 and 17, with dire warnings. In 30:15 the two "daughters" of the leech may refer to that small creature's suckers. Some commentators suggest here a connection to Lilith, the bloodsucking night demon of men's fears from Mesopotamia. A barren womb, antiquity's symbol of women's unfulfillment of their social and biological functions, is compared to the ever-hungry underworld of Sheol, whose greed is never satisfied. In 30:19 attraction between the sexes is viewed as being as mysterious as other natural phenomena concerning movement of a small thing through or across a larger expanse (eagle through the sky, snake on a rock, ship through the sea) and so may be a symbolic reference to the sexual act itself. The word "girl" (NRSV) refers to a young woman of childbearing age.

In 30:20 the image of eating is used euphemistically to refer to the "appetites" of the adulteress, who sees no wrong in fulfilling herself. This image recalls the invitation to partake of stolen water and secret bread issued by Woman Folly in 9:17. Other typical female stereotypes occur in 30:23 as things to be abhorred: the unloved woman who finally succeeds in marrying and the slave woman whose sexual services to the husband succeed in undercutting her mistress's status. One is clearly reminded of the conflicts between the barren wife and the fertile co-wife of lesser status, such as those that take place between Sarah and Hagar in Genesis 16.

***Conclusion.*** After the lengthy poems in Proverbs 1–9 comparing Woman Wisdom to Woman Stranger, the adulteress, and Woman Folly, much of the overt female imagery disappears in the proverb collections of chaps. 10–30 that focus on concrete examples from everyday life. Still, the male authors and collectors made their view of women felt by what they chose to include and leave out. While there are many proverbs about the misfortune of living with a quarrelsome woman, there are no balancing sayings about the dreadful plight of being matched to an abusive, violent man. While fools, scoffers, drunkards, and sluggards are roundly condemned, it is primarily from the perspective of their interactions with other men in society. Little is said about the devastation a drunkard might wreak on his family or the damage a liar or an adulterer might do to the household at large. Deprived of full social standing and power, women with miserable, vicious husbands might be just as capable as the wife of Prov. 31:10–31 and still have it come to nothing if the heads of the household chose to squander resources. Doubtless, forms of social control for women in such situations existed: close kin might choose to exert their influence to improve the situation, but all of these considerations are lost as the sages give a picture of domestic ills from one perspective only.

Similarly, from the book of Proverbs one would think that no young man could walk down the street without receiving licentious propositions from women on all sides. The adulterer is considered stupid to risk reputation and life in such behavior, but the worst imagery—that of death and the Pit—is reserved for the female partner in the act. The custom of arranged marriages, with women assigned to inferior roles, created the conditions that might make women want to participate in such behavior, but nothing is said of this nor of the regulations regarding inheritance, which might force a woman to prostitution. The sages view their society and its ills through the narrow focus of the privileged male, so the picture presented is a lopsided and partial one at best.

### The Mother's Torah (chap. 31)

The final chapter of the book returns to the strong female figures who opened the work in chaps. 1–9, but here they are in human rather than metaphorical dress. The chapter is divided into two sections: vv. 1–9, the instruction of the mother of King Lemuel, and vv. 10–31, a composition in praise of the Woman of Worth.

*Proverbs 31:1–9.* Although the instruction form occurs in chaps. 1–9 and 22–24, Prov. 31:1–9 is the first and only occurrence of an instruction attributed to the mother rather than the father. Various proverbs have indicated the mother's role in teaching children, but here a concrete example is finally presented. Interestingly, it does not deviate from the treatment of the standard wisdom themes (duties of rulership, warnings against intoxication, defense of the helpless) and shows that the elite mother, if this passage is indeed by a woman, has internalized the male fear of women so prevalent throughout the book (31:3a).

What accounts for this fear, especially as it appears here in a royal context? Political marriages were the rule in ancient times, and wives and daughters were given and taken to cement alliances. Foreign wives often existed in the courts of their husbands with a "support" group brought with them from their native country. Such a group might easily form the nucleus of a political faction capable of "seducing" a weak-willed king from the interests of his own country in favor of humoring his wife. The Deuteronomistic historian envisions something of this sort when he blames Solomon's foreign wives for that king's departure from the proper worship of the god of his fathers (1 Kings 11:1–8). Other examples of the power exercised by royal wives occur in 1 Kings 15:13; 19:1–3; 21:1–16; 2 Kings 9:22; 11:1, and are generally viewed in a negative light. The fears of Lemuel's mother were not without political and historical foundation, though the passage here may also refer to the folk idea that sexual relations with women are debilitating to men, an idea still endorsed in athletics, theater, and opera in modern times.

Though the queen mother warns against too much indulgence in strong drink in 31:4–5, her prohibitions are contextual. In 31:6–7, she notes that intoxicants can be a blessing to those who are suffering and hopeless. That Lemuel's mother intends this behavior only as a last resort is clear from 31:8–9: drugs are no lasting remedy for social injustice, and it is up to the king to champion the helpless.

*Proverbs 31:10–31.* The words usually translated "a capable," "perfect," or "good" wife mean literally "a woman of worth," for the term for "woman" and "wife" is the same in Hebrew. "Worth" is a term more often applied to men, as in the phrase usually translated "mighty man," and denotes persons at the height of their powers and capacities. The poem is an acrostic; that is, each line begins with a letter following the order of the Hebrew alphabet (cf. Psalms 9–10; 25; 119; Lamentations 1– 4). Comparison of the capable wife to rare jewels in 31:10 reminds one of Woman Wisdom in 3:15 and 8:11. Again as with Woman Wisdom, the man who possesses her will lack for nothing (31:11–12). Her industry is far-reaching: she works at traditional female tasks herself (vv. 13–14, 19, 22, 24), directs others (vv. 15, 27), shows compassion to the poor (v. 20), and speaks and teaches the "wisdom of loving-kindness/covenant love" (v. 26). In all, she is the living embodiment of Woman Wisdom's teachings and attributes and does not rely on simple appearances (vv. 25–26, 30).

The family unit pictured here is an elite one, in keeping with the sages' social background and goals. The wealth of the woman and the forethought with which she provides for the future well-being of her home are more than a simple reflection of the milieu of the sages, however. Just as Woman Wisdom began the book with promises of wealth, happiness, honor, and long life as the reward for following her prudent teachings, the Woman of Worth and her fine household represent the concrete fulfillment of those earlier promises and so make a fitting conclusion to the work. While there is evidence here of possibilities that only elite women could realize in their everyday lives (the purchase of land, for example, in v. 16), it is likely that this picture of rosy contentment and good fortune is held up as a goal to which all wives, regardless of their social status, ought to aspire. As seen earlier, the success of this woman is viewed from the perspective of what she provides for her husband and children. It is her fulfillment of the roles in the home assigned to her by society that causes her to be praised in the very gates of the city where Woman Wisdom first raised her cry.

## BIBLIOGRAPHY

Camp, Claudia V. *Wisdom and the Feminine in the Book of Proverbs.* Bible and Literature 11. Sheffield: Almond Press, 1985.

——. "Wise and Strange: An Interpretation of the Female Imagery in Proverbs in the Light of Trickster Mythology." *Semeia* 42 (1988), 14–36.

Crenshaw, James L. *Old Testament Wisdom: An Introduction.* Atlanta: John Knox Press, 1981.

Fontaine, Carole R. "Proverbs." In *Harper's Bible Commentary,* edited by James L. Mays, pp. 495–515. San Francisco: Harper & Row, 1988.

Lang, Bernhard. *Wisdom and the Book of Proverbs: An Israelite Goddess Redefined.* New York: Pilgrim Press, 1986.

Newsom, Carol A. "Woman and the Discourse of Patriarchal Wisdom: A Study of Proverbs 1–9." In *Gender and Difference in Ancient Israel,* edited by Peggy L. Day, pp. 142–160. Philadelphia: Fortress Press, 1989.

Rad, Gerhard von. *Wisdom in Israel.* Nashville: Abingdon Press, 1972.

Vawter, Bruce. "Prov. 8:22: Wisdom and Creation." *Journal of Biblical Literature* 99 (1980), 205–216.

# ECCLESIASTES

*Carole R. Fontaine*

## Introduction

### Date, Setting, and the Identity of the Author(s)

Although traditionally attributed to Solomon (Eccl. 1:1), Ecclesiastes could not have been written by him. The language of the book contains late words and grammatical forms borrowed from Aramaic and Persian. Scholars place the composition of the book sometime between 250 B.C.E. and the Maccabean revolt of 167 B.C.E. Because the author has adopted the fiction of kingly background and speaks as a wisdom sage, he probably belonged to the elite of Jerusalem.

The Hebrew title of Ecclesiastes, *Qohelet*, comes from the word meaning "to gather, assemble" and displays a grammatically feminine form, though it is highly unlikely that this sage was female. The name may refer to the author's role as a teacher who assembled students or perhaps to his role as a collector of wisdom forms. He may have taught in a school in Jerusalem, even though he often seems a renegade in his attitudes toward traditional wisdom teachings. The contradictions observed throughout the book have raised questions about its unity. Some scholars believe that Ecclesiastes quotes traditional positions to which he then replies with his own contrasting view. There is clear evidence of at least one other voice besides the main author's in 12:9–14, where the epilogue departs from first-person speech.

### Form and Contents

The work belongs to wisdom literature, although it differs from Proverbs and Job in significant ways. In structure, it uses typical wisdom forms: collections of proverbs, parables, anecdotes, reflections, and wisdom poetry. The theme of "vanity" or futility summarizes the author's reflections, and seven times he exhorts his hearers to enjoy life, since death is the inevitable end for humanity (2:24–26; 3:12–13, 22; 5:18–20; 8:15; 9:7–10; 11:7–10). Even wisdom has little power to prevent the ultimacy of death and hence is limited in value (2:12–17). Male experience is assumed as the starting point, and the author's words are directed to a male audience. Unlike in Proverbs, where Wisdom, personified as Woman, is accessible and loving, for Ecclesiastes it is far off (7:23–24). Unlike Job, who never questioned that God was involved, Ecclesiastes' God is distant, unknowable, and possibly indifferent (3:11, 18; 5:1–2; 6:1–2; etc.).

## Comment

### The Great Experiment (1:2–3:22)

As part of his royal fiction, Ecclesiastes describes his endeavors to discover the meaning of life. After opening with a poem that describes the monotony of nature and the impossibility of anything new or memorable, he speaks of his tests of pleasure, status, and intellectual pursuits. None of these was found sufficient to give meaning to life—no matter how many slaves, concubines, singers, pleasure gardens, and fountains he acquired, he still found no meaning in his possessions. His search for wisdom ended similarly, leading him to hate his life (2:17).

Significantly, the author never speaks of entering a meaningful relationship and so lives in a world where he is the only true subject. Nature, women, and other social inferiors remain objects for his use, so naturally he suffers the boredom of the elite who exist in a world populated only by themselves. Callous dismissals of the plight of the oppressed are symptoms of the same self-centered, elite male worldview (4:1–3; 5:8–9). With such thought, it is no wonder he concludes that it is better never to have been born (4:3; 6:1–6). Given women's traditional association with "nature" and their role in childbearing, the misogyny expressed (7:26) is no surprise. Ecclesiastes has no use for the contributions women are allowed to make to society: for him children are lazy usurpers who will forget the man who labored so hard for the goods he leaves behind (2:18–19).

Ecclesiastes' book is beset by contradictions, however. Given life's futility, the best course is to enjoy what life one has to the fullest, because the dead know nothing (3:9–22; 9:4–6, 10). Hence, some association with women is inevitable (3:5–6, where v. 6, concerning "throwing away" and "gathering stones together," is a veiled reference to sexual intercourse). Women, culturally designated as providers of sustenance, entertainment, and sexual services, are required for a man to enjoy his life and "seize the day." Interestingly, this advice echoes a much more ancient text, the *Gilgamesh Epic* from Mesopotamia. There Siduri, the divine tavernkeeper, a wise woman herself, admonishes Gilgamesh to forsake his heroic quest for immortality and accept human mortality. In the face of death, she too counsels for the enjoyment of life, including the pleasure of relationships with wife and children.

### Partnership—Pleasure or Peril? (4:1–11:10)

Given Ecclesiastes' disillusionment with life and people, his sudden praise of partnership in 4:9–12 represents another surprising twist. Although he views companionship solely from the perspective of what it can do for the ego in control, he judges it good to have help. A friend can provide aid, warmth at night, and protection. He quotes a proverb familiar from Mesopotamian wisdom (4:12b, the threefold cord) to sum up his view that two are better than one.

"The woman who brings death," a familiar figure in scripture, reappears in 7:26–29. Ecclesiastes' remarks are so virulent that they were quoted in the fifteenth-century Inquisitors' witchhunting manual, *Malleus Maleficarum*, to sanction torture of women accused of witchcraft. Warnings to young men against involvement with "undesirable" women are common in ancient Near Eastern wisdom. However, Ecclesiastes' condemnation makes little distinction between "good" and "bad" women, since he claims never to have found a female who met his high standards. He may also be alluding here to his inability to find a suitable wife, since "find a woman" in Hebrew may also refer to the taking of a wife. Some scholars suggest that he is once again quoting a traditional argument which he then refutes (cf. 2:13–14), but there is little evidence here that Ecclesiastes disagrees with the conventional misogyny he may be quoting.

Another reverse occurs in 9:9. Is this the same author who issued warnings in 7:26–29, or is he simply bowing to the inevitability of marital entanglements? When Ecclesiastes counsels the enjoyment of life's simple pleasures, he always notes that this is one's "portion" from God and, as such, is sealed with divine approval. In the face of death, which stretches on endlessly, people ought to savor the joys of being human.

### The Significance of Ecclesiastes for Women

While the author's view of women is unappealing, there are certain wholesome trends within his thought that deserve attention. Ecclesiastes grounds his philosophy of life firmly in his personal experience. He contradicts some of the most basic tenets of biblical faith—his idea of an uninvolved, distant God is fairly unorthodox, though not totally new (cf. Job)—and even finds wisdom itself to be of limited use. Such revisioning of the basic givens of his tradition authorizes similar moves today, and his guardedly positive valuation of the pleasures of the natural world and the body is a precursor of feminist theology. As unpleasant as some of his attitudes toward women might be, he is the creature of his times, echoing the ancient warnings of the sages even as he advocates celebrating life. This infuriating yet courageous little book witnesses to the integrity of a tradition that does not try to suppress such unorthodox male voices.

# BIBLIOGRAPHY

Crenshaw, James L. *Old Testament Wisdom: An Introduction.* Atlanta: John Knox Press, 1981.

———. "Qoheleth in Current Research." *Hebrew Annual Review* 7 (1983), 41–56.

Fox, Michael V. *Qohelet and His Contradictions.* Journal for the Study of the Old Testament Supplement Series 71. Sheffield: Almond Press, 1989.

Gordis, Robert. *Koheleth—The Man and His World.* 1951. Reprint. New York: Schocken Books, 1968.

Murphy, Roland E. "Qoheleth's 'Quarrel' with the Fathers." In *From Faith to Faith,* edited by G. Y. Hadidian, pp. 235–245. Pittsburgh: Pickwick Press, 1979.

———. *The Tree of Life: An Exploration of Biblical Wisdom Literature.* The Anchor Bible Reference Library. New York: Doubleday, 1990.

Rad, Gerhard von. *Wisdom in Israel.* Nashville: Abingdon Press, 1972.

# SONG OF SONGS

*Renita J. Weems*

## Introduction

Readers attempting to read the Song of Songs for the first time are invariably astonished to discover that such sexually provocative language and imagery can be found in the Bible. Contained in the eight brief chapters of this little-read book are some very titillating romantic speeches between a woman and her suitor. Their exchanges about their love, passion, desire, and longing for each other can hardly be matched by classical secular romance writings. Indeed, Song of Songs' contents seem to stand in stark contradiction to other portions of the Bible, both Old and New Testaments, where human sexuality in general is regarded as requiring careful governing and female sexuality in particular, serious restraint. It is no surprise, therefore, that the matter of the Song's place within the Bible has been and continues to be the subject of considerable debate and speculation. To see the Song of Songs, however, as some have, simply as a collection of love poems celebrating human sexuality is in the end to fail to appreciate the book's unique social and ideological significance. In fact, in the Song of Songs human sexuality is explored and delighted in so as to make some very specific assertions about female sexuality, to counter some definite notions about beauty, and to insist in a rather dramatic manner on a woman and a man's right to love, irrespective of prevailing cultural norms, whomever their heart chooses.

Besides its erotic contents, two striking characteristics help set the Song apart from the rest of the Bible. First, nowhere in the book's eight chapters is God mentioned. The book of Esther is the only other book in the Bible that compares in this regard; and although it does not mention God, Esther does presuppose God and worship in its references to praying, fasting, and the celebration of the feast of Purim. That the Song of Songs does not contain any direct reference to the deity and therefore does not seem to offer any direct insight into divine law or sacred history contributes to the impression that the book is one of the most secular of all the biblical writings.

The second distinguishing characteristic is that the protagonist in the Song is the only unmediated female voice in scripture. The voice and thoughts of the anonymous woman are conveyed to the reader not through a narrator's voice (as, e.g., in Esther or Ruth) but through monologues, soliloquies, and love songs. Nowhere else in scripture do the thoughts, imaginations, yearnings, and words of a woman predominate in a book as in the Song of Songs. To the extent that the Song, as a part of the canon, does express religious insight, that too is mediated through a woman.

### The Book of Love Songs

The Hebrew title of the book provides a helpful clue to the kind of literature contained within it. Most commentators translate the Hebrew literally—though flatly—"the Song of Songs." Careful attention to the form of the book suggests, however, that the book's title, also known in English as "The Song(s) of Solomon," might be better translated "The Song of Many Songs," or "The Song Comprised of Songs." The syntax also allows for one other way of translating the title, as a superlative: "The Most Excellent of Songs."

The book is a collection of beautifully composed love songs, or a chorus of poems. The exact number (14, 18, 28, or 31?) depends on the literary criteria used to divide the book into units. While the Bible is full of examples of history and theology set to song (e.g., the Song at the Sea in Exodus 15, Hannah's Song in 1 Samuel 2, the book of Psalms, the Magnificat in Luke 1:46–55), the Song of Songs finds its closest parallels in ancient Near Eastern love poems, where the poetry is noted for its frankness, openness, tenderness, desperate longing, and bold erotic outbursts between the lover and the beloved.

## Author and Date

The attribution to Solomon in 1:1 is in all likelihood an editorial gloss and was probably inserted either to suggest that King Solomon, a renowned composer (1 Kings 5:12), wrote these songs himself or inspired their composition, perhaps as a result of his notorious fondness for foreign wives (1 Kings 11:3) or to associate the book with a tradition of thinkers, the wisdom circle, who would have been responsible for the book's preservation and transmission through the centuries and whose origins most likely date back to Solomon's reign.

Despite the attribution to Solomon, one is struck by the amount and quality of speech credited to women in the Song. The emotions and experiences of the female protagonist and the Jerusalem daughters are at the center, not the periphery, of the poetry. That their emotions and experiences ring authentic and their words represent the only unmediated female voices in the Bible have led more than one scholar to speculate whether the poet might be a woman. There is no compelling evidence to the contrary. The sophisticated nature of the poetry, coupled with imagery that implies a familiarity with patrician culture (e.g., the reference to her own vineyard in 1:6, the royal wedding procession in 3:6–11; the scattered references to fine spices, fruits, perfumes, and fruits), suggests that the author may have been associated with a group of intellectuals (e.g., wisdom circle). Indeed, a likely author of the Song of Songs may well have been one of Solomon's many foreign wives (1 Kings 11:1–3) who, as a member of the ruling elite, would have probably been at least modestly educated.

While the archaic grammatical and linguistic forms found in the book suggest that some version of the book dates back to the early period in Israel's history, lyrical compositions are notoriously difficult to date. Indeed, much of their appeal is owing to their seemingly timeless, universal application to the human situation. Although there is little reason to doubt that the lyrical heritage of the Song dates back as early as the time of Solomon's reign or earlier, the theme of the lovers' insistence on the right to love each other irrespective of social norms fits best within a later period in Israel's history when the lyrics of the Song could have served as a rejoinder to attempts to restrict social relations along ethnic, class, and geographical lines.

## Structure and Contents

The book's unusual perspective, the presence of different speakers, the identification of varying themes—to name a few literary features—have prompted unusually divergent proposals for understanding the social, religious, and literary context of the Song of Songs. The book has been viewed as a dramatization of a cult ceremony reenacting an ancient fertility rite uniting the deity and the nation in a sacred marriage; as a single love poem unified by the repetition of key phrases, words, and motifs; and as an allegory, where the original meaning of the book idealizes, from the Hebrew perspective, the love of God for Israel and, from the Christian perspective, the love of Christ for the church. Opinions vary, and no consensus has emerged.

The presence of speakers, dialogue, and audiences indeed does give the poetry of the Song an unmistakably dramatic tone and has prompted some modern readers to conclude that the Song is a drama. As a genre, however, drama suggests unity and a discernible plot. Close examination of the Song of Songs shows that only after considerable rearrangement and structural impositions and only by ignoring a number of other features of the book (e.g., shifts in setting, moods, and perspectives) might one claim literary uniformity and consistent characterization within the book.

The most salient clue to the book's organization may be the shifts in speakers—despite the occasional uncertainty about the identity (3:6–11) and gender (6:13b) of the speakers. Consider the Jerusalem daughters, for example. Sometimes supportive (6:1), sometimes skeptical (5:9; 6:13), and sometimes celebrative (1:4b) of the lovers' affaire, theirs is the only voice that repeatedly intrudes itself into this otherwise private dialogue between the woman and her suitor. And while admittedly their interjections do not necessarily offer a discernible structural design to the book, they do function within the poetry to buttress, goad, inquire, and provoke the emotions, words, and thoughts of the two lovers. In fact, what one finds in the Song of Songs is one of those rare cases where form and content cohere. The wide range of emotions, the abrupt changes in settings, and the shifts from one speaker to another only accentuate the pathos of the poetry with its focus on the passionate, bewitching, vacillating, and unpredictable character of human love.

## Comment

### The Rhetoric of Love, Sex, and the Erotic

Poets, like prophets, rely on metaphors, because they are frequently trying to talk about the most elusive of human experiences—peace, hope, joy, community, death, faith, and so on. The poet of the Song of Songs finds herself having to rely on metaphors even more in her attempt to describe the most elusive of all human experiences: love. The language is often as bewitching as the imagery, alternating between ambiguity (8:8–10) and explicitness (2:4–7), reality (1:5–7) and fantasy (5:2–8), the literal (3:6–11) and the metaphorical (4:16). It insists that the reader experience in reading what the lovers experience in their romance: the elusive yet visceral nature of passion. Love dictates its own rhetoric.

Because love defies easy definition, the poet does not place in the mouths of the two lovers in the Song of Songs abstract discourses about the nature of love, nor impartial assessments of the other, nor precise descriptions of what the two lovers look like. Instead, the two lovers describe love and their vision of each other in poetic images (e.g., fruits, flowers, animals) that capture how they experience love sensually. Theirs is a "joyous capitulation to the senses," where the two lovers delight in each other's taste (2:3; 4:11; 5:1), touch (7:6–9), smell (1:12–14; 4:16), and the sound of each other's voice (2:8, 14; 5:16). They present an experience of love that elaborates unashamedly and unapologetically on the physical pleasures of love. Throughout the book, in their praises of each other's body (4:1–7; 5:10–16; 6:4–10; 7:1–5), the lovers rhapsodize about those parts of the body that one explores and luxuriates in during sexual intercourse (e.g., lips, teeth, hair, neck, thighs, breasts, navel, vulva). Unfortunately, the distance between ancient and modern culture prevents modern audiences from being able to appreciate many of the details of the poet's imagination and references (e.g., 2:15; 6:13b).

Modern readers are the poorer for it. Nevertheless, the poetry that is straightforward is nothing less than erotic.

The lovers talk openly and repeatedly about their love, their lovemaking, their longing and desire for each other. The modern reader with modest sensibilities is tempted to "rescue" this erotic language and view the love spoken of here as in fact platonic and pristine. Erotic literature, however, such as the Song of Songs, stands in stark contrast to pornographic literature. The latter, it has been argued, stresses sensation without feeling. The woman in touch with her sensuality, however, is a woman empowered.

Certainly the female protagonist in the Song of Songs stands out in biblical literature as a woman who insists on her right to initiate love, to feel, to enjoy, and to explore the power of her sexuality. She feels good about herself and basks in her beloved's desire for her. In fact, her love and praise for her beloved (as well as his for her) are so forward, so uncompromising, so urgent that it almost sounds argumentative. Might this be, beneath the surface of the rhetoric of sexuality, a clue to the book's purpose? Might their expressions of love be filled with such frankness, such insistence, because theirs is a love affaire, the author assumed, that would have met with protest from the typical Israelite audience? It seems that the poet assumed that her audience needed to be persuaded of the suitability of this woman and man's love for each other.

### The Social World Inscribed in the Song of Songs

From the historian's point of view, love poetry is perhaps the most beguiling of all compositions. Its appeal is owing to its seemingly timeless, universal relevance. Yet love poetry, like all literature, emerges out of very particular social and material settings: that is, love poetry simultaneously preserves and promotes certain views about social reality and seeks either to challenge or to defend the way in which people are socially constituted. In short, love poetry is beguiling but not guileless.

Just beneath the surface of this otherwise beautiful chorus of love poems is an almost imperceptible yet unmistakable debate. The candor of the sexual speeches, the sometimes skeptical tone of the Jerusalem daughters (5:9; 6:13a), the beloved's repeated refrain to the Jerusalem daughters (2:7), and her occasionally defensive remarks (1:6; 6:13b), among other things, lend a polemical tone to the entire book. The fundamental assumption here is that poets, like ancient and modern speakers, design their messages with a specific audience in mind: to instruct, build upon, defend, challenge, or correct prevailing assumptions. In other words, literature is inescapably political. In the case of the Song of Songs, the subtle defensive tone of the book hints that the poet understood that some aspect(s) of the lovers' relationship were in contradiction to prevailing norms. She builds on her assumptions about her audience and exploits their own utopian desires, as she attempts to uncover and debunk the respectable prejudices of her audience in her defense of their right to love one another.

What might be some clues within the rhetoric of the poetry of subtle yet underlying polemic?

1. There is first the matter of the woman's physical appearance. The protagonist assumes, whether correctly or incorrectly, that her blackish complexion, which she claims was the result of having been put to labor by her brothers in her vineyard, made her the object of the stares of her female companions, the Jerusalem daughters (1:5–6). Whether the women stare at her out of admiration, prejudice, or curiosity one can only guess from other statements in the poetry. But the protagonist's remarks about her own black skin contrast with those of the Jerusalem daughters, who in 7:1 are skeptical of what the male suitor sees in the Shulammite, a woman who besides her dark color evidently had the misfortune to have small breasts as well (8:8). From their skeptical comments one begins to understand that there are reasons why the beloved and her lover devote considerable amounts of space to praising one another's physical appearance (4:1–7; 5:10–16; 6:4–10; 7:1–5). Over and again the beloved suitor insists that his lover is beautiful, irresistibly so (1:9–11, 15; 4:1, 9; 6:4, 9)—despite what others may think. Is this simply the extravagant gush of lovesick lovers? Perhaps not.

Commentators generally steer away from attributing any ethnic import to the woman's dark complexion, preferring rather to see the protagonist as perhaps the victim of class prejudice. The argument is that in ancient Oriental culture the light-complexioned woman who had the luxury of remaining indoors during the day was preferred over the dark-complexioned woman who was constrained to labor outdoors in the sun. There is one hint, however, that ethnicity may be at issue. Michael Goulder has argued that the reference in 7:1, commonly translated the "daughter of nobility" (NRSV: "queenly maiden"), actually refers to the protagonist's hometown of Nadiv in Arabia.

2. The often-repeated refrain, "I adjure you, O daughters of Jerusalem, . . . do not stir up or awaken love until it is ready!" (2:7; 3:5; 8:4) has been interpreted in various ways. Marcia Falk argues convincingly that here the protagonist tries to dissuade her audience, the Jerusalem daughters, from interfering with the love that she fantasizes about, presumably not until it has had the opportunity to materialize. With that in mind, she proposes a better translation: "O women of the city, swear by the wild field doe not to wake or rouse us till we fulfill our love." This translation certainly captures the underlying tension between the protagonist and the Jerusalem women.

3. The lovers are always having quick departures and hasty escapes. They must continually seek one another out (5:6), never quite fulfilled (5:8), never quite satisfied by their time together. As certainly as she beckons him to her, the beloved must shoo him away (8:14), perhaps for his safety, perhaps for hers (5:7). The only way she imagines that their love might win the approval of society would be for them to have been sister and brother or otherwise (ethnically?) related. Then neither in the streets nor in her mother's chambers would their kisses be despised (8:1). Evidently something prevents their love affaire from being public and forces their rendezvous, whether real or imagined, to be carried on in clandestine settings. Even there they are hasty, secretive, and often interrupted.

4. Three times the woman contends that her beloved suitor belongs to her (2:16; 6:3; 7:10). Taken alone, her statement might be properly seen as mere assertion: as far as she is concerned the two belong together. But when viewed within the context of the other defensive statements, her words become insistent. In fact, in one refrain she insists that her beloved's

desire is for her only, despite what others may think (7:10).

The point here is that the love poetry in the Song of Songs is not innocent of controversy. To interpret it simply as a paean to human sexuality and love is not only to modernize the book but to ignore certain other suggestions within the book that something more complex and subtle is beneath the surface. It is not simply the beauty of love and the wholesomeness of human sexuality in the abstract that the lovers insist on. It is the beauty of *their* love for each other and their irresistible attraction to each other that they insist on. They are two lovers whom society, for inscrutable reasons, sought to keep apart, perhaps because they were from different classes, from different ethnic backgrounds, or of a different color.

That the polemical tone underlying these poems is often overlooked by modern readers says as much about the poet's ingenuity as it does about modern readers' obtuseness. Casting her argument in the form of love poetry rather than outright disputation speeches (e.g., Deutero-Isaiah) or a protest novel (e.g., Jonah) was a shrewd rhetorical strategy: the poet was able to arrest the attention of her audience and win their imaginative consent because through love poetry she was able to appeal to the universal urge in an audience for reciprocated love and fulfilling intimacy despite their prejudices.

### Religion, Sexuality, and Culture

It is one thing to speculate about the ways in which the Song of Songs may have originally functioned as literature within ancient Israel. It is another thing to talk about the manner in which the Song functions within the canon. There it ceases to be a critique of culture alone and becomes a critique of scripture as well. Within the context of the Old Testament, the Song of Songs has been seen by some as a commentary or midrash on other portions of scripture which undermine human sexuality in general and female sexuality in particular. An obvious story that the Song counterbalances is the creation story in Genesis 2–3. As a result of the event in the garden, there is a rupture in creation, disharmony between woman and man, an imbalance in social relations, the subjugation of the woman, and, by implication, the demise of mutual sexual fulfillment. Without the Song of Songs, the prevailing stories in the Bible about women would be those where women are penalized and scandalized for their sexuality, confined to procreation without fulfilling sex, and forgotten because of their submission to repressive gender roles. With the Song, women find in the Bible permission to initiate, enjoy, and long for the erotic. The Song of Songs advocates balance in female and male relationships, urging mutuality not domination, interdependence not enmity, sexual fulfillment not mere procreation, uninhibited love not bigoted emotions. It adjures us not to disturb love but to allow relations to ripen into full bloom following their own course, not to impose on relationships our own biased preconceptions about what is appropriate and inappropriate sexual behavior, who makes a suitable mate and who does not. It is a text that deserves repeated reading and reflection by modern audiences.

## BIBLIOGRAPHY

Falk, Marcia. *Love Lyrics from the Bible, The Song of Songs: A New Translation and Interpretation.* San Francisco: Harper-Collins, 1990.

Goulder, Michael D. *The Song of Fourteen Songs.* Journal for the Study of the Old Testament Supplement Series 36. Sheffield: JSOT Press, 1986.

Lorde, Audre. *Sister Outsider.* Trumansburg, N.Y.: The Crossing Press, 1984.

Pope, Marvin H. *Song of Songs.* Anchor Bible 7C. Garden City, N.Y.: Doubleday & Co., 1977.

Trible, Phyllis. "Love's Lyrics Redeemed." In her *God and the Rhetoric of Sexuality*, pp. 144–165. Overtures to Biblical Theology. Philadelphia: Fortress Press, 1978.

Weems, Renita J. *Marriage, Sex, and Violence: Ancient Israelite Rhetoric and Audience.* Minneapolis: Fortress Press (forthcoming).

# ISAIAH

## Susan Ackerman

Appearances, the cliché tells us, can be deceiving. In the Bible this is nowhere more true than in the book of Isaiah. This book, with its sixty-six chapters, is the longest composition in the prophetic corpus. One might thus reasonably expect it to contain the most complete record of a biblical prophet's life and thought. Instead, the sixty-six chapters of Isaiah, which appear to be a unity, are, in the consensus of modern scholars, an amalgam. Within this amalgam are found the words of two, or perhaps even three, different prophets: First Isaiah, Second Isaiah, and, if a third existed, Third Isaiah.

## Introduction: First Isaiah

### The Oracles of First Isaiah (chaps. 1–12; 28–32)

First Isaiah was a prophet active in the last four decades of the eighth century B.C.E. (ca. 742–701) in Jerusalem, the capital of Judah (the Southern Kingdom). He is, broadly speaking, associated with chaps. 1–39 of the book. A more precise reckoning, however, would limit First Isaiah's corpus to chaps. 1–12 and 28–32. Chapters 36–39 are almost identical to 2 Kings 18:13–20:19 and seem to be copied from the account in 2 Kings. Chapters 34–35 are in message, tone, and style most like Isaiah 40–55, oracles of Second Isaiah from the mid-sixth century (ca. 540 B.C.E.). Similarly, chaps. 24–27 seem most at home in the late sixth century, when Isaiah 56–66 was composed. Chapter 33 also is a late composition. Finally, while the majority of the prophecies in chaps. 13–23 are from First Isaiah's time (except 13:1–22; 21:1–10; and perhaps 23:1–18), their message is not particularly revealing of First Isaiah's thought. Some may not even be the work of the prophet. Only chaps. 1–12 and 28–32 will be considered here.

### First Isaiah's Age and Message

The earliest prophecy in chaps. 1–12 and 28–32 is found in 6:1–13, which is dated to 742 B.C.E.,

"the year of King Uzziah's death" (6:1). This passage records First Isaiah's commissioning as a prophet. Of particular note is the setting, for First Isaiah describes seeing Yahweh, the God of Israel, enthroned in the inner sanctum of the Jerusalem Temple. In a later period, and perhaps in First Isaiah's time, access to this area was restricted to priests. Although the sources never explicitly claim this office for First Isaiah, the evidence of 6:1–13 is suggestive.

Certainly First Isaiah, whether priest or not, was someone closely connected to the aristocracy of Jerusalem and Judah. Indeed, the major portion of the prophet's ministry was devoted to serving as a kind of secretary of state to Kings Ahaz (ca. 734–715 B.C.E.) and Hezekiah (ca. 715–687). Early in Ahaz's reign, for example, in 734–733, Judah was threatened by a coalition of Syria and Israel (the Northern Kingdom), both of whom wished to depose Ahaz and force Judah to join in battle against Assyria, the dominant power in the Near East (Isa. 7:1–2). When Ahaz resolved to resist this threat by allying himself with Assyria (2 Kings 16:7–9), First Isaiah responded by counseling the king to ignore both the Syrian/Israelite menace and the security of an Assyrian alliance (7:3–8:15). Instead, Ahaz should remain neutral and uninvolved.

After this crisis, First Isaiah seems to withdraw from public life (8:16–17), perhaps because Ahaz failed to heed the prophet's counsel and did make a treaty with the Assyrians. First Isaiah reemerged only after Ahaz's death in 715 B.C.E. Shortly thereafter, during a second Assyrian crisis in 713–711 and 705–701, he delivered to King Hezekiah advice similar to that which he had earlier given to Ahaz. While neighboring states urged Hezekiah to join in rebellion against Assyria, First Isaiah counseled a policy of neutrality. To enter battle against the imperial army of Assyria, he argued, was to invite certain destruction. Those who would do so "make a covenant with death" and "an agreement with Sheol" (28:15).

First Isaiah realized both in 734–733 and in 713–711, 705–701 B.C.E. that the best policy for a weak and insignificant state like Judah in times of crisis was to melt into the background, staying out of sight of the world's great imperial powers. More important to the prophet, however, than this kind of pragmatic consideration were theological concerns. First Isaiah believed that not only were foreign alliances politically counterproductive for Judah; they were religiously inappropriate. Judah, First Isaiah

maintained, should rely on God alone. Nowhere is this made more clear than in the great Immanuel prophecy (7:10–17), in which the child Immanuel, whose name means "God is with us," is presented to King Ahaz as a sign that Yahweh served as Judah's ally. In the prophet's mind royal attempts to replace this divine allegiance with foreign support were blasphemy.

When Ahaz did commit such blasphemy, First Isaiah responded (8:5–8) by invoking the name of Immanuel a second time. On this occasion "God is with us" signified judgment, describing how the deity, because of Ahaz's sinful alliance with Assyria, would send God's agent into Judah for retribution (see also 1:2–5:24a). Moreover, Assyria, First Isaiah argued, was this agent of God's chastisement, "the rod of my anger" (10:5). Still, Assyria's punishment of Judah would not be absolute (see 1:9, 24–26; 8:9–10; 10:12, 27b–32; 14:24–27; 29:1–8), given the prophet's belief that God had chosen the dynasty of David, as represented by Ahaz and Hezekiah, to rule Jerusalem for eternity (9:2–7; 11:1–9).

## Comment: First Isaiah

### The Daughters of Zion

In the traditional ordering of both the Jewish and Christian canons, Isaiah is the first book of the "classical" prophets. It is thus in Isaiah, and more specifically in First Isaiah, that many readers initially encounter a rhetorical device frequent in prophetic literature: the singling out of women as particularly responsible for behaviors the prophets deemed unacceptable within the Yahwistic community (Isa. 3:16–24; 4:1; 32:9–14; cf., e.g., Hosea 1–3; 4:13; Amos 4:1–3; Ezek. 8:14; Jer. 7:18; 44:15–19, 25). Oracles of this type tend especially to describe ways in which a prophet believed women had been religiously apostate. The result, according to the prophet, was divine punishment of the entire community.

A variant motif, also encountered initially in First Isaiah and then elsewhere in the prophetic books, personifies Jerusalem, also called Zion, as a female apostate or "harlot" (Isa. 1:21–23; 3:25–26; cf., e.g., Isa. 57:6–13; Jer. 4:30; 13:20–27; 22:20–23; Lam. 1:8–9; Ezek. 16:1–63; 23:1–4, 11–49). Indeed, the identification of women, in particular the women of Jerusalem/Zion, with Jerusalem/Zion itself was made so

facilely that a prophet could slip almost without notice from describing one to the other. Isaiah 3:16–4:1, for example, begins by castigating the daughters of Zion in 3:16–24, then switches in vv. 25–26 to condemning woman Zion, before returning its attention to Zion's women in 4:1. Such easy identification encouraged the prophets to claim that the "harlotries" of Zion personified as a woman, like the apostasies of women in general, render the entire population subject to judgment.

This kind of imagery can hardly be anything but offensive to feminist readers. It is not surprising that many omit these oracles from their study or, in more extreme cases, reject the tradition and its misogyny altogether. Yet there are ways to confront the "harlotry" prophecies and to mitigate the insult. For example, a reader might propose to read these prophetic oracles without the prophet's judgmental eye. That is, she might look at a prophet's descriptions of women's religious activities without concurring with the prophet's evaluation that those religious activities were wrong. In so doing, she can sometimes uncover significant information about women's religious life in Israel and Judah.

If one strips from Isa. 32:9–14 its overlay of

prophetic polemic, for instance, one uncovers positive images of women's role in the cult. In this poem First Isaiah condemns Jerusalem's women for being complacent while celebrating the annual fall vintage festival. This accusation of women's complacency within the context of a Yahwistic feast is, to be sure, disquieting. But what underlies the accusation is a hint that women apparently played a role in the celebration of the wine harvest. Note that Judg. 21:16–24 describes how unwed maidens danced in the vineyards at the fall vintage festival in Shiloh.

The passage in Judges suggests that the particular responsibility of women at the vineyard feast involved the making of music. Another hint that singing and dancing were the responsibility of women at the fall vintage festival is found in Isa. 5:1–7. This composition, in fact, is often called the Song of the Vineyard. As it stands, the song is an allegory in which God is described as lovingly tending a vineyard, namely, Israel and Judah (v. 7), which yielded only wild grapes, that is, bloodshed and outcries (vv. 4, 7). In composing this allegory, the prophet seems to quote an actual song of the vintage festival, especially in vv. 1–2. This vintage song, addressed as it is to a male "beloved," originally would have come from a woman's mouth.

Music making was an important female ritual at other points in Israelite cultic life. Indeed, by pursuing further a nonbiased reading of Isa. 32:9–14, one discovers that a second arena of female music making within the cult was keening in situations of lament. In 32:11–12 the women who were condemned for their complacency while celebrating the vintage festival are told that as punishment, the vineyards will fail. Their response, the prophet predicts, will be to engage in typical Israelite mourning rituals: to strip and make themselves bare, to gird sackcloth on their loins, and to beat their breasts, wailing in lamentation. While there is a disquieting polemic here, the underlying imagery provides evidence that women specialized in mourning within the Israelite cult.

Further evidence for women's role in Israelite mourning rituals is found in Isa. 3:16–4:1. This passage begins by describing the daughters of Zion as "haughty" and characterizes them as being concerned solely with perfumes, jewels, and similar items of luxury (3:18–23). The prophet warns that such ostentatiousness will not be tolerated by Yahweh, who instead, according to 3:24, will turn the perfumes of the daughters of Zion to stench, their fine girdles to hemp rope, their elaborate hairstyles to baldness, and their rich robes to sackcloth. This polemic concludes in 3:26 with a description of Zion, personified as a woman, ravaged and sitting on the ground.

The misogyny here seems unrelenting. Note, however, that what Yahweh substitutes for the rich robes of Zion's daughters is sackcloth, which, as noted above, was the typical garb of mourning in ancient Israel. The baldness that replaces the women's elaborate hairstyles also seems to have been required in Israelite mourning rituals (Lev. 21:5; Isa. 15:2; Jer. 7:29; 16:6; 41:5; 47:5; 48:37; Micah 1:16), even though the authors of Deuteronomy (Deut. 14:1) objected to the practice. Sitting on the ground as does the ravaged Zion in 3:26 was similarly a typical rite of Israelite lamentation (Isa. 47:1; Ezek. 26:16), one that continues today in Jewish tradition. What underlies the highly denigrating polemic of 3:16–4:1, then, is positive imagery describing women as mourners. Passages such as 2 Sam. 1:24; Jer. 9:17–21; Ezek. 32:16; and 2 Chron. 35:25, all of which refer to women's roles in lamentation, confirm that ritual keening and related mourning activities were primarily (although not exclusively) the responsibility of women.

These passages illuminate a late Isaianic text from the sixth century, 24:7–12, which describes how the joy of the vintage festival will be replaced by mourning in a time of judgment. Although no gender-specific language identifies either the rejoicers or the mourners, it is tempting, in light of Isa. 3:16–4:1; 5:1–7; and 32:9–14, to associate both the joyful music of the vineyard feast and the mournful keening of lament in Isaiah 24 with women's singing and dancing. Isaiah 16:10–11 (cf. Jer 48:33, 36) might be similarly analyzed.

There are two final oracles of religious "harlotry" in Isaiah that can be stripped of polemical language in order to find positive information about women's religious life beneath a negative veneer. Here, though, the task is more difficult, because Isa. 1:21–23 and 57:3, 6–13 use denigrating images of women while offering little in the way of redemptive language. In 1:21–23 Jerusalem is described as the "faithful city" who "has become a harlot" (1:21), failing to defend the rights of those to whom Yahweh extends special protection, the orphan and the widow (1:23). Even more striking is

57:3, 6–13, a sixth-century Isaianic oracle. In this poem Jerusalem is personified as a sorceress, an adulteress, and a harlot (emended text, v. 3) and is accused of engaging in fertility rituals (v. 8; cf. Isa. 1:29), in rites of child sacrifice (v. 9a, reading "you anointed the child sacrificial victim with oil"), and in necromancy (v. 9b).

The prophecies accusing the personified Jerusalem of apostasy indict all the city's inhabitants and not just the women. Still, the personification of the apostate city as female troubles a feminist consciousness. Moreover, many modern readers may be tempted to side with these condemnations of the female city. Today's sensibilities no more allow for the practices censured in 1:21–23 and 57:3, 6–13 than did the sensibilities of the ancient prophets. This does not mean, however, that the ancient men and women who participated in such non-Yahwistic religious practices felt the same. Instead, the very fact that the people of Jerusalem engaged in these activities implies that for them such behaviors were spiritually fulfilling, more fulfilling even than the practices prescribed by the Yahwistic cult.

This is an especially important point to keep in mind when considering women's religious life in ancient Israel and Judah. The Yahwistic cult, as it is presented in the Bible, is one that was almost exclusively in the hands of men. Despite certain evidence to the contrary (such as that on music making and mourning presented above), the reality for women was that opportunities for spiritual expression within the biblical tradition were sparse. There was little choice for a woman who wished to participate fully in a religious life but to avail herself of ritual behaviors that thrived outside the priestly and prophetic purview. When read in this light, poems like Isa. 1:21–23 and especially 57:3, 6–13 serve not so much as evidence of female apostasy, but as testimony to the fact that the heavily male orientation of biblical religion forced many women to seek spiritual fulfillment elsewhere.

## The Female Prophet of Isaiah 8:3

The preceding analysis of Isa. 1:21–23 and 57:3, 6–13 is dependent on the work of Jo Ann Hackett, who has used anthropological models in order to describe women's religious powerlessness in Israel and Judah during times when the Yahwistic cult was stable and highly centralized. According to Hackett, women in Israel and Judah were likewise relatively powerless politically during periods of a stable and highly centralized government. Conversely, during periods of either religious or political dysfunction, women did have the opportunity to wield power in religion and in government. First Isaiah acknowledged this in an oracle that describes a period of anarchy that he predicted would come to Jerusalem (3:1–15). One feature of this coming anarchy, according to the prophet, is "my people . . . women rule over them" (v. 12, although note that some ancient versions reflect "usurers" [noshim] instead of "women" [nashim]).

First Isaiah dreaded this future period of anarchy when women would rule, which suggests that the prophet lived in the opposite kind of society, one with centralized and stable communal organizations. First Isaiah's focus on such long-lived institutions as the Temple and the Davidic monarchy also suggests a certain stability in the Judah of his day. This is particularly true for Jerusalem, the only great urban center of the eighth century that was able to withstand the multiple Assyrian crises of 734–733 and 713–711, 705–701 B.C.E. Although a full description of the city's social organization during this period is impossible, given the limited date, First Isaiah's Jerusalem does seem to have been the kind of stable and centralized society in which, according to Hackett's thesis, women were marginalized.

But what of Isa. 8:3, in which First Isaiah reports a visit to a female prophet? Is this not proof that, contrary to our hypothesis, women could function as religious leaders during times of social stability?

There are reasons for thinking not. In Isa. 8:3 the role of the female prophet is restricted to having sexual relations with First Isaiah and bearing as a result a son. The female prophet, that is, was First Isaiah's wife. Since this woman takes no action in the narrative other than to bear children (she seems also to be the mother of Shear-jashub, mentioned in 7:3), one can surmise that her title was honorific, derived from her husband, as the wife of a king is called a queen. The female prophet of 8:3 is in this sense the exception that proves Hackett's rule: living as she did in a time of centralization and relative stability, she could not be a prophet who controlled religious or political power. Indeed, the female prophets who did wield significant and independent power, Miriam,

Deborah, Huldah, and Noadiah, all lived in periods that, it can be argued, were characterized by some degree of social upheaval and even instability (although, again, the data are limited).

## Introduction: Second and Third Isaiah

### Second Isaiah's Age and Message

Isaiah 34–35, 40–55 are the work of an anonymous prophet usually called Second Isaiah. Second Isaiah wrote nearly two hundred years after First Isaiah, ca. 540 B.C.E. The people of this time had witnessed a calamity of almost incomprehensible proportions: the fall of Judah and Jerusalem in 587 B.C.E. at the hands of the Babylonian empire. Second Isaiah speaks to a group in exile in Babylon, where certain upper- and middle-class members of Judean society had been taken by their conquerors (2 Kings 24:12–16). This audience surely had doubts concerning its status as God's chosen people and even the existence of God within the heavenly pantheon. Second Isaiah's message answers these doubts by assuring the people both that Yahweh still has compassion for them and that Yahweh, despite the triumph of Babylon over Judah, is still sovereign in the heavens and over history.

The earliest oracle in Second Isaiah, 40:1–11, begins without preamble by proclaiming God's compassion. In vv. 1–2, Yahweh commands the lesser beings present in the heavens to "comfort, comfort my people . . . speak tenderly to Jerusalem." The comfort, however, is to involve far more than words, for in v. 3 a herald proclaims that a highway of Yahweh shall be prepared in the wilderness. This is a promise of restoration: the highway through the wilderness is the path back from Babylon to Judah. The language here recalls the story of the Israelite exodus from Egypt and suggests a similar miraculous journey to the "promised land" (see also 35:1–10; 41:17–20; 43:14–21; 48:10–22; 49:9c–11; 51:9–11; 52:11–12).

Why, though, did God, who cares enough to promise comfort and even restoration, allow the people to suffer so in the first place? Here, too, 40:1–11 provides an answer. The second half of v. 2 tells Jerusalem that "her iniquity is pardoned, she has received from Yahweh's hand double for all her sins" (RSV). The prophet suggests that the destruction of Judah and the exile were necessary punishments for the people's transgressions. God's compassion was never absent from the people, but God's sense of justice required that the nation's iniquities be punished (see also 42:18–25; 50:1–3).

Yet why was the suffering so extreme that the community was required to pay "double for all her sins" (40:2)? Second Isaiah replies that the people's suffering is in some way redemptive for all nations. The covenant community Israel is able to and should bear the sins of foreigners and by so doing bring blessings to the entire world. This seems at least to be the point of the renowned (and much debated) Servant Songs (42:1–4; 49:1–6; 50:4–9; 52:13–53:12), which describe the vicarious suffering of God's servant (interpreted here as the people Israel; see 49:3) as that which redeems the nations and restores them to wholeness or *shalom* (53:5).

Such a theology is based on the assumption that Yahweh is the sovereign of history who has a plan for all creation (48:1–22). This leads Second Isaiah to proclaim a message of Yahwistic universalism, which, although not without antecedents in preexilic literature, is asserted in such a daring way in Second Isaiah as to make it seem revolutionary. For example, the prophet applies the title Messiah (the anointed one of God), which was previously reserved for Israelite and Judean kings, to the Persian conqueror Cyrus (41:2–4, 25–29; 44:28; 45:1–13; 46:8–11). The reason is that Cyrus functions as Israel's redeemer by overthrowing Babylon in 539 B.C.E. and issuing an edict allowing the exiles to return home (Ezra 1:2–4).

Even more astonishing is Second Isaiah's explicit claim of monotheism: "Thus says Yahweh . . . 'I am the first and I am the last; besides me there is no god'" (44:6; see also 41:4; 43:10; 44:8; 45:5–7, 14, 18, 22; 48:12). There are preexilic antecedents for such a theology, but it is in Second Isaiah that one first encounters theoretical monotheism. Second Isaiah describes Yahweh as the sole creator of all the earth (40:12–31) and dismisses the idols of the nations as nothing (41:21–24; 44:9–20; 46:1–13). The prophet can even anticipate the day when all the nations of the earth will convert to the worship of the God of Israel. This is a powerful, almost audacious, message, shot through with unbridled optimism. It is this unrestrained optimism, proclaiming God's goodness and greatness and the imminent redemption of both the covenant community and the nations, that underlies all of Second Isaiah's message.

## A Third Isaiah?

Isaiah 24–27 and 56–66 date from the period after 538 B.C.E., the year in which Cyrus issued his edict of return. These oracles come from Jerusalem and describe the experiences of those who took advantage of Cyrus's offer. The returnees, who had expected a glorious restoration as envisioned by Second Isaiah, found themselves frustrated by innumerable hardships, in particular famine and a resulting poverty. The oracles of Isaiah 24–27, 56–66 are testimonies to increasing pessimism and even despair. As despair and frustration quickened, the returnees begged God for a miraculous resolution to their unhappy situation. From this perspective, it is but a short step to apocalyptic language, in which the present age is doomed to cataclysmic destruction (24:1–23; 26:1–19; 27:2–11; 65:17–25; 66:1–24).

The author of these oracles of despair and, ultimately, nascent apocalypticism is difficult to determine. It may be best to attribute them to a group, the "followers" or the "school" of Second Isaiah. Such a designation recognizes Isaiah 24–27, 56–66 as dependent on Second Isaiah's prophecies and even in dialogue with them. At the same time, it establishes a break between the unguarded optimism of Second Isaiah and the increasing frustration experienced by the postexilic community. Other scholars, however, prefer to speak of an individual author, Third Isaiah, or even of an older and disillusioned Second Isaiah. But the question remains unanswered. All one can be sure of is that Isaiah 34–35, 40–55 and 24–27, 56–66 speak from a shared understanding of God's sovereignty in the cosmos and speak to the same issue of God's relationship with the people Israel.

## Comment: Second and Third Isaiah

### The Woman Zion

Isaiah 34–35, 40–55 and 24–27, 56–66 also use a shared vocabulary of female imagery. Both personify Jerusalem/Zion as a woman. Such a personification is hardly unfamiliar, as it is found already in First Isaiah (1:21–23; 3:25–26), but in First Isaiah Zion the woman was scorned as an apostate and a harlot. In the sixth-century Isaianic materials the images of the woman Jerusalem/Zion are, with only one exception (57:3, 6–13; cf. 47:1–15), positive.

Isaiah 66:7–16 is an oracle that celebrates the future restoration of Jerusalem. The poem begins in vv. 7–8 with imagery appropriate to rejuvenation: a description of childbirth. The mother who gives birth is none other than Zion the city, who brings forth as her children the renewed nation. In biblical tradition women had been cursed with pain in childbirth since the expulsion of Adam and Eve from Eden (Gen. 3:16). Zion's delivery, however, is accomplished before the onset of birth pangs or labor. The absence of such pain in 66:7–8 thus hints at a return to paradise (see also 51:3). As mother Zion gives birth to the nation, she simultaneously brings forth a new Eden.

This positive depiction of the woman Jerusalem/Zion is developed further as the poem continues. In 66:11a the city, having given birth in vv. 7–8, now lovingly tends to her newborn. Her peoples are told that they will suck and be

sated "from her consoling breast . . . from her full-laden bosom" (author's translation). Jerusalem as devoted young mother appears again in v. 12b, where the city's sucklings (reading with the ancient Greek translation) are promised that they will "be carried upon her hip and bounced upon her knees" (author's translation; see also 49:22; 60:4, 9). In v. 13 this mother city is even compared to God, as together they effect the miraculous rebirth and rejuvenation of the people.

However positive the imagery of the female Jerusalem/Zion in 66:7–16, one might argue that the poem, in reflecting a hope for an Edenic future, does not accurately reflect the prophetic attitude toward sixth-century Jerusalem or toward the sixth-century women she represents (cf. First Isaiah, who castigated the women and city of his day but simultaneously dreamed of a virtuous city and virtuous females in the future: 1:24–26; 2:2–4; 4:2–6; 29:1–8). But in fact the exilic Isaianic prophecies do extend their positive descriptions to the city of their day. Thus in 49:14, Zion, in pain because of her destruction in 587 B.C.E., is depicted as an anguished daughter of God. This imagery recalls that of Lamentations, which similarly describes the ravaging of the woman Zion (see especially Lam. 1:1–22). Second Isaiah, however, ultimately rejects these images of anguish by assuring Zion that despite her desolation she is still the offspring whom Yahweh loves and, more important, the child whose suffering will be ended. An end to Zion's current suffering is promised also in 51:17–52:2, where Jerusalem/Zion, here depicted as a forsaken mother (51:18) and wife (52:1), is commanded to rouse herself and shake off her shackles. She is reassured that despite her captivity she is "the holy city" and one who will soon adorn herself with "beautiful garments" in order to celebrate the restoration that the edict of Cyrus makes possible (52:1).

One is tempted to suggest that Jerusalem's beautiful garments in 52:1 are wedding garb. Certainly marriage imagery is dominant in other sixth-century Isaianic poems that rejoice in Jerusalem's restoration: 49:7–26; 54:1–10; and 62:1–12. Isaiah 49:7–26, after assuring daughter Zion that she will be comforted, compares the glory of the renewed city to the jewels with which a bride adorns herself on her wedding day (v. 18). Similarly, 62:4 promises the city that on the day of her redemption she will no more be called "Forsaken" and "Desolate," but instead will be known as "My Delight Is in Her" and "Married." The next verse expands the marriage metaphor by promising Zion that "as the bridegroom rejoices over the bride, so will your God rejoice over you" (62:5).

Isaiah 54:1–10 likewise speaks of Zion as the bride of Yahweh. In this poem, however, the primary imagery is not that of a wedding but rather of a marriage gone sour that now experiences reconciliation. Thus Jerusalem/Zion is described as a wife who was previously abandoned and left barren by her husband, Yahweh, but who is now reclaimed by a deity who promises untold progeny and everlasting love.

This description of Jerusalem/Zion as a forsaken wife who is reclaimed in the marriage relationship is again an example of the positive imagery of the female city that one finds in the sixth-century Isaianic corpora. According to John Sawyer, even more remarkable here is that in presenting a positive image of Jerusalem as an abandoned wife, Second Isaiah suggests that it is God the husband who bears primary blame for the breakup of the marriage. Such seems to be the point of 54:6, for example, where metaphoric language compares Jerusalem to "a wife forsaken and grieved in spirit," one who was as "the wife of a man's youth when she is cast off." Indeed, only one short phrase in 54:1–10 suggests that the wife Jerusalem/Zion is at all to blame for her husband's desertion ("the shame of your youth, and the disgrace of your widowhood," v. 4).

The exegete must be very cautious here,

however, not to read modern paradigms that view spouses as equal back into ancient Israel. That culture assigned authority within marriage to the male, including the prerogative of divorce (Deut. 24:1–4). A husband, in this case God, was within his rights to abandon his wife without becoming subject to criticism within the society. Moreover, it is surely not the case that the sixth-century Isaianic oracles are consistently critical of God when masculine imagery is used. There are innumerable passages in Isaiah 34–35, 40–55 and 24–27, 56–66 that use male imagery of God in a positive way (God as loving husband in 62:4–5, for example). Still, it is striking in 54:1–10 that the deity is cast as a penitent male and the female is depicted as aggrieved.

## God as Woman

A number of images in the sixth-century Isaianic oracles describe God by drawing on feminine imagery. In 42:14, the imagery of labor and childbirth is assimilated to God. This verse is embedded within a hymn of creation (42:5–17), the point of which is to celebrate both Yahweh as the creator of old and Yahweh as the author of a new creation through which the exilic community will be redeemed. Appropriately, the deity describes this chaotic process of creating anew in the language of childbirth: "Now I will cry out like a woman in labor, I will gasp and pant" (42:14).

Passages can also be found in both Isaiah 34–35, 40–55 and 24–27, 56–66 that allude to the motherhood of God. In 45:9–10 a series of rhetorical questions compares Yahweh to a potter, a father, and a mother, implying that God is all three. In response to daughter Zion's lament in 49:14 that Yahweh has forgotten her, Yahweh poses a question: "Can a woman forget her nursing child, or show no compassion for the child of her womb?" (49:15a). This question suggests that Yahweh's love for Zion should be compared to a mother's devotion to her offspring. As the poet implies, both these loves are unfailing. Yet even if the love of a human mother should wane, Yahweh the divine mother assures Zion: "I will not forget you" (49:15b). As profound as the love of a human mother is for her child, Yahweh the divine mother transcends even this in Yahweh's love for the city.

Isaiah 66:12–13 similarly makes a comparison between an earthly mother, Jerusalem, and Yahweh the divine mother. In v. 13 Yahweh promises to comfort the people "as a mother comforts her child." In v. 12 the nature of this comfort is made clear, as the activities of mother Jerusalem, who carries and bounces on her knees the suckling community, are described. This imagery of Jerusalem's motherliness in v. 12 is metaphorically extended to v. 13, which suggests that Yahweh the mother carries and amuses the nursing Israel. Similarly, in v. 9, following the oracle of Zion giving birth in vv. 7–8, birth imagery is assimilated to the deity, so that Yahweh identifies with Zion's delivery.

Phyllis Trible has argued forcefully that maternal imagery is used of God also in Isa. 27:11b. This text, embedded within an oracle of judgment, says of Yahweh, "he that made them will not have compassion on them, he that formed them will show them no favor." The verbs "to make" and "to form," although not explicitly female, are elsewhere used in conjunction with God's activity in the womb (Jer. 1:5a; Job 31:15). The use of the word "compassion" (*rachamim*), which is related to the Hebrew word for womb (*rechem*), convinces Trible that an allusion to God as mother is intended.

In Isa. 46:3–4 the conjunction of the verb "to make" and the noun "womb" also suggests an allusion to God as mother. Even more vivid in these verses is the picture of Yahweh as Israel's nurse and midwife. God is said to be the one who, like a midwife, has lifted up Israel from the womb and who, like a nurse, has carried the people from the day of its birth. Moreover, the loyalty of God the nurse will not falter: the people are promised "until old age I will bear [you] . . . I will bear [you] and I will save [you]" (v. 4).

## Conclusions

In Isaiah 34–35, 40–55 and 24–27, 56–66 one encounters an abundance of positive female imagery. Can this bounty be explained?

Many have tried. Mayer Gruber, for example, has suggested that the positive female images are introduced deliberately to accommodate women worshipers who had previously felt excluded from a male-dominated religion. Leah Bronner prefers to argue that the loss of monarchy, Temple, and homeland led the sixth-century Isaianic authors to seek metaphors in the one social unit that still functioned, the family. Hence, she suggests, the emphasis on marriage, childbirth, and motherhood, images all drawn from the domestic sphere.

Bronner is probably correct in viewing the social dysfunction of the sixth century as the impetus for the positive female imagery of Isaiah 34–35, 40–55, and 24–27, 56–66, but Hackett's thesis would suggest that Bronner is wrong in focusing on a retreat to the domestic sphere. Rather, in the sixth century as in other times of social upheaval, Hackett would argue that women could exercise power in the public area. The positive portrayals in the exilic Isaianic materials of that which had been previously denigrated (Zion) or ignored (motherhood, childbirth, and the like) may be responses to a temporary increase in female status. When social stability returned, misogyny unfortunately reemerged. Still, there remains in Isaiah 24–27, 34–35, and 40–66 a legacy of positive female imagery unparalleled in other prophetic books and indeed almost anywhere in the Bible.

## BIBLIOGRAPHY

Bronner, Leah. "Gynomorphic Imagery in Exilic Isaiah (40–66)." *Dor le Dor* 12 (1983–1984), 71–83.

Clifford, Richard. *Fair Spoken and Persuading: An Interpretation of Second Isaiah.* Theological Inquiries. Ramsey, N.J.: Paulist Press, 1984.

Darr, Katheryn Pfisterer. "Like Warrior, Like Women: Destruction and Deliverance in Isaiah 42:10–17." *Catholic Biblical Quarterly* 49 (1978), 560–571.

Gruber, Mayer. "The Motherhood of God in Second Isaiah." *Revue Biblique* 90 (1983), 351–359.

Hackett, Jo Ann. "Women's Studies and the Hebrew Bible." In *The Future of Biblical Studies: The Hebrew Scriptures*, edited by R. E. Friedman and H. G. M. Williamson, pp. 141–164. Atlanta: Scholars Press, 1987.

Kaiser, Otto. *Isaiah 1–12, A Commentary.* Old Testament Library. Philadelphia: Westminster Press, 1972.

———. *Isaiah 13–39, A Commentary.* Old Testament Library. Philadelphia: Westminster Press, 1974.

Muilenburg, James. "Isaiah: Introduction and Exegesis." In *The Interpreter's Bible*, edited by G. A. Buttrick, 5:381–773. Nashville: Abingdon Press, 1956.

Sawyer, J. F. A. "Daughter of Zion and Servant of the Lord in Isaiah: A Comparison." *Journal for the Study of the Old Testament* 44 (1989), 89–107.

Trible, Phyllis. "Journey of a Metaphor." In her *God and the Rhetoric of Sexuality*, pp. 31–59. Overtures to Biblical Theology. Philadelphia: Fortress Press, 1978.

# JEREMIAH

*Kathleen M. O'Connor*

## Introduction

The book of Jeremiah is about catastrophe and survival, destruction and rebuilding, grief and joy. Its themes echo and contradict one another to create a poignant symphony of tragedy and hope. Images of women abound in the book, but often in ways that stereotype, belittle, and blame them for the disaster that befalls the nation. Yet if women approach the book critically, they may find that its sufferings mirror their own pain and its hope promises them a different future.

### Development and Authorship

Because the book contains a mixture of literary materials that seems to lack order or design, the book can overwhelm readers. Poems of Jeremiah intermingle with stories about him and with prose sermons attributed to him. Chronological headings are out of order; verses repeat themselves unexpectedly in different contexts; messages of hope coexist with threats of doom. The result is a literary soup that demands a revelatory recipe, but no simple description of its ingredients is possible.

For most of the twentieth century, interpreters believed that the book contained three separate written documents or literary sources, combined by editors who were influenced by the book of Deuteronomy. These sources included poetry of Jeremiah, stories about him by his scribe Baruch, and sermons attributed to him by the editors.

Scholarship at the end of this century challenges this consensus. One interpreter denies involvement of Deuteronomistic editors and ascribes the book largely to Jeremiah and Baruch. A second scholar claims, instead, that anonymous members of the community collected prophetic materials over a long period of time and assigned them to Jeremiah. A third commentator insists that, although Jeremiah's words form the heart of the book, readers cannot recover them, because later additions to Jeremiah's preaching obscure his original words.

### Jeremiah

In light of this discussion, it becomes clear that interpreters disagree about the ability of readers to encounter Jeremiah himself in the text. Opinions vary from seeing the text as a reliable report of his life to understanding him as a fictional character. Ancient writers, however, sought to convey the significance of events, and to do so they shaped their material freely.

What the book of Jeremiah does is to present a portrait of the prophet that mixes fact and interpretation inextricably. Though it seems likely that Jeremiah's words and deeds underlie the text, it is difficult to determine what is historical information and what is interpretation. Nevertheless, it is certain that the community recognized the message of this prophet as a living word. They remembered, cherished, and adapted it as they were driven into exile and lived in hope of return. It was probably during this period of expectation of return or shortly after the return that the book achieved final form. Its purpose was to help the people make sense of their tragedy, recover their identity, and move toward the future.

### Historical Context

Jeremiah's prophecy is the product of fiercely troubled times. The events it records begin during the reign of King Josiah in 626 B.C.E. (1:2) and end with King Jehoiakin's death in exile sometime after 582 (52:34). During these years the nation-state of Judah experienced turmoil from within and from without. Egypt and Babylon vied for control of the country. In 605, Judah finally became a vassal state of Babylon. This arrangement allowed the Babylonians to extort high taxes from Judah, to place a puppet king on the throne, and to interfere in internal affairs.

Three times Judah revolted, and each time Babylon invaded (597, 587, and 582). With each invasion, leading citizens and members of the upper classes were deported to Babylon (39:1–10; 52:1–30). In the invasion of 587 Babylon destroyed Jerusalem. After a long siege, the army breached the city walls, destroyed the palace and the Temple, deported the king and his family, and killed many of the nation's leaders. By 582 B.C.E. life in the land had been severely disrupted.

In the period before Babylonian control, Jeremiah prophesied Judah's imminent destruction. Unless the people repented of their idolatry and injustice, disaster would befall them. When disaster did occur, Jeremiah advised them to submit to Babylon because that nation was God's instrument. After the nation's fall, however, the prophet's message turned to words of hope.

### Structure

Despite the lack of order among the book's smaller units, its large divisions are easily discernible: chaps. 1–25, accusations against Judah and Jerusalem; chaps. 26–29; 34–45, narratives concerning the prophet; chaps. 30–33, little book of consolation; chaps. 46–51, oracles against the nations; chap. 52, epilogue from 2 Kings 24–25.

## Comment

### Harmful Gender Language

The abundance of female imagery in the book creates the impression that Jeremiah was particularly sensitive to the realities of women. Female figures personify the nation and the city of Jerusalem. Women's suffering symbolizes the pain of the entire people. Yet Jeremiah's use of female language is double-edged at best. On the one hand, its presence indicates awareness of women's painful circumstances. On the other, it uses women as symbols of wickedness, blames them for the fall of the nation, and exploits their experiences by applying them to men.

*Bride, adulterer, and prostitute (2:1–4:4).* After Jeremiah's call narrative (chap. 1), a collection of originally separate poetic and prose passages introduces Jeremiah's preaching (2:1–4:4). These passages indict the nation for its sin and infidelity. One of the unifying features of these passages is the motif of woman as unfaithful sexual partner. Even though some passages feature male figures (2:14–19; 2:26–28; 4:1–4), female images tie the units together in a potent rhetoric of blame.

The first poem (2:1–3) shapes readers' perceptions of what is to follow. The divine husband recalls his wife's past loyalty. "I remember the devotion of your youth, your love as a bride" (2:2b). Mournfully he recalls their honeymoon in the wilderness, her devotion, and the protection he provided for her. The nostalgic tone of this poem indicates that the marriage is over. Subsequent poems (2:4–13, 14–19) ask what went wrong with the relationship and charge the nation with abandonment (vv. 11, 13, 17).

Accusation intensifies in 2:20–25. This poem transforms the bride into an adulteress and a prostitute. Though the word translated "whore" (2:20) probably refers to a promiscuous unmarried woman, the broken bridal relation of 2:1–3 indicates that adultery is the woman's sin. The former bride has now broken free of her covenant relationship. "For long ago you broke your yoke" (2:20). On every hill and under every tree she "plays the whore" (2:20b).

The poet piles images on top of one another in an effort to describe her sins. She is like a "degenerate" vine (2:21). Her infidelity makes her so dirty and defiled that, even with lye, she cannot wash herself clean (2:22). Like a female camel or wild ass in heat, she goes in headlong pursuit of idols (2:23–24). In this line, animal imagery merges with harlot language to label female sexuality as wild, disgusting, and uncontrollable. The woman cannot help herself. "It is hopeless, for I have loved strangers, and after them I will go" (2:25).

Her divine husband interrogates her about her rebellion (2:29–32). Cruelly he tells her that in order to bring her around he has struck down her children. Then he mocks her for her fickleness. "Can a girl forget her ornaments, or a bride her attire?" (2:32; see 4:30). The implied answer to the question is no; such forgetfulness is inconceivable. A girl is far too attached to adornments to forget them, but though women are mightily bound to frivolous things, Israel easily forgets its God.

In the following poem the woman's promiscuity infects others (2:33–37). She is not content to seek lovers herself; she teaches her harlotry to "wicked women" (2:33). Worse yet, she callously destroys the nation's poor. "On your skirts is found the lifeblood of the innocent poor, though you did not catch them breaking in" (2:34). In strangely twisted imagery, the poet chooses a woman to portray the nation's despicable treatment of the poor. Yet in ancient Israel women were often as powerless and as little esteemed as the ill-treated poor.

In the next poem (3:1–5), the husband refuses on legal grounds to take back his twice-divorced and rejected wife. According to Deut. 24:1–4, a woman divorced from a second husband cannot return to the first. Their reunion would bring guilt upon the land (Deut. 24:4). Since in Israelite society a divorced woman had little hope of survival, this poem depicts the fate of the nation in terrifying terms. In Jeremiah's poem, even if the divine husband wishes to take back his wife, the law prevents him from rescuing her.

Other passages continue the metaphor of the unfaithful woman as cause of the land's contamination. A prose passage (3:6–11) accuses the Northern Kingdom of Israel of polluting the land with harlotry, but Judah bears even greater guilt. She too played the whore (3:8), and "because she took her whoredom so lightly, she polluted the land" (3:9). For the prophets, the moral quality of human life directly affected the well-being of the land. Judah's whoring disturbs the flocks, the herds, and the people (3:24), and it brings drought upon the land (3:3; 13:25–27; 14:1–6).

In this collection of poetry the root metaphor is that of marriage as symbol of covenant relationship. Jeremiah did not create this metaphor but borrowed it from the prophet Hosea (1:2–3:19). The sources of both prophets' language, however, were the institutions of marriage and prostitution in ancient Israel. Married women had few rights, were considered the property of their husbands, and, unlike men, were severely punished for infidelity.

Jeremiah's use of the marriage metaphor, however, is not entirely negative. By describing the covenant in terms of a common human experience of intimacy and love, it makes covenant understandable and appealing. Moreover, it evokes compassion for God by portraying the deity as vulnerable and injured by human sin. In one poem God treats women better than the society does, because he urges his divorced wife to return (3:1–5). Yet negative implications of this language overcome its advantages. Jeremiah uses marriage language less to speak of divine-human intimacy than to dramatize the wife's infidelity. The marriage metaphor exalts men because it uses them alone as appropriate symbols of the divine. It brands women because it uses them and their sexuality as symbols of wickedness and treachery.

***Daughter language.*** Jeremiah also uses women as symbols of evil by personifying nations and cities as women. Personification is a literary device that represents things as people. Because Hebrew nouns for cities and countries are feminine grammatical forms, it is easy for poets to personify them as women. With a cluster of "daughter" phrases, Jeremiah personifies Judah and Jerusalem: "daughter my people" (4:11; 6:26; 8:11, 19, 21, 22; 9:1, 6; 14:17; author's translation); "daughter Zion" (4:31; 6:2, 23); "virgin daughter" (31:21; 49:4; NRSV: "virgin"); and "daughter" of other nations (46:11, 19, 24; 48:18; 50:42; 51:33).

Sometimes these terms intensify blame and accusation. The poet urges the "faithless daughter" to return (31:21–22). God promises to send shepherds to destroy the lovely daughter (6:2–3). "Daughter Egypt shall be put to shame" (46:24). At other times daughter language carries more positive connotations. The father laments the dying of his daughter (8:11, 19, 21–22; 9:1; 14:17; see 4:31).

No matter how daughter language is used, however, it reflects a patriarchal world where a daughter's value is ambiguous at best (6:26). It arises from the bride-price she will bring or from alliances families might make through marriage arrangements. Even when this language expresses tender regard for the daughter, it conveys a structure of relationship in which males represent God and females again symbolize erring nations and cities.

***Queen of heaven (7:18 and 44:15–28).*** The book's denouncement of women becomes most emphatic in a prose sermon about idolatry

(44:15–28). This sermon develops ideas that first appear in Jeremiah's Temple sermon (chap. 7). There Jeremiah accuses entire families of participating in idolatry by worshiping the queen of heaven. "The children gather wood, the fathers kindle fire, and the women knead dough, to make cakes for the queen of heaven" (7:18).

Chapter 44 reinterprets and expands these accusations. It accuses women alone of worshiping the queen, whereas it reduces the husbands' offense to failure to control their wives (44:15–19, 24–25). Hence, chap. 44 makes women the direct cause of the nation's collapse (vv. 20–23, 26–30). Following the pattern of the story of Eve (Genesis 3), the passage claims that death and disaster stem from women's disobedience. (See below for consideration of positive aspects of this story.)

***Circumcise your hearts (4:4).*** Jeremiah orders the men of Judah to circumcise themselves to God, "Remove the foreskins of your hearts" (4:4). At first glance, this command appears to transform a male ritual into a spiritual event that might include women. It does not. Instead, Jeremiah's command urges the circumcised men of Judah to live covenant ritual wholeheartedly.

**Problematic God language.** Jeremiah's favorite titles for God are male terms that come from the social realities of the ancient world. They include father (3:4, 19; 31:9), judge (12:2–3), king (8:19; 10:7), and most often, Yahweh of Armies, often translated Lord of Hosts. In patriarchal societies these figures could be benevolent or domineering. Whatever their mode of exercising authority, however, they controlled the lives of everyone under them.

When Jeremiah uses these titles, they portray God's authority, justice, and power. The problem for women is that Jeremiah lacks equivalent titles for God drawn from women's lives. Hence, Jeremiah implicitly teaches that men represent God and women do not. Moreover, these titles reinforce hierarchical human relationships.

The book's frequent portrayal of God as violent punisher of the people compounds the problem (e.g., 5:10, 15–17; 6:12, 19; 8:17). Of particular concern is the language of chap. 13, where God rapes the female nation because of her sins. "It is for the greatness of your iniquity that your skirts are lifted up and you are violated" (13:22). "I myself will lift up your skirts over your face . . ." (13:26). God language mirrors human relations, and it implicitly justifies human behavior. Much, but not all, of Jeremiah's God language justifies violence against women and subordinates them to their human kings, judges, and fathers.

## Importance of the Book for Women: Women's History

These criticisms of the book of Jeremiah in relation to women do not tell the whole story. Despite its male-centered perspectives and its harmful prejudices against women, the book also contains literary, theological, and political resources that may benefit women. It provides glimpses of the actual lives of women in the past. It contains poetic imagery that portrays both God and women in a positive light. It includes stories and themes that may comfort women and give them hope for a better future.

Behind Jeremiah's images of wives, prostitutes, divorced women, mourners, mothers, worshipers, and victims of war stand real women. To meet them, even through the smokey veils of ancient literature, reminds contemporary women of their painful history and cries out for a different future for themselves and their daughters.

***Mourners (9:17–22).*** At times of death and defeat, women acted as professional mourners, though perhaps primarily within the confines of the home. The mourning women's task was to weep and wail as an expression of the family's grief. Their official weeping did not substitute for the tears of others. Its purpose was to aid the expression of grief by setting loose everyone's tears over the death of a loved one.

Jeremiah employs images of professional mourning women to dramatize the tragic fate of the nation. "Consider, and call for the mourning women to come; . . . let them quickly raise a dirge over us, so that our eyes may run down with tears" (9:17–18). Jeremiah summons the mourners to weep and wail. But the corpse is not a deceased person; the corpse is the nation. "Teach to your daughters a dirge, and each to her neighbor a lament" (9:20), he urges. "Death has come up into our windows" (9:21).

***Queen of heaven (44:15–28).*** It seems certain that Israelite women worshiped the queen of heaven. Women were excluded from full participation in temple worship, and the predominant Israelite conception of God was masculine. The queen provided them with a female deity who offered them protection and prosperity (44:17).

The queen's identity is not clear. She probably combines features of two or more fertility goddesses of the ancient Near East. It is even possible that women understood her to be connected in some way with the God of Israel. If that were the case, they would have intended no idolatry. It is difficult to explain why chap. 44 blames women for this worship, although 7:18 accuses entire families. Perhaps over time worship of the queen decreased among men and grew among women, or perhaps chap. 44 reflects a changed society in which misogyny had increased.

From the perspective of women today the queen's worshipers of chap. 44 appear in a positive light. They are resourceful, independent women with their own subculture. When they stopped worshiping the goddess, they "lacked everything" and were "consumed by sword and famine" (44:18–19). On the basis of this experience, they became religious agents, taking worship into their own hands, as are many women today.

*Child sacrifice.* Another form of idolatry that the book criticizes severely is the practice of child sacrifice (7:31–32; 19:5; 32:35). Scholars know neither the extent of child sacrifice nor the role of women in it. Women may have resisted it or enabled it. Either way the practice is likely to have caused them great fear and suffering. Women's lives were usually centered on their children, and their status and sometimes even their future depended on them.

*Childbirth.* Women in childbirth appear frequently in Jeremiah (4:31; 6:24; 13:21; 20:14–18; 22:23; 30:6; 48:41; 49:24; 50:43). The abundance of childbirth imagery may indicate once again that the prophet was particularly sensitive to women, or it may reveal that childbirth created such fear among men that it could serve aptly as a symbol of the nation's approaching calamity. What captures the poet's attention is not the joy of giving birth; it is the panic, pain, and distress of women as labor comes upon them—"anguish," "a cry," "gasping for breath, stretching out her hands" (4:31).

By making childbirth a symbol of death, Jeremiah inverts its meaning (but see 31:8). He applies the pain of women to men, to warriors, and to the nation. Like a woman giving birth, men will be overcome by pain. "Why then do I see every man with his hands on his loins like a woman in labor?" (30:6). Jeremiah appropriates women's unique contribution to life and applies it to men as a metaphor of death.

*Women in wartime.* Throughout history women and children continue to suffer acutely during wartime. Jeremiah, however, uses the terrors women experience in war to highlight the coming disaster. War will affect women of every class. Royal women will be taken into exile (38:22–23); wives of landowners will be turned over to enemies (6:12); poor women will survive to face chaotic struggles in Judah during the aftermath of the Babylonian invasion (40:7).

Widows created by war will represent the reversal of the promises to Abraham and Sarah. "Their widows became more numerous than the sand of the seas; I have brought against the mothers of youths a destroyer at noonday" (15:8). The mother of seven, once deemed blessed, will instead be cursed because war will sweep away her offspring (15:9). With a traditional curse, Jeremiah asks God to make widows of the enemies' wives (18:21). He prophesies a famine in Jerusalem so extensive that parents would eat the flesh of their children (19:9). Whether this actually happened in Jerusalem is not certain, but the famine was great (38:9; 52:6; cf. Lam. 2:20; 4:10).

## Failed Leadership

A feminist reading of the book of Jeremiah needs to attend not only to those passages in which women figure explicitly but also to passages that offer models for women's struggles. For example, Jeremiah's critique of failed leadership may offer a model for modern women engaged with religious leaders and institutions who too frequently ignore or deny women's words, talents, and experiences.

During Jeremiah's time the community suffered from conflicting claims for its leadership. In poetry and prose Jeremiah chastises prophets, priests, and kings both for their injustice and for their failure to listen to the word of God (6:13–15; 14:13–18; 20:1–6; chaps. 22–23; 26; 27–28; 36–39). Prophets deceive the people with words of peace when peace is not at hand (6:14; 8:11). A king builds a grand palace and ignores the cause of the poor and the needy (22:13–17). A priest imprisons Jeremiah in the Temple and lies to the people (20:1–6).

The struggle over leadership became particularly acute during the exile when kingship was defunct and the exiles needed direction for the future. Who has the word of God? became a vital question. The conflict appears in many of the stories in the latter half of the book. In chap. 26 priests and prophets sentence Jeremiah to death for his preaching. In chaps. 27–28 Jeremiah confronts the prophet Hananiah in a dispute over which of them had the true revelation for the community. In chap. 36 the king destroys the scroll of Jeremiah's prophecy and forces him and Baruch to go underground. Perhaps women can take courage from Jeremiah's relentless fidelity in the face of opposition and persecution.

## Suffering

The theme of Jeremiah's suffering forms a thread that unites the disparate materials of the book. His sufferings begin in the story of his prophetic call, where God tells Jeremiah that the people will fight against him (1:19). Enemies seek his life (11:19, 21), and even his own family turns against him (12:6). A priest beats him and puts him in the stocks in the Temple (20:1–6). Kings reject his prophecy (chaps. 26 and 36), threaten his life, and imprison him (chaps. 37–38). Although he was rescued from death twice—by Ahikam, a member of the nobility (chap. 26) and by Ebed-melech, a court official of African descent (chap. 38)—his career ends tragically. Some of his own people force him, against his wishes, to flee with them to Egypt (chap. 43).

Jeremiah's afflictions are not merely physical. Poems called the confessions (11:18–12:6; 15:10–21; 17:14–18; 18:18–23; 20:7–13) portray him as a prophet besieged by anguish, loneliness, and doubt. The confessions are prayers, written in the first person, that generally follow the same literary pattern as psalms of lament. In the laments speakers complain to God about their sufferings. They beg for God's intervention in their affairs, and in the midst of their predicaments, they praise God for their anticipated rescue.

Jeremiah uses this prayer form to complain bitterly about attacks from his enemies (11:19; 18:19–23; 20:10), about his prophetic mission (15:15–17; 17:15–16; 20:7–9), and, above all, about God's mistreatment of him (12:1–2; 15:18; 20:7). He lays charges against God for the evil he sees around him (12:12). He blames God for the loneliness of his life (15:17) and for the hatefulness of his mission (20:8–9). He calls God a "deceitful brook," "waters that fail" (15:18), and accuses God of seducing and deceiving him (20:7).

Jeremiah's laments arise from the unique difficulties of his prophetic mission. In the midst of them, he raises an angry fist to God, accuses God of treachery and deceit, and even tries to escape his mission. Yet despite his outbursts of anger and disappointment, the relationship between them remains intact. Indeed, Jeremiah's expressions of anger serve as a vehicle of his fidelity. The confessions end by praising God, who "has delivered the life of the needy from the hands of evildoers" (20:13).

The connection of the confessions to Jeremiah's own life is a matter of dispute among scholars. Some think these prayers are the work of a later editor who saw in Jeremiah a symbol of the suffering people. The people too are taken captive, dragged from their land, and deprived of their Temple. They are beaten, imprisoned, and face death as a people, and, like Jeremiah, they cry out to God in anger and despair. In exile they too would put God on trial for treachery and injustice.

If this understanding of the confessions of Jeremiah is correct, then they may also serve as a model for the outcry of all women who find their words rejected by religious authorities, their bodies battered and abused, wondering if God has abandoned and betrayed them. With Jeremiah, suffering women can cry, "Why is my pain unceasing?" (15:18). And like Jeremiah, women's expressions of anger and doubt reveal their fidelity to the God who "delivers the needy from the hands of evildoers" (20:13).

## Lamentation and Weeping

Grief, lamentation, and weeping pervade the book. Rachel weeps for her children (31:15); the mourning women weep for the nation (9:17–19); even animals and the earth weep (9:10). Jeremiah weeps because God's flock has been taken captive (13:17). God commands Jeremiah to cry out, "Let my eyes run down with tears night and day, and let them not cease, for the virgin daughter—my people—is struck down with a crushing blow" (14:17).

Even God weeps in this book. In two poems (8:18–21; 9:1–3), the weeping figures of Jeremiah and God become indistinguishable. "O that my head were a spring of water, and my eyes a fountain of tears, so that I might weep day and night for the slain of my poor people" (9:1). This merging of the two figures is a poetic device to show that the prophet speaks and acts for God. God cries out, "My joy is gone, grief is upon me, my heart is sick" (8:18). "For the hurt of my poor people I am hurt, I mourn, and dismay has taken hold of me" (8:21). God is not distant from the people's suffering in these poems of weeping; God identifies with them. The people's pain is God's pain.

In seeming contradiction to the God who punishes and destroys, the God of these poems laments and weeps with the people. God anguishes over the people's fate like a mother yearning to save her children from their self-destructive ways. "Shall I not punish them for these things?" (5:9, 29). She wonders how she has failed them. "Have I been a wilderness to Israel, or a land of thick darkness?" (2:31).

Jeremianic themes of weeping and lamentation call upon common human experience, but it is women who are particularly familiar with weeping and grief—grief for their children, for their loved ones, for themselves, for the world. Jeremiah's weeping may help women recognize and express their own unnamed grief, and perhaps it may help them place their sufferings before God, not a God who threatens and punishes but a weeping God who takes up women's pain and weeps with them.

## Hope (chaps. 30–33)

Only shreds of hope appear in this book to counterpoise the deep river of devastation, grief, and despair that pervades most of it (3:14–18; 12:14–17; 16:14–15; 17:24–26; 22:2–4; 23:5–8; 24:4–7; 29:10–14; 42:7–12). In a collection of prose and poetry called "the little book of consolation" (chaps. 30–33), joy overtakes grief, singing replaces weeping. The book of consolation gathers up many themes of destruction and death sounded elsewhere in the book and reverses them to proclaim healing and new life. Poems in this unit feature women in positive ways. The poems include women explicitly among the returnees and present them as symbols of the restored society.

***Wholeness restored (30:8–31:6).*** The prophet sets forth a dream world that completely reverses the reality in which his captive audience lived. His promises are designed to set them on the tiptoes of hope. On some future day God will remove the yoke of bondage from their neck (30:8) and bring them back from the

places to which they have been scattered (30:10–11). God will heal the incurable wound of the outcast woman Zion (30:12–17). "For I will restore health to you, and your wounds I will heal, says Yahweh, because they have called you an outcast: 'It is Zion; no one cares for her!'" (30:17).

Poems in the book of consolation circle about the theme of return. One promises that after the humiliation of defeat, God will restore the nation's honor and turn weeping into merrymaking (30:18–22). "Out of them shall come thanksgiving, and the sound of merrymakers" (30:19). The nation will increase and prosper (30:19), and their rulers will come from their own people (30:21). In another poem, virgin Israel will take her tambourines and "go forth in the dance of merrymakers" to celebrate the rebuilding of the nation (31:4). This poem compares virgin Israel to Miriam and the women who sang and danced with tambourines after the escape through the sea (Ex. 15:21). Once again God sets captives free, and as religious agents women celebrate the event in worship.

***The return (31:7–14).*** The new beginning is both certain and imminent. To welcome it, another poem begins with a command to "sing aloud with gladness" (31:7–14). For the first time in the book, north no longer refers to the direction from which the invading armies will come (1:13; 6:22); here it is the place from which the exiles will return (31:8). Unlike the army coming in terror and cruelty, the returnees will come home in a procession of the weak and the vulnerable. They will form a great company of the blind and the lame, women with children, and women giving birth (31:8). In this poem childbirth does not symbolize death but the new life that will repopulate the decimated nation.

In this paradise, yet to be realized, everyone will share in the joy and abundance of life. The people will "be radiant over . . . the grain, the wine, and the oil, and over the young of the flock and the herd; their life shall become like a watered garden, and they shall never languish again" (31:12). Women and men, young and old, priests and people—all will know comfort and laughter, abundance and satisfaction (31:13–14). The transformed society imagined in these poems provides a social vision that includes everyone not only in worship but also at the banquet of material life. For everyone will share in "the grain, the wine, and the oil" and the benefits of the "flocks and the herds" (31:12, 5). The society will satisfy the basic human needs of all, and it will be characterized by justice, harmony, and peace.

*Rachel, mother of Israel (31:15–22).* In another poem announcing the return, the comforting of Rachel, mother of Israel, symbolizes that new society (31:15–22). The poem depicts Rachel weeping bitterly for her lost children. Like any mother who loses her children, "she refuses to be comforted for her children, because they are no more" (31:15). God speaks to the bereaved mother, "Keep your voice from weeping, and your eyes from tears . . . they shall come back from the land of the enemy; there is hope for your future" (31:16–17). The reader is left to imagine Rachel's joy at this heart-stopping news. Her children are not dead. God will bring them back to her.

The poem then turns to the child, Ephraim, repentant of his sins and forgiven by a merciful God. God's attachment to Rachel's son is as strong as the mother's own: "I am deeply moved for him; I will surely have mercy on him" (31:20). Since the Hebrew word for mercy comes from the same root as the word for womb, God too is the mother of the people in this poem (see Trible).

Rachel's poem closes with an enigmatic line. God promises the "faithless daughter" Israel to create "a new thing on the earth: a woman encompasses a man" (31:22). Literally translated, the second line reads, "a female surrounds a warrior," but its meaning for the poem is not clear. Perhaps it refers to future sexual relationships in which women will be active agents in the procreation of a restored people. Perhaps it speaks of a society at peace so that women will be capable of protecting warriors. Or perhaps it anticipates role reversals of a different sort. What is clear is that the surprising new role of women symbolizes a changed order of relationships in a reconstituted and joyous society.

*New covenant (31:31–34).* A fundamental aspect of that restored society is that in it everyone "from the least to the greatest" will live in covenant relationship. In this most famous Jeremianic passage (31:31–34) God promises to make a new covenant with the whole of Israel. This promise refers not to the New Testament but to a renewal of Israel's covenant with its God. In the past, Israel had broken covenant repeatedly. In the future, the entire

people will live wholeheartedly in covenant relationship. God will make this possible. "I will put my law within them, and I will write it on their hearts; and I will be their God, and they shall be my people" (31:33).

Although this passage employs marriage imagery (31:32), it assures the people that God has not abandoned them, no matter what their infidelities. God has been with them through their sufferings and wishes to be one with them in a covenant of mutual knowledge and commitment. Moreover, in this covenant no one can claim special revelation or superior intimacy with God. All will know God from the least to the greatest. Inherent in this vision is an egalitarian claim that challenges religious domination by the chosen few. It contains a resource for women's hopes of a new order of social relations based on mutuality and interdependence.

*Humans and the earth.* The hierarchical dualism that makes humans sovereigns over the earth rather than its partner is not found among the prophets. For Jeremiah, people are part of the earth, and its fate depends on their fidelity. Borrowing language of Gen. 1:3, he prophesies the return of the earth to chaos because of human sin (4:23–28; see chap. 14). God reverses this vision in 31:35–37 by promising never to cast off Israel unless creation were to cease and the heavens could be measured.

The way a society treats the earth often correlates with the way it treats women. Traditionally women are linked with the earth as subordinate to men. Jeremiah's poetry challenges this assumption. The earth and all its inhabitants are God's creation and the survival of the individual depends on the whole.

## God Language

Although the book portrays God primarily in male terms, God escapes the narrow confines of patriarchal imagery in some passages. God weeps, laments, and cries out over the fate of the people (8:19–9:3); God is a healer who restores health to the people (30:17; 33:6); God is a potter who shapes, destroys, and reforms the people so that they are capable of right relationship (8:1–12). God is a mother attached to her child through unbreakable bonds of love (31:20). God is the covenant maker who abhors injustice and religious arrogance (7:1–15) and seeks covenant relations of mutuality and justice (31:31–34). These divine images provide women with theological bases to claim a place for themselves within the Jewish and Christian faiths.

## BIBLIOGRAPHY

Ackerman, Susan. "'And the Women Knead Dough': The Worship of the Queen of Heaven in Sixth Century Judah." In *Gender and Difference in Ancient Israel,* edited by Peggy L. Day, pp. 109–124. Minneapolis: Fortress Press, 1989.

Bird, Phyllis. "'To Play the Harlot': An Inquiry Into an Old Testament Metaphor." In *Gender and Difference in Ancient Israel,* edited by Peggy L. Day, pp. 75–94. Minneapolis: Fortress Press, 1989.

Carroll, Robert P. *Jeremiah.* Old Testament Library. Philadelphia: Westminster Press, 1986.

Follis, Elaine R. "The Holy City as Daughter." In *Directions in Biblical Hebrew Poetry,* edited by Elaine R. Follis, pp. 173–184. Journal for the Study of the Old Testament Supplement Series 40. Sheffield: JSOT Press, 1987.

Holladay, William L. *Jeremiah.* 2 vols. Hermeneia. Philadelphia and Minneapolis: Fortress Press, 1986, 1989.

McKane, William. *A Critical and Exegetical Commentary on Jeremiah.* Vol. 1. International Critical Commentary. Edinburgh: T. & T. Clark, 1986.

Trible, Phyllis. "Journey of a Metaphor." In her *God and the Rhetoric of Sexuality,* pp. 31–59. Overtures to Biblical Theology. Philadelphia: Fortress Press, 1978.

# LAMENTATIONS

*Kathleen M. O'Connor*

## Introduction

The book of Lamentations is a heartbreaking cry of pain and grief by the survivors of a war. The book's sorrow echoes through the wars of the ages and stands as testimony to war's horror and futility. Women figure prominently in the book's description of war's atrocities and serve as symbols of the pain of the people.

### Setting and Purpose

The Babylonian invasion of Jerusalem lasted from 589 to 587 B.C.E. In its wake, the city lay in ruins: the palace and Temple had been destroyed, many people had been killed, and leading citizens of the city had been deported to Babylon. In the war's aftermath, the survivors faced bitter memories of the war's miseries, including a devastating famine that racked the city. Beyond the enormous problems of physical survival that the war created were seemingly insurmountable emotional and spiritual dilemmas. To the remnant in Jerusalem it seemed that God had forgotten them, turned against them, or abandoned them forever. The five poems of Lamentations are the people's heartbroken response to this interlocking set of disasters.

### Authorship

A long tradition ascribes Lamentations to the prophet Jeremiah. A preface to the Septuagint, the Greek translation of the book, names him as its author, and the Septuagint places Lamentations after the book of Jeremiah in the canon. Like the book of Jeremiah, Lamentations uses the lament form to grieve over the fate of the people. A near contemporary of the prophetic book, in many ways Lamentations evokes the spirit of the "suffering prophet." It is not likely, however, that Jeremiah is the book's author, because the language and spirit of its poetry are too different from that of the prophetic book. Furthermore, the Hebrew text of Lamentations makes no mention of Jeremiah, and the Hebrew canon locates the book among the five scrolls (*megillot*).

Instead, one or more anonymous authors composed the laments for public recitation by the people. It is possible that survivors recited them at the site of the destroyed Temple to pour out their grief over the disasters that had come upon them (Jer. 41:5). Because laments help people to weep over their tragedy and thus release their pain, Lamentations is truly the work of the people. Since women acted as official mourners in Israel, a woman may have been among the book's authors, but there is no evidence to support this suggestion.

The book continues to have a liturgical life in the Jewish and Christian communities. Jews recite Lamentations on the ninth of Ab to commemorate the fall of the Second Temple in 70 C.E., and Christians use parts of the book during Holy Week services.

### Literary Forms

The primary literary form used in Lamentations is the lament. Laments are liturgical prayers or psalms in which the speakers complain to God about their circumstances and beg for release. The speaker may represent an individual or the community. Typical elements of the lament form appear in each of the five poems of Lamentations: a series of complaints, a statement of guilt, a request for God's favor, and a petition against enemies. Significantly absent from all five laments, however, are the statements of praise conventionally found in psalms of lament (e.g., Psalm 22). This omission suggests that the people's devastation and confusion were so severe that they could not bring themselves to praise God directly. Nonetheless, the mere use of a lament is an act of fidelity, because the purpose of the form is to address God in the midst of inexplicable suffering.

Incorporated into three of the laments is another literary form that intensifies the expression of sorrow and despair in the poems. It is the dirge, or death wail, used during funeral processions (1:1; 2:1; 4:1). A "limping" rhythm, three beats followed by two beats, characterizes the dirge. Known as *qinah* meter, this rhythm occurs throughout the poems of Lamentations, emphasizing the people's grief at the death of the nation.

### Literary Arrangement

Beyond the structure of the lament form, the individual laments of the book exhibit further literary structuring not apparent in English translations. Each poem corresponds in some way to the twenty-two-letter Hebrew alphabet. Four poems (chaps. 1–4) are acrostics, in which the first letter of succeeding verses creates the Hebrew alphabet. Chapter 3 intensifies this acrostic form by devoting three verses to each letter of the alphabet. Although chap. 5 is not an acrostic, it too is an alphabetic poem in that it contains twenty-two lines. These alphabetic designs reveal that the poems are not haphazard outpourings but carefully controlled, artistic creations. Their tight structuring creates the effect of confining the experience of overwhelming chaos, thus making the people's tragedy appear survivable.

Careful literary arrangement extends to the book itself. The other four chapters make a frame around chap. 3, the only poem of the book that expresses hope in an extended way (vv. 21–66). This framing device emphasizes the theological centrality of chap. 3 and thus highlights the community's movement toward hope even in its darkest hour.

## Comment

Despite the evocative beauty of Lamentations, there are reasons for women to be cautious when they approach it. Biases against women appear in the book's imagery and in its structure.

### Ambiguous Gender Imagery

The poems in chaps. 1, 2, and 4 use a variety of female images to depict Judah and Jerusalem. These images are fluid, weaving in and out of one another to create the impression that several women are present in the poem. Yet the female representations of Judah and Jerusalem merge into one figure, "daughter Zion," who personifies Jerusalem. In these three chapters a narrator speaks about her, and she speaks herself in 1:12–22 and 2:11, 20–22.

*Daughter Zion.* Personification is a literary device that gives to things qualities of persons. Since cities and countries are feminine grammatical forms in Hebrew, it is easy to understand how biblical poets came to symbolize cities as females. Perhaps there may even be remnants of the ancient notion of a city's protective goddess involved in Zion's title, but if so, evidence that she represents a deity has disappeared in Lamentations. The personification of Jerusalem as daughter Zion comes from the name of the mountain in the center of the city upon which the Temple was built. Zion was the place where God chose to dwell.

The title "daughter Zion," therefore, appears at first to provide contemporary women with a female biblical symbol of high dignity. She is God's beloved daughter. She is an eloquent spokeswoman for the people's grief, and like many speakers in the psalms, she expresses her sorrow with language of intense feeling (1:16, 20; 2:11). Ultimately she discards the role of victim (chap. 1) to become God's adversary, challenging divine mistreatment of herself and her people (2:20–22).

That the authors of Lamentations would give daughter Zion so prominent a role in the book suggests that they were aware of women's sufferings and valued them highly enough to employ them as metaphors of the community's pain. Nonetheless, the poetic figure of daughter Zion carries nuances that are harmful to women. Although the title "daughter" conveys divine tenderness toward Zion, the term also portrays women as subordinate to the deity, symbolized as male. Furthermore, Lamentations (especially chap. 1) depicts daughter Zion as the object of scorn, as the cause of her own suffering, and as a woman who collaborates in her own abuse.

### The menstruating woman (1:1–11, 17).

The book's opening verse captures the reader's sympathies by comparing the devastated Jerusalem to a widow. In the ancient world the term "widow" referred not merely to a bereaved wife but specifically to a wife whose husband's death deprived her of economic support. She is an innocent victim of circumstances. Lamentations 1:2, however, transforms the innocent widow into a loose woman whose "lovers have abandoned her." This shift of imagery implicates her in her own suffering.

Subsequent verses feature daughter Zion and blame her explicitly for her tragedy. She suffers "for the multitude of her transgressions" (1:5). She has "sinned grievously, so she has become a mockery" (1:8). "Her uncleanness was in her skirts; she took no thought of her future" (1:9).

Language in some of the verses brings connotations to the poem not evident in English translations. The Hebrew word for "uncleanness" (1:9) refers to ritual impurity, which could have several origins. Among the possibilities specific to women are uncleanness from menstruation (Lev. 15:19–30) or from adultery (Num. 5:19). Daughter Zion's uncleanness arises from adultery, which she commits with careless disregard for the future (1:9). Menstrual uncleanness, nonetheless, is an aspect of daughter Zion's shame in chap. 1. Among her enemies she has become a "filthy thing" (niddah, 1:17). The Hebrew word used here has the general meaning of "impurity" but often refers specifically to menstruation. In 1:8 a similar word, translated "mockery" (nidah), may create a pun on niddah. The woman has become a mockery because she is menstruous and unclean. In this chapter, therefore, a natural condition of the female body becomes a metaphor of shame and humiliation.

Daughter Zion's shame involves her body in still another way. "All who honored her despise her, for they have seen her nakedness" (1:8). In ancient Israel the exposure of the body caused profound disgrace, and stripping may have been part of the punishment of prostitutes or newly taken slaves. In this poem the occasion for daughter Zion's nakedness is not specified, but her degradation and bodily humiliation are clear.

### The abused woman (1:12–27).

In the second half of chap. 1 daughter Zion herself begins to speak. Theologically, chap. 1 aims to explain the disaster that befell the community: the sin and infidelity of the people, not God's failure, brought tragedy. As daughter Zion gives voice to her sufferings, she describes herself in language that today calls to mind the circumstances of battered women. She is abused, beaten, and tortured by the one whom she trusted. She bitterly laments her sorrows and names their source. God inflicted them "on the day of his fierce anger. From on high he sent fire; it went deep into my bones; he spread a net for my feet; he turned me back; he has left me stunned, faint all day long" (1:12–13). Daughter Zion blames herself for the excesses of her abuser and, like contemporary victims of domestic violence, appears to have no self-esteem left. "Yahweh is in the right, for I have rebelled against his word" (1:18).

To assign responsibility to humans, the poet of chap. 1 uses the metaphors of adulteress, menstruant woman, and abused woman. As a consequence, the poem symbolically blames women alone for the destruction of the city, and it teaches disdain for women and for their bodies. Most disturbing of all, chap. 1 indirectly justifies abuse of women by portraying God as the abuser.

## Gender Imagery in the Book's Structure

The book's gender biases appear also in its structure. When the authors wish to blame the people or to speak of their humiliation, they use female symbols (chaps. 1, 2, and 4). When they want to speak of hope (3:55–66) and to petition God directly for help (5:1–19, 22), female symbols disappear. In chap. 5 the speaker is not a woman but the collective voice of the community. In chap. 3, the theological heart of the book, the speaker is male. The NRSV obscures the male voice by translating 3:1, "I am the one who has seen affliction." This translation implies that daughter Zion is still speaking from chap. 2, but the one who announces that God's mercies "are new every morning" (3:23) and claims that God has "taken up my cause" (3:58) is not daughter Zion but a "strong man" or "warrior" (geber, 3:1). It is he who represents the emerging Jerusalem, confident of God's steadfast love (3:22).

## Women's History

As symbolic figures, women convey mixed messages in Lamentations, but when the book speaks of real women, it tells of their history in painful and illuminating ways. The book brings into the open hidden victims of war who suffer long after the war's end. Some verses mention women's sufferings alongside those of men and other social groups. Young women have gone into captivity with young men (1:18). Both are slaughtered without mercy (2:21). Young girls and elders grieve over Zion's destruction (2:10). Other verses attend specifically to the plight of women. The male speaker grieves over "the fate of all the young women in my city" (3:51). "Mothers are like widows" (5:3). "Women are raped in Zion" (5:11).

But the war's effects on women appear most sharply in graphic vignettes about the famine. The famine touched everyone (4:9; 2:19), but its impact was greatest on mothers and young children. "Infants and babes faint in the streets of the city" (2:11). Mothers listen to their babies cry for food and watch them die on their breasts (2:12). "Children beg for food, but no one gives them anything" (4:3–4). Unlike the jackals, who "offer the breast and nurse their young," Israel has become cruel (4:3).

Hunger leads to horror when the poems accuse mothers of cannibalism. The speaker of chap. 4 reports that "the hands of compassionate women have boiled their own children; they became their food" (4:10). To describe the terrible consequences of divine punishment, daughter Zion hurls an accusation at God, "Should women eat their offspring, the children they have borne?" (2:20).

Most mothers can imagine no greater horror than that their children would die at their own hands. If women did participate in cannibalism, it was probably not to feed themselves but to feed other starving children. Though the poets may have been aware of women's pain during these sad events, that is not their chief concern in reporting them. Their primary interest is to show how devastated is a people whose children cannot survive.

The cannibalism of which women are accused in these laments, however, may be more symbolic than actual. The authors of Lamentations may have adapted a curse from Deut. 28:53–57, which described what would happen if Israel violated the covenant. If that is the case, the poets have modified the Deuteronomic curse at women's expense. Whereas Deuteronomy promises that both men and women will eat the flesh of their children, Lamentations reports that women alone fulfilled the curse.

## Women's Prayer

Besides offering women glimpses of the painful lives of their foremothers, Lamentations also provides women with a rare female voice in biblical liturgical prayer. Although daughter Zion accepts and participates in her own abuse, she also articulates her own pain and ultimately demands that God redress what seems to be divine injustice.

She complains about the way passersby treat her suffering as if it were trivial, urging them: "Look and see if there is any sorrow like my sorrow" (1:12). She blames God for her suffering (1:13–15). She weeps for her isolation, for the abuse she has received, and for the desolation of her children at the hands of her enemy (1:16). She finally begs God to avenge her against her enemies and to afflict them as she has been afflicted (1:21–22). In chap. 2 she abandons self-recrimination altogether and shouts in outrage at God for killing the young women and men of the city, for "slaughtering them without mercy" (2:21).

Hence, daughter Zion's prayer may help contemporary women in their prayer. Daughter Zion's voice evokes the pain of women who have lost their children, who know sexual abuse, who are victims of war and famine. To pray with daughter Zion is to join with the struggles of women around the globe. It is to reject victimhood by embracing the anger that can provide energy to transform relationships. It is to pour out the "heart like water before the presence of Yahweh" (2:19).

Daughter Zion insists that if God really saw the plight of her people, God would do something about it. She demands that God "look" and "consider to whom you have done this" (2:20). See "how distressed I am" (1:20). It is as if all this pain occurred because God was careless, but if God saw the affliction of the beloved daughter Zion, the divine heart would change. Such is the confidence with which she prays. She assumes, as do all speakers of biblical laments, that God values her life and that God will hear and act on her behalf.

By praying with her, women may be able to give voice to their pain and despair, and, by voicing it, by expressing their anger, they may be able to move beyond circumstances of impasse to announce in their own lives, God's "mercies never come to an end; they are new every morning" (3:22).

## BIBLIOGRAPHY

Guinon, Michael D. "Lamentations." *The New Jerome Biblical Commentary*, edited by Raymond E. Brown et al., pp. 558–562. Englewood Cliffs, N.J.: Prentice-Hall, 1990.

Hillers, Delbert R. *Lamentations*. Anchor Bible 7A. Garden City, N.Y.: Doubleday & Co., 1972.

Kaiser, Barbara Bakke. "Poet as Female Impersonator: The Image of Daughter Zion as Speaker in Biblical Poems of Suffering." *Journal of Religion* 67 (1987), 164–182.

Westermann, Claus. "Lamentations." In *The Books of the Bible*, vol. 1, *The Old Testament/The Hebrew Bible*, edited by Bernhard W. Anderson, pp. 303–318. New York: Charles Scribner's Sons, 1989.

# EZEKIEL

## Katheryn Pfisterer Darr

## Introduction

### Ezekiel and His Times

Ezekiel was deported to Babylonia in 597 B.C.E. and was called to be a prophet in his fifth year of exile. At a crucial period in Judah's history, he struggled to convict his people of their sinfulness, to justify God's actions, and to articulate a vision of Israel's future.

Ezekiel elaborated on the female imagery of earlier prophets; the result is some of the Bible's most misogynistic texts. He flatly condemned certain women for their religious practices and stressed the priestly belief that during their monthly periods females were a potential source of ritual impurity for males. For these and other reasons, many contemporary women have criticized Ezekiel, wary of the consequences of his message for women. Further study of the book may not dispel such concerns; it can, however, help readers understand why Ezekiel spoke as he did.

***Historical background.*** Both Egypt and Babylonia vied for power as the once-mighty Assyrian empire verged on collapse late in the seventh century B.C.E. The situation was precarious for Assyria's vassals, including Judah: Should one support Babylon or pledge loyalty to Egypt?

With an Egyptian defeat at Carchemish (605 B.C.E.), Syria-Palestine fell under Babylon's control. A subsequent clash between Egyptian and Babylonian forces ended indecisively, however (601 B.C.E.); and when the Babylonians retreated, King Jehoiakim of Judah rebelled against Nebuchadrezzar, his Babylonian overlord, no doubt expecting Egypt's assistance. But in 597, Nebuchadrezzar besieged Jerusalem; and Jehoiachin, Jehoiakim's successor, surrendered. Nebuchadrezzar placed Zedekiah on

the throne, deporting to Babylonia not only Jehoiachin and other members of the royal family but also political, military, and religious leaders, including Ezekiel the priest, son of Buzi.

Little is known of the exiles' living conditions. A substantial community was settled at Tel-abib, near the Chebar River. References to Ezekiel's house suggest that the deportees were not forced into work camps. Of course, some exiles may have been imprisoned along with Jehoiachin and his household. It seems likely, however, that most were permitted to practice their trades and support their families. Back in Jerusalem, the prophet Jeremiah wrote a letter advising the deportees to build houses and plant gardens (Jer. 29:5). Assuming that he actually knew of their circumstances (and Jeremiah 29 suggests that communication flowed between the two regions with relative ease), Jeremiah's advice is evidence that the exiles were free to do these things.

Their suffering and anxiety should not be minimized, however. Not only had they been thrust into an alien environment, leaving behind family, friends, and possessions, but also they lived with uncertainty about their own futures and the fate of their homeland. Frightened and desperate for divine guidance, the exiles sought a reassuring word from Yahweh. They received no comfort, however, from the priest/prophet Ezekiel.

***A priest called to prophesy.*** Biographical information about Ezekiel is sparse. He was from a priestly family and perhaps had served in the Jerusalem Temple. He was married, but no children are mentioned. Ezekiel seems eccentric, given to unusual actions and behaviors. In the past, some scholars have claimed that he suffered from psychological and/or physiological disorders, but his behavior had precedents within Israel's early prophetic traditions. If his conduct was extreme, it reflected the extremity of his times.

Unlike Jeremiah (Jer. 1:6), Ezekiel did not resist the call to prophesy (3:1–3). On the contrary, when God ordered him to eat a scroll inscribed with words of "lamentation and mourning and woe" (2:10), he found it "sweet as honey." One cannot read the book without being struck by Ezekiel's utter determination in the face of hostile defiance (2:3, 6; 3:7), despondency (20:32), and—worst of all—apathy (33:31–32), to convince the exiles that the God against whom they and their ancestors had sinned was bringing them to justice, purging them of impurity, and demonstrating divine sovereignty throughout the world.

## The Book of Ezekiel

*Structure.* The book has three large sections. Introduced by an account of Ezekiel's first vision of Yahweh's glory (1:1–28) and his prophetic call (2:1–3:11), the first section (chaps. 1–24) consists mainly of condemnations and judgments concerning the past and present people of Israel. The second section (chaps. 25–32) contains oracles against foreign nations and rulers, and the third (chaps. 33–48) consists primarily of prophecies about Israel's future restoration.

Fourteen passages in the book are dated: 1:1, 2 (a double date); 3:16; 8:1; 20:1; 24:1; 26:1; 29:1; 29:17; 30:20; 31:1; 32:1; 32:17; 33:21; and 40:1 (also a double date). These dates, ranging from July 594 B.C.E. (or 593) to April 571, are for the most part in chronological sequence and contribute to the book's well-structured appearance.

*Narrative summary of the book's contents.* Seven days after Ezekiel's vision of Yahweh's enthroned glory and his call to prophesy, God appoints him watchman over Israel. (Watchmen, stationed upon hills or high walls, scanned the horizon for enemies and alerted fellow citizens of danger.) Henceforth he must warn the wicked of their impending fate and call the backsliding righteous to repentance (3:16–21). Immediately, however, Yahweh restricts both his movement and his speech. Ezekiel cannot himself reprove his rebellious community; he can speak only when God opens his mouth. The apparent contradiction between a mandate

to function as Israel's watchman and these physical limitations is not easily resolved, but perhaps 3:27 intends to convince his audience that Ezekiel's words are in fact *God's* words—a reliable message from Israel's sovereign deity, spoken through an authentic prophet.

A series of sign-acts (actions that are themselves a divine message to the prophet's audience and serve to reinforce his words) portend the tragic future of God's people (4:1–5:4; see also 12:1–20; 24:15–24). The sign-acts are followed by three judgment oracles, each indicting a larger group of offenders: Jerusalem's citizens (5:5–17); the inhabitants of Israel's mountains (6:1–14); and the "four corners of the land," that is, Judah's entire population (7:1–27). Chapters 8–11 detail Ezekiel's visionary tour of Jerusalem's Temple compound, the site of various abominable acts. Yahweh orders that the city's wicked residents be slaughtered. When Ezekiel cries out against the enormity of the annihilation, God forswears compassion. The tone is severe, the message clear: Jerusalem deserves the devastation that lies ahead. By the end of the vision, God's glory has abandoned the city to its fate (11:22–25).

Ezekiel's accusations and threats are no less extreme throughout the remainder of the first section. Although he occasionally moves beyond doom to speak of Israel's restoration (e.g., 16:53–63; 20:33–44), these texts scarcely ameliorate the savagery of his attacks against male and female prophets (chap. 13), those exiles engaging in ostensibly illicit forms of worship (chap. 14), Jerusalem (e.g., chap. 16), Zedekiah (e.g., chap. 17), Israel's princes (e.g., chap. 19)—indeed, all of Israel throughout its history (chaps. 20; 23). Relentlessly Ezekiel insists that the exiles cannot base their hopes for release and national deliverance on Israel's past relationship with Yahweh or on Jerusalem's privileged status. On the contrary, the people have rebelled against God from the beginning, and Jerusalem's sin exceeds Sodom's. When Yahweh causes the death of Ezekiel's beloved wife, he is forbidden to express his grief through normal mourning rituals. His quiet anguish becomes a portent of the exiles' own inability to mourn when the Temple is destroyed (24:15–24). With Jerusalem's demise, however, Ezekiel's speech restrictions end (24:25–27; 33:21–22).

Although oracles against foreign nations appear also in the first section (21:28–32) and the third (35:1–15), most are found in chaps. 25–32. Chapter 25 condemns Judah's malicious neighbors—Moab and Philistia as well as

Ammon and Edom—but the remainder of the section is devoted to oracles against Tyre (26:1–28:19) and Egypt (29:1–32:32), two powers that tempt Israel to subvert Yahweh's will. The origin of oracles against foreign nations may lie in war oracles commissioned by ancient Near Eastern rulers against their enemies. In Ezekiel, however, they affirm Yahweh's worldwide sovereignty, warn Israel of the consequences of arrogant pride, and serve as a transition to the oracles of restoration.

After Jerusalem's fall (33:21), Ezekiel's message shifts from judgment to deliverance. He has not changed his opinion about the people's guilt (36:31–32). Nonetheless, he promises that in the future, God will be Israel's "good shepherd" (34:15), the people will enjoy peace and prosperity in a rejuvenated homeland (36:8–12), and, in his exquisite vision of the valley of dry bones, the whole house of Israel will be "re-membered" and restored to life (37:1–14). A final cosmic battle, begun when the forces of Gog attack Israel, will demonstrate God's sovereignty and holiness to all the nations (chaps. 38–39). The remainder of the book (chaps. 40–48) recounts Ezekiel's great vision of Israel's rebuilt Temple, reestablished cult, and rejuvenated, well-ordered homeland.

**The history of the book.** Although some scholars argue that Ezekiel was personally responsible for virtually the entire book in its final form, other critics believe that the work took shape over a period of years stretching beyond his death. According to this view, Ezekiel's original oracles, which he may have collected and expanded during his lifetime, were subsequently gathered, arranged, and supplemented by editors who completed the book some years after the Babylonian exile had ended, that is, after 538 B.C.E.

## Understanding and Interpreting Ezekiel

**Presuppositions underlying Ezekiel's message.** Ezekiel's severity is comprehensible only in light of the presuppositions and convictions whence his words proceed. Steeped in a God-centered worldview, Ezekiel could not regard crucial events in Judah's history simply as fate or as the result of a chance confluence of unfavorable events. At least four basic convictions undergird Ezekiel's oracles. First, he was convinced that the events of 597 were just the beginning of his people's suffering. Certain Judeans, the prophet Hananiah among them

(Jer. 28:1–4), believed that conditions would improve soon, but Ezekiel insisted that *his* was God's authentic word.

Second, Ezekiel insisted that Judah's destruction was God's doing. He denied that the nation's plight signaled Yahweh's weakness relative to Babylonian deities. Neither would he accept the complaint that "Yahweh does not see us, Yahweh has forsaken the land" (8:12). God was in control of history, he argued; the situation could not be blamed on divine impotence or abandonment.

Third, Ezekiel maintained that Yahweh's actions against Judah were not the capricious deeds of a disinterested God. On the contrary, they were the deity's response to human sinfulness. Fourth, Ezekiel insisted that Yahweh's punishment was proportional and just. Indeed, he declared that Israel had incurred sufficient guilt to merit exile from its land centuries earlier (20:23–24). Only God's concern for the divine reputation ("name") had delayed the nation's destruction until the present day. His companions might complain that "the way of the Lord is unfair" (18:25, 29; 33:17, 20), but Ezekiel defended the justice of God's actions. He insisted, moreover, that Israel's future restoration be understood as the result of Yahweh's determination to see the divine plan for Israel fulfilled rather than as a reward for human righteousness.

**Priestly perspectives in Ezekiel.** In his language about God, his diagnosis of Israel's moral and religious maladies, and his vision of the future, Ezekiel was influenced by priestly thought and language. Scholars have noted, for example, the particularly close relationship between Ezekiel and portions of the so-called Holiness Code (Leviticus 17–26). Central to priestly theology is the holiness of God. Ezekiel attests both to the importance of this divine attribute and to its significance for Israel and the nations. In his visions he attempts to describe God's "glory," that is, the divine holiness made manifest. Turning to history, he insists that Yahweh sought to sanctify Israel but the nation repeatedly acted in ways that render it unclean and profane God's holy name. Even the priests are guilty of profaning what is sacred (22:26). Such impurity threatens the relationship between Yahweh and Israel, but the latter is incapable of cleansing itself. Only God can purify this people, manifesting divine holiness before the nations (36:22–23). Ezekiel's magnificent vision of Israel's future Temple, cultus, and land (chaps. 40–48) attends with meticulous detail to the conditions necessary to maintain Israel's holiness when God's glory again dwells in its midst.

Although the nation cannot purge itself, Ezekiel urges individual Israelites to assume responsiblity for moral conduct. Embedded in chap. 18, for example, are a number of requirements for righteous and just living (18:5–9, 10–13, 14–18). That the instructions are addressed to males is clear from references to adultery with another man's wife and to sexual intercourse with a menstruating woman. Modern readers may wonder that intercourse with a woman during her monthly period is grouped with other offenses and instructions of a seemingly more serious nature. From a priestly perspective, however, such intercourse rendered a man unclean (see Lev. 18:19); and impurity threatened not only the individual but also the whole people of God.

***Prophetic influences and issues in Ezekiel.*** Ezekiel was influenced by his prophetic prede-cessors. He knew at least some of the oracles of Hosea, Isaiah, and Jeremiah, and he elaborated on Hosea's and Jeremiah's use of marital imagery to depict the relationship between God and Israel. Ezekiel actually performed actions his predecessors had predicted for the future (compare Isa. 7:20 and Ezek. 5:1–4) or cast in figurative language (compare Jer. 1:9 and Ezek. 3:1–3).

Other aspects of Ezekiel's book link him with the so-called former prophets, especially Elijah and Elisha. Like Elijah, he experienced the powerful "hand of Yahweh" (Ezek. 3:14; 1 Kings 18:46). Like Elisha, he saw events beyond his actual range of vision (Ezekiel 8–11; 2 Kings 5:25–27).

Ezekiel's predecessors also performed sign-acts (e.g., Isaiah 20), one purpose of which was to reinforce a prophet's words. Determining whether a prophet was trustworthy was no easy task in Israel's world. Ezekiel, like his predecessors, had to compete with prophets whose oracles contradicted his own (see, e.g., 13:10–12).

## Comment

### God's Sinful People and Their Punishment

***Oracles against royalty (19:1–14).*** Two indictments of Judah's royalty contain female imagery. In 19:2–9 and 10–14, Ezekiel invites his audience to perceive the lamented "princes of Israel" through the selective lens of two images: a lioness who raises her cubs, only to see them ensnared and carried off; and a vine uprooted from fertile soil, hurled into the desert, and destroyed. Despite the shift in imagery, these two sections are linked themati-cally, as well as by the catchphrase "your mother" (19:2, 10).

Because Ezekiel customarily addresses his dirges to the one being lamented, it follows that 19:2–14 is directed to one (or more) of Judah's princes. That his first words are about "your mother" suggests her significance: on the one hand, the lioness is an active agent, choosing to advance first one cub and then the other and teaching them to hunt. When they are captured, their undoing is seen through her eyes. On the other hand, in 19:10–14 the focus remains fixed on the "mother" vine. She does not merely observe her children's demise. On the contrary, her own destruction—sudden, shocking, and absolute—is inextricably linked with the downfall of her towering (i.e., prideful) offshoot.

In constructing this lament, Ezekiel has—with his usual literary deftness—presented an image positively, only to expose the negative or vulnerable characteristics lurking beneath the surface. In 19:2–9, he initially draws on positive associations with lionesses—their strength, pride, and nobility. Because of her maternal attention and training, the cubs become strong young lions and successful hunters—a pre-requisite, after all, for survival. But with the notice that both young lions have devoured humans (19:3, 6), the imagery's connotations of pride and nobility recede and other character-istics—rapacity and violence—predominate (see also Ezek. 22:25; Zeph. 3:3; Prov. 28:15). Similarly, vv. 10–14 begin on a positive note, affirming that "your mother," like a vine planted in well-watered soil, is fruitful, has many strong offshoots, and is (ostensibly) assured of continued health and growth. Suddenly, however, Ezekiel undermines the imagery's sense of security and longevity. The plant is uprooted, hurled to the ground, desic-cated, defoliated, seared by flame, and trans-planted to dry desert land—the antithesis of its former, fertile environment.

These observations, coupled with the mournful phrase "What a lioness was your mother among lions" (19:2), suggest that

Ezekiel 19 laments the mother's loss (both her *experience* of bereavement [vv. 2–9] and her *demise* [vv. 10–14]) more than the princes' undoing. But who or what does the mother represent? Some scholars have sought her identity among historical women, suggesting that she is Hamutal, mother of Jehoiahaz and Zedekiah or—at least in v. 10—Nehushta, the queen mother exiled with her son, Jehoiachin (2 Kings 24:12). Although the poem admits such speculation, one should remember that poetic imagery can convey multiple meanings. "Mother" also can be understood to represent Judah, the Davidic dynasty, and especially Jerusalem—home of Judah's royalty and the entity Ezekiel elsewhere depicts both as female and as a mother.

***Oracles against women's religious activities (8:14–15; 13:17–23).*** Transported to Jerusalem in a vision, Ezekiel witnesses four abominations in or near the Temple itself, Judah's most sacred space. North of the gate leading to the Temple's inner court, he sees "the image of jealousy, which provokes to jealousy" (8:3), identified by some commentators as a statue of the goddess Asherah (see 2 Chron. 33:7, 15). He watches as the seventy-member national council secretly burns incense before engraved images of unclean animals. Prior to the fourth and worst offense—twenty-five men turning their backs on Yahweh's altar to worship the sun—Ezekiel sees certain women sitting at the entrance of the Temple's north gate and "weeping for Tammuz."

The cult of the Mesopotamian god Tammuz, or Dumuzi (whose name may mean "the Quickener of the young [in the mother's womb]" or "the good young one," i.e., the god manifest in the birth of healthy, well-formed offspring), was primarily a women's cult. Mesopotamian in origin, it both celebrated nature's seasonal fertility and mourned its loss. Tammuz was manifest in trees' rising sap, in the date palm and its fruits, in the grain used to make bread and beer, and in ewes' milk (Jacobsen, pp. 73–74). He was, surviving texts make clear, much beloved by his devotees, who imagined him as partly human in nature, a youthful, charming lad married to the goddess Inanna. During the fourth month of each year (called Tammuz in his memory), when spring's new life waned in the heat of summer, women mourned his death. Their poetic laments, distinguished by a sense of heartfelt grief, bereavement, and longing for the deceased, expressed the sorrow of those whose love for Tammuz was like the love of a sister for her brother, a bride for her bridegroom, or a mother for her cherished son.

Ezekiel's outrage stems from his conviction that weeping for Tammuz, like the three other abominations, is idolatrous—the ascription of power and offering of devotion to a deity other than Israel's God. It is quite possible, however, that other Judeans of the period did not regard the Tammuz cult as inconsistent with Yahwism. Is Ezekiel's fury further inflamed by the proximity of these women—potential sources of impurity—to the Temple? That he places their ritual weeping in the sixth month, rather than the fourth, has been explained as a cultic variation practiced by Judean women (because spring arrived later in their geographical region?) or as Ezekiel's attempt to depict all of Jerusalem's past and present sins within the confines of a single visionary experience, irrespective of their original temporal locus.

In his famous essay "Toward the Image of Tammuz," Thorkild Jacobsen assesses the cult's ethical and religious values. That it was a women's religion, as Ezek. 8:14 suggests, is crucial to his analysis, since he believes that the cult was "conditioned by the specific psychological horizon of the ancient Mesopotamian woman." "Though Tammuz is a male god," Jacobsen writes, "proper manly virtues such as one finds exemplified and celebrated in, for instance, the early epical texts—courage, resourcefulness, steadfastness—are in him almost conspicuously lacking" (p. 91). Instead, the deity is adored because of his youthful lack of responsibility, his utter dependence and vulnerability. The love his devotees feel for him is not an unselfish, mature emotion, however. Rather, it is a form of self-love that fastens upon another out of need. Despite their extravagant expressions of devotion, Jacobsen believes that the females' fascination with Tammuz is in fact infatuation—immature, needy, unwilling to let go. His evaluation should be challenged for its polarization of "proper manly virtues" at one extreme and its caricature of women's ostensibly "emotional" nature at the other. Moreover, in emphasizing ancient women's "psychological horizon," he has largely overlooked their physiological horizon, by virtue of which they experienced, more intimately than could males, those aspects of the divine power manifest in the deity called Tammuz—the quickening of new life, birth, and lactation.

In 13:17–23, Ezekiel condemns "the daughters of your people, who prophesy out of their own imagination" (v. 17). Already he has revealed his primary complaint against these women: whatever their activity (and its precise nature is, unfortunately, obscure), it is their own doing, not Yahweh's. By their acts, Ezekiel charges, these women deceive their clients, so that the innocent fear for their lives while the guilty are reassured that all is well. Such activity clearly flies in the face of Ezekiel's own self-understanding, according to which God commissioned him to call the wicked to repentance and warn the righteous of sin's penalty. The women's fate is certain, Ezekiel asserts. After freeing their victims, God will bring their lies and divination to an end.

The arm cushions or pads and veils or bonnets worn by these women were apparently aids in revealing the future. Perhaps the barley and bread referred to in 13:19 also were used for divination (Greenberg) rather than as payment for their services (Zimmerli). If they were active in Babylonia, then it is possible that these women were influenced by the magical methods of Babylonian diviners. Magic was part of ancient Israel's society, however, despite the Bible's negative attitude toward it. It is reasonable to assume that in periods of crisis, especially, Judeans resorted to every possible means to gain some reassurance about the future, some sense of control over their lives (see also the story of Saul and the Endor diviner in 1 Samuel 28). In the end, one cannot be certain that Ezekiel's characterization of the women's activity is accurate, for he sought to discredit those intermediaries whose methods and messages conflicted with his own.

### Oracles against Jerusalem (chaps. 16; 23; 22:1–16).
Two lengthy oracles depict Jerusalem (chaps. 16 and 23) and Samaria (chap. 23) as Yahweh's adulterous wives. Ezekiel 16 tells the story of Jerusalem, an abandoned infant rescued by God. After she grew to sexual maturity, Yahweh married her, lavishing on her beautiful clothes and fine food. But Jerusalem betrayed her husband, constructing phallic images from his silver and gold (the masculine pronoun is, in this context, appropriate), sacrificing God's children to these images and offering her sexuality to strangers—Assyrians, Babylonians, and Egyptians—at every crossroad. She was worse than common prostitutes, Ezekiel charges, because she paid her lovers rather than being paid by them (16:34). Therefore, Yahweh threatens, her lovers will gather a mob to stone her, stab her, and burn her houses

(the metaphor slips a bit). Beyond her mutilation and murder, however, lies restoration. Jerusalem will be filled with shame, but Yahweh will reunite with her in an eternal covenant.

In chap. 23 wanton Jerusalem is joined by her sister, Samaria (the capital city of northern Israel, destroyed by the Assyrians in 721 B.C.E.). Yahweh tells Ezekiel a story about Oholah (Samaria) and Oholibah (Jerusalem). During their youth in Egypt, both women engaged in promiscuous sexual activity, flagrantly bestowing on their lovers the intimacies properly reserved for their future husbands. Eventually Yahweh wed the two sisters, and they bore children. But Oholah, seduced by the Assyrians' beauty and vigor, reverted to her former, lascivious ways. As punishment, Yahweh handed her over to her Assyrian paramours, who stripped and abused her, captured her children, and put her to the sword. Despite her sister's fate, Oholibah committed harlotries of her own. Indeed, her lewdness exceeded Oholah's. Therefore, God threatens, her former lovers will attack her, carrying off her children and burning whatever remains.

Ezekiel's choice of female imagery for Jerusalem and Samaria was not a poetic innovation. Cities frequently were personified as females within the Hebrew Bible and in other ancient Near Eastern texts as well. Neither was he the first to adopt marriage, with its demand for female (but not male) sexual fidelity, as a metaphor for the relationship between Yahweh and a city (the embodiment of its inhabitants). However, Ezekiel developed marital/adultery imagery more fully than had Hosea, Isaiah, or Jeremiah.

The violence inflicted on these two "women" raises disturbing questions. Should one simply accept the enraged husband's explanation of why his wives deserved to be murdered? For Ezekiel, the enormity of Jerusalem's destruction required that the people's sins be depicted as proportionately heinous, lest the justice of God be doubted. Nevertheless, his use of female imagery is problematic, for he depicts female sexuality as the object of male possession and control, presents physical abuse as a way to reclaim such control, and then suggests that violence can be a means toward *healing* a broken relationship. It is true, of course, that in chaps. 16 and 23, the women are representative of all the cities' inhabitants, male and female. But the inclusive nature of gender-specific imagery is easily forgotten. Consider, for example, Ezek. 23:46–48. In the words "Thus will

I put an end to lewdness in the land, *so that all women may take warning and not commit lewdness as you have done"* (23:48, emphasis added), one discerns a later editor's effort to admonish *women* (but not men) to refrain from illicit sexual behavior. The original imagery's inclusiveness has collapsed into a threat intended for women alone. Finally, one suspects that female sexual imagery and the violence that so often accompanies it—imagery that clusters around crises in Israel and Judah's history—reflect both unease with female sexuality and a concomitant desire to keep it under male control. Ezekiel 23:48 suggests that such attitudes had implications for women living in biblical times, but their effects are not confined to the distant past. Whether one regards the Bible as sacred literature or simply as a literary classic, it has had a deep and abiding influence on our culture.

Yet another indictment of Jerusalem appears in Ezek. 22:1–16. Unlike in chaps. 16 and 23, female imagery is not prominent in this oracle. Its author does, however, cite abominations that Jerusalem's male citizens have committed against, or with, females.

The oracle begins with Yahweh's command that Ezekiel judge "Bloodshed City," as Jerusalem is called, making known its abominations. It has committed acts of violence and idolatry, hurrying its own destruction to the delight of enemy nations (22:2–5). The city's inhabitants—murderers, abusers, slanderers, and thieves—treat father and mother contemptuously, in violation of Israel's earliest laws. They oppress aliens, widows, and orphans—persons lacking the legal standing and material means to defend themselves. The city's inhabitants commit adultery, engage in incestuous acts of sexual intercourse with daughters-in-law and half sisters, and rape women who are in their menstrual periods (thereby compounding violence with ritual uncleanness). In typical fashion, Ezekiel juxtaposes acts of immorality, impurity, oppression, and greed to assert that the people have sinned in every sphere of their lives—public and private. They have, in short, "forgotten" God (22:12). Yahweh therefore promises to exile Jerusalem's inhabitants, although their presence among the nations will profane God (since it might be construed as evidence that Yahweh is incapable of maintaining Israel in its land; see 36:20). The threatened punishment of Jerusalem's citizenry is less severe than that envisioned in chap. 9, where six executioners were ordered to "cut down old men,

young men and young women, little children and women" (9:6), that is, everyone not previously marked for survival (v. 4).

## The Future of God's People

Within Ezekiel's great vision of restored Israel (chaps. 40–48), female imagery and women have little role to play. Unlike his anonymous prophetic successors, the so-called Second and Third Isaiahs, he does not adopt wife/mother metaphors to depict Jerusalem's future restoration. Such imagery suited Ezekiel perfectly when he was lambasting Jerusalem and Samaria for their abominations and shamelessness. Because of his inability to express grief, the untimely death of a human woman—Ezekiel's own wife—became a presage of the people's unspeakable dismay over the loss of Temple and offspring during the city's destruction. But when Ezekiel looks beyond doom to Israel's divinely ordained future, human women rarely intrude. Only once does an ancient image of female fertility appear on the horizon, transforming everything it touches.

***Restrictions on priests (44:22–25).*** At issue in this passage are the concept of holiness and its maintenance, when, in the future, Israel's cultic objects, rituals, and personnel are to be acceptable and holy to God. The priests serving before God's altar are commanded to observe laws of purity more rigorous than those required of their nonpriestly counterparts. On the one hand, care must be taken that they do not inadvertently communicate "holiness" to the people (44:19). On the other hand, the priests themselves must not be defiled. Accordingly, laws regulate and protect the priestly sphere of holiness. In 44:25–27, for example, priests are forbidden contact with a corpse, unless the deceased was a parent, child, brother, or unmarried sister (proper behavior when a priest's wife dies is not specified). Similarly, priests' sexual relations must be carefully regulated. They cannot marry women who have previously had sexual intercourse, even though their husbands are now deceased. Rather, they must marry Israelite virgins. The only exception to this rule allows marriage to widows of priests, who are eligible because they already are part of this special sphere of holiness (44:22). The same issue is addressed somewhat differently in Lev. 21:7.

*The waters of life (47:1–12).* Ezekiel describes a miraculous stream that trickles forth from the Temple platform and grows as it flows eastward. Traversing Israel's Arabah region, the desiccated land lying west of the Jordan River, its now abundant waters fructify the earth, which brings forth a great profusion of fruit-bearing trees. When the stream empties into the Dead Sea, that foulest of water is transformed, becoming fit for the teeming fish that will fill it.

In this marvelous description of desert-turned-Eden (see also 36:35), female imagery is by no means explicit. However, ground water is an image of female fertility (see Song 4:15; Psalm 87; Jer. 31:12; Isa. 51:1–3). It is not irrelevant, for example, that Israel's ancestors frequently encounter their future brides at a well, since well water symbolizes the virgin's (as yet untapped) fecundity. Did the amniotic fluid that bursts forth just prior to birth suggest the imagery's appropriateness? Ezekiel did not choose to develop female dimensions of the life-giving, healing issue whose course he followed in our passage. But they remain, as it were, an undercurrent, part of water imagery's network of cultural connotations.

## Conclusion

The book of Ezekiel enriches scripture with its architectural majesty and literary artistry. During a critical period in Judah's history, Ezekiel and his followers wrestled with questions about human sinfulness, God's response to individuals and nations, and the shape of Israel's future. One can only respect their absolute refusal to surrender faith in Yahweh, despite the incapacitating losses they suffered. But the violence frequently attending Ezekiel's use of female imagery, his presuppositions about women's ritual impurity, and his characterization and utter condemnation of certain women's religious practices raise serious questions for readers. Understanding why this priest spoke as he did may ameliorate such concerns somewhat, but beyond historical understanding lies the need to assess the book's contemporary relevance. Because Ezekiel's presuppositions

differed from those of many modern readers, they will undoubtedly conclude that his word concerning, for example, violence and murder as a means of restoring a troubled marital relationship, is not the final word. Rejecting aspects of Ezekiel's message does not mean, however, that one should excise offending passages from the canon. On the contrary, ongoing dialogue with Ezekiel's difficult texts is important, not because one affirms their assertions but rather because they compel the reader to confront and think through important questions.

## BIBLIOGRAPHY

Adler, Elaine June. "The Background for the Metaphor of Covenant as Marriage in the Hebrew Bible." Ph.D. dissertation, University of California at Berkeley, 1989.

Darr, Katheryn Pfisterer. "Teaching Troubling Texts: Ezekiel's Justifications of God." *Journal for the Study of the Old Testament* (forthcoming).

Galambush, Julie. *Jerusalem in the Book of Ezekiel: The City as Yahweh's Wife.* Society of Biblical Literature Dissertation Series 131. Atlanta: Scholars Press, 1992.

Greenberg, Moshe. *Ezekiel 1–20.* Anchor Bible 22. Garden City, N.Y.: Doubleday & Co., 1983.

Jacobsen, Thorkild. "Toward the Image of Tammuz." In *Toward the Image of Tammuz,* edited by William L. Moran, pp. 73–101. Harvard Semitic Series 21. Cambridge, Mass.: Harvard University Press, 1970.

Klein, Ralph W. *Ezekiel: The Prophet and His Message.* Studies on Personalities of the Old Testament. Columbia, S.C.: University of South Carolina Press, 1988.

Zimmerli, Walther. *Ezekiel 1.* Edited by Frank M. Cross, Klaus Baltzer, and Leonard Jay Greenspoon. Translated by Ronald E. Clements. Hermeneia. Philadelphia: Fortress Press, 1979.

———. *Ezekiel 2.* Edited by Paul D. Hanson with Leonard Jay Greenspoon. Translated by James D. Martin. Hermeneia. Philadelphia: Fortress Press, 1983.

# DANIEL
# AND ITS ADDITIONS

*Toni Craven*

## Introduction

In the Hebrew Bible, Daniel consists of six short stories written by unknown authors *about* Daniel and his companions (chaps. 1–6) and four apocalyptic visions written in the first person that fictitiously claim to be *by* Daniel (chaps. 7–12). In the Greek Bible, Daniel is expanded to include two prayers and three stories (the deuterocanonical or apocryphal additions): The Prayer of Azariah and The Song of the Three Jews (sixty-eight verses inserted between 3:23 and 3:24 into the story of Shadrach, Meshach, and Abednego's brush with martyrdom in Nebuchadnezzar's fiery furnace); Susanna (sixty-four verses found *before* chap. 1 in some versions of Daniel, including the oldest extant Greek text of Daniel, and as chap. 13 in others); The Priests of Bel (14:1–22); and The Dragon (14:23–42).

The first six chapters, written partly in Hebrew (1:1–2:4a) and partly in Aramaic (2:4b–7:28), are a collection of loosely connected, edifying, entertaining short stories about Daniel and his three companions. These young men, exiled from their Judean homeland, demonstrate loyalty to their own heritage, advance politically, and prosper in foreign settings even though their religious values are at odds with those of the ruling authorities.

Three stories about Daniel and the three companions are tests of loyalty. First is the food test that Daniel (=Belteshazzar), Hananiah (=Shadrach), Mishael (=Meshach), and Azariah (=Abednego) undergo during their three years of training in the Babylonian court of Nebuchadnezzar (1:1–21). Second is the fiery furnace in which Shadrach, Meshach, and Abednego face martyrdom at Nebuchadnezzar's hands on account of their decision to worship the God of Israel (3:1–30). In its Greek version, this story is expanded to include a brief connective narrative about an angel of God who comes down to drive the flames from the furnace (vv. 23–27) and two prayers (that of Azariah, who praises God's wisdom and justice and confesses the sinfulness of his own nation [vv. 1–22]; and that of the three, who together sing a song of praise and thanksgiving to God for saving them from the raging fire [vv. 28–68; cf. Psalm 148]). Third is Daniel in the lions' den, in which Daniel is endangered on account of his decision to kneel in prayer three times a day despite Darius's decree (6:1–28).

Three stories are displays of wisdom: Daniel's interpretation of Nebuchadnezzar's dream of a crumbling statue of various metals (2:1–49); Nebuchadnezzar's testimonial letter about his madness (4:1–37); and the writing on the wall at Belshazzar's feast and its interpretation (5:1–31).

According to the first six chapters, Daniel and his companions were taken as youths into the Babylonian exile in 606 B.C.E. (see 1:1), where they matured as faithful Jews and capable courtiers. Purportedly telling of events that occurred in the courts of Babylonia and Medo-Persia during the sixth century B.C.E., these six short stories teach that faithfulness and obedience to God's law are rewarded by success for those separated from their homeland. Good triumphs over all adversity.

Vocabulary, knowledge of Persian and Hellenistic customs, and fundamentally inaccurate descriptions of major sixth-century historical events and personages make it improbable that these chapters come from the sixth-century Babylonian exile. Though there is room for debate, Daniel 1–6 seem best to fit the need of the third-century diaspora community to resist assimilating too much Greek culture into Judaism.

The visions in chaps. 7–12 (written in Hebrew, except for chap. 7, which is in Aramaic) are a series of four revelations concerning the course of world history. In the apocalypses (Greek for "unveiling" or "revelation"), Daniel is the recipient (not the interpreter as in chaps. 2; 4; 5) of secret revelations. Daniel learns of divine actions soon to occur through symbolic visions explained to him by an angel (chaps. 7; 8) and direct revelations told to him by an angel (chaps. 9; 10–12). All the apocalypses are retrospective prophecies that present past historical events as if they are still to happen. The events described make it likely that chaps. 7–12 were composed and combined with chaps. 1–6 toward the end of the oppressive reign of the Seleucid king Antiochus IV Epiphanes, who persecuted the Jews of Jerusalem and Judah (175–164 B.C.E.). Because the visions inaccurately describe the death of Antiochus (see 11:40–45), it is probable that they were composed sometime late in his reign before his actual death of an undiagnosed disease at Tabae in Persia (164 B.C.E.; see 1 Macc. 6:1–16). The point of all the visions is that God will soon intervene to destroy all evil so that those who stand firm in their faith will triumph.

Daniel 13–14 have a highly complicated history and exist in two different Greek versions, the Septuagint and the so-called Theodotion. The Prayer of Azariah and The Song of the Three are virtually identical in the two Greek versions; there are considerable differences in the wording and content of the two versions of the story of Susanna; and there are minimal differences between the versions of Bel and the Dragon. The five additions are not quoted or even alluded to until the middle of the second century C.E., though it is likely that much of their material was composed during the second century B.C.E. Sometime around 250 C.E., for reasons now unknown, the Septuagint of Daniel was replaced in the Christian church by the Theodotion Greek text. In Jerome's Vulgate, The Prayer of Azariah and The Song of the Three were inserted between Dan. 3:23 and 3:24, and the three stories were appended to the end of the book: Susanna (chap. 13), The Priests of Bel, and The Dragon (chap. 14).

In Bel (14:1–22), Daniel persuades Cyrus that the Babylonian god Bel (= Marduk) does not consume the daily sacrifices by putting ashes on the sanctuary floor so that the king sees the footprints of the priests and their families who enter through a secret trap door and consume the food themselves. In The Dragon (14:23–42), Daniel convinces the king that the dragon is a worthless god because when fed pitch, fat, and hair it burst and died. Angered that they have lost their priests, Bel, and the dragon, the people demand that Daniel be thrown into a lions' den (see chap. 6). In this apocryphal version Daniel spends six days with seven lions, but he is unharmed because God sends Habakkuk from Judah with food.

## Susanna

In the Septuagint, Susanna is followed by Bel and the Dragon. In Theodotion, Susanna begins the book. Most translations (including the NRSV) follow the text of Theodotion and the practice of Jerome's Vulgate in making the story chapter 13. Susanna is a narrative about God's raising up a champion of faith who triumphs over adversity. The identity of the champion is affected by the story's attachment to the book of Daniel in the Greek versions. By association attention is drawn to Daniel, though he is not introduced until v. 45 and is at best a secondary character in Susanna. In its earliest form Susanna was probably an independent story, dating possibly from the Persian period.

Susanna's protestation of her innocence (vv. 42–43) and the present narrative explanation that "the Lord heard her cry" (v. 44) and so "stirred up the holy spirit of a young lad named Daniel" (v. 45) highlight the heroism of the woman.

Like the food test (chap. 1), the fiery furnace (chap. 3), and the lions' den (chap. 6), the story of Susanna (chap. 13) is a test of courage and loyalty to the law, a woman's courage and loyalty. Like Nebuchadnezzar's dream (chap. 2) and madness (chap. 4), and the writing on the wall (chap. 5), the story of Susanna contains a display of Daniel's wisdom in solving what is sometimes called one of the earliest detective stories. Unlike Daniel 1–6, Susanna is not set in a royal court nor are foreigners the menace. There is no pressure in this story to worship other gods. Susanna presumes that the Jewish community is self-governing, able to execute those who broke its religious laws.

Babylon is the setting (v. 1; cf. chaps. 1–5; 7–8), and the scene is the garden of Joakim (v. 4), a wealthy Jewish exile married to beautiful, God-fearing Susanna. Two wicked old judges lust for Susanna, whom they daily watch walking in Joakim's garden. Each secretly develops a passionate desire for sexual intimacy with her (note the range of terms "to seduce/embrace," vv. 11, 39; "lie with," v. 37; "so give your consent and lie with us," v. 20; and "being intimate with," v. 54). Admitting their desire to each other, the judges plot to find an occasion on which they can seduce Susanna.

One hot afternoon Susanna instructs her two maids to prepare a bath for her in the garden (v. 17). When the maids retire, the elders appear and demand that Susanna lie with them (v. 20), saying that if she refuses, they will testify that they saw her with a young man (v. 21).

Susanna courageously chooses to call out for help, saying, "I will fall into your hands, rather than sin in the sight of the Lord" (v. 23). As she cries out, the elders also shout, and one of them runs to open the garden gate, so as circumstantially to convict her. Servants in Joakim's household rush out and hear the concocted story about the young man and Susanna. Believing the elders, they are very much ashamed of their mistress (v. 27).

The next day Susanna is tried and sentenced to death (vv. 28–41). She protests her innocence to God (vv. 42–43), who hears her prayer (v. 44) and stirs a young boy named Daniel to speak out in her defense (v. 45; this identification of Daniel as a youth is the legitimation for placing the story before chap. 1). Though declaring the judges guilty of giving false evidence from the start (v. 49), Daniel examines each separately, asking each under which tree he saw Susanna and her lover. One answers, "under a mastic tree" (*schinon*), and is told he will be "cut in two" (*schisei*, vv. 54–55, a play on words in the Greek). The other says, "under an evergreen oak" (*prinos*) and is told he will be "split in two" (*prisai*, vv. 58–59). According to the law (see Deut. 19:16–19), the judges are sentenced to the fate they planned for Susanna (vv. 60–62).

Ironically, according to the story's present conclusion, Susanna receives no credit for her courageous loyalty to the law (as did Shadrach,

Meshach, and Abednego after their brush with death in the fiery furnace [3:28] and Daniel as he was delivered from the lions' den [6:23]). "Hilkiah and his wife *praised God* for their daughter Susanna, and so did her husband Joakim and all her relatives, because she was found innocent of a shameful deed. And from that day onward *Daniel had a great reputation* among the people" (vv. 63–64). God is praised and Daniel's reputation increases because "she was found innocent of a shameful deed."

The importance of Susanna's voice in the narrative's conclusion is not noted. To judge that she was found innocent only because the boy Daniel spoke in her defense would be comparable to saying that Daniel survived the lions' den in Bel and the Dragon only because Habakkuk came to him (14:33–39). But twice the text says more. Before the judges, "Susanna groaned and said, 'I am completely trapped. For if I do this, it will mean death for me; if I do not, I cannot escape your hands. I choose not to do it; I will fall into your hands, rather than sin in the sight of the Lord.' Then Susanna cried out with a loud voice" (vv. 22–24a). Condemned to death, "Then Susanna cried out with a loud voice, and said, 'O eternal God, you know what is secret and are aware of all things before they come to be; you know that these men have given false evidence against me. And now I am to die, though I have done none of the wicked things that they have charged against me!'" (vv. 42–43). So it happened that, "The Lord heard her cry. Just as she was being led off to execution, God stirred up the holy spirit of a young lad named Daniel" (vv. 44–45). She proved her innocence and dedication to the law when she decided not to sin with the elders (v. 23). Though seemingly trapped in a situation in which social convention allowed men of age and rank to determine her fate, she found a voice to refuse the elders and to cry out to God. God heard her prayer. But in the end, the narrative overlooks her and credits Daniel.

The story of Susanna raises questions for sensitive readers. Why was the community silent in exempting the judges from condemnation sooner if it was known that "this is how you have been treating the daughters of Israel, and they were intimate with you through fear" (v. 57)? Why did her mother (compare Edna's encouragement of her daughter Sarah in Tobit 7:16), father, husband, maids, and servants (note the opportunity in vv. 26–27) fail to speak in Susanna's defense? Her righteous parents "had trained their daughter according to the law of

Moses" (v. 3), but they did not defend her innocence nor did this law protect her or other women, even if in the end it is this same "law of Moses" by which the judges were condemned (v. 62). No one but a boy stirred by God believed in Susanna. No one but God listened to her own words.

Law did not entitle Susanna to speak publicly in her own defense; only the elders testified (vv. 36–41). Nonetheless, her choice not to satisfy the lust of the elders was informed by the law of Moses (v. 3). Susanna knew it meant death to give in to the elders even if she could not escape their plot (v. 22). Prayer was her only recourse in the story. "Through her tears she looked toward Heaven, for her heart trusted in the Lord" (v. 35). When the assembly condemned her to death, she defended herself to God (vv. 42–43). Her words and the fact that "the Lord heard her cry" (v. 44) free her.

Susanna decided her own fate when she refused the elders (vv. 22–23). Though "completely trapped" (v. 22), she chose to cry out in the garden rather than be intimate with the elders (vv. 22–24). Her complaint to God about her unfair condemnation (vv. 42–43) changed things. God listened and delivered her. Her protest distinguishes her from other biblical women victimized sexually by patriarchy. Susanna is not without a voice in the face of rape as were Dinah (Genesis 34), Bathsheba (2 Samuel 11), and Tamar (2 Samuel 13). She is not quiet about the unfairness of her death sentence as was the daughter of Jephthah (Judges 11). More like Hagar (Genesis 21) and Rebekah (Genesis 25), Susanna raises her voice to God to protest unfairness. Susanna wrests a blessing from God by refusing to break the law and protesting the unfairness of her fate.

To allow the story to increase only Daniel's reputation is to miss the importance of Susanna's actions and the association of this story with other books titled by the names of women, notably Ruth, Esther, and Judith. Even though appended to the book of Daniel, "Susanna" is still remembered as the title of this story.

Susanna, the daughter of Hilkiah and the wife of Joakim (vv. 1–2, 29), is the only woman named in the entire book of Daniel. All other female references are through role designations. Susanna's unnamed mother, designated both as one of her "parents" (13:3, 30) and the "wife" of Hilkiah (13:63); Susanna's "two maids" (13:15,

17–19, 36); the "daughters of Israel" (13:57); and a "daughter of Judah" (13:57) are the only Jewish females mentioned in the fourteen chapters. Unnamed foreign women in Daniel include a Babylonian "queen" (5:10–12), "wives" of Medo-Persian officials (6:24), and "wives" of the priests who serve Bel in the Persian court of Cyrus (14:15, 20, 21). Susanna is distinguished from all other women in Daniel by virtue of her name and the fact that by her own courage she surmounts the powerlessness her female status accorded her in an otherwise male-dominated world. Susanna's story tells how a woman *within* the covenant community faced death and triumphed over adversity when threatened—not by powerful foreign officials but by supposedly trustworthy Jewish leaders. Susanna, like Daniel, Shadrach, Meshach, and Abednego, honors God's sovereignty by valuing faithfulness more than life itself. She champions prayer and the finding of one's own voice in refusing evil and choosing good. Good triumphs because of God's attention to her cry.

## BIBLIOGRAPHY

Craven, Toni. *Ezekiel/Daniel.* Collegeville Bible Commentary 16. Collegeville, Minn.: The Liturgical Press, 1986.

Fewell, Danna Nolan. *Circle of Sovereignty: Plotting Politics in the Book of Daniel.* Nashville: Abingdon Press, 1991.

Hartman, Louis F., and Alexander A. Di Lella, "Daniel." In *The New Jerome Biblical Commentary*, edited by Raymond E. Brown et al., pp. 406–420. Englewood Cliffs, N.J.: Prentice-Hall, 1990.

Moore, Carey A. *Daniel, Esther and Jeremiah: The Additions.* Anchor Bible 44. Garden City, N.Y.: Doubleday & Co., 1977.

Nickelsburg, George W. E. *Jewish Literature Between the Bible and the Mishnah: A Historical and Literary Introduction.* Philadelphia: Fortress Press, 1981.

Towner, W. Sibley. "Daniel and Additions to Daniel." In *The Books of the Bible*, vol. 1, *The Old Testament/The Hebrew Bible*, edited by Bernhard W. Anderson, pp. 333–347. New York: Charles Scribner's Sons, 1989.

Viviano, Pauline A. "The Book of Daniel: Prediction or Encouragement?" *The Bible Today* 21/4 (July 1983), 221–226.

# HOSEA

*Gale A. Yee*

## Introduction

The book of Hosea is a much-examined work among feminist biblical scholars because the prophet Hosea is the first to employ the metaphor of husband for the deity, casting Israel in negative female imagery as God's adulterous wife. This imaging reflects the historical situation of ancient Israel, where gender relationships were asymmetrical: the man occupied the more privileged position in this society, and the woman was subject to him. What is important for women is that this socially conditioned relationship deeply affects the theology of the book of Hosea. This theology interprets the divine as male and the sinful as female. Using this imagery, the prophet describes God's legitimate punishment as physical violence against the wife by her husband. The problem arises when the metaphorical character of the biblical image is forgotten and a husband's physical abuse of his wife becomes as justified as is God's retribution against Israel.

### The Structure of the Book

The book is structured in three sections, each highlighting a particular metaphor of the God-Israel relationship.

Hosea 1–3 focuses on the husband-wife metaphor. The bitter experiences of Hosea's marriage to his promiscuous wife, Gomer, and the birth of their three children (chap. 1) give the prophet deep insight into the covenantal relationship between God and Israel (chap. 2). Hosea imagines this relationship as a marriage, and Israel's worship of Canaanite deities as adultery. God's eventual reconciliation with his "wife," Israel, seems to provide a model for Hosea's own reunion with Gomer (chap. 3).

The second and largest section, chaps. 4–11,

contains the bulk of Hosea's oracles against Israel's politics and cult. The final chapter summarizing and concluding this section, chap. 11, employs the parent-son metaphor for the God-Israel relationship. God is the loving, caring parent, while Israel in its breach of covenant is the rebellious son.

In the third section, chaps. 12–14, the prophet takes up the husband-wife metaphor again. The repentant wife returns to her husband and to the land. Symbolizing the wife and her reunion with her husband, the land that had formerly been devastated blossoms forth into a fruitful, luxurious plantation.

### The Historical Context of the Prophet and His Wife

***The political and religious climate.*** One of the eighth-century prophets, Hosea preached in the Northern Kingdom of Israel. His ministry extended from the end of Jeroboam II's reign, ca. 750 B.C.E. until 725 B.C.E., just prior to the fall of the Northern Kingdom to the Assyrians in 721. This era was a politically tumultuous one. The prosperous and peaceful rule of Jeroboam came to an end with his death in 746. From then on, the nation was plagued by several assassinations of its kings, court intrigue, imprudent political alliances, the Syro-Ephraimite war, and incursions into Israelite territory by the Assyrian leader Tiglath-pileser III.

Besides contending with the political instability of the nation, Hosea struggled with what he saw as perversions in the religion of Israel. Hosea accused the wife/Israel of chasing after her lovers, the Canaanite *baals* (2:7–8, 13). Baal, whose name means "master" or "husband," was the Canaanite storm god responsible for bringing the life-giving rains. For an arid climate like Israel's, such rains were crucial for survival. Grounded in the agricultural seasons of the year, the Canaanite religion placed a strong emphasis on fertility in all areas of life, not only in the cultivation of crops and the breeding of flocks but also in the birth of children. Hosea accused the people of praying to Baal and other Canaanite deities for their material welfare, abandoning Yahweh altogether or placing him alongside Baal. For Hosea, the important questions were these: Who is the giver of all good things? Who is the Creator God who brings forth fertility from barrenness? In Hosea's mind the absolute answer was Yahweh himself.

***Canaanite influence on Israelite religion.*** One gets the impression from reading the book of Hosea (as well as other prophets and the whole Deuteronomistic History from Judges through 2 Kings) that a pristine worship of Yahweh had become tainted with the Canaanite religion of the land Israel had conquered. In interpreting the book, however, one must keep in mind that the monotheistic theology represented there is the one that *eventually* became normative for Israel. Monotheism, the belief in a single God and the denial of the existence of any other god, was not always practiced in Israel. The religion described in the biblical texts represents only a part, albeit an important one, of the rich pluralism in Israelite religious belief and practice. Rather than a static, fully formed religion, the religion of ancient Israel was influenced in its formation by other cultures. Particularly important for understanding Hosea is the recognition that the religion of ancient Israel had a strong heritage in the Canaanite religion itself. Although Yahweh was the primary deity, the early Israelite religion included the worship of several other gods. The veneration of Canaanite deities like El, Baal, and perhaps even the goddess Asherah was accepted or at the very least tolerated in the early stages of Israel's religious development. A number of complex factors, such as the centralization of cult, the rise of the monarchy, the increased use of writing, which disseminated normative views, and a growing religious self-definition vis-à-vis other cultures, led to an evolving monotheism and a rejection of Israel's Canaanite heritage. The worship of Baal, which was once a legitimate part of Israelite religion, was now condemned by Hosea.

Although worship of Canaanite deities was most likely a long-established practice in ancient Israel, Canaanite religious rituals are very difficult to reconstruct on the basis of the biblical text alone. Because of its polemic against the religion, the biblical text presents a biased and even distorted picture of Canaanite rites.

***The phenomenon of so-called cultic prostitution.*** One alleged Canaanite practice that is specifically relevant to the book of Hosea is that of cultic prostitution. As was mentioned above, fertility in all areas of life and the harmonious world order that resulted from it were major concerns of the Canaanite religion. Much has been learned about this religion from the Ras Shamra tablets discovered some fifty years ago on the coast of Syria. In these mythological texts, the storm god Baal was killed by Mot, the god of barrenness and death. In its prescientific milieu, this belief explained the hot, dry period between May and September when no rains fell on the land. Baal's sister-lover, the goddess Anat, came to the rescue by slaying Mot and bringing Baal back to life. Their passionate sexual intercourse, the Canaanites believed, initiated the rainy season that began in October.

Many scholars think that this mythic drama was rehearsed every year in a religious New Year festival that took place in October, even though the festival itself is not described in the Ras Shamra tablets. Supposedly, part of this festival was a "sacred marriage" in imitation of Baal and Anat, during which Canaanite men, from the king on down, had ritual sex with cultic prostitutes to bring about fertility in their land, flocks, and families. The religious intent behind these fertility cults was very serious indeed, nothing less than the survival of the people in a hostile climate. Human nature being of a piece, however, some worshipers may have frequented these cultic prostitutes for less than religious reasons. In the minds of many interpreters, these rituals often degenerated into full-scale orgies at the sanctuaries and high places. Allegedly, it was these services that were so offensive to Hosea (see 4:11–19; 9:1–3). Some critics even regard Hosea's wife, Gomer, and other Israelite women (see Hos. 4:14) as cultic prostitutes themselves.

Nevertheless, a number of scholars have recently questioned the phenomenon of cultic prostitution not only in Canaan but in the rest of the ancient Near East. No substantive textual or archaeological evidence exists to verify that such a class of prostitutes ever existed or that such sexual rites were ever performed. The testimonies of ancient authors, such as the Greek writers Herodotus and Strabo, used by some to support cultic prostitution, are in reality quite unreliable because they were written at a far later date and are markedly tendentious.

Furthermore, the standard translations that describe Gomer as "a wife of harlotry" (1:2) and Israel as one "who has played the harlot" (2:5) are misleading. The Hebrew noun for "prostitute," *zonah,* is a cognate of the verb *zanah,* the primary meaning of which is "to engage in sexual relations outside of marriage." *Zanah* is a more inclusive term covering a range of sexual transgressions from *adultery,* involving a married woman, *fornication,* involving an unmarried daughter, sister, or widow committed under levirate law (see Deut. 25:5–6), to *prostitution,* involving women soliciting sex as a profession.

Gomer is a "wife of harlotry," but not because she is a prostitute; she is never labeled a *zonah,* the technical term for a prostitute. Rather, she is a "woman/wife of harlotry" (*'eshet zenunim*) because she is habitually promiscuous. Her adulterous acts are evaluated pejoratively as being *"like* a harlot," although she is not a prostitute by profession. Instead of "wife of harlotry," a more accurate translation would be "wife of promiscuity" (=promiscuous wife), which avoids identifying Gomer as a prostitute. Similarly, "to play the harlot" is more correctly rendered "to be promiscuous."

The translation of "cult prostitute" for the Israelite daughters described in Hos. 4:14b is likewise inaccurate. The Hebrew word customarily translated "cult prostitute" is *qedeshah,* not *zonah,* which designates a common prostitute and has no specialized connection with cultic activity. *Qedeshah* (literally, "holy one") does have particular associations with the cult. However, the service these female cult functionaries actually performed within Israelite sanctuaries is very difficult to reconstruct on the basis of the biblical text or even the Ras Shamra tablets. Although in the prophet's mind their rituals involved sexuality, it would be a mistake to accept this at face value. The biblical text is simply too polemical, revealing more about the prophetic mind that leveled the accusation than about the actual observances in the cult itself. Until more intelligible and less polemical evidence surfaces, it would be

better to translate *qedeshah* as "hierodule" rather than "cult prostitute." "Hierodule," a word taken from Greek and meaning "temple servant," would preserve the cultic force of the word but remain neutral regarding the sexual aspect, if any, of the woman's ministry.

***Marriage and adultery in ancient Israel.*** Since Hosea's distinctive metaphor for the Yahweh-Israel relationship was one of husband and wife, it is important to have an understanding of Israel's institution of marriage and its laws regarding adultery. Two primary features of this marriage were its patrilineal, patrilocal kinship structure and its honor/shame value system.

The kinship line of descent in ancient Israel was patrilineal: the transmission of family name and inheritance followed the male line. Marriage arrangements as well were patrilocal. A wife was brought to live with her husband in the household of her father-in-law. By its patrilineal and patrilocal customs, ancient Israel privileged the male. Marriage arrangements involved female mobility and male stability. The young woman had to leave the household of her birth and enter into the unfamiliar and sometimes hostile domicile of her husband, adapting herself to it as best she could. Love and romance were not major factors in the joining of a couple in wedlock. The father often used the marriages of daughters to forge or strengthen alliances with other households and larger clan groups. Furthermore, if the husband was polygamous, his wife had to contend with the other wives, who vied for the husband's attention and the resultant status it could bring, particularly through the birth of sons.

In a labor-intensive agricultural society such as Israel's, the birth of children was crucial for survival. Sons were especially valued because they were the beneficiaries of the father and did not leave the household. In fact, they brought into the household additional human resources in the persons of wives and the potential children they would bear. The wife's primary contribution to the household was her sexuality, bearing legitimate sons to carry on the family name and keep land and property in the household. The sexuality of wives and daughters was therefore carefully guarded and controlled.

Embedded within this patrilineal, patrilocal kinship structure was an honor/shame value system. Honor was one's reputation, the value of a person in his or her own eyes *and* in the eyes of his or her social group. Unlike our modern-day concept of shame as something negative, in ancient Israel shame was a positive concern for one's reputation or honor.

The values of honor and shame were particularly divided along gender lines. The male embodied the positive value of honor in his manliness, courage, his ability to provide for his family and defend their honor, and his assertion of sexual masculinity. The female embodied the positive value of shame in her concern for her reputation. This concern manifested itself in her meekness and timidity, her deference and submission to male authority, her passiveness, and her sexual purity. A man failing to exhibit courage or defend the family honor, or a woman failing to remain sexually pure, would equally be rendered *shameless* and therefore *get shamed* by the community. Both genders would have failed to consider their personal reputations and that of their household; they would not *have had shame*. However, the individual causes of their *shamelessness* differed according to their gender.

In the patrilineal kinship structure, a large measure of a man's honor rested on a woman's sexual behavior, whether it be his wife's, daughter's, sister's, and/or mother's. Men had various strategies, such as insisting that women remain veiled in public, segregating them, restricting their social behavior, to keep their women (and by extension, themselves) honorable. If a woman was sexually shameless in any way, it would be revealed publicly that her husband, father, brother, or son failed to preserve the family honor by his inability to control her. The male would consequently lose his honor or reputation in the community.

Adultery was therefore a first-class offense in a society that operated under patrilineal and honor/shame-based social systems. In the first place, it violated a man's absolute right to the sexuality of his wife and placed his paternity in question, something very threatening and disruptive in a society governed by a patrilineal kinship structure. Second, adultery resulted in a considerable loss of honor for the husband and his household. His "shameless" wife defied his authority, revealing his failure to control his woman in his duty to maintain the honor of the family.

Two types of punishment for adultery seem to have been applied. The first was the stoning of both parties to death (Lev. 20:10; Deut. 22:22). In practice, however, the punishment was often incurred only by the woman (see Genesis 38; John 7:53–8:11). According to the law, the couple had to be caught in the act by witnesses for the death penalty to be applied (Deut. 19:15). This, of course, was not always feasible. Moreover, the woman was more vulnerable than the man to the accusation, because she could later become visibly pregnant from the union. The second type of punishment is the one recorded in Hosea, that of publicly stripping the adulteress naked and exposing her shamelessness (Hos. 2:2–3; cf. Ezek. 16:37–39).

An implicit double standard existed in the biblical evaluation of a man who broke wedlock. Extramarital activity, which would have been inexcusable for the wife, was tolerated for the husband in many cases. A man was not punished for having sex unless an engaged or a married woman was involved *and* he was caught in the act (see Deut. 22:23–29). Engaging the services of prostitutes was acceptable (see Gen. 38:12–23; Josh. 2:1–7; 1 Kings 3:16–27). This double standard underscored the issues of honor and paternity that so characterized the ancient Israelite society, making the woman the primary offender in adulterous acts.

## Comment

### God as Faithful Husband, Israel as Faithless Wife (chaps. 1–3)

In Hos. 1:2 Yahweh commands Hosea, "Go, take for yourself a promiscuous wife and bear children of promiscuity, for the land has been promiscuous away from Yahweh" (author's translation). Hosea then marries Gomer, the daughter of Diblaim, and has three children by her: a son Jezreel, a daughter Not-Pitied, and another son Not-My-People (1:3–9). Each child represents allegorically the deteriorating state of the nation. Gomer's licentiousness brings dishonor not only to Hosea himself but to his whole household. Hence, their offspring become "children of promiscuity" (see also 2:4–5).

The prophet's marriage to a promiscuous woman becomes an act symbolizing that "the land has been promiscuous away from Yahweh." The land (people) has wantonly turned away from Yahweh to worship the Canaanite storm god Baal (see 2:8, 13, 17). The tragic human story of the prophet interconnects with the metaphorical tale of Yahweh and Israel, so that the two stories become essentially one. The prophet creates in this fusion the powerful marriage metaphor to articulate the special covenantal relationship between God and Israel.

Nevertheless, because the metaphor originates in a particular historical period with its own cultural ideas about marriage, it presents theological problems for present-day women. These theological problems are particularly present in chap. 2, which details the covenantal relationship as a broken marriage. As was stated above, in ancient Israel the wife was the primary offender in an adulterous affaire and the "victim" was her dishonored husband. Hence, the religiously pluralistic nation condemned by the prophet metaphorically becomes the faithless wife, Gomer, and Yahweh becomes the dishonored husband, Hosea. Being bracketed by the human story of Hosea's marriage (chaps. 1 and 3), chap. 2 pushes the marriage metaphor to dangerous limits, whereby Yahweh's legitimate punishment of Israel for breach of covenant is figuratively described as threats of physical violence against the wife.

The first cycle of threats in chap. 2 begins with Yahweh/Hosea enjoining his children to plead with their mother that she might forswear her promiscuity: "Or I will strip her naked and expose her as in the day she was born, and make her like a wilderness, and turn her into a parched land, and kill her with thirst" (2:3). This escalating series of threats also includes the children who are infected by their mother's shamelessness (2:4–5a). Their dishonor lies not only in the mother's sexual transgressions but also in her attributing to her lovers the material sources of her well-being (2:5b). On the religious level "the lovers" refer to Canaanite deities thought to bring fertility. On the human level they imply the great dishonor of the husband, who apparently could not provide for the material and sexual needs of his own wife and control her behavior. Both the religious level and the human level converge in chap. 2.

Yahweh engages in a three-part strategy to curb his "wife's" actions. This strategy reflects the social methods of the patrilineal, honor/shame culture described above to control women's sexuality. The first thing the husband does is segregate his wife from her lovers:

Therefore I will hedge up her way with thorns;
and I will build a wall against her,
so that she cannot find her paths.

She shall pursue her lovers, but not overtake them;
and she shall seek them, but shall not find them.

(2:6–7a)

This enforced seclusion has as its aim the wife's recognizing her utter dependence on her husband, something of which she seemingly is unaware (2:7b–8). The divine isolation of Israel from her lovers apparently serves as a model for Hosea's sequestering of Gomer in 3:3–4. However, it is the human behaviors of Israelite husbands toward their wives that are represented as God's actions, not vice versa.

The second part of the husband's strategy is a series of physical and psychological punishments against the wife. He will withhold food and clothing from her (2:9). He will humiliate her by exposing her genitalia before her lovers. No one will be able to rescue her from his power (2:10). He will put an end to her laughter and festivals (2:11). He will destroy her vineyards and orchards, making wild animals devour them (2:12). From his point of view, her public physical humiliation and punishment compensate for his own public loss of honor "when she offered incense to them [the Baals] and decked herself with her ring and jewelry, and went after her lovers, and forgot me" (2:13).

The third part of the husband's strategy to control his wife is the most insidious one, because the implications of such a strategy for actual battered wives tend to be ignored, as the reader becomes caught up in the joyous reconciliation between Yahweh and Israel. After the wife has been suitably punished, after she has endured various forms of abuse, the husband will seduce his wife, bring her into the wilderness, and speak tenderly to her (2:14).

On the religious level, the "wilderness" of Sinai is the place where Yahweh and Israel first pledged themselves in a covenantal relationship and where, in some traditions, they enjoyed their one and only period of marital bliss. It will be in the wilderness again where Israel will respond to Yahweh "as in the days of her youth, as at the time when she came out of the land of Egypt" (2:15). Israel will recognize Yahweh, not Baal, as her true husband (2:16). God, in turn, will forgive her transgressions and betroth her to him again forever (2:19–20). In love once more, the couple will renew their covenant/marriage vows, inaugurating a period of cosmic peace, harmony, and bounteous fertility (2:18–22). Moreover, the critical question of paternity is decided in 2:23. Yahweh/husband acknowledges his children as his own and renames them, indicating a new covenantal order. Jezreel now symbolizes the sowing of his mother back into the land. Yahweh will have pity on his daughter, Not-Pitied, and will declare to Not-My-People, "You are my people."

As beautiful and profound as these religious images are, the human level on which they are based is very problematic for women. Studies have shown that many wives remain in abusive relationships because periods of mistreatment are often followed by intervals of kindness and generosity. This ambivalent strategy reinforces the wife's dependence on the husband. During periods of kindness, her fears are temporarily eased so that she decides to remain in the relationship; then the cycle of abuse begins again. Moreover, the one-sided images of the father's restored relationship with his children in Hosea belie the trauma real children experience when witnessing their father physically abuse their mother.

Hosea's metaphor of the marriage between Yahweh and Israel gives an entrée into the divine-human relationship as no other metaphor can. It engages the reader in a compelling story about a God who is loving, forgiving, and compassionate, in spite of Israel's sinfulness. However, growing out of a social structure and value system that privileged the male over the female, this metaphor makes its theological point at the expense of real women and children who were and still are victims of sexual violence. When the metaphorical character of the biblical image is forgotten, a husband's physical abuse of his wife comes to be as justified as God's retribution against Israel.

Given its difficulties, is this metaphor still appropriate in describing the divine-human relationship for the modern reader? What are the criteria for determining the appropriateness of a particular metaphor? One can assess its appropriateness by asking a number of questions. To whose experience does the metaphor speak, and whose experience does the metaphor exclude? Whose experience does the metaphor describe positively, and whose experience does it describe negatively? Is the metaphor fair and just in its representations? Certainly, the male violence embedded in the text of Hosea as it stands should make readers, both male and female, wary of an uncritical acceptance of its marriage metaphor. Moreover, the imaging of God as male/husband becomes difficult when one forgets the metaphor God is *like* a husband

and insists literally that God *is* a husband and therefore always male.

Because of the variety of human religious experiences, various metaphors are needed to represent them. Are there other metaphors in the book of Hosea that present different insights into the divine-human relationship? Although not as well known as the marriage metaphor, the image of parent and son in Hosea 11 is such a metaphor.

## God as Loving Parent, Israel as Rebellious Son (chaps. 4–11)

Chapter 11 summarizes and concludes the second major section of the book of Hosea, chaps. 4–11. It begins thus:

> When Israel was a child, I loved him,
>   and out of Egypt I called my son.
> The more I called them,
>   the more they went from me;
> they kept sacrificing to the Baals,
>   and offering incense to idols.
>
> (11:1–2)

Thematic echoes from chap. 2, such as God's love for Israel (2:19–20; cf. 3:1), Israel's exodus from Egypt (2:15), and its idolatry of Canaanite gods (2:8, 13), can be found in these opening verses of chap. 11. However, the metaphor expressive of God now is the one of the caring parent rather than the loving husband. The metaphor of Israel is of the rebellious son, instead of the adulterous wife.

In first-person narrative, Yahweh describes a series of nurturing gestures performed on Israel's behalf:

> Yet it was I who taught Ephraim to walk,
>   I took them up in my arms;
>   but they did not know that I healed
>     them.
> I led them with cords of human kindness,
>   with bands of love.
> I was to them like those
>   who lift infants to their cheeks.
>   I bent down to them and fed them.
>
> (11:3–4)

In contrast to chap. 2, which views God explicitly as husband, it is important to note that, although the prophet does not call Yahweh "mother" in chap. 11, he does not call Yahweh "father" either. Teaching a son to walk, holding him in one's arms, healing him, leading him, and bending down to feed him are all activities that *both* parents can perform, although one can argue that the primary caregiver during childhood is the mother. Emphasized in the parental metaphor is the nurturing, sustaining love of Yahweh. Just as the wife/Israel "did not know" that it was her husband Yahweh who provided for her (2:8), the son/Israel "did not know that I [Yahweh] healed them" (11:3). Instead, he persists in his rebelliousness. The son thus disowns himself from his parent, just as the wife/Israel divorces herself from her husband (2:2a). He will be banished to the lands of Egypt and Assyria "because they have refused to return to me" (11:5).

According to Deuteronomic law, both parents could condemn a stubborn, rebellious son before the elders of the city, whereupon he would be stoned to death (Deut. 21:18–21). This legal background throws into relief the theological intent of 11:8:

> How can I give you up, Ephraim?
> How can I hand you over, O Israel?
> . . . . . . . . . . . . . . . . . .
> My heart recoils within me;
> my compassion grows warm and tender.
> (11:8)

A rare glimpse of the emotional turmoil of God on the verge of destroying the son is presented here. Yahweh's abhorrence regarding the son's death penalty gives way to a growing compassion. Ultimately, the mother/father-God makes a decision:

> I will not execute my fierce anger;
> I will not again destroy Ephraim.
> (11:9a)

Though the parent has the legal right to have the son killed, compassion for and bonding with the child prevents God from doing so. Yahweh transcends human legal institutions which enforce the death sentence for disobedient sons: "for I am God and no mortal, the Holy One in your midst, and I will not come in wrath" (11:9b).

The mother/father-God desires the son's repentance in turning from his evil ways. In chaps. 4–11, the summons to repentance has been strategically placed in 6:1–3 and 10:12 before this climactic chapter. These passages prepare for the son's eventual repentance at the end of chap. 11, where the mother/father-God welcomes him back from the lands of his banishment:

> When he roars,
> his children shall come trembling from
> the west.
> They shall come trembling like birds from
> Egypt,
> and like doves from the land of Assyria;

and I will return them to their homes,
says Yahweh.
(11:10b–11)

## God as Faithful Husband, Israel as Faithful and Fruitful Wife (chaps. 12–14)

In the third and final section, chaps. 12–14, the prophet takes up the marriage metaphor of chaps. 1–3 once again. There the punishment of the wife was geared to bring about her repentance and return to her husband. The same theme of repentance for the son who comes to his senses after his banishment appears in chap. 11. Hence it is fitting that the last chapter of the book open with a summons to repent:

> Return, O Israel, to Yahweh your God,
> for you have stumbled because of your
> iniquity.
> Take words with you and return
> to Yahweh.
> (14:1–2a)

Responding to Israel's repentance, Yahweh makes a number of declarations in 14:4: "I will heal their disloyalty," he says, just as the mother/father-God healed the son (11:3); "I will love them freely," just as Yahweh/husband expressed his passionate, tender emotions to his repentant wife (2:19–20; 3:1).

Concerning the wife/Israel in chap. 2, Yahweh had proclaimed that he was going to "sow her for myself in the land" (2:23). Hosea 14:4–7 develops this image by describing the luxuriant growth of Israel in the land, which follows upon this sowing. The metaphors of fertility in 14:4–7 are culled from the tradition of Hebrew love poetry that has its written form in the Song of Songs. As the woman is "a lily among brambles" for her lover (Song 2:2), so shall Israel "blossom like the lily" as Yahweh pours forth his dew upon her (14:5). This outpouring reinforces the fact that Yahweh, not Baal, is the bringer of life-giving rain. In Song 2:3, the woman describes her lover

> as an apple tree among the trees of the wood,
> so is my beloved among young men.
> With great delight I sat in his shadow,
> and his fruit was sweet to my taste.

Likewise in Hos. 14:7, Yahweh declares that Israel "shall again live beneath my shadow" and compares himself to a tree that protects Israel and delights her with its fruit:

> O Ephraim, what have I to do with idols?
> It is I who answer and look after you.

I am like an evergreen cypress;
  from me comes your fruit.
        (14:8, author's translation)

In Hosea 14 the prophet documents the lush fruitfulness that springs forth in the covenantal rejoicing of Yahweh and Israel. He concludes his story of the husband and wife on a very propitious note—or almost a propitious one. What gives one pause is the qualifier of Yahweh's declaration of love in 14:4 (emphasis added): "I will love them freely, *for my anger has turned from them.*" The reader vividly recalls the descriptions of the God/husband taking out his wrath on the wife in chap. 2. Remembering the physical price the wife had to pay to regain her husband's favor, one becomes ambivalent about the beautiful metaphors of the wife's abundant fertility. They are built on a series of images that are all too real and painful for many women. There is perhaps another way of looking at this concluding chapter that is more healing and affirming of women. The well-known female personification of God's own wisdom, Woman Wisdom herself, is also described as a life-giving tree:

She is a tree of life to those who lay hold
    of her;
  those who hold her fast are called happy.
        (Prov. 3:18)

The metaphor of the tree for Woman Wisdom in Hos. 14:8 gains further support in the next and final verse of the chapter:

Those who are wise understand these
    things;
  those who are discerning know them.
For the ways of Yahweh are right,
  and the upright walk in them,
  but transgressors stumble in them.
        (14:9)

For the wise and discerning, for the abused and the pained, God the husband gives way to the Wisdom of God, Woman Wisdom as the tree of life. Happy are those who embrace her and receive their fruit from her!

## BIBLIOGRAPHY

Andersen, Francis I., and David Noel Freedman. *Hosea.* Anchor Bible 24. Garden City, N.Y.: Doubleday & Co., 1980.

Bird, Phyllis. "'To Play the Harlot': An Inquiry Into an Old Testament Metaphor." In *Gender and Difference in Ancient Israel,* edited by Peggy L. Day, pp. 75–94. Minneapolis: Fortress Press, 1989.

Oden, Robert A., Jr. "Religious Identity and the Sacred Prostitution Accusation." In *The Bible Without Theology: The Theological Tradition and Alternatives to It,* pp. 131–153, 187–193. New Voices in Biblical Studies. San Francisco: Harper & Row, 1987.

Pitt-Rivers, Julian. "Honour and Social Status in Andalusia." In *The Fate of Shechem or the Politics of Sex,* pp. 19–47. Cambridge: Cambridge University Press, 1977.

Setel, T. Drorah. "Prophets and Pornography: Female Sexual Imagery in Hosea." In *Feminist Interpretation of the Bible,* edited by Letty M. Russell, pp. 86–95. Philadelphia: Westminster Press, 1985.

Smith, Mark S. *The Early History of God: Yahweh and the Other Deities in Ancient Israel.* San Francisco: Harper & Row, 1990.

Weems, Renita J. "Gomer: Victim of Violence or Victim of Metaphor." *Semeia* 47 (1989), 87–104.

# JOEL

*Beth Glazier-McDonald*

## Introduction

### Authorship and Date

Nothing is known with certainty about the prophet Joel. Because the cultic element in the book is pronounced—the blowing of the shofar (ram's horn), solemn assembly at the Temple, invoking of the fast, and frequent mention of priests and sacrifices—some regard the oracles as a collection of temple liturgies and Joel as a Jerusalem priest.

The date of Joel's prophecy is likely between 515 and 500 B.C.E. References to the Temple indicate a time after 515 B.C.E., when the Second Temple was dedicated. The threat to Edom in 3:19 must predate the reference to Edom's destruction in Malachi (ca. 475–450 B.C.E.). Further, since Joel 2:32 explicitly quotes Obadiah 17, Joel's dependence suggests a slightly later date than Obadiah, which is probably to be dated to the early postexilic period.

### Joel and the Day of Yahweh

The theme that binds Joel's prophecy together is the Day of Yahweh, when Yahweh would intervene in the historical arena to establish universal sovereignty. It was a day associated with judgment and curse, both for the nations and for sinful Israel. For the faithful, however, it was the day of their vindication and blessing.

In the first part of the book, Joel vividly describes drought (1:15–20) and locust plague (2:2–11), using those natural disasters as a conceptual springboard by which he moves into various images of the coming Day of Yahweh. Like others in the biblical tradition, Joel regards locust and drought as God's chastisement for breach of covenant obligations, indeed, as a sign that Yahweh is coming to sit in judgment. He therefore calls his people to repent and so avert Yahweh's wrath (1:14; 2:12–17). Their positive response wins both a reprieve from the Day and the prospect of material blessing (rain, abundant crops), but the matter does not end there. As harbingers of Yahweh's Day, the locusts signal a threat to the nations that have oppressed Yahweh's people. They will be gathered to the Valley of Jehoshaphat (3:2), where there will be a final conflict in which Yahweh confronts them and the evil they represent (3:9–15). They will be destroyed, and faithful Israel will live in a Jerusalem where Yahweh reigns (3:21).

## Comment

### Judah, Locusts, and God (1:2–2:17)

Joel compares the invading locusts to the sound and fury of an advancing enemy army in order to compel his religiously insensitive community to react to the seriousness of their situation and its significance to their relationship with Yahweh (2:1). The prophet employs a repetitive, accumulating structure to emphasize the scope of the calamity (see 1:4, 10, 12, 17–20; 2:2–11). Indeed, all inhabitants (1:12), the fields and its produce (1:10–12), the flocks and herds (1:18–20), are affected by the invading locusts. To represent the grief of the people at the devastation of their country, Joel invokes the image of a young woman mourning her husband (1:8) in widow's weeds of sackcloth (see Amos 8:10).

Joel's rallying cry is to "return" wholeheartedly to Yahweh (2:12). Interestingly, although Malachi (3:7) assures his hearers that returning to God will evoke the responsive turning of God, for Joel repentance is no guarantee of deliverance. There is only a chance that Yahweh will turn from the present dire policy and pour out a blessing (2:14).

As a practical implementation of the repentant attitude, the people are summoned to a great penitential assembly (1:14; 2:15). No one is exempted. The radically comprehensive terms in which the gathering of the community is described without respect to age or social condition (2:16) is a measure of the danger facing the community. Indeed, the crisis is so severe that normal privilege is suspended. Thus, although the newly married husband was exempt from military and other service for a year "to be happy with the wife whom he has married" (Deut. 24:5), the newlyweds must forget their personal joy and join in the nationwide supplication to God.

### Reversal of Judah's Destruction (2:18–32)

Apparently Joel's pleas for repentance were heeded, and Yahweh responded to the people's changed attitude by showering them with material blessings (2:19-26): "I will repay you for the years that the swarming locust has eaten" (2:25). Three additional blessings to be dispensed at a subsequent time (2:28), but "before" the coming of Yahweh's Day (2:31), are described in 2:28-32: the outpouring of the spirit (2:28-29), cosmic signs (2:30-31), and salvation on Zion (2:32). Whereas in the past the gift of prophecy was the prerogative of a few, in the future it will be an inclusive gift (see Num. 11:29). Distinctions of age (old men and young men, 2:28), gender (sons and daughters,

2:28), social class (male and female servants, 2:29) will be swept away in this common spiritual endowment. For women the future will be the inverse of the present. Now subservient to men, "in those days" they will stand equally with men (2:28-29). Joel asserts, however, that in the coming Day of Yahweh, deliverance is not universal. Only those who acknowledge Yahweh and are acknowledged by God will be gathered to safety in Jerusalem (2:32).

### Judgment of the Nations (chap. 3)

The necessary complement to the blessing of Judah and Jerusalem is terrible judgment on the nations. Gathered into the Valley of Jehoshaphat ("Yahweh will judge"), also called the Valley of Decision (3:14), there will be a final battle in which the enemies of Yahweh and Israel will be subdued (3:9-15). In preparation for the conflict, the idyllic picture of Isa. 2:4 and Micah 4:3 is reversed; tools of peace are beaten into weapons of war (3:10). But the actual battle is Yahweh's, whose coming is accompanied by cosmic upheaval (3:15).

The renewed intimacy among Yahweh, people, and land is seen not only in the outpouring of material blessing (3:18) but also in the inviolability of the holy city (3:17) and in the perpetual occupation of the land (3:20). Yahweh dwells in Zion (3:17, 20).

### BIBLIOGRAPHY

Ahlström, Gösta W. *Joel and the Temple Cult of Jerusalem.* Supplements to Vetus Testamentum 21. Leiden: E. J. Brill, 1971.

Wolff, Hans Walter. *Joel and Amos.* Translated by Waldemar Janzen et al. Hermeneia. Philadelphia: Fortress Press, 1977.

# AMOS

## Judith E. Sanderson

❧

## Introduction

Amos came from the town of Tekoa in the hills of the Southern Kingdom, Judah, to deliver his message of doom to the Northern Kingdom, Israel (1:1; 4:1, 4; 7:10). The first prophet whose oracles have been preserved, Amos preached while Jeroboam II was king in Israel and Uzziah in Judah, or sometime between 790 and 745 B.C.E. Amos's socioeconomic status is hard to pin down. Since he is variously and cryptically described in 1:1 and 7:14–15 as a breeder (or herder?) of sheep and of large cattle, as "following the flock," and as a dresser of sycamore trees (which do not grow around Tekoa), one can only speculate. Was he a migrant farmworker and herder, or was he the wealthy owner of herds and orchards? His oracles show him to have been an accomplished poet in strong solidarity with "the poor of the land" (8:4).

The book can be outlined according to form or content. In form, poetic oracles (1:2–6:14) are followed by four first-person vision reports (7:1–9; 8:1–3) surrounding a third-person narrative (7:10–17), which are followed in turn by poetic oracles (8:4–14; 9:7–15) surrounding another first-person vision report (9:1–4). Hymn fragments appear in 4:13; 5:8–9; and 9:5–6. In content, the book opens with oracles against foreign nations, accusing them of a variety of war crimes and climaxing with an oracle against Israel (1:2–2:16). Most of the book is devoted to the evils within Israel and the destruction God will bring as judgment (3:1–9:10), but it concludes with a brief promise of restoration (9:11–15).

Amos's chief concern was twofold: the affluence of the powerful (3:15; 4:1; 6:1, 4–6) resulting from their oppression of the poor (3:9–10). This exploitation, which Amos described very graphically (2:6–8; 5:11–12; 8:4–6),

had reached such proportions that justice and righteousness were utterly perverted (6:12), religion had become a comfortable ritual divorced from God's demands for justice (2:8; 4:4–5; 5:21–24; cf. 3:14), and monarchy and priesthood were corrupt (7:10–17). All this so clearly flew in the face of God's purpose for Israel (3:2) that God had brought various punishments designed to call the people to repentance (4:6–11). Since these warnings had been ignored, God would now bring total destruction to the entire nation, described in chilling detail, both literal (3:11–12; 5:3, 16–17; 6:7–11; 7:9, 11, 17; 8:3; 9:8, 10) and figurative (5:2, 18–20; 8:8–14; 9:1–6, 9).

For women today this book presents problems on two levels. First, specific texts relating to women challenge readers to try to understand what Amos intended, a process that may involve critique of interpretive traditions and/or the biblical text itself. Several such texts will be dealt with below. Second, the impact of the book read as a whole calls for a critique, if not of Amos's own understanding, since that is no longer accessible, at least of the lack of balance in what has been preserved of his oracles. Amos saw clearly the present suffering of the economically and legally exploited masses, the present luxury of the wealthy and comfortable few, as well as the future suffering of those wealthy, when God's day of wrath would bring war and exile. Unfortunately he saw less clearly when it came to the situation of women.

Amos specifically condemned wealthy women for oppressing the poor (4:1) but failed specifically to champion the women among the poor. Yet both the analogy of modern times and the witness of the Bible itself strongly suggest that women were disproportionately represented among the poor in Israel. The modern feminization of poverty is evident in statistics showing that women suffer disproportionately from poverty with all its ramifications: inadequate but high-cost housing, low and unstable salaries, poor nutrition, and the struggle to care for children with too few resources. The recurring concern throughout the Bible for widows, often linked with the fatherless and resident aliens, as exemplifying the most vulnerable and exploited segment of society (e.g., in laws: Ex. 22:21–24; prophecy: Isa. 1:17; wisdom: Prov. 15:25; liturgy: Ps. 94:6; and narrative: Genesis 38) shows that other biblical writers were aware of the plight of at least one group of women—those who had no man to provide for them financially and legally. Yet no word has survived that would indicate that Amos demonstrated any such awareness of the special sufferings and exploitations of women. As Amos singled out wealthy women—a small group—for special condemnation, a balanced analysis would also have singled out poor women—a much larger group—for special defense and a show of that solidarity of which he was so clearly capable.

In addition, Amos's sweeping condemnation of wealthy women must be approached with suspicion. Again, both the analogy of modern times and the witness of the Bible itself show that patriarchal thinking enables the power and the sinfulness of women to be greatly exaggerated. Far too often in both biblical texts and the interpretive tradition, women, whether literal or metaphorical, are scapegoated or even seen as personifying evil (e.g., in laws: Num. 5:11–31; prophecy: Ezekiel 16; wisdom: Proverbs 5 and 7; and narrative: Judges 16; 1 Kings 21). While it is especially common to blame women for sexual sins, Amos and Isaiah (Isa. 3:16–4:1) both broadened the picture of their culpability. A survey of modern commentaries on Amos 4:1 reveals the alacrity with which women are blamed for societies' evils, their relative powerlessness is disregarded, and their accountability for sin is seen as greater than their circumstances would allow. As the widespread wife battering in wealthy U.S. homes becomes less hidden—to name only one limitation on the power, wealth, and safety of "wealthy" women—one is forced to ask what life was like for "wealthy" women in ancient Israel. If the gusto with which some commentators demean the women in 4:1 is any guide, then Amos's words themselves merit suspicion.

Further, though Amos twice predicted the suffering of the few wealthy women in the coming time of war and exile (4:2–3; 7:17), he ignored the much more wide-ranging suffering that the same war and exile would bring to the many poor women. Had Amos condemned the wealthy, championed the poor, and threatened future suffering without distinction according to sex, there would be no complaint. The problem for modern readers arises in his choosing to condemn what he interpreted as the luxury of a minority of women in scathing terms while ignoring the oppression of a majority of women. It is ironic that while Amos could see a very few wealthy women oppressing and could foresee those few women being judged, he could neither see the many poor women being presently trampled on nor foresee their suffering the rape, pillage, and exile of the military defeat he predicted. This imbalance of the book as a whole has only fueled the fires of misogynistic interpretation.

## Comment

### "They Have Ripped Open Pregnant Women in Gilead" (1:13)

In reading Amos's descriptions of warfare past or future, one must read between the lines and imagine what was happening to the women, since he usually did not focus on the special sufferings that women endure in time of war. Some of his graphic word pictures facilitate the inclusion of women in the scene, however, as when he accused Damascus of having "threshed Gilead with threshing sledges of iron" (1:3; cf. Isa. 41:15). While his general references sometimes can easily be understood as including women, as when he speaks of "entire communities" going into exile (1:6, 9), he sometimes refers exclusively to men, especially those in power (1:15; 2:3).

Sometimes the fate of females is mentioned from a patriarchal perspective, as in 7:17, where Amos threatened Bethel's powerful and corrupt priest Amaziah with punishment that would affect his wife, his sons and daughters, his property, and finally himself. When Amos predicted the death of his sons and daughters, in line with the corporate sense of guilt and punishment common to the Bible, he considered the children's deaths both a punishment *for* Amaziah's sin and a punishment *of* Amaziah himself. Thus, for Amos the guilt or innocence and the fate of the children themselves were not an issue.

Amos's threat that Amaziah's wife would "become a prostitute in the city" is one of his very few explicit references to the special sufferings war brings to women. It is unclear whether he envisioned her being used as a prostitute by the invading army (with the emphasis on the military compulsion of conquerors) or acting as a prostitute to earn enough to keep herself alive (with the emphasis on the economic compulsion resulting from the exile or death of both her husband and sons). Amos's reference to the city may suggest the former emphasis by naming the headquarters of the occupying soldiers or the latter emphasis by obliquely establishing her culpability (cf. Deut. 22:23–27). In either case, it is again clear that Amos saw her plight not for its effect on her but as a fair punishment of her husband, and perhaps even an especially ironic case of poetic justice. Any husband would have been dishonored, but a priest even more so, given the prohibition against priests' marrying prostitutes (Lev. 21:7, 14). Regardless of Amos's intent, one of the special forms of devastation that war brings to women is clear to careful readers.

Only once, regarding the Ammonites' ripping open of pregnant Israelites (1:13), did Amos's recognition of the devastating results of war for women elicit any sense of compassion or any call for retribution. The small and less productive land of the Ammonites and the fluidity of their border with the fertile Israelite region of Gilead may have given them a special motive for such acts of terror in their frequent border raids. Nonetheless, Amos's accusation indicates nothing special about the ferocity of the Ammonites, since it was apparently one of the conventional ways of referring to the activities of war in general (2 Kings 8:12; 15:16; Hos. 13:16). Some scholars find the motive in a determination either to decrease the next generation of enemy soldiers or to emasculate the fathers ritually. While such theories are plausible, it is interesting to see that they focus the attention entirely on the males, whether unborn sons or fathers, and ignore the slaughter of the mothers. Yet throughout history it has been commonplace for soldiers to lash out at women in uncontrolled acts of violence including rape, sexual mutilation, and murder. Specifically, in

ancient times conquered women were customarily raped and carried off as booty; women already pregnant were butchered on the spot, as were small children who could not make the journey. While they were unfortunately not extraordinary acts, Amos considered the Ammonites' atrocities against pregnant Israelite women at least worthy of God's judgment of conquest and exile.

## "You Cows of Bashan . . . Who Crush the Needy" (4:1)

One must also read between the lines to imagine the situation of the women when reading Amos's descriptions of oppression and poverty. Most of his very graphic portrayals show the exploitation of poor people seen as a whole (e.g., 2:6–7a, 8; 8:4–6) or the idle luxury of wealthy people seen as a whole (e.g., 3:15; 6:1, 4–6). The role of women is mentioned specifically only once, or perhaps twice.

The situation depicted in 2:7b is disputed because of the ambiguity of the Hebrew and the paucity of the information given: literally, "a man and his father go/walk to the girl, so that my holy name is profaned." If the verb refers to sexual intercourse, this would be the only time it does so, and, further, it would fail to indicate the willingness or unwillingness of the girl in the matter. The identity of the girl is not stated, nor is her status or relationship to the two men indicated. Most translations and commentaries envision a specific father and son engaging in sexual intercourse with "the girl," understood to mean "the same girl." Some speculate that the girl was a common prostitute, and others a "cult prostitute," the latter arguing that the sin of the two men was a cultic one (Hos. 4:14; Deut. 23:17). Others envision a slave, making the sin a socioeconomic one: even a girl sold into slavery by her father had the right to be designated for either her master or his son exclusively (Ex. 21:7–11; Lev. 19:20–22). The cultic interpretation, it is argued, would fit well with the context in 2:8, while the socioeconomic interpretation would fit well with 2:6–7a. Yet Hebrew has specific words for common prostitutes, for "consecrated women" (the traditional idea that they were prostitutes seems to result from Hosea's polemical use of sexual metaphors), and for servants or slaves, any of which Amos could have used here. Instead he chose a word that means simply "young female (of marriageable age)." There are ten passages where this word does refer to slaves or servants, but in each of those cases it occurs in the plural and with a possessive pronoun indicating the relationship of the slaves to their mistress or, in one case, master (e.g., "her attendants," Ex. 2:5). Other scholars see a different scenario: after a man had sexual intercourse with an (unidentified) girl, thereby obligating himself to marry her, his father then intruded into their relationship and in effect broke the command against sexual involvement with one's daughter-in-law (Lev. 18:15). Does Amos's vagueness reveal his lack of concern for women's experience? Or is it rather a case of idiomatic Hebrew that no longer conveys the specific meaning it had for ancient Israelites? In any case, Amos said nothing at all about the profession or status of the girl, nor her willingness or unwillingness, nor the results of the males' actions for her, choosing rather to focus solely on the profanation of God's name. The girl got lost in the theological accusation.

A fourth interpretation tries to do justice to the oddity of the Hebrew by understanding it as a denunciation of a generic "everyman" for following his father throughout generations in walking to a shrine to worship "the" female deity, who needed no further identification to Amos's audience. If this is what Amos intended, then no human female was in view here at all.

In 4:1–3 the Hebrew is also puzzling, but according to the most common interpretation, in referring to the "cows of Bashan . . . who crush the needy" Amos was denouncing the upper-class women of the capital city for idly luxuriating while oppressing the needy. Two aspects of these verses may sound much more misogynistic to modern readers than they were originally intended. Amos may well have meant to deliver a stinging denunciation of what he understood to be the women's attitudes and behavior toward the poor, but yet without any intent gratuitously to insult their bodies or their relationships with their husbands, as commentators often assume. "You cows of Bashan" was almost certainly not meant as derogatorily as it sounds in English, though the precise nuance in Amos's mind is not clear. It was common to apply animal metaphors to human beings; whether this was positive or negative depended completely on the context. In erotic literature, where the mood was exuberantly positive, a woman could be likened to "a mare among Pharaoh's chariots," a man to "a gazelle or a young stag," and a woman's breasts to "two fawns, twins of a gazelle" (Song 1:9; 2:9; 4:5; 7:3). "Bull," "ram," and "young lion" were used in

the Bible to designate leaders, nobles, and warriors (e.g., Ps. 68:30; Nah. 2:13). In prose passages such metaphors are usually obscured in English translations, which retain the sense but not the figure of speech (e.g., in 2 Kings 24:15 "the rams of the land" is translated "the elite of the land"). While most such cases use the male animal to refer to male human leaders, Amos 4:1 may well indicate that the female animal could be used to refer to wives of such leaders, in which case Amos was probably thinking primarily of their social status.

Bashan was a mountainous area east of the Jordan River, renowned for its lush wheat fields, pastures, and valuable breed of cattle, and providing a very positive image of prosperity in the Bible. In Ps. 22:12 the enemies are called "strong bulls of Bashan" either because they owed their great strength to having metaphorically grazed on Bashan or because they were strong enough to plow the rich basalt there (see Deut. 32:14; Ezek. 39:18). Other prophets looked forward with longing to the time when all Israelites would again "feed in Bashan and Gilead as in the days of old" (Micah 7:14; cf. Jer. 50:19). Thus it seems likely that Amos was not ridiculing these women for being well fed and comfortable but was denouncing them for having achieved their position by exploiting others and for continuing to use their position to oppress.

It is also unclear that, as commentaries often assume, Amos's point in referring to their asking their husbands for a drink (4:1b) was to show that their attitudes and behavior were blameworthy not only to the poor but also to their husbands. Quite possibly the husbands would be drinking with them (the Hebrew reads simply "Bring, so that we may drink," with no indication of who "we" are), and some evidence suggests that the roles of husbands and wives were not so strictly circumscribed as they are in many modern minds. This may simply be a condemnation of any luxury enjoyed by those who "crush the needy," in line with 6:1, 4–7, similar to Amos's condemnation of all worship engaged in by those who pervert justice and righteousness (5:21–24). It may be, then, that as strongly as Amos intended to denounce these women's attitudes and behavior toward the poor, he did not add gratuitous insults concerning their physical appearance or their proper role in marriage. These insults have perhaps been imported into the passage by commentaries.

How valid is the point Amos made? It is true that all women do not suffer the same kind or degree of oppression in a patriarchal society.

Some who enjoy borrowed wealth and power appear to be basking in the wealth and prestige of their husbands, and as long as their husbands are alive and treat them well—two major qualifications—they are able to maintain a certain degree of precarious security in their relationship to their husbands and thus are insulated somewhat from the harmful effects of male dominance that most women experience. How ironic as well as tragic if these women use their borrowed—and often temporary—power to oppress less fortunate people. On the other hand, one must ask, How clearly was a male Israelite able to assess the actual situation of women, and how accurately did he portray the degree of power or even of security that they actually enjoyed? And if his assessment of their power was skewed, how accurate could his understanding of their attitudes and sinfulness be?

While one cannot discern with certainty all the nuances of Amos's own attitudes toward these women, it is at least clear that he was holding them responsible for what he understood to be their unjust treatment of the poor. While Amaziah's unnamed wife was to be punished for her husband's sin, these women were to suffer for their own sin. Clearly, then, despite the fact that most biblical instruction (e.g., Ex. 19:15) and legislation (e.g., Ex. 20:17; 21:22–25; Lev. 19:29), as well as many blessings (e.g., Psalm 128) and prophetic denunciations (e.g., Hos. 4:14; Ezekiel 18), address only the men of Israel, Amos believed that women were accountable for ethical obligations similar to those incumbent upon men.

## "Let Justice Roll Down Like Waters" (5:24)

Amos expressed as clearly as any Hebrew prophet God's demand for justice, God's disgust with worship that ignored economic realities, and God's love and concern for those who were exploited. He demonstrated as well a clear understanding of many of the forces that prevented justice in Israel: greed, desire for opulence and idleness, false sense of security, reliance on placating God with offerings, dishonesty in business dealings, and corruption of the legal system.

Women today are building on the kind of insight that Amos showed and developing a more consistent critique of society than is evidenced in the book named for him. This more thoroughgoing analysis leads to both a more specific and a more structural sense of justice than was possible in Amos's day. Understanding

that women in every group and all members of oppressed groups are victimized in varying degrees by the structures of society, many women are committed to an ever-deepening understanding of the interactions of sexism, classism, racism, militarism, and nationalism that enslave and oppress so many. A clearer grasp of the structures at work will enable a more balanced understanding of poverty and exploitation, revealing, for instance, not only the special vulnerability of women to economic exploitation resulting from classism, racism, and/or militarism but also the tragic irony of women's using borrowed power to oppress those of a poorer class. Such an understanding will enable Amos's vision to speak to this generation of women and men alike and will flesh out that vision more profoundly than Amos himself was in a position to do. As Amos felt so strongly the evil of breaking a "covenant of brotherhood" (1:9, RSV), many women today feel especially strongly the evil of breaking the covenant of sisterhood, of that solidarity that should exist among women of all classes and of all peoples.

## BIBLIOGRAPHY

Andersen, Francis I., and David Noel Freedman. *Amos*. Anchor Bible 24A. Garden City, N.Y.: Doubleday & Co, 1989.

Bird, Phyllis. "'To Play the Harlot': An Inquiry Into an Old Testament Metaphor." In *Gender and Difference in Ancient Israel*, edited by Peggy L. Day, pp. 75–94. Minneapolis: Fortress Press, 1989.

Brownmiller, Susan. *Against Our Will: Men, Women and Rape*. Toronto: Bantam Books, 1975.

Hayes, John H. *Amos: The Eighth-Century Prophet: His Times and His Preaching*. Nashville: Abingdon Press, 1988.

Hiebert, Paula S. "'Whence Shall Help Come to Me?': The Biblical Widow." In *Gender and Difference in Ancient Israel*, edited by Peggy L. Day, pp. 125–141. Minneapolis: Fortress Press, 1989.

Hobbs, T. R. *A Time for War: A Study of Warfare in the Old Testament*. Wilmington, Del.: Michael Glazier, 1989.

Mays, James Luther. *Amos, A Commentary*. Old Testament Library. Philadelphia: Westminster Press, 1969.

Wolff, Hans Walter. *Joel and Amos*. Translated by Waldemar Janzen et al. Philadelphia: Fortress Press, 1977.

# OBADIAH

*Beth Glazier-McDonald*

## Introduction

### The Message

Obadiah has the distinction of being the shortest book in the Hebrew Bible—twenty-one verses. It is a concentrated attack on Edom (Esau), whose "violence" against "brother" nation Judah (Jacob) will result in his being cut down and wiped out on Yahweh's Day (vv. 10, 18). This vengeance, Obadiah feels, is well deserved because when the Babylonians conquered Jerusalem (587 B.C.E.), the Edomites "stood aside" (v. 11) and later looted the defenseless city, turning fleeing Judeans over to the Babylonians (vv. 11, 13, 14). Obadiah's message is clearly summed up in the taunt the prophet hurls against Edom: "As you have done, it shall be done to you; your deeds shall return on your own head" (v. 15b).

### Authorship and Date

Nothing is known of the prophet Obadiah. It is often assumed that he was one of the remaining prophets of the Jerusalem cult and that his book was a liturgical composition used in lamentation ceremonies for the survivors of the Babylonian destruction. However, the prophecy's concrete historical orientation, in contrast to the more general tone of cultic compositions, suggests only that he borrowed traditional themes to develop his pronouncements.

A date in the late exilic or early postexilic period is feasible for Obadiah. Indeed, the vehemence of Obadiah's denunciation suggests that the memory of the Babylonian conquest was fresh in his mind and perhaps also the early Arab incursions into Edom, which led to the gradual expulsion of Edomites from their land.

## Comment

### The Destruction of Edom (vv. 2–9) and Edom's Wrongdoing (vv. 10–14, 15b)

Verses 2–9 are found almost verbatim in Jer. 49:7–22, and the relationship between the two passages has been much discussed. It is suggested that both prophets may have drawn on a third source of preexilic oracles against Edom.

All human communities use symbolic models to express various kinds of social and national relations. Frequently in ancient Israel these models were drawn from the sphere of family relationships. The kinship of Israel/Jacob and Edom/Esau is grounded in the patriarchal traditions of chapters 25–29 and 32 of Genesis and emphasized in passages like Deut. 23:7. Indeed, Judah is expressly called Jacob (Obadiah

10) to recall their brotherhood and kinship obligations and to stress the heinous character of Edom's guilt. Although brotherhood is a model that implies a standard of expected conduct (the repeated phrase "you should not have" [vv. 12–14] is especially striking), it is interesting that the narrative material on brothers in Israel's patriarchal society stresses conflict as an almost inevitable part of the relationship (Cain and Abel; Isaac and Ishmael; Jacob and Esau; Joseph and his brothers; the sons of David). And just as conflicts between brothers affect the larger family circle, so the actions of Edom/Esau against Judah/Jacob are affecting Judean society (vv. 12–14) and will affect Edom itself (vv. 15b, 18).

## The Day of Yahweh (vv. 15a, 16–21)

Most scholars reverse the two halves of v. 15, placing 15b, which deals with Edom's destruction, with vv. 10–14. Verse 15a introduces the account of the Day of Yahweh, which is continued in vv. 16–21.

Embedded in the traditions concerning the Day of Yahweh is the belief that Yahweh's universal dominion demands recompense and requital. That Obadiah links this "Day" with the terrible "day" of Jerusalem's destruction (vv. 8, 15a), suggests that Yahweh's retributive effort is motivated by the catastrophe of 587 B.C.E.

Further, Edom's reversal of fortune and Judah's rehabilitation (described as a reunion of North and South, an expansion of boundaries until all ancient territory is recaptured, vv. 17–20) are Yahweh's work, mediated through an obedient people living on a restored Mount Zion (v. 21).

## BIBLIOGRAPHY

Wolff, Hans Walter. *Obadiah and Jonah: A Commentary.* Translated by Margaret Kohl. Minneapolis: Augsburg Publishing House, 1986.

# JONAH

*Marsha C. White*

## Introduction

Jonah ben Amittai was a prophet during Jeroboam II's reign (see 2 Kings 14:25). The book of Jonah, however, is a work of fiction with factual references that create the illusion of reality. The story's timelessness makes it notoriously difficult to date, but the presence of certain biblical quotations and allusions requires that the book be dated after the sixth century B.C.E. The author may have been associated with the wisdom teachers, a group that exercised broad freedom in questioning established patterns of thought (see Job and Ecclesiastes). Like the author of Job, he chose an obscure figure from the past to be the main character in a theological tract that probes the nature of God's justice. His tactic, though, was to unhinge the audience's expectations by creating a wonderland in which a prophet tries to run away, foreigners act like Israelites, and the most wicked city imaginable repents on a massive scale. By destabilizing his hearers, possibly people whose rigid notion of divine justice had led them into self-righteous despair, the author prepared them to receive a radical message of God's compassion. The story exhibits the enigmatic quality of a Zen koan and goes beyond gender differences in its depiction of a comically sympathetic hero.

## Comment

### God's Greatness (1:1–2:10)

The prophetic call comes to Jonah in typical fashion (1:1–2), but he is told to proclaim judgment against Nineveh, the capital of the Assyrian empire, which overran Israel in the eighth century B.C.E. and was famous for its gross cruelty. The first of many incongruities arises: What language shall he use? By what authority shall he speak? Can the people really be expected to listen?

Prophetic reluctance is a common motif in the Hebrew Bible (cf. Moses, Elijah, and Jeremiah), but Jonah's abrupt flight in the opposite direction (1:3) is more than resistance; it is a bizarre response to a strange request. His attempt to run from God's presence parodies Ps. 139:7–10, which states the impossibility of such escape.

God intervenes, hurling a "great wind" that stirs up a "great storm" (1:4). The sailors respond appropriately: in fear they cry out to their gods and heave the cargo overboard. Meanwhile, Jonah inexplicably has gone down into the ship's hold, where he has fallen into a deep sleep (1:5). The wording of the captain's request in 1:6 anticipates the king of Nineveh's decree (3:9). Upon determining that Jonah is the cause of their misfortune, the sailors want to know who he is (1:7–8). Jonah identifies himself as one who fears "Yahweh, the God of heaven, who made the sea and the dry land" (1:9), a confession that provides the interpretive key to the first half of the story. Yahweh is the sovereign God, creator and master of all. The "dry land" has special associations with the creation of the cosmos (Gen. 1:9, 10) and the creation of Israel (Exodus 14). The disparity between Jonah's confession and his behavior raises the issue of his motivations.

In answer to the sailors' fearful question, Jonah requests to be thrown overboard, which could be understood either as a magnanimous gesture or as a suicide attempt (1:10–12; cf. 1:5 and 4:3, 9). Again, Jonah's behavior is perplexing. The foreign sailors ignore Jonah's request and try to row to shore. When their attempt fails, they incongruously pray to Yahweh in traditional Israelite language (1:13–14), effecting an ironic reversal of Jer. 26:15. When the sea stills, the sailors "greatly fear" Yahweh and offer sacrifices and vows, which were standard Israelite practices (1:15–16).

God intervenes a second time, appointing a "great fish" to swallow Jonah (1:17). The fish saves Jonah from drowning and brings him back to where he started, unceremoniously vomiting him onto the "dry land." The psalm in 2:1–9 is a later insertion, imputing a piety to Jonah at variance with the rest of the story.

## God's Goodness (3:1–4:11)

***The power of repentance (3:1–10).*** God's determination that Jonah proclaim against Nineveh is unrelenting, and this time Jonah gives in (3:1–3a). Nineveh appears as a legendary "great city," whose projected overthrow for its evil recalls Sodom and Gomorrah (Genesis 19). Jonah's terse message allows the Ninevites time in which to do something about their sentence, suggesting the possibility of repentance (3:3b–4).

The response by people and king alike is instantaneous: immediately they proclaim a fast, put on sackcloth, and sit in ashes, thereby performing the traditional Israelite ritual of penitence (3:5–6). The incongruity of foreigners practicing Israelite customs has been anticipated by the sailors, to which is added the startling abandonment of evil by a latter-day Sodom.

The king's decree extends the remarkable penitence even to the animals, evoking a ludicrous picture of hungry cattle and sheep dressed in sackcloth and crying out to God (3:7–8). The story's series of surprising events climaxes here, which highlights the central theme of repentance. The theology derives entirely from Jeremiah: the phrase "all shall turn from their evil ways" (3:8b) is an idiomatic expression unique to Jeremiah. "Who knows?" (3:9) echoes the captain's "perhaps" (1:6), used by Jeremiah for the possibility of Judah's repentance. The juxtaposition of "relent" and "turn back" (3:9) appears elsewhere only in Jeremiah.

The summary of the climactic events (3:10) is also a précis of Jeremiah's thinking on repentance. Although there was precedent in the story of the golden calf for God's relenting of punishment (Ex. 32:12–14) and eighth-century prophets called on Israel to return to God (e.g., Amos 4:6–12), it was Jeremiah who coined the term "repent" and developed its covenantal implications. The book of Jonah can be seen as an illustration of the axiom set forth in Jer. 18:7–8, in which God promises to renounce punishment decreed against a nation if it turns away from its wickedness. The passage hyperbolically generalizes to any nation a principle that in fact applied only to Israel. Only Israel was bound in a covenant relationship to Yahweh. Only Israel could turn away from Yahweh and be punished, and only Israel could turn back to Yahweh in repentance. The fantastic and utterly impossible depiction of Nineveh's repentance is therefore intended as a message to Israel: if the very essence of evil was able to "return" to God, then surely so could God's own people. This turning will be matched by a similar turning on God's part. The symmetry between the people's renunciation of evil and God's renunciation of punishment is a hallmark of Jeremiah on repentance.

***God's compassionate response (4:1–11).*** Jonah's anger at the sparing of Nineveh (4:1–2) is an unexpected reaction to an incredible event. In contrast to the biblical heroes who interceded on behalf of those doomed to destruction (Abraham in Genesis 18, Moses in Exodus 32) and all the prophets who labored unsuccessfully to bring Israel back to Yahweh, Jonah is greatly displeased by the overwhelming reponse to his few words. Finally he reveals the reason for his incomprehensible behavior. He had known from the beginning that God would forgive the Ninevites, and this offends his sense of justice.

Significantly, Jonah quotes an ancient liturgical confession of God's attributes, which appears originally in Ex. 34:6–7. The attribute formula carefully balances God's mercy with God's justice in view of human sin. Some versions of the formula stress the attribute of mercy (e.g., Psalm 103), while others stress the attribute of justice (e.g., Nahum 1:2–3). In Exodus the context of Israel's apostasy with the golden calf followed by divine forgiveness and covenant renewal (Exodus 32–34) weights compassion over judgment in the original. Indeed, the name Yahweh implies graciousness and compassion (Ex. 33:19). However, the version in the book of Jonah goes even further. In place of the judgment clause is the renunciation of punishment; Yahweh is the gracious and compassionate God who "relents from punishing"

(4:2). Mercy no longer tempers justice but overrides it entirely. The effect of withholding the reason for Jonah's flight until late in the story is to underscore the changed formula. The new formula becomes a punch line that resolves all prior suspense, calling attention to the radical nature of God's compassion.

Jonah's outlandish death wish (4:3–11) parodies the genuine despair of Moses (Num. 11:15) and Elijah (1 Kings 19:4). The lesson of the evanescent plant is designed to shame him for his refusal to pity anyone but himself. God's way is to feel for the creatures God brought into the world and to do everything possible to spare them.

### Repentance and Compassion

The central theme of the book of Jonah is the efficacy of repentance and God's compassionate response. The book is not a universalistic sermon against a narrow-minded and particularistic Israel. Rather, the picture of perfect Gentile piety is an impossibly absurd backdrop against which the drama between God and Jonah takes place. The reader both identifies with and condemns Jonah, demanding a reassessment of the religious community's relationship with God that pertains equally to men and women.

### BIBLIOGRAPHY

Darr, Katheryn Pfisterer. "Jonah." In The Books of the Bible, vol.1, The Old Testament/The Hebrew Bible, edited by Bernhard W. Anderson, pp. 381–384. New York: Charles Scribner's Sons, 1989.

Magonet, Jonathan. Form and Meaning: Studies in Literary Techniques in the Book of Jonah. Sheffield: Almond Press, 1983.

Sasson, Jack M. Jonah. Anchor Bible 24B. New York: Doubleday & Co., 1990.

Trible, Phyllis. Studies in the Book of Jonah. Ann Arbor, Mich.: University Microfilms, 1963.

# MICAH

## Judith E. Sanderson

## Introduction

Micah, a younger contemporary of Isaiah, lived sometime between 742 B.C.E. (Jotham's accession, 1:1) and 687 (Hezekiah's death). A native of the town of Moresheth in the Judean foothills, Micah attacked the wealthy and corrupt leaders of Jerusalem, including the rulers, landowners, judges, priests, and prophets, for their exploitation of the common people, with whom he felt solidarity.

Apart from the editorial superscription (1:1) the entire book is written in very creative poetry using a variety of genres. The first major section, 1:2–3:12, begins by predicting the destruction of Samaria and ends by predicting that of Jerusalem because of its violence and oppression. The second section, 4:1–5:15, begins with a total reversal, the symbolic exaltation of Jerusalem as the center of worldwide peace depicted in terms highly meaningful to women (4:4), and continues the theme of restoration after disaster. The final section, 6:1–7:20, opens with God's lawsuit against Israel

and God's demand for justice, kindness and loyalty, and a wise life in communion with God (6:8, deservedly the most famous verse in Micah; the traditional "walk humbly" is neither the best translation nor the most helpful word to women; see the comment on Zeph. 3:12). It then reverts to a condemnation of specific crimes of oppression and an indictment of the entire people, ending with expressions of repentance and God's forgiveness. Some scholars attribute all or almost all of the book to Micah himself, while others date portions, particularly from chaps. 4 to 7, to the late preexilic, exilic, and postexilic periods, on the grounds of subjects and style.

While only one woman—Miriam—is named in the entire book, Micah showed his special concern for the women who suffered exploitation by the rich (2:9; contrast Amos). Nevertheless, the impact of the language and imagery of the book as a whole is detrimental to the perception of women by women and men alike.

## Comment

### "As the Wages of a Prostitute She Gathered Them" (1:7)

Throughout the book, nations and cities, especially Jerusalem, are personified as women. Because of the book's message of sin and judgment, this personification leads to extremely negative images of women. Since the words "city" and "land" belong to the feminine gender in Hebrew, they necessarily were spoken of with feminine pronouns, which are often retained in English translations despite the existence of neuter pronouns in English (e.g., 1:6: "her stones . . . her foundations"). Further,

some evidence may suggest that Israel inherited from the Canaanites the image of capital cities as female gods married to the male patron god of the city. If this is true, it would have been even more natural for male writers to extend the use of the feminine beyond grammar to imagery as well. Hence, "her wages" in the first half of 1:7 easily led to depicting Samaria as a prostitute in the second half of the verse (cf., e.g., Jer. 3:1–3). It also led in 4:10 to the image of the suffering of Jerusalem ("daughter Zion") as the pains of childbirth (cf. Jer. 4:31). The negative connotations are sometimes clearer in

Hebrew than in English: five times in 1:11–15 "the inhabitants" is actually a feminine singular noun. Thus, in 1:11 a woman ("the inhabitants of Shaphir") is called to pass on "in nakedness and shame" (cf. 4:11). On the other hand, sometimes the imagery was not originally as negative as it now sounds. In 1:16 the call to the woman to shave off her hair should not be understood, as in the modern world, as humiliation for a woman who has slept with the enemy but rather as a symbol of mourning (cf. Amos 8:10).

This metaphor determines the speakers in 7:8–10, where Jerusalem speaks as a woman to her enemy, represented as another woman, about God, represented as a man, and in 7:11–13, where God responds as a man to the woman. Then 7:14–20 is addressed to the man, God. Though it is not always clear in English, every verb and every occurrence of the words "you" and "your" in Hebrew must be either masculine or feminine. Thus Hebrew grammar and poetic imagery work together to perpetuate the notion that God is male and the people, whether Israel or Jerusalem, is collectively female. Even worse, God is a good and just and forgiving male, while the people is at worst an evil and corrupt female and at best a repentant female.

## "I Sent Before You Moses, Aaron, and Miriam" (6:4)

Micah 6:4 is the only reference in the prophets to Miriam by name (Jer. 31:4 alludes anonymously to her tambourines and dance, as in Ex. 15:20–21). Surprisingly, the same is true for Aaron, and even Moses is mentioned only in Isa. 63:11–12; Jer. 15:1; and Mal. 4:4. Micah 6:4 is notable for several reasons. First, it makes a statement that is both clear and significant: all three were sent by God to lead the Israelites. Second, the implication of vv. 4–5 is that these three divine commissions were as significant as the liberation from slavery and that they belong to God's "saving acts" in the wilderness. Third, the verse serves as a contrast to 7:20. In that verse only two men of ancient memory are mentioned, Jacob and Abraham, while here a woman is named as the equal of two men.

There are also two features notable by their absence in 6:4. The first is any explanation or description of the three figures. This lack indicates that each was well known in Israel when this passage was written (by contrast, Balak and Balaam are both identified in the following verse; Jacob and Abraham are not

identified in 7:20). Their fame is especially important in the context, a recitation of God's saving acts designed to evoke gratitude in the hearts of its listeners. Such a recitation would intentionally highlight those persons who had played a major role in the national memory. The second feature significant for its absence is any identification of Miriam by her father or husband, the usual way that women in the Bible are identified. Instead, only her own name is given, so that she stands in her own right as an independent woman. In fact, the Bible never mentions her marital status. She is not said here to be related to Aaron and Moses. The tradition that the three were siblings (only in Num. 26:59 and 1 Chron. 6:3; cf. Ex. 15:20) seems to have been a late one, indicating not familial relationship but rather the significant cultic leadership of all three.

The importance of this verse is its implication that Miriam was remembered at the time of its writing as a very important leader sent by God during the wilderness period, in spite of the fact that in the Bible as we now have it tantalizingly little about her has been preserved. Whether this verse goes back to Micah or a later writer, at least the three major traditions preserved in the Bible concerning Miriam—and perhaps more—must have been common knowledge. Miriam led the women in singing, playing the tambourines, dancing, and celebrating God's victory at the Reed Sea (Ex. 15:20–21); she led a challenge against Moses' authority, in consequence of which she was temporarily struck with leprosy (Numbers 12; cf. Deut. 24:9); and she died and was buried in Kadesh just prior, as the biblical chronology now has it, to the sin for which Moses and Aaron were both said to have died (Num. 20:1).

## BIBLIOGRAPHY

Burns, Rita J. *Has the Lord Indeed Spoken Only Through Moses? A Study of the Biblical Portrait of Miriam.* Atlanta: Scholars Press, 1987.

Fitzgerald, Aloysius. "The Mythological Background for the Presentation of Jerusalem as a Queen and False Worship as Adultery in the Old Testament." *Catholic Biblical Quarterly* 34 (1972), 403–416.

Hillers, Delbert R. *Micah.* Hermeneia. Philadelphia: Fortress Press, 1984.

Mays, James Luther. *Micah, A Commentary.* Old Testament Library. Philadelphia: Westminster Press, 1976.

# NAHUM

Judith E. Sanderson

## Introduction

Nothing is known about Nahum except that he came from the town of Elkosh and that he presumably spoke his gloating words in Jerusalem between the year 663 B.C.E., when the Egyptian capital, Thebes, fell (3:8–10), and the year 612, when Nineveh fell. His name means "Comfort" or "Comforter," which was ironic from Nineveh's viewpoint (see 3:7) but quite appropriate from Judah's (see 1:12–13, 15). The "devastation, desolation, and destruction" (2:10) of Nineveh, the capital of the Assyrian empire, the most powerful, feared, and hated empire of the world, meant consolation for Judah.

A second irony of this book is that its message of revenge and violence is couched in exceptionally artistic poetry, among the most vivid in the Hebrew Bible. Following the title (1:1), the book opens with what appears to be the first half of an acrostic poem (in which each line begins with a successive letter of the Hebrew alphabet), now somewhat mutilated (vv. 2–8). This poem depicts God in historical terms as an angry and avenging warrior destroying enemies while protecting Israel (vv. 2–3a, 7–8) and in mythological terms as a storm god soaring through the skies and wreaking havoc on nature (vv. 3b–6; see also the comment on Habakkuk). The prophet then interprets this picture as a threat to the enemy but comfort and peace for Israel (1:9–15). Chapter 2 graphically describes the utter defeat of Nineveh. Verse 7 should probably be understood as referring to the stripping of the statue of Nineveh's female deity Ishtar and her deportation along with her loudly lamenting female priests (RSV is preferable to NRSV here; cf. 1:14; and see Isa. 46:1–2 for the deportation of Babylon's two chief gods, both male). In Nahum 2:13–3:7 God speaks directly to Nineveh, describing divine wrath and retaliation. As Thebes, Egypt's great capital, had fallen to Assyria, it was now Nineveh's turn to fall (3:8–10). Further taunts follow in 3:11–17 regarding the quick surrender of Assyrian fortresses and soldiers, the futility of preparations for the siege, and the rapid disappearance of Assyrian officials throughout the empire. In closing, the joyful applause of all the nations is heard in 3:18–19.

The point of each of the three chapters is epitomized in its closing reference to messengers or news delivered. The "one who brings good tidings" to Judah in 1:15 is able to do so because of God's power to defeat all enemies, extolled in chap. 1. In contrast, "the voice of your [Nineveh's] messengers shall be heard no more" conveying imperial commands and demanding tribute (2:13), after the battle described in chap. 2. And the international significance of Nineveh's defeat is clear in 3:19: "All who hear the news about you clap their hands over you. For who has ever escaped your endless cruelty?" This closing verse helps to explain the vengeful spirit of the book. Nineveh, as the capital of the Assyrian empire, had recently been the richest and most powerful city in the world, because of imperial conquest and the seizure of tribute. Its armies had committed atrocities in many lands, including Thebes (3:8–10; all who could not walk into exile, including infants, would have been killed on the spot). They had forcibly deported many peoples from their own lands and resettled them hundreds of miles away in order to establish better control over the far-flung regions of the empire. (Nahum 2:12 expresses metaphorically what is described historically in

217

2 Kings 17:1–6, 24 and 18:13–16). As so many had suffered so deeply at Nineveh's hands, they now clapped their own hands in joy and in a sense of vindication.

## Comment

### "I Will Lift Up Your Skirts Over Your Face . . . and Make You a Spectacle" (3:5–6)

In the face of massive violence against women in modern Western societies, it is very difficult for women to read biblical stories of men's violence against women and even worse to read biblical imagery of God's violence against women, as in Nahum 3:4–7. Even though one realizes that all language about God is meta-phorical and that God can be imaged only through human analogies, it is nevertheless painful to read God's activities of judgment portrayed as sexual violence. There are two parts to Nahum's depiction of God's judgment: the image of Nineveh as a prostitute and the image of its defeat as sexual humiliation at the hands of God. How can readers understand and respond to these images? Four questions are involved: What was the actual situation in Israelite society that made these images meaningful? How did Nahum use these images to express something about Nineveh and about God? What is the actual situation in today's society that colors our hearing of these images? What would these images express to today's society about God? Throughout this discussion male pronouns will be used for God and female pronouns for cities and lands, as the only appropriate language for exploring these metaphors. Perhaps this very exploration will demonstrate the dangers of both uses of pronouns.

To understand the function of this passage for the author and his audience, one must determine what can be known about both prostitution and sexual violence in ancient Israel and how they were perceived by males, including the author. The role of a prostitute is an ambivalent one in any society. The more stringently the sexuality of most women is controlled by fathers and husbands—and thus the less available most women are for the sexual gratification of men—the more urgently is felt the need for women whose sexuality is not controlled by men and thus stand outside the normal social order. On the other hand, given the double standard common to patriarchal societies, the blame for sexual activities attaches to the female only. Thus, prostitutes' activities are deemed to be a necessary evil

for the society, which means that while the women must be tolerated, they are despised and represent fair game for vitriolic verbal attacks. The attacks in several prophetic works in the Bible against metaphorical prostitutes (e.g., Hosea 2; Jer. 13:27; Ezekiel 16; 23) may suggest the attitudes of many Israelites toward actual prostitutes. While prostitution could not be eliminated from the society and prostitutes could not be literally cast out, they were treated as outcasts and thus marginalized. Although it was not illegal for males to resort to prostitutes, nevertheless men could be warned in the strongest possible tones of the evil consequences, ethically, ritually, and practically, of doing so. In these very dramatic warnings, prostitutes were endowed by their critics with enormous power to mislead, to deceive, in fact to victimize males, partly by means of their finery in clothing and cosmetics.

The other aspect of this imagery is sexual violence as retaliation. Though the violence and humiliation of stripping naked appear preparatory to sexual assault, in the ancient world forced sex with a prostitute would not have been understood as rape. Rape in a thoroughgoing patriarchal society is forced sexual intercourse with a woman who belongs to a man. The typical prostitute did not belong to a man; hence, force used against her would not have been deemed rape. Instead, since she was viewed as flaunting her sexuality for her own material gain and in a deceptive way, for a man to demean her sexuality would be viewed as appropriate retaliation. Commentators are reading too much into the prophetic descriptions of the degradation of prostitutes when they understand them as revealing the accepted legal practice in Israel. Since prostitution was not illegal, all that can be said definitely is that these imagistic passages reveal the patriarchal attitudes of scapegoating and despising these women.

The second question is: How did Nahum use these images to express something about Nineveh and about God? What aspects of prostitution and of sexual violence seemed to him analogous to God's opinion and treatment of Nineveh? What Nahum shares with other biblical writers who use sexual activity metaphorically is that the blame is always placed on the woman, for two reasons. The first is the double standard mentioned above, and the second is that when male–female relations are used to image God's relations with humans, God is always pictured as male and humans always as female (see also 3:8–10, where Thebes is a woman; and see the comment on Micah regarding cities and lands as grammatically feminine and metaphorically female). Yet the metaphor of the prostitute functions differently here than in most other biblical passages. Elsewhere the prostitute is God's own people, whether Israel (Hosea) or Judah/Jerusalem (Jeremiah and Ezekiel), and the underlying image is that of marriage between God and his people, whereby he has an exclusive right to his wife's sexuality. His wife has wronged him by giving herself to others, so that she is seen first as adulterous, with the emphasis on her unfaithfulness, and ultimately as a prostitute, with the emphasis on her habitual promiscuity. In the case of Isa. 23:15–18 regarding Tyre and Nahum 3:4–7 regarding Nineveh, however, there is no underlying sense that the woman belongs to Israel's God. Rather, Nineveh was dedicated to Ishtar (whose two chief characteristics, incidentally, were her erotic and warlike nature). Thus it is not unfaithfulness to God — or to any husband — that is in view here but rather habitual promiscuity with a variety of nations ("the countless debaucheries of the prostitute" or, more literally and neutrally, the greatness of her promiscuity, Nahum 3:4).

Female sexuality in general was seen as dangerous to men (e.g., Proverbs 7), but a prostitute's sexuality was seen as even more so, for two reasons. First, her sexuality was not controlled by a man (the victims of the "loose woman" in Proverbs 7 are so numerous [v. 26] because her husband is "on a long journey" [v. 19]); and, second, she was perceived as a brazen, mercenary predator out solely for her own gain and loyal to no one but herself (see Jer. 3:3; Ezek. 16:30–31; Prov. 23:27–28). Another metaphor for her dangerous power was that of witchcraft ("mistress of sorcery," Nahum 3:4; cf. Isaiah 47 against Babylon). Just as Jehu expressed his contempt for Jezebel by accusing her of promiscuity and sorceries (2 Kings 9:22), so Nahum applied the same two words to Nineveh (compare the connection in English between sexual charms and magical charms). In Nahum's patriarchal imagination Nineveh had seduced and then deceived many political and military allies, including Judah (2 Kings 18:31–32 provides a sample of her honeyed words).

"Enslaves" in 3:4 should perhaps be understood as "betrays" or "ensnares." In any case, her seduction had brought nothing but trouble to her allies, presumably because, after she made treaties with them, she either failed to deliver the promised help or perhaps even worked against them (Second Chronicles 28:16–21 exemplifies Nahum's attitude toward Assyria's "help"). Nahum presumably missed the special irony of his personification of Nineveh as a woman. Assyria was profoundly hated because of its brutality in conquest, which was planned and executed by men. When women were involved at all, far from being perpetrators of the bloodshed, they were part of the booty (3:1), suffering the special treatment reserved for women captives, rape. Surely there is something perverse about Nahum's personification.

To continue with the image, Nineveh would be punished for her deception and disloyalty to her clients, and the punishment would fit the crime, as is regularly the case in the Bible. As Nineveh's crime was depicted as sexual — flaunting her sexuality ("gracefully alluring," 3:4) in order to seduce nations — so her punishment would be sexual — being forcibly stripped naked before those nations. As her fine clothing was viewed as a major source of her seductive power, it was that fine clothing which was violently removed. According to one of the more likely interpretations of 2:7, Nahum had already described the stripping of Ishtar's statue; here he applied the same verb metaphorically to the city herself. Hosea was the first to use this imagery. In Hos. 2:2–3 God threatened to "strip her [Israel] naked and expose her as in the day she was born" (cf. Isa. 3:16–17). In Hos. 2:9–10 God's purpose was stated more explicitly: "I will uncover her [Israel's] shame [i.e., genitals] in the sight of her lovers." There God was the jealous husband who would prove that he was stronger than her lovers by punishing his unfaithful wife with impunity in their presence; thus he would humiliate her and, to a lesser degree, them. Jeremiah, probably a contemporary of Nahum, had God explicitly link exposure with violation in 13:22 ("your skirts are lifted up, and you are violated"), while 13:26–27 made God's purpose of humiliation — this time of the woman alone — explicit: "I myself will lift up your [Jerusalem's] skirts over your face, and your shame will be seen." Ezekiel, writing somewhat later, would picture Jerusalem being exposed by God first and then by her lovers (16:36–40; see also Isa. 47:2–3 about Babylon). All of these prophets were making a point similar to Nahum's: the appropriateness of the punishment. Since Nahum had depicted Nineveh's treachery in terms of female sexuality, it felt quite fitting to him to depict its punishment in terms of the sexual violence of a man against a woman. As her sexual conduct had been "shameless," she would now be treated "shamefully."

The third question is: What is the situation in today's society that colors our hearing of these images? Women's sexuality is consistently seen as a marketable commodity, as their source of power, and as their chief attribute, all of which diminishes and devalues the wholeness of women. This may suggest that the use of women's sexuality as a religiously informing metaphor is inappropriate. No aspect of God's relationship with humankind can be represented in the modern world by an image that depends on a destructive view of women's bodied selves.

Further, a growing awareness of the social factors that lead women and girls into prostitution suggests caution in the old stereotypes of prostitutes as powerful and evil seducers of men. Far from seeing prostitutes as glamorous and dangerous, it is now easier to see them in their true light, as victims of patriarchal social and economic systems. Whereas in the comments above the focus was on patriarchal perceptions of prostitutes, here the focus is on feminist understandings of prostitutes in all times and places. Since in patriarchal societies women are seen as actually or ideally dependent on men for support, girls tend neither to be trained for jobs whereby they can support themselves nor to be taught attitudes and traits of self-reliance and assertiveness in other than sexual ways whereby they may attract a man to support them. Thus, when for any reason a woman does not find a man or loses the man she had, she often finds no way to support herself except through her sexuality (see the comment on Amos 7:17). In addition, women and girls who are in economically or emotionally vulnerable situations are often tricked or forced into life as prostitutes. What is true to a certain extent in modern Western societies was much more so in ancient societies, where women could neither inherit property (see Numbers 27 and 36 for a significant but closely circumscribed exception) nor be trained for independent trades.

In addition, an increased knowledge of the history of women warns against accusations of sorcery, even when metaphorical. Nahum's use of that metaphor against Nineveh not only reveals the patriarchal fear of the power of women's sexuality but also recalls the accusations of witchcraft that have brought suffering and death to millions of women throughout the centuries.

Finally, a new definition of rape—and with it, of other forms of sexual violence—becomes appropriate as societies become less patriarchal. No longer seen as a crime against the man to whom the woman belongs, rape is now understood as a crime against the woman herself. Thus, any form of sexual violence against a woman is repudiated as a violation of her personal integrity and well-being and is repugnant to all who wish women well. As the full personhood of women becomes more and more accepted, there is a new sense that violence against women is never justified, regardless of the provocation. Just as battering is not justified when supper is late, so sexual violence is not justified in the case of adultery or prostitution.

The fourth question is: What would these images express to today's society about God? Current struggles to achieve more egalitarian styles of marriage both in reality and in the collective imagination call into question the appropriateness of the marriage metaphor as it appears frequently in the Bible for the relationship between God and humans, whereby God is always the husband. The prophets used that metaphor so frequently and so extensively because it offered several distinct advantages over other metaphors taken from human relationships. While these advantages must be taken seriously in analyzing other prophetic passages (see the comments on Hosea, Jeremiah, and Ezekiel), it is clear that they are not a factor in Nahum, since the relationship between God and Israel is not the issue here. Thus there is no alleviation of the harmful effects of the sexual imagery here. Given Nahum's anger, it seemed appropriate to him to suggest that since Judah was one of Nineveh's disappointed clients, Judah's God was now retaliating for her perfidy to Judah. Judah was a customer enticed, seduced, deceived, now spurned, and thus angry and vindictive. The degree of anger and the desire for revenge are understandable if Judah had depended on Assyria for defense and had been betrayed. But the image Nahum used to vent that anger is dangerous to women's health, lives, and well-being and must be recognized as such. In a society where violence against women is epidemic, it is extremely dangerous to image

God as involved in it in any way. The danger is of two kinds. What would it mean to worship a God who is portrayed as raping women when angry? And if humans see themselves in some way as the image of God, what would it mean to reflect that aspect of God's activity on the human level? To involve God in an image of sexual violence is, in a profound way, somehow to justify it and thereby to sanction it for human males who are for any reason angry with a woman. No wonder, then, that these biblical passages are seldom used for preaching and teaching.

One can appreciate the anger Nahum expressed against the ruthless tyrant of his day and can appreciate his desire to use a metaphor that graphically expressed the biblical notion that God's punishment fits the crime in very appropriate ways. In today's world one must insist, however, that this anger and this concept of God's punishment be expressed in ways that do not demean women and women's sexuality and do not promote violence against women. It is dangerous enough that God is depicted as male while human beings are female. The danger is greatly compounded when God is depicted as a male who proves his manhood and superiority through violent and sexual retaliation against women.

## BIBLIOGRAPHY

Bird, Phyllis A. "The Harlot as Heroine: Narrative Art and Social Presupposition in Three Old Testament Texts." In *Narrative Research on the Hebrew Bible*, edited by Miri Amihai, George W. Coats, and Anne M. Solomon. *Semeia* 46 (1989), 119–139.

Gebhard, Paul Henry. "Prostitution." In *The New Encyclopaedia Britannica*. 15th ed. Vol. 15, pp. 75–81. Chicago: Helen Hemingway Benton, 1977.

Smith, John Merlin Powis, et al. *A Critical and Exegetical Commentary on Micah, Zephaniah, Nahum, Habakkuk, Obadiah and Joel*. International Critical Commentary. Edinburgh: T. & T. Clark, n.d.

# HABAKKUK

*Judith E. Sanderson*

## Introduction

Habakkuk's name occurs in 1:1 and 3:1, where he is identified as a prophet, but no further information is provided about him. From the description of the Chaldeans (Babylonians) in 1:6, one can surmise that he was speaking in Judah as the Babylonians were beginning the creation of their empire, toward the end of the seventh century B.C.E.

Most of the book is in poetry, but in three very different genres: a dialogue between Habakkuk and God (1:2–2:5), a series of five woes (2:6–20), and a psalm complete with liturgical instructions (3:1–19). While the forms suggest different occasions of writing if not different authors, the themes of the various parts give a certain unity to the book. The overarching theme is patient confidence that, regardless of present appearances, human violence will ultimately be defeated by divine violence. The dialogue consists of two complaints by Habakkuk, each followed by a response from God. Some reading between the lines is necessary to follow the thread of the conversation. First Habakkuk complains that God has done nothing to end the violence and injustice within Judah (1:2–4), to which God responds that the exceedingly violent conquest of Judah and its neighbors by the

Babylonians will be more than Habakkuk could have dreamed (1:5–11). Next Habakkuk complains that since the Babylonians are even more violent and evil than the Judahites, God must put a stop to their conquests (1:12–17). Speaking as a military guard of a city (2:1), Habakkuk proposes to station himself on the rampart to watch for God's answer, which is prefaced by God's instructions to write the answer large enough that it may be easily visible (2:2–3). The answer itself (2:4–5) is somewhat enigmatic but at least suggests the patience and confidence in God's ultimate victory that are the themes of the book. There follow a series of five taunts against the Babylonian oppressors, each ironically introduced with the word "Alas for" or "Woe to," and each showing the appropriateness of the punishment coming to the wicked. The ending of the woe section, 2:20, may well have been the original ending of the book. But the psalm (chap. 3) contributes to the theme of the book by narrating a theophany, that is, a direct manifestation of God (3:3–15) experienced by one who pleaded with God to act again as in former times (3:2) and who afterward is first horrified but then comforted and empowered to wait for God's victory (3:16–19).

## Comment

For women struggling to find new models of relationships that avoid violence and dominating power, two of the most distressing aspects of the Bible are the prevalence of violence and the image of the divine warrior-king. As short as Habakkuk is, it is replete with violence and domination, culminating in the theophany in chap. 3 of God warring against the whole earth and all its nations. How are the

predictions of violence and the picture of God as warrior to be understood?

### "The Violence Done to Lebanon Will Overwhelm You" (2:17)

It may be helpful to trace the course of violence throughout the book. In its three short chapters Habakkuk contains the word "violence" six times (1:2, 3, 9; 2:8, 17a, b), which is 10 percent of all the occurrences in the Bible. More than that, almost every verse gives a picture of violence even when the word is not used. The first perpetrators of violence are right before Habakkuk's eyes in Judah, bringing wrong-doing, destruction, strife, and lack of law enforcement (1:2–4). God's answer to Habakkuk's lament is that the Babylonians will bring violence on a much larger scale, as they plunder the entire region, sneering at kings and defenses, confident in their own might (1:5–11). Implicit in these verses is that the Babylonians' violent conquest will be God's way of punishing the Judahites for their own violence. Habakkuk's second complaint, "Your eyes are too pure to see evil, and you cannot look at wrongdoing" (1:13) echoes his previous question, "Why do you make me see wickedness and look at wrong-doing?" (1:3, author's translation). Habakkuk is objecting that if violence within Judah is bad, it should not be punished by worse violence from people who worship their own might (1:11, 16). God's only answer is found in 2:3–5: wealth and arrogance will not last, and the righteous will faithfully wait until the end comes for the violent oppressors. This brief response is followed first by Habakkuk's five taunts confidently mocking the oppressors, repeating the word "violence" three more times, and then by the vision of God's violent appearance. It is the woes that show that the Babylonians, whom God uses to punish Judah, will themselves be punished for their own violence.

The idea that God's punishment fits the crime, a common feature of biblical theology, is often conveyed by repetition of words and phrases. When Habakkuk complains that within Judah "justice does not go forth to prevail" and that "justice goes forth perverted" (1:4, author's translation), God's response is that the Babylonians' own "justice . . . will go forth from themselves" (1:7, author's translation). In other words, if the Judahites refuse to live by God's justice, they will be forced to experience Babylonian "justice," where might makes right (cf. 1:11). This would be recognized by an Israelite as an appropriate method of punishment. But that is not the end of the story. The Babylonians will then be punished by violence themselves, since they have achieved God's purpose but in an ungodlike manner. Thus the first woe (2:8) shows by repetition the next stage: "Because you have plundered many nations, all that survive of the peoples shall plunder you." The fourth woe (2:17) likewise shows the

reversal of violence as punishment. In this verse, while the perpetrators of the final stage of violence are not stated, the nature of the previous Babylonian destruction is suggested: killing of animals and humans is explicit, and the violence to Lebanon and to the earth certainly includes destruction of forests and other natural resources.

Thus, a major point of the book is that while humans bemoan the lack of justice in human relations, God is aware of the situation and indeed is responding, acting in unexpected places, among nations, peoples, and groups where one might not first expect God to be operating.

## "You Drove Your Horses, Your Chariots to Victory" (3:8)

Thus far God's judgment has operated through the violence of human beings. Contrary to Habakkuk's indignant claim, God may indeed be able to "look at wrongdoing" (1:13) and use it for divine purposes, even to the extent of being the one who "rouses" the enemy (1:6). But thus far God has not been portrayed as directly involved in the violence. This changes in the psalm in chap. 3, where God appears as a warrior conquering the earth.

To understand this imagery it is necessary to see that the Israelites pictured their God in images that came from the portrayals of other gods in the ancient Near East. Baal, the Canaanite storm and fertility god, was depicted as a warrior whose voice was thunder, whose arrows were flashes of lightning, whose breath was the wind, who defeated the power of chaos, Sea (also known as River), and whose coming shook the whole earth in storm. The Israelite God was often depicted similarly as the storm god whose lightning brought destruction (Hab. 3:4, 9, 11) but whose rains brought prosperity (e.g., Psalm 29), and as the warrior who used Sea/River as a weapon against the Egyptians to liberate the Hebrews (Hab. 3:8, 15; cf. Ex. 15:1–21). God comes from Teman, Mount Paran, through Cushan and Midian (3:3, 7; cf. Sinai, Seir, and Edom in Deut. 33:2 and Judg. 5:4–5), all in the south, where Sinai was. These references to the sea and the south allude to the two events foundational for Israel, the exodus and the encounter with God at Sinai. Just as one of Baal's titles as storm god was Rider on the Clouds, so Israel often imaged its God riding through the skies in a chariot, the main vehicle for warfare, as in Hab. 3:8 (cf. Deut. 33:26; Ps. 18:10; 68:4, 33;

104:3; Isa. 19:1). In the military retinue came other gods clearly subject to Israel's God: Pestilence and Plague in Hab. 3:5 (Plague was a Canaanite god), elsewhere "myriads of holy ones, . . . a host of his own . . . they marched at your heels, accepted direction from you" (Deut. 33:2–3; cf. Ps. 68:17). The earth quaked and all nature and peoples along God's route were profoundly upset, as in Hab. 3:6–12 (cf. Judg. 5:4–5; Psalm 114; Ex. 15:14–16).

But if all this picture language came from the Canaanite culture, what was the point of it for the Israelites as they thought of and worshiped their own God? The most important verse in Habakkuk 3 is v. 13, which states the purpose of God's appearing as a warrior and storm god: "You came forth to save your people." As God had acted at the Reed Sea to liberate the Hebrew slaves from the Egyptian oppressors, so God would act again to bring the Babylonian oppressors to judgment and the Israelites to peace and freedom. In other words, chap. 3 is a pictorial way of saying what chaps. 1–2 have already said: God is in ultimate control of the world and of history and is the one who first rouses the Babylonians (1:6) to punish Judah and then uses Babylon's victims to punish the Babylonians themselves (2:6–17). Whereas the Babylonians worship their own military might (1:11, 16), the theophany empowers the psalmist to find strength in God (3:19). The deity who can be pictured riding a war chariot through the skies accompanied by the warrior gods Pesti-lence and Plague and wreaking havoc in their path can equally be pictured enthroned in a holy temple in such majesty and splendor that utter silence is the only response from all peoples of the earth (2:20).

Understanding an image as it was used by biblical writers is not the final word. Many question the continuing appropriateness of some biblical images for God, particularly those depicting violence. The challenge comes both to explore the Bible to discover images already offered but seldom used today and also to explore life in today's world to discover images for God from modern culture just as the biblical writers used images from ancient cultures.

## BIBLIOGRAPHY

Bergant, Dianne. "Yahweh: A Warrior-God?" *The Bible Today* 21 (1983), 156–161.

Christ, Carol P. "Feminist Liberation Theology and Yahweh as Holy Warrior: An Analysis of Symbol." In *Women's Spirit Bonding,* edited by Janet Kalven and Mary I. Buckley, pp. 202–212. New York: Pilgrim Press, 1984.

Eszenyei Széles, Mária. *Wrath and Mercy: A Commentary on the Books of Habakkuk and Zephaniah.* Translated by George A. F. Knight. International Theological Commentary. Grand Rapids: Wm. B. Eerdmans Publishing Co., 1987.

# ZEPHANIAH

## Judith E. Sanderson

## Introduction

Zephaniah preached in Jerusalem during the reign of Josiah (640–609 B.C.E.), one of the kings most renowned for his political and religious reform in Judah.

Chapter 1 depicts God's "great day" of anger (1:7–10, 14–16, 18; cf. 2:2–3; 3:8, 11). While the beginning and end speak of the devastation of the whole earth (1:2–3, 18), the heart of the chapter describes the sin and judgment of Judah and Jerusalem (1:4, 8, 10–12). Comparison of 1:5 with Jeremiah 44 may suggest that one or more female deities were among "the host of the heavens" being worshiped. Chapter 2:1–3 focuses again on Judah, warning its inhabitants to seek God, righteousness, and humility, in the hope of being delivered from divine wrath. Zephaniah then predicts destruction for surrounding nations: the four Philistine cities to the west of Judah (2:4–7), Moab and Ammon to the east (2:8–11), Ethiopia far to the south (2:12), and Assyria far to the north, especially its capital Nineveh (2:13–15; cf. the book of Nahum). Chapter 3 reverts to Jerusalem, identifying the city not by its own name but by the name of its God and describing the evil especially of its leaders (3:1–7). Zephaniah's vision again broadens in 3:8–10 to God's judgment of all the nations, followed by their conversion. The book ends with the happy future of Jerusalem after the arrogant have been removed and only the faithful remain (3:11–20). (For the image of God as warrior-king [3:14–20], see the commentary on Habakkuk.)

## Comment

### "Zephaniah Son of Cushi . . . [Great-Great-Grand]son of Hezekiah" (1:1)

Women who have been studying the Bible in the last few decades have become increasingly aware of two factors that are relevant to the question of Zephaniah's identity. First, as women today have been discovering or rediscovering the roles that women played in ancient Israel, they have also become increasingly sensitized to the presence in the Bible of various other groups who are marginalized in modern Western societies, such as black Africans. Zephaniah's genealogy is traced back four generations (1:1) and contains a tantalizing reference in this regard. His father's name was Cushi, which is an adjective meaning "Ethiopian" everywhere else in the Bible (except in Jer. 36:14, where the word also appears to be a man's name in a genealogy). Some have speculated, therefore, that Zephaniah's father was an Ethiopian, like other figures in the Bible such as Moses' wife (Num. 12:1) and Ebed-melech, the king's official who saved Jeremiah's life (Jer. 38:7–13; 39:15–18). The distinctively Hebrew names of Cushi's three ancestors may make that unlikely, unless he was adopted (contrast the chronology in Jer. 36:14). In any case, the suggestion sometimes made, that Cushi was a black *slave* in Jerusalem, perhaps in the Temple, may reveal more about the social location of the interpreter than of Cushi. Since the black skin of Ethiopians was proverbial (see Jer. 13:23), Cushi may have been so named because his skin was exceptionally dark for an Israelite. At least it can be said that Zephaniah showed a disproportionately great interest in Ethiopia, referring to the land in 3:10 and to the people in 2:12, whereas all the rest of the prophets put together make such references only twenty-one times. This might suggest the influence of Zephaniah's Ethiopian ancestry on his thinking and imagination. (Some scholars, however, attribute 3:9–20 to a later writer.)

Second, women interpreters have become increasingly aware that the life situation of biblical authors—not only their sex and race but also their nationality, class, and educational, professional, social and other opportunities—profoundly influenced their outlook, interests, and writings. Furthermore, the relationships of prophets with kings and other leading figures were both highly conflictual and highly significant for Israelite history and for biblical theology and ethics. Thus, another tantalizing aspect of his genealogy—and of his social location—is the possibility that Zephaniah's great-great-grandfather Hezekiah was the king of Judah by that same name (at the end of the eighth century). Since King Hezekiah was the great-grandfather of Josiah, the king when Zephaniah was active, that identification is chronologically quite possible. It is not necessary, however, especially since three other figures are named Hezekiah in the Bible, indicating that it was not an unusual name. On the other hand, only one of the fourteen other prophetic books traces a prophet's ancestry back more than one generation (Zechariah's father and grandfather are named). The fact that Zephaniah's ancestry is traced back four generations suggests that his family connections were viewed as especially noteworthy. This has been interpreted in two ways, focusing either on the first or the last name in the series. Some have argued that the purpose of listing the three Hebrew names of his ancestors was to prevent any misinterpretation of the first name: his father Cushi was fully Israelite rather than foreign. Others have argued that the focus was on the last name: his great-great-grandfather Hezekiah was the king of Judah.

If Zephaniah was of royal descent, how might that have affected his preaching? It may be significant that, although Zephaniah seems mainly to have been speaking to the powerful elite (and that in very harsh tones), there is no indication that he condemned their affluence or their exploitation of the poor (the unspecified "violence and fraud" of 1:9 and "oppressing city" of 3:1 are as close as he came in what has been preserved). Zephaniah did use three words in 2:3 and 3:12 that are often best translated "poor" or "oppressed," but the NRSV is probably right in translating them here as "humble" and "lowly," given the strong emphasis throughout these chapters on arrogance (see below) as well as the juxtaposition of righteousness and humility in 2:3. Thus it may be that he was a member of the upper class himself and did not feel solidarity with those less fortunate (contrast, e.g., Micah, Amos, and Jeremiah). Another possibility also exists. Perhaps the fact that Zephaniah showed greater interest in perversions of Israel's worship than in social justice indicates his close relationship to Temple and cult.

Regardless of the uncertainties about Zephaniah's social location, it is at least clear that what has been preserved of his preaching shows no interest whatsoever in women as distinct from the society as a whole. His book never alludes to any women, named or unnamed, individually or as a group, in any context, positive or negative.

## "A People Humble and Lowly" (3:12)

As a book written by males, the Bible naturally describes sin and righteousness in ways appropriate to male experience. Many of those in a dominant position in society need to hear a call from God to give up their arrogance and self-sufficiency, learning a humility that will value others as much as self and that will rely on God rather than self for guidance and help. Such language is often inappropriate to the experience of women and of members of minorities, many of whom need rather to hear a call from God to give up their low self-esteem and dependence, learning a pride that will value the self as much as others and that will rely on God for empowerment to take responsibility for their own actions. One small step toward re-imaging sin is to translate biblical denunciations with "arrogance," which is clearly always bad, rather than "pride," leaving room for that legitimate pride which many males take for granted but many females did not learn as children. Another step is to consider carefully the nuances of the arrogance that a given biblical writer denounces in order to determine the appropriate nuances of the humility for which he calls.

Zephaniah provided some clues about his understanding of arrogance and humility. In 2:8–11 he accused Moab and Ammon of arrogance that took the form of taunting, reviling, boasting, and scoffing against God's people. He promised them a destruction like that of Sodom and Gomorrah. Though he did not describe those cities' sin, he perhaps had in mind an image similar to that in Ezek. 16:49–50, where Sodom is accused of arrogance in conjunction with a prosperity that did not help the needy. Zephaniah also accused Nineveh of an extreme sense of security and self-sufficiency that refused to recognize any other city's existence (2:15).

Closer to home, Zephaniah expressed Judah's arrogance as a complacent confidence that God would neither bless nor harm the people (1:12), as shamelessness (2:1), as a refusal to listen to anyone, accept any correction, or trust in God (3:2), and as an exultant haughtiness (3:11; "exultant" is another ambiguous word, used to describe both Nineveh's arrogance [2:15] and Jerusalem's future rejoicing [3:14]). Conversely, he called for a humility that would involve doing God's commands and seeking righteous-ness (2:3), fearing God and accepting correction (3:7), and seeking refuge in God's name (3:12). The promise for the future of these humble people was that they would be "renowned and praised among all the peoples of the earth" (3:20)—surely a far cry from a self-effacing inability to appreciate one's own worth and to take responsibility for one's beliefs and actions. While Zephaniah's idea of sin and goodness cannot provide the final word for women, it may not be as inimical to women's experience as the title of this section, a quotation taken out of context, might suggest.

## BIBLIOGRAPHY

Eszenyei Széles, Mária. *Wrath and Mercy: A Commentary on the Books of Habakkuk and Zephaniah.* Translated by George A. F. Knight. Grand Rapids: Wm. B. Eerdmans Publishing Co., 1987.

# HAGGAI

*Beth Glazier-McDonald*

## Introduction

### Historial Overview

The passage of the Babylonian empire to Persian control under Cyrus in 539 B.C.E. had momentous consequences for the Jews. Perhaps motivated by the belief that contented subjects were less likely to rebel, Cyrus permitted exiled peoples to return home, rebuild temples, and reestablish cults. Unfortunately, the circumstances under which the resettlement of Jerusalem was begun were distinctly adverse. The pioneers experienced droughts, poor harvests, poverty, inflation, and social tensions. The question of property rights quickly surfaced, becoming a source of friction between returning Jews and those who had never gone to Babylon but were now living on land that had once belonged to the exiled families.

In 520 B.C.E., as Darius was consolidating his hold on the empire, the Persian authorities sent Zerubbabel, grandson of King Jehoiachin, to Jerusalem. His appointment should be viewed as an integral part of Persia's policy of installing loyal representatives in critically important areas. Zerubbabel was accompanied by other Jews, including the high priest, Joshua. Among their objectives, Zerubbabel and Joshua were to rebuild the Temple, a task completed amid great rejoicing in 515 B.C.E. Although Zerubbabel seems to have become the subject of political expectations on the part of some Jerusalemites who hoped that he would submit to being crowned king of Judah, he quietly drops out of the biblical record at this point. Some suggest that the Persians considered this royalist stance to be a threat to their hegemony and removed him. It is also possible that Zerubbabel's disappearance testifies to the growing power of the high priest in religious and civil affairs and to the Temple's centrality.

### Authorship, Date, and Message

Very little is known about Haggai. Although the book is steeped in temple tradition, it is unlikely that he was a priest, since he seeks priestly guidance concerning a matter of ritual cleanness (2:10–13). He was active for about four months during the second year of Darius I's reign (520 B.C.E.). It is likely that he preceded his contemporary Zechariah, since Temple rebuilding work, the crux of Haggai's prophecy, is presupposed in Zechariah.

The book of Haggai contains four oracles, each introduced with a date and the formula, "the word of Yahweh came by the prophet Haggai" (1:1; 2:1; 2:10; 2:20). These oracles were compiled by an editor who added the background information that places them in their historical setting. The short collection represents the editor's choice of oracles that most profoundly influenced the Temple's reconstruction. There is no mention of women in these oracles; however, the reorganization of religious and social life in postexilic Judah certainly had implications for women, especially in connection with marriage (see the commentaries on Malachi and Ezra-Nehemiah).

Haggai believed that all the trouble experienced by the community in Judah could be blamed on its failure to rebuild the Jerusalem Temple. In his eyes the solution was simple: restore that house and the new era would finally dawn.

# Comment

## Command to Rebuild the Temple (1:1–15)

Like his prophetic predecessors, Haggai draws a close connection between the people's sin and Yahweh's judgment. The people sinned because they did not rebuild the Temple; Yahweh judged that sin by sending drought and economic deprivation (1:9–11). Renewed prosperity could result only from a rebuilt Temple, the seat of Yahweh's life-giving, community-sustaining presence (1:8).

The effectiveness of Haggai's preaching is witnessed in the immediate and overwhelming response of the community, its leaders and people (1:12–15). Barely three weeks had passed since the prophet's first appeal, and the work of restoration was already under way. It is noteworthy that other texts, roughly contemporary with Haggai, express a much more ambivalent attitude toward the Temple rebuilding (see Isaiah 56–66) and suggest that the actual historical situation was more complex than the editor of Haggai reveals.

## Assurance of Yahweh's Presence (2:1–9)

Haggai's words of encouragement were necessitated by the disappointment people experienced when they recognized that their feeble efforts would produce nothing so physically majestic as Solomon's Temple (2:1–3). Haggai promised that, despite current appearances, the restored Temple would exceed the glory of its predecessor (2:9), and he assured the people that their actions in the present would initiate a glorious future in which Yahweh would rule and the wealth of the nations would flow into Jerusalem (2:6–8).

The religious and social conditions of the postexilic period gave rise to a number of prophetic visions of a time of well-being and transformation. Although Haggai does not refer specifically to women in connection with these transformations, the roughly contemporary book of Joel does (see Joel 2:28–29).

## Priestly Ruling, Prophetic Interpretation (2:10–19)

These verses take the form of priestly instruc-tion on clean and unclean things. Responding to questions posed by Haggai, the priests affirmed that uncleanness has a greater infectious power than the consecrated, or clean (2:12–13). Haggai then uses this priestly ruling to reemphasize the connection between the people's sin and the lack of community well-being (cf. 1:1–11). Indeed, he reminds the people that their failure to respond to God's will by rebuilding the Temple was the source of the uncleanness pervading all areas of their life (2:16–17). Further, he points out that when the people "turned to" Yahweh, responding to the command to restore the Temple, Yahweh turned to them, assuring the community of material blessing (2:18–19).

## Future Hope and Blessing (2:20–23)

It is clear that the Temple restoration affects not only Israel's life (2:19) but the course of human events (2:22). The idea of "shaking" heavens and earth in 2:21 (cf. 2:6) is used to portray God's entrance into the sphere of human history in a final act of judgment and salvation. Haggai then announces Yahweh's readiness to place Zerubbabel, the Davidic descendant and governor of Judah, on the throne as ruler of the earth.

It is important to recognize that Zerubbabel is not an independent actor; his role is dependent on Yahweh's establishment of universal dominion. Only then will Yahweh's chosen one become the "signet" (seal on which the owner's name was engraved) through which the deity's sovereignty will be exercised and with which the divine intention will be stamped into the earth.

## BIBLIOGRAPHY

Meyers, Carol L., and Eric M. Meyers. *Haggai, Zechariah 1–8.* Anchor Bible 25B. Garden City, N.Y.: Doubleday & Co., 1987.

Petersen, David L. *Haggai and Zechariah 1–8, A Commentary.* Old Testament Library. Philadelphia: Westminster Press, 1984.

# ZECHARIAH

*Beth Glazier-McDonald*

## Introduction

Although little is known of Zechariah, he appears to have been both a prophet and a priest. A contemporary of Haggai, his first word is dated October/November 520 B.C.E., the night visions from January/February 519, and his final word from November/December 518. For those disheartened by the slow, painstaking work of rebuilding the Temple, Zechariah was a prophet of hope, offering the encouragement of changes soon to take place. He saw the completion of the Temple as the decisive turning point that would inaugurate the new age of Yahweh's salvation, of well-being and prosperity, of military and political deliverance, of the ingathering of God's still-scattered people (8:7–8). With the completion of the Temple, Yahweh would dwell among the people in Jerusalem, a city that would become not only the center of the world enlightenment but the object of universal pilgrimage (8:21–23).

### Zechariah 1–8

The major part of Zechariah's prophecy is couched in eight night visions full of symbols and images reminiscent of Ezekiel: riders patrolling the earth on different-colored horses (1:8–17), a flying scroll (5:1–4), wickedness personified as a woman in a basket (5:5–11). Here in a series of visions of the world under Yahweh's control, the reader sees apocalyptic (literature "revelatory" of the end time) in a developing stage. Typical of the style, the prophet is instructed about the future by an interpreting angel with direct access to the heavenly councils. Consequently, Zechariah does not so much deliver Yahweh's words as report revelations given him through angelic mediation, a significant movement away from prophecy in its traditional form. Indeed, Zechariah views the past as a time when the deity

proclaimed the future through prophets, but that period has ended. They are now called "the former prophets" (7:7). The presence of angels aiding Yahweh emphasizes the transcendence of God and may be modeled on the political reality of the imperial communications networks employed by Babylonian and Persian rulers to control their empires.

### Zechariah 9–14

As the reader passes from Zechariah 1–8 to Zechariah 9–14, an entirely different atmosphere is encountered. Here there are no visions; the angels disappear. The name Zechariah is not found, as it is in chaps. 1–8, and the prophecy is not dated. No allusion is made to Temple building or to the leadership of Zerubbabel and Joshua, and there are no reflections of the Persian period, under the shadow of which the first eight chapters were written. The emphasis on ethical matters, so characteristic of the early chapters, is totally lacking. New subjects are introduced. Tyre and the Philistines are threatened with punishment; the leaders of Judah, diviners, and prophets are denounced; Jerusalem is captured by the nations and subsequently delivered; and reference is made to "your sons, O Yavan" (9:13), a term designating Greece. Taken together these features have led to the recognition that chaps. 9–14 are not the work of the sixth-century prophet Zechariah. Often referred to as "Deutero-Zechariah," as if ascribed to one author, chaps. 9–14 are, rather, a collection of anonymous and late prophecies dating from the early Hellenistic period. Their general theme is the "apocalyptic" victory of God over all nations, leading to universal peace. The inevitability of this victory becomes a fact towering above all contradictory present appearances. Yahweh is going to win.

Interestingly, in spite of the differences between Zechariah 1–8 and 9–14, certain theological affirmations pervade all this material: the centrality of Jerusalem as Yahweh's abode and as the place of the nations' worship (1:12–16; 9:8–12), God's cleansing and renewal of the community (5:1–11; 13:1–2), and a universal kingdom open to all (8:20–23; 14:16–19). Therefore, although Zechariah 1–8 and 9–14 are clearly from different and later hands, these similarities may suggest that continuing development of a Zechariah tradition.

## Comment

### The Woman in the Ephah Basket (5:5–11)

The eight visions in Zechariah 1–8 delineate the ways in which the restoration of Jerusalem is prepared for: activity in heaven (1:7–17), the overthrow of Israel's enemies (2:1–4), the measuring of Jerusalem (2:5–9), validation of leadership (3:1–10; 4:1–14), moral cleansing (5:1–4; 5:5–11), and the establishment of Yahweh's rule through the agency of the Davidic prince Zerubbabel (6:1–15).

The seventh vision describes the removal of idolatrous worship from the land. A woman called "Wickedness" (risha‘, also a technical term for idolatry) is imprisoned in an "ephah," a barrel-shaped grain container holding approximately five gallons. Significantly, ephah also designates a Mesopotamian cult room. Thus, the woman "Wickedness" (=idolatry) may represent a goddess in her shrine and so symbolize non-Yahwistic worship. Another option is to view the woman as human, representing foreign women (in this case Babylonian wives brought back from exile by returning Judeans), so often portrayed in the Bible as purveyors of alien culture, threatening Yahwism's integrity (Ex. 34:16; Ezra 10; Mal. 2:10–16). Synthetically, the figure bottled up in the ephah may be both a foreign woman, denoting the explicit historical danger of foreign cultural integration, and a goddess, the result of such integration, that is, idolatry.

Two women with "wings like a stork" (5:9) are detailed to carry the ephah and its contents to Shinar, a poetic reference to Babylon (Gen. 11:2; Isa. 11:11). There they will build a "house," that is, a temple for her. There is irony in the suggestion that "Wickedness" (=idolatry) is relegated to Babylon, the place from which it originated and the only place fit for it. It is unlikely that these winged women are attendants of the goddess. Bottled up, both she and any attendants are impotent, according to Yahwistic thought. The Hebrew word for stork (chasidah) is closely related to the word for "devoted," "faithful" (chasid). Thus, foreign women, representing the destruction of Yahwism's integrity, are now counterbalanced by "faithful" Judean women, whose work at Yahweh's behest has a restorative, cleansing effect on the community.

### The End of Prophecy (13:2–6)

Zechariah 9–14 vividly describes the end time, when in a great battle Yahweh's (and Judah's) enemies will be overthrown (12:3, 7–9; 14:1–7), when idolatry and prophecy will be repudiated (13:2–6), when life will be characterized by material abundance (9:17), and when Yahweh's sovereignty will be recognized (14:16–21).

An intriguingly negative view of the prophetic enterprise is presented in 13:2–6. Some scholars argue that these verses refer to idolatrous prophets. Others contend that since all that the prophets foretold was on the brink of fulfillment, and since Yahweh would soon be present in the Temple, prophets were no longer necessary to mediate God's word to the community. The latter interpretation is especially problematic since there was a vivid expectation for prophecy to return in the future (Mal. 4:5–6). Indeed, Joel stresses the inclusive nature of the prophetic gift in the coming Day of Yahweh (2:28–29). Perhaps the postexilic age saw the emergence of groups like levitical singers, who claimed prophetic authority (2 Chron. 20:14–19; 29:30) but were not worthy of it, according to supporters of traditional prophets. These traditionalists thus denigrated all attempts at contemporary prophetic activity while asserting its reappearance just prior to the arrival of Yahweh's Day (Joel 2:28).

### BIBLIOGRAPHY

Mason, Rex. The Books of Haggai, Zechariah and Malachi. The Cambridge Bible Commentary. Cambridge: Cambridge University Press, 1977.

Meyers, Carol L., and Eric M. Meyers. Haggai, Zechariah 1–8. Anchor Bible 25B. Garden City, N.Y.: Doubleday & Co., 1987.

Petersen, David L. Haggai and Zechariah 1–8, A Commentary. Old Testament Library. Philadelphia: Westminster Press, 1984.

# MALACHI

## Beth Glazier-McDonald

❧

## Introduction

The book of Malachi concludes the collection of the Twelve Prophets and sheds welcome light on the little-known conditions of life in post-exilic Judah. It reflects the weaknesses of a community disheartened by the nonfulfillment of the promises of past prophets: priestly laxity in temple service (1:6–2:9), the people's careless indifference in acts of worship (3:6–12), widespread divorce and intermarriage (2:10–16). Although Malachi harshly condemns priests and evildoers, he shows deep concern for the hard-pressed faithful, assuring them of God's love (1:2–5) and of God's certain coming to fulfill all their hopes (3:1–5; 3:16–4:6).

### Authorship, Date, and Form

Nothing is known of the person(s) behind the oracles in the book of Malachi. Although "Malachi"="my [Yahweh's] messenger" could be a proper name (perhaps taken by the prophet at the time of his call), many think that the term is a late editor's attempt to identify the book's author with the promised messenger of Mal. 3:1.

A comparison of the terms in which Malachi speaks with the conditions of Judah in the Persian period leaves no doubt that his prophecy, generally speaking, belongs to the age of Nehemiah and Ezra. The priesthood was lax (1:6–8); intermarriage was prevalent (2:10–16); the people were remiss in tithing (3:8); and there was a distinct lack of social justice (3:5). These abuses are precisely those that Nehemiah and Ezra set out to reform. It is the opinion of a majority of scholars that Malachi belongs in the period between 470 and 450 B.C.E.

It is widely agreed that the contents of the prophecy fall into six clearly marked sections that, generally speaking, imitate the form of an oral debate (1:2–5; 1:6–2:9; 2:10–16; 2:17–3:5; 3:6–12; 3:13–4:3). Each unit is introduced by a statement of Yahweh or the prophet (e.g., 1:2), which is then challenged by the priests or people (1:2b) and finally defended by Yahweh in words of reproach or doom (1:3–5).

## Comment

### Jacob and Esau (1:2–5)

Jacob and Esau figure here not as individuals but as symbols of the nations descended from them. Geographically Edom (Esau) was Israel's neighbor and, traditionally, Israel's twin (Gen. 25:22–26). Because of this close relationship, similar treatment by Yahweh might have been expected. However, whereas Yahweh loved Jacob, Esau was detested, and Malachi refers to some recent desolation of Edom's territory as proof of that statement. Although no reason is given for the hatred of Edom, Malachi's animosity is likely rooted in Edom's participation in the Babylonian destruction of Judah in the sixth century B.C.E. (see Obadiah).

### Indictment of Priestly Negligence (1:6–2:9)

Because the maintenance of holiness and the keeping of the law were essential to the survival of the community, priests were necessary to the people. But often they perceived themselves as a privileged class accepting the honors of their position while inwardly mocking the cultic practices it was their duty to perform. Thus, the priests are accused of having a poor interior disposition (1:13), offering sacrifices of inferior quality (1:8, 13), profaning Yahweh's altar (1:7), and misleading the people who come to them for guidance (2:8–9). Indeed, the priests have corrupted the levitical covenant which Yahweh is determined to uphold (2:4). Therefore, Yahweh acts in judgment (2:9). But priestly punishment is not merely a penalty for a covenant breach; it is also a necessary preparation for future renewal (3:1–5).

## Rejection of Intermarriage and Divorce (2:10–16)

It is no coincidence that Mal. 1:6–2:9 and 2:10–16 are juxtaposed. In each section a covenant is corrupted (2:8) or desecrated (2:10) by the actions of the group addressed (priests, people). Here Malachi confronts the people with a double abuse that has social and religious consequences: marriage to foreign women and divorce of legitimate wives. These issues are inextricably linked. Although polygyny is a recurrent feature in narratives describing the premonarchic period, by the eighth century monogamous marriage was clearly the more typical practice; consequently, the incidence of divorce increased. That the Persian period witnessed an upsurge in intermarriage and divorce may be attributed to the depressed condition of Jews returning from exile. Desirous of upgrading their economic and social status, many men chose to marry women from wealthy, foreign families. Often characterized as inherently religious, women tended to stick to their own religions rather than integrating the values and beliefs prevalent in their new environment. Thus, the society-threatening aspect of intermarriage, the loss of common loyalties, should not be lightly dismissed (see Ezra 9:2; 10:3; Neh. 13:23–30).

What is undeniable is that in Mal. 2:10–13 the prime pitfall of intermarriage is not loss of ethnic purity but the resultant incorporation into the Yahweh cult of the rites of other gods (see 2:13, where "weeping" may have been part of a foreign fertility rite performed in the post-exilic period). The reference to "profaning the covenant of our ancestors" (2:10) alludes to the covenant detailed in Ex. 34:15–16 (cf. Deut. 7:3–4), in which Israel agreed not to intermarry, since the marriage of an Israelite male to a

foreign woman would result in a turning away from Yahweh to follow her gods. It is striking in Malachi that a foreign woman is explicitly called a "daughter of a foreign god" (2:11), that is, a foreign cult worshiper, and is further described as luring her Judean husband to her cult and god (cf. Neh. 13:23–30). Ironically, the book of Ruth, also a product of the Persian period, is a counterexample of the religious faithfulness of non-Judean women and their importance in the upbuilding of Israel.

Divorce, the consequence of the desire to intermarry, is explored in Mal. 2:14–16. Although 2:16 is commonly translated, "'I hate divorce,' says Yahweh, the God of Israel . . . ," in line with the legislative terminology in Deut. 24:1–4 this verse should be rendered, "'For one who divorces because of aversion,' says Yahweh, the God of Israel, 'thereby covers his garment with wrongdoing.'" "To cover with a garment" means to claim a woman as wife, afford her the protection of marriage (see Ruth 3:9). In Malachi, that the garment (lebush) is itself covered (with wrongdoing) suggests the wife's loss of protection in divorce. Interestingly, the Hebrew word lebush designates the outermost garment, on which stains are most visible. Thus, one who divorces his wife airs his dirty linen for all to see and so publicly humiliates his wife. The threefold description of the Judean wife in 2:14 as "the wife of your youth," "your companion," "your wife by covenant" (see 2:10, "the covenant of our ancestors," by which the Israelites and, through them, succeeding generations agreed not to intermarry) emphasizes both the intimateness of the marriage bond to which Yahweh has served as witness and the deceitful behavior of the spouse. The consequence of such reprehensible conduct is graphically described as sterility (2:15). That the prime object of marriage was to ensure the survival of the family by providing male successors is indisputable. Malachi intimates, however, that the seeking of progeny through intermarriage will always be a fruitless enterprise. To those who intermarry and thus turn away from Yahweh and their Judean wives, the germination of further life will be denied.

## The Approach of Yahweh's Day (2:17–3:5)

Malachi's expectation for the coming Day of Yahweh is expressed here and in 1:11. Both sections deal with priest and cult, and both advance the thesis that prevailing conditions will be transformed; the future will be the inverse of the present. From the complementary parts of this single vision, it becomes evident that there is movement from a general formulation (1:11) to one that is more specific (3:1–5). According to Mal. 1:11, the manner in which sacrifices are offered and those who offer them will be changed. These thoughts are particularized in 3:1–5, where the Levites (sacrificers) are purified (3:3), which results in offerings pleasing to Yahweh (3:4). Further, in 1:11 proper sacrifice will be offered everywhere, and Yahweh's name will be great among the nations. In 3:1–5, the lens narrows to the postexilic community in Jerusalem. Thus Malachi affirms that the renewal that begins with the nations (1:11) culminates in the transformation of Yahweh's own people, the postexilic community (3:1–5; 3:13–4:3).

### Elijah, Reconciliation, and Yahweh's Day (4:3–6)

Many scholars consider these verses to be later additions, providing a summarizing admonition from a "legalistic" editor (4:4) and a secondary attempt to identify the messenger promised in 3:1 (4:5–6). Thematically and linguistically, however, they need not be considered of later origin, but as the conscious literary product of Malachi himself.

Malachi 4:4–6 is the climax of the prophecy. All Malachi's major themes are found here: the stress on the law (4:4; see also 2:6–8; 3:7); the coming figure whose task it is to prepare for Yahweh's appearance (4:5; see also 3:1); the Day of Yahweh (4:5; see also 3:1–5; 3:17–4:3), when Yahweh will judge and destroy the evildoers (4:6; see also 3:5; 3:18–4:1; 4:3); the emphasis on "turning to Yahweh," repenting to avert God's wrath (4:6; see also 3:7). Moreover, in these final verses, Malachi sets his message in a picture that is enriched by Israel's fuller tradition. His claim that Elijah is the coming messenger serves to equate the hearers of his prophecy with the disobedient, vacillating people of Elijah's time, whose allegiance to Yahweh was similarly in danger of being dissolved. Implicit in this analogy is the hope that Elijah will be able to elicit from Malachi's contemporaries the same recognition of Yahweh's greatness and power that he did from his own (1 Kings 18:39) and so avert God's wrath (see 4:6).

### BIBLIOGRAPHY

Fischer, James A. "Notes on the Literary Form and Messsage of Malachi." *Catholic Biblical Quarterly* 34 (1972), 315–320.

Glazier-McDonald, Beth. *Malachi, The Divine Messenger.* Society of Biblical Literature Dissertation Series 98. Atlanta: Scholars Press, 1987.

# THE APOCRYPHA

*Eileen M. Schuller*

## Introduction

Although the term "apocrypha" (literally "hidden," "set aside") can be used in a number of different and quite confusing ways, in this article it serves to designate a collection of fifteen books. All of these are works of religious literature of the Jewish community, written from approximately the third century B.C.E. to the first century C.E. Some modern editions of the Bible do not include the Apocrypha; others place it as a separate unit between the Old Testament and the New Testament (or occasionally after the New Testament). In Catholic editions of the Bible these books are grouped with others of similar type in the Old Testament (e.g., Tobit and Judith come after Nehemiah; the Wisdom of Solomon and Sirach after the Song of Songs; and the additions to Daniel and Esther are included within the respective canonical books).

The existence of the Apocrypha as a distinct entity is a reflection of the long, complex process of forming the canon, that is, the list of books judged to be normative for the community. There is much that is not known about the reasons and the process whereby certain books were included as "sacred scripture" and others were excluded. To simplify a vastly complex question, one can say that the books of the Apocrypha were not included in what became the Hebrew canon of twenty-four books. The Greek Bible of the early Christian church included this broader selection of books, which also came to be part of the Latin Bible (the Vulgate) used throughout the Middle Ages—though scholars such as Jerome in the fourth century were still conscious of the distinction between those books that were included in the Hebrew canon and those that were not. At the time of the Reformation, Protestants adopted the shorter Hebrew canon and either omitted the Apocrypha entirely from their Bibles or retained it for "example of life and instruction of manner" but not "to establish any doctrine" (the Anglican Thirty-Nine Articles, 1562). At the Council of Trent (1546) Catholics affirmed the canonicity of most of the Apocrypha (with the exception of 1 and 2 Esdras and the Prayer of Manasseh). The Orthodox churches accept all the apocryphal books as canonical (as well as a few others, such as 3 Maccabees and Psalm 151).

In terms of types of literature, content, language, and date of composition, the Apocrypha is a very diverse collection. There are narratives (Judith, Tobit); books that continue the biblical wisdom tradition (Sirach, also known as Ecclesiasticus, and the Wisdom of Solomon); works of history (1 and 2 Maccabees, 1 Esdras); psalms and prayers (the Prayer of Manasseh, Baruch); apocalyptic visions (2 Esdras, also called 4 Ezra); and additions to the Hebrew books of Esther (including royal letters and the prayers of Mordecai and Esther) and Daniel (the stories of Susanna, Bel and the Dragon, and the Song of the Three Youths). Many of these books were originally composed in Hebrew (e.g., Sirach, Baruch, 1 Maccabees) or perhaps Aramaic (Tobit) but have only survived in Greek translation; others (the Wisdom of Solomon, the Prayer of Manasseh) were certainly written in Greek.

The books of the Apocrypha are crucial for an understanding of Second Temple Judaism. They provide information about the events of history (particularly the crucial period from 180 to 140 B.C.E. that marked the overthrow of Greek domination and the rise of the Hasmonean kings). The many prayers, hymns, and psalms in these books give evidence of rich piety and devotion, and several of these works illustrate how the powerful influence of Greek language and ideas was simultaneously resisted and absorbed by Judaism in this period.

## Women in the Apocrypha

The apocryphal books provide fascinating sources of information about Jewish women in the Hellenistic and Roman periods. However, given the diversity of the Apocrypha (literature in a variety of genres, written over a span of almost four hundred years, from Palestine, Egypt, and other centers of the Diaspora), one cannot expect uniformity of interest in women or evaluation of women's role and status. The texts chosen for comment are meant to provide some sense of the diverse and even contradictory ways in which women appear in the Apocrypha.

### 1 Esdras

Scholars have long puzzled over the origin and purpose of 1 Esdras. Much of the book is a translation (though different from the standard Greek translation, the Septuagint) of 2 Chronicles 35–36, all of Ezra, and a small segment of Nehemiah (7:73–8:12). Of particular interest is a section not found elsewhere (3:1–5:6), a story that tells how the Persian king Darius permitted the rebuilding of the Second Temple as a reward for Zerubbabel, who won a contest among the king's guards by giving the best answer to the question "What is the strongest thing?"

The tale of a contest of wits at the royal court is probably part of ancient folklore in the Near East and not necessarily Jewish in origin. In 1 Esdras, however, the traditional version has been reworked so that the winner is the Jew Zerubbabel, who has received his wisdom from the God of Israel (4:59–60). The first guard argues that wine is the strongest; the second proposes the king; then Zerubbabel presents a double argument: women are the strongest, but truth is strongest of all. In the original form of the story, the argument in favor of women formed the climax.

The argument developed by Zerubbabel is one of the earliest statements of the male-perceived dilemma "you can't live with them, you can't live without them." The power of wine and of the king is real, but ultimately it is women who give birth to these very kings and to the "men who plant the vineyards from which comes wine" (4:16). Women make clothing; women bring men glory, and so not only in the sexual realm but also in the economic and social realms there is no way to escape the fact that "men cannot exist without women" (4:17). Yet these same men fall apart when they see a beautiful woman, as vividly illustrated by the power the concubine Apame exercises over even the mighty king Darius as he would "gaze at her with mouth agape" (4:31). In fact, the "curse" of Gen. 3:16 is reversed, for "women rule over you" (4:22). This dependence, however, allows the male formulator of this argument to blame women when men perish or sin, since they are vulnerable because of the love of a woman. Thus, in this unpretentious folkloric story, one has access to a popular statement from a male perspective of the relationship between the sexes.

### The Letter of Jeremiah

According to certain biblical laws that reflect both ancient taboos and priestly concerns, menstruation and childbirth render a woman ritually unclean for a period of time and thus unable to engage in cultic activity. This understanding is assumed, though more by implication than direct argumentation, in the Letter of Jeremiah, a brief work that purports to be written by the prophet Jeremiah to the people going into exile in Babylon but was probably composed sometime in the Hellenistic period. In a ten-part treatise, the author attempts to convince the reader of the absolute impotence of idols and the folly of worshiping them. As part of his argument that "they are not gods; so do not fear them" (v. 16), he offers as proof the fact that sacrifices to idols are touched by women during menstruation or at childbirth (v. 29); that women set out the offerings, therefore fulfilling a priestly/cultic role (v. 30); and that women are involved in a ritual activity involving "burning bran for incense" (v. 43), which the author describes in terms of cultic prostitution (though it is far from certain what is really going on here). In contrast, for the author of the Letter of Jeremiah, worship of the true God of Israel does not permit such involvement of women.

### Historical Retellings

A different type of insight is provided by a number of passages in the Apocrypha that retell the sacred history of Israel and provide a glimpse of how that history was remembered in the Second Temple period. The final section of the Wisdom of Solomon (chaps. 10–19) retells events from the day of creation to the exodus in order to illustrate the saving activity of Lady Wisdom/Sophia. In the book of Sirach, chaps. 44–50, there is a long poem in praise of "famous men, our fathers in their generations" (Sir. 44:1) from Adam until the current high priest, Simon (ca. 200 B.C.E.). In both retellings, the women who were part of the biblical tradition — Eve, Sarah and the other matriarchs, the midwives who enabled the Hebrew babies to survive, Miriam, Deborah and Jael, Esther, prophets such as Huldah — are not included. The only women who appear in the lengthy poem in Sirach are in conjunction with King Solomon, whose downfall is attributed not to idolatry as in the books of Kings but to the fact that "you brought in women to lie at your side, and through your body you were brought into subjection" (Sir. 47:19). Furthermore (though the passage is not entirely clear), Sirach gives the first indication that the Genesis story of the Garden of Eden was now interpreted in a way that put the blame on Eve ("from a woman sin had its beginning and because of her we all die," 25:24). If this is how scripture was being taught to young men in the wisdom schools of Jerusalem and Alexandria, their views about women were being shaped in a specific way.

## Sirach

Over one hundred verses of the book of Sirach deal in some way with women (e.g., 3:2–6; 9:1–9; 19:2–4; 22:3–5; 23:22–26; 25:1, 8; 25:13–26:18; 36:26–31; 40:19, 23; 42:6, 9–14) and provide some of the most positive as well as the most negative statements about women in the tradition. Jesus the son of Sira (50:27, the only author of an apocryphal book whose name is known) was a scribe and an instructor of young men from the upper class in a school in Jerusalem around 180 B.C.E. His book is a collection of teachings, grouped according to topic and expressed in the form of proverbs and admonitions, all designed to give instruction in how to act in order to succeed in an increasingly complex, cosmopolitan world. This book is firmly rooted in the broader wisdom tradition, though Sirach is the first to make a close identification between this ancient wisdom and the law revealed to Israel (24:8–12, 23).

As is traditional in this type of wisdom discourse, Ben Sira treats women solely in terms of their relationship to men as wife, mother, daughter, adulteress, and prostitute. His perspective is unapologetically male and upper class, shaped by the instructional genre in which he works. How much this reflects the reality of women's lives in Jerusalem at this time is a difficult question, though occasionally issues are raised that go beyond what is found in Proverbs; these may give some insight into the changing Hellenistic milieu that brought increased freedom and public access for women, for example, the warning about dining with another man's wife (9:9), the criticism of a drunken wife who brings public shame (26:8), or the situation where a man's wealth comes from marriage to a rich woman (25:22). Distinctive to Sirach is the special concern for the daughter and the shame she is potentially able to bring to her father before and after her marriage (7:25; 22:1–5; 26:10–12; 42:9–13).

## Lady Wisdom/Sophia

The figure of Lady Wisdom (Sophia in Greek), which first appears in Proverbs (especially Prov. 8:22–31), is to be found in three books of the Apocrypha — Sirach, Baruch, and Wisdom of Solomon — texts that provide a crucial bridge between Proverbs and the wisdom tradition of the New Testament. As in Proverbs, there is the paradox of a tradition negative to women in the concrete but open to describing wisdom itself with bold and innovative female language.

The book of Sirach, at least in the Greek form in which it has come down to us, is structured by a series of poems about Wisdom: two poems at the beginning praising Lady Wisdom's availability and bounty (1:1–20; 4:11–19), a hymn at the end about the young man's search for Wisdom (51:13–22), and, in the center, Wisdom speaking in self-praise (24:1–34). The first poems echo many of the older ideas of Proverbs, presenting wisdom as universal and accessible, given by God to all (1:10) so that she might reveal her secrets (4:18). Lady Wisdom relates to the young male students as a mother and as a wife, nurturing and feeding them "with the bread of understanding . . . the water of wisdom" (15:2–3). The final poem (51:13–22) is extant also in Hebrew, in a more original form, as part of a collection of psalms found in Cave 11 at Qumran; in this version, the relationship of the young man and Wisdom is suggestively erotic: "She came to me in her beauty . . . I kindled my desire for her."

In the center of the book, Wisdom herself speaks from the heavenly realm: "I came forth from the mouth of the Most High . . . I dwelt in the highest heavens" (24:3–4). Yet she wanders about, making a circuit of the vault of the heavens, seeking a dwelling place on earth. In contrast to a comparable fragment of poetry preserved in 1 Enoch 42:1–2, where Wisdom finds no dwelling and is forced to return to the heavens, in this poem God assigns her to Israel and she takes up her abode in Zion. Her invitation to eat and drink still extends to all (24:19–21), yet she is also identified specifically with "the law which Moses commanded us" (24:23). A very similar poem in Bar. 3:9–4:4 concludes with the direct statement "she is the book of the commandments of God, the law that endures forever" (4:1).

In the Wisdom of Solomon, under the influence of Greek philosophy, Wisdom is described in a more abstract and philosophical manner: "She is a pure emanation of the glory of the Almighty" (7:25), "in her there is a spirit that is intelligent, holy, unique, manifold, subtle, mobile . . ." (7:22). She is sought as mother (7:12) and bride (8:2) because, though distinct from God and beloved by God (8:3), she is able to save (9:18). This salvific role of Wisdom, so closely identified with that of God as to be virtually indistinguishable, is exemplified in the latter chapters as sacred history is retold. First, Wisdom is the active and guiding force: "She protected the first-formed father of the world . . . when the world was flooded . . . wisdom again saved it . . . when a righteous man was sold, she did not desert him but delivered him from sin. . . ." Then, with no perceptible change of focus, the subject switches to the second person, the masculine "you" of God, "when they were thirsty they called upon you . . ." (11:4).

In these texts from the Apocrypha, even more than in Proverbs, Lady Wisdom/Sophia seems to be more than simply a literary personification of cosmic order, or a divine attribute. The specific portrayal of Wisdom often echoes and is shaped by language and themes from contemporary Hellenistic hymns to the goddess Isis (to give only one example, Wisdom saves Noah "by a paltry piece of wood" [10:4] just as Isis guides the path of sailors). There is much that is not known about how this tradition functioned theologically or what purposes it served within a school such as Ben Sira's. But the fact remains that it is within wisdom poems such as these that one sees

glimpses of the divine, present and active in the world, as a female figure.

## 1 and 2 Maccabees

The books of 1 and 2 Maccabees are major sources of historical information about the second century B.C.E. and its traumatic events: the rise of Antiochus Epiphanes I, struggle over Hellenization, persecution of those faithful to the Torah, desecration of the Temple, establishment of a resistance movement under Judas Maccabeus and his brothers, recovery of freedom and rededication of the Temple, and (in 1 Maccabees) the establishment of Simon Maccabeus as ruler, initiating the Hasmonean dynasty that was to last for one hundred years. First Maccabees, written originally in Hebrew, is very pro-Hasmonean; 2 Maccabees, a summary of a five-volume work in Greek (now lost) by Jason of Cyrene, focuses more on the Temple and God's miraculous deliverance.

The history recorded is definitely a male world. Men are the actors, and, for the most part, women are absent. Occasionally their presence is noted at moments of crisis when women fulfill a role of lamentation and supplication (1 Macc. 1:26–27; 2 Macc. 3:19). However, both books (1 Macc. 1:60–61; 2 Macc. 6:10) preserve the tradition that women were among the group of pious Jews "devoted to the law" who suffered martyrdom rather than submit to the decrees of Antiochus. "According to the decree, they put to death the women who had their children circumcised" (1 Macc. 1:60); in the parallel account in 2 Maccabees (as in a late retelling of the story in 4 Macc. 4:25), the women seem to have circumcised their sons themselves (though in later rabbinic law this was expressly forbidden).

First Maccabees recounts that "many in Israel stood firm . . . [and] chose to die rather than to be defiled by food" (1:62–63), whereas 2 Maccabees 7 gives a specific incident, the lengthy and gruesome account of the torture and death of seven brothers whose deaths—from the theological perspective of the author—assure victory for Judas Maccabeus and the whole community. It is difficult to determine what in this story stems from genuine historical memory. Second Maccabees includes the unnamed mother, although the wording of the introduction ("it happened also that seven brothers and their mother were arrested," 7:1) may hint that the mother was not always part of the tradition. The mother watches the torture and death of her seven sons in a single day and encourages them to remain steadfast, confident that God "will in his mercy give life and breath back to you again" (7:23). She is praised as "especially admirable and worthy of honorable memory," for, "filled with a noble spirit, she reinforced her woman's reasoning with a man's courage" (7:20–21). The chapter ends with the brief and stark statement: "last of all, the mother died, after her sons" (7:41); she does not share in the glory of martyrdom. In the final analysis, as the youngest son says so clearly in his dying words, deliverance from the wrath of the Almighty comes "through me and my brothers" (7:38).

## Tobit

The book of Tobit is one of the most popular stories of the Apocrypha, a finely crafted narrative, rich in piety and moral teaching. The book was written in Aramaic, perhaps as early as the mid-third century B.C.E. (though some date it to the second century), probably in the Diaspora (i.e., among Jews living outside Palestine).

The story, set in the eighth century B.C.E. in Nineveh, where Tobit and his people have been taken captive by the Assyrians, treats religious questions about the suffering of the innocent and the justice of God. Two parallel scenes of distress are presented and slowly brought together and resolved. First there is Tobit, who, though a model of piety and virtue, is blinded as a consequence of his good deed of burying the dead. Then there is Sarah, his niece, who is afflicted with a demon that has already destroyed seven husbands on her wedding nights. Resolution comes as Tobit sends his son Tobias to a distant city in Media to collect some money owed him. God provides an angelic companion, Raphael, who will save and heal both sufferers. In Media, Tobias meets Sarah and falls in love with her; thanks to the potion provided by Raphael, the power of the demon Asmodeus is destroyed, and the marriage consummated. After collecting the money, Tobias and his bride return home, where Raphael again supplies the potion that cures Tobit's blindness. The book ends with a hymn about Jerusalem that moves the focus of attention beyond the personal, to the deliverance of the community.

Readers have often commented on the strong feminine element in this book. Not only are Sarah and Tobit presented as parallel figures, but the minor female characters are more developed than in many biblical narratives and are always given a name. For example, in contrast to Genesis 22, where Sarah plays no part when Abraham sets off with their son, here the reader sees Anna weeping and hears her lament and reproach when Tobit decides to send their son to a distant land (5:17–18; 11:5–6). In addition, Tobit's grandmother, Deborah, is named (1:9) and credited with teaching him intricate details of the law. The fine balance between men and women is maintained in attention to details such as the burial of Tobit and Anna (14:11–12) and Tobias's father-in-law and mother-in-law (14:13). Within the world of the story, women are assumed to have considerable freedom of activity (Sarah goes out to meet the guests; both Raguel and his wife, Edna, set their seal on the marriage document). Though many details may reflect the exigencies of a marriage arranged under unusual circumstances, the book is an important source of information about marriage customs (e.g., the dowry given by the bride's father to the bridegroom in 10:10; the document in 7:13, an early form of the *ketubah* [the marriage contract] or a betrothal agreement).

In a scene that is a common motif in literature of this period, Tobit, on his deathbed, gives final words of advice and instruction to his son. He exhorts him to honor his mother "for she faced many dangers for you when you were yet unborn" (4:4) and commands him to take a wife from his own tribe; however, there is no lengthy warning about the dangers and snares of wicked women out to lead innocent young men astray—a theme common in many testaments from this period.

The view of marriage in this book is surprisingly romantic: "She was set apart for you before the world was made" (6:17); "he loved her very much and his heart was drawn to her" (6:18—though they have not yet met!). Tobit's blessing on his wedding night is the earliest text that applies the creation story of Genesis 2 to marriage: "Blessed are you, O God of our ancestors . . . you made Adam and for him you made his wife Eve as a helper and support . . . grant that she and I may find mercy and that we may grow old together" (8:5–7).

A closer look at the figure of Sarah points to issues that emerge when the story is approached from a feminist perspective. As noted above, the narrator skillfully presents Tobit and Sarah as parallel figures: the action takes place "on the same day" (3:7); both are pious and suffer unjustly; both are reproached by those around them (the words of Anna [2:14–15] and the maids of Sarah [3:8–9]); both are saved by Raphael and his potion from the fish; even the cause of Tobit's blindness from bird droppings may suggest the work of a demonic force associated with birds (*Jubilees* 11:11; Mark 4:4, 15) and thus a parallel to Asmodeus's attack on Sarah. Both pray to God: while Tobit in despair can envision only that God will take his life, Sarah's prayer looks to other alternatives ("If it is not pleasing to you, O Lord, to take my life, hear me in my disgrace," 3:15) and so provides an opening for the action of the story.

In the development of the two characters, the patriarchal outlook of the narrator and his society becomes obvious. Tobit's reputation for righteousness is established by enumerating at length his acts of piety (1:5–8, 16–18); of Sarah's, all one learns is her own claim in her prayer ("You know, O Lord, that I am innocent," 3:14). Her innocence is based solely on her having preserved her virginity. Sarah reveals little of how she feels about seven husbands dying in their marriage bed; even when she is driven to consider suicide, her concern is for the disgrace she will bring on her father (3:10). Although Sarah plays an active role in meeting the guests, she is largely silent. She prays to God and answers "Amen" to Tobias's blessing on her wedding night; beyond this, once Tobias appears, Sarah does not speak again in the narrative. Indeed, as the action draws to a close, the world of the narrative becomes increasingly male. Sarah and Anna are expressly excluded at the moment of revelation, when the angel Raphael tells his true identity (12:6), and there is no mention of Sarah's death.

## Judith

Like the books of Esther and Ruth, the book of Judith takes its name from the woman who is the story's central character. In contrast to Esther and Ruth, in this book there is no figure of an uncle or a newly discovered male relative to guide the action or to rescue by marriage. Judith alone is the heroine, the one who saves through her piety, initiative, and courage. As the people had been delivered in days long past from Pharaoh "through the hand of Moses," so now the people are rescued from an equally invincible foreign ruler "through the hand of a woman" (Judith 8:33; 9:10; 12:4; 13:14, 15; 16:5).

In no other book is a woman praised so explicitly and profusely. From her first introduction in the story she is surrounded with words of praise: "beautiful in appearance, and . . . very lovely to behold . . . no one spoke ill of her, for she feared God with great devotion" (8:7–8). Her high status and esteem within the Jewish community predate this present crisis, for Uzziah acknowledges that "from the beginning of your life all the people have recognized your understanding, for your heart's disposition is right" (8:29). After the climactic deed, the book concludes with a paean of praise: "O daughter, you are blessed by the Most High God above all other women on earth" (13:18) . . . "you are the glory of Jerusalem, you are the great boast of Israel, you are the great pride of our nation!" (15:9). Indeed, Uzziah promises this woman: "Your praise will never depart from the hearts of those who remember the power of God" (13:19).

Praise and remembrance of Judith did live on throughout the centuries. Versions of the story circulated in Aramaic and Hebrew, though the book was not part of the library at Qumran, nor was it mentioned by Philo or Josephus, nor accepted by the rabbis into the Hebrew canon. In its Greek form, the book of Judith was well known in the early Christian church, where Judith was praised as a model of chastity and was presented as evidence that "women, empowered by God's grace, have performed deeds worthy of men" (*1 Clement* 55.3.4). The story was immensely popular in medieval art, poems, and dramas, with over 150 plays alone from the Middle Ages surviving. And, from the nineteenth century on, Judith has appeared as the queen of hearts on playing cards!

The modern era has been more ambivalent about the story of Judith. Painters have transformed her into a courtesan; moralists and pietists are shocked by her decision to lie and murder in order to accomplish an admittedly noble purpose; feminists criticize her blatant use of physical beauty and sexual wiles. Given its apocryphal status, the book is not part of the core of Protestant or Jewish religious instruction, and in the Catholic community the story is not read as part of the set cycle of scripture readings (though one small selection, 8:2–8, can be selected for feasts of widowed saints).

It is difficult to determine a date for the composition of Judith with any specificity. Some of the names and events seem to point to the Persian period, but, if so, the story has been reworked in light of the persecution under Antiochus Epiphanes and the victory of Judas Maccabeus. In its final form, the book comes from the late second or the early first century B.C.E. Most scholars assume a Hebrew or an

Aramaic original, but it is possible that the book was initially composed in the semiticized Greek in which its survives.

The story is divided into two parts: chaps. 1–7 and 8–16. In the first seven chapters the scene is set. The opening words prepare the reader for a work of history: "It was the twelfth year of the reign of Nebuchadnezzar, who ruled over the Assyrians in the great city of Nineveh" (1:1); later it is explained that the Jews "had just returned from exile" (4:3). Yet none of this makes sense historically—any reader would immediately recognize that Nebuchadnezzar ruled in Babylon, not Assyria, and at the time when the people went into exile, not at their return. From the very first verses one is alerted that this work is not what it appears to be, and one is thus prepared for irony and double entendre in what follows.

The stage is that of world history: empires and battles, the might and arrogance of Nebuchadnezzar out to conquer the world. Judea and Jerusalem are initially mentioned only in passing as two of the nations who defy the power of Nebuchadnezzar and refuse to join his war of conquest against Arphaxad and the Medes. Throughout the first three chapters the reader is overwhelmed with the seemingly invincible power of Nebuchadnezzar and his general Holofernes. One by one all the nations are destroyed or submit as vassals, leaving Judea to face the Assyrian giant alone.

The response to crisis here as later in the story is twofold: both human initiative and recourse to God with prayer and fasting. The Jews prepare to defend themselves at the mountain passes at Bethulia (the specific geographical place is unknown), while turning to God in prayer and lamentation with fasting and sackcloth and ashes. "The Lord heard their prayers and had regard for their distress" (4:13; cf. Ex. 2:23–24). This is the only sentence in the book where God is the active subject. Deliverance is already assured; it will come—but how?

Once again the story seems to digress, or at least to take up a subplot about Achior, the leader of the Ammonite contingent. This pagan is put in the position of explaining Israel's history and theology to Holofernes and is then handed over to the people whom he has described so well. In all this, the tension is heightened as Achior explains that if the Jews have not sinned, "their Lord and God will defend them and we shall become the laughingstock of the whole world" (5:21). But how will this deliverance come about, particularly if a mighty

army is to be reduced to a laughingstock in the process? Holofernes prepares for attack by blocking off the water supply to force the city into submission. In desperate circumstances Uzziah and the elders of the city give God five days in which to act; after that they agree to surrender.

Until this point, the story has been a traditional one of war and conquest. The main actors have all been male: Nebuchadnezzar, Holofernes, Achior, Uzziah, and the elders of Bethulia. Yet women are explicitly recognized as part of the community: along with children, cattle, aliens and slaves (4:10–11), the women put on sackcloth and ashes, and there is traditional concern voiced for the suffering of women and children from siege and thirst (7:14, 22, 28). Women are participants in the decision of the community to surrender ("all the people, the young men, the women, and the children," 7:23). Yet clearly the men are the leaders; they pray at the Temple, begging "the God of Israel not to allow their infants to be carried off and their wives to be taken as booty" (4:12). Uzziah, having been asked by the entire community to surrender, responds explicitly to the men: "Courage, my brothers" (7:30). As the first section of the book draws to a close, the men take their posts on the walls, the women and children are sent home, and all await disaster.

The author has structured the story so as to create the maximum element of surprise as the figure is presented who will completely change the tide of events: "Now in those days Judith heard about these things" (8:1). (Since ancient scrolls probably did not have a title, this is the first hint of a heroine!) Judith is carefully introduced and given the longest genealogy (some sixteen names) of any woman in the Bible. She is a widow, of exemplary piety, attentive to fasting and prayer, beautiful, and independently wealthy, with her own maid in charge of her estate (8:10). Curiously, she seems to have been absent when the community decided to set a time limit and then surrender. Now Judith, taking the initiative, sends her maid to summon the elders. In a lengthy speech she presents an alternate reading of the situation, a radically different theological perspective that judges not that destruction is inevitable but that "the Lord scourges those who are close to him in order to admonish them" (8:27). Uzziah replies patronizingly, acknowledging the truth of her words and her wisdom in the past, even as he restricts her present response: "Now since you are a God-fearing woman, pray for us, so that the Lord may send us rain to fill our cisterns" (8:31). Judith announces her intention to respond not with prayer but with action: "I am about to do something that will go down through all generations of our descendants" (8:32). Once again, at the end of chap. 8, the men retire to their posts, but now two women, Judith and her maid, go forth to act and save the city.

The action of the narrative is deliberately slowed as Judith turns to God. Her extended prayer gives only tantalizing hints of what action she might be planning: it is to involve deceit ("by the deceit of my lips strike down," 9:10, 13), and the cryptic reference to her ancestor Simeon who avenged the rape of Dinah (9:2) suggests that it will involve violence. Judith prays neither for guidance as to what to do nor for the intervention of an angel (contrast 2 Macc. 15:23). Rather, from the "God of the lowly, helper of the oppressed, upholder of the weak, protector of the forlorn, savior of those without hope" (9:11), she asks only for "strength to do what I plan" (9:9).

In addition to her wisdom and piety, Judith now draws upon her beauty as she adorns herself with the finest clothing and perfumes. At each step of her journey her beauty is praised: by the elders as she leaves the city (10:7), by the sentries and soldiers as she enters the Assyrian camp (10:14, 18), and by Holofernes as she comes into his presence (10:23). But she who is "beautiful in appearance" is also "wise in speech" (11:21, 23). Her conversations with Holofernes are masterpieces of irony and double entendre, as she convinces him that "God has sent me to accomplish with you things that will astonish the whole world" (11:16). Wisdom and piety come together as she establishes a pattern of prayer and ablutions that allow her unquestioned movement in and out of the Assyrian camp.

Of the five allotted days, three pass by and little seems to happen. On the fourth, Holofernes, who has been "waiting for an opportunity to seduce her" (12:16), summons Judith to a banquet. Now the plot moves quickly. Left alone in the tent with the drunken Holofernes, Judith utters two brief petitions to God for strength and cuts off his head. She and her maid, carrying the head of the proud leader ignominiously in their food bag, return to Bethulia.

Judith continues in charge until victory is complete. She is the one who directs the pursuit and final slaughter of all the Assyrians who flee in panic upon discovering the headless corpse of their general. Just as the beginning of the story established the magnitude of the crisis by the leisurely description of Assyrian might and Judean terror, so now a sense of the magnitude of the victory is captured by repeated and lengthy descriptions of praise and rejoicing over three months of feasting. As Moses sang a song of triumph after the deliverance from Egypt, so Judith, as mother of the people, sings the song of her victory, giving praise to God "great and glorious, wonderful in strength, invincible" (16:13). Then Judith returns to Bethulia, withdraws from the public domain, lives unmarried and independently, honored and respected by all, to an old age when she dies in peace.

The fact that Judith is a woman is an essential part of the purpose and theology of the story on three different levels. Following the biblical pattern of symbolizing the nation as a woman, Judith embodies the whole Jewish people, crushed by foreign rulers but ultimately vindicated and victorious through their piety and prayer. On another level, it is essential that Holofernes, the embodiment of foreign arrogance and might, is not only killed, but killed by a woman and so forced to endure the ultimate disgrace (compare Judg. 9:52–54, where Abimelech begs his servant to kill him with the sword "so people will not say about me 'A woman killed him'"). Thus the cry of Bagoas on discovering the headless corpse: "One Hebrew woman has brought disgrace on the house of King Nebuchadnezzar" (14:18). Three times the author emphasizes the gender factor with the phrase "by the hand of a female" (9:10; 13:15; 16:5). Theologically, the choice of a "weak" woman as the instrument of salvation highlights the power of God, as Judith acknowledges in her prayer: "Your strength does not depend on numbers, nor your might on the powerful. But you are the God of the lowly, helper of the oppressed, upholder of the weak, protector of the forsaken, savior of those without hope" (9:11). Not only is Judith a woman; she is a widow, in biblical thought the poorest and most defenseless of all groups of women (e.g., Ps. 68:5; 146:9; Deut. 10:18). It is specifically as a widow that she lays claim to divine help: "O God, my God, hear me also—a widow" (9:4).

Yet the author of the book prevents a simplistic equation of woman/widow = weak = object of divine favor. Judith is portrayed as wealthy and well respected, the very antithesis of the traditional widow. Although Judith is clearly modeled after female figures such as Miriam and Jael, the author leads one to associate

Judith also with male figures such as Moses, who delivered the people; Samson, who prayed for strength (Judg. 16:28; cf. Judith 13:7); and David, a youth armed only with his slingshot, who cut off the head of the giant (1 Samuel 17).

Judith provides an example of a female who challenges and overcomes both the male enemy and the male establishment within her own community. She is presented as a model of faith and wisdom, combining traditional prayer and piety with radical human initiative and unconventional action. In parallel situations of oppression, as in Latin America today, the story of Judith is remembered and retold by women as a paradigm for women's involvement in the struggle to liberate their people. In much of North American culture, women are more attuned to other aspects of the story, such as Judith's independent control of her estate and the role of her maid "who was in charge of all she possessed" (8:10).

There are still aspects of the narrative, however, that raise questions from a feminist perspective. At the most basic level, this book serves as a caution against the simplistic assumption that every woman portrayed, or even praised, in the Bible necessarily provides a model for women to emulate. Whatever lessons are to be learned, it is surely not that women should be liars, murderers, and *femmes fatales!* Similarly, few women today would want simply to emulate Judith either in her withdrawal from sexual activity in her long widowhood or in her blatant exploitation of sexual wiles and beauty to seduce and ensnare Holofernes. Though the heroine is a woman, it has rarely even been suggested that the author of the book was a woman. (It is hard to image a woman speaking as Judith in praise of the violence of her ancestor Simeon, omitting to include Dinah by name, and casually recalling that "you gave their wives for booty and their daughters to captivity," 9:2–4.) In some ways, this is still very much a man's story.

In the book of Judith, one has an exceptional woman acting in exceptional circumstances. Whenever her story is retold, her own prediction is actualized: "I am going to do something which will go down through all generations of our descendants" (13:9), so that her "praise will never depart from the hearts of those who remember the might of God" (13:19).

## BIBLIOGRAPHY

Archer, Leonie. *Her Price is Beyond Rubies: The Jewish Woman in Graeco-Roman Palestine.* Journal for the Study of the Old Testament Supplement Series 60. Sheffield: Sheffield Academic Press, 1990.

Craven, Toni. *Artistry and Faith in the Book of Judith.* Society of Biblical Literature Dissertation Series 70. Chico, Calif.: Scholars Press, 1983.

Metzger, Bruce M., ed. *The Oxford Annotated Apocrypha.* Expanded edition. New York: Oxford University Press, 1977. Contains an excellent introduction to the Apocrypha as a whole.

Moore, Carey A. *Judith.* Anchor Bible 40B. Garden City, N.Y.: Doubleday & Co., 1985.

Nickelsburg, George W. E. *Jewish Literature Between the Bible and the Mishnah: A Historical and Literary Introduction.* Philadelphia: Fortress Press, 1981.

# EVERYDAY LIFE
## Women in the Period
## of the Hebrew Bible

*Carol L. Meyers*

## Introduction

An important aspect of the foundational role of the Bible in Western culture is the way biblical figures are regarded as role models for later generations. The men and the women of scripture are viewed, perhaps erroneously, as being somehow closer to God than those in the post-biblical world. Considering the lives of women in the period of the Hebrew Bible thus bears on the continuing role of the Bible and its human characters in Western tradition. Would or should women today want to emulate their Israelite forebears?

Another consideration that arises when one contemplates the lives of our biblical ancestors is the very validity for later generations of the way matters of gender are treated in scripture. In the modern world, the values of egalitarianism with respect to women and men are widely held. Yet many biblical texts presuppose a form of social organization that is apparently hierarchical when it comes to gender relationships. One way to deal with such disparities between the Bible and the often opposing perspectives of contemporary life is to recognize the very different social reality that existed in biblical antiquity. That is, examining the daily lives of people in a distant land millennia ago may help us understand why some scriptural ways of presenting women seem meaningless or even unacceptable in comparison with our late-twentieth-century outlook.

Investigating the lives of women in the biblical world may be highly significant for

members of today's religious communities. Yet even beyond that, recovering the modes and dynamics of daily existence of such women is part of a larger task. The last two and a half decades of Western feminism have demonstrated that traditional ways of viewing Western culture are severely flawed. They have consistently omitted the contributions of women, and they have failed to consider what the lives of roughly half of the population were like amid the unending succession of wars and other highly visible and male-dominated political events that have been the focus of most historical writing. But now such imbalances in assessing our cultural heritage are being redressed by feminist scholarship. Consequently, investigating the lives of women in the biblical world that shaped much of subsequent Western life is a critical part of today's agenda of attempting to make visible all those humans long hidden by the dominant male-oriented perspectives on our past.

### The Bible as a Source for Women's Lives

The Hebrew Bible is a voluminous document. Consequently, one might assume that it is full of data that can be used to reconstruct patterns of daily life in biblical times, especially relating to women. Although this is true to a certain extent, there are serious problems in using the Bible for the task of examining the lives of women. A number of those problems deserve attention.

To begin with, the Bible as a whole is androcentric, or male-centered, in its subject matter, its authorship, and its perspectives. One example of how it focuses far more on men than on women is in the simple matter of personal names. The Hebrew Bible mentions a total of 1,426 names, of which 1,315 are those of men. Thus, only 111 women's names appear, about 9 percent of the total. The enormous gap between the number of women's and of men's names signals the male-centered concerns of biblical literature.

As for the Bible's authorship, all the authors identified by name (e.g., prophets) are male. Presumably, so are the anonymous ones, though perhaps some female ones can be posited (as for the Song of Songs). But of even greater concern for our task is the fact that the biblical perspective is so predominantly male. Not only are individual women largely ignored; but also the issues pertaining to women's lives tend to appear in only minor or tangential ways.

This last point may be more a reflection of a second major bias than of an explicitly discriminatory stance. That is, as a story of ancient Israel, the Hebrew Bible's focus is on the public and communal life of the people. Since that life was dominated by men—kings, warriors, priests, prophets, and sages—the more private or domestic arena of daily life receives proportionately little direct attention. Even when these things are mentioned, as in some biblical laws, the issues that are treated are those that involve special problem areas and do not reveal the nitty-gritty of women's routine daily activities.

Not only does male bias raise problems for using the Bible as a source for women's lives; so does the closely related fact that the Bible is a formal text. Recent ethnographic research shows that what appears in a people's official documents may diverge from the dynamics of their everyday social lives. This disparity between normative text and daily existence is particularly characteristic of matters of gender. That is, there is a gap between what the documents depict and what happens in real life.

Thus, for example, the Bible may indicate male dominance in various legal arrangements, such as the transfer of property, but that would not necessarily mean that in the dynamics of individual male-female interactions women were subjugated to men. Nor can it be assumed

that dominance in a specific matter was a sign of general dominance. These are important points. They mean that neither narrative descriptions nor legal prescriptions in the Hebrew Bible can be assumed to have a one-to-one relationship to reality. In fact, women probably had control over many important aspects of their life activities, even though scripture would lead us to believe otherwise.

## Extrabiblical Resources for Reconstructing Women's Lives

Clearly it is difficult to use scripture alone in order to see the everyday lives of women in the biblical past. Fortunately there are other avenues of inquiry that can assist in this enterprise. Other kinds of information, from the ancient world and also from more recent times, can be enormously valuable in recovering patterns of life and modes of gender interaction in societies that can no longer be directly observed.

One vital resource is the information provided by archaeological excavations. The materials recovered through archaeological fieldwork provide the opportunity to re-create the material environment in which both women and men lived. We can see the dwellings they inhabited, the tools and vessels they used, the precious items they acquired, and the public structures (temples, palaces, fortifications) that figured in the lives of some few of them. Furthermore, through the use of sophisticated analytical techniques, information about diet, technology, and other life-sustaining features of daily life is increasingly available. However, such data must be used carefully. Artifacts, no matter how plentiful, are not "gender noisy"—they do not reveal the gender of the persons who used them.

Archaeological remains are thus silent witnesses to the biblical past when it comes to matters of gender. Yet they can be given a voice if they are interpreted in light of what is known about other societies that exhibit similar features of economic life and that exist under similar environmental constraints. This is where the results of ethnographic fieldwork carried out with sensitivity to feminist research interests become critical. The insights into women's roles and the dynamics of gender relationships in societies analogous in key ways to ancient Israel fill in some of the spaces between the clues in the biblical text and those in the archaeological record.

## Women's Lives in Israelite Villages

Ancient Israel began and sustained its national life as a farming people. To be sure, images of pastoralism are attached to the narratives about the matriarchs and patriarchs—the proto-Israelites—in the book of Genesis. Yet during all of Israel's settled existence in the promised land, its economy was firmly based on agriculture. Indeed, Palestine has virtually no natural resources apart from its relatively mediocre soils, rocky hillsides, and insecure water supplies. Israel's precarious survival was intimately connected to the hard work and technological skills of the farm families that lived in tiny highland villages in the biblical period. The way of life in these villages probably remained fairly constant throughout Israel's history.

Daily life centered on what can be called the "family household," which was the basic unit of society. This designation is useful because it indicates that the family involved more than just the people related by marriage and descent who lived together; it also denotes that the family's viability was linked to the building(s) that housed it, its tools and utensils, its livestock, and its fields and outbuildings. Indeed, the family household was clearly an economic unit as much as a biological one. It produced and processed virtually all of the food, clothing, and implements (with the exception of metal items) necessary for survival in the highlands of Palestine. Other forms of social and political organization, such as tribe or monarchy, may have operated at a regional or national level. Yet the family household remained the determinative location for most Israelite women, men, and children. Their daily lives and activities took place within its physical and social boundaries.

Nowhere in the Bible is the human composition of the Israelite family household spelled out. Accustomed as we are to thinking of a typical nuclear family in terms of two parents and their offspring, we tend to project that image backward onto the biblical world. In fact, in the millennium or so of the period of the Hebrew Bible, families were complex and changing configurations of persons related by descent and marriage. The spatial arrangements in domestic buildings in rural villages indicate that, at least in some periods, families must have been multigenerational. That is, a senior couple would have resided with their adult sons, their unmarried daughters (for daughters left home upon marriage), their sons' spouses, their grandchildren, and perhaps also an orphaned niece or nephew or a widowed sibling.

These extended families, contrary to romantic images, were actually quite difficult to sustain in terms of interpersonal relationships—the more people, the more opportunities for disagreements and tension. Yet they existed because they served an important function in providing enough labor and technological skills for a household unit to survive. Considering all the tasks necessary for economic self-sufficiency, the efforts of a conjugal pair alone were not always sufficient. Thus the stresses of a complex family had to be carefully managed in order for the viability of a family household to be preserved.

### Women at Work: The Economic Role

Because so much is known about the agricultural economy of Israelite villages, the participation of women in the productive chores of the family household can be reconstructed with considerable confidence. Although there was some regional variation, most households survived by growing grains (mostly wheat but also some barley), olives (as a foodstuff and for oil), and grapes (as fruit and for wine) in varying proportions. A number of other orchard and garden crops—figs, dates, nuts, seeds, legumes, vegetables, and leeks—supplemented the basic diet.

In addition, specialty crops such as flax were produced in a few locations. Each family also kept a small number of animals—sheep, goats, probably some cows and oxen. These animals were a source of dairy products, and they served to supplement the diet occasionally (perhaps mainly on feast days) with animal protein. They also provided some assurance of food supply in case of crop failure, served (in the case of oxen) as draft animals, and were a source of skins and wool for making clothes and other textile or leather items.

The nature of cropping patterns, in relation to the climate and terrain that characterized Israelite farms, represents what is known as intensive agriculture. Sometimes it is also called plow agriculture, because cereal crops grown in plowed fields were the mainstay. The role of women in such systems is fairly well understood. They were involved in outdoor farmwork, just as are women in less advanced agricultural regimes (horticultural societies), where women and men contribute almost the same number of hours per day to farming tasks. It is unlikely that Israelite women did the actual plowing or that they were involved in start-up operations such as clearing land (cutting trees and moving rocks), digging cisterns, and building terraces. Yet planting, weeding, and harvesting activities certainly depended on women's involvement.

This kind of field labor typically takes four to five hours a day of a woman's time. Not all of this time was spent in fields far removed from the woman's home, however. Women's tasks to some extent had to be compatible with child care. Thus, the gardening work—cultivating fruit trees, vines, vegetables, and herbs as opposed to field crops—occupied a significant portion of women's outdoor time. Those commodities were grown in plots adjacent to the living quarters, which made it easier for women to tend to both children and crops.

However, the work load of Israelite women, in their intensive agricultural system, went far beyond the crop production processes. For one thing, the growing season in Palestine does not last throughout the year. Consequently, foodstuffs had to be converted into forms that could be stored for use in the months following harvest. The plethora of store-jars and storage pits discovered in Israelite dwellings attests to the extensive efforts that went into transforming grains, olives, fruit, and herbs into forms that would not spoil and that would be available out of season. Women were responsible for many, if not most, of these food preservation tasks. They did much of the threshing, drying, pounding, and pitting of foodstuffs to ensure a year-round food supply.

Another major factor in the daily schedule of Israelite women was that their staple crops required not only preserving activities but also processing ones. Cereal crops, the dietary mainstay of an intensive agricultural regime, require a complex and time-consuming series of operations to make them edible. Grains must be soaked, milled, and ground; then the flour must be mixed, set to rise, and baked. Only then is bread, the staff of life, available as family fare. One estimate places the time spent by women in such grain processing at almost two hours a day! And this is just for grain. Add to this the time required for preparation of other foodstuffs, including dairy foods. Take into account also that the routine care (feeding, milking) of domestic animals, which were often stabled in the ground floor of people's homes, was also a

woman's responsibility. It then becomes clear that a woman's daily routine included an array of courtyard or indoor tasks as well as outdoor ones.

Agricultural tasks and the preserving and processing of foods, however, were not the sum total of the economic role of women in Israelite family households. Their indoor tasks included also the responsibility for making most items of clothing used by a family. The material remains of such activities—spindle whorls and loom weights—in Israelite settlements attest to the family-by-family production of cloth. Women are almost universally responsible for such tasks, and Israelite women were unlikely to have been an exception. They were thus often occupied with the complex and time-consuming aspects of providing clothing, which included the shearing of wool or preparation of flax, the carding and spinning of thread, the weaving of cloth, and the sewing of garments. Some of this work (such as sheepshearing or the working of leather) may have been done by men, but the bulk of it was accomplished by female labor, except perhaps when certain households specialized in producing luxury textiles for market purposes (as happened in several regions during the late monarchic period). On the average, several hours a day for much of the year would have been invested in some aspect of clothing manufacture.

In addition to textile production, other kinds of household vessels or implements were probably made by women's hands. Commercially available pottery in cities may have been produced in men's workshops. Yet there is a strong probability, based on ethnographic parallels, that village potters serving tiny local communities were women or that some pots were made by the women (though perhaps fired communally) of each household. The same can be said for basketry. Only metal implements and tools required outside specialists.

This overview of women's economic contributions to the family household can be summarized by emphasizing two salient features. The first is the extraordinary, at least in comparison to modern life, amount of time involved in carrying out life-supporting daily activities. The time required for indoor, courtyard, and outdoor work, with some seasonal variation, was surely more than ten hours a day. The second, perhaps less noticeable but highly significant in terms of gender relations, is the degree of technological expertise involved in many if not most of these tasks. Whereas male farmwork is often characterized by activities requiring sustained efforts and physical strength, women's labor features a series of sophisticated and intricate operations. Many female (and male) jobs were simple and repetitive. But many more female tasks involved skill, experience, and planning.

In the division of labor by gender characteristic of agricultural systems, it is not efficient for both men and women to become proficient at the full array of operations necessary for survival. Both the intricacy and the time-consuming aspects of women's farm labor thus meant that Israelite women exercised control over critical aspects of household life. The diversity of activities and the expertise required had important implications for women's other roles—as mothers and as wives.

## Procreation and Parenting: The Maternal Role

The survival of individual households as well as the corporate territorial claims of ancient Israel were dependent on women for productive labor and also for population growth. Large families clearly made the farming enterprise more viable, and an emphasis on having many children is characteristic of societies based on intensive agriculture. Biblical injunctions to "be fruitful and multiply" surely served the interests of Israelite villagers and of society as a whole.

There can be little doubt that both men and women welcomed and rejoiced in the birth of children. Although some biblical customs and texts give the impression that male children were favored over female ones, that preference should be viewed in relation to the specific needs of a society in which the transfer of family lands was effected patrilineally—through the male line. Surely the labor of daughters was no less valuable than that of sons, considering the array of tasks facing female members of a household. Thus, the sense of girls being disadvantaged may not have been all-pervasive. This is possibly one example of how the male bias of scripture may hide or distort a daily reality.

However welcomed children were by both parents, the prospect of multiple pregnancies carried grave risks for women. To begin with, the infant mortality rate was high; as many as half of the children born may have failed to reach adulthood. This meant that women had to have almost twice as many pregnancies as

the number of children desired. Suppose that a family with four children seemed optimal; seven or eight live births would be needed to achieve that number. Given the risk of death in childbirth in ancient Israel, as in any pre-modern society, it is no wonder that the esti-mated average life span for women in ancient Israel, based on the analysis of skeletal remains found in tombs or graves, was about thirty years. Men, spared the dangers of the reproduc-tive process, lived an average of ten years longer.

The rigors of childbearing notwithstanding, choosing to remain childless was hardly an option. Women responded to their own maternal impulses and to the larger family and societal needs. Thus, having children and caring for them were integral parts of every woman's life (except if she was barren). The variety and com-plexity of a woman's economic role were surely matched by the demands of her maternal role.

Although older children would certainly have helped, as would have grandmothers and childless aunts, the mother undoubtedly assumed the chief responsibility for the care of small children. Still, the child-care component of a woman's workday did not for the most part compete with her other obligations. In agri-cultural households, the tending of small children is subsumed into the routine of sub-sistence tasks. With more of a woman's time than a man's being spent within the household and its contiguous gardens and courtyards, women spent more time than did men with children of both genders. Until boys were old enough to accompany fathers into the fields and keep up with their strenuous activities, they along with their sisters were cared for mainly by mothers.

For this reason, and in the general if not total absence of any formal or institutionalized education, the socialization of young children was accomplished largely by women. This is hardly a trivial task in societies in which schools are not present; it was certainly a fun-damental aspect of the transmission of culture, technology, and values in ancient Israel. This educative role is not directly visible in scrip-ture, where the presence of sages and elders gives the impression of a male monopoly on the teaching and inculcating of traditional practices and beliefs. Yet the day-to-day interactions of mothers with children in the household were of foundational significance in passing most aspects of Israelite culture from one generation to the next. Indeed, the very notion in Proverbs that "wisdom," which includes pragmatic as well as lofty sagacity, is female may be rooted in the broad role of mothers in caring for and socializing their children (see, e.g., Prov. 4:1–9; 6:20; 8:1–36; 31:10–31).

The relationship of mothers to offspring was critical for the early years of the children, but it did not stop with early childhood. Because of the complex, multigenerational population of many households, and because of the multiplicity of tasks involved in family life, the role of women as mothers included managing the tasks of those junior to her. The *raison d'être* for large families was the labor-intensive nature of the agricultural economy of ancient Israel. No woman alone could carry out all the household activities relegated to females. Thus women, particularly senior ones in an extended family, assumed managerial responsibility. They not only taught younger family members—children but also daughters-in-law or nieces—how to perform certain tasks; they also assigned jobs and saw that they were accomplished.

A woman's success in running a complex household, along with her husband's ability to accomplish his array of tasks, depended on the existence of well-established parental authority. Whereas some ancient Near Eastern societies apparently favored men over women in the relegation of authority over offspring, Israel exhibited parity of mothers and fathers in this respect (e.g., Ex. 20:12). This meant the continuing parental control of adult children, not just toddlers, in multigenerational households; such strong parental authority can be seen in certain biblical laws (e.g., Deut. 21:18–21). The household, with its family laws, in fact served as the primary locus of community justice.

Women thus figured prominently as authority figures in intrafamily matters. Their authority over children may also have extended beyond their own households. Women in agrarian household settings probably exercised some control over the marital arrangements of their offspring. The Bible calls the household "mother's household" rather than the usual "father's household" in several passages concerned with marriageable daughters (Gen. 24:28; Ruth 1:8; Song 3:4; 8:2). These instances may be a signal that, at least for female children, mothers were involved in interfamily arrangements. Such a role took women out of their own domestic contexts and gave them input into matters affecting land and property. It gave them direct influence over aspects of life that transcended their own immediate milieu.

## Women and Worship: The Religious Role

As an extension of both their economic and maternal roles, women played a large part in the specifically religious or ritual features of family life. When it comes to ritual, the Bible is largely focused on public, communal practices; yet there are clear indications, in both the scriptural and archaeological record, of domestic religious practices. Family celebrations of either local or national significance punctuated the annual calendar. As organizers and participants in household-based festivals, and also as individual worshipers, women took part in a multifaceted spiritual life. Women's modes of prayer may even have influenced some of the formal liturgical expressions preserved in the Psalter. Indeed, there were probably few gender-based restrictions, except for the possibility of serving as priests. But then, that hereditary office was not available to most men, either.

In addition to their regular sacral activities, carried out in the households as well as in the villages and cities of ancient Israel, some women also held special expertise in public performance. Sometimes this was in the sad task of carrying out funerary rites; women were the reciters, and probably the composers, of traditional laments for the dead (Jer. 9:17; 2 Chron. 35:25). In addition, as dancers, singers, and musicians, women performed at major public events (see Judg. 21:21). The cultural high point of such performances is represented by the great hymns sung by women in celebration of Israel's victory over hostile forces through divine intervention (see Ex. 15:20–21; Judges 5; 1 Sam. 18:6–7).

## Women as Wives: The Marital Role and Gender Identity

There has been much debate in biblical scholarship about the legal relationship between women and men as married couples. (See the commentaries on Leviticus and Deuteronomy.) Were women the property of their husbands? Were they mere chattel to be disposed of? Did male heads of household have unmitigated control over female family members? The patrilineal structure of Israelite society, the fact that men controlled most economic assets, and the way women appear as dependents in many legal contexts—all these factors make such questions valid. Yet it is not simple to answer them. The kinds of information provided in this essay suggest that the impressions of gender hierarchy based on biblical texts must be weighed against the growing knowledge about ancient Israel's social reality.

While the verdict is hardly in on such matters, several observations are in order. One is that there are no absolute statements in the Hebrew Bible of categorical male supremacy over women. Even the last line of Gen. 3:16, traditionally viewed as a mandate for male dominance, is perhaps better understood in the context of that verse as a whole, and especially in its relation to the preceding line: It deals with sexuality in the context of a sanction for increasing the birthrate, not with general social dominance. Indeed, the household context of women's lives was so rich in its relational and occupational dynamics that the category "woman" was of little significance. Females were mothers, daughters, sisters, wives; and they were also bakers, cooks, weavers, managers, teachers, worshipers, and so on. All of these roles involved some combination of social, economic, and biological functions. Only when separated from households might sexuality, and thus the category "woman," emerge as a salient factor in their identity. For most women, life apart from households was not a possibility, and so belonging to an abstract category according to sex was of little relevance.

Closely related to the relative insignificance of sex as a category of personal identification is the concept of gender unity that appears in the Hebrew Bible, especially in the creation stories of Genesis (see Gen. 1:27; 2:23–24). With some notable exceptions, especially in the book of Judges, the goals and strategies of those women visible in the Bible are not peculiarly feminine; they are part of the general goals of family and community. The Western dichotomizing categories of female submissiveness or passivity as opposed to male aggression or action simply do not apply to the Israelite concept of gender. The ideal of male and female as "one flesh," extraordinary as it may seem, goes beyond its explicit mention in Gen. 2:24; it emerges in many of the narrative and poetic depictions of male–female pair-bonding contained in scripture. It is even possible to view legal materials that seem unfavorable to women as not concerned with women as such but rather with trying to promote family and territorial stability in a patrilineal context. In this sense, ancient Israel may have been virtually unique in the ancient world. It is worth contemplating that the unity and asexuality of the Israelite deity bore some relationship to the human community made in the image of that God. That is, while God is presented largely through male imagery, the prevailing monotheism of scripture, along with the nonsexual nature of divine creativity and the occasional female metaphors for God, may have contributed toward the relative social unity of male and female in household settings.

## Women in Urban Settings

Most ancient Israelites lived in agricultural settlements throughout the biblical period. The family household remained the fundamental societal form in the village context. Yet the larger social and political structures of Israel were not static; the Israelite tribal league gave way to a nation state. The profound changes that accompanied state formation were most felt in urban centers and especially in Jerusalem, the capital. Those changes would have had a profound impact on matters of gender. A monarchy, and a centralized government with its bureaucracy of male officials, meant that status and privilege were accorded far more to men than to women. A market economy with the availability of basic goods and luxury objects (such as processed foods, pottery, clothing, jewelry), and also services performed outside the household, would have diminished aspects of female contributions to daily life.

Much more could be said about the effect of state formation on gender valuations and roles. Yet those effects would have been of relatively minimal importance in rural settings, given the extreme geographical isolation of highland villages in the fractured landscape of Palestine. Mainly in the cities, in the centers of public life, would tendencies toward gender polarization emerge, but in fact there were very few such cities. Most places called "city" were really overgrown towns, and people's lives were still tied to the agricultural hinterland. In some larger centers, and specifically in Jerusalem, features of the urban life that accompanied political change, more than the actual existence of monarchic government, would have impacted in major ways on women's lives.

It is neither possible nor appropriate, proportionately speaking, to give as much consideration here to urban women's lives as to the lives of their country sisters. Urban women were in a minority; probably up to 90 percent of Israelites lived in village settings throughout most of the biblical period. However, since Jerusalem especially plays such a central role in the formation of scripture, a few comments are in order.

Probably the most important point is the altered economic role of women. In cities, most households were not self-sufficient units. If husbands were not farmers but rather were soldiers or bureaucrats or priests or craftsmen or shopkeepers, their wives hardly played the same kind of essential economic role that they did in agricultural villages, even if they were involved to some degree in several of these specialized occupations. At the same time, city households tended to be smaller, nuclear. Thus the full range of female authority exhibited in agrarian households was circumscribed in urban families. Furthermore, the changing economic conditions were accompanied by socioeconomic stratification. Some people became rich and privileged, and others were disadvantaged. For the former, leisure time became available. Another consequence of the predominance of nuclear families was the greater risk for women to be left on their own, should husbands predecease them and should their families of origin be inaccessible.

For all these reasons, and no doubt many others, city life meant that some women were released—from unending toil, from household authority, from a family with males—more than was possible in villages. Women thus unencumbered posed different possibilities for gender identification and thus categorization than did their rural sisters. Gender differences became more sharply defined when the complementarity and mutual dependence that characterize agricultural households diminished. Yet the emphasis on family integrity persisted even in cities. It surely helped sustain Israelites and their national identity during the sixth-century exile. And in the last centuries of the period of the Hebrew Bible, when even Jerusalem was reduced to a town of only several hundred inhabitants, it provided the basis for a virtually complete return to nonurban life.

## BIBLIOGRAPHY

Bird, Phyllis. "The Place of Women in the Israelite Cultus." In *Ancient Israelite Religion: Essays in Honor of Frank Moore Cross*, edited by Paul D. Hanson, Patrick D. Miller, Jr., and S. Dean McBride, pp. 397–419. Philadelphia: Fortress Press, 1987.

Bossen, Laurel. "Women and Economic Institutions." In *Economic Anthropology*, edited by Stuart Plattner, pp. 318–350. Stanford, Calif.: Stanford University Press, 1989.

Ember, Carol R. "The Relative Decline in Women's Contribution to Agriculture with Intensification." *American Anthropologist* 85 (1983), 285–304.

Frymer-Kensky, Tikva. "The Ideology of Gender in the Bible and the Ancient Near East." In *Dum-e2-dub-ba-a: Studies in Honor of Åke W. Sjöberg*, edited by H. Behrens, D. Loding, and M. Roth, pp. 185–191. Philadelphia: University of Pennsylvania University Museum, 1989.

Meyers, Carol. *Discovering Eve: Ancient Israelite Women in Context*. New York: Oxford University Press, 1988.

——. "Historical Approaches to Patriarchy in the West: A Consideration of Judeo-Christian Tradition." In *Foundations of Gender Equality*, edited by A. Zagarell (forthcoming).

——. "'To Her Mother's House'—Considering a Counterpart to the Israelite Bêt 'Ab." In *The Bible and the Politics of Exegesis*, edited by David Jobling, Peggy L. Day, and Gerald T. Shepherd, pp. 39–51, 304–307. New York: Pilgrim Press, 1991.

Pressler, Carolyn Jo. "The View of Women Found in the Deuteronomic Family Laws." Doctoral thesis, Princeton Theological Seminary, 1991.

Silverblatt, Irene. "Women in States." *Annual Review of Anthropology* 17 (1988), 427–460.

Stager, Lawrence E. "The Archaeology of the Family in Ancient Israel." *Bulletin of the American Schools of Oriental Research* 260 (1985), 1–36.

# MATTHEW

## Amy-Jill Levine

## Introduction

Probably written around 85–90 C.E., the Gospel of Matthew addresses an originally Jewish congregation that has begun to incorporate Gentile members. Antioch in Syria is often proposed as the setting, but recent studies suggest that the Gospel may have had a Palestinian, specifically a Galilean, origin. Emphasizing Jewish concerns such as Jesus' descent from King David, the fulfillment of biblical sayings, and retention and interpretation of Pentateuchal law, Matthew locates the church within the context of Israel's salvation history. The Gospel portrays Jesus as having limited his earthly mission to Jews; following the resurrection, the mission is extended to all. Within this new ethnically mixed movement, neither Jew nor Gentile is privileged; judgment is based not on race, class, or ethnicity, but on doing the will of heaven.

Traditionally, Matthew's Gospel was viewed as an eyewitness account as well as a source for the other three canonical stories of Jesus. Today, both views are largely rejected. Although some scholars still support the priority of Matthew, most believe that Matthew utilized a variety of sources: the Bible (i.e., what was eventually labeled the Old Testament by the church); Mark's Gospel; a collection composed primarily of Jesus' sayings (called Q, from the German word for "source," *Quelle*), which was also used by Luke; and additional material unique to this Gospel (called M). The Gospel begins with Jesus' genealogy, an account of his infancy, his baptism by John, and an extended temptation narrative (1:1–4:16). Then follow several series of miracle stories, controversies, and other narratives, among which are interspersed five teaching discourses: the Sermon on the Mount (chaps. 5–7); missionary teachings (chap. 10); parables concerning the realm of heaven (chap.

13); instruction to and about the church (chap. 18); and predictions of the end time (chaps. 24–25). The teaching materials continue into the passion narrative, and the text concludes with a brief account of a resurrection appearance to the eleven disciples in Galilee.

Both the narrative and the instructional materials highlight persons removed from religious and political power in both the Roman and Jewish systems. Indeed, the Gospel decries various structures that cause social oppression. For example, Matthew defines the family unit in terms of mothers and children rather than, as might be expected, fathers (cf. 12:50; see "Everyday Life: Women in the Period of the New Testament"). The evangelist attempts to eliminate all relationships in which one group exploits or dominates another. Thus, in the Gospel rulers like Herod and Pilate are found wanting in comparison with relatively powerless people like Joseph and Pilate's wife; and residents of Jerusalem, those with political power, are contrasted with those who live on the margins of cities and those who, like Jesus and the disciples, have no permanent home. Matthew condemns those who are complacent about the divine will, believe descent from Abraham guarantees their salvation, and refuse to act upon the good news of the gospel. In turn, men and women who demonstrate their faith not merely by saying "Lord, Lord" but by doing the will of heaven (7:21) are those welcomed into the new realm that Jesus inaugurates. Faith manifested in action defines Matthew's understanding of "higher righteousness." Members of the church are to be more faithful to the Mosaic law than are the Pharisees and scribes; they are to do more than what the law literally demands, even if their deeds may strike their neighbors as unwarranted or unexpected. In the face of the demands of heaven, radical action is necessary.

Among the Gospel's specific demands, Matthew emphasizes the importance of service (see especially 23:8–12). In particular, women frequently represent both the ideal of service that Jesus requests of his disciples (20:26–27) and the model of fidelity that the church requests of its members. But this service is not equated with women's stereotypical duty as servant to spouse or children. Rather, women who appear apart from husband, father, or son assume positive, active roles in the Gospel (8:14–17; 9:20–22; 12:42; 13:33; 15:21–28; 21:31–32; 25:1–13; 26:6–13; 27:55–61; 28:1–10). While Matthew has not designed a community in which women and men have entirely equal roles, the Gospel recognizes the contributions made to the growth of the church by women as well as by others removed from positions of power (foreigners, lepers, the possessed, and the dispossessed).

## Comment

### Genealogy and Nativity (1:1–25)

Matthew begins with material, much of it not attested elsewhere, on Jesus' family background, childhood, and early struggles with temptation. Marked by a series of quotations from the earlier scriptures, this material depicts Jesus as the Messiah destined for Israel. By means of characterization, prophetic commentary, and plot, the opening of the Gospel also foreshadows Jesus' later ministry to the disenfranchised, his new interpretation of the law, and his opposition to those in leadership positions.

Beginning with a genealogy, Matthew emphasizes Jesus' Hebrew ("son of Abraham") and royal ("son of David") lineage. Within the list of ancestors, the evangelist has unexpectedly inserted the names of five women: not the matriarchs, but Tamar (Genesis 38), who posed as a prostitute and seduced her father-in-law, Judah; Rahab, the prostitute from Jericho, who betrayed her city to the Hebrews (Joshua 2; 6); Ruth, the Moabite who married Boaz after placing him in a compromising position one night on the threshing floor (Ruth 3); the "wife of Uriah," Bathsheba, who committed adultery with David; and Mary, who became pregnant before her marriage to Joseph but while betrothed to him in a legally binding relationship (Matt. 1:18).

Some of the explanations that have been offered for the inclusion of these women in the genealogy are unsatisfactory. It is unlikely that the focus on extramarital sexual activity was intended to combat Jewish charges of Jesus' illegitimate birth, since such charges come from a time later than the composition of the Gospel. Neither are the women to be seen as sinners (see Matt. 1:21) in need of the redemption Jesus brings to all, as some of the early church fathers suggested; sexuality was not, in Matthew's time, automatically equated with sin. Moreover, other sources from this period, both Jewish and Christian, did not regard these women as sinners. Rahab and Ruth were Gentiles, so their presence, along with that of Uriah the Hittite, foreshadows the welcome of Gentiles into the church (see Matt. 8:5–13). But this explanation, although correct, is insufficient. In early Jewish tradition, Rahab and Ruth were considered proselytes, and Tamar and Bathsheba are usually considered to be Hebrews. Nor can a Gentile association explain Mary's presence.

The genealogy is best interpreted as presenting examples of "higher righteousness": Tamar acts when Judah unjustly refuses; Rahab recognizes the power of the Hebrew God and so protects the scouts; Uriah (who is named in the genealogy, whereas Bathsheba is not named) — unlike David — displays fidelity to his commission and his fellow soldiers; and Ruth, following Naomi's advice, moves Boaz to action. They demonstrate Matthew's recognition of those removed from positions of power. Judah, the king of Jericho, David, and Boaz — all of whom had the power to act but who either failed to empower others or succeeded in exploiting them — are taught the lesson of higher righteousness by Tamar, Rahab, Uriah, and Ruth. These individuals also acted in a manner not expected by the social mores of their times, in order to further divine purposes; so will Jesus. Additionally, the genealogy highlights women who were initially removed from traditional domestic arrangements: unmarried, separated from their spouse, widowed, or prostitutes. Although the genealogy ultimately associates all the women with men, it also indicates that marriage is not (contrast 1 Timothy) the prerequisite for righteous action or salvation.

Unlike Luke's nativity account, which

emphasizes women's active roles, Matthew's depicts Mary as entirely passive. This presentation is consistent with Matthew's insistence that familial connections are to be restructured in the new community that Jesus creates. Mary's passivity serves to undercut the privileged position she acquires by being Jesus' mother. Here, Joseph is the model of higher righteousness. Like the unconventional figures in the genealogy, he does what he considers proper even though his action is neither legally necessary nor socially expected. Joseph first resolves to divorce Mary quietly and so, apparently, to avoid her being charged with adultery or assumed to be the victim of rape. His accepting Mary and naming the child (see 1:21) socially legitimates both mother and son; Joseph is Jesus' legal father by means of adoption.

The character of Joseph predominates in the nativity and infancy accounts, but feminine images encircle the stories of the conception and birth. For instance, Mary conceives by the Holy Spirit, a term that is grammatically neuter in Greek but feminine in Semitic languages such as the Hebrew of the Bible and Jesus' native Aramaic. The Spirit will reappear to acknowledge Jesus' divine role (3:16–17), to serve as the source of his powers (12:28), and to be the final test for entry into the age to come (12:32). The combination of the originally feminine Spirit and Jesus' lack of a human father (note the passive verb "was born" in 1:16) indicates the restructuring of the human family: outside of patriarchal models it is not ruled by or even defined by a male head of the house.

Matthew explains the virgin birth as the prophetic fulfillment of Isa. 7:14. Although the Hebrew version of Isaiah states simply that a "young woman" has conceived, the Greek version of this passage (the Septuagint), which Matthew follows, translates the term for "young woman" as *parthenos*, or "virgin." This verse in the Septuagint was probably interpreted as predicting that a virgin would, at some later time (presumably after her marriage), conceive a child in the normal manner. Only Christian interpreters seem to have read Isa. 7:14 as a messianic prediction; there are no parallels in any other Jewish writings of the biblical or Hellenistic periods to the Messiah's being conceived in this manner.

According to the Gospel, Mary maintained her virginity "until she had borne a son" (1:25); nothing is said of her subsequent sexual activity

and thus the question of her perpetual virginity. Matthew 1:25 serves as a guarantee only for Jesus' unusual conception.

## The Infancy Narrative (2:1–23)

Beginning in chap. 2, the evangelist demonstrates concern for those removed from the political system by contrasting the disenfranchised with the elite and by distinguishing those who stay put and remain complacent from those who are displaced or who lack permanent homes. The literally well-placed "Herod and all Jerusalem" are arrayed against the displaced holy family and the Gentile magi who travel to and from Bethlehem.

The scene is set to recapitulate the story of Moses (Ex. 1:8–2:10). In each case an evil king orders the deaths of male Hebrew babies, and in each case one special child is saved. Whereas Exodus focuses on such women as the midwives, Pharaoh's daughter, and Moses' sister, Matthew emphasizes Joseph: he receives the warning dreams, and by moving his family first to Egypt and then to Galilee, he displays higher righteousness. Although Mary is passive, her role as mother is recognized and so accorded value: the magi recognize "the child with Mary his mother" (2:11); Joseph is commanded to take "the child and his mother" (2:13; see also 2:20, 21). This concern for the maternal role is confirmed in the fulfillment quotation about "Rachel, weeping for her children" (2:18; see Jer. 31:15). It also serves as a contrast to the negative value given to Archelaus, who reigned "in place of his father" Herod (2:22). Thus, the infancy material defines the role of father according to the model established by Joseph: he serves his family rather than rules over them and others.

## Baptism and Temptation (3:1–4:25)

Concerns for both "higher righteousness" and the condemnation of those who would rule rather than serve continue as the Gospel begins the account of Jesus' ministry. The message of John the Baptist, who serves as Jesus' prophetic forerunner, indicates that individuals cannot remain smug in their faith or rely on privileged position for salvation. To the Pharisees and Sadducees who wished to participate in his baptism of repentance he asserts that Abrahamic descent will not save them from divine wrath (3:7–10). For Matthew, proper actions rather than biological lineage determine one's relationship to heaven. Jesus is the "beloved Son" (3:17) because he submits to baptism even though John would have prevented him from doing so. In submitting, in recognizing John's authority, he fulfills "all righteousness" (3:15).

Such obedience to the will of heaven is not easily accomplished, as the temptation indicates. When the devil wants Jesus to prove his identity as "Son of God" by performing miracles, Jesus indicates that true sonship consists in following the scriptural word. His willingness to deny himself comfort (4:3–4), safety (4:5–7), and power (4:8–10) for the sake of the realm of heaven foreshadows the response to his call by the first four disciples (4:18–22). The two sets of brothers enter into a new family centered on Jesus; they leave everything (cf. 19:27): their boats, their nets, and—for the sons of Zebedee— even their father. Thereby they form the basis of the new community that Jesus will gather: a family defined by service to others and commitment to Jesus. Baptized, having overcome the devil and having gathered his first disciples, Jesus is ready to preach his gospel and seek new members for his family.

## The Sermon on the Mount (5:1–7:29)

Just as Moses, having survived the persecution in Egypt and having overcome the temptation to apostasy in the wilderness, ascended Mount Sinai to deliver divine instruction to the Hebrews, so Jesus, having been to the wilderness, ascends a mountain and delivers a law. And just as the first law was given to a community of homeless slaves, so Jesus' interpretation of that law addresses the descendants of those fugitives. Of particular concern, as the Beatitudes indicate, are those who have been disenfranchised and those willing to forgo leadership and elitist positions. Although women are not directly mentioned as part of the audience and therefore of the missionary focus (cf. 14:21; 15:38), and although the demands of the sermon are addressed to men, women's situations nevertheless may be seen as included in Jesus' message.

Of special relevance to women are the injunctions regarding adultery and divorce (5:27–32; cf. 19:2–12). For Jesus, as well as for the evangelist, adultery involves not merely the physical act but also the desire for it. By collapsing the distinction between thought and action, this extension of the law against adultery to include lust suggests that no one should be regarded as a sex object. The burden is here placed on the man: women are not seen as responsible for enticing men into sexual misadventures. Matthew's Jesus also insists that the Mosaic ruling concerning divorce (Deut. 24:1–4) was a temporary concession to human weakness. Members of Matthew's community will have permanent marriages of the sort suggested by Gen. 2:24 (cf. Mark 10:2–9; Luke 16:18; Rom. 7:2–3; 1 Cor. 7:10–11). A remarried divorced woman will be considered an adulteress, and whoever marries her will be an adulterer. Yet Matthew adds to Mark's legislation (Mark 10:10–12): divorce is permitted only in cases of "unchastity" (porneia). What the term specifically indicates remains debated. It is probably not a reference to adultery, since the immediately preceding discussion of adultery employs different vocabulary. Matthew may be referring to marriages between forbidden relations (see Lev. 18:6–18), perhaps those contracted by Gentiles who subsequently joined the church. Sexual purity and legally contracted betrothals are essential to the Matthean view of marriage, as the earlier picture of Joseph's concern for Mary's reputation indicates.

Scholars have often suggested that the injunction against divorce establishes for women an economically secure position. However, since Jewish women had marriage contracts which would have made divorce economically prohibitive for most husbands, so strict a teaching was not needed to protect them from being cast aside. Nor is there evidence that the injunction was meant to stop an increasing divorce rate in order to preserve the family. Finally, it is unlikely that eliminating the possibility of divorce would be beneficial to women trapped in loveless or violent marriages. These injunctions might best be seen as having a theological rather than a social motivation, attempting to reestablish the relationship between woman and man as it existed between Eve and Adam before the Fall. The Edenic model takes precedence over the Mosaic. If Jesus himself believed that time would end in his generation (16:28), elimination of divorce would be less of a hardship than might otherwise be imagined. For Matthew, living fifty years after the crucifixion and addressing Gentiles as well as Jews, certain accommodations may have been warranted. Thus, to Jesus' unequivocal elimination of divorce as recorded by Mark, Matthew adds an exception in the case of unchastity.

## Healings of Marginal Individuals (8:1–17)

Following the sermon, Jesus shows that he is the Messiah of deed as well as of word. Chapters 8 and 9 consist of ten miracle stories and several controversy accounts. By focusing primarily on the interaction between Jesus and those who are outcasts of or marginal participants in the Jewish cultic establishment—lepers (8:1–4), Gentiles (8:5–13), women (8:14–15), demoniacs (8:16, 28–34; 9:32), tax collectors (9:9–13), sinners (9:11–13), the cultically impure (9:20–22), and even the dead (9:23–26)—Matthew shows the inclusivity of the new community.

At the beginning of chap. 8, the evangelist groups together the healings of the leper, the centurion's servant, and Peter's mother-in-law. The leper represents those removed from full participation in the Temple and thus from a major aspect of the public practice of religion because of disease; the centurion is restricted to the Court of the Gentiles; the woman has her own religious responsibilities and privileges, including those in the Court of the Women, but even she cannot enter the Temple's inner court. All three are granted miracles with symbolic import. Jesus' command to the now-cured leper indicates the preservation of Mosaic law: the leper's reincorporation into Jewish society requires that the priest proclaim him to be cured, and Jesus insists as well that the leper offer the appropriate temple sacrifice (see Lev. 14:2–32). Jesus' initial reluctance to help the centurion and the eventual healing of his servant (or perhaps son) from a distance (see 15:21–28) foreshadow the Gentile mission but retain Jesus' focus on his fellow Jews (cf. 10:5b–6; 15:24). The healing of Peter's mother-in-law (Matt. 8:14–15; cf. Mark 1:29–31; Luke 4:38–39) indirectly reveals the Gospel's interest in moving toward a more equal social structure. Matthew 8:14–15 is the only healing in the Gospel in which Jesus takes the initiative, and the woman literally rises to this occasion: getting up from her bed, she "serves" (*diakonei*, 8:15) him. If her action has ecclesiastical connotations, then Matthew has depicted the church's first deacon. It is, however, unlikely that an office is suggested by this term: "to serve" is, for Matthew, primarily a matter of attending to one's physical needs (4:11; 25:44; but cf. 20:26–28). Like the women at the tomb who "provide for" (the term is the same as "to serve") Jesus (27:55–56), Peter's mother-in-law follows the model Jesus sets (20:26–28). Ironically, although instructed to "serve," the Twelve are never described as doing so. That Peter had a mother-in-law also indicates that at least one disciple had a wife. The mother-in-law's presence in his home may suggest that she had moved in with her daughter (who is never mentioned), which would confirm Jesus' concern in 15:1–20 that parents receive necessary support from their children. Peter's own willingness to give up his family for Jesus' sake will be recalled in 10:37–39; 19:27–30. But the ultimate irony is that whereas the unnamed mother-in-law rises from her bed to serve Jesus, Peter will sleep when Jesus needs him most (26:36–46).

## The Bridegroom (9:14–17; see also 22:1–14)

Continuing the contrast between those who manifest "higher righteousness" and those who remain complacent with their present, incomplete level of religiosity, Matthew next introduces a controversy between the disciples of Jesus and those of the Baptist. Jesus employs the image of the bridegroom to explain his disciples' unexpected behavior (9:15). Unlike the Pharisees and the Baptist's disciples, Jesus' followers do not engage in ritual fasting. The comment that one does not fast while the bridegroom is present need not be seen as sanctifying the institution of marriage, since the passage speaks of the bridegroom's being taken away. Nor need it lead to an analogy of men as caretakers for either their wives or for the church and so lead to a justification either for inequality in marriage or for restricting women from the pulpit. The bridegroom is not a husband (a permanent role) but rather a celebrant (a transitional role). The focus of the imagery is on the joy of the groom and on the special celebration that marks the encounter with Jesus (cf. Matt. 25:1–13).

## The Ruler's Daughter and the Woman in the Crowd (9:18–26)

An abbreviation of Mark 5:21–43 (cf. Luke 8:40–56), the next incident returns to the Gospel's interest in women's status. Matthew lacks Mark's strong parallelism between the twelve-year-old girl approaching the expected age of both menses and marriage and the woman's twelve years of exaggerated vaginal bleeding, but the First Gospel nevertheless indicates both that women are a part of the community Jesus addresses and that Jesus will not be deterred from his mission by the prospect of becoming ritually unclean. Paralleling the

Gentile centurion of 8:5–13 and the Canaanite mother of 15:21–28, the Jewish father wants his child to live. And the hemorrhaging woman, like Peter's mother-in-law, manifests faith in action. She approaches Jesus, and he in turn heals her (note the mention of her act of faith—touching the fringe of his cloak—9:20–21; cf. 14:36). Each approach is consistent with the social situation of the supplicant: the ruler makes a public request; the cultically impure woman (see Lev. 15:25–33) comes up from behind Jesus and seeks to touch him secretly. But the woman, doubly marginal through gender and bleeding, is depicted as fully worthy of a miracle; her healing is accomplished, and her faith is proclaimed in public.

## Disruption of Families (10:34–39; see also 12:46–50; 19:29–30)

Having presented Jesus' own mission to serve, to heal, and to teach, the evangelist adds missionary instruction (Matt. 10:1–42) to those who would continue this ministry. The discourse is addressed to the twelve apostles, but the instructions are apparently programmatic for missionaries connected to Matthew's church. Whether such missionaries were accompanied by spouses, or even whether women were included in the evangelist's model (cf. Priscilla and Aquila, Junia and Andronicus in Rom. 16:3, 7) is unknown. One result of their teaching, however, will be domestic discord. Men and women brought into the church will not only find healing and teaching; they will also face, at the very least, familial disruption: "a daughter against her mother, and a daughter-in-law against her mother-in-law" (10:35). Matthew's concern for the new family constituted according to Jesus' preaching may thus take the place of the original family torn apart by religious dissension. For Matthew, all human relationships are to be subordinated to loyalty to Jesus (10:38–39).

Discussion of the true family continues in 12:46–50 (cf. 13:54–58; 15:4–7; 19:19). Decreasing the harshness of Mark 3:31–35 (cf. Luke 8:19–21), Matthew insists that biological relationships are to be replaced by new mothers, brothers, sisters (12:46–50): the men and women who do the Father's will. The only "father" is the one in heaven; no earthly father is mentioned in the context of this new social experiment. These instructions do not mean that the earthly family is to be slighted. Matthew 15:4–7

and 19:19 assert that one must honor and indeed provide for both father and mother.

## Wisdom Sayings (11:16–30)

At the conclusion of the instruction on evangelizing, Matthew, unlike Luke and Mark, presents no separate mission of the Twelve. Jesus' comments on the wisdom tradition may suggest why a mission is lacking: the people of the towns are receptive neither to Jesus nor to John the Baptist, the representatives of Wisdom.

The comment that Wisdom (sophia) is "justified [or, "vindicated"] by her deeds" (11:19; cf. Luke 7:35) need not be seen as indicating leadership roles of real women in the community. The passage rather stresses the connection between Jesus, the new manifestation of the divine on earth (see 1 Cor. 1:21, 24, 30), and personified Wisdom, the traditional image of the divine presence (see Job 28; Proverbs 8–9; Sirach 24; Wisdom of Solomon 7–8). In 11:25–30, Jesus assumes Wisdom's roles: mediating knowledge, demonstrating intimacy with the deity, providing comfort. Yet Jesus is not made feminine by this association. Instead, by assuming her roles, he represents Sophia as a man.

## The Queen of the South (12:42)

Consistent with other Q material (e.g., Matt. 24:41), this next saying about a woman (cf. Luke 11:31) parallels a saying concerning men: the inhabitants of Nineveh. The "queen of the South," who is to be identified as the queen of Sheba (1 Kings 10:1; 2 Chron. 9:1) is, like each of the Ninevites, a Gentile who will receive a more favorable final judgment than the Jewish towns. The woman's role as a witness in a lawcourt is unexpected, but it shows that Matthew elevates those who do not exploit positions of power and condemns attitudes of complacency. The queen is a helpful example of Matthew's agenda, since even though she is herself a royal figure, she acknowledges greater Wisdom, and she travels to its site: the court of Solomon.

## The Parable of the Yeast (13:33)

By teaching in parables, Jesus assumes Wisdom's role. The third of seven parables gathered in chap. 13 is the only one presenting a woman as a main character. Paralleling the immediately preceding parable of the mustard seed, Matt. 13:33, about the woman making bread, reinforces the sexual division of labor that was probably practiced within the community: men work outside; women, inside. But the parable may also be seen as reinforcing certain literary and social conventions. First, the mention of three measures of flour (cf. Luke 13:21) recalls the amount Sarah kneaded for the heavenly messengers (Gen. 18:6; see also Judg. 6:19; 1 Sam. 1:24; Hos. 7:4). This was approximately a bushel and was thus the largest amount of dough a person could knead. The bread produced could feed about one hundred people. Here work traditionally associated with women is recognized as having value. Second, against the prevailing negative image of leaven (Ex. 12:15–20; 23:18; 34:25; Lev. 2:11; Matt. 16:5–12; 1 Cor. 5:6–8; Gal. 5:9; but cf. Lev. 7:13–14; 23:17) is a positive picture of its use. The final point is that the message of the *basilea* ("realm"), although hidden like a small bit of leaven in a mound of dough, will become—through this woman's effort—the bread of life.

### Rejection in Nazareth (13:53–58)

At the completion of the parables, the family of Jesus is again invoked (cf. 12:46–50). The comments of those in Nazareth (cf. Mark 6:1–6a) indicate the failure of some to grasp Jesus' message; in this way they fulfill Jesus' citation of Isa. 6:9–10 (Matt. 13:14–15). The people question the source of Jesus' wisdom and deeds by identifying him as the son of the builder and Mary and by mentioning his brothers and sisters. They believe one can be judged by one's biological family, and in this case the family's background would not portend such powers. For Matthew, however, one is judged by one's deeds (see 7:21; 25:31–46). Matthew identifies Jesus as the son of a builder rather than, as in Mark 6:3, a builder himself. Joseph is not mentioned apart from the nativity accounts, and the canon never explains his absence.

### The Death of the Baptist (14:1–12)

Interest in true and false families as well as in Jesus' identity continues in 14:1–12 (cf. Mark 6:14–29; Luke 9:7–9). Herod Antipas suggests that Jesus is not the son of a builder but is John the Baptist raised from the dead. Because John condemned his illegal marriage to Herodias, the wife of his brother Philip (Lev. 18:16; 20:21), Herod imprisoned him. Herodias's daughter (Matthew does not mention Salome by name) dances for Herod's birthday, and he is so pleased

with her performance that he foolishly promises her anything. The ill-fated dance may be contrasted with the wisdom sayings in 11:17, where the children refuse to dance. Further, while the daughter requests and receives the head of the Baptist on a plate, and so is served a perverse meal, the refusal of the children is directly linked to the rejection of the Baptist, who "came neither eating nor drinking" (11:18). As Wisdom is justified by her deeds (the Lukan variant reads "children"), so Herodias, who prompts her daughter's request and who finally receives the head, is condemned by hers. The story indicates the influence women might wield in politics and thus foreshadows the unsuccessful attempt by Pilate's wife to rescue Jesus (27:19). Women's entry into the political sphere is depicted in a generally negative manner: they can pervert what is not necessarily harmful, and they can worsen but not improve what is already bad. This depiction is consistent with Matthew's overall agenda. Service, rather than power exercised over another, is the mark of true discipleship. The entry of women, indeed of anyone, into secular politics cannot for Matthew provide either social or spiritual redemption.

### Feeding and Eating (14:13–15:20; 15:32–38)

The perverse image of John's head on a dish is replaced by the feeding of the five thousand (14:13–21); the meal of horror gives way to the foreshadowing of the messianic banquet. The explicitly noted presence of women and children at the miraculous meals (14:21; cf. 15:38) contrasts with the presence of Herodias and her daughter at Herod's feast. Not included among the five and four thousand men but mentioned "in addition" to them (14:21; 15:38b), the women and children indicate both Matthew's male-centered perspective and the appeal of Jesus' message. Their presence will be evoked in the next chapter, as Jesus performs a miracle not for the Jewish community but for a Gentile woman and her daughter.

References to feeding, women, and children again combine in 15:1–20, the discussion of the oral tradition. Like Jesus, the Pharisees practiced the interpretation of biblical law in order to determine how best to live the life heaven desired. Responding to the Pharisees' complaints against his disciples, Jesus suggests that the leaders are themselves unfaithful. While they are commanded to honor father and mother (Ex. 20:12; Deut. 5:16) and not to speak evil of them (Ex. 21:17; Lev. 20:9), they permit the dedication of property to the Temple and so remove its potential to support fathers (15:5b). The reference to the mother in this verse is not included in many early manuscripts, perhaps in order to create a better parallelism to the mention of the deity.

## The Canaanite Woman (15:21–28)

The roles of parents and children are complicated in the next story, when the ethnic factor is introduced. During his ministry, Jesus limits his mission and message to the house of Israel (see 10:5b–6). Nevertheless, he does come into contact with Gentiles. The episode of the Canaanite woman recalls that of the centurion (8:5–13). These healings—the only two in the Gospel explicitly concerning Gentiles and accomplished from a distance—indicate both that the Gentile supplicants are worthy of Jesus' beneficence and that the Gospel will eventually be extended to all peoples.

Unlike Mark's account (7:24–30), Matthew's does not present Jesus entering Tyre and Sidon; rather, the woman leaves her native land to meet Jesus. Further, she is not identified as a Syro-Phoenician (Mark 7:26) but as a Canaanite. Her presence recalls the original struggle between the Hebrews and the indigenous population of the land. By meeting Jesus both on his own turf and on his own terms, the Canaanite woman acknowledges the priority of the Jews in the divine plan of salvation.

The woman's faith is portrayed in the extended dialogue with Jesus. Whereas Mark's version records no titles, the woman in Matthew's account addresses Jesus as "Son of David" (15:22b; cf. 9:27; 20:30) and thereby recalls the reference to the monarchy in the genealogy, associates herself with the Jewish crowds who later acclaim Jesus (21:9, 15), and distances herself from the leaders who will not (22:41–45). But, Jesus ignores her, and the disciples wish her to be sent away (cf. 10:5b–6; 15:24). The woman overcomes Jesus' reluctance by turning to her advantage his language about taking the children's food and throwing it to the dogs. Instead of taking offense at his identification of her with the dogs, she redirects his comment and again appeals to Jesus as "Lord." The woman asserts her claim and demonstrates her faith not by protesting the insult to her ethnic group but by arguing that both Gentiles (dogs) and Jews (children) are under the same authority.

Her comments are made even more profound by the lack of relational terms identifying her: like other women who approach Jesus, she is not characterized as under the authority or the protection of a husband. The reference to bread in this story recollects the women and children in the two feeding narratives as well as the woman in the parable (13:33). Again, the bread serves as a positive symbol, in contrast to the leaven of the Pharisees and Sadducees. These comparisons confirm Matthew's artistry as well as emphasis on the marginal and the disempowered.

## The Church as a New Family (16:13–20; 18:1–35)

Unique to Matthew among the canonical Gospels is the mention of the grammatically feminine term *ekklesia*, or "church." Punning on the nickname "Peter," which means "rock," Matthew establishes a separate institution apart from the Temple or synagogue which will define Jesus' followers. As the instruction on the church (18:1–35) makes clear, life among these followers is marked by humility, forgiveness, and service. Matthew 18:1–5 presents little children (cf. 11:25; 19:13–15; 21:16) as the ideal members of the new movement. Familial imagery reappears and, again, ideal discipleship is defined by lack of power.

## A Mother's Wish (20:20–28)

All is not harmonious in the *ekklesia*, however, for there is a struggle for supremacy among the disciples. In the parallel passage in Mark 10:35–45 (cf. Luke 22:24–27), James and John request positions of honor for themselves; here Matthew places the request on the lips of their mother. Although this shift improves the brothers' presentation by removing from them such a prideful request, it does offer a negative view of their mother. Further, Jesus repudiates the woman by addressing his response directly to the disciples, and he repudiates her agenda by emphasizing service, not supremacy (20:25–28).

## Palm Sunday (21:1–11)

Jesus' entry into Jerusalem is accompanied by political images such as the allusions to David and other kings, but it also presents subtle feminine images, from the female donkey who carries Jesus to the quotations from Zech. 9:9 and Isa. 62:11 concerning "daughter Zion," which Jesus is said to fulfill. He is a king, but a humble one who comes to the people. The familial language counterbalances the royal acclamation: Jesus' mission is to create a new family of heaven, not an earthly kingdom.

## Tax Collectors and Prostitutes (21:28–32)

Consistent with the Gospel's interest in restoring to full dignity those marginalized or stigmatized by the prevailing social system, Jesus proclaims that members of two despised groups—tax collectors and prostitutes—epitomize the new faithful. Tax collectors, as agents of the occupation government of Rome, were seen as traitors. Prostitution was perceived to be dishonorable at best, sinful at worst (see Lev. 19:29; Deut. 23:17–18; Prov. 2:16–22; 29:3). Yet these individuals heed Jesus' message. Unlike the "chief priests and elders" (21:23) ensconced in the Temple and secure in their status, the tax collectors and prostitutes, who accepted John the Baptist's message (21:32), will be welcomed into the realm of heaven.

## The Woman with Seven Husbands (22:23–33)

Within the city, conflicts with Pharisees fade, and the Sadducees and high priests—both Temple officials—become the antagonists. Amid such controversies as the concern for paying taxes (22:15–22), the question of the great commandment (22:34–40), and the issue of the Christ's identity (22:41–46), Matthew includes the Sadducees' question about levirate marriage at the resurrection (cf. Mark 12:18–27; Luke 20:27–40). Based on Deut. 25:5, levirate marriage (from *levir*, Latin for brother-in-law) states that a childless widow should be married to her husband's brother in order to bear a child who will carry the dead husband's name. The Sadducees' inquiry is not an innocent quest for theological clarification. Since they do not believe in resurrection, the question is designed to trick Jesus into either condoning a woman's having multiple husbands or denying the afterlife. Jesus overcomes the question by explaining its incorrect premise: resurrected individuals are like angels and therefore are not married (22:31–33). Marriage, particularly with its sexual component, is appropriate to this world but not to the resurrected life. Gender roles ("married and given in marriage") define earthly

relationships only. While divorce is not permitted except under specific circumstances, the realm of heaven offers a life beyond marriage. Jesus' comment to the Sadducees may thus be compared to his statement about eunuchs (19:12). Upon the disciples' observation that without a divorce clause marriage may not be expedient, Jesus speaks of those who make themselves eunuchs for the realm of heaven. The language need not be taken literally. Matthew's point may be that individuals of special grace have forsworn sexual relationships in order to devote themselves to spiritual concerns (cf. 1 Cor. 7:5–7).

## Lament for Jerusalem (23:37–39)

Similar to the use of the wisdom metaphor in 11:19, Matt. 23:37 (cf. Luke 13:34) has Jesus compare himself to a mother hen. In the context of the chapter's exaggerated complaints against Pharisaic hypocrisy and elitism, the feminine metaphor of gentleness and concern for children is apt. Moreover, the extended metaphor casts Jesus in the role of public mourner, a role traditionally assigned to women (cf. 28:1), and draws a connection between him and Rachel (Matt. 2:18). Both matriarch and Messiah mourn their doomed children.

## The End of the Age (24:1–51)

Maternal metaphors continue into the fifth discourse. Signs of destruction are described as "birth pangs" (24:8). The reference graphically indicates the inevitability as well as the increasing intensity and pain associated with the end time. Matthew 24:19 (cf. Mark 13:17–18; Luke 21:23) specifically concerns the problems faced by pregnant women and nursing mothers: not only will they too undergo the tribulation in fleeing and finding refuge; they will have the added physical burdens unique to women. That women are included as equals in all facets of the end time is further noted in the Q saying, "Then two men will be in the field; one is taken and one is left. Two women will be grinding at the mill; one is taken and one is left" (24:40–41 RSV; cf. Luke 17:34–35). The parallel placement of the women at the mill and the men in the field suggests both that those in Matthew's community will continue their normal pursuits as they wait for the end of the age and that the sexual division of labor also will continue. Salvation is granted equally to men and women, but membership in Matthew's church does not eliminate traditional gender roles.

## Judgment and Salvation: The Ten Virgins (25:1–13)

Unique to Matthew, the parable of the ten "bridesmaids" (NRSV; literally, "virgins") continues the Gospel's concern for women at the final judgment (cf. 24:19, 41). Here the focus is not on mothers but on "virgins" (probably referring to young women of marriageable age). Because we know little about first-century wedding customs, the virgins' role is unclear. The women may be wedding guests or, more likely, servants waiting for the groom to return to his home. This latter interpretation draws a connection to the immediately preceding parable of the good servant (Matt. 24:45–51) and so retains the evangelist's interest in paralleling stories about men and women. In either case, evident is the insistence that women bear responsibility for their own salvation. Indeed, as unmarried persons, these women are not distracted by family interests and so perhaps can more easily recognize their religious responsibilities.

Other characteristics of the parable pose particular problems regarding women's roles. First, the bride herself is absent in the better early manuscripts. Second, the women lack solidarity: those with oil refuse to help those without. However, the reluctance of the wise young women is explainable. Were they to share their oil, there would be no light for anyone. The third problem is that the women all fall asleep (25:5), an act that is condemned implicitly in 25:13 (cf. 26:40–41, 43, 45). Finally, this is the only parable in the Gospel in which the evangelist provides a judgment of the characters; only the women are described as either wise or foolish.

Although misogynistic implications may exist in the parable, Matthew ultimately depicts the women in a positive manner. The parable is consistent with the major Matthean themes of doing one's own good works, dedicating one's life to Jesus, and being prepared for the end time. Because the women are to light the way for the bridegroom, they fulfill both the demand for service and the command that their light should "shine before others, so that they may see your good works" (5:16). The good works, specifically mentioned in 25:31–46, consist of service to the poor, the imprisoned, the hungry. Jesus identifies himself with such people, and to serve them means to serve him and so perform the will of heaven. Both men and women are exhorted to do these things, and both bear the responsibility for complying.

## The Passion Narrative (26:1–27:66)

Paralleling Mark 14:3–9 and John 12:1–8, Matt. 26:6–13 (cf. Luke 7:36–50) describes the anointing of Jesus prior to his death. The action has a twofold meaning: Jesus equates it with the rituals that accompany burial (26:12) and so acknowledges women's traditional role. But anointing the head is also a sign of a royal commission, and thus the woman is cast here in the untraditional position of priest and/or prophet. Like the other evangelists, Matthew emphasizes the costliness of the ointment. The economic notice is consistent with the identification of Joseph of Arimathea as a "rich man" (27:57) and the beatitude about the "poor in spirit" (5:3) rather than simply the poor (cf. Luke 6:20b). The rich are welcome in the church, as long as their money is appropriately used (i.e., in service to others). As in Mark, the Matthean Jesus proclaims that the woman's prophetic action will be preached universally. As in Mark as well, her name is never recorded and her presence in the house of the leper is unexplained.

The disciples' complaint that she has wasted the funds that might have been given to the poor contrasts the woman's true understanding of Jesus' fate with their focus on earthly—albeit important—matters. The disciples' lack of true understanding continues throughout the passion narrative, where it is juxtaposed with the various depictions of women as aware, sympathetic, and loyal.

This service at the leper's house may be contrasted with the following scene of the Last Supper (26:17–29). As the woman prepared Jesus for burial in a meal setting, Jesus now has to prepare his disciples for his departure. Both scenes also recount the unexpected: the woman's funds aid Jesus rather than the poor, and Jesus is betrayed by a disciple. Absent from the Last Supper and from Gethsemane, women continue to function as foils for the disciples. While Jesus is tried by the high priest, Peter denies him in the courtyard. On two of three occasions, these denials are prompted by women who recognize Peter as one of the disciples; the third accusation is made because of Peter's Galilean accent (26:69–75). The women of Jerusalem thus appear to have direct familiarity with Jesus and his followers. The fidelity and awareness of women continue into the trial before Pilate. Only Matthew (27:19) presents the governor's wife as interceding on Jesus' behalf during the trial. Like Joseph and the magi, she has been warned in a dream that Jesus is righteous (a favorite Matthean term).

The many women at the cross and burial (27:55–61; cf. Mark 15:40–47; Luke 23:49–56; John 19:25b–27) confirm the contrast with the fallible apostles. Like Peter's mother-in-law, they act as disciples ("followers") offering service (*diakonia,* 27:55) to Jesus. Sitting opposite the grave, they hold a vigil rather than, as in Mark, merely observe the place of burial. They may also be contrasted with the guards, who are bribed to say that they slept while the disciples stole the body. Just as women mediate both a man's entry into this world by giving birth and, in many traditions, his exit by participating in funerary rites, women frame the life of Jesus: they are present in his genealogy and the story of his birth, and they are the primary witnesses to his death and resurrection.

## Easter Witnesses (28:1–10)

Seeing the earthquake and the angel, the guards are struck senseless. But the women, guided by the angel, who, like Jesus, understands their fear, continue to act faithfully. They witness the empty tomb, and they follow precisely the instructions to report quickly the news of the resurrection. Although they are not included in the reference to "his disciples" (28:7) or mentioned as present at the Great Commission (28:16–20), the angel's words (28:7) and the

meeting with Jesus (28:9–10) indicate their substantive role in the Easter mission. Indeed, it is Jesus who first greets them, and they in turn are the first to worship him. Matthew records of the Eleven that "some doubted" (28:17), but of the women only their legitimate fear and their joy are reported. These independent, motivated women are both the first witnesses to the resurrection and the first missionaries of the church.

## BIBLIOGRAPHY

Anderson, Janice Capel. "Matthew: Gender and Reading." *Semeia* 28 (1983), 3–27.

Gundry, Robert H. *Matthew: A Commentary on His Literary and Theological Art.* Grand Rapids: Wm. B. Eerdmans Publishing Co., 1982.

Kingsbury, Jack Dean. *Matthew.* Proclamation Commentaries. Rev. ed. Philadelphia: Fortress Press, 1986.

Levine, Amy-Jill. *The Social and Ethnic Dimensions of Matthean Salvation History.* Lewiston, N.Y.: Edwin Mellen Press, 1988.

Meier, John P. *The Vision of Matthew: Christ, Church, and Morality in the Gospel of Matthew.* Theological Inquiries. New York: Paulist Press, 1979.

Schweizer, Eduard. *The Good News According to Matthew.* Atlanta: John Knox Press, 1975.

Senior, Donald. *What Are They Saying about Matthew?* Ramsey, N.J.: Paulist Press, 1983.

# MARK

## Mary Ann Tolbert

❦

## Introduction

The Gospel of Mark, perhaps the earliest of the four canonical Gospels, has received little attention through most of Christian history. Some of that lack of interest may be attributed to the view of Augustine, a fourth-century theologian, that Mark was an abbreviation of the Gospel of Matthew (a view still held by a few modern writers). It is undoubtedly also the result of the strange story the Gospel relates: a secretive Messiah chooses twelve disciples who in the end betray, flee, and deny him; he preaches a message of service, sacrifice, and humility that even his own disciples never seem to understand; he is put to death by Roman officials who are apparently forced into this action by envious Jewish religious leaders; and his resurrection is announced to women followers at an empty tomb who respond by saying "nothing to anyone, for they were afraid" (Mark 16:8). Indeed, this conclusion to Mark's "good news" about Jesus Christ (Mark 1:1) has been so unacceptable to many Christians that they added several alternative endings to a number of the ancient manuscript copies of the Gospel text. While contemporary scholarship almost universally judges the original Gospel narrative to have ended at Mark 16:8, some old manuscripts contain twelve more verses (16:9– 20), a few add one extra verse, and others combine, with variations, both of these two additions.

Nevertheless, the central role of women in this final episode of the Gospel has raised the question of the importance of women throughout the narrative. In harmony with all of the canonical Gospels, Mark's women characters are not included among Jesus' twelve specially designated disciples (3:13–19). However, Mark's presentation of the disciples' blatant failure to understand Jesus' message (see, e.g., 6:51–52; 7:17–18; 8:14–21, 32–33; 9:31–32; 10:13–14) coupled with their dismal performance during

Jesus' time of need in Gethsemane (14:32–50) makes Mark's twelve into a considerably less admirable group than is the case in the other three New Testament Gospels, all of which strive with mixed success to rehabilitate the disciples' image, at least after the resurrection. Indeed, in Mark the only faithful group of followers to be found at the cross and the tomb are women, who, though identified as followers and ministers since Jesus' early days in Galilee, only enter the story actively as a group at the cross after the downfall of the male disciples (15:40).

Moreover, these faithful women at the cross continue a predominant Markan pattern, for with the exception of Herodias and her daughter (6:17–28) and possibly Jesus' mother (3:31–34), all the women characters in Mark are depicted positively, as persons who either come to Jesus in faith for healing (5:21–34; 7:24–30), perform loving acts for him (14:3–9), stand as examples of piety to be emulated (12:41–44), or speak the truth when a disciple does not (14:66–69). This almost universally positive portrayal stands in striking contrast to the dominantly negative portrait of the twelve male disciples in Mark. It forms the basis for the claims of many feminist scholars that the Christian community reflected by Mark's Gospel must have contained strong women leaders and role models, since the Gospel itself so clearly uses women characters in such a fashion. To set the context for studying these women in Mark, it is necessary to look at the ancient world that nurtured and produced the author and first audiences of the Gospel.

### The Greco-Roman World of the Gospel of Mark

To understand the Gospel of Mark, one must recognize that it comes from a historically ancient and culturally distant world. Its original audience was Greek-speaking and probably mostly illiterate. Literacy was uncommon among members of the middle and lower strata of ancient society, from whom most of the early Christians came. Literary works generally had to be read aloud by the few who were educated in order for the greater masses to hear them (see Col. 4:16; 1 Thess. 5:27; Rev. 1:3). The pervasiveness of illiteracy meant that texts intended for general audiences, like the Gospel of Mark or for that matter any of the New Testament documents, had to be written primarily for the ear to hear rather than for the eye to read. In order for understanding to be achieved, the ear needs to hear important points more than once. This means that repetition is one of the major features of ancient texts. In addition, ancient authors needed to provide listening helps for their audiences, like summaries, key words, foreshadowing, plot synopses, prologues, and epilogues. Since these techniques are rare in modern literature, modern readers of ancient texts may miss these listener-oriented guidelines and consequently miss some of the points that an ancient audience would have heard.

The author of this strange Gospel is unknown, although church tradition has associated the Gospel with a follower of Peter in Rome named Mark. Given the very negative portrayal of Peter in the text, this association seems unlikely. Since literacy among women had risen slightly during the period when the Gospel was written, it is not impossible that the author was female. Whoever the author was, he or she wrote in a very plain and unpolished Greek style, explaining all Hebrew or Aramaic words and many Jewish customs (e.g., 7:3–4; 12:18). This might indicate that the text was intended for a middle- or lower-class audience from an area fairly far removed from Palestine, though this cannot be proved.

Like most of the early Christians, Mark's audience probably lived in the large, multinational urban areas around the Mediterranean basin. While the exact place of composition of Mark is also unknown, church tradition has associated the Gospel with Rome or, less often, with Egypt. These urban centers of cultural exchange and mixing were fertile ground for the new mystery and salvationist religions (like Christianity), and just about any of these cities may have been the home of the author. Most of the people who flocked to these cities in the latter part of the first century C.E., when Mark's Gospel was probably written (between 60 C.E. and 75 C.E.), were looking for the improved

financial and social situation that urban living promised. However, in separating from their native traditions, lands, and family kinship groups, they often found instead social alienation, disease (resulting from crowded living conditions and poor sanitation), and famine (because the Romans never succeeded in supplying large urban areas with sufficient food). Mark's depiction of Jesus as one who calls into existence a new family, based not on blood relations but on doing the will of God (3:33–35), as well as his emphasis on Jesus' abilities as a healer of diseases and a multiplier of bread and fish (6:35–44; 8:1–10), would obviously have struck resonant chords in such people.

These social ills afflicted all the inhabitants of the urban areas in which Christianity flourished, but women in first-century Greco-Roman society occupied social roles distinct from those of men. What little is known about the way women's social roles were defined in the ancient world suggests that proper behavior for women was almost the direct opposite of proper behavior for men. Male honor depended, in public, on winning contests of wit, strength, or rhetoric among male peers and, in private, on asserting authority over women of their class and over men and women of lower status. For women, winning honor was virtually impossible, and any public display was strongly discouraged; they could, however, avoid shame by submitting to the authority of male superiors. Of course, gender is never alone as a social factor, for class, race, economic standing, and so on, are always part of the picture—then as now. Ancient women of the Roman aristocracy had significantly greater power than male slaves, though male slaves may have had greater power than female slaves (if slaves could be properly said to have "power" at all in ancient times). Especially in ancient Mediterranean society, class played a major role in defining one's status in the cultural hierarchy, and a woman's class was determined by that of her father, husband, or other close male relative. In light of this, Mark's depiction of unaccompanied women, frequently unidentified by any male relation, coming to Jesus and speaking with him in private (7:24–30; 14:3–9) and even more shockingly in public (5:25–34) is important. Women ignored the social rules of modesty only if they were already among the "shamed" (e.g., slaves, freed slaves, prostitutes, actresses) or were willing to be viewed that way. By such stories the author may have either challenged some of the restrictive cultural rules defining proper female behavior or possibly indicated the "outcast" status of some of the women attracted to Christianity. What kind of story was the author of Mark trying to present by such challenges to the social status quo or such depictions of those attracted to Christianity? What was this "good news" all about and to whom was it directed?

## Hearing the Gospel Story of Mark

Since the Gospel of Mark is a literary presentation, a story, of the life of Jesus from his baptism through his death to his empty tomb, the primary sources for understanding it must come from what remains of the literary production of ancient society. Unfortunately, what remains is very little indeed! Most of the writings produced by ancient Mediterranean cultures did not survive the manuscript transmission process developed during the Middle Ages. Hence, the texts still in existence today from the Greco-Roman world are only a tiny remnant of a much larger body of material actually produced and now lost forever. This loss has proved especially problematic for the interpretation of the New Testament Gospels because no exact parallel to them is to be found in the limited material still in existence.

Nevertheless, by recognizing the *popular* nature of the New Testament writings—by recognizing, in other words, that they were written in the "common" language of commerce and trade for widespread audiences from the broad middle strata of ancient society—some help can be drawn from other writings sharing a similar *popular* heritage. Examples of one other popular literary type have survived into the modern world: the ancient novel. While Mark is clearly not itself an ancient novel, it may share with that genre some of the stylistic devices and literary conventions that are common to ancient popular literature generally. (1) The novels are filled with anticipations, repetitions, and recapitulations of material, so that the audience is never in suspense about what is to happen. (2) Characters in the novels are fashioned as "types" who illustrate concepts or ethical principles rather than as the realistic figures such as are found in modern writings. (3) The novels end with extended recognition sequences in which the fundamental nature of all the characters is revealed and all the important persons and issues are identified. These stylistic conventions make sense of the many repetitions in the Gospel of Mark, the unchanging nature of its characterization of many groups from the

disciples to the Jerusalem religious leaders, the late placement of Jesus' self-revelation concerning his identity in the trial narrative (14:61–62), and the Roman centurion's confession of him as "son of God" at the crucifixion (15:39).

In ancient drama the audience was often given a summary of the plot of the play before the action itself began so that everyone would know what was coming, including how it was all to end. The ancient popular novel accomplished the same task by means of dreams and oracles that outlined or prefigured the plot or even by means of the author's direct interruption into it. Since ancient audiences were mostly *hearing* the material, they needed to be constantly oriented to what was taking place. While the Gospel of Mark does not have dreams or oracles, it does contain two long parables, the sower (4:3–9) and the wicked tenants (12:1–12), which appear to perform the same orienting function for the hearers of the Gospel story. In the parable of the sower, Jesus tells of the response of four types of ground to the seed sown in it, and he then follows the parable itself with an allegorical explanation. In the explanation (4:14–20) the seed is identified as the "word," and the various types of ground are groups of people with quite varying responses to hearing this word. One group, the hard ground of the path, never hear the word, because Satan removes it from them. A second group, the rocky ground, initially hear the word with joy but when persecutions arise on account of the word, they all fall away. A third group, the thorny ground, have the word choked out by riches and the cares of the world. Finally, a fourth group, the good ground, hear the word and bear abundant fruit.

In looking at the Gospel of Mark as a whole, one recognizes that Jesus is the preacher of the word of God and all the people and groups who hear him respond to the word he preaches in one of the four ways the parable describes. Thus the parable of the sower, repeated twice in Mark 4 for emphasis and taught in an easily memorable form, provided an ancient audience with the four categories of response they needed to know in order to understand what was happening between Jesus and his hearers throughout the Gospel. For example, the scribes, Pharisees, and Jerusalem religious leaders never really hear Jesus' message but instead call him a blasphemer from the first time they hear him (2:7) until their final condemnation of him (14:64); they respond as the hard ground of the path. The twelve disciples, especially as represented by

Peter (whose name in Greek means "rock"), James, and John, initially react positively and immediately to Jesus' call to them (1:16–20), but when persecutors come to arrest Jesus they all flee (14:43–50), and Peter eventually denies Jesus three times (14:66–72); they respond as the rocky ground. Herod, who hears John the Baptist gladly but has him beheaded rather than violate an oath made before guests (6:14–29); Pilate, who knew Jesus was innocent but ordered him crucified because he wanted to please the crowds (15:6–15); and the rich man who had obeyed all the commandments but could not bring himself to sell his many possessions to follow Jesus (10:17–22), all glimpse the truth but in the end refuse to act on it because concerns about reputation, worldly power, or wealth stand in the way; they respond as the thorny ground. Finally, there are many within the Gospel story who, mostly anonymously, come to Jesus in faith, are healed (or saved) by that faith, and often then go out to preach to others (e.g., 1:40–45; 2:1–12; 5:1–20; 5:25–34; 7:25–30; 9:14–29; 10:46–52); these anonymous ones illustrate the fertile ground which bears abundant fruit. It is to this final group that most of the women characters in the Gospel belong. Their anonymity, courage, generosity, and ministry, as well as their concrete healing, witness to their position among the fruitful elect of God's kingdom.

But the parable of the sower aided an ancient audience in following only part of the story of the Gospel of Mark, the interactions between Jesus and those he met. Why Jesus had been sent out by God in the first place, why he was killed, and what response God would make to that act of murder is summarized for the audience in the second long parable in the Gospel, the parable of the wicked tenants (12:1–12). That parable tells the story of a person who lovingly created a vineyard and then went away, renting it out to tenants. When the rent came due, the tenants refused to return to the owner what was required. After sending several servants, whom the tenants treated violently or killed, to request the fruit, the owner decided to send his last emissary, his own beloved son, thinking that the tenants would respect the son and obey him. However, when the tenants realized that they were meeting the only son, they seized him and killed him, hoping to make the vineyard fully theirs. After such a hideously wicked act, the only course open to the owner of the vineyard was to come and destroy the present tenants and install others, faithful ones, in their place. For an ancient and even for a modern audience, the import of the parable is clear, especially given the connection in Mark 12:12 of the wicked tenants with the Jerusalem religious leaders. The parable relates allegorically the story of God's dealings with the world that God had lovingly created and then given into the care of human tenants, who decided to violate the terms of their contract. All the prophets and messengers God had sent to call the people to repentance and obedience had been treated violently or killed. Finally, as a last loving chance for these evil tenants, God sent the beloved son, hoping that they would revere him. But in absolute confirmation of their implacable wickedness, they murder the son instead. With their terrible viciousness proved beyond doubt, all God can now do is destroy them.

For the Gospel of Mark and the early Christians who heard it, the crucifixion of Jesus stood as the crowning atrocity that sealed the fate of those in political and religious authority. In response to their murder of Jesus, God would now destroy this present human world and install a new order. This belief that the present world is about to end is called *apocalyptic*. The Gospel of Mark is permeated with apocalyptic thought. Although Jesus and all of his followers can expect only persecutions, crosses to bear, and suffering under this present order because of the perversity of those holding power and authority, the good news is that this present order is about to end and a new world is about to come into being. In the Gospel of Mark, Jesus' call to his followers to accept suffering is based on the conviction that the time for such suffering is extremely short. Bearing up under suffering and pain for years is not what is intended, for that would be a masochistic message far removed from Mark's view of God's fruitful kingdom. However, in the brief time remaining for this present evil world, those who would follow Jesus must be willing to risk their lives, security, possessions, reputation, and hopes for human glory. These requirements explain the inability of many people who hear Jesus' message—including his own disciples—to be fruitful (after all, three of the four possible responses to the word end in failure). Most people faced with these alternatives respond with fear, either for their lives or for their prerogatives of power and status. Only those who have nothing to lose or do not count it as a loss, who lack desires for fame, glory, status, wealth, power, and authority, are likely to respond with joy and faith to the "good news" that Jesus preaches. But for them the word brings release from illness and demons now and the hope of eternal life in the future. With this overview of the story of the Gospel of Mark in mind, the various roles women characters fulfill in the narrative may become more understandable and distinct.

## Comment

### Women Among the Healed

Most of the individual women depicted in the Gospel qualify by their actions as examples of the fourth type of response to the word, the good ground that bears the fruits of faith. For Mark, one of the clearest indications of this fruitfulness is healing, which stands as a concrete manifestation of the restored wholeness of the individual. In the ancient world, illness and disfigurement were most often thought to be visited upon people by evil or demonic spirits, who inhabited all corners of the human world. Jesus' power over such beings is absolute and unchallenged in Mark. Far more than a demonstration of Jesus' abilities, for Mark healings also often involve the prerequisite of faith on the part of the one seeking healing. As Jesus says several times (5:34; 10:52), their faith makes them well, and their "wellness" is a manifestation of God's kingdom, the way human beings were intended to be by the loving God who created the vineyard.

***The woman who ministers to Jesus (1:29–34).*** The first woman to appear in the Gospel of Mark becomes the second person Jesus heals as he begins his ministry in Galilee. She is identified by the name of a male kinsman, a proper social convention for the period, and her domain is the house of two of Jesus' new disciples, Simon and Andrew. Women of honorable families were often encouraged or even required to remain in the private realm of the house to protect their modesty (i.e., to restrict their potential contact with males outside the family unit or "shameful" females) and thus their husband's or male kinsman's reputation. Given the later expressions of the disciples' valuing of reputation (9:34) and glory (10:35–37), it is fascinating to recognize that the initial description of Simon's house and Simon's mother-in-law conforms to the code of male honor. Indeed, the male family members intercede with Jesus on behalf of the sick woman, again a proper social convention. But at this point conventional behavior ceases, for Jesus, a male outsider to the family, goes to the sick woman and touches her, and the fever flees

from her. Moreover, she responds to this irregular action by *ministering* to them all. Some English versions translate the verb designating her action as "serve," which is acceptable as long as the same translation has been used for this word in its first appearance in the story in Mark 1:13, but some of those translations render the first occurrence as "the angels *ministered* to him." Translating the same Greek word as "minister" when angels are the subject but "serve" when a woman is the subject downplays her action. The author of Mark, by using the same word for the action of angels and the action of the healed woman, obviously equated their level of service to Jesus. What the angels were able to do for Jesus in the wilderness, the woman whose fever has fled now does for him in her home. In addition, that evening after the Sabbath is over, the door of her house becomes the threshold for healing for all in the city who are sick. While faith is not mentioned as an element in her healing, her response to what has happened to her indicates her fruitfulness.

***The woman in the crowd (5:24b–43).*** If the healing of Simon's mother-in-law begins in a staunchly conventional tone, the next healing story involving a woman is anything but conventional at its outset. The episode is set in public, on the way from the sea of Galilee to Jairus's home, where his little daughter lies near death. Jesus is surrounded by a large crowd of people, pressing against him as he walks. That a woman, who at least at one time had some wealth (5:26), should be in such a public place evidently unaccompanied by protectors and that she should dare to touch a strange man without his consent are extraordinary events in an ancient cultural context. Either the degree of her desperation or, as Mark has Jesus say, the depth of her faith makes such unheard-of actions possible.

Unlike Simon's mother-in-law, this woman is not identified by male kin, making her status uncertain. She has had money, which suggests a higher status, but she has now had to spend it all on useless physicians. They caused her to undergo much suffering while making her condition, a constant hemorrhaging, worse rather than better—a situation with which most women, whether ancient or modern, can probably sympathize. In a Jewish context, her bleeding placed her in a state of perpetual cultic impurity (see Lev. 15:25–30) that would not only have prevented her from participating in cultic activities but would also have infected anyone who touched her, lay on a bed in which she had slept, or sat on a chair she had vacated. It may be that this twelve-year curse of impurity, besides having drained her finances, had also isolated her socially from friends and kin. In a Greco-Roman social context, her appearance in public without companions may have indicated a "shamed" status, but the only explanation given by the Gospel is her disease. Her illness, then, has placed her outside the religious community and perhaps also outside the honorable human community.

Moreover, her healing occurs completely at her own initiative: she has heard reports about Jesus and says to herself that if she can only touch his garment, she will be healed. Of course, given her unclean condition, her touch would also transfer her impurity to Jesus. Her action would thus be doubly audacious, a violation of social codes for proper female behavior *and* a violation of religious law. Jesus takes no active part whatsoever in her healing, confirming the truth of his later statement that *her faith* has made her well. The moment she touches him, her bleeding stops and she feels in her body that she is whole. Only after this main action of the episode is concluded does Jesus cease his passive role in the story; he perceives that something in his body has changed as well and asks the crowd who touched him. The disciples' query to him about the futility of such a question in the midst of a pressing crowd is noteworthy, because it indicates that the woman's touch was one of faith, an action distinctly different from the jostling of the crowd.

In contrast to her earlier boldness, she comes forward at Jesus' word, falling at his feet "in fear and trembling," to confess her act. The shift from audacity to timidity in her behavior begs for an explanation. Her earlier "shameful" boldness in approaching Jesus was acceptable from one who was already banished from honorable society; but with her healing she may be reinstated in the religious and social community. Consequently, her timorous deference reflects her renewed conventional status as a woman in the male world of honor and shame. Jesus confirms her reincorporation by providing her with what she lacked at the open-

ing of the episode, kinship with a male: "*Daughter*, your faith has made you well" (5:34). Jesus now becomes her kinsman, and her subordinate behavior signals her return to reputable society. Although Jesus has indicated that he is fashioning a new family order, one based not on blood ties but on doing the will of God (3:31–35), evidently even in this family some of the conventional subordinate roles of women in relation to dominant males may still adhere.

The story of the woman in the crowd is placed in the midst of another story, the healing of Jairus's little daughter (5:21–24a, 35–43), and the placement may be especially significant in light of the conclusion of the woman's episode. Jairus comes to Jesus as a concerned father of high social standing in the Jewish community to intercede in behalf of his "little *daughter*," who is close to death. Jairus is an excellent example of the responsibility of dominant males to protect and care for the women of their household, in this case a daughter, in the public realm outside the home. Jesus' address to the woman as "daughter" after she is healed invokes the same cultural convention: the woman is now under the protection of a new "father," Jesus, who has the power to heal her and to intercede for her in the public realm. Her twelve years of illness constituted a social death in which she was barred from community and kin, a situation not all that removed from the actual death of the twelve-year-old daughter of Jairus, whom Jesus was also able to revive and reincorporate into the human and family circle (5:41–43).

### The foreign woman and her daughter (7:24–30).

Whereas the woman in the crowd was separated from her religious and kinship community by her illness and the impurity it caused, the woman in Mark 7 is an outsider because of her nationality and her religious beliefs. She is "a Syrophoenician by birth," meaning a Phoenician from Syria. Jesus, trying unsuccessfully to find privacy from the pressing crowds, is traveling through the region of Tyre (7:24) in Phoenicia just north of Upper Galilee, then a predominantly Jewish area. This woman was born even farther north in Syria, and she is clearly identified as a Gentile or a "Greek" (probably more a religious label than a racial one). Beyond these national and religious affiliations, this woman is given no other markers of status: no male kinsman or economic level is mentioned. The only other thing the audience is told about the woman is that she is the mother of a demon-possessed daughter.

She approaches Jesus in a house, the customary setting for reputable women, because she has heard about him. She falls at his feet (the very same deferential position adopted by the woman in the crowd after her healing) and begs Jesus to drive the evil spirit from her daughter. Like Jairus, who also bowed down before Jesus to make his request, she is interceding in behalf of her child, not herself; but unlike Jairus, she is not a Jewish male of high status who can speak openly to Jesus in public. Moreover, Jesus' response to her is strikingly different from his response to Jairus, whom he had willingly joined at once to go to the sick child. To this foreign woman, Jesus expresses his refusal to accede to her request in a disdainful metaphor, which compares her and her daughter to little dogs who are not to be fed the children's bread.

Since Jesus has already healed a foreigner, the demoniac from the Decapolis (5:1–20), the woman's nationality and religious affiliation alone are insufficient to explain his negative response or the disparagement with which it is delivered. While her nationality, religion, and gender distinguish her from Jairus, only her gender differentiates her from the demoniac. Although she behaves with due deference in a private setting, her very action, daring to approach a strange man in behalf of her family, was an unconventional and, evidently to Jesus, unacceptable act. The protection and care of an honorable family were the responsibility of the father or other senior male relative (see 1:29–34; 5:21–24a, 33–34, 35–43; 9:14–27). Consequently, even though the foreign woman's setting and posture were conventional, the request itself—coming from a woman—was shameful, drawing both Jesus' refusal and his disdain.

However, the story does not end here. The woman compounds her shameful behavior by boldly, and successfully as it turns out, contesting Jesus' metaphor. Indeed, she is the *only* character in the entire Gospel of Mark to best Jesus in an argument. Although a Gentile, she prefaces her response with a very pious and exalted title of address to Jesus, "Yes, Lord," and continues on to stand his metaphor on its head, but "even the dogs under the table eat the children's crumbs." Acknowledging her clever and daring retort, Jesus tells her that her original request has been granted and the demon has left her daughter, which upon her arrival home she discovers to be true.

Her unconventional behavior, which initially draws the dominant male's wrath, by its increasing boldness, cleverness, and basic moral correctness eventually subverts that wrath into agreement. Jesus has already taught others that religious customs should not stand in the way of doing good for those in need (see 2:23–28; 3:1–6). Now *he* must be taught that social conventions should not do so either. Furthermore, an ancient audience may have heard in Jesus' metaphor and the woman's revision of it an additional element that English translations hide. Jesus calls the woman and her daughter "little dogs" (*kynaria*, the diminutive of *kyon*, "dog"). In the fourth century B.C.E. a philosophical movement associated with Diogenes Sinope began in Greece that was highly critical of current social and cultural conventions and political institutions. Adherents of the movement not only brashly criticized and satirized established social customs, but some of them also chose to shun all conventions in their style of living and behaving. Because of their aggressive, rude, and sometimes shameless behavior, they were called *kynes*, "dogs," a name they adopted to describe their philosophical movement—in English the "Cynics." The foreign woman's unconventional behavior and its challenge to customary social roles that stand in the way of helping those in need make her description as a "cynic" (or in this case a "little cynic") quite appropriate.

## Women as Examples of Faithful Acts

Besides demonstrating by their healings their affiliation with the fruitful ground of the parable, women characters in the Gospel of Mark also function as examples of correct forms of cultic practice and exemplary actions, which Jesus recommends to the disciples. Like the healed women, these women are anonymous figures who act out of love or devotion with no underlying craving for fame, reputation, or honor.

***The poor widow's offering (12:41–44).*** On a long day of controversies and teachings in the Temple, just before telling his disciples about the signs of the coming end of the world, Jesus watches a poor widow throw two coins into the Temple treasury. Widows need not be poor, as this one was (and some wealthy widows might have been very influential members of early Christian communities); however, their status was often tentative, because their husbands, their major source of protection and identity, were dead. While sons, other male relatives, or family wealth could provide some measure of security, widows were traditionally considered subjects of special moral concern because of their generally defenseless legal and financial position. In the scene immediately preceding this one, Jesus condemns the scribes for, among other things, consuming the homes of widows (12:40), which probably refers to the practice of appointing some supposedly well-reputed and pious man to oversee the affairs of a widow, only to have the individual use the estate for his own gain.

The widow who comes to the treasury, then, is not only disadvantaged by poverty but also by her vulnerable status, which makes her almost invisible in the legal, religious, political, and social eyes of her society. Jesus had been watching many rich people put in large sums of money, when he observed the widow throw in the tiny amount of a "penny." However, to his disciples he asserts that the widow's offering is greater than any of the others because she has given all that she has, "her whole living." Besides indicating that what matters to God is the nature of the act of giving itself rather than the gross amount given, Jesus' saying also underlines the ultimate or total nature of the financial sacrifice made by the widow. For one whose only protection from complete destitution is the little money she possesses, to give *all* of it to the Temple is to consign herself to disaster; yet this she does without fanfare or desire for glory, but out of faith. Such indifference to conventional human desires for security, wealth, and status stand as a very appropriate introduction to Jesus' teaching on the coming end of the world, for at that time faith in God and not faith in human wealth and status will establish one's membership in the saved elect of the coming kingdom.

### The woman who anoints Jesus (14:3–9).
Immediately preceding Jesus' teaching concerning the end of the world, the story of the widow's offering presents an example of the radical quality of giving required for proper religious practice in the short time remaining before the end. Immediately following his teaching, another anonymous woman's act of extravagant regard for Jesus stands as an example of loving compassion to one in need wherever the gospel is to be preached. The woman comes up to Jesus as he is eating a meal in the home of Simon the leper at Bethany and breaks a flask of expensive, aromatic ointment and pours the ointment over his head. She is not provided with any kinship or other status identification; all that is known about her is that she has the resources to purchase very expensive

perfume. Although evidently not a guest herself, her presence at the meal occasions no surprise from those eating. They are upset at the "wastefulness" of her act, not at her being there, even though meals with male guests were not customarily attended by women, except those serving the meal or entertaining the guests. This anonymous woman may have functioned in either of those capacities. It may have been the practice occasionally to hire or invite local prostitutes for the pleasure of male guests, but there is no indication in Mark's story that this woman was of that profession. Nevertheless, the whole setting of this story is odd, for while Jesus is often described in the Gospel of Mark as staying in someone's house, only rarely is the host identified. In this case, the host is Simon *the leper*. Lepers were, for obvious reasons, social outcasts, contact with whom brought ritual impurity as well as the danger of contagion. To share a meal with a leper in his home was certainly an unusual situation. Most commentators assume that Simon's leprosy has been cured, although the text does not say so. Some of the indignation the woman's act incites may derive from the understandable feelings of a family that had itself experienced great distress expressing concern for others in the world who are poor and in need. Whether Simon is cured or not, Jesus is clearly violating conventional social standards by eating there, but he is also obeying his own rule that the sick and not the whole are those in need of the physician's presence (2:17).

The woman never speaks in the story, though Jesus and the other guests speak to and about her. The reasons for her actions are interpreted only through Jesus' words. The act of anointing the head with oil was a widespread rite in the ancient Near East signifying selection for some special role or task. Kings were often anointed with oil as part of their coronation ceremony; prophets also sometimes employed the rite. Indeed, the Greek word *christos*, "Christ" is a translation of the Hebrew word for "Messiah," which means "the anointed one." Hence the woman's action could be taken as a symbolic announcement of Jesus' status as the Christ. Having an anonymous servant woman "crown" the Messiah would fit very well with Jesus' continuing teaching in Mark about the first being last and the last first, or the leader of all needing to be the slave of all. However, Jesus does not interpret her action explicitly in this manner; instead, he says that she is anointing his "body beforehand for burying." Jesus as the anointed one is Jesus as the crucified one for Mark: the special role Jesus is to fill is one that leads inevitably to death. This woman is treating his living body to the gentle ministrations and loving care his dead corpse will never receive, and he is grateful.

But what of the objection that such an act is wasteful? Surely the poor are in desperate need, and the money used for the oil, almost a year's wages for most workers, could have mitigated some real suffering in the world. Are Jesus' words about the poor always being available, while he will not be, a rather easy dismissal of the legitimate complaint of others at the table? Perhaps not, for what Jesus suggests here is that helping the poor is a constant requirement of the moral life, but it does not substitute for personal acts of love for individuals in particular need—nor vice versa. To give money to benefit the poor but to refuse to comfort and assist the one right beside you is as wrong as ignoring the agony of the poor of the world in order to concentrate on personal concerns. *Both* public acts of almsgiving *and* private acts of sympathy and compassion are part of the religious life—neither one substitutes for the other—and one should not be harassed for doing either. The irony of arguing about which kinds of loving use of money are the most moral or "right" is underscored by the passage immediately following this story, in which Judas, a male disciple of Jesus, is promised money to betray his teacher to the chief priests (14:10–11). Using money to purchase evil is so dominant in this corrupt world that exchanging money for good in whatever way one can should always be valued and remembered, and thus this anonymous woman's lavishly loving act, says Jesus, will be told across the world "in memory of her." Of course, Judas's act will also be told across the world, but the memory it will evoke will be a very different one, for it would have been better for that man had he not been born (14:21).

## Women Depicted in a Negative Light

Although most of the women portrayed in the Gospel of Mark are illustrations of the good ground that bears much fruit, there are a couple of interesting exceptions: Jesus' mother Mary and family, who are associated with mildly negative situations, and Herodias and her daughter, who are implicated in a profoundly wicked plot. Since these characters are exceptions to the general pattern, looking at their stories may help to clarify the overall themes Mark is developing.

*Jesus' mother Mary and family (3:20–35; 6:1–6).* Relatively early in the Gospel, Jesus' own kin are brought into the narrative in a rather negative way. In Mark 3:20–21, his family (the Greek is literally "those near him") goes out to capture him because people are saying that he is insane. While this group may have included also some of his disciples, the actual persons named are "his mother and his brothers" (3:31). The problem appears to be that Jesus' very success at healing and preaching drew huge crowds to him that prevented him from even being able to eat. The situation was so out of control that some were beginning to argue that Jesus was insane or was possessed by a demon. The charge itself permits Jesus to point out to the scribes that Satan could not possibly cast out Satan, for no divided house or kingdom can stand. Consequently, his ability to cast out Satan demonstrates his identification with God. When his family finally arrives to call him, he implicitly rejects their relationship to him by explicitly naming those sitting around him in the crowd who do "the will of God" as his "brother, and sister, and mother" (3:35).

Since the action of Jesus' mother and brothers may legitimately be viewed as an attempt to help or protect him, why are they shut out by Jesus? Some assistance in answering this question may be found in the other episode in the Gospel that deals with his family and neighbors, Mark 6:1–6. Jesus and his disciples have returned to his own country, and he begins to teach in the synagogue on the Sabbath. His neighbors and friends are at first astonished and then angry at his words and acts; after all, is this not the carpenter they knew, whose mother, brothers, and sisters are right there in the town? Jesus himself is amazed at their rejection of him and remarks that prophets are given honor *except* in their own homes and lands and among their own families. In both stories the problem arises because Jesus' family and neighbors refuse to see him in any way but the old relationships of conventional blood ties and social connections. Although they hear his words of wisdom and witness his mighty acts of healing, they still choose to relate to him out of the patterns of the past. To bring home the insane son of Mary is a protective act, but to try to seize the Christ, the Son of God, is folly and unfaith. Jesus' mother, brothers, and neighbors are so immersed in the world of conventional social relationships that they are blind to the new age and new family Jesus himself is establishing. Their ties to the status quo block any of the fruits of faith from developing.

### Herodias and her daughter (6:14–29).

Like Mary, Jesus' mother, but unlike the anonymous healed women or women examples, Herodias is a named individual, and the story about her and her daughter is one of the most intriguing in the Gospel of Mark—not in the least because it is the only story in the Gospel that does not include Jesus as the central character. The plot of the episode revolves around two men, Herod and John the Baptist, and two women, Herodias and her daughter. Herodias held a grudge against John because of his vocal disapproval of her marriage to Herod the tetrarch of Galilee, one of the sons of King Herod the Great. Herod had taken Herodias as his own, even though she had been married to his brother Philip, and the immorality of such "wife swapping" had drawn John's condemnation. However, when Herodias tried to kill John, her husband Herod stopped her by imprisoning John in a kind of protective custody. Since Herodias had no direct means to accomplish her aim against her husband's wishes, she had to bide her time until an opportune moment arrived and then take on the ancient female role of the trickster to satisfy her blood greed. That moment came during Herod's fateful birthday banquet. Herod, celebrating with his friends, became so charmed by the dancing of Herodias's daughter that he promised her anything, up to half of his kingdom. But it was not half his kingdom that Herodias wanted, and the child, after consulting with her mother, asked instead for the head of John the Baptist on a platter. Unwilling to take back his oath before all his male guests, Herod reluctantly granted the request and had John's head brought in on a platter like the final course of the grand meal, a grotesque scene that has provided abundant material for plays, operas, and paintings through the centuries. Mark fashions Herod himself as a type of the thorny ground. He begins well by protecting John but then fails when his own honor and reputation are at stake before his guests; the cares of the world choke out the seed sown in him.

Yet, even though the actual order to kill John comes from Herod, the narrative places the real blame for his death on Herodias, just as the Gospel will later place the blame for Jesus' crucifixion on the Jews rather than on Pilate, who actually ordered it. Herodias was a woman of great status and wealth as the wife first of Philip and then of Herod, but her characterization in the story is an example of both the limits of power for even aristocratic women and the negative manner in which their actions in the public realm were viewed. She personifies the terrible mischief routinely unleashed on the world by powerful and wicked people. More than Herod or Pilate, Herodias stands with the high priests and Jerusalem religious leaders as the epitome of evil for the Gospel of Mark. That a woman occupies that ignominious position as well as men suggests some caution in evaluating the overall role of women in the Gospel.

## Women in the Passion Narrative

The story of Jesus' passion, that is, his arrest, trial, crucifixion, and resurrection, begins in chap. 14 and continues until the end of the Gospel at 16:8. Women play a major role in this material, especially after Jesus' death on the cross. The depiction of these women builds on the patterns the Gospel has developed in earlier chapters: most women of the good ground are anonymous, act boldly without letting traditional customs or conventions prevent their faithful service, seek no fame or status for themselves, and show the fruitfulness of faith in the kingdom. However, when women are blinded by conventional standards, as is the case with Mary, or are grasping after power, as is the case with Herodias, even they can be evaluated negatively by Jesus or the author. The first woman character in the passion narrative, the woman who anoints Jesus, has already been discussed; the other women are the maid of the high priest and the women at the cross and the tomb.

### The maid of the high priest (14:66–72).

The passion narrative in Mark functions similarly to the closing recognition sequences in other ancient popular literature: the true identity and affiliation of all the characters come to light. The maid of the high priest plays a crucial role in an episode illuminating one of those characters, Peter. Earlier in the evening, Jesus had predicted that all of the disciples would flee and (to Peter's vehement objections) that Peter himself would deny Jesus three times before the cock crowed twice (14:27–31). Indeed, Peter's very objections to Jesus' predictions demonstrate a boastful and prideful denial of the Messiah's teaching! Nevertheless, when Jesus is arrested, all of the disciples do flee, one even running away naked to escape, but Peter has courage enough to follow the armed crowd at a distance back to the house of the high priest where Jesus is to be interrogated. While Jesus is being questioned about his true identity by the high priest in the chamber above, Peter, warming himself by the fire in the courtyard below, faces similar questions begun by the maid of the high priest. This question-and-answer format was a very common feature of recognition scenes in Greek literature from Homer on and would have been expected and understood by an ancient audience. Moreover, by placing the interrogation of Jesus (14:55–65) within the story of the questioning of Peter (14:54, 66–72), the author suggests that both interrogations are being conducted *at the same time*, one in the chamber above and the other in the courtyard below.

The maid of the high priest is not explicitly called a slave, though she may well have been, but a young girl who is somehow associated with the family of the high priest. Her presence in the courtyard among groups of bystanders suggests her lowly status, for no woman or girl of honorable rank would be permitted access to such places. She speaks to Peter in public and indeed draws public attention to herself and Peter (14:69), another clear sign of her "shamed" or lowly status. The two connected scenes of Jesus and the high priest and Peter and the young girl are parallel recognition scenes. However, Jesus' acceptance of his true identity and Peter's rejection of it make the scenes opposites, type and antitype. While Jesus bravely says "I am" to the high priest's question about his identity as "the Messiah, the Son of the Blessed One," Peter denies three times (finally even under a self-directed curse) his true identity as a follower of Jesus. The reversal evident between the two scenes extends to the questioners as well: while Jesus is questioned by the high priest, a Jewish male of very high status and power, who rejects the truth of Jesus' words, Peter is questioned by a young servant girl of lowly status, who insists on truth in the face of his repeated lies. In typical Markan fashion, the anonymous, lowly, and marginal character stands for truth while the high status, powerful character rejects the truth or tells lies. In speaking the truth, Jesus is condemned to death; by telling lies, Peter saves his life—but "those who want to save their life will lose it, and those who lose their life for my sake, and for the sake of the gospel, will save it" (8:35).

### The women at the cross and the tomb (15:40–16:8).

After the twelve chosen disciples have either fled, betrayed, or denied Jesus, and after he has died alone, surrounded only by

the mocking crowds, the author introduces a group of women, three of whom are identified by name, Mary Magdalene, Mary the mother of James and Joses, and Salome. The women have witnessed the crucifixion from afar, and the two Marys also go on to witness Joseph's burial of Jesus. Although the author says that these women have been followers of Jesus and ministers to him from his days in Galilee, this reference in 15:40 is the first time in the entire Gospel this large group of female followers has been mentioned. While it is strange that such constant and faithful followers of Jesus should be omitted from earlier episodes, it comes as a hopeful sign to know that some of Jesus' followers have remained true to him, especially since the twelve male disciples have proved to be such thoroughly rocky ground. Actually, with the exception of Pilate and the centurion, all the characters in the closing verses of the Gospel are new to the story. Joseph of Arimathea is a member of the Jewish council, *all* of whose members had earlier condemned Jesus to death. Thus, Joseph is a former enemy of Jesus who now has compassion on the body and asks for the privilege of burying it, an act that rightfully should have been carried out by Jesus' own absent disciples (cf. 6:29). Even though the women keep their distance from the public sites of the crucifixion and burial, as proper women would, they are at least present, demonstrating by that fact alone their superiority to the male disciples. Such faithful constancy from women should come as no surprise to the audience of the Gospel, given the positive way women have generally been portrayed throughout the narrative. In their first presentation in the story, these women followers already show themselves to be better disciples of Jesus than the rocky twelve who have fled, betrayed, and denied him.

Consequently, at the beginning of the last episode in the Gospel of Mark, the visit by the women to the empty tomb, the audience might have reason to hope that Jesus will finally be well served by some of his human followers. After the Sabbath the two Marys and Salome purchase spices to go to the tomb and anoint him. But what do they expect to find at the tomb? The purchase of spices suggests that they expect to find a corpse; yet, if they had followed Jesus since his days in Galilee, they would have heard his predictions that after three days he would rise from the dead (8:31; 9:31; 10:33–34). Perhaps, then, the spices are to be used to anoint the risen Christ. Are these women faithful followers awaiting the risen Christ or dejected mourners determined to bury the dead decently? The exact reason for their visit remains ambiguous until the final verse of the Gospel. Yet the women are named in the story, a rather ominous feature that associates them with Jesus' mother Mary and Herodias. Moreover, one of them is also identified by relation to her son. Hence, all three are depicted as conventional women of some status.

When they arrive at the tomb, they find the stone rolled away and a young man in white sitting on the right side, the customary dress and posture of divine messengers. He proclaims to them the wonderful news of Jesus' resurrection and then orders them to go and tell his disciples, even Peter, that Jesus is going before them to Galilee. The women, however, like the Twelve before them, flee from the tomb in trembling and astonishment, saying nothing to anyone, for they are afraid. The news of the resurrection, like the earlier word to the male disciples of the coming end of the world and the kind of discipleship it requires, has once again fallen on rocky ground that does not bear fruit. It is not clear whether the author intends the naming of the women—and the expectation of conventional social roles that such naming represents in the Gospel—to explain their failure to act boldly and courageously on their divine commission. But it is the case in Mark that women who behave conventionally or concern themselves with social status, power, or customary roles have *not* been those whose faith has proved fruitful. The "good news" Jesus has been preaching of a different world on the horizon demands followers who are willing to act outside the constraints of society, religiously and socially. The two Marys and Salome, like the twelve men earlier, are evidently not of that quality.

To end the Gospel on such a resounding note of failure is very upsetting from a modern perspective. After observing Jesus' continual struggles to make his male disciples understand his teachings and seeing their ultimate failure, readers want so much for someone in the story to prove faithful to Jesus. It is devastating to watch those who have already demonstrated more faithfulness than the Twelve fail as well! But from an ancient perspective the very point of the Gospel of Mark may rest with this painful ending. Ancient writing was intended to *do*

things, to make people act or believe or change their behavior, not just to entertain them with a suitably concluded literary experience. Certainly the Gospel of Mark was not written simply to entertain its audience, for a Gospel that argues so ardently about the imminent coming of the end of the world has no time for mere aesthetic pleasure. The expectations raised and then crushed by the end of the Gospel are intended to move the hearers of the Gospel to action. If the women do not carry the message, is there anyone else who can? Is there anyone else who has heard Jesus' preaching, seen his healings, watched his crucifixion and burial, and listened to the wondrous announcement of the resurrection? The audience of the Gospel has heard all of this. At the end and indeed *by means of* the end itself, the audience of the Gospel of Mark, both women and men, are challenged to become themselves faithful disciples, carrying the message to the world, doing what some characters in the Gospel have not proved worthy to do because of their subservience to social conventions or their desires for status, wealth, fame, or power. The ending of Mark intends to arouse the emotions of its hearers on behalf of Jesus and the "good news" he came to preach. It intends to make faithful hearers and readers into faithful disciples and followers, for very little time remains until this present evil world is wiped away and God's fruitful kingdom is established.

## BIBLIOGRAPHY

Hägg, Tomas. *The Novel in Antiquity.* Berkeley, Calif.: University of California Press, 1983.

Kelber, Werner. *Mark's Story of Jesus.* Philadelphia: Fortress Press, 1979.

Rhoads, David, and Donald Michie. *Mark as Story: An Introduction to the Narrative of a Gospel.* Philadelphia: Fortress Press, 1982.

Thurston, Bonnie Bowman. *The Widows: A Women's Ministry in the Early Church.* Minneapolis: Fortress Press, 1989.

Tolbert, Mary Ann. *Sowing the Gospel: Mark's World in Literary-Historical Perspective.* Minneapolis: Fortress Press, 1989.

Winkler, John. *The Constraints of Desire: The Anthropology of Sex and Gender in Ancient Greece.* New York: Routledge & Kegan Paul, 1990.

# LUKE

*Jane Schaberg*

## Introduction

### Warning

The Gospel of Luke is an extremely dangerous text, perhaps the most dangerous in the Bible. Because it contains a great deal of material about women that is found nowhere else in the Gospels, many readers insist that the author is enhancing or promoting the status of women. Luke is said to be a special "friend" of women, portraying them in an "extremely progressive" and "almost modern" fashion, giving them "a new identity and a new social status." But read more carefully.

Even as this Gospel highlights women as included among the followers of Jesus, subjects of his teaching and objects of his healing, it deftly portrays them as models of subordinate service, excluded from the power center of the movement and from significant responsibilities. Claiming the authority of Jesus, this portrayal is an attempt to legitimate male dominance in the Christianity of the author's time. It was successful. The danger lies in the subtle artistic power of the story to seduce the reader into uncritical acceptance of it as simple history, and into acceptance of the depicted gender roles as divinely ordained.

This Gospel also contains challenge and promise, however, because close reading of it can be an empowering education. It stimulates valuable questions rather than provides final answers, and points to issues that demand rethinking. Those whose study of Luke is informed by contemporary critical methods and by the concerns of women will fully appreciate this new promise.

It is necessary to distinguish different aspects of the text (historical, ideological, theological, and literary) and the different levels of transmission. The reader is challenged to recognize the ambivalence of the tradition, both to enter into the text to appreciate it, and to stand apart from it in order to assess its truth and helpfulness. Insights valuable for the building of an egalitarian society and of a theology that preserves and respects women's experience are indeed present in Luke. But learning to untangle and free them from the harmful elements of the tradition is a difficult task.

The author of Luke is interested in the education of women in the basics of the Christian faith and in the education of outsiders about Christian women. The Gospel attempts to meet various needs, such as instructing and edifying women converts, appeasing the detractors of Christianity, and controlling women who practice or aspire to practice a prophetic ministry in the church. One of the strategies of this Gospel is to provide female readers with female characters as role models: prayerful, quiet, grateful women, supportive of male leadership, forgoing the prophetic ministry. The education that the study of Luke offers today involves a conscious critique of this strategy. It is not at all the education Luke had in mind!

### Narrative Summary

This Gospel is organized into eight parts. It begins with a prologue (1:1–4) setting forth the purpose of the work. The author, a third-generation Christian, has researched and written "an orderly account" of the events concerning Jesus, in order to reassure Theophilus (probably a Christian convert being instructed in the faith) and other readers about the instruction they received. An infancy narrative (1:5–2:52) then parallels the annunciations of conception, the births, and the childhoods of John the Baptist and Jesus.

The third part (3:1–4:13) entails preparation for Jesus' ministry—John the Baptist's preaching, the baptism of Jesus, his (all-male) genealogy, and his resistance to temptation by the devil. The fourth part, Jesus' ministry in Galilee (4:14–9:50), includes his teaching, exorcisms and healings, choice of followers and companions, opposition from religious leaders, and predictions and foreshadowings of suffering and glory. Jesus in Luke is a masterful, emotionally restrained figure, empowered by God and focused on God.

The fifth part is a lengthy account of Jesus' journey to Jerusalem (9:51–19:27). It details a period of intensive training in discipleship: its demands, powers, and dangers. Much of his public teaching (often by parable) takes place at meals and is about table community and/or the distribution of wealth. In the sixth part (19:28–21:38) Jesus enters Jerusalem hailed as "the king," and he teaches in the Temple. His now-deadly opposition is primarily from the chief priests, scribes, and elders, who fear his popularity.

The seventh section (22:1–23:56a), the passion narrative, begins with the Last Supper and ends with the burial of Jesus. The apostles are given final preparation for leadership and (except for Judas) are not depicted as failing Jesus. He is portrayed as strong in the face of death and innocent (his innocence recognized by Pilate, Herod, a criminal crucified with him, and the centurion). The people at first fail by following their leaders in calling for his crucifixion, but there is a mass repentance after his death. The final portion of the Gospel concerns the vindication of Jesus (23:56b–24:53). It contains narratives of the empty tomb, appearances of the resurrected Jesus, the commissioning of witnesses, and his ascension to heaven.

Unlike the other three canonical Gospels, the story told by this evangelist continues in a narrative of the foundation and spread of the Christian movement from Jerusalem to Rome. Because the Acts of the Apostles is implied in its prologue to be the second volume written for Theophilus, and because the style of the author of Acts appears to be that of the third evangelist, almost all scholars hold that the same person wrote both volumes. If this is so, they should be read together. In fact, when they are, it can be seen that the Gospel of Luke lays the basis for Acts' pictures of the church, of salvation, and of the meaning of the Christ.

Acts, in turn, is the author's own commentary on the Gospel story and its concepts and tendencies.

## Source Theory

In the prologue the author says that this Gospel builds on the written work of others, who themselves utilized the traditions of "eyewitnesses and servants of the word," and on the author's own careful investigation. This is not, then, the work of an eyewitness or a servant of the word, nor is it the first "orderly account" of the story of Jesus. The theory most commonly accepted, and followed provisionally in this article, is that the author of Luke used the Gospel of Mark (with some omissions, e.g., of Mark 6:45–8:26), a source called Q (available also to the author of the Gospel of Matthew), and sources—probably oral and written—called L (material available only to Luke). Source analysis provides essential clues about the workings of the author's mind, the audience's makeup, and important historical and theological issues.

Of special interest here will be the L material, since much of it features women. The following passages focusing on women are often classified as part of L: sections of the infancy narrative (chaps. 1–2, featuring Elizabeth, Mary of Nazareth, Anna); the raising of the son of the widow of Nain (7:12–17); the forgiven prostitute who anoints Jesus (7:36–50); Galilean women followers of Jesus (8:1–3); Martha and Mary (10:38–42); the woman crying out from the crowd (11:27–28); the bent woman (13:10–17); the parable of the sweeping woman (15:8–10); the parable of the persistent widow (18:1–8); the daughters of Jerusalem (23:27–32); women at the cross (23:49); women preparing spices (23:56).

It has been proposed that Luke may have had access to a women's source—a collection of stories and teachings perhaps written or preserved by women and providing insight into women's experience of the Jesus movement. Scholars have wondered whether 7:11–17; 7:36–50; and 8:2–3 might not have been at one time a narrative collection reflecting the early community's concern about the question of women. Others have asked if the story of the bent woman, "daughter of Abraham" (13:10–17), was once connected with Luke's infancy narrative (see 1:5, where Elizabeth is said to be "of the daughters of Aaron," and 2:36, where Anna the prophet is called "the daughter of Phanuel"). There is evidence that much of the material concerning women is traditional, not part of Luke's own editorial work. But if it originally came from a women's source or sources, it cannot be taken as simply expressing the viewpoint or reality of early Christian women. Luke responds to concern about the role of women by incorporating and editing material, subtly making the point that women must be restricted. Some of the material, however, bears traces of women's greater involvement and leadership. Perhaps it is related to the "old wives' tales" 1 Tim. 4:7 warns against, or was produced in circles like that of the widows 1 Tim. 5:2–16 attempts to control.

## Distinctive Characteristics

Some of the distinctive characteristics of Luke provide clues about its author, date, and intended early audience and about the context in which women are depicted.

*History and eschatology.* Luke is precise about the broad historical and political context of the story of Jesus, marking events with references to specific Roman and Jewish rulers (1:5; 2:1; 3:1–2). The period of Israel (from creation to John the Baptist) is seen as leading up to the period of Jesus (from his ministry to his ascension); the period of the church under stress (from the ascension to the "parousia" or return of the risen Christ) stretches ahead indefinitely in a mission to all nations. Imminent expectation of the parousia and the final inbreaking of the reign of God is modified in Luke by the sense that the reign is already "among you" (17:20–21) and by emphasis on the work to be done before the end (21:12–13). This appears to be a document from the generation that has confronted and accepted the fact of the delay of the parousia. Accommodations are being made to ongoing life in the Roman Empire.

*Romans and Jews.* There is evidence that the author had detailed knowledge of the Roman siege of Jerusalem in 70 C.E. (21:20, 22; cf. 13:35a). Rome's military triumph is interpreted as punishment for Israel's rejection of its Christ (19:39–44), a harsh anti-Jewish polemic that continues today. Roman involvement in the execution of Jesus has been downplayed in this Gospel, and responsibility has been shifted so heavily onto Jewish leadership that the impression is given that "the Jews" killed Jesus (22:54; 23:23–26; 24:20; cf. Acts 2:22–23; 3:17; 7:52–58). This historically inaccurate and

unjust depiction is due in part to a desire to show the reader that the founder and his movement were not revolutionary and therefore were not dangerous to the state. Those who are repentant in Israel form the nucleus of the people of God and are presented as a tiny minority within a people called "prophet killers" (11:47–51; 13:34; Acts 7:52). Jewish messianic hopes are said to be "fulfilled" as Luke depicts Christianity as the logical and legitimate continuation of Judaism and thus as a lawful religion in the Roman Empire. The split between synagogue and church is evidently wide, and most of the followers of Jesus for whom this Gospel is written are Gentiles in a predominantly Gentile setting.

*Wealth and poverty.* This is often called "the Gospel of the poor," just as it is called "the Gospel of women," meaning that Luke's concern for the marginalized and oppressed is apparent. It is important to analyze the link between these concerns, since most of the poor in every age are women and the children who are dependent on them. In this Gospel the economically destitute are called blessed (6:20; cf. 4:18), and a reversal of their situation by God is expected (1:53; 16:19–31). Luke seems to be particularly interested in the help given by Jesus to disabled beggars (18:35–43; Acts 3:1–10) and the hungry (14:13–14, 21). The disciples are called to leave "all" to join Jesus (5:11, 28; 18:22), which is tantamount to joining the poor, becoming poor as Jesus is.

Women do follow Jesus in this Gospel, but not at such a cost; they are benefactors, giving out of their evidently retained wealth (8:2–3). They are like a bridge to what seems to be Luke's primary interest in this regard: interest in the rich. All the rich are repeatedly warned by parable and by short sayings (7:24; 12:13–21; 16:14) that they can be lulled into false security and callousness, ruled by their possessions. They are told that if they hope to participate in the reign of God (i.e., in what God is doing for the poor), they must be transformed and share with the poor by loans and outright gifts (6:30–35; 12:33).

The Jerusalem community in Acts functions like those explicitly called disciples in the Gospel: it is demanded that they give up private ownership and eradicate Christian poverty (Acts 2:44–45; 4:32), and for the most part they meet that demand. But for the rest—the women followers in Galilee and others, and the later believers outside Jerusalem—adjustments are made to the normal workings of society. Some have, some do not; those who have are urged to be voluntarily generous. The radical friendship life-style sometimes called "primitive communism" is not promoted for all. An unrelieved tension exits in this Gospel between the ideal and the accommodation, the radical attitude toward wealth and the moderate attitude.

## Date and Authorship

The New Testament Gospels are anonymous; that is, they do not name their authors. Tradition going back to the end of the second century C.E. attributes this Gospel to one Luke, a companion of Paul on his journeys, a physician (Col. 4:14; Philemon 24; 2 Tim. 4:11). Indirectly, Paul's own authority is invoked in the writings of his supposed companion. Many scholars conclude, however, that internal evidence does not support this claim. The theology of Paul in Acts is unlike that of Paul's own letters: there is no evidence of professional medical knowledge, and—most important—Luke-Acts supports values similar to those of other New Testament works from the end of the century, the pastoral epistles (1 and 2 Timothy, Titus), which also lay claim to the authority of Paul.

By the end of the first century and into the second, Paul's name was used to encourage the organization of churches in Asia Minor into patterns of patriarchal domination and submission, assimilating the radicalism of the Jesus movement and the early Christian missionary movement into what some have called "love

patriarchalism." In that process of assimilation, inequalities inherent in social, economic, and political hierarchies and in differentiated roles were to be willingly accepted by those said to possess inner equality "in Christ," and those with power were to wield it nonabusively. In Luke's writings this process of acceptance is reflected and promoted.

The author of Luke, probably a Gentile Christian, was well educated in Hellenistic literature and rhetoric, familiar enough with the Greek translation of the Hebrew Bible to be able to imitate its style, skilled and artistic in the use and blending of sources, and theologically creative. It is not impossible that the author was a woman. Women of wealth or status in this period were able to be educated, and some were writers. Female authorship is improbable, however, mainly because of the Gospel's attitude toward women. Further, the narrator speaks as a man (in the Greek of 1:3). But in fact the author's identity is an open question that raises other questions.

Because of the use of Mark as a source, references to the destruction of Jerusalem (70 C.E.), and reflections of some political and social trends of the 80s, the Gospel of Luke is usually dated around 85–90 C.E. It was written after Colossians and Ephesians, with their household codes, and probably before the Pastorals (written at the turn of the century), with their even more blatant prescriptions subordinating women. Antioch in Syria, the third-largest city in the Roman Empire, is often identified as the place of composition.

## Comment

### Issues of Special Concern

*Women in Luke.* The number of women depicted in Luke and the emphasis on their presence in the narrative are surprising. Women characters are taken over from Mark and from Q, and many others are found only in Luke's special source (L). The technique called "pairing" is very noticeable. One version of a story or teaching refers to a man and the other to a woman, reinforcing the message and encouraging women as well as men to identify with the characters. This pairing occurs most often in the discourse of Jesus—for example, the man who plants the mustard seed and the woman who takes leaven (13:18–21 Q); the man who searches for the lost sheep and the woman who

searches for the lost coin (15:4–10 L). Some healings form pairs: the widow's only son and Jairus's only daughter (7:12; 8:42); Sabbath healings of the bent woman and the man with dropsy (13:10–17; 14:1–6). There are two lists of the names of Jesus' followers: one of the male apostles (6:12–19) and one of women (8:1–3).

There is also a noticeable tendency in this Gospel to defend, reassure, and praise women. Luke refers to widows more frequently than do the other Gospels (2:37; 4:25–26; 7:12; 18:3, 5; 20:47; 21:2–3), often in passages that presuppose their economic helplessness in a male-dominated society. The "sinner" who anoints Jesus is contrasted with the Pharisee (7:36–50). The bent woman is given the unusual designation "daughter of Abraham" (13:16), affirming her dignity. The "impure" woman with the flow of blood is praised for her faith (8:48). Mary of Bethany is defended against the complaint of her sister Martha and is affirmed in her choice of the "good portion," listening to the word of Jesus (10:38–42).

Mary the mother of Jesus is often considered Luke's model of obedient, contemplative discipleship (1:38; 2:19, 51). She is not defined by her biological motherhood but blessed for her belief (1:45), as are all who "hear the word of God and obey it" (11:27–28). The harsh contrast seen in Mark 3:31–35 between Jesus' mother and brothers and his true family of disciples is changed in Luke to a saying that seems to praise the former (8:19–21). The women who travel with Jesus and the Twelve and serve them from their possessions (8:3) are models of sharing. These are the loyal ones who are among those who see the crucifixion (23:49) and the burial (23:55) and who have "a vision of angels" (24:23) at the empty tomb, which they do report to the Eleven and all the rest (24:9; contrast Mark 16:8).

**Comparisons.** Luke emphasizes Jesus' ministry to women, but whether this emphasis is regarded as enhancing or restricting the position of women depends on the angles from which the evidence is examined and on that to which it is compared. It is important to analyze why certain aspects are stressed and others not and who benefits—to analyze, that is, the sexual politics of the Gospel. Attention must be paid not just to the number of women but also to what they are doing and saying, and to what they are not doing and not saying.

*Women in Judaism.* The claim is often made that women in Luke (and in the ministry of the historical Jesus) are much more liberated than Jewish women of the first century C.E. Jesus is considered a revolutionary "feminist" pitted against his religious environment and heritage. Later Christian restriction of women is then often seen as rooted in necessary capitulation to Jewish or Jewish-Christian tradition. This position, which can be embedded in and foster an attitude of anti-Judaism, is not supported by recent research on women in the various types of first-century Judaism.

Inscriptions, papyri, and archaeological data as well as literary sources indicate that there was great diversity. Some Jewish women were leaders in synagogues, were financially independent landowners and businesswomen, and acquired religious education, even devoting their lives to the study of Torah. Others were legally disadvantaged and powerless. The comparative situation of women in ancient Judaism and early Christianity is not yet clear, but it is clear enough that no simple contrast favoring Christianity can be drawn.

*Roman women.* Luke restricts the roles of women to what is acceptable to the conventions of the imperial world. The capitulation, in other words, is more to repressive forces within the Roman Empire than to forces within Judaism. Evaluation of Roman law concerning women shows that in the classical period even the small numbers of wealthy Roman women of the upper classes were "emancipated" only in a very restricted, vicarious sense. They were without real decision-making authority and leadership. The expanded role for women in the ministry of Jesus and in early Christianity was looked on with suspicion, as involving un-Roman religious activities, magic, and permissiveness dangerous to family and state. Motivated by the desire that Christian leaders and witnesses be acceptable in the public forum of the empire, the world of men, Luke blurs traditional and historical traces of women's leadership and exaggerates the leadership by men.

*Women in the other New Testament Gospels.* In terms of sheer quantity, Luke has more material about women: forty-two passages, of which twenty-three are unique to Luke. But careful comparison must be made of the quality of female roles and functions and of the liberating potential of each Gospel. A few examples follow. Luke has no women who challenge Jesus or initiate a mission to the Gentiles. The story of the feisty Syrophoenician woman in Mark 7:24–30 is part of Luke's great omission of Markan material; there is no counterpart in Luke to the Samaritan woman of John 4. The Johannine Martha and Mary have more significant and powerful roles than the Lukan Martha and Mary. The interpretation of Mark's abrupt ending at 16:8 is pivotal to any evaluation of the treatment of women in that Gospel: by condemning the women who flee from the empty tomb and are silent, Mark is urging women to break their fearful silence. Luke, on the other hand, fosters women's silence in the Gospel as a whole, although the women at the tomb do speak out. Matthew's treatment of leadership as shared (16:19; 18:18) is theoretically more egalitarian than Luke's treatment. Furthermore, the women at the tomb in Matthew not only receive a commission, but as they run to tell the disciples, the risen Christ appears first to them (28:1–10).

*Historical women in the early Christian movement.* Luke's depiction of women must be placed alongside reconstructions of the early Christian movement, which indicate that the movement was truly egalitarian in its initial stages, with women in positions of leadership and authority (see, e.g., Romans 16). The roots or sources of the experiment in inclusive community remain a historical puzzle, but Jewish egalitarian movements based in apocalyptic and wisdom traditions seem likely keys.

*Internal comparisons.* Finally, the Gospel's depiction of women must be compared with its depiction of men, especially with respect to those elements constitutive of character: name, speaking and being spoken to, action, and responsibility. The women of the Gospel must also be compared with the women in Acts, where most scholars agree that the author's interests are more apparent.

With respect to characters named and unnamed, a few statistics are instructive. There are 10 women named in the Gospel of Luke. As characters in the story, 39 named men appear, but the proper names of 94 more are mentioned (76 in the genealogy alone), a total of 133 men. The named men outnumber the named women by more than 13 to 1. In Acts, 7 women are named, of whom only 1 (Mary the mother of Jesus) is mentioned also in the Gospel. Luke has 10 unnamed women with parts to play and 2 groups of women. Of unnamed males in the Gospel, there are 40 individuals and 27 groups (one consisting of 5,000 men). So these individual men outnumber the women 4 to 1, and male groups outnumber the female groups by almost 14 to 1. In Acts there are 3 unnamed women characters and 13 groups of women. In the teaching of Jesus in Luke, women are mentioned 18 times, contrasted to the 158 times men are mentioned. In Acts, in the teaching of the apostles women are mentioned only once.

The conclusions are obvious. First, the impression of "many" women in this Gospel is conditioned by expectations of finding none or very few and by the impression, documented by psychologists, that numbers of women in mixed groups seem (to both men and women) much larger than they actually are. One male critic speaks of "a surplus of women" in the communities in Acts. Second, there is a drastic reduction of interest in women in Acts, where Luke's own perspective is more visible.

Statistics again provide an interesting picture of who speaks and who is spoken to in Luke's writings. In Luke, women speak 15 times. Their words are given 10 times and are not given 5 times. In Acts, women's speaking is reduced to 5 instances, their words given 3 times, not given 2 times. Women, then, are gradually silenced. In contrast, an attempt to count the hundreds of times that men, including Jesus, speak leads one to realize the virtual din of male voices.

In Luke, women as groups and individuals are spoken to 15 times, 9 times by Jesus (to defend, correct, and praise them). In Acts, women are spoken to 6 times, 5 times by the apostles. No sermon in Acts is addressed to women. The 2 individual women of Acts spoken to in direct speech are condemned and silenced (Sapphira in Acts 5, like her husband Ananias, is silenced effectively by death; the slave girl in Acts 16 who has been annoying Paul is silenced by an exorcism). A quick reading shows that men are spoken to constantly, with affirmation as well as condemnation. These analyses drive home the fact that both works are androcentric (male-centered), but Acts much more so than Luke.

With respect to women's action and responsibility, Acts shows us the roles Luke affirms for women in the early Christian community, and looking back at the Gospel of Luke through the lens of these roles clarifies the author's position. With the exception of Priscilla, who is recognized as a missionary (Acts 18:18) and teacher (Acts 18:26) in full partnership with her husband Aquila, the primary female role in Acts is that of "mother" to the fledgling community, one who out of her wealth provides home, hospitality, and material aid to believers. The women of Acts are also "receiving women," beneficiaries of the preaching and healing powers of men. Only men decide the affairs of the church in Acts.

In the Gospel, women are also nurturers. Luke never calls them "disciples" or "apostles." In fact, Luke insistently speaks of the twelve males chosen in 6:13 as "the apostles," even though the term has a wider use elsewhere in the New Testament. As in the other Gospels, there is no call narrative in which Jesus summons a woman to follow him. Instead, Luke presents a pattern of women healed or exorcised, who then serve "them" (the male disciples and Jesus, 4:38–39; 8:2–3). No women are commissioned as apostles in Luke (contrast Mark 16:7).

A comparison of Luke 18:28–30 with its probable source, Mark 10:28–30, shows that Luke made important changes that confine discipleship to men. (Inclusive-language translations obscure this aspect of Luke's intention.) Luke's addition of "wife" (with no corresponding addition of "husband") to the list of what must be left for the sake of the kingdom of God means that the disciples are imagined as men. Only in Luke's version of the parable of the marriage feast is "marrying a wife" given as an excuse for refusing the invitation (14:20). Even though in the Gospel women are present during Jesus' ministry, at the cross, burial, and empty tomb, in Acts 1:21–22 the replacement of Judas as witness to the resurrection must be drawn from the males who accompanied them from the baptism of John to the ascension.

Luke thinks of a woman's proper attitude as that of a listener, pondering what is not understood, learning in silence. The women in this Gospel as in Acts can be called a "hearing community." The only questions asked by a woman are the questions of Mary of Nazareth (1:34; 2:48). The only christological insight expressed by a woman is that of Elizabeth, who recognizes that Mary is pregnant with her "Lord" (1:43). No women in Luke, by word or action, identify Jesus as Messiah or Son of God. Anna the prophet (2:38) is given no speech. Only the woman with the flow of blood, who progresses from denying that she touched Jesus to giving thanks (8:45–47), makes a public proclamation of his power; but her words are not quoted, and, moreover, Luke shifts emphasis from her to Jesus.

In the Gospel as in Acts, receptive women are nurturers of men. A woman's blessedness is not restricted to being the mother of a great son (11:27–28), but emphasis on biological motherhood is replaced by an emphasis on what might be called spiritual motherhood, a role perhaps even more confining. Luke is concerned to evoke in the audience the question, "What shall we do?" (3:10, 12, 14; 10:25; 18:18). The proper answer is that one should "hear the word of God and do it" or "keep it" (2:19, 51; 6:47, 49; 8:15, 21). But "doing" is different for men than for women. In contrast to the role approved for women, full discipleship in this Gospel involves "the power and authority" to exorcise, heal, and preach (9:1–6; 10:1–16). Women can be assumed to be present when the risen Jesus appears to "the Eleven and their companions" (24:33), announces a worldwide mission of proclaiming repentance and forgiveness, and promises "power from on high" (24:47–49). Women can be assumed to be present when the Holy Spirit is said to fill those assembled at Pentecost (2:1–4; cf. 1:14). But Luke shows only the men empowered to speak and act and bear responsibility within the movement.

## Androcentrism

Since the Gospels are male-centered, women have had to read as though they were men in order to hear themselves fully addressed and challenged. This effort can lead to misreadings that have harmful consequences. For example, many of women's deepest concerns, fears, weaknesses, and needs are not addressed in the Gospel—nor indeed in the whole biblical tradition. As Valerie Saiving has pointed out, pride and the will-to-power are not the principal temptations for women, who are more apt to accept for themselves the roles prescribed by society and tradition—believing in their inabilities and inadequacies, acquiescing in their own powerlessness, failing to act responsibly, sacrificing rather than developing their own selves. Women, to whom no authority or power is given in this Gospel, can doublethink their way only with great difficulty and danger into texts that criticize the techniques and results of power grabbing, and call for repentance. For example, just before Jesus commissions the Twelve at the Last Supper, he warns them about the abuse of power (22:24–27). He counters their desires to be "greatest" with his own example: "I am among you as one who serves." Luke has not seen the loose ends left flying: the "leader" should be "as one who serves." But the only followers who "serve" in this Gospel narrative are women (4:39; 8:3; 10:40), and they are not appointed leaders. A real temptation for women, it can be argued on this basis, is to remain unauthorized, unempowered.

Several passages from Luke's Gospel if seen through the eyes of a battered woman can be read to condone violence. Luke omits Mark's prohibition against divorce but retains the prohibition of remarriage after divorce, with no exceptions (Luke 16:18; cf. Mark 10:10 and Matt. 5:31–32). This prohibition (addressed only to men) may have been experienced as protecting some women in antiquity and later from being replaced and dismissed into lives of humiliation and poverty, or as freeing the divorced for the ascetic life (a life-style Luke appreciates; see 20:34–35). But interpreted in rigid fashion, this prohibition has also often condemned women and men to the alternative of an intolerable bondage or a life of isolation and sexual repression.

Luke 6:29 (Q) counsels offering the other cheek; 6:27 expands the command to love one's enemies by doing good to them, blessing them, praying for them. In 9:23 Luke adds the word "daily" to the saying of Jesus about taking up the cross. That addition extends the symbolism of the cross and depoliticizes it, altering the emphasis from martyrdom to sacrificial living, which women have understood differently from men. In 24:26, one of Luke's major themes appears: that it was necessary that the Messiah suffer (13:33; 17:25; 22:37; 24:7) and "enter into his glory" (see 2:49; 4:43; 24:44; Acts 14:22). Why must his suffering happen, according to Luke? Because it manifests the coherence of God's plan and work of salvation and because it corresponds to the will of God. While these texts are not meant to glorify suffering or victimization, they have been so used.

Luke 4:18–20 quotes Isa. 61:1; 58:6 to announce that Jesus' ministry is to the oppressed. But this Gospel has no scene that illustrates release for an abused woman, freeing her from low self-esteem, guilt, and masochism as well as from the brutality and intimidation of another—freeing her, in effect, from such texts as those mentioned above. This Gospel does have, however, stories such as that of the woman bent over for eighteen years with "a spirit of infirmity" (RSV, 13:10–17), which some women have read as allegories of their oppression and release.

An examination of the parable of the Good Samaritan (10:29–37 L) illustrates difficulties a woman encounters reading self-consciously as a woman. It is a story about the world of men, who travel, rob and beat, pass by, have compassion for a fellow traveler (even one who is an enemy). The male experience is presented here as universal human experience. But if there may be "places in the world a woman can walk," the dangerous, isolated road from Jerusalem to Jericho is certainly not one. Without altering the dynamics of the story, most women cannot easily imagine themselves *as women* in the ditch, or passing by, or even having such an opportunity to help as the Samaritan does. Efforts to enter the parable in this way, to read as a woman, either complicate it with the theme of sexual violence or dissolve it into an abstract statement about being a neighbor. Many other passages in Luke—such as the parable of the prodigal son/father (15:11–32, which

can be read as the parable of the missing mother, who is never mentioned) and Luke's passion narrative (in which male political and religious powers crush the innocent, while the women watch)—are occasions to confront androcentrism, to explore precisely how women have read themselves into the texts, and to recognize the urgent need for women's own parables, women's own narratives.

## Five Passages

Against this background of the role of women in Luke, one can examine in more detail passages unique to Luke that focus on women.

*The origins of John the Baptist and Jesus (chap. 1).* Three women appear in this section (Elizabeth, Mary of Nazareth, and Anna) in roles far more powerful than the roles of women in the rest of the Gospel. This is the only section in which women are given speeches that are not followed by the women being corrected. It is likely that Luke has permitted powerful women characters here in the narrative mainly because the context is the traditional women's role of bearing and raising children. However, even here, in the parallel accounts of the birth, circumcision, naming, and maturing of John the Baptist and of Jesus, the major focus of Luke's interest is the sons, not the mothers.

Elizabeth is the barren woman whom God makes fruitful (like Sarah, Rachel, Hannah, and others). Barrenness canceled what was regarded as a woman's main function in life, the bearing of children—especially sons—to her husband; it denied her the highest status and security a woman might achieve. Barrenness was thought of as the woman's fault (as here in 1:7), a punishment for sin or at least a result of God's "forgetting" the woman (1 Sam. 1:11). Luke 1:6, however, insists that both Zechariah and Elizabeth are righteous. Nevertheless, Elizabeth can still call her barrenness "my disgrace among men" (RSV, 1:25; cf. Gen. 30:33). God mercifully intervenes to take away this disgrace. At the scene of the visitation with Mary, Elizabeth, though not given the title, functions as a prophet. "Filled with the Holy Spirit" she praises Mary as "blessed among women," for her belief (1:42). Elizabeth makes the first and only christological confession by a woman in this Gospel: "Why has this happened to me, that the mother of my Lord comes to me?" (1:43). "Lord" is for Luke here and in many other places a

Christian title for Jesus, affirming his transcendent dominion.

Mary is directly in touch with the heavenly world in her dialogue with the angel Gabriel (as are the women at the tomb, spoken to by two supernatural men [24:4–7]). Luke depicts Mary as the model female believer. Almost—but not quite—commissioned as a prophet or disciple, she is the only woman to whom Luke has given a full speech of proclamation, the Magnificat. Elsewhere Luke takes pains to present a positive picture of her. In Acts 1, Mary makes her last New Testament appearance in the upper room in Jerusalem, where the Eleven "were constantly devoting themselves to prayer, together with certain women," including her.

The widow Anna, the only woman in the Gospel called a "prophet," is said to have publicly "returned thanks" to God and to have continually spread abroad the word about the child (or about God; the Greek is ambiguous) "to all who were looking for the redemption of Jerusalem," a phrase that has a revolutionary ring. Unlike Simeon, however, Anna is given no canticle and the Spirit is not said to be with her, though it is three times said to empower Simeon (2:25, 26, 27), who has two canticles. What is stressed, besides Anna's silent witness, is the great length of her widowhood and her continual presence fasting and praying in the Temple (presumably in the outer court, the only part of the precincts women were allowed to enter). This portrait of Anna may provide a trace of the important ministry of widows in the early church, but it does not elaborate on the nature of that ministry.

The conception of Jesus by Mary merits special attention. Matthew's account of Jesus' origin is very different from Luke's, but a close reading shows that the two accounts contain many points in common. If Matthew and Luke wrote independently of each other, these agreements stem from the older tradition they inherited and worked with. Both Matthew and Luke report that the parents of Jesus were Mary and Joseph, who was of Davidic descent. They agree that Mary's pregnancy occurred between their betrothal and the home-taking or completion of the marriage (Matt. 1:16, 18; Luke 1:27). They agree also that Joseph was not the biological father of Jesus (Matt. 1:18–19; Luke 3:23). In both Gospels, an angel announces the role of the Holy Spirit in this pregnancy (Matt. 1:18, 20; Luke 1:35), gives the child the name Jesus (Matt. 1:21; Luke 1:31), and predicts his role in the history of Israel (Matt. 1:21; Luke 1:32–33). Matthew and Luke both consider Mary a virgin (Matt. 1:23, by implication; Luke 1:27). Both allude to Deut. 22:23–27, the law concerning the seduction or rape of a betrothed virgin (Matthew in his description of Joseph's dilemma; Luke in 1:17, 48). They insist that the birth of Jesus took place after his parents had come to live together (Matt. 1:24–25; Luke 2:5–6), in Bethlehem during the reign of Herod the Great (Matt. 2:1; Luke 2:4–6; 1:5). Both evangelists speak of Jesus as accepted from the very beginning by the just and pious of Israel (Matt. 1:19; Luke 1:41–45; 2:25–32, 36–38).

It is traditionally and commonly claimed that both Matthew and Luke agree also that Jesus was "virginally conceived"—conceived, that is, by the direct act of God, without male sperm or intercourse, like a new creation from nothing, with Mary the nurturing "vessel." If this idea is indeed found in Matthew's and Luke's infancy narratives, these are the only two places it is found in the New Testament. An audience acquainted with stories from the Jewish traditions would not be prepared to think of a virginal conception, since in those traditions divine paternity does not replace human paternity. An audience acquainted with stories of the marvelous or miraculous conceptions of heroes, immortals, and benefactors of humanity in Greco-Roman biographies would think either of divine *and* human paternity or of the divine mating with the virgin, in literal or symbolic penetration (the sacred marriage).

Theologians today differ widely in their interpretation of the meaning that "virginal conception" is meant to convey and in their conclusions about its importance. Homage given to the mother of Jesus as "the Virgin Mary" (maternal but not erotic; honored for the nonuse of her sexuality) and development of her image and legend in Christian imagination and devotion have made her a figure that functions in many ways like a goddess, Christianity's adaptation of the feminine dimension of the divine. Luke 1 is the major New Testament source for that development, which has had both positive and negative effects on women's spirituality, self-understanding, and political empowerment.

In contemporary New Testament scholarship, the tendency is to find the virginal conception clearly asserted in Matthew and less clearly (if at all) in Luke. It has been claimed that Luke 1 *can* be read as *not* about a virginal conception. Read in and for itself, without the overtones of the Matthean account (so the argument goes), every detail of it can be understood as referring to a child to be conceived in the usual human way. Gabriel appears to Mary who is at that time a virgin and tells her she will conceive a son. Her question in 1:34 stresses that she and Joseph are in the period of betrothal and not having sexual relations. The question gives Gabriel an opening to speak about the character of the child to be born. Gabriel's statement in 1:35 about the Holy Spirit "coming upon" and "overshadowing" Mary is a figurative way of speaking about the child's special relation to God, not implying the absence of human paternity (cf. Gal. 4:29, where Isaac is called "the child who was born according to the Spirit").

Conception with Joseph as the biological father is an idea not expressly denied in Luke 1 or 2; however, it *is* denied in 3:23: Jesus is only the "supposed" child of Joseph. The reader who understands Luke 1 to be about a normal conception is thus faced with another alternative: the biological fatherhood of some unnamed person and the illegitimacy of Jesus. It is possible that both evangelists inherited a tradition of the illegitimacy of Jesus and transmitted it very differently. Both evangelists, it must be pointed out, stress the Messiahship and holiness of this child (Matt. 1:21, 23; Luke 1:31, 35), in spite of or perhaps because of his origins.

When Luke's account is viewed as preserving and working with a tradition of Jesus' illegitimacy, several of its details fall into place. For example, in the dialogue between Gabriel and Mary, Gabriel's response (1:34) is not an explanation of how the pregnancy is to come about but is a statement of reassurance, urging trust. The verbs "come upon" and "overshadow" promise empowerment and protection (cf. Acts 1:8; Luke 9:34). These verbs have no sexual or creative connotations. Mary's question "How?" is sidestepped and remains unanswered. This scene echoes aspects of the commissioning or call of prophets. But Mary is commissioned to be a mother, not a prophet. Her response is to consent freely to motherhood (1:38). With this expression of her consent in faith, Luke creates the positive portrait of Mary as model believer.

At the same time, Mary's characterization of herself as the "slave" of the Lord is the text most responsible for the impression of her as a passive character, the antithesis of a liberated woman. Is this Luke's way of setting her up as the model for submissive feminine behavior and of articulating an acceptance of patriarchal belief in female inferiority, dependence, and helplessness? Slaves held the lowest social position within the Israelite, Jewish, and Christian communities and were without rights at law, unable to own property, or have a family or a genealogy in the proper sense. The term "slave" has a shock value that can be felt by those today who are aware of their heritage of slavery and who are anguished by the slavery that exists in our world. Luke, however, surely intends the term to have a positive value here. It must be seen in connection with Jewish use of the honorary title "slave of God," applied to a few outstanding men of Israelite history (Moses, Joshua, Abraham, David, Isaac, the prophets, Jacob) and to one woman (Hannah). The word associates Mary also with Jesus, portrayed as among the disciples "as one who serves" (22:27), though not called "slave," and with the female slaves on whom God's Spirit would be poured out "in the last days" making them prophets (Acts 2:17–18, citing Joel 2:28–32).

In Luke 1 as a whole, there is a "step parallelism" between the stories of John the Baptist and Jesus. For example, whereas for the Baptist a prophetic destiny is predicted (1:17; cf. 1:76), Jesus' destiny is royal (1:32–33). In the conception of the Baptist, the humiliation of his mother Elizabeth as a barren woman is overcome. In the case of Jesus, what is overcome is his mother's deeper humiliation, the violation of a betrothed virgin. In this context, Mary's canticle, the Magnificat (1:46–55) is powerfully appropriate.

The Magnificat is the great New Testament song of liberation—personal and social, moral and economic—a revolutionary document of intense conflict and victory. It praises God's liberating actions on behalf of the speaker, which are paradigmatic of all of God's actions on behalf of marginal and exploited people. The powerful memory is evoked of God's deliverance of Israel throughout its history. Key themes for the Gospel that follows are introduced here, especially the proclamation of good news to the poor (4:18–19; cf. Isa. 61:1–2). Mary's song is precious to women and other oppressed people for its vision of their concrete freedom from systemic injustice—from oppression by political rulers on their "thrones" and by the arrogant and rich. In the transformed social order that is celebrated, food is provided for the hungry. The spiritual realm is understood as embedded in socioeconomic and political reality. Focus is on the might, holiness, and mercy of God, who has promised solidarity with those who suffer, and who is true to those promises.

God is "magnified" for effecting changes—now, in history.

The Magnificat has many allusions to Hannah's song (1 Sam. 1:11; 2:1–10) and was probably written in the circles of the Jewish Christian 'anawim ("poor" in a spiritual and often literal sense). Here it celebrates Mary's own vindication by God, who protects her and her child, recognizing this child as God's Son and Messiah. Her experience of reversal anticipates the resurrection. The point is not that the girl who utters the Magnificat is lowly, humble, and insignificant in comparison to the mighty God. It is rather that God has looked on her "humiliation" (1:48) and has "helped" (1:54) her and the child. Mary preaches as the prophet of the poor. She represents their hope, as a woman who has suffered and been vindicated.

However, the author's picture of Mary is ambiguous, and some aspects of her role already hint at the restriction of women seen in the rest of the Gospel. In chap. 1, while she is evangelist and prophet, she is without an explicit commission to preach. Her submission to the word of God is total. In the second chapter she is the model listener (2:19), a dependent, contemplative heroine (2:33–35, 51) who never initiates any action. Hers is what Luke considers a woman's perfect response to the word of God: obedient trust and self-sacrifice.

The dominant mood of Luke's first chapter is one of celebration and serenity, and the narrative atmosphere is one of delicacy and restraint, in contrast to the story of danger and moral dilemma in Matthew 1. Any potential scandal of the tradition of Jesus' origins, like the scandal of his death, has been defused in Luke's Gospel. If Luke knew of an illegitimacy tradition, it has been muted and almost silenced here. The annunciation scene is too beautiful, too positive, and too indirect to convey that difficult message. Rather, Luke's subtlety opens the story of Jesus' conception to miraculous, supernatural interpretations, especially for readers of Gentile background. Luke conveys the "good news" of the power and respectability of the Christian faith.

Still, this scene, in which a betrothed virgin is visited by the angel of God and told of her forthcoming pregnancy and of God's empowering protection of her, is the only biblical instance of God's direct interest in such a woman. The tradition affirms that the child to be born will be God's, because the Holy Spirit is ultimately responsible for his conception. The pregnancy is no accident or mistake, but divinely ordained. The Magnificat is not the song of a victim but one that proclaims liberation with tough authority.

**The sinner (7:36–50).** Accounts of a woman anointing Jesus appear in all four Gospels: Mark 14:3–9; Matt. 26:6–13; John 12:1–8; Luke 7:36–50. Critics are puzzled about exactly how the accounts are related. What seems likely is that one event lies behind them, an event that was changed radically in the telling, and to which Mark's version is in some respects the most faithful. Some elements of Luke's account apparently derive from a pre-Lukan stage (e.g., the anointing of feet, the parable of the two debtors, perhaps the story of a prostitute touching Jesus), and some are the products of Luke's creativity. What is certain, however, is that Luke's version, in which the anointing woman is a sinner, is the one most people remember. Luke's "brilliant" and dangerous artistic ability is evident in what has been called one of the great episodes in the Lukan Gospel. Until feminist criticism began to probe the differences among the accounts and show special interest in Mark's, it was Luke's that overpowered the other three in the popular Christian imagination. Further, in all four Gospels, Jesus is physically anointed only by a woman. But his baptism was early interpreted as his anointing by God with the Holy Spirit. This tradition overshadowed any human anointing as the source of Jesus' authority and identity as the Anointed One ("Christ").

A comparison of all four accounts, laid side by side, is necessary to a critique of Luke's. In the other three Gospels, anointing by a woman is a prelude to the passion of Jesus in Jerusalem. In Luke, however, a woman anoints Jesus during his ministry up north in Galilee at the house of Simon the Pharisee. Luke has moved the story backward from where it was found in the Markan source. It is possible that 7:36–50 is meant to illustrate how Jesus is a "friend of tax collectors and sinners" (7:35; cf. 5:32) and how the Pharisees rejected "God's purpose" (7:30). It is also possible that Luke means it to illustrate the type of woman who became part of Jesus' entourage (8:2–3). In any case, placement of the story of the sinner before the list of women on the road with Jesus is responsible for an extremely important distortion in the imagination of Western Christianity: the characterization of Mary Magdalene as a prostitute. She, mentioned in 8:2, is identified in later Western Christian interpretation as the anonymous "sinner" in 7:37. But there is no warrant for this identification in the text. As Eastern Christianity recognized, 8:2 and 7:37 are about two different women.

No name is given the woman in Mark and Matthew; in John she is Mary of Bethany. Luke calls her "a woman in the city, who was a sinner." It is likely that Luke means the audience to identify this woman's sin as notorious sexual activity, prostitution. Her action in Mark and Matthew consists of bringing an alabaster jar of expensive ointment and pouring it on the head of Jesus, as prophets anointed kings (1 Sam. 15:1; 16:13; 1 Kings 1:45; 19:15–16; 2 Kings 9:1–13; and the eschatological prediction in Dan. 9:24). In John, the woman takes a pound of expensive ointment, anoints Jesus' feet, and wipes them with her hair. Luke's "sinner" wets Jesus' feet with her tears, wipes them with her hair, kisses his feet and anoints them with ointment. Normally, feet were not anointed with perfume, except for the feet of the dead. Washing the feet was an act of hospitality, but kissing them was usually an act of gratitude for pardon. Unbound hair may be the mark of a "loose woman" (Num. 5:18 Septuagint; *Mishnah Sotah* 1:5); in Corinth, however, it was associated with women prophesying (1 Cor. 11:5–6).

Reaction in Mark, Matthew, and John is protest over waste. In these Gospels Jesus defends the woman, saying that the anointing is his embalming for burial. That interpretation of her deed as a prophetic acting out of the anointing of his corpse corrects and depoliticizes the claim to royalty (which was probably the point of the earliest account), by means of the prediction of suffering. Mark 14:9, followed by Matthew, has Jesus predict that wherever the gospel is preached in the whole world, "what she has done will be told in memory of her." In Luke's version, however, the anointing itself is not central. Rather, focus is on the emotional extravagance of the woman's actions, on Jesus' acceptance of the touch of such a person, and on her being forgiven.

Jesus tells the parable of the two debtors who are forgiven, the one forgiven more loving more. Then the parable is applied to the woman, who has shown Jesus more love than has Simon, the inadequate host. Love, in the logic of the parable, is both cause and result or sign of divine forgiveness. The woman embodies that love. Because of the emotional quality of her action and its lavish sensuousness, her love has a strong erotic dimension, though its essence may be thought to be grief and

gratitude. One male commentator thinks the scene exhibits "a touch of hysteria" on the part of a woman who seems unable to express "her more or less clear self-knowledge intellectually."

The prophetic and political aspect of the event behind Mark's story and John's (and whatever love that might have involved) is lost in Luke. Jesus, not the woman, is shown to be a prophet (cf. 7:16; 24:19), who knows intimately the human heart and the mind of God who has forgiven her sins. In Luke the anointing also bears no relation to the death of Jesus; it is reduced to a display of unusual affection on the part of an intruding woman. A social outcast takes on herself the role of servant in gratitude to Jesus. But by erasing the female prophet from the Markan source, Luke has refused to honor her memory. Given the emphatic nature of Mark 14:9, Luke's editing displays real arrogance. Politically, prophetically, what she has done will *not* be told in memory of her.

***Women traveling with Jesus (8:1–3).*** Luke mentions two groups who were with Jesus as he traveled through cities and villages in Galilee: the Twelve, and "some women who had been cured of evil spirits and infirmities." From the second group, three are named: Mary called Magdalene; Joanna the wife of Chuza, Herod's steward; and Susanna. These and many other women are said to have "provided for them [or, "served them"] out of their resources." These deceptively simple verses raise many questions—on the historical level about the makeup and life-style of the Jesus movement and on the redactional level about Luke's depiction of the involvement of women, who are never explicitly called "disciples."

One of the names in Luke's list and the verb that describes the women's activity are drawn from other Synoptic traditions. Mark 15:40–41 tells of many women looking on from afar at the crucifixion, who had followed Jesus when he was in Galilee and provided for him. Luke appears to be using this Markan verse but also to have other information. A comparison of the names of women at the crucifixion and empty tomb in the four Gospels shows that the name of Mary Magdalene is constant—based on a strong, unshakable, widespread memory—and suggests that the names of others were remembered in different communities. The tradition that seven demons were exorcised from Mary Magdalene is found also in Markan Appendix 16:9, with no indication that this links her with prostitution. Only Luke's Gospel gives us the names Susanna and Joanna. As the wife of the manager of Herod Antipas's estate, the latter is the first of many women of wealth and status mentioned by Luke (Acts 13:50; 17:4; 17:12; 15:24; 25:13).

The Greek verb translated in Mark 15:41 and in Luke 8:3 as "provided for" is *diakoneo:* to serve, wait on, minister to as deacon. Whereas in Mark 15:41, followed by Matt. 27:55, the women are providing for or ministering to Jesus alone, in Luke 8:3 the object of their attentions is Jesus and the Twelve. The women are cast in a nonreciprocated role of service or support of the males of the movement. Since in Luke-Acts the Twelve are the major witnesses and leaders, the women's role is subordinate. The wording of 8:2–3 implies that they are acting out of gratitude for being healed, unlike the Twelve.

On the historical level, several questions are prompted by these verses. Did women (with or without husbands) travel with Jesus and the other males in an itinerant, charismatic ministry, dependent on hospitality in various Galilean cities and villages? Or, since the area is small, and since only the male disciples are said to have left their homes to follow Jesus (18:28), did the travel for the women consist of day trips from home bases? Scholars often remark that the practice of including women in such a ministry was scandalous. If this is true, why did that scandal leave no mark on the traditions, and why was the practice never explicitly defended? Unfortunately, these questions cannot be answered on the basis of present knowledge of the activities and life-styles possible for Jewish women in the time of Jesus.

In the various lists of women, some are identified by their relationship to husbands or sons (for example, Joanna in 8:3), but other women are listed without such an identification. Were they unmarried, divorced, or widows? Although Luke narrows the term "apostle" to refer to the Twelve, in this Gospel seventy(-two) disciples are also appointed and sent out two by two, returning with joy in their success (10:1–20). Women are not mentioned in this connection, so most readers have imagined male partners. But is this an instance of the erasure of women who may have traveled in pairs or with male counterparts? The silent disciple on the road to Emmaus, for example, could be thought of as a woman (24:13–35). Some commentators have demonstrated that women can be read into the texts of Luke where disciples are mentioned (e.g., at the Last Supper)—a practice that probably gives us a more accurate historical

picture—but it is important to be clear that the resulting picture is not the one Luke intends. The separate lists of male and female followers of Jesus in the Synoptic Gospels stand in contrast to the integrated list of church leaders in Romans 16. Does Luke think of the women as a distinct and separate community within the movement, analogous perhaps to the women gathered at the synagogue by the river in Philippi (Acts 16:13) or to the Therapeutrides, female contemplatives discussed by the Jewish philosopher Philo?

Many different opinions are found in the commentaries concerning the type of work or service (*diakonia*) the women may have done. Some scholars see it as domestic (shopping, cooking, sewing, serving meals), the work of a traditional wife. Some see it, in line with the mission of the Twelve and the seventy(-two), as involving preaching about the kingdom, although women are not explicitly commissioned to preach in the New Testament. The term *diakonia* referred in the early Christian community not to domestic chores but to eucharistic table service and to proclamation of the word (Rom. 11:13; 15:31; 1 Cor. 12:5; 2 Cor. 4:1; 5:18; Acts 6:1, 4). There may be a tradition behind Luke 8:2–3 and Mark 15:41 that women were significant figures in the table community and the intellectual activity that marked the original movement. (The example of Priscilla [Acts 18:26] shows that a woman could be accepted later as an important teacher.)

Other scholars think of the women in Luke 8:2–3 as wealthy philanthropists, "benefactors." However, this does not fit with the widely accepted suggestion that most members of the earliest movement were from the ranks of the poor. Luke's redactional interest, in placing women followers only in financial support roles, cannot be taken as historical memory. The fact that Luke presents the women as providing or serving out of their "resources" is important for an understanding of Luke's perspective on wealth and discipleship, as well as the perspective on women. That they (still) have resources means that they are not among the destitute poor. Nor are they disciples in the mind of Luke, since disciples are called to sell "all" and distribute to the poor (18:22; 14:33; see below, however, on 12:33). The women thus are shown aiding the poor (disciples and Jesus), but as patrons from outside their ranks.

Apart from divestiture of wealth (a practice adopted according to Luke by the early church; see Acts 4:32–5:11), Luke shows special interest in the right use of possessions or resources by the wealthy (12:15–21; 16:19–31; 19:1–10). Although the saying appears in a sermon to the disciples, the command to "sell your possessions, and give alms" (12:33) seems to be exemplified in the behavior of the women in 8:2–3. These women have "purses that do not grow old," which Luke opens wide to the men of the movement. Luke's depiction of a female-supported, male-led organization has been mirrored down the centuries by many Christian organizations.

There is an unintended ironic parallel between the women in 8:2–3 and the widow in 21:1–4, who dropped into the Temple treasury "all that she had to live on." This scene follows the saying condemning scribes who "devour widows' houses" (20:47). Thus, Jesus is not praising the widow's action but lamenting it. Despite this overt meaning of the story, however, her story turns out to be that of the women in Luke's vision of the church as well. Unlike wealthy women who may have contributed financially as well as otherwise to the early phases of a movement in which they were historically full members, the women in Luke-Acts are inadvertently described as supporting a nonegalitarian system that subordinates and exploits them.

**Martha and Mary (10:38–42).** Popular literature and traditions associated with Martha give evidence that many women have long been uncomfortable with this familiar story, which pits sister against sister. A glance at different commentaries will show that there is no agreement about its basic meaning. Jesus is a guest at the house of Martha, who is "distracted with much serving" (diakonia). Sitting at his feet listening to his "word" is Mary, who is silent throughout. Martha says, "Lord, don't you care that my sister has left me to serve (diakonein) alone? Tell her then to help me" (author's translation). Her question echoes that of the disciples in the sinking boat in Mark 4:38 (a story Luke does not relate): "Teacher, don't you care if we die?" Unlike the response of Jesus in the storm at sea, which indicates that Jesus *does* care (he calms the storm), here he gently chides Martha and leaves things as they are. Her request denied, Martha is silenced. She is the loser, with whom the reader is not supposed to identify, but with whom many readers do.

The textual variant found in some manuscripts at v. 42 ("few things are necessary, or only one") is often understood incorrectly as a comment on the menu for a meal and Martha's excessive preparations. However, the shorter reading, "one thing is necessary," is probably more original. Nothing is said about a meal. The "one thing" that is necessary is the "better part" Mary chooses. The implication is clear, that Martha's part is lesser. One traditional interpretation sees the two women as abstract principles or types. For example, they are said to represent active and contemplative life-styles, or justification by works and justification by faith, or Judaism and Christianity. Another approach pays attention to the fact that the protagonists are women and attempts to read the story in terms of female careers or priorities or jealousies. Some see here a feminist manifesto of the rights of women to theological education. Jesus defends Mary's right to study with him. His action is often contrasted — incorrectly — with the denial of the right of Jewish women to study Torah. But no such rule existed in Jesus' day, and so to oppose Jesus to Judaism in this way is simply inaccurate.

Recently the narrative has been read by Elisabeth Schüssler Fiorenza as reflecting debate at the end of the first century C.E. both over the roles of women and over emerging offices in the house-churches, some of which were founded and led by women. As has been noted above, in Christian usage, diakonia became a technical term referring to eucharistic table service, proclamation, and ecclesial leadership. In the story of Mary and Martha, however, Luke distinguishes diakonia (Martha) and "listening to the word" (Mary) as two distinct roles. Mary's choice of the latter over the former is praised and defended by the Lord. Luke, Schüssler Fiorenza argues, is thus prescribing for the church of the time, not describing a condition that prevailed then or earlier.

It has long been seen that there is some connection between this story and Acts 6:1–6. In the latter passage there is also a separation of the two tasks of diakonia (preaching and table service) and the subordination of the latter (cf. 1 Tim. 5:17 and 3:8–13). It is clear, however, from the description of the preaching ministry of those devoted to table service (6:8–7:60), that in the tradition Luke is using, diakonia still refers to both ministries. "Service" (diakonia) and "the word" are not really split apart, as they are in the story of Martha and Mary, the two sisters who do not even speak to each other. With that split, the diakonia of women is reduced and discredited. Finally, it disappears:

Acts does not mention any *diakonia* of women, but only of men (1:17; 6:1; 11:29; 12:25).

Several additional points of contrast should be noted between Mary's *diakonia* of the word and that of various male characters. "The word" is preached by both the Twelve and the Seven in Acts, but it is only listened to by Mary, who never speaks even to question. Her study is totally receptive and passive, not creative learning. In contrast, the missing twelve-year-old Jesus is found in the Temple "sitting among the teachers [not at their feet], listening to them and asking them questions" (Luke 2:46). The next verse mentions his answers, not his questions. The Gerasene demoniac sits healed at the feet of Jesus, begs to stay with him, but is sent away to proclaim what God has done for him (8:35–39). Mary's position at the feet of Jesus is like Paul's brought up at the feet of Gamaliel (Acts 22:3), but Paul's subordination to his teacher is temporary; in contrast, Luke tells of no subsequent independent teaching or other leadership by Mary.

The disciples and apostles in Luke learn often in dialogues (e.g., 5:1–11; 8:4–15; 9:10–11), but Mary is silent. Her attitude is that of a disciple, but she is not a disciple. She is only an audience. What she has heard and learned at the Lord's feet is private; it does not instruct and shape the whole community.

In contrast to their fate in Luke, Martha and Mary of Bethany, evidently well remembered in the early church, appear in quite a different light in John 11:1–45; 12:1–8. There, both are loved by Jesus, and they are not in competition with each other. Martha, who serves at table, makes the central christological confession of this Gospel, of Jesus as the Christ (cf. the confession of Peter in the Synoptics), and Mary, who also enters into dialogue with Jesus, performs the prophetic action of anointing Jesus' feet. In John's portrait of the two sisters, *diakonia* of the table and of the word remain integrated.

Luke does not present Jesus saying, "I permit no woman to teach or preach" or "Women must be silent" or "Only men can be apostles or disciples or deacons." In the world of Luke, Jesus is not a "divider" (see 12:13). Approved women are shown choosing for themselves the passive role, which the Lord in Luke calls "the better part" (10:42). Martha, who serves unaided, is called "distracted," "anxious" and "troubled" about things that are not necessary. Her request for Mary's help is understood as a spiritual threat to her "sister."

But if Luke 10:38–42 is called on to authorize women's solid theological education, this text can perform a subversive function — subversive, that is, of Luke's intent, which is to undermine the leadership of women. The educated woman sees through the text, sees its different levels and sees Luke's strategy. Most important here is recognition of the tone of affection and concern and perhaps exasperation, as in the repetition, "Martha, Martha. . . ." This is the kindly voice of "love patriarchalism." But if one listens — as this passage urges — to the "word of the Lord," but in one's own experience and that of other women, one may hear behind the text another voice encouraging women's leadership and reconciliation.

***Women at the cross and empty tomb (23:49; 24:1–12).*** In the final three chapters of this Gospel, women all but disappear. This is so because the reader enters the world of male politics, violence, and bonding, but also because Luke is describing last preparations and authorization of male figures for future leadership. The near disappearance of women is achieved in three ways. First, the women become part of a crowd. Second, compared to Mark's treatment, their role is reduced in significance as those of male characters gain power and become more positive. Third, they are erased as the essential, designated witnesses. Luke's description of the final events is important for understanding the narrative of the women at the empty tomb.

At the Last Supper in Luke, Jesus sits at table "and the apostles with him" (22:14). They are the nucleus of the eschatological community. The Eucharist is Jesus' legacy, given to them. Jesus confers on the Twelve a kingdom in which there will be continued table community and in which they will "sit on thrones judging the twelve tribes of Israel" (22:30). No women are mentioned as present at this scene, or at the Mount of Olives, or at the hearings before the sanhedrin, Pilate, and Herod.

As elsewhere in Luke, the editing of Mark and the addition of new material present the disciples in a more favorable light. It is stressed that they have "stood by" Jesus in his trials so far (22:28) and that they will stand by him to the end. Simon will be tested, but Jesus prays that his faith not fail and that he will in the end strengthen his "brothers" (22:31–32). Some have read these verses as a special commissioning of Peter (cf. Matt. 16:17–19; Mark 1:17; John 21:15–19). Unlike the other Gospels (Mark 14:27; Matt. 26:31; John 16:32), Luke contains no prediction that all the disciples will lose faith and be scattered. They do not abandon Jesus when he is arrested.

At a crucial point, the "people" fail in their support of Jesus by following their leaders, the chief priests and rulers (23:13, 18). But this failure is not complete. On the road to The Skull (23:33), Jesus is followed by Simon of Cyrene, carrying the cross of Jesus like a disciple (9:23; 14:27). Also following is "a great multitude of the people, and of women who were beating their breasts and wailing for him" (23:27, author's translation). The construction and grammar of this sentence, with "who" in Greek referring only to the women, indicate that Luke has added "of the people and" to a source fragment dealing only with the women; this type of addition will be made again in 23:49. The daughters of Jerusalem (23:28), not to be identified with the Galilean women who appear in 23:49, are possibly professional mourners. Representing the city destroyed in 70 C.E., they are warned to weep rather for themselves and their children. The coming destruction will be so terrible that barren women will be considered "blessed." Contrasted now with their scoffing rulers, "the people" stand by watching the crucifixion (23:35).

After the death of Jesus, Luke mentions a mass repentance (23:48). Then, in contrast to the other Gospels, which name the small number of witnesses important to the Christian community, Luke describes another crowd: "And all his acquaintances and the women who had followed him from Galilee stood at a distance and saw these things" (23:49, RSV). The important participle at the end of the sentence is feminine plural: the women who had followed him from Galilee "saw." The Greek again shows that Luke has added others (here, "all his [male] acquaintances") to a tradition dealing only with women (cf. Mark 15:40). Most commentators think that the phrase is meant to include at least some of the apostles, but Luke cannot state that they were present if it was widely known that they were not. According to Mark and Matthew, only women followers of Jesus witnessed the crucifixion. In John, four women are joined by the male "beloved disciple." Mark, emphasizing the importance of the women's witness to the crucifixion, burial, and empty tomb, names them three times in the space of a few verses (Mark 15:40, 47; 16:1) and remarks that they had followed and served (*diakonein*) Jesus in Galilee. In contrast, Luke

neither names them nor mentions their service at this point in the narrative.

After the body of Jesus is wrapped and laid in a tomb by Joseph of Arimathea, "the women who had come with him from Galilee followed, and they saw the tomb and how his body was laid. Then they returned, and prepared spices and ointments" (23:55–56). The plan of these Jewish women is to give him a proper burial once the Sabbath is over. (Note that the "acquaintances" have disappeared from the narrative.)

It is sometimes argued that the tradition of women finding the tomb of Jesus empty is late apologetic, not based on historical memory. One reason given for this position is that no mention of an empty tomb is made in the earliest preaching fragment that Paul hands down, 1 Cor. 15:3–7; cf. Acts 13:28–31. Further, Phil. 2:8–11, the Gospel of John, and the epistle to the Hebrews may reflect an earlier mode of speaking about Jesus' ultimate destiny, in terms of exaltation instead of bodily resurrection. However, because of the strong agreements here among the four Gospels, in contrast to the variety in their accounts of resurrection appearances, and because the tomb tradition involves the witness of women (an unlikely choice if invented), many scholars are inclined to treat the narrative as having a historical core. Unfortunately, it may be impossible to reconstruct the Galilean women's experience and interpretation of the death of Jesus, the empty tomb, and his appearances. But their witness is the bedrock of Christian faith.

Luke's account of the empty tomb is quite different from the narratives found in the canonical Gospels and in the apocryphal *Gospel of Peter*. Most important, in Luke the women are not commissioned to go tell the disciples that they will see the risen Jesus in Galilee. Instead, reference is made to a prediction of the passion and resurrection made by Jesus to them in Galilee. Strangely, however, this prediction does not match any in Luke's Gospel (9:22, 44; 18:32–33) but rather is closest to the non-Markan tradition found in Matt. 20:19. Nevertheless, the women remember, and in spite of not being commissioned, they do tell "all this" to the Eleven and the rest.

At this point Luke finally names the women: Mary Magdalene, Joanna, and Mary the mother of James. Other women are said to have been with them (24:10). The first two appear also in Luke 8:2 and the third in Mark 16:1. Only the name Mary Magdalene is found associated with the empty tomb in all the canonical Gospels and in the *Gospel of Peter.* Luke says that the report of the women seemed to the apostles "an idle tale," and they did not believe them (24:11). The Greek term applies to the wild talk of a person in a delirium, hysterical nonsense. The reader, of course, knows that the women's report is true, and the disciples, as the risen Jesus will later say, are "foolish" and "slow of heart" (24:25). But Luke's point is not to contrast believing, faithful women with disbelieving, unfaithful men. Nothing is said about the women believing, although they do remember, and the men have not been unfaithful. The point seems instead to be that the faith of the men who are Jesus' successors is not based on the word of women, on indirect testimony. Nor is it based on the empty tomb: Peter verifies that it is empty, but the sight creates amazement, not faith (24:12; cf. 24:24). Rather, in this Gospel, faith that Jesus has been raised is based on appearances and teachings of the risen Lord: to Simon (24:34), to the two disciples going to Emmaus (24:31), to the Eleven and their companions (24:41-43, 46, 52). But in Luke the risen Jesus does not appear to women. Their witness is not essential to the Christian faith.

In this Gospel, as in 1 Cor. 15:3-8, there is no appearance to Mary Magdalene or the other women who had been at the cross; contrast Matt. 28:9-10; John 20:11-18; Markan Appendix 16:9, where the first appearance is to her. It is impossible to know for sure what traditions were available to Luke. Perhaps Luke was ignorant of any accounts of appearances of Jesus to women. However, the links with John 20:3, 4, 5, 6, 10 in this section of the special Lukan material can lead one to speculate that Peter's race to the tomb may have been followed in Luke's source L, as it is in John, by the tradition of an appearance to Mary Magdalene. But since Acts stresses that only men can witness officially to the resurrection (1:21-26) and lead the Christian community, we can surmise that if Luke had a tradition of an appearance to Mary Magdalene or to another woman, it would have been suppressed in the interests of this perspective on leadership and power, which overarches Luke's entire work.

## Conclusions and Open Questions

The oppressive dynamics of the Gospel of Luke have been explored here far more than the liberating elements. Luke is read as showing and exercising pressure on the minority group of Christians in the cities of the Roman East to conform to traditional gender expectations and roles. When that pressure is recognized, one begins to see how influential Luke has been in the creation of Christian assumptions, ideals, and institutions that do not affirm women but instead relegate them to the margins of the community and especially of its leadership. The artistic beauty of this Gospel, in its elegant structure, style, and portraits, is in part at the service of this pressure to conform. If one asks about the truth of women's historical participation in the Jesus movement, the truth of women's experience and full potential, then in this case beauty is not truth, nor truth beauty. The reader learns to be suspicious of such beauty and to resist certain ways Luke has led women and men to imagine themselves, and led them to act, dream, think, and pray.

Luke's Jesus is the prophet of the Wisdom of God (7:33-35), but he does not call a community of equals. Women are included in Jesus' entourage and table community, but not as the equals of men. Women speak prophetically (e.g., 1:47-55), but they suffer as prophets no one hears (24:11). Women are models of "listening to the word," but their prayer and study, unlike that of Jesus or of other male characters, does not lead beyond itself to decisive action or to their being recognized as teachers in their own right. With unintended irony, this Gospel contains an exhortation to fearless and irrefutable confession (21:15) and yet silences women. The text excoriates those who reject and murder the prophets, yet itself "kills" female prophecy. It hands on the tradition of the healing of the bent woman (13:10-17), while it praises the posture of female inferiority and passivity.

Once the negative side of this ambivalent tradition is recognized and worked with, the reader is freed in relation to the text. What is positive and promising in Luke's Gospel can be explored with enthusiasm and even respect. Reading with new eyes against Luke's intent may bring to light egalitarian traditions preserved in the sources of this Gospel. Rethinking elements of the markedly God-centered Christology of Luke, and of Luke's insights about poverty and wealth, may prove helpful in creating inclusive visions bent on eliminating rather than glorifying suffering. But enthusiasm for Luke-Acts, the most massive work in the New Testament, is enthusiasm for a formidable opponent, not for an ally. Freedom in relation to this work is freedom to answer back, when the silenced find their voices.

## BIBLIOGRAPHY

D'Angelo, Mary Rose. "Women in Luke-Acts: A Redactional View." *Journal of Biblical Literature* 109 (1990), 441–461.

Fiorenza, Elisabeth Schüssler. "A Feminist Critical Interpretation for Liberation: Martha and Mary: Luke 10:38–42." *Religion and Intellectual Life* 3 (1986), 21–35.

———. *In Memory of Her: A Feminist Theological Reconstruction of Christian Origins.* New York: Crossroad, 1983.

Fitzmyer, Joseph A. *The Gospel According to Luke.* Anchor Bible 28, 28A. Garden City, N.Y.: Doubleday & Co., 1981, 1983.

Parvey, Constance F. "The Theology and Leadership of Women in the New Testament." In *Religion and Sexism,* edited by Rosemary Radford Ruether, pp. 139–146. New York: Simon & Schuster, 1974.

Quesnell, Quentin. "The Women at Luke's Supper." In *Political Issues in Luke-Acts,* edited by R. J. Cassidy and P. J. Scharper, pp. 59–79. Maryknoll, N.Y.: Orbis Books, 1983.

Saiving, Valerie. "The Human Situation: A Feminine View." *Journal of Religion* 40 (1960), 100–112.

Schaberg, Jane. *The Illegitimacy of Jesus.* New York: Crossroad, 1990.

Tannehill, Robert C. *The Narrative Unity of Luke-Acts: A Literary Interpretation.* Vol. 1. Philadelphia: Fortress Press, 1986.

# JOHN

### Gail R. O'Day

## Introduction

### The Distinctiveness of John

The New Testament contains four distinct Gospel portraits of the life, ministry, death, and resurrection of Jesus. All four share many crucial elements; for example, all tell the stories of the feeding of the five thousand and Jesus' walking on water. All contain lengthy accounts of the passion and death of Jesus. There are, however, important differences among them. For example, in the Synoptic Gospels, Jesus' public ministry begins in Galilee, and Jesus moves out of Galilee into Judea only once, in the journey to Jerusalem that culminates in his death. In John, however, Jesus' ministry alternates between Galilee and Jerusalem. He makes three trips to Jerusalem (2:13; 5:1; 7:10) in contrast to the one trip of the Synoptics. In the Synoptic Gospels, Jesus' public ministry lasts one year, whereas John narrates a three-year public ministry. In the Synoptic Gospels Jesus often speaks in parables; in John he rarely does.

It is important to resist the temptation either to harmonize these four accounts in order to create one story out of four or to subordinate one Gospel account to the others. All four Gospels attempt to bring the good news of the story of Jesus to the faith needs of a particular community. Each Gospel grapples with the meaning of Jesus' identity and mission in its own way. The church therefore needs to allow each Gospel to have its say about Jesus in its own voice.

The formative issue for the Gospel of John seems to have been the question, Who is Jesus? The Gospel narrative is an attempt to provide fresh answers to this question. It seeks to move the reader away from overly confident assumptions, false certitudes, and complacency about Jesus' identity. It offers each reader of the Gospel the opportunity to discover Jesus for himself or herself. This purpose, to lead the reader to his or her own experience of Jesus, accounts for the distinctive literary style of John. The "I am" sayings (e.g., 6:20, 35; 8:12; 11:25) provide fresh alternatives to the more traditional titles for Jesus. The intricate blend of narrative and discourse, the use of figurative language, and the extensive dialogues between Jesus and other characters all combine to open the story to the reader's own experience.

### Historical and Social Setting

The author of the Gospel of John, like the authors of the other Gospels, is anonymous. The name "John" was attached to this Gospel by the church, and its author was identified as the apostle John. However, there is no evidence to suggest that the Gospel was actually written by this apostle. Indeed, the Gospel names "the beloved disciple" as the guarantor of its tradition (19:35; 21:20–24) but does not give this disciple a name. That the guarantor of this tradition is identified by his relationship to Jesus ("beloved") and not his name is a reminder that the community offers a distinctive voice in relation to other apostolic witnesses. Neither does the Gospel of John provide a clear indication of its place of composition; it is written in Greek, which was spoken throughout the Mediterranean world.

The Gospel does provide some indirect clues to its date of composition. The story of the blind man and the Pharisees in chap. 9 shows that a key issue for John and his community was their relationship to the synagogue. Chapter 9 (vv. 18–23, 34, 35) points to a break between the Jewish synagogue and those Jews who claimed Jesus as the Messiah. Scholars have determined that this break probably occurred in the 80s or 90s, so one could date the composition of John to that period.

The break between the synagogue and Jews who confessed Jesus as Messiah is crucial for understanding the social setting of John. At times the Gospel of John speaks of "the Jews" in very negative language (e.g., 8:44). The contemporary reader must place these references in the context of the break with the synagogue and try to imagine what that break meant to John's community. It was metaphorically, and often quite literally, a rupture in a family. These new Christians were faced with an impossible choice: they could claim Jesus as the Messiah and be forced to leave the synagogue and the community that had nurtured them and given them life; or they could remain in the synagogue and deny what they believed to be the fullness of God's gift to the world. The intense language that John uses about "the Jews" is fraught with the pain of this choice. John does not speak of the Jewish people when he says "the Jews," but he uses "the Jews" as a symbol for powers and authorities who oppose and (as he describes them) are "blind" to the witness of Jesus (e.g., 9:39–41).

John's words about "the Jews" have been misused in order to support Christian anti-Semitism. Nothing could be farther from John's original use of this term. When John used the term, it was insider language—one member of the family speaking in pain to another member of the family. When contemporary Christians take over John's language and use it against the Jews, it becomes outsider language—one group speaking in judgment against another group. When contemporary Christians appropriate

John's language about "the Jews," therefore, it should not be directed against any Jewish community, historical or contemporary. Instead, contemporary interpreters can best capture the original intent of John's language by applying its critique to those powers and authorities *within the Christian community itself* who oppose and do not recognize the witness of Jesus.

## Structure and Contents

The Gospel of John, unlike the other Gospels, begins not in story but in *song.* John 1:1–18, known traditionally as the Prologue to John, consists of a hymn to the Word of God become flesh (1:14). Details about John the Baptist are interspersed throughout this hymn (1:6–8, 15), but the primary purpose of John 1:1–18 is hymnic celebration of the grace that believers have received from God through Jesus (1:16).

The Prologue also provides a clue to the overall structure of the Gospel. Verses 11–12 read, "He came to what was his own, and his own people did not accept him. But to all who received him, who believed in his name, he gave power to become children of God." These two verses help to explain the break in the narrative that occurs between chap. 12 and chap. 13. Chapters 1–12 narrate Jesus' coming to "what was his own" and his reception by "his own people." Jesus' teachings are offered to a broad public in chaps. 1–12. Chapters 13–21, particularly chaps. 13–17, narrate Jesus' teaching and ministry to those who "believe in his name," to his disciples. Chapters 1–12 are sometimes called the Book of Signs because they narrate the miracles and dramatic acts in Jesus' public ministry. Chapters 13–21 are sometimes called the Book of Glory because they narrate the passion of Jesus.

## Comment

Women play significant roles in the Gospel of John. This significance is evident both in the number of stories in which women appear and in the theological importance of those stories. The opening miracle in Jesus' ministry occurs at a woman's initiative (2:1–11). Women are Jesus' main conversation partners in three stories that reveal Jesus' identity and vocation and the nature of faithful discipleship (4:4–42; 7:53–8:11; 11:1–44). Jesus' passion is watched over by the women from its preparation (12:1–8) through Jesus' death (19:25–27) and resurrection (20:1–18). Men do not have a monopoly on

witness and discipleship in John; rather, the Gospel of John narrates a faith world that would not exist without women's participation in it.

### The Wedding at Cana (2:1–11)

John 2:1–11 is the opening event in Jesus' ministry. In 1:35–51, Jesus gathers his first disciples, and in 2:1–11 he attends a wedding with them (2:2). Jesus' mother is also in attendance (2:1). This is the first mention of Jesus' mother in John.

John 2:2 indicates that Jesus "was invited" to

the wedding. He is not the host of the wedding feast but a guest like everyone else. Jesus' ministry thus opens with Jesus as the recipient of a gesture of hospitality. The beginning of his ministry is played out in an intimate, personal, familial setting.

Jesus' mother is the catalyst for the miracle in this story. When the wine at the wedding feast runs out, Jesus' mother informs him of this lack. The conversation between Jesus and his mother is important. When Jesus' mother speaks to him in 2:3, she asks nothing explicit of him, but Jesus' response in v. 4 makes clear that her words contain an implied request. She assumes that her son can remove the scarcity. Jesus' words to his mother in 2:4 seem harsh to the modern ear: "Woman, what concern is that to you and to me? My hour has not yet come." His words are not an act of rudeness to his mother, however, but are an important assertion of Jesus' freedom from all human control. Verse 4 insists that Jesus' actions will not be dictated by anyone else's time or will. Not even Jesus' mother can control what he does or who he will be.

That one should not read 2:4 as rudeness is confirmed by Jesus' mother's response in v. 5. Despite Jesus' seeming rebuff of her, his mother tells the servants with utter confidence that Jesus will do something. His mother is thus a model disciple: she trusts that Jesus will act and allows him to act in freedom.

The miracle that Jesus performs is appropriate to the personal setting of the wedding. Turning water into wine is an act of turning scarcity into abundance, of repaying the initial hospitality offered him. Jesus' first miracle in John takes place in the presence of friends and family, not in the presence of powers and authorities. This opening to Jesus' ministry shows that the miraculous life-giving power of God is at work even (and perhaps, especially) in the intimate daily places of human lives.

The imagery of this wedding scene is picked up in 3:25–30. John the Baptist describes his joy at the coming of Jesus in the language of bride and bridegroom. Once again, intimate, personal language provides the language of faith.

## Jesus and the Samaritan Woman (4:4–42)

Prior to this story of Jesus' visit to Samaria, Jesus' activity has centered on the people and places of official Judaism (e.g., 2:13–25; 3:1–21). When Jesus travels to Samaria (4:4), he moves away from official Judaism, because at the time of Jesus, Jews and Samaritans were bitter enemies (see 4:9). The source of the enmity between them was a dispute about the correct location of the cultic place of worship, a problem the Samaritan woman herself puts before Jesus (4:20). Although the break between Jews and Samaritans is first narrated in 2 Kings 17, the most intense rivalry began about 300 B.C.E. The Samaritans built and worshiped at a shrine on Mount Gerizim, a shrine that competed with the Temple in Jerusalem. This shrine eventually was destroyed by Jewish troops in 128 B.C.E.

When Jesus meets the Samaritan woman at the well, then, he meets someone who provides a striking contrast to all that has preceded. When Jesus speaks with Nicodemus in John 3, he speaks with a male member of the Jewish religious establishment. In John 4 he speaks with a female member of an enemy people. Nicodemus has a name, but the woman is unnamed; she is known only by what she is—a foreign woman.

The conversation between Jesus and the woman is thus a scandalous conversation, a scandal noted by the woman herself. She responds to Jesus' request for water with the words "How is it that you, a Jew, ask a drink of me, a woman of Samaria?" (4:9). The woman knows that a Jewish man should not talk with a Samaritan woman. Moreover, a Jew should not consider drinking water from a Samaritan vessel (4:9). The scandal is noted also by Jesus' disciples when they arrive at the well (4:27). They are amazed that Jesus speaks with the woman; Jewish rabbis (see 4:31) did not speak in public with women.

The disciples want to ask Jesus why he is speaking with her, but their question remains unvoiced. Their protests reflect traditional cultural and social conventions and expectations; however, Jesus will not be limited by such conventions and restraints. He breaks open boundaries in his conversation with the Samaritan woman: the boundary between male and female, the boundary between "chosen people" and "rejected people." Jesus' journey to Samaria and his conversation with the woman demonstrate that the grace of God that he offers is available to all. Jesus and his ministry will not be bound by social conventions. This conversation challenges the status quo by offering the water of life (4:13–14) to a Samaritan woman.

Perhaps it is not surprising that commentators on this text have more readily accepted the offer of the gospel to the Samaritans, a despised people, than they have accepted the offer of the gospel to the woman, a despised sex. This resistance to Jesus' boundary breaking in his conversation with the woman takes two main forms. First, many commentators raise questions about the woman's moral character. Second, many commentators express doubts about the woman's ability to engage Jesus in serious conversation. Both strategies attempt to delegitimize the woman as a conversation partner for Jesus and hence as a recipient of the gospel.

The popular portrait of the woman in John 4 as a woman of dubious morals, guilty of aberrant sexual behavior, derives from a misreading of John 4:16–18. In these verses, the Samaritan woman tells Jesus she has no husband (4:17). Jesus responds to the woman's words by telling her the story of her life (4:18). The text does not say, as most interpreters automatically assume, that the woman has been divorced five times but that she has had five husbands. There are many possible reasons for the woman's marital history, and one should be leery of the dominant explanation of moral laxity. Perhaps the woman, like Tamar in Genesis 38, is trapped in the custom of levirate marriage and the last male in the family line has refused to marry her. Significantly, the reasons for the woman's marital history intrigue commentators but do not seem to concern Jesus. Nor does Jesus pass moral judgment on the woman because of her marital history and status. All such judgments are imported into the text by interpreters. When interpreters speak of the woman as "a five-time loser" or a "tramp" (as has been the case in recent scholarship), they are reflecting their own prejudices against women, not the views of the text.

When one sets aside the prejudicial misreading of John 4:16–18 and reads the story on its own terms, one sees that the conversation about the woman's husbands serves two purposes. First, it illustrates Jesus' ability to see and know all things. This is an important theme in John (e.g., 1:48–50; 2:24). Second, it is a moment of revelation for the woman, a moment when she is able to see Jesus with new eyes. She responds to Jesus' announcement of her marital status with the words "Sir, I see that you are a prophet" (4:19). This exchange between Jesus and the Samaritan woman about her husbands thus does not delegitimize the woman because of her supposed immorality but instead shows the woman's growing faith.

The woman's recognition of Jesus as a prophet leads her to ask him the most pressing theological question that stands between Jews and Samaritans (4:20): Where is the proper place to worship God? Yet many commentators have dismissed the woman's words to Jesus as a psychological ploy, as a classical act of evasion to change the subject from the embarrassing truth about her morals. Commentators doubt whether this *woman* would have been able to understand the substance of Jesus' words to her. Once again we see presuppositions about women (women's intellect and interests) skewing a faithful reading of the text. The text presents the woman as a character who is unafraid to stay in conversation with Jesus, who recognizes that a prophet is the perfect person of whom to ask her question. The woman is the first character in the Gospel to engage in serious theological conversation with Jesus. At the end of the conversation about worship (4:20–26), the woman's faith grows again, as she begins to think about the possibility of Jesus being the Messiah (4:29).

The outcome of the story of John 4:4–42 itself offers a persuasive counterbalance to any attempts to diminish the woman's identity and role. When Jesus' disciples return from the city (4:27), the woman leaves Jesus and goes into the city to testify to her townspeople about Jesus (4:29). On the basis of the woman's testimony (4:30, 39), many of the Samaritan villagers believe in Jesus and go to meet Jesus for themselves. To witness to Jesus—to see Jesus and tell others about that experience—is one of the primary marks of discipleship in John. John the Baptist witnessed to Jesus and led some of his own disciples to Jesus (1:29–37). Jesus' first disciples witnessed to him, and the number of his followers grew (1:40–49). Now the Samaritan woman witnesses to Jesus, and through her words many come to faith. When the Samaritan villagers hear and see Jesus for themselves, the woman's witness is superseded (4:42). That is the appropriate pattern of discipleship and faith. The witness that leads to Jesus is replaced by one's own experience of Jesus. The Samaritan woman is thus a witness and disciple like John the Baptist, Andrew, and Philip.

## Scribes, Pharisees, and Women (7:53–8:11)

The story traditionally known as "the Woman Taken in Adultery" has a complicated textual history. The passage is missing from the earliest Greek manuscripts of John. When the passage is found in manuscripts, it appears in several locations. After 7:52 is the best-attested location, but some manuscripts place the passage after John 7:36, or at the end of the Gospel of John. This complicated textual history influences the way the passage is printed in most English translations (note the brackets that surround John 7:53–8:11 in the NRSV) and has occasioned much scholarly debate. The scholarly consensus holds that the story is an authentic piece of Jesus tradition, but opinion is divided on whether or not the story belonged originally to the tradition of the Gospel of John.

When reading John 7:53–8:11, then, the interpreter finds a situation unique to the New Testament—a well-known Jesus story that is told and retold in the life of the church, but whose textual and canonical status is up for debate. This presents a challenge to the interpreter: while one can comment on the contents and theology of this particular passage, one cannot really move from there to talk about how this passage fits in the larger scheme of John. In many ways, then, John 7:53–8:11 is a story without a time or place, a story to be read on its own terms without sustained reference to its larger literary context.

Just as popular interpretation reads John 4:16–18 as a judgment against the Samaritan woman, popular interpretation of 7:53–8:11 reads this text as a judgment against the woman. In the most prevalent reading of this text, which can be traced back to Augustine, Jesus is the embodiment of grace and the woman is the embodiment of sin. A careful reading of the story, however, shows that this narrow polarity between Jesus and the woman distorts the text.

The story consists of three scenes. The action of the story begins when the scribes and Pharisees bring the woman who has been caught in adultery to Jesus and ask him to judge her case (8:3–5). The second scene of the story begins in 8:6b when Jesus bends down and writes on the ground with his finger. He writes on the ground to indicate his unwillingness to spring the trap that has been set for him. The scribes and Pharisees continue to press him for an answer, so in 8:7 Jesus stands and addresses them directly. The last scene of the story begins in 8:8, when Jesus bends down and writes on the ground again. The crowd departs while Jesus writes on the ground (8:9). In 8:10 Jesus stands up again and speaks to the woman twice. When

he finishes speaking to her, she is free to go, just as the rest of the crowd did.

A careful reading of this story shows that Jesus' focus is not on the woman alone but is evenly divided between the scribes and Pharisees and the woman. Jesus bends down and writes twice and twice stands to address his conversation partners. Indeed, what is striking about this story is that Jesus treats the woman as the social and human equal of the scribes and Pharisees. Jesus speaks to both sets of characters about sin. His words to the scribes and Pharisees, "Let anyone among you who is without sin be the first to throw a stone at her" (8:7), envision the past, the way the crowd has lived until this moment. His words to the woman, "Neither do I condemn you. Go your way, and from now on do not sin again" (8:11), envision the future, the way the woman could live from now on. Jesus invites both the scribes and Pharisees and the woman to begin life anew in the present moment. They are invited to give up old ways and enter a new way of life.

When the scribes and Pharisees brought the woman who had been caught in adultery to Jesus, they dehumanized her, turning her into an object for debate and discussion. Interpretations of John 7:53–8:11 that focus exclusively on the woman and her sexual behavior as sin continue to dehumanize and objectify her. The text does not isolate the woman's sin, nor does Jesus single out the woman as "sinner." Rather, the text identifies all the characters as in need of and receiving an invitation to new life. Jesus does offer grace and mercy to sinners in this story, but the offer is extended equally to scribes, Pharisees, and women.

### Mary, Martha, and Jesus (11:1–44)

One usually thinks of 11:1–44 as the story of the raising of Lazarus, but Jesus' raising of Lazarus actually occupies a very small part of this story. Of the forty-four verses that constitute this story, only seven of them take place at Lazarus's tomb (11:38–44). The miracle of the raising of Lazarus is the climax of this story, but it is not its center. The story centers on the conversations Jesus has as he travels to Lazarus's tomb. These conversations help the reader to see that the raising of Lazarus is not a freak act of nature but is the demonstration of God's power for life. Jesus' main conversation partners as he travels to Lazarus's tomb are Mary and Martha, Lazarus's sisters.

The opening verses of this story contain many references to the family of Lazarus, Mary, and Martha. Lazarus and his illness are mentioned first in 11:1, but the town in which Lazarus lives, Bethany, is identified as "the village of Mary and her sister Martha" (v. 1). The sisters are more well known than their brother. Verse 2 tells us why Mary is so well known. She is the one "who anointed the Lord with perfume and wiped his feet with her hair." On the one hand, this reference is curious, since the anointing does not take place until the next chapter (12:1–8). On the other hand, this reference testifies to the powerful place Mary occupied in the tradition of the early church. One could not speak of this Mary without remembering the story of the anointing (cf. Mark 14:9).

The action of this story begins with the initiative of Mary and Martha. They send Jesus a message about Lazarus's illness (11:3). Their message bears a striking resemblance to the words of Jesus' mother in 2:3 about the wine shortage. In both cases the women do not explicitly request anything of Jesus; they simply present Jesus with the facts. Yet in both cases the reader senses that these women address Jesus with the confidence that he will know what to do. The motivation for Mary and Martha's address to Jesus, and perhaps the source of their confidence in him as well, is their knowledge of his love for Lazarus. Like the story of Jesus and his mother in chap. 2, this is a story about intimates.

John 11:5 shows that Mary and Martha were correct about Jesus' love: Jesus loves the whole family. Yet Jesus' actions in response to that love are puzzling. Instead of rushing to the assistance of this beloved family, Jesus stays away longer (11:6). Jesus is not insensitive to the family's needs, but he understands that this family drama belongs to a larger story. Lazarus's illness is part of the story of the glory of God (11:4). This illness is not an isolated event but is part of Jesus' ministry and mission (11:15). When Jesus finally heads for this family in Bethany, he does so knowing that his return to Judea carries with it the possibility of his own death (11:8). Jesus' own future and the future of this family are inextricably linked.

When Jesus arrives at Bethany, Lazarus has been buried for four days (11:18). Men and women from the Jewish community have come to mourn with the two sisters (11:19). When word of Jesus' approach reaches this grieving family and community, Martha goes first to meet him, while Mary stays at home (11:20).

This detail is reminiscent of the story of Mary and Martha in Luke 10:38–42. Luke and John both may be preserving memories of the same family.

The conversation between Martha and Jesus is the theological heart of this story. Martha's opening words to Jesus express both complaint and confidence, "Lord, if you had been here, my brother would not have died. But even now I know that God will give you whatever you ask of him" (11:21–22). Martha's bold and robust faith empowers her to speak forthrightly to Jesus. Even in the face of her brother's death, she still trusts Jesus to make God's gifts available.

Jesus tells Martha that Lazarus will rise again (11:23). Martha understands those words as a statement of the Jewish belief in the resurrection at the last day (11:24); however, this is not the resurrection of which Jesus speaks. In 11:25 Jesus tells Martha, "I am the resurrection and the life." The victory over death that resurrection represents is available in the present moment in the person of Jesus, not simply in some distant future. Through faith in Jesus, death loses its power and life gains new power (11:26a). Jesus thus challenges and transforms Martha's (and the reader's) traditional understandings of life and death. Jesus places this promise of new life before Martha and asks her, "Do you believe this?" (11:26b).

Martha responds to Jesus' question with a confession of faith (11:27). Yet Martha's confession is spoken in conventional language about Jesus, "the Messiah, the Son of God, the one coming into the world." Her confession rings more of the old than it does of the radical new life offered by Jesus. Martha thus embodies here the central question of this Gospel: Will the faithful continue to contain Jesus within their own predetermined categories, however well-intended those categories may be, or will believers allow Jesus to shatter those categories and thus offer them the radical fullness of his grace?

Martha returns home and quietly summons Mary to Jesus (11:28). Mary speaks to Jesus with the same forthrightness that Martha did (11:32). In addition to her forthrightness, Mary also places her grief before Jesus. She and the Jews who have followed her continue their weeping in Jesus' presence. Their weeping touches Jesus (11:33), and he is finally ready to go to Lazarus's tomb (11:34), where Jesus also weeps (11:35). Jesus' tears may be a sign of his love for this family, as some in the crowd suppose (11:36), but that is not all they signify. Jesus weeps also because of the destructive power of death that is still at work in the world. Once again one sees the intersection of the intimate and the cosmic: the pain of this family reminds Jesus of the pain of the world.

At Lazarus's tomb Jesus orders the stone to be taken away (11:39). Martha tries to stop him, reminding him of how putrid the four-day-old corpse will smell. Martha's dilemma at Lazarus's tomb is the dilemma of all believers: Can one let go of the limits that one places on what is possible in order to embrace the limitless possibilities offered by Jesus? Jesus reminds Martha of what he said earlier, "Did I not tell you that if you believed, you would see the glory of God?" (11:40). Jesus' words hold sway, the stone is rolled away, and Jesus calls Lazarus from death back into life (11:41, 43–44).

Jesus' conversations with Mary and Martha transform this story from a miracle story about the raising of Lazarus into a story about the fullness of new life that is possible to all who believe in Jesus. The initiative of these women in sending for Jesus, their bold and robust faith, the grief and pain that they bring to Jesus, their willingness to engage Jesus in conversation about life, death, and faith, and their unfaltering love for Jesus are marks of the life of faith for John. Martha and Mary model how people are to live as they struggle to free themselves from the power of death that defines and limits them and move to embrace the new promises and possibilities of life available through Jesus.

## The Anointing of Jesus (12:1–8)

The family of Martha, Mary, and Lazarus returns to prominence in the story of the anointing in 12:1–8. In the interval between the raising of Lazarus and this story, the chief priests and the Pharisees have determined that Jesus must be killed (11:53). The upcoming feast of Passover seems a good time to capture him, because as an observant Jewish male, Jesus will probably come up to Jerusalem for the feast (11:55–57). Jesus does indeed return to Judea as Passover approaches. He comes to Bethany to dine with those he loves in the face of his own impending death.

All three family members are mentioned explicitly in this story. Martha, like the Martha in Luke 10:40, serves the meal. Lazarus dines at table with Jesus (12:2). Mary, who is mentioned last (12:3), has the central role in the story.

Mary's anointing of Jesus is narrated in one long sentence in Greek (although the NRSV punctuates it as two sentences): "Mary took a pound of costly perfume made of pure nard, anointed Jesus' feet, and wiped them with her hair. The house was filled with the fragrance of the perfume" (12:3). The anointing is an act of pure extravagance, underscored by the comment that the house was filled with the fragrance of the perfume. Mary has anointed Jesus so lavishly that all present can participate in it. This is the second time a scent has been connected with this family. In 11:39 Martha worried about the odor of Lazarus's rotting corpse. Here, however, the odor is the marvelous fragrance of nard. The odor of death has been replaced by the odor emanating from Mary's extravagant love.

Judas protests the anointing (12:5–6), but his protest does not diminish Mary's act. Rather, it reaffirms the extravagance of her gesture – she has spent almost a year's wages for Jesus. Judas tries to establish a situation of either/or love: either you love Jesus or you love the poor. Jesus refutes Judas by affirming the kind of both/and love Mary has shown: one can love both Jesus and the poor (12:7–8).

This story of the anointing anticipates three crucial parts of the remainder of the Gospel of John. First, as Jesus' words to Judas suggest, the anointing anticipates Jesus' death and burial. Jesus will be anointed again when he is laid in the tomb (19:38–42). At his death, however, Jesus will be anointed in secret by men who are afraid to make public their faith (19:38–39). In this story, Mary unashamedly anoints Jesus in front of all who dined with him. Mary's declaration for Jesus is not deferred until after his death but is offered to Jesus while he lives.

Second, this anointing, in which Mary anoints Jesus' feet rather than his head (cf. Mark 14:3; Matt. 26:7), anticipates the footwashing in John 13:1–20, which has two meanings. One meaning is very familiar: the footwashing models service and discipleship (13:12–16). The second meaning is less familiar: to participate in the footwashing is to participate in Jesus' suffering and death (13:3–11). Mary's anointing of Jesus anticipates both of these meanings. It is an act of service, but it also participates in the events of Jesus' passion. Mary does for Jesus now what Jesus will do for his disciples later.

Third, Mary's anointing of Jesus anticipates the love commandment that Jesus will give his disciples, "I give you a new commandment, that you love one another. Just as I have loved you, you also should love one another" (13:34–35). The depth of Mary's love for Jesus is signaled by the extravagance of her gift. Mary is the first person in the Gospel to live out Jesus' love commandment.

In chap. 11 Mary modeled the robust faith that makes it possible to embrace Jesus' gift of new life. In this story Mary models what it means to be a disciple: to serve, to love one another, to share in Jesus' death.

## Jesus' Mother and the Beloved Disciple (19:25–27)

John 19:25–27 narrates the scene at the foot of Jesus' cross. All four Gospel accounts of Jesus' death agree that it is the women who keep vigil at Jesus' death. Jesus predicted that all the followers would abandon him at his death, scattering to their own homes (16:32), but the women stand firm. In the face of death and the fear of reprisals, the women do not run away. They gather for the death watch (19:25). The tradition does not speculate on the reasons for the women's faithfulness; it simply reports it as fact.

In the Synoptic Gospels the women watch Jesus' death from afar, but in John they stand near the cross, so near that Jesus is able to speak to his mother. Verses 26–27 focus on Jesus' mother and the beloved disciple, who stands with her. This disciple is unnamed in the Gospel and is identified solely on the basis of Jesus' love for him. Like Mary in chap. 12, the disciple returns Jesus' love by being present to Jesus in his need.

Jesus speaks parallel sentences to his mother and the beloved disciple. To his mother he says, "Woman, here is your son" (19:26); to the disciple, "Here is your mother" (19:27). The precise symmetry of Jesus' words reinforces the symbolism of this exchange. Both Jesus' mother and the beloved disciple function as symbolic figures. As Jesus' birth mother and as someone who has been a witness from the beginning (2:1–11), Jesus' mother represents the continuation of Jesus' earthly ministry. The beloved disciple represents the Johannine community and is the symbolic connection between the Jesus tradition and the life of the faith community. In this moment at the foot of Jesus' cross, the past (Jesus' mother) and the future (the beloved disciple) meet. At his death, Jesus ensures continuity between the past and the future.

At the heart of Jesus' ministry is the creation of a new family of God. The creation of this family is symbolized here when the beloved disciple takes Jesus' mother to his own home (19:27). Jesus was rejected by "his own" (1:11), but the beloved disciple's reception of Jesus' mother signals the possibility of a future marked by acceptance, not rejection. The new family that is born at the foot of the cross is marked by love and trust.

In many of the stories from John, the heart of the gospel is lodged in language of intimacy and family. Jesus' mother, the family of Mary, Martha, and Lazarus, and the beloved disciple are all bound to Jesus with the intimate bonds of love. The Gospel of John is frequently criticized for making Jesus seem distant and removed from the everyday realities and struggles of human life. Many of the stories in this Gospel, however, especially those whose principal character is a woman, call such criticisms into question. In these stories Jesus is shown in intimate, loving relationship with family and friends.

## Mary Magdalene and the Risen Jesus (20:1–18)

All four Gospels agree on one vital detail about Easter morning: in the early morning hours, when it was still dark, women went to Jesus' tomb. The specifics of that early morning visit vary from Gospel to Gospel (how many women were at the tomb, who greeted them at the tomb, how they responded to what they saw and heard), but the presence of the women is a constant. As with the women's vigil at Jesus' crucifixion, the tradition does not speculate about this further display of faithfulness by the women. It simply accepts it as an essential part of the story of the resurrection.

The story of Mary Magdalene in chap. 20 is the most detailed of the four stories about women at Jesus' tomb. It divides into two scenes: 20:1–10 (Mary at the empty tomb) and 20:11–18 (Mary and the risen Jesus).

Verses 1–10 establish Mary Magdalene as the first witness of the empty tomb. When she arrives at the tomb, she sees that the stone has been rolled away (20:1). She runs and reports the news to Peter and the beloved disciple (20:2). She offers what appears to be the only logical explanation of the data: someone has taken Jesus' body out of the tomb, and it cannot be found. Mary's confusion reflects the world-shattering dimension of the empty tomb. Until the community encounters the risen Jesus, there are no categories through which to understand the empty tomb. The preresurrection world cannot make sense of an empty tomb with any theory except grave robbing.

On the basis of Mary's words, Peter and the beloved disciple run to the tomb (20:3–4). Both men enter the tomb (20:5–8), but only the response of the beloved disciple is recorded. Verse 8 says that he "saw and believed." His faith is only incipient faith, however, because the story goes on to say that they did not yet know about the resurrection (20:9). The male disciples, like Mary, could find no words out of their prior experiences to describe the empty tomb. Yet Mary bore witness to the tomb even in her confusion; Peter and the beloved disciple kept silent.

The second scene (20:11–18) begins with Mary alone again at the tomb, weeping. She, like Peter and the beloved disciple before her, now looks into the tomb. She is greeted by two angels. The angels address her: "Woman, why are you weeping?" (20:13). The greeting "woman" is the same word that was used by Jesus to address his mother in 2:4 and 19:26 and will be used by the risen Jesus to address Mary in 20:15. Mary's answer to the angels resembles her initial announcement to Peter and the beloved disciple (20:2), but with one important difference. Her words are more personal in 20:13. She speaks of "my Lord" (not "the Lord"); she says, "I do not know" (not "we do not know"). Her words to the angels are spoken out of her personal grief, not simply out of her confusion.

After Mary answers the angels, she turns around (to face the garden) and sees Jesus, "but she did not know that it was Jesus" (20:14). The conversation that takes place between Jesus and Mary at the tomb is one of the most poignant and artfully drawn scenes in all of scripture. The reader knows what Mary does not know— that the man she assumes to be the gardener is really Jesus (20:15). The power of the scene comes from the reader's anticipation of Mary's moment of recognition.

Jesus speaks to Mary, repeating the angels' question about her weeping and asking an additional question, "Whom are you looking for?" (20:15). These questions are the first words spoken by the risen Jesus. His question, "Whom are you looking for?" mirrors the first words he spoke in his ministry. When the followers of John the Baptist approached Jesus, he asked them, "What are you looking for?" (1:38). This question is an invitation that introduces one of the marks of discipleship in John: to look for Jesus. The repetition of that question in chap.

20 establishes continuity between Mary and the first disciples of Jesus.

Jesus' questions to Mary do not penetrate her grief and confusion. Her world is determined by the seemingly harsh reality of the empty tomb, and so she begs the "gardener" for assistance: "Sir, if you have carried him away, tell me where you have laid him, and I will take him away" (20:15). Because Mary still has no categories with which to grasp the significance of the empty tomb, she assumes that the solution to the mystery of the missing body lies within her control. If the gardener would tell her what she needs to know, she would take care of the situation.

The word the "gardener" speaks changes Mary's world forever. The risen Jesus calls Mary by name, and when she hears her name spoken in his voice, she turns around again. But this time she sees Jesus, her teacher, not the gardener (20:16). Once again the intimate and the cosmic conjoin: through the intimacy of Mary's name, the reality of the resurrection is revealed.

When Mary listens to the voice of the risen Jesus, her perspective on the events in the garden changes. She no longer understands the empty tomb as a manifestation of death, but as testimony to the power and possibilities of life. In the parable of the shepherd in John 10, Jesus said, "[The shepherd] calls his own sheep by name and leads them out. . . . The sheep follow him because they know his voice" (10:3–4). Jesus called Lazarus by name to summon him from the tomb (11:43), and now his voice summons Mary to new life.

Mary may have attempted to embrace Jesus after she recognized him, because he says to her, "Do not hold on to me, because I have not yet ascended to the Father" (20:17a). Jesus' words may strike some readers as unnecessarily harsh, as a cruel rebuke to Mary's expression of joyous recognition. To read these words as cold and harsh is to misread them, however, and to overlook their import.

Jesus' command, "Do not hold on to me," is the first postresurrection teaching. When he speaks these words, Jesus teaches Mary that he cannot and will not be held and controlled. One cannot hold Jesus to preconceived standards and expectations of who he should be, because to do so is to interfere with Jesus' work and thereby limit what Jesus has to offer. If Mary had stopped Jesus from ascending to God, holding him with her in the garden, the Easter story would be incomplete. Jesus' prohibition to Mary thus actually contains the good news of Easter: Do not hold on to me, but let me be free so that I can give you the fullness of what I have to offer.

Jesus' prohibition is followed by a positive exhortation, "But go to my brothers [and sisters] and say to them, 'I am ascending to my Father and your Father, to my God and your God'" (20:17). Instead of holding on to Jesus and keeping him static, Mary is exhorted to spread the news of the resurrection and ascension and of the new life with God and one another that is now available to all. Those who follow Jesus have become members of the family of God and Jesus.

Mary heeds Jesus' words and goes to the disciples with the announcement, "I have seen the Lord" (20:18). Her announcement of the presence of the risen Jesus is the core of the Easter gospel. Her confusion and sadness at the empty tomb have been transformed by her encounter with Jesus into the witness of Easter. Mary is the first Easter witness in both senses of the word "witness." She is the first to see the risen Jesus, and she is the first to tell others what she has seen. She is the first disciple of the risen Jesus.

### John and Women's Experience

The seven passages discussed above show the pivotal place women occupy in the unfolding of the story of Jesus in the Gospel of John. In addition to these passages, however, there are general theological themes in the Gospel that need to be highlighted. While these themes do not deal with or address women specifically, consideration of them from the angle of women's concerns offers a fresh perspective on John that might otherwise be overlooked.

*The language of love.* Chapters 13–17 are known as the Farewell Discourse, because here Jesus speaks to his disciples just prior to his arrest, trial, and death. Jesus prepares his disciples for his departure from them and for their life in his absence. What Jesus envisions as the future for his disciples is the present reality for the reader of the Gospel, because the contemporary church lives without the physical presence of Jesus and is sustained by Jesus' words. Jesus' words in chaps. 13–17 offer a vision of the new life that is possible for all who follow him.

At the heart of this vision is the community's love for one another: "I give you a new commandment, that you love one another. Just as I have loved you, you also should love one another." This vision of love receives its most explicit statement in 13:34–35; 15:12; and 15:17, but the language of love runs throughout the Farewell Discourse (e.g., 14:15, 21, 23–24; 15:8–9).

When the commandment to love one another is compared with the abundance and variety of ethical teaching in Matthew and Luke, the ethics of John are often found wanting. For example, in Matthew and Luke Jesus commands that one love one's enemies, but in John, Jesus commands only one thing: Love one another as I have loved you. To find the ethical demand of this commandment too easy and somehow inferior, however, is to be deceived by the simplicity of its wording and the sharpness of its focus. It is also to dismiss the language of love and mutuality as not being serious ethical categories.

The commandment to love one another is essentially sectarian; that is, its primary focus is on the life of the Christian community. That focus does not provide grounds for dismissing the ethical seriousness of the commandment. Indeed, the history of the church and of individual communities of faith suggests that to love one another may be the most difficult thing Jesus could have asked. There are many circumstances in which it is easier to love one's enemies than it is to love those with whom one lives, works, and worships day after day.

John 13:35 states, "By this everyone will know that you are my disciples, if you have love for one another." Love for one another is to be the identifying mark of the Christian community in the world. How can the church be an effective witness to Jesus' love if it cannot enact that love among its own members? The love Christians are commanded to have for one another will continue the work and presence of Jesus after his death and resurrection.

The language of love is a different ethical language from the language of discipleship found in the Synoptic Gospels. It is language of fullness rather than language of emptying. One will give one's life for one's friends as an act of love (15:13), not as an act of self-denial and sacrifice, as it is understood in the Synoptic Gospels (e.g., Mark 8:34). In John, one gives out of the abundance of one's love, not out of the denial of one's self.

The Johannine language of the fullness and abundance of love is very important for women, because a one-sided emphasis on emptying and self-denial has led many women (and some men) to subscribe to an ethos of perpetual self-sacrifice and the meaninglessness of self. The Gospel of John provides a much-needed balance to this ethos. Fullness and the sharing of love characterize discipleship and faith. The Christian community is known by how much its members love one another, not by how much they deny themselves. The ultimate sign of this love remains the giving of one's life, but it will be given in fullness of self, not in denial.

The Gospel of John makes clear that the Christians' love for one another derives from and is modeled on Jesus' love for his followers. Jesus loves his followers by making God known to them (14:10–11), giving them God's word (17:14), embodying God's love (17:23), calling many and varied sheep into his fold (10:16), calling his followers "friend," not servant (15:14–15), and laying down his life for his friends (10:17–18). All of these ways, not exclusively the last, model how the community of Jesus' followers is to love one another.

*The vine metaphor.* In John 15:1–11 Jesus paints a picture of the Christian community with his metaphor of the vine and its branches. The metaphor is quite vivid: Jesus is the vine, those who love Jesus are the branches, and God is the vine grower who tends the vine, pruning and trimming branches so that they bear fruit.

Two aspects of this metaphor are striking. First, the vine metaphor characterizes the Christian community as a community of interrelationship, mutuality, and indwelling. This mutuality is conveyed by the use of the verb "abide," which occurs ten times in 15:1–11. To "abide" means to remain and suggests constancy of presence. The term "abide" describes Jesus' relationship to God (15:10), Jesus' relationship to the community (15:4, 9), and the community's relationship to Jesus (15:1, 7). In their mutuality, Jesus and God anticipate the possibilities of life for the community.

Individuals in the community will prosper only insofar as they recognize themselves as members of an organic unit. No individual is a free agent, but is one branch of an encircling and intertwining vine whose fruitfulness depends on abiding with Jesus: "Just as the branch cannot bear fruit by itself unless it abides in the vine, neither can you unless you abide in me. I am the vine, you are the branches. Those who abide in me and I in them bear much fruit, because apart from me you can do nothing" (15:4–5).

The life envisioned in this metaphor stands in striking contrast to contemporary Western models of individualism, privatism, and success based on individual accomplishment. This metaphor assumes social interrelationship and accountability. In the vine metaphor, an individual is fruitful only as he or she abides with others in Jesus' love. The mutuality envisioned by the vine metaphor is a sign of the presence and work of God: "As the Father has loved me, so I have loved you; abide in my love" (15:9).

Second, the metaphor of the vine provides a radical nonhierarchical, perhaps even antihierarchical image for the composition and constitution of the church. One branch is indistinguishable from another; no branch has pride of place. All branches are rooted together in the one vine, and only as a result of their common root can they bear fruit. The task of assessing fruitfulness falls to God alone (15:2), not to any of the branches. As the vine grower, God works to prune and shape the vine so that it produces the maximum fruit. God decides what is dead wood and determines where and when to prune back a dead stick to find green wood and the promise of new life. Since God and God alone is the vine grower, all branches are equal before God. The future of the vine, of the church, is entrusted to God, not to any of the branches. There is no bishop branch, elder branch, or church bureaucrat branch with special status in this vine. One cannot distinguish between clergy and laity in this vine.

Jesus is the vine of the church, out of, into, and around which all the branches grow. The vine metaphor is a powerful image of the church: the center vine out of which the branches grow is identifiable, but the mass of intertwining branches is indistinguishable. One cannot tell which branch sprouted first, which branch is longest, where one branch stops and another branch begins. Hierarchy among members is impossible in the vine of the church, because all members grow out of the same vine and are tended equally by the one vine grower.

*Father language for God.* The question of the appropriate language to use for God is an important and painful one for many women. Until recently the church almost exclusively used male pronouns and images for God, overlooking both the rich variety of names and images for God in the biblical and historical material and the political and theological assumptions that lay behind this language. The exclusive use of male language for God is not a neutral or objective act, simply reflecting the "reality of God" (as proponents of such usage would argue). Rather, all decisions about the language with which people speak about God involve political and theological choices, because language shapes how people understand their relationship to one another and to God. Many women feel excluded from a faith community that allows no visible place for women in its public language.

Father language for God is particularly painful for many women because of the burden of patriarchy it frequently carries. "Father" has become a synonym for God in much of the church, but to use father language that way simultaneously reduces the power of father language and diminishes the richness of other parts of the Christian tradition. When Father becomes a synonym for God, one loses the specificity of that language in the stories and books of the Bible in which it first appears. A vibrant image of God is replaced by a theological absolute.

God is called Father more times in John than in any other book in the New Testament (over one hundred times), and to attempt to eliminate that term in the interests of inclusive language would destroy the particularity of the Johannine vision. Just as it is false to the richness of the Christian tradition to use father language as generic language for God, it is equally false to the tradition to speak about God in general terms that flatten the vitality and depth of biblical metaphor and language. God is Father in John, and the church's job is to move beyond the assumption that Father is simply a synonym for God and discover what father language in John contributes to a fuller understanding of God and the Christian life.

Father language in John is essentially relational: God is Father because Jesus is God's Son. This language, then, is not primarily the language of patriarchy but is instead the language of intimacy, relationship, and family. From the very beginning of the Gospel, the explicit purpose of Jesus' ministry has been to create a new family of God: "But to all who received him, who believed in his name, he gave power to become children of God, who were born, not of blood or of the will of the flesh or of the will of man, but of God" (1:12–13). The promise in these verses is that a new family will be born, a family that is determined by faith, not by flesh and blood relationships. People who have no families, who come from destructive families, or who are alienated from their birth families can belong to a new family by virtue of becoming children of God. This promise of a new family receives its most poignant expression in Jesus' words in John 14:18: "I will not leave you orphaned." All who believe are offered a family and a home (see also 14:1–3).

The language of birth and family continues throughout the Gospel: e.g., 3:3–10; 8:31–47; 14:1–3, 18–24; 16:20–24; 19:25–27; 20:17. Moreover, as has already been noted, many of the pivotal events in Jesus' ministry occur in the presence of those whom he loves. Jesus' announcement to Mary of the good news of Easter is couched in the language of family: "But go to my brothers [and sisters] and say to them, 'I am ascending to my Father and your Father, to my God and your God'" (20:17). At Jesus' ascension, the creation of the new family is fully under way: Jesus' followers are now called his brothers and sisters, children of God.

The intent of this discussion of language is not to minimize the male language of God in John but to show how the church's almost exclusive focus on the maleness of that language as what is essential and normative actually distorts the function of that language in John. John speaks of God as Father not in order to reinforce patriarchy (recall the nonhierarchical image of the vine in John 15:1–11) but in order to evoke a new world in which intimate relations with God and one another are possible.

## BIBLIOGRAPHY

Brown, Raymond E. *The Gospel According to John*. Anchor Bible 29, 29A. Garden City, N.Y.: Doubleday & Co., 1966, 1970.

Kysar, Robert. *John*. Minneapolis: Augsburg Publishing House, 1986.

O'Day, Gail. *The Word Disclosed: John's Story and Narrative Preaching*. St. Louis: CBP Press, 1987.

Ringe, Sharon. "Homiletical Resources on the Gospel of John: The Gospel as Healing Word." *Quarterly Review* [Nashville] 6 (1986), 75–103.

Schneiders, Sandra. "Women in the Fourth Gospel and the Role of Women in the Contemporary Church." *Biblical Theology Bulletin* 12 (1982), 35–45.

Yee, Gale A. *Jewish Feasts and The Gospel of John*. Wilmington, Del.: Michael Glazier, 1989.

# ACTS

## Gail R. O'Day

## Introduction

The Acts of the Apostles is a unique book in the literature of the New Testament. It is neither gospel nor epistle, although it shares characteristics with both of those types of writing. Acts and the four Gospels are all narratives; that is, they are essentially stories. Acts and the New Testament epistles share a common subject matter, the life and struggles of the early church. The story the four Gospels tell does not include the story of the church, however; nor do the epistles present the life of the church in story form. Acts is the only New Testament book to tell the *story* of the *church*.

### Authorship and Date

The reader of Acts is better able to understand both its literary form and its theological purposes if he or she remembers that Acts is not a freestanding volume in the New Testament. Acts is the second volume of the story begun in the Gospel of Luke. The opening verses of Acts contain a statement of the relationship of Luke and Acts as a two-volume work: "In the first book, Theophilus, I wrote all that Jesus did and taught from the beginning until the day when he was taken up to heaven . . ." (Acts 1:1–2). The author of Acts identifies himself as the same person who wrote "the first book," the Gospel of Luke. It is therefore conventional to refer to the author of Acts as "Luke" and to refer to the two books as Luke-Acts in order to emphasize their unity. Luke and Acts are separated from each other in the canon because of the practice of grouping the four Gospels together. Since Luke and Acts were written by the same author as two parts of the same work, they can be dated together, approximately 90 C.E. (For additional discussion of the authorship of Luke, see the commentary on Luke.)

The title "Acts of the Apostles" was given to the second volume of Luke by the later church and is somewhat of a misnomer. "Apostle" in Luke-Acts is restricted to the twelve apostles. Paul is therefore not an apostle in Lukan terms, yet Paul is the central character of Acts. The title reflects the later church's interpretation of this book and should not be read as a key to Luke's intentions in Acts.

### Narrative Overview

Acts is often perceived as the first document of Christian history and hence as a source for the history of the early church. Acts is not primarily history, however. Although it may contain historical facts, it is not an objective chronicle of the early church. Acts' ambiguous relationship to early Christian history becomes apparent when one compares the Paul of Acts to the Paul of his own letters. Acts' version of events differs from Paul's own at significant places (cf. Acts 9:3–30 and Gal. 1:13–17; Acts 15 and Gal. 2:1–10). Acts should be understood primarily as a story of the early church as told by Luke and colored by Luke's interests and theological stance.

Acts 1:8 provides a key to the narrative movement and structure of Acts: "But you will receive power when the Holy Spirit has come upon you; and you will be my witnesses in Jerusalem, in all Judea and Samaria, and to the ends of the earth." Chapters 1–7 narrate the spread of Christianity (under the guidance of the Holy Spirit) in Jerusalem and Judea. Chapters 8–12 focus on Samaria and surrounding areas, and chaps. 13–28 narrate the movement of the gospel to the "ends of the earth," that is, Rome.

Acts thus narrates the movement of the church from its origins in Jerusalem to a broader world stage. The two main characters responsible for this movement are Peter and Paul, and Paul receives the lion's share of attention. The two pivotal events in the movement of the gospel away from Jerusalem are the conversion of Saul (Paul) in Acts 9 and Peter's baptism of the Gentile Cornelius in Acts 10. These events are so important to Acts that they are recounted more than once. The Cornelius story is repeated in Acts 11:1–18, and Paul retells the story of his conversion in Acts 22 and 26.

## The Purpose of Acts

By presenting the stories of Jesus and the church as two parts of one continuous story, Luke accords theological significance to the church. The period of the church, the time between the ascension of Jesus and his return (Acts 1:11), is not understood simply as a waiting period, but is a fruitful time in its own right. Neither is the period of the church to be esteemed for its antiquarian value, because the church is the basis and vehicle for the ongoing proclamation of the gospel. Luke's purpose in writing Acts is not to point backward to the church's past but to use the story of the church to point forward to the ongoing witness of the gospel.

This witness is accomplished through the presence and work of the Holy Spirit in the church. The Holy Spirit that descended on Mary at Jesus' conception (Luke 1:35) and anointed Jesus in Nazareth (Luke 4:18) now descends on the church (Acts 2:1–4) and guides the activities of apostles and disciples (e.g., Acts 4:31; 8:29; 15:8; 19:21). Luke tells the stories of Jesus and the church in a way that makes the work of the Spirit visible.

As noted, Luke's primary concern in Acts is

with the mission to the Gentiles, the movement of the church outward from the confines of Palestine to the expanses of the Roman Empire. Paul testifies before imperial functionaries, the governors Felix (Acts 24) and Festus (25:6–12) and King Agrippa (26:1–32), in order to show that "this was not done in a corner" (26:26). An angel even tells Paul that he will stand before the emperor in Rome (27:24).

Luke structures the story of Acts to show the successful witness of Christianity in the Roman world. At the end of Acts, Paul is in custody in Rome, yet the last verse of Acts is one of triumph and promise. It describes Paul as "proclaiming the kingdom of God and teaching about the Lord Jesus Christ with all boldness and without hindrance" (28:31). In reality Paul was martyred in Rome, but Luke leaves both Paul's fate and Acts open-ended in order to emphasize the ongoing life of the gospel witness rather than the fate of its proclaimers. Luke paints a picture of a church that can thrive in the Roman Empire and be a factor in world history.

## Acts and Women

Women have a limited role in the accomplishment of Luke's purposes in Acts. Luke frames Acts around the ministries of Peter and especially Paul, because they embody for him the movement of the gospel from Jews to Gentiles. The ministries of all other teachers and leaders, male and female, are diminished as a result of this emphasis. It is important therefore to remember that Acts does not contain a representative picture of church leadership. In addition, Luke's desire to present a picture of Christianity that would win favor in the Roman Empire led to a further diminishment of women's roles in Acts. Women were second-class citizens in the Roman Empire; public leadership roles were all held by men (see "Everyday Life: Women in the Period of the New Testament"). Luke shapes his treatment of women in Acts to conform to this Roman model.

## Comment

Luke includes women in Acts' story of the church in two distinct ways. First, the narrative contains scattered references to women as a group (e.g., Acts 5:14). These references show how Luke perceives the general role and function of women in the early church. Second, Acts narrates five stories that feature individual

women (Acts 5:1–11; 9:36–43; 12:12–17; 16:11–40; 18:1–4, 18–28). These stories about individual women balance the general references by providing the reader of Acts with a concrete glimpse (albeit one determined by Luke's purposes in Acts) of what life was like for some women in the early church. (For a statistical picture of the number and type of appearances of women in Acts, see the commentary on Luke.)

## Women Believers in the Early Church

After Jesus' ascension (Acts 1:9–11), a group of believers gathered in an upper room in Jerusalem to pray (1:13–14). The group that met together consisted of men and women. The men are all identified by name; they are the eleven remaining disciples (1:13). Of the women who gather in the upper room, however, only one is identified by name, "Mary the mother of Jesus" (1:14). The mention of Mary serves a theological purpose for Luke because it establishes continuity between the birth of Jesus and the birth of the church.

The anonymity of the remaining women in the upper room suggests that women do not have equal standing with men in this gathering. Acts 1:21–26 makes the disparity between men and women even clearer: only a man can be elected to replace Judas as the twelfth apostle. Luke attaches symbolic importance to both the "twelve" and the term "apostle." First, Luke is concerned to portray the church as the new Israel, and the twelve apostles thus represent the twelve sons of Jacob, the twelve tribes of Israel. Symmetry with the Old Testament story demands that the Twelve be men. The Twelve also need to be men in order to correspond to Roman models of leadership.

Second, "apostle" is a technical term for Luke, used almost exclusively to refer to the Twelve, not to church leaders in general. (The one exception to this usage is Acts 14:14.) This is a much narrower understanding of "apostle" than is found elsewhere in the New Testament. The term "apostle" occurs only in the sections of Acts that focus on the Jerusalem church. Once the focus of Acts shifts to the Gentile mission, "apostle" drops from the narrative. "Apostle" thus refers to those men who carry the ministry of the historical Jesus into the emerging church. It describes a very limited ministry that excludes all women and most of the men in Acts.

In addition to this initial gathering of disciples, Luke makes other group references to women as members of the church. The context of Acts 2:1–4 suggests that women were among those present when the Holy Spirit descended on the church at Pentecost. In summary descriptions of both Jewish and Gentile converts, Luke mentions women. In response to signs and wonders performed by the apostles in Jerusalem, "yet more than ever believers were added to the Lord, great numbers of both men and women" (5:14). When Paul travels to Greece, women are numbered among those who join him in Tyre (17:4), Beroea (17:12), and Athens (17:34). The social standing of these Greek women is important to Luke: they were "leading women" (17:4), of "high standing" (17:12). With the exception of Damaris (17:34), these women believers are unnamed and thus undifferentiated.

Acts 21:5 also documents the presence of women as full participants in a Christian community, but the NRSV translation masks this fact. The NRSV translation of 21:5 reads, "and all of them, with wives and children, escorted us outside the city." The Greek word for "woman" and "wife" is the same (gyne), and there are neither linguistic nor contextual grounds for preferring "wives" to "women" in this verse. The more accurate translation is "and all of them, with women and children. . . ." The NRSV prejudices the reading of the verse when it translates gyne as "wife," because it describes women as secondary participants, present only because they accompanied their husbands. Acts 21:5 actually describes the inclusiveness of the Christian community at Tyre. Men, women, and children pray with Paul and bid him farewell (21:6).

## Asides About Women

Some of Acts' more suggestive glimpses into the lives of women in the church surface when the main focus of the story is elsewhere. For example, Acts 8 and 9 tell the story of Saul's persecution of the church. The initial description of Saul's ravaging of the church notes that Saul dragged off "both men and women" and "committed them to prison" (8:3). At a later stage in the persecution, Saul asks the high priest to provide him with letters for the synagogues in Damascus, "so that if he found any who belonged to the Way, men or women, he might bring them bound to Jerusalem" (9:2; see also 22:4).

These details about Saul's persecution of the church suggest that female Christians were as dangerous as male Christians to Saul. Since women were persecuted as vigorously as men were, women must have been understood as full members of the community. Acts 13:50 contains an interesting twist on the persecution motif, because there Luke reveals that women could also be equal participants in the opposition to the church.

Another suggestive reference to a group of women believers is found in an aside about Paul's visit to Philippi. When Paul and his companions were looking for a place to worship on the Sabbath, "[they] went outside the gate by the river, where [they] supposed there was a place of prayer; and [they] sat down and spoke to the women who had gathered there" (16:13). In Philippi Paul found a Sabbath gathering composed *exclusively of women*. Luke offers no comment on this gathering apart from this mention of it in relation to Paul's itinerary. Even this brief reference, however, opens up a whole new way of envisioning the lives of first-century Christian women. Were there other gatherings of women that have gone unreported? This Sabbath gathering suggests that as early as the first century, women believers sought ways to hear their own voices and stories in worship, freed from the dictates of the male-dominated church.

## Women and Ministry in the Early Church

Luke mentions women also in relation to two ministries of the early Christian communities. The first is the ministry to widows. Neglect of some widows in the daily food distribution is the precipitating factor in the disagreement between Greek-speaking Jews ("Hellenists") and Aramaic-speaking Jews ("Hebrews") (Acts 6:1). In this disagreement, the community's care of the widow is assumed.

The positive side of this ministry to widows is that it shows the early church's care for those who were without their own economic resources. The ministry to widows continues the Old Testament imperative to care for the widow, the orphan, and the sojourner. This ministry also has a downside, however. First, it helps to perpetuate women's economic dependence on the church. Second, the group that is formed in Acts 6:3–6 to assist in the supervision of this ministry of service consists of seven men. The twelve apostles (6:2) perpetuate their model of leadership in this new group. Women are the objects of ministry in Acts 6:1–6, not agents of ministry.

The distinction the apostles make in 6:2 between the ministry of the word and the ministry of waiting on tables is also a mixed event. Elsewhere in the New Testament, widows will become the agents for the ministry of service to other widows (1 Tim. 5:9–16). Luke never explicitly labels this service by women as ministry in Acts (see the discussions of Tabitha and Lydia below), but the hierarchy of ministerial responsibilities in this text had important repercussions for women. In the subsequent history of the church, the ministry of the word will be understood as men's ministry, and

ministry of service will become the acceptable arena for women's ministry.

The second ministry involving women in Acts is the prophetic ministry. In Acts 21:8 Paul visits Philip (one of the seven appointed in Acts 6:5), who has "four unmarried daughters who had the gift of prophecy" (21:9). This notice is the only comment Luke makes on these women and their ministry. Unlike the prophet Agabus (21:11) and the prophets at Tyre (21:4), the content of the daughters' prophecies is not given. The prophetic activity of both men and women is a sign of the Spirit at work in the church (Acts 2:17–18), but in telling his story of the church, Luke almost completely ignores women's prophetic ministry. No additional women prophets are named in Acts, even though other New Testament writings attest to women's prophetic activity (e.g., 1 Cor. 11:5). These four virgin daughters, children of a well-known church leader, may have been so renowned in the tradition that Luke could not avoid mentioning them when he discussed the church at Caesarea. The reality of women's prophetic activities in the church may have constrained Luke from suppressing all mention of it, but he did succeed in keeping this ministry at the margins of his story of the church.

On the one hand, then, Luke's summary descriptions of the constituency of early Christian communities testify to the conversion of women and their membership in communities of faith. On the other hand, these general statements about women occur infrequently in Acts, which suggests that women's participation in the church was an incidental item for Luke, attention to which is not sustained with any intentionality throughout the sweep of the narrative. At times (e.g., in the case of women's prophetic ministries in the churches), Luke tells only a fraction of women's stories. As was noted in the discussion of Saul's persecution of the church and the gathering of women at Philippi, the most suggestive images of women's experience surface when details of women's lives form the backdrop of narratives seemingly unrelated to women's concerns.

## Ananias and Sapphira (5:1–11)

The first story in Acts in which an individual woman figures prominently is the story of Ananias and Sapphira. This story, in which two Christians are struck dead as a direct result of their deception of the community, is perhaps the most infamous story in Acts. It offends modern sensibilities and defies any rational or psychological explanations. The harshness of this story can be neither softened nor explained away. It is a difficult story and the reader's best option is to attempt to read the story on its own terms and discern its function in Acts.

As shocking as the story of Ananias and Sapphira is, it is not without precedent in the Bible. This story parallels the Old Testament stories of Achan (Josh. 7:1–26) and Saul and the Amalekites (1 Samuel 15). In each of these stories, the central character knowingly disobeys God by keeping back some of the war booty, and this deception leads to his demise. Achan is killed at God's command, and God renounces Saul as king because of Saul's disobedience. This renunciation ultimately leads to Saul's death.

In Acts 5:1–11 the couple's deception of the community is established in the opening verses (5:1–2a). This introduction highlights Sapphira's involvement: "with the consent of his wife . . . with his wife's knowledge. . . ." Luke's intent in 5:1–2 is to stress the complicity of both partners in the deception, but he has inadvertently provided an intriguing detail about Ananias and Sapphira's marriage. Ananias does not make unilateral decisions for the household but instead consults with his wife about the sale and disposition of the property. Although this is not Luke's main purpose, 5:1–2 shows Sapphira as having an equal voice in the economic management of her marriage.

The story proper employs a Lukan technique found also in the Gospel, the pairing of male and female characters (e.g., Luke 2:25–35 and 2:36–38; Luke 15:3–7 and 15:8–10). The structure and content of the scene featuring Ananias (Acts 5:2b–6) and that featuring Sapphira (5:7–11) are remarkably similar. Both are accused of lying to the Holy Spirit (5:3–4, 9). Upon hearing the accusation, both fall down and die (5:5, 10a). Both are carried out of the room by young men and buried (5:6, 10b). Ananias remains silent throughout the story and Sapphira speaks once (5:8).

The story of Ananias and Sapphira is a cautionary tale, intended to warn the Christian community of the dangers of deceiving the Holy Spirit and lying to God. The sharing of property provides the occasion for the deceit, but the story's warning is more general. The story itself signals the response that Luke wants to evoke in his readers, "And great fear seized the whole church and all who heard of these things" (5:11). Both Christians and non-Christians who hear this story are to stand in awe of the power of God to avenge deceit against the Holy Spirit. The pairing of male and female characters shows that Luke intends both men and women to learn the lesson of this story. It is probably not coincidental that the first general reminder that both men and women joined the church immediately follows this story (5:14).

## The Raising of Tabitha (9:36–43)

The story of the raising of Tabitha (Dorcas) also follows the Lukan pattern of pairing stories with male and female characters. In Acts 9:32–35 Peter heals Aeneas, a paralytic man who has been bedridden for eight years (9:32). Peter's raising of Tabitha (9:36–43) immediately follows the Aeneas story. The story in which the man is the central character is briefer and less colorful than the Tabitha story. Both stories have a similar function in Acts, however: to portray Peter as a miracle worker in the line of Elijah and Elisha and Jesus and to win converts to Christianity (9:35, 42).

Tabitha is an important person in the Christian community at Joppa. Her death affects the disciples so much that they send two men to bring Peter to her bedside (9:38). Indeed, Tabitha is identified as a "disciple." She is the only woman explicitly identified as a disciple in Acts, and 9:36 is the only occurrence of the feminine form of "disciple" (mathetria) anywhere in the New Testament.

Tabitha's value to the Joppa community comes from her "good works and acts of charity" (9:36). This phrase warrants careful attention. The expression "acts of charity" is more accurately translated as "almsdeeds," that is, almsgiving, and neither this expression nor "good works" are used to describe anyone else's service in Acts. Verse 39 provides a specific example of Tabitha's "good works": she has made clothes for the widows of Joppa. The word "ministry" (diakonia) is not used to describe Tabitha's work, although Luke does refer to men's care of widows as diakonia in Acts 6:1 and 4.

When Luke's description of Tabitha is read carefully, it becomes clear that Tabitha is valued as a philanthropist, a woman, seemingly a widow herself, who takes care of the needy widows in Joppa out of her own resources. She spends her own money to care for the widows, not the church's money. It is no wonder that the widows weep when she dies (9:39) and are among the first to be shown that their benefactress has been restored to life (9:41). Tabitha is the proper society matron, doing works of charity and sewing clothes for the less fortunate.

Tabitha's service to the community of women at Joppa is indeed to be valued as a model of discipleship. One has to wonder, however, why when men take care of widows, Luke calls it "ministry" (6:4) but when Tabitha performs the same services Luke calls it "good works."

### Rhoda at the Gate (12:12–17)

The story of Rhoda is a brief interlude in the story of Peter's escape from prison. Peter has been imprisoned by King Herod and is being kept under maximum security (12:4, 6). Despite Herod's extreme security measures, Peter is rescued from his imprisonment by "an angel of the Lord" (12:7–11). Once Peter is out of prison, he goes "to the house of Mary, the mother of John whose other name was Mark" (12:12). Many believers had gathered at Mary's house to pray for Peter's deliverance (12:5, 12). When Peter knocks at Mary's gate, her maid Rhoda answers (12:13).

The description of Mary and her house in 12:12–13 reveals two details about Mary's standing in the Jerusalem community. First, her identification as John's mother indicates that her son is more well known than she is. Her offspring is her distinguishing feature. Second, Mary has a house large enough to hold a gathering of believers and to be separated from the street by a gate and courtyard. Her privileged economic position is further attested by the reference to her maid, Rhoda.

The story of Rhoda and Peter is a masterful piece of storytelling, full of comedy and suspense. It is comic when Rhoda, overwhelmed with joy at the sight of Peter, runs to announce his arrival without letting him in (12:15). Yet the story is also suspenseful, because the reader wonders whether Peter will be reapprehended while he waits to be admitted to his own community.

The response of the gathered community to Rhoda's news recalls the reception the women received in Luke 24. In both stories, women have important news to communicate, truth about the power of God to overcome seemingly unconquerable obstacles; yet in both instances the women's words are dismissed. The women's announcement of the empty tomb is rejected by the eleven apostles as "an idle tale" (Luke 24:11). Rhoda's announcement that Peter is standing at the gate is taken first as a sign of Rhoda's mental instability ("You are out of your mind"), then as a sign of her delusion ("It is his angel," 12:15). In both instances, the women were

without any intrinsic authority that would grant credence to their messages. In Luke 24, the women dared to bring news to the inner circle of the eleven apostles. In Acts 12, Rhoda has even less authority because of her social status as a servant. The women's attempts to convey the good news are thwarted by the resistance of their listeners.

### The Women at Philippi (16:11–40)

The story of Paul's visit to Philippi contains many references to women. As noted earlier, Paul's first experience of the Philippian church is a Sabbath gathering of women (16:13). This Sabbath gathering is the setting in which Paul meets Lydia, a Gentile woman who worships God but is not a member of the Christian community (16:14). She listens to Paul at the women's gathering, and eventually she and her household are baptized (16:15). Lydia offers her home as a center for Paul and the other missionaries. The story of Paul and Lydia is in many ways the abbreviated counterpart to the story of Peter and Cornelius in Acts 10. Lydia is the first official European convert in the same way that Cornelius was the first official Gentile convert. Luke's male/female parallelism is again operative.

Lydia is a businesswoman who sells purple cloth, which was a luxury item for the wealthy (cf. Luke 16:19). Her business therefore put her in contact with the elite of Philippi. Her offer of her home as a missionary center and the information that she was the head of her household (16:15) suggest that Lydia is wealthy herself. Once again Luke draws attention to a wealthy woman who acts as benefactor to a growing Christian community. Lydia embodies Luke's ideal of women's contribution to the church: to provide housing and economic resources. Acts 16:40 suggests that Lydia's house quickly became a center of the Philippian church, but Luke does not credit Lydia with any leadership role in that development.

The next woman Luke encounters in Philippi lives in a completely different world from that inhabited by Lydia. She is an unnamed slave girl whose owners exploit her gift of divination to make money for themselves (16:16). When Paul passed this woman in the streets of Philippi, she proclaimed him to be a man of God (16:17). Her words announce the truth about Paul and Silas, but her repeated utterances annoyed Paul. He therefore silences her in the name of Jesus (16:18). Paul could have attempted to convert the slave girl but instead only silences her. The silencing of the woman may reflect Luke's discomfort with the prophetic voice of women in the church. The scene can be read as emblematic of Luke's silencing of women prophets throughout Acts.

Once Paul silences the slave girl, she is forgotten. The focus of the story shifts to the loss of income her owners suffer because of her silence. The slave owners have Paul and Silas thrown in jail, which leads to a miraculous escape from prison similar to Peter's in Acts 12. The slave girl vanishes completely from the purview of the narrative. What becomes of her life after Paul silences her divination? Is she returned to the slave market once her economic value to her owners disappears? The slave girl is only a commodity to her owners, and she is treated no better by Paul and the story itself. Luke shows no interest in the slave girl as a human being. She is only a narrative prop to show the power of God at work in Paul.

## Priscilla and Aquila (18:1–4, 18–28)

When Paul encounters Priscilla and Aquila, Luke is faced with telling the story of a well-known female Christian leader. Priscilla and Aquila, wife and husband, were important missionaries in Corinth and Ephesus. Their expulsion from Rome suggests that they were active in the church in Rome as well (18:2).

Luke does not spend much time on Priscilla and Aquila, because as always, his main focus is on Paul. What he does write, however, provides insight into women's leadership roles in the church, information hitherto lacking in Acts. Priscilla and Aquila are always mentioned as a pair. Sometimes Aquila is mentioned first (18:2), sometimes Priscilla (18:18, 26). This suggests that the two were genuine partners in ministry and that Priscilla was not Aquila's subordinate (see also Rom. 16:3–4; 1 Cor. 16:19). Acts 18:3 leaves open the possibility that Priscilla also worked alongside Aquila and Paul making tents.

The importance of Priscilla and Aquila to Paul's missionary work is demonstrated when Paul takes the two of them with him on a sea journey to Ephesus (18:18). Paul leaves them in charge of the missionary activities in Ephesus (18:19–21). Acts 18:26 shows Priscilla and Aquila teaching Apollos "the Way of God." First Corinthians 16:19 suggests that the home of Priscilla and Aquila became a center of the church at Ephesus.

The references to Priscilla and Aquila in Paul's own letters (Rom. 16:3–4; 1 Cor. 16:19) reveal both the high esteem he felt for them and their indispensability to his ministry and the ministry of the church in Asia Minor. Paul's high assessment of Priscilla and other women leaders runs contrary to Luke's own more ambivalent assessment of women's leadership. For example, Luke never identifies the work of Priscilla and Aquila as ministry, but his description of what they do leaves no doubt that Priscilla was a missionary and teacher. In other parts of the Acts narrative, Luke studiously avoided discussing women's leadership, but he could not avoid this subject in the story of Priscilla because she was too well known. He did try, however, to tell her story with as much restraint and decorum as possible.

## Acts and Women's Experience

This article has focused on women in the church in Acts, but Acts provides another type of information about first-century women. Many of Luke's stories provide glimpses into the social world of women. Luke's scattered references to women range from the Ethiopian queen Candace (8:27) to the servant Rhoda (12:12). A riot in Ephesus is caused by the Christians' disruption of the city's worship of the goddess Artemis (19:23–41). The economic status of women in Acts varies from the total economic dependence of the slave girl and some widows to the economic independence of many women. The story of Ananias and Sapphira provides a glimpse into a first-century Jewish marriage, as does the story of Priscilla and Aquila. The varieties of women's experience that are hinted at in Acts remind the contemporary reader not to generalize about "women in the early church." Even in a book such as Acts, where women's experience is largely background material, the complex character of women's lives emerges. The stories in Acts shed much light on the class differences among women in the early church. Class and social location was at least as critical to the day-to-day lives of women in the first century as gender.

*Women's roles.* The most positive portraits of women in Acts, those images that Luke may be offering as models for his female readers, are of wealthy women and women who learn from apostles and disciples. Wealthy women who function as patrons of the developing Christian communities were obviously of critical importance to the early success of Christianity. The church depended on the economic largess of women, particularly widows. Luke explicitly draws these women to the community's attention. With the exception of Rhoda (a wealthy woman's maid) and Mary (Jesus' mother), all the women named in Acts are wealthy. Even Priscilla and Aquila had the economic resources to sponsor a house-church. The anonymous women in Acts are those without economic means.

Luke's picture of women in the church thus fits with the conventions of the Greco-Roman world. Women can be ministered to and women can give money to support the churches. Because of Luke's theological and apologetic concerns to win acceptance of Christianity as a factor in world history and a participating institution in the Roman Empire, Luke ignores the leadership roles held by women in the church. This amounts to a *de facto* silencing of many of those women. The closing sections of Paul's letters, particularly Romans and 1 Corinthians, give evidence of the extensive leadership by women in the church, but in Acts, Luke mentions only one female teacher, Priscilla.

The reasons for Luke's narrowing of women's roles are twofold. First, as mentioned earlier, Acts is the story of Paul, who embodies the movement of the gospel to the world stage. All characters are secondary to Paul. Second, and more significant for the picture of women in Acts, propriety and decorum are essential virtues for Luke. Luke's sense of decorum means that women in the early church cannot be portrayed in ways that would be embarrassing or threatening to men in the Roman Empire. Men occupied public leadership roles, not women. The importance of decorum is evident also in the civility that characterizes Paul's relationship to the Roman state in Acts. Luke is above all a "gentleman's gentleman," and Acts is his book.

*Women's futures.* Even given Luke's particular agenda, however, glimpses of women's lives and experience slip into the story and work against Luke's aims. Most of these glimpses of women's lives occur in offhand descriptive remarks (e.g., Acts 16:13) and in details about women that are simply taken for granted (e.g., the description of Ananias and Sapphira's marriage and the story of Priscilla). Such details reside below the level of conscious literary strategy, and their presence in the narrative works to subvert Luke's priorities. These glimpses of women's experience that move outside Luke's attempts to control the picture of the early church—and women in the early church—contain the seeds of hope for women readers of Acts as they work to construct a fuller picture of the church.

It is important to note also that the heart of Acts' theology, the universal appeal of the gospel and its spread to the Gentiles, has possibilities for contemporary women's lives in the church that also subvert Luke's attempt at control. The decisive event in the movement of the gospel to the Gentiles is the story of Peter and Cornelius (Acts 10). Peter has a series of dreams in which God instructs him to go to Cornelius. The governing metaphor of these dreams is that cultic distinctions of clean and unclean have been superseded by the power of the gospel. The dreams and Peter's subsequent meeting with Cornelius lead Peter to say, "I truly understand that God shows no partiality" (10:34). The dissolution of cultic distinctions between clean and unclean refers to Jews and Gentiles, but the implications are farther reaching. When Luke's theology is played out in a different context, this dissolution of cultic distinctions provides the theological grounds for removing cultic classifications of women as unclean or impure. Women and men can stand as equals before the impartial God of Acts.

## BIBLIOGRAPHY

Cassidy, Richard J. *Society and Politics in the Acts of the Apostles.* Maryknoll, N.Y.: Orbis Books, 1987.

D'Angelo, Mary Rose. "Women in Luke-Acts: A Redactional View." *Journal of Biblical Literature* 109 (1990), 441–461.

Fiorenza, Elisabeth Schüssler. "A Feminist Critical Interpretation for Liberation: Martha and Mary: Luke 10:38–42." *Religion and Intellectual Life* 3 (1986), 21–35.

Gaventa, Beverly Roberts. *From Darkness to Light: Aspects of Conversion in the New Testament.* Overtures to Biblical Theology. Philadelphia: Fortress Press, 1986.

Haenchen, Ernst. *The Acts of the Apostles.* Translated by Bernard Noble and Gerald Shinn. Revised by R. McL. Wilson. Philadelphia: Westminster Press, 1971.

Johnson, Luke T. *Luke-Acts: A Story of Prophet and People.* Chicago: Franciscan Herald Press, 1981.

Pervo, Richard. *Luke's Story of Paul.* Minneapolis: Fortress Press, 1990.

# ROMANS

*Beverly Roberts Gaventa*

## Introduction

### Contents

Paul's letter to Christians in the powerful city of Rome opens not only with an identification of the writer (1:1) and the addressees (1:7), but with a concise summary of the gospel itself (1:1–6). The gospel concerns God's Son, Jesus Christ, through whom Paul's work among the Gentiles has been authorized. The thanksgiving that follows (1:8–15) reveals that Paul himself has not yet been to Rome, although he knows the reputation of the church there. The thanksgiving also specifies that Paul's work is with the Gentiles ("both to Greeks and to barbarians," 1:13–14). With 1:16–17, the introduction culminates in an initial statement of the letter's central point: In the gospel God acts with power to save all human beings, first Jews and then also Greeks. If the gospel reveals God's salvation, it also reveals God's wrath. In 1:18–3:20 Paul relentlessly argues that all human beings, without exception, are sinful in that they rebel against the very power and priority of God. The sin of Gentiles (i.e., all persons who are not Jews) consists of their refusal to acknowledge God, while the sin of Jews consists of their refusal to abide by the very law of God in which they themselves take pride. Even the advantage of God's gifts to the Jewish people does not change the fact that they, like all human beings, are "under the power of sin" (3:9).

In 3:21 Paul returns to the central point already introduced in 1:16–17. Through the faithfulness of Jesus Christ, God reveals God's own righteousness and thereby reclaims humanity from the deadly grip of sin. Since this act of salvation is God's doing, human beings have no right to boast of their own accomplishments (3:21–31). Like Abraham and Sarah (chap. 4), who could not imagine the possibility of a child

born in their old age, humanity finds that God has not only raised Jesus from the dead but has made righteous the ungodly. The extravagance of God's act of reconciliation leads to a comparison between Adam and Christ. Both lives affect every human being, yet Adam's act of rebellion brings sin and death, while Christ's act of righteousness brings a new and gracious life of reconciliation (chap. 5). In this life the Spirit of God rules in place of sin, and the Spirit empowers hope even in the face of suffering and pain. Indeed, by means of the Spirit, believers see on the horizon God's final act of salvation for all of creation (chap. 8). Paul's bold statement about God's unfathomable generosity prompts some predictable questions. First, if God justifies sinners, does that mean that God actually encourages sin? The answer is no, because God's justification means freedom from sin and freedom for a new obedience (6:1–7:6). Second, does this gospel of God's free righteousness mean that the law of Moses is evil? Paul insists that the law is a good gift from God, but sin uses it to bring about death (7:7–25). Third, since most Jews do not believe that Jesus is the Messiah, does God reject Israel and thereby reveal God's own faithlessness to the ancient covenant? Chapters 9–11 strenuously deny this conclusion, insisting instead that God is faithful and that Israel's final salvation remains secure in God's hands.

The call to transformation in 12:1–2 marks an important shift in the letter, as Paul explicitly takes up the implications of the righteousness of God for daily life. Chapters 12 and 13 address the relationships between Christians and other human beings and the relationships between Christians and civil authorities. The next section, 14:1–15:13, addresses relationships among Christians, with the behavior of Christ as the example of an active tolerance. Paul concludes the letter with comments about his own plans and his need for support from believers at Rome (15:14–33), followed by an extended set of personal greetings (chap. 16). These personal greetings seem out of place in a letter to a church Paul has neither founded nor visited. Since the letter apparently did circulate in ancient times without these greetings, some scholars have suggested that chap. 16 actually belongs to another letter. However, Acts 18:2–3 places Prisca and Aquila (Rom. 16:3) in Rome earlier, raising the possibility that they may have been among those banned from Rome by Claudius (see below) and may have met Paul during their exile. If Paul knew only a few such individuals, he might have referred to each one in order to establish his slender ties with Roman Christians.

## Occasion and Purpose

Certain features of Romans distinguish it from Paul's other letters and make it difficult to determine why the letter was written. The longest of Paul's letters (thus its place at the beginning of the collection of letters), Romans is also the only one addressed to a church Paul did not found. By contrast with the polemical tone that is found in the Corinthian correspondence, Galatians, and Philippians (see, e.g., 2 Cor. 12:11–13; Gal. 3:1; Phil. 3:2–4), Romans seems cool and dispassionate. Here Paul offers a sustained theological defense of his own positions and makes little specific reference to the church in Rome. These distinctive features prompted earlier generations of scholars to see Romans as a summary of Paul's thought, unlike his other letters that were written to address specific communities and problems. Two considerations argue against that understanding of the letter: (1) the absence from this letter of several theological issues (such as baptism and the Lord's Supper) that are important in his other letters, which makes it unlikely that Paul intends this as a summary of the gospel; and (2) the improbability that Paul (or any other Christian of the first century) had either the leisure or the inclination to write a systematic theology or a theological essay without a concrete pastoral goal in view.

The earlier consensus has broken down, replaced by a bewildering array of suggestions about Paul's aims in this letter. The suggestions fall into two general categories: (1) those that

see in Paul's own situation a reason to seek the help of believers in Rome, and (2) those that see within the church in Rome a problem that Paul feels compelled to address, making it in fact a pastoral letter like the others. Within the first category, some scholars argue that Paul's upcoming trip to Jerusalem dominates his thinking. As 15:25–29 indicates, Paul is preparing to go to Jerusalem, where he will present to Jewish Christians money that has been offered for them by Gentile Christians. While a famine in Israel may have created the need for this offering (cf. Acts 11:27–28), Paul understands its acceptance by Jerusalem Christians as acceptance of his ministry among Gentiles and, more important, as acceptance of the unity of Jew and Gentile. For that reason, he writes to Roman Christians to seek their prayers on behalf of his trip to Jerusalem. A second approach within this same category sees the occasion for the letter in Paul's mission to Spain. According to 15:22–29, Paul anticipates traveling from Jerusalem to Rome and then to Spain. For this new venture, he seeks the support, presumably material as well as spiritual, of Roman Christians. The letter then functions to introduce Paul and his understanding of the gospel, with the hope that Christians in Rome will be willing to lend their support to Paul's project. On this reading, the restrained style of Romans is attributable to the fact that Paul is not involved in polemic, and the content primarily introduces Paul's thought in an effort to secure the needed spiritual and financial support for his work.

The second category, those approaches that understand Paul to be addressing some problem within the church in Rome, takes its starting point from an incident related by the Roman historian Suetonius, who writes that the Roman emperor Claudius expelled the Jews from Rome on account of a disturbance caused by a certain "Chrestus." Since Chrestus is almost certainly to be identified with "Christos," or Christ, this reference may mean that conflict broke out within the large Jewish population of Rome over the proclamation of Jesus as the Christ. As a result, Claudius probably expelled Jewish Christians in 49 C.E., making the Christian community in Rome overwhelmingly Gentile. With Claudius's death in 54 C.E., the expulsion was revoked and Jewish Christians returned to Rome. Conflict followed as Jewish Christians expected to resume leadership within the Christian community, while Gentile Christians saw no reason to yield to their returning sisters and brothers. According to this scenario, or a variation on it, Paul's letter addresses a group of Christians whose conflict runs along ethnic lines (although some Jews may well have identified themselves with Gentile points of view and vice versa). The letter itself sets out to foster the reconciliation of Jewish and Gentile Christians. The content of the letter then is understood to be intimately connected with the situation itself. Paul's restrained style reflects the fact that he has not yet been to Rome and has no relationship on which to draw.

One striking feature of this debate regarding the occasion of Romans is the degree to which proponents of various positions build their arguments on different parts of the letter. As the discussion above already reveals, those who see the occasion of the letter in Paul's own situation emphasize his comments about his itinerary in the letter "frame," the opening and closing remarks (1:1–15; 15:14–33). On the other hand, those who see the letter addressing conflict in the church in Rome stress the "body" of the letter, especially the sections that deal with conflict between Jews and Gentiles. Every proposal regarding the purpose of Romans struggles to understand the relationship between the letter frame and the content of the letter.

While certainty regarding the purpose of a letter as complex as Romans remains unlikely, a few conclusions can be drawn. Paul writes to a congregation of strangers. Even if he knows some important individuals within the congregation (16:1–24), he must carefully identify himself and the major contours of the gospel he preaches. As Paul writes, he is planning an immediate visit to Jerusalem, where he intends to present a gift of aid for Christians in that city and for which plan he seeks the prayerful support of Christians in Rome. Following that trip to Jerusalem, he will move on to Rome, where he hopes to "share the gospel," and then to Spain, where a new stage in his mission will begin (15:22–29). Given the content of the letter, with its emphasis on God's radical grace for all people, Jew and Gentile (1:16; 3:21–26), Paul may also have in mind a conflict within the church in Rome. Whether he knows that conflict rages at present or whether he anticipates it on the basis of his experience is less clear. Based on the itinerary he identifies, the letter was probably written sometime between 55 and 57 C.E., and probably from Corinth, since he refers to his host Gaius (see 1 Cor. 1:14).

## Theological Significance

Although Romans stands first among Paul's letters because of its length, one might argue that Romans belongs first because of its place in the history of Christian theology. Through the interpretations of such theologians and church leaders as Augustine, Martin Luther, and Karl Barth, Romans has exerted incalculable influence in Western Christian theology. The male dominance of that history of interpretation, taken together with the fact that this letter makes few direct references to women, might prompt the conclusion that Romans has little significance for the lives of women. Such a conclusion would be premature and indeed unfortunate, however, for within Paul's interpretation of the "righteousness of God" lies a powerful and liberating word for women and for men. When Paul refers to the righteousness of God, he refers both to a characteristic of God (that is, God *is* righteous) and to the implications of that characteristic for human beings (that is, God freely gives to human beings the gift of God's own righteousness). As Paul works through this notion in Romans, at least four themes emerge that have direct implications for women: the "impartiality" of God, sin as rebellion against God, the radical nature of God's grace, and the solidarity of humankind with the rest of creation.

When Paul speaks of God as impartial, as he does in 2:11, he draws on a traditional Jewish conviction. To claim that God is impartial is not to say, as in contemporary American English, that God is merely evenhanded or that God is detached from human affairs. Instead, God's "impartiality" refers to the fact that God evaluates without reference to the usual human values of wealth, power, or religious status. In the Hebrew Bible, the claim that God is impartial forms a basis for admonitions to protect the widow, the orphan, the outsider (see, e.g., Deut. 10:17–19; 2 Chron. 19:7; Ps. 82:1–4). Paul radicalizes those convictions, applying them not only to Gentiles who live within Jewish communities but to all people without exception. If God is not partial to the rich over against the poor, to the child with a family over against the orphan, then God is also not partial to the Jew over against the Gentile. Without reference to any social or economic factor that usually conveys special privilege, God both judges and redeems each human being. In Paul's argument in Romans, this insistence on God's impartiality serves to overturn traditional judgments about the greater value of Jews over against

Gentiles, but women may find in it a significant way of addressing the value judgments that still elevate men over women. To understand that God is impartial is to claim that all human beings have the same value in God's sight and, therefore, that humans should view one another in the same way.

A second theme of Romans is the universality of human sin. In 1:18–3:20 Paul argues explicitly that sin pervades the lives of each and every human being. In 5:12, Paul refers to sin entering the world and going through the world, personifying sin as if it were an independent being or had a personal existence. While sin manifests itself in human lives in a vast number of ways, ranging from the sexual acts itemized in 1:26–27 to the religious pride of 2:17–24, Paul sees in each of these manifestations a single sin: humanity lives in rebellion against God (they "worshiped and served the creature rather than the Creator," 1:25). What Romans offers women is an opportunity to reflect on the ways in which they participate in the human condition of rebellion against God. In some instances that rebellion may take the form of pride, perhaps a religious pride that presumes to know God's will and God's favor. In other instances, rebellion may take the form of low self-esteem, even a self-negation that implicitly denies that the creature in fact derives from God. Contrasts drawn in very generalized terms about the principal sin of men as pride and the principal sin of women as self-negation fail to perceive the depth of the situation Paul portrays. Such analyses—whether or not they are accurate—limit sin to the sphere of human relations. Paul would insist that whatever form sin takes, it arises from a common human rebellion against God.

A third theme of Romans is the radical nature of God's grace, which operates in spite of the universality of human rebellion against God. Again and again the letter drives at this theme. The Christ event reveals that God's righteousness is for all human beings (1:16–17) and that righteousness works through God's grace (3:24). God's grace has proved to be even more powerful than human sin, for the grace inaugurated by Jesus Christ has brought life for all people, regardless of their sinfulness (5:12–21). Even where God's grace appears to have failed, as in the case of Israel, the future triumph of God will reveal that God's grace has not failed; indeed, the future will reveal that God's grace is for all people (11:25–36). This radical understanding of God's grace means that no human being can *achieve* God's favor or pleasure, for that favor is already abundantly granted in Jesus Christ; one need not work for what one already has. Especially for women, all too often socialized to believe that they must serve everyone else's needs and ignore their own, that they must constantly work to accomplish "enough" for their families or communities or employers or God, this statement comes as an instance of God's grace, a firm reminder that God's love is universal, irrevocable, and irresistible.

A fourth theme of Romans concerns the solidarity of humankind with the remainder of creation. While this theme appears in only a small portion of the letter, its significance for women, particularly in the context of the current ecological crisis, warrants attention. Already in 1:18–23, Paul presupposes a connection between humanity and the remainder of creation. Because God is visible in the created world, the human race should have acknowledged God and given God thanks. This statement imagines a vital link between humanity, the remainder of creation, and the God who creates. That link becomes explicit in 8:18–39, where Paul refers to the "eager longing" of "the creation," as it looks forward to God's final triumph. Creation "groans" along with human beings, who wait for their redemption. Unlike the dualistic philosophies and religions (such as Gnosticism) that understand creation to be essentially evil, Paul here asserts a fundamental continuity between humanity and its earthly home. That continuity can stimulate not only a fresh appreciation of the relationship between humanity and the rest of creation but a commitment to treat creation as itself a gift of God.

## Comment

### Natural and Unnatural Acts (1:18–32)

Within the context of his initial discussion of humanity's rebellion against God, Paul refers to the "degrading passions": "Women exchanged natural intercourse for unnatural, and in the same way also the men, giving up natural intercourse with women, were consumed with passion for one another" (1:26b–27). In order to understand what Paul means by this negative reference to homosexual relations, it is necessary to see the logic of the passage. The passage fundamentally concerns the relationship between God and humanity; it is not primarily a passage *about* homosexuality. It begins with an assertion of God's wrath against human sin (1:18); despite the clear evidence of creation, in which God is revealed to humanity, humankind has nevertheless refused to honor God (1:19–21). Indeed, humanity persists in making gods of themselves and denying the reality and power of God the creator (1:25). As a result of this rebellion ("therefore," v. 24; "for this reason," v. 26; "since they did not see fit to acknowledge God," v. 28), God allowed human beings to pursue their own desires ("God gave them up," 1:24, 26, 28). Those specific behaviors identified in 1:26–32, then, are the *result* of human sin. Rather than identifying homosexuality (or wickedness, evil, deceit, and so forth) *as* sin, Paul's analysis is that these actions stem from and are symptomatic of the fundamental human sin of denying the reality and power of God. That does not mean that homosexuality serves in this passage merely as an example and that lying or cheating would have suited Paul's purposes just as well as the example chosen. Since the passage as a whole revolves around the issue of creation (God as creator, humankind as created by God, the creature-creator relationship), Paul chooses homosexual behavior because, as he sees it, homosexuality runs counter to the creation of male and female and their roles in the ongoing created order. Since sexual relations between men and women are fundamental to God's creation, especially as the narratives of Genesis depict that creation, Paul regards sexual relations that contradict that pattern as unacceptable.

As contemporary readers grapple with conflicting information and volatile viewpoints regarding homosexuality and with the complicated question of how the Bible plays a role in contemporary decision making, it is important to acknowledge forthrightly that Paul understands homosexuality to be a violation of God's intention for creation. That acknowledgment, however, must be coupled with an awareness that in Rom. 1:18–32 Paul begins an extensive examination of the nature of human sin. Persons who are heterosexual and conclude from this passage that they are justified in judging or condemning persons who are homosexual will find themselves condemned in turn by Paul's statement in 2:1: "Therefore you have no excuse, whoever you are, when you judge others; for in passing judgment on another you condemn yourself, because you, the judge, are doing the very same things." If, in Paul's mind, homosexual behavior is a symptom of rebellion against God, so is self-righteousness. To use this passage to justify the exclusion of persons who are homosexual would be the grossest distortion of Romans and its claims about God's radical and universal grace.

## Circumcision and Uncircumcision (2:25–29)

As elsewhere in his letters, Paul here employs the terms "circumcision" and "uncircumcision" to refer to Jews and Gentiles respectively. The use of these categories raises questions for women, because the categories are exclusively male and would appear to exclude women from consideration. The issue that arises is whether Paul writes with only men in mind; that is, does the fact that he uses "circumcision" and "uncircumcision" mean that he thinks only of male experience? In one sense, the answer to that question is probably yes, to the extent that most people think primarily in terms of their own experience. On the other hand, three factors weigh heavily against concluding that Paul writes only for and about men. First, he clearly understands women to be part of the community of faith in general and the Roman community in particular (see the names of women in chap. 16). Second, for Paul and for many of his contemporaries, circumcision was perhaps the most important distinguishing characteristic of Judaism. Not only was circumcision associated with Abraham (see Gen. 17:9–14; Rom. 4:1–12), but during the Maccabean revolt it had become a significant symbol of loyalty to the Jewish people precisely because the Seleucids had forbidden the practice (see, e.g., 1 Macc. 1:41–64; 2 Macc. 6:1–11). While Jews were not the only peoples who practiced circumcision, they understood it to be essential to their ethnic and religious identity. That historical circumstance probably means that the use of these terms is a shorthand way of referring to Jews in general, rather than only to male Jews. Third, in this particular part of the letter, Paul introduces a distinction between external signs and internal observance (2:27–29). The physical language of circumcision and uncircumcision supports this distinction and thus may have been chosen in part because of its utility in the argument rather than because it is gender specific.

## Adam and Christ (5:12–21)

In this passage Paul introduces a convoluted set of comparisons between Adam and Christ. Women may sense their exclusion from this text, first, because of its use of the term "man" (5:12, 15–19) and, second, because of the male characters, Adam and Jesus Christ, through whom all of human history is being interpreted. Regarding the first concern, the Greek word *anthropos*, which means human being or person rather than male, appears consistently in this text. Presumably it is for that reason that translators of the NRSV have revised some parts of the passage so that, for example, 5:12 reads, "and so death spread to all because all have sinned," rather than "and so death spread to all men because all men sinned" (RSV). Perhaps "man" was left as the translation of *anthropos* when referring to Adam and to Jesus Christ because those two historical figures were men. Unfortunately, that translation decision obscures the important connection in the text between the individual persons (Adam and Jesus Christ) and the collective person (all humanity). Regarding the second concern, it is difficult to imagine that Paul, a product of his age, could have chosen for this argument any representative figures other than two males, Adam and Jesus, or that he could have spoken in general terms, such as "the human." More important, foundational to Paul's understanding of the gospel is the conviction that God acted through a very particular human being, a Jewish male, through whose death and resurrection God inaugurates a new era. To attempt to obscure any aspect of Christ's identity would be to undermine what theologians refer to as the "scandal of particularity."

## A Married Woman (7:1–6)

In the context of a discussion about the way in which the gospel carries with it freedom from sin and from the law Paul uses an analogy about the marriage relationship. In the analogy, he speaks of a married woman being "bound by the law to her husband as long as he lives" and being freed from the law upon her husband's death. If she lives with another man while her husband is still alive, she will be called an adulteress. Following her husband's death, she can marry another man without being termed an adulteress (7:2–3). This passage appears to understand a woman solely in terms of her husband and her freedom simply as a function of his longevity. Nothing is said of the husband's obligation to faithfulness or the husband's being termed an adulterer. The passage stands in tension with Paul's comments about the marriage relationship in 1 Corinthians 7, where he invokes considerable mutuality in marriage relations (see, e.g., 1 Cor. 7:2–4, 10–16, 34). Unlike 1 Corinthians 7, however, where Paul clearly intends to provide instruction about marriage (within a framework of intense expectation about Jesus' immediate return; see 1 Cor. 7:29–31), Paul intends Romans 7 to provide not a teaching about marriage but an analogy. The point toward which the analogy moves appears in 7:4–6, where Paul concludes that believers have died to the law and now belong to Christ. To use this passage to construct an understanding of marriage is to misperceive its function in the letter and to misconstrue Paul's attitude toward women.

## Groaning in Labor Pains (8:18–25)

This section of the letter portrays the anguish and the confidence with which believers, together with all of creation, await the final triumph of God (8:18–39; see above under "Theological Significance"). Although confident that God will be victorious, believers live in the present age, which is characterized by suffering and decay. As part of his depiction of the expectations of all of creation, Paul writes that "the whole creation has been groaning in labor pains until now" (8:22). This vivid use of imagery that derives from the experience of giving birth warrants attention. Here Paul draws on a convention of the Hebrew Bible in which birth pains serve as a metaphor for the period of strife and travail that ushers in a new age (see, e.g., Isa. 13:8; Jer. 4:31). Variations on this metaphor appear in other early Christian writers as well (Mark 13:8; John 16:21; Rev. 12:2). What makes the use of the metaphor especially significant is that Paul elsewhere speaks of himself as being in labor pains with the Galatians, who must come to birth again as Christians (Gal. 4:19), and as being with the Thessalonians as a nurse would be with her own children (1 Thess. 2:7). Even if he is employing conventional expressions, the application of it to himself suggests that one way in which Paul thinks of himself is not only as a father to believers (1 Cor. 4:15) but also as their mother. That maternal role is connected with the gospel itself, which ushers in a new age by means of "groaning in labor pains."

## A Living Sacrifice (12:1–2)

On the basis of the claims that Paul has made in Romans 1–11 about the grace and the righteousness of God, he turns in 12:1 to an explicit discussion of ethical matters. Romans 12:1–2, then, serve as an introduction to and a basis for the ethical instructions that follow. For women who are accustomed to patterns of submission to the desires of others and of denying their own worth, the language of this passage seems to reinforce those expectations. Many women have seen themselves as "living sacrifices" and have experienced that as profoundly destructive.

Such an interpretation of this text constitutes a significant misreading of Paul's words. Verse 1 anticipates the response of human beings, male and female, to the "mercies of God." Those mercies demand not a meager offering but a complete response, in which the whole person (the *soma*, or "body") is handed over to God. Verse 2 explicates this offering. Believers are not to be "conformed to this world," but "transformed by the renewing" of the mind; that is, the thoughts and actions of believers do not simply repeat those of the world at large in this time and place, but they are transformed. By means of the renewal of their minds, itself a gift from God, believers are enabled to discern God's will and live in conformity with it, despite the pressures to conform with "this age." This call for transformation understands that transformation to have its origin and its goal in God. To see this passage as reinforcing the submission of any human being to another human being profoundly distorts its importance.

## God Has Welcomed Them (14:1–15:13)

As the culmination of the ethical exhortation of this letter, Paul writes an extended discussion on the relationship among groups with varying, even conflicting, religious practices. Paul does not identify these groups, but they may coincide more or less with the ethnic divisions referred to earlier (see above under "Occasion and Purpose"). The "weak" are those who believe that they must abstain from certain foods, including especially those that may be unclean according to Jewish dietary law (see also 1 Corinthians 8 and 10). Probably many Jewish Christians belonged to this group, along with those Gentiles who agreed with them. The "strong," by contrast, are those who believe that they may eat anything, since Christ has abrogated the law. This group would consist primarily of Gentile Christians, although some Jewish Christians may have identified with them. (Note, however, that Paul only introduces the term "the strong" in 15:1.) While these specific disagreements pertain to the circumstances of the first Christian generations, the way in which Paul adjudicates the issues is instructive. The God-centered (theocentric) character of the letter as a whole obtains here as well. All people belong to God and are accountable *only* to God for their actions (14:7–12). Though convinced himself that all foods are permitted, Paul insists that believers not behave in ways that will be detrimental to their sisters and brothers. He also claims that those who act with the conviction that they are wrong, who act with a bad conscience, are in fact wrong before God (14:13–23). Paul concludes this section with an appeal to the behavior of Christ, who pleased others rather than himself and who welcomed all people, both Jew and Gentile (15:1–13).

What Paul advocates here goes well beyond the flaccid tolerance that merely endures differences as a necessary evil while waiting for the final vindication of one's own position. To "welcome one another" (15:7; see also 14:1) is to seek actively to know and to understand another's reasoning and another's judgments, based on the theological assumption that all people belong to God and that God may be served in a variety of ways. This passage, in its historical context, concerns conflicting religious practices that apparently stemmed from varying ethnic groups. Its significance for women and men today may go well beyond that context, to include the bewildering array of conflicts among women and between women and men. Reconciliation begins when all are able to acknowledge with Paul that "whether we live or whether we die, we are the Lord's" (14:8).

## Women in Ministry (16:1–16)

In form, this part of the conclusion to Romans is largely conventional. Letters of the period typically include a recommendation of the person who would deliver the letter (see, e.g., 1 Cor. 16:15–17) and a set of greetings (as in 1 Cor. 16:19–20; 2 Cor. 13:12; Phil. 4:21–22). As noted above (see "Contents") one unusual feature of this set of greetings is that Paul gives an extensive list of individual names and sends that list to people in a city he has not yet visited. Probably he hoped that these individuals would pave the way for the reception of his letter and its content.

A second unusual feature of this set of greetings is the prominence of women within it. First comes Phoebe, whom Paul recommends and who is probably to be the bearer of the letter itself. He describes Phoebe as "a deacon of the church at Cenchreae" and a "benefactor of many and of myself as well." Although Paul writes at a time prior to the official establishment of church offices, the fact that Phoebe is a "deacon" (not a "deaconess" as the RSV erroneously translates) surely means that she serves in some significant leadership role in the congregation at Cenchreae. That she is a "benefactor" (or, better, "a patron") signals that Phoebe is a person of some wealth and power and that she has used those assets on behalf of Paul and other Christians. Among the persons Paul greets in Rome, nine women appear: Prisca, Mary, Junia, Tryphaena, Tryphosa, Persis, the mother of Rufus, Julia, and the sister of Nereus. Paul singles out several of them for comments: Prisca (and Aquila) for her work with Paul and for risking her life; Mary for her hard work; Junia as an apostle; Tryphaena, Tryphosa, and Persis for their labor. Nothing in Paul's comments justifies the conclusion that these women worked in ways that differed either in kind or in quantity from the ways in which men worked. Indeed, all of the individuals listed appear to be engaged in tasks of ministry, a fact that needs to be taken into account in any assessment of the roles of women in early Christianity.

## BIBLIOGRAPHY

Achtemeier, Paul J. *Romans*. Interpretation. Atlanta: John Knox Press, 1986.

Bassler, Jouette. *Divine Impartiality: Paul and a Theological Axiom*. Society of Biblical Literature Dissertation Series 59. Chico, Calif.: Scholars Press, 1982.

Brooten, Bernadette J. *Women Leaders in the Ancient Synagogue*. Brown Judaic Studies 36. Chico, Calif.: Scholars Press, 1982.

Cranfield, C. E. B. *A Critical and Exegetical Commentary on the Epistle to the Romans*. 2 vols. International Critical Commentary. Edinburgh: T. & T. Clark, 1975, 1979.

Dunn, James D. G. *Romans*. 2 vols. Word Biblical Commentary. Waco, Tex.: Word Books, 1988.

Hays, Richard B. "Relations Natural and Unnatural: A Response to John Boswell's Exegesis of Romans 1." *Journal of Religious Ethics* 14 (1986), 184–215.

Meyer, Paul W. "Romans." In *Harper's Bible Commentary*, edited by James L. Mays, pp. 1130–1167. San Francisco: Harper & Row, 1988.

# 1 CORINTHIANS

## Jouette M. Bassler

### Introduction

Paul founded the church in Corinth around 51 C.E. First Corinthians—actually the *second* letter Paul wrote to this church (see 1 Cor. 5:9)—provides an account of this early work (chaps. 1–3), but it is highly rhetorical and yields few concrete details beyond the names of the first converts (1:14–16). The dramatic account in Acts 18:1–18 is more detailed, but the historical reliability of that book is uncertain. Nevertheless, there one learns of various individuals who participated in the founding of the church, including Priscilla (Prisca) and Aquila, a missionary couple with whom Paul stayed in Corinth (see also 1 Cor. 16:19). Acts also suggests a mixed church of Jews and Gentiles, but Paul's letter seems to presuppose only a pagan (Gentile) background (1 Cor. 12:2). The social makeup of the church, however, was clearly diverse (1 Cor. 1:26–29), and this may have been a factor in some of the disputes there.

Between Paul's departure from the church and the writing of 1 Corinthians, there was a lively exchange of information and a number of important developments took place. Paul sent Timothy to Corinth to remind them of his teachings (4:17); Paul wrote the Corinthians a letter with instructions which they misunderstood (5:9–13); Chloe's people (her slaves, relatives, or associates) brought Paul news of divisions within the church (1:11); and a delegation of three men arrived from Corinth and were with Paul when he wrote this letter (16:17–18). These men were probably the bearers of a letter from the church (7:1) in which the Corinthians raised questions concerning, or challenging, Paul's earlier instructions. Paul wrote 1 Corinthians from Ephesus (16:8), probably in 54 C.E., in order to respond to these developments. In this letter he addresses a variety of issues, but some consistent underlying patterns are discernible.

The church in Corinth, or a significant number of its members, was convinced that already they fully enjoyed the spiritual benefits of the resurrection. Whether this idea derived from the preaching of Apollos, from the Corinthians' misunderstanding of the sacraments (10:1–5), or from their own spiritual experiences and theological speculation, it had serious consequences for the moral and communal life of the church. There was, for example, an attitude of freedom from earthly norms (5:1–8; 6:12–20), an excessive interest in some spiritual gifts (chap. 14), an apparent contempt for those with lesser gifts (chap. 12), and an emphasis on the individual rather than the communal benefits of these gifts (chap. 14). In addition to these developments, there was a crisis concerning the church's relationship to Paul (4:18; 9:1–3; 14:37), and addressing this problem acquired a natural priority.

Whatever else lay behind the factions in the church, belonging to Apollos or Cephas (1:12) meant rejecting Paul's authority (see 4:6). If Paul hoped effectively to address the problems in the community, he first had to reclaim this authority. He thus opens the letter by defending his message and his work in Corinth. God, he argues, has reversed the world's polarities. Folly is wisdom and wisdom is folly; and the crucified Messiah (1:23), the trembling apostle (2:3), and the socially misfit Corinthians (1:26–29) define and embody God's true and saving wisdom.

Paul uses a number of metaphors to describe and defend his founding labors in this church, and these cross lines of gender and social status. He was their wet nurse (3:2), the farmer who planted them (3:6–9), the master builder who laid their foundation (3:10–15). He was their only "father" (4:14–21), but he is also their "brother" (1:11). He is a servant of Christ (4:1), foolish, weak, and reviled (4:9–13). He also knows himself to be, however, empowered by God (4:19–21; see 1:25; 2:5), and thus with some confidence he begins to deal with the problems in this church.

His comments in chaps. 5–6 address issues that have come to him by oral report (5:1). Unlike the issues that the Corinthians themselves raise (see below), which primarily concern matters of spirituality and theological knowledge, Paul's informants report on social ills afflicting the church: lawsuits (6:1–11) and sexual immorality (chaps. 5; 6:12–20). Such conduct is particularly abhorrent to Paul, who views the baptized Christian as spiritually united with Christ. This spiritual union makes the deeds of the body more—not less—important, for what is done with the physical body is mapped onto the body of Christ. "Do you not know that your bodies are members of Christ? Should I therefore take the members of Christ and make them members of a prostitute?" (6:15). Here Paul assumes that the offending Christians are male. Whether this reflects accurately the circumstances or simply the fact that Paul cannot easily map the female body onto Christ, in this discussion the Christian who fully explores the slogan "All things are lawful" (6:12) is assumed to be male. The prostitute is merely a vehicle for sexual freedom; Paul shows no theological or pastoral interest in her.

Chapters 7–16 are primarily devoted to issues raised in the Corinthians' letter. (Points where Paul explicitly responds to these issues are signaled by the phrase, "Now concern-

ing . . ."; see 7:1, 25; 8:1; 12:1; 16:1.) Paul treats each issue separately but with a consistent emphasis on the relational and communal aspects of Christian life: husband and wife must have concern for each other (chap. 7); one's actions are to be regulated by their impact on the brother or sister (chaps. 8–10); spiritual gifts are to be employed for communal edification and not personal satisfaction (chaps. 12–14). Paul emphasizes a unity that transcends the Corinthians' diversity, reminding them of the baptismal liturgy that proclaims the unification of Jews and Greeks (Gentiles), slaves and free, in one body of Christ (12:13). The omission here of any reference to the unification of male and female is noteworthy (cf. Gal. 3:28). If this is deliberate, as seems likely, it is probably related to developments within this church, where male-female relations have become a point of controversy (see below).

The extensive discussion of the resurrection in chap. 15 does not seem to be in direct response to a report about or question from the Corinthians. It is instead Paul's way of attacking the theological issue that has generated problems for this church. Here he reminds them that the resurrection—the final, definitive spiritual transformation—remains an event *of the future*. Their claims to spiritual perfection are premature. The present calls for steadfastness (15:58), not spiritual arrogance. The final point Paul touches on concerns preparations for the collection, which bonds the Corinthians with other churches and points them to material issues of *this* world. Paul closes the letter, as is usual, with travel plans and greetings. The "holy kiss" (16:20) reflects the liturgy of the early church and symbolizes the communal spirit that Paul is encouraging in Corinth.

## Comment

### Sex and Spirituality (7:1–40)

In this chapter, Paul begins to respond to the issues the Corinthians raised in their earlier letter. His obvious concern to present arguments that are balanced in their treatment of women and men is striking. The nature of the issues addressed (sex, marriage, divorce) does not adequately explain this. Women were probably prominently involved in raising questions about these issues, forcing Paul to break out of his normal mode of addressing a community exclusively through its male members. Only in

this chapter, for example, is the Christian kinship term "sister" paired with "brother" (7:15). Elsewhere in Paul's letters members of the community are collectively addressed as "brothers."

As Paul responds to the Corinthians' written questions, he frequently quotes from or alludes to their letter to him. This, of course, posed no problem for the Corinthians, who would have immediately recognized Paul's references to their own words. For the contemporary reader, however, it generates serious problems. Where is Paul quoting the Corinthians' opinions and where is he citing his own? Where does his particular wording of an argument derive from *their* phrasing of the question and where does it reflect and accurately convey his own particular emphases? These issues must be constantly kept in mind as one reads Paul's response here.

The distance from the situation that evoked these comments generates another problem as well. Several categories of women are mentioned: "wives" are paired with "husbands" in a natural way (7:2–4), and "the unmarried" are mentioned with "the widows" (7:8). A third group, "the virgins," is distinguished in a natural way from married women, but they are also distinguished from "unmarried women" as if they were a separate group (7:34). It is possible that Paul and this community had developed a special vocabulary for describing various groups of women, and one cannot assume that all of these terms bore their "natural" meaning. This makes the interpretation of Paul's comments more difficult now than it was for the original readers.

***Sex, marriage, and divorce (7:1–24).*** Paul begins his comments with an abrupt statement that defines the primary issue here to be sex and not marriage: "It is well for a man not to touch a woman." There is a growing consensus that these words do not represent Paul's own opinion but are a quotation from the *Corinthians'* letter. (To indicate this, the NRSV now encloses the words in quotation marks; compare the text of the older RSV.) What gives weight to this conclusion is the way Paul continues the argument, for with a qualifying "but" he introduces instructions that effectively undermine the quoted statement: "But because of cases of sexual immorality, each man should have [sexual relations with] his own wife and each woman her own husband." (Note the similar pattern of quoted statement followed by qualifying argument in 6:12; 8:1; and 10:23.) Even when Paul agrees to temporary periods of abstinence for special devotion to prayer, he does not present this with any enthusiasm but as a "concession" to the preferences of the Corinthians (7:5–6).

The Corinthians, or some of them, seem to be encouraging a rigorous asceticism even for married couples. Though Paul does not explicitly say so, this attitude probably derives from the Corinthians' conviction that they already enjoy the spiritual status and benefits of the resurrection. Already they participate in the reign of God (4:8) with a status like that of the angels (13:1), and some, at least, advocate a life-style that conforms to this perceived reality. They may know some words of Jesus (see, e.g., Luke 20:34–36) that lend support to their position. (Indeed, this may account for Paul's concern to identify where possible his own advice with commands of the Lord [7:10, 12, 25].) They probably point to the example of Paul's unmarried state and may even trace their position on asceticism back to Paul's own teaching. The curious way that Paul argues in this chapter, qualifying rather than contradicting their positions, suggests that he may well have said something in Corinth in support of the celibate life. The Corinthians, however, with their customary zeal, have transformed Paul's personal and practical preference into a general principle required of everyone who would be considered truly spiritual. It is this absolutism that Paul resists, and the tack of his argument is to maintain the practical advantages of celibacy while insisting that it is not the only option for Christians and certainly not one to be imposed on married couples (7:7; see also vv. 8–9).

The quotation cited above ("It is well for a man not to touch a woman") presents the issue of celibacy solely from the male perspective. Paul, however, not only contradicts the premise of this statement but in both the content and balanced format of his response insists on the two-sidedness, the mutuality of sexual relations within marriage. Whether one can extrapolate from this to conclude that Paul viewed the entire marriage relationship as one of equality and mutuality is difficult to answer in light of his comments in chap. 11 (and possibly chap. 14; see below). Nevertheless, the sense of mutuality in at least *this* area of married life is exceptional for a man of his time and culture.

On the other hand, Paul's insistence on sexual relations within marriage, however mutual they might have been, is predicated on a concern for self-control (7:2, 5; see also vv. 9, 36–37). He seems to view marriage exclusively and negatively as a means of sexual containment, and there are no references to love or procreation. Indeed, sex within marriage, for all its mutuality, is defined in rather joyless terms: it is a "debt" or "duty" that must be paid ("conjugal rights" in the RSV and NRSV); each spouse has "authority" (power) over the other's body; thus to be married is to be "bound" (7:27, 39). This seems to be, at least in part, a consequence of the questions or statements to which Paul is responding and the context in which he makes them. The Corinthians have asked him about sexual relations in marriage, not about marriage in general, and his comments follow hard on the heels of a discussion of sexual immorality (chaps. 5–6). Moreover, his lack of interest in procreation surely stems from his conviction that the world already stands in the shadow of the end (7:29–31).

He does, however, convey a sense of the pervasive holiness of marriage that embraces children and can somehow touch even unbelieving marriage partners (7:14). He also views marriage as a deep commitment. It involves a concern for the spouse so profound that it competes with the Christian's devotion to the Lord (7:32–35). It is striking that Paul can say this without any obvious trace of criticism. To be sure, because of this aspect of marriage he recommends the unmarried life as more suited to the times. The old world, as he thinks, is passing away, and its dissolution will be marked by trauma and crisis. Under these circumstances, undivided devotion to the Lord is advantageous, so Paul recommends unmarried life. But he does not challenge married couples to revise their priorities. Paul recognizes that concern ("anxiety") for the spouse is a part of the fabric of marriage and cannot be retracted.

Though Paul insists that consummated marriages are not the place to practice celibacy, his basic conviction is that for those for whom it is an option, the celibate life has concrete, practical advantages. Thus in 7:8–9 he affirms that for the unmarried and widows (or perhaps "widowers and widows") "it is well for them to remain unmarried." In saying this he is probably again citing, and this time agreeing with, the Corinthians' own position on the matter. As before, however, he immediately introduces a qualification, though this one is not as all-inclusive as the one concerning marriage partners: "But if they are not practicing self-control, they should marry." This comment is once again negatively motivated by a concern for sexual immorality. The basic premise—that unmarried women can *and should* remain that way—is, however, strikingly innovative. In a culture defined by patriarchy, Paul not only insists that within a marriage women and men are equal sex partners but also sanctions for women a life without marriage, and thus a life permanently free from all the hierarchical strictures of that relationship. Paul thus opens wide the door to social independence for those women gifted with celibacy.

The desire for the celibate life-style seems to have encouraged many of the Corinthians to seek divorce, and Paul addresses this aspect of the issue in 7:10–16. For the first and only time in this chapter Paul's response takes the form of a command: Neither wives nor husbands should divorce their spouses. Paul attributes this prohibition directly to the Lord (see Mark 10:2–12 and Matt. 19:3–9), yet even so he permits a partial exception: "But if she does separate [from her husband], let her remain unmarried or else be reconciled to her husband" (7:11). But even if the spouse is an unbeliever—and the motivation for divorce in *this* case is even greater (see 2 Cor. 6:14–18)—Paul insists that the preferred course of action is for the married couple to remain as they are. The holiness of the believing spouse will consecrate the marriage and the children and *may* even effect the salvation of the unbelieving partner (7:16). Remarkably enough, Paul seems to imply that peace is more important than possible conversion. If the unbelieving partner agitates for divorce, the believer is to permit it—for the sake of peace (7:15).

Throughout this evenhanded discussion of women and men, Paul mentions the role of the man (husband) first. In the discussion of divorce, however, he mentions the wife first (7:10) and the exception clause is applied only to the case of the woman (7:11). (In the sayings of Jesus on divorce, the wife is discussed second [Mark 10:11–12] or not at all [Matt. 19:9].) This reversal of emphasis could indicate that the pressure for divorce within the Corinthian community is coming primarily from the women, who, one could surmise, are encouraged to seek freedom on a social level commensurate with their freedom in Christ (Gal. 3:28). Paul does not forbid this (7:11a), but neither does he encourage it. Throughout his advice to this community, Paul proclaims a conservative ethic: Remain as you are. The advantages of the single, celibate state are not so great as to demand universal compliance or social disruption. Paul concludes this section of the letter by discussing this general principle in some detail (7:17–24), and as he does so he reverts to the male perspective that is more characteristic of his letters.

*Virgins (7:25–40).* Paul's use of the phrase, "Now concerning . . . ," in 7:25 indicates that he is responding to a related but separate question from the Corinthians. It concerns a group called the "virgins," and because both the Corinthians and Paul treat this group separately, something other than the question of marriage for the "unmarried" (7:8–9) must be at stake.

Paul reverses his earlier sequence and here presents the general principles first (7:26–35). He repeats the point mentioned earlier (remain as you are, v. 26) and now buttresses it with comments concerning the passing of the age (7:26, 29, 31). In view of the rapidly approaching end and the divided loyalties that marriage creates for the Christian, it is better for a virgin to remain as she is. Thus far Paul's advice is not markedly different from that he gave earlier to the unmarried. He even provides a similar exception clause: "But . . . if a virgin marries, she does not sin" (7:28). Nevertheless, his later comments (7:36–38) seem to presuppose a somewhat more complex situation. Most translations obscure the difficulties by translating "virgin" as "fiancée" or "betrothed," but the strangeness of the situation comes out with a more literal translation of the text.

> But if anyone thinks he is behaving disgracefully toward his virgin, if his passions are strong and so it has to be, let him do what he wishes, he is not sinning. Let them marry. But whoever stands firm in his heart, and has no necessity, but has authority concerning his own will and he has determined in his own heart to keep his virgin, he will do well. So then, the one who marries his virgin does well and the one not marrying will do better. (7:36–38, author's translation)

Several things are striking here. First, the sense of mutuality so prominent in Paul's earlier discussion is completely absent. The man alone determines whether to marry "his virgin," and no thought is given to her passions, her wishes, or the determination in her heart. Second, Paul is obviously concerned to reassure the Corinthians that marrying a "virgin" is no sin (7:28, 36). This means that someone in the community is suggesting it *is* a sin to marry a virgin, and that adds a new note to the discussion. It is not behaving disgracefully toward the virgin, but *marrying* her, that seems to elicit this charge. This suggests that something more is at stake than meets the eye.

Finally, the way Paul refers to the men and their virgins is decidedly strange. For some time the prevailing opinion has been that Paul is referring to fathers with virgin daughters of marriageable age, but the text does not really support that interpretation. Most translations now reflect the idea that engaged couples, caught up in the Corinthians' enthusiasm for asceticism, have sworn to remain in this state of celibate engagement but now are having second thoughts. But "his virgin" is a strange way to refer to a man's fiancée. It suggests at the very least that, for the Corinthians, virginity rather than espousal has become the defining characteristic of the relationship. This suggests a third interpretation of this text.

Corinthian men and women have perhaps voluntarily entered special celibate relationships, "spiritual marriages" (the NEB refers to "partners in celibacy") to symbolize what they understand to be their current spiritual status. Perhaps the virgins symbolize the entire community's relationship to the returning Christ, for Paul speaks later of his desire "to present [the church] as a chaste virgin to Christ" (2 Cor. 11:2). The situation is similar to the celibacy within marriage that Paul rejected earlier (1 Cor. 7:1–7), but in this case the "spiritual marriage" that Paul approves is understood *from the beginning* to be a special, symbolic relationship. The Corinthians may consider the symbolism to be so sacred that it is a sin to break it. Details of the situation are simply not clear. Paul's response, however, *is* clear and clearly one-sided. The man, whether fiancé or virgin-partner, should not be pressured by the community (or even by his virgin!) into remaining in this perpetually chaste relationship. If he has the gift to sustain it, well and good. If not, marriage is no sin.

Paul rounds off his discussion in 7:39–40 by returning to some points he made earlier (cf. 7:8, 9, 13): Married women should not divorce their husbands and while widows may marry, they will be better off (*Good News Bible:* "happier") if they do not. These somewhat redundant comments about women provide an artificial sense of balance to 7:36–38, which focuses exclusively on men's behavior. Paul's concern here for women's happiness also stands in some tension with his earlier lack of concern for the virgins' preferences. In the context of Paul's earlier advice, the final verses also serve as a reminder to the celibate partners that if the relationship is transformed into a normal marriage, the change is permanent. Whereas "real" married partners can engage in temporary periods of celibacy (7:1–7), their mirror opposites, the celibate couples, cannot enjoy temporary periods of "marriage."

***Summary.*** The Corinthians, it seems, were limiting the options of "spiritual" Christians to celibacy within marriage or no marriage (and thus no sexual intercourse) at all.

Though he may have once extolled to the Corinthians the advantages of celibacy, Paul is determined to resist this imposition of a single standard on all members of the community. He argues for options. There is more than one way to live a holy life. A marriage with full and mutual sexual activity is holy (7:14–15), and celibate life is holy too (7:34). Yet even as he argues against the view that celibacy is the *only* way, Paul cannot deny that, in his opinion, it is the *better* way. Nevertheless, he knows that this world is not the heavenly realm of sexless angels and only some few in it are gifted for celibacy. For the others, frustrated sexual passion is a more serious threat to one's spiritual life than the distractions of marriage. So Paul affirms marriage with as much enthusiasm as his own gifts and insights allow, but these gifts do not permit him really to celebrate its possibilities.

## Women, Veils, and Worship (11:2–16)

Paul's comments in these verses are as obscure as any he makes. So convoluted is Paul's argument and so enigmatic are the terms he uses that it is impossible to determine exactly what activity lies behind these comments, why it is taking place, and what Paul objects to about it. Indeed, the lack of clarity and the tortuous logic may signal that Paul himself is not exactly sure what is going on. At any rate, he does not seem to be responding here to an issue raised in the Corinthians' letter. Probably the information came to him in an oral report; how knowledgeable the informant was one cannot say.

Paul begins by commending the church for maintaining the traditions he has established, but then he launches immediately into extensive criticism of some behavior in the worship service that does not follow these traditions. The offensive activity seems to involve the wearing—or not wearing—of veils, though various hairstyles are also mentioned in the course of the argument (11:14–15). As in chap. 7, Paul presents the implications of the issue for both women and men in a balanced way, yet it is unmistakably clear that the concrete problem (whatever its precise nature) arises with the women and not the men. Women are praying and prophesying in church with uncovered heads, and Paul objects to the practice with surprising vigor. More seems to be at stake than customs of dress or hairstyle, but it is hard to evaluate the precise meaning of the women's

actions without knowing more about the cultural context. Did Jewish or Greek customs on veiling prevail in the church? Were the veiling practices for a public or a private space followed there? These cultural questions cannot be answered, but Paul provides some clues about the *theological* issues at stake.

Paul refers first to the way *men* pray (11:4), but he mentions this only in order to provide rhetorical balance to the argument. There is no problem with their behavior; they are, it seems, praying and prophesying with heads properly uncovered. Yet these comments and the comment about cropped hair (11:6) make it clear that by removing their veils the women are dressing—at least in part of their attire—*like the men*. One can postulate that this came about because the women of this church took seriously the baptismal affirmation used in Paul's churches: "There is no longer Jew or Greek, there is no longer slave or free, there is no longer male and female; for all of you are one in Christ Jesus" (Gal. 3:28). The distinctions between women and men are no longer valid, especially when both are inspired by one and the same Spirit (1 Cor. 12:11), and the women symbolize this by removing a distinctive feature of female dress during the worship service: their veils. Paul himself passed on, and perhaps formulated, the baptismal statement, but this application of it obviously alarms him. This church had a tendency to overemphasize the present reality of salvation, with grave consequence for its moral and social stability, and this activity probably seemed to Paul to be another instance of that tendency.

Paul's response to these developments takes the form of an elaborate play on words that tends to obscure rather than clarify the meaning of the passage: "But I want you to understand that Christ is the head of every man, and the man is the head of a woman, and God is the head of Christ" (11:3, author's translation). It is likely, as many argue, that "head" here means "source" and not rank or authority. (Later, for example, in 11:8–9 Paul's argument is developed explicitly in terms of source.) It is also likely, though the Greek is more ambiguous on this point, that Paul speaks here of the relationship between men and women in general (based on the story of the creation of Eve from Adam's "rib" in Genesis 2), and not (as the NRSV presents it) the specific relationship between husband and wife. But if Paul is not intending to suggest a hierarchical relationship between man and woman (or husband and wife), he does clearly suggest that the man is closer to the godhead than the woman. (Exactly how that supports Paul's views on veils is not as clear as one would wish!)

This presupposition reappears in 11:7, when Paul asserts that "a man ought not to have his head veiled, since he is the image and reflection [RSV: "glory"] of God; but woman is the reflection [RSV: "glory"] of man." This argument is based on a misreading of Gen. 1:27, which actually asserts that all humankind—both women and men—was created in the image of God. Several scholars have noted that Paul does not *deny* that women are created in God's image. But Paul also does not affirm it, and this silence is significant. By stating that woman is (only) the *reflection* of man, Paul implies again her derivative and secondary status and then he confirms this by insisting with emphatic parallelism that woman was created from and for the sake of man, *and not* vice versa (11:8–9).

This argument is developed with discouraging symmetry, with the man and the woman presented as a contrasting rather than a co-ordinate pair (cf. chap. 7!). Since Paul opens this argument by asserting that a man "ought not" to wear a veil, one expects him to complete the contrast by insisting that a woman *ought* to wear one. That, after all, is the obvious rhetorical goal of this passage. Instead he says (when the Greek is translated in the most reasonable way) that "a woman ought to have *authority over* her head, because of the angels" (author's translation). One expects insistence on an act that symbolizes derivative status: veiling the head. Instead Paul asserts the woman's authority over her head. He seems to be contradicting his own logic.

Paul continues to undo his earlier argument with a statement of mutuality that borders on equality: "Nevertheless, in the Lord woman is not independent of [perhaps: "not different from"] man or man independent of [perhaps: "different from"] woman" (11:11). He follows this with a clear rebuttal of the derivation sequence he has just established: "For just as woman came from man [see 11:8], so man comes through woman" (11:12). Finally, he presents a statement that relativizes every argument in which superior status is based on derivation: "All things come from God." Without warning Paul has reversed directions in his argument, affirming the mutuality of existence and equality of origin that he earlier denied. And without warning he reverses direction again. Abandoning any attempt to present a reasoned argument

for his position, abandoning also the sense of equality he has just encouraged, Paul concludes by simply asserting that veiling of women is proper, natural (since women's long hair is nature's way of providing a veil), and customary in all the churches of God.

It is hard to know what to make of this. Some scholars respond by dismissing the entire argument as a later insertion into the letter, but there is little evidence to support this. Paul probably wrote it, but his argument is inarticulate, incomprehensible, and inconsistent. Affirming Pauline authorship does not, however, sanction the use of these chaotic verses to define Paul's normative view of women. One senses *conflicting* views within Paul shutting down the rational process, and where reason fails, emotion and tradition take over: "But if anyone is disposed to be contentious—we have no such custom, nor do the churches of God" (11:16). The only thing that remains constant in the argument is the uncontested assumption— shared, apparently, by both sides—that women's participation in worship is functionally equal to that of men. The issue Paul addresses concerns only the mode of dress (or hairstyle) the women adopt while praying or prophesying in church. The *right* to pray or prophesy—and this involves a prominent role in the service (see 14:3–5, 24–25, 29–33)—is bestowed by the Spirit and cannot be contested (12:4–11).

It is only veils that are at issue here, but veils are a highly symbolic article of dress. All the participants in this ecclesial drama were acutely aware of this. It is perhaps not surprising then that it was not the uncontested assumption of functional equality that prevailed in the later church, but the message of secondary, derivative status conveyed by the firmly reimposed veils (see Eph. 5:22–24; 1 Tim. 2:11–15).

## Silence! (14:34–35)

These two verses, usually printed as part of a paragraph that extends from 14:33b to 14:36, are strange by any reckoning of the matter. Though Paul responds conservatively and restrictively to the question of veils in chap. 11, one is still unprepared for these verses and their absolute insistence on the silence of women in the church. How can women exercise their acknowledged right to pray and prophesy (chap. 11) if they must keep absolute silence? How can women like Euodia and Syntyche (Phil. 4:2–3), Prisca (Rom. 16:3; 1 Cor. 16:19), Mary (Rom.

16:6), Junia (Rom. 16:7), and Tryphaena and Tryphosa (Rom. 16:12) function as co-workers in the churches if they cannot speak in those churches? How can Phoebe fulfill the role of deacon (Rom. 16:1–2) if she cannot speak out in the assembly? Something is seriously amiss here.

Various solutions to this dilemma have been proposed. Some have suggested that the praying and prophesying described in chap. 11 were done in the home, while silence was imposed on women in the church. Nothing, however, in chap. 11 suggests a domestic setting, and chap. 14 rather clearly establishes worship services as the appropriate setting for prayer and prophecy. Others see a contrast between inspired speech (chap. 11), which Paul permits, and uninspired chatter (chap. 14), which he does not. Yet the language of the injunctions in chap. 14 rather clearly—and emphatically—covers all forms of speaking. Some assume that Paul applies the command of silence to married women, while granting the holy, unmarried women (7:34) the right to participate actively and vocally in worship. But Paul does not signal, as he does in chap. 7, that different groups of women are being addressed.

Some ascribe the differences to a change in Paul's attitude. In chap. 11, Paul presupposes full participation of women in the worship services, but his growing concern over the chaotic practices in Corinth leads him in 14:34–35 to an unfortunate reversal. In the interest of order, various groups, including the women, are commanded to silence (14:28, 30, 34–35). The words to women, however, have an absolute quality not found in the words to the other groups. Indeed, they are presented as universally valid, which is inconsistent with an ad hoc development in Corinth.

Another approach is to assume that these words are not Paul's. There are two possibilities here. As we have seen, Paul frequently quotes the excessive positions of the Corinthians only to correct them (6:12; 7:1–2; 8:1, 4–6). A rather tenacious line of interpretation thus ascribes 14:34–35 to the Corinthian church, and Paul's emphatic disagreement with this position is signaled in v. 36. There is much to commend this view. It eliminates the tension between the views expressed here and in chap. 11, and it corresponds to Paul's established mode of argumentation in this letter. Yet the proposal is not totally convincing. There is, for example, no clear signal here that Paul is quoting the Corinthians (compare 7:1; 8:1, 4); the other quotes are

not as lengthy as this one; and elsewhere Paul's rebuttal is more clearly marked. A second possibility, though more radical, avoids these problems.

In the early New Testament manuscripts, the verses in question do not always appear at the same point in the argument. In most manuscripts they are found as traditionally printed: after the assertion that God is a God of peace. In some manuscripts, however, they appear after the final words of this chapter. The most likely explanation for this is that the words on women's silence were originally what is called a marginal gloss—comments added in the margin of a manuscript by a later reader. Following a fairly common practice, copyists of this manuscript, uncertain as to the origin of the gloss, incorporated the words into the text of the letter, some inserting them in one place, others in another. The fact that the attitude expressed in these verses corresponds not to Paul's expressed views but to the views of the later church (1 Tim. 2:11–12; 1 Peter 3:1–6) supports this hypothesis of a later addition.

The inclusion of these verses in the text of Paul's letter is particularly unfortunate, for their strong wording affects the way the rest of Paul's comments on women are read. They reinforce, for example, the conservative tendencies of chap. 11 and obscure the more liberating aspects of Paul's statements about women. The fact that the verses could be so readily received as Paul's own words reflects not only the ambiguity of Paul's position (see especially 1 Cor. 7:36–38; 11:7–9) but also the impact of the more overt misogyny of the deutero-Pauline letters. It is difficult enough to assess Paul's own words on women. When later views invade the picture, the task becomes hopelessly complex.

## BIBLIOGRAPHY

Fee, Gordon D. *The First Epistle to the Corinthians.* New International Commentary on the New Testament. Grand Rapids: Wm. B. Eerdmans Publishing Co., 1987.

Fiorenza, Elisabeth Schüssler. "Neither Male Nor Female: Galatians 3:28—Alternative Vision and Pauline Modification." In her *In Memory of Her: A Feminist Theological Reconstruction of Christian Origins,* pp. 205–241. New York: Crossroad, 1983.

Macdonald, Margaret Y. "Women Holy in Body and Spirit: The Social Setting of 1 Corinthians 7." *New Testament Studies* 36 (1990), 161–181.

Meeks, Wayne A. "The Image of the Androgyne: Some Uses of a Symbol in Earliest Christianity." *History of Religions* 13 (1974), 165–208.

Pagels, Elaine H. "Paul and Women: A Response to Recent Discussion." *Journal of the American Academy of Religion* 42 (1974), 538–549.

Perkins, Pheme. *Ministering in the Pauline Churches.* Ramsey, N.J.: Paulist Press, 1982.

Scroggs, Robin. "Paul and the Eschatological Woman." *Journal of the American Academy of Religion* 40 (1972), 283–303.

Wire, Antoinette Clark. *The Corinthian Women Prophets: A Reconstruction Through Paul's Rhetoric.* Minneapolis: Fortress Press, 1990.

Yarbrough, O. Larry. *Not Like the Gentiles: Marriage Rules in the Letters of Paul.* Society of Biblical Literature Dissertation Series 80. Atlanta: Scholars Press, 1985.

# 2 CORINTHIANS

*Jouette M. Bassler*

## Introduction

The second letter in the Christian canon from Paul to the church in Corinth is rather disjointed, reflecting the unstable relationship between the apostle and this church and raising as well some questions about the literary integrity of the letter. A number of unsettling events occurred after the writing of 1 Corinthians: Paul visited Corinth to deal with a growing crisis in the church, and the visit—described by Paul as painful—resulted in a traumatic confrontation with at least one member of the church (2:1–11); following this visit he wrote an emotional, "tearful" letter of reproof (2:3–4, 9); he sent Titus, perhaps as the bearer of the tearful letter, to Corinth and Titus returned with comforting news of a reconciliation of the church with Paul (7:5–16); some Christian missionaries—Paul calls them "false apostles" and, more ironically, "superapostles"—arrived in Corinth and by direct accusation and subtle innuendo turned the church against Paul (11:1–15). Sometime during this growing crisis, Paul suffered some life-threatening experience, perhaps imprisonment, in the province of Asia (1:8–10).

Second Corinthians contains a defense against the accusations leveled against Paul and an attack on the perpetrators of these accusations. Paul's tone is at times magnanimous, confident, and even joyful (7:16); at other times, however, it is bitter, sarcastic, and even threatening (10:1–2; 13:2). The shift in tone is so great that many scholars wonder whether the entire letter could have been written at the same time—that is, whether 2 Corinthians was originally one letter. It has often been proposed that 2 Corinthians contains parts of two or more letters (chaps. 1–9 and chaps. 10–13) that were written at different times and reflect

different stages in the tumultuous relationship between Paul and this church. There is, however, some disagreement on the sequence of these letters. Does the mood of reconciliation that pervades chaps. 1–9 reflect a happy resolution to the conflict evident in chaps. 10–13? Or do chaps. 10–13 reflect a flare-up of the situation that Paul thought was resolved when he wrote chaps. 1–9? The debate on this continues.

In its present form, the letter opens on a note of praise to God for the comfort Paul has received in his affliction. Both his physical peril in Asia (1:8–11) and his emotional distress over the church (7:5–13) have, for the moment at least, been resolved. Not all the accusations raised against him, however, have been completely laid to rest, so Paul defends his recent activities, especially his decision not to return immediately to Corinth, against charges of vacillation or callousness (1:12–2:13; 7:5–16). He interrupts this discussion of his recent travels with a rather rambling defense of his apostolic ministry. Echoes of conflict can be heard here. Paul has no legitimating letters of recommendation (3:1); others are "hucksters" of God's word (2:17); some pride themselves on outward appearances (5:12); and Paul makes an explicit plea for reconciliation (6:12–13; 7:2–3). The dominant mood, though, is one of pride, joy, and above all confidence in the church (7:4). These statements of confidence provide strong grounding for the exhortations concerning a collection for the Jerusalem church that fill chaps. 8 and 9 and end on a note of nearly ecstatic thanksgiving (9:15).

Beginning in chap. 10, however, the tone of confidence and reconciliation is replaced by a hurt and caustic mood as Paul directly counters the attacks that have been leveled against him by the false apostles and expresses real concern about his future relations with this church (12:20–21; 13:2–3). Repeatedly Paul cites the charges against him: he is weak and humble in person and only bold in his letters (10:1, 10; 11:20–21); he has not forthrightly accepted money for his work but has used guile to fill his pockets (11:7–11; 12:14–18); he has not adequately displayed the miracles and wonders that were regarded as signs of a true apostle (12:11–13); and he is deficient in the area of "visions and revelations" (12:1–10). Paul refuses to apologize for these "weaknesses," for through them God's power is more perfectly revealed (12:9). He closes the letter with stern warnings about what to expect at his next visit (chap. 13).

The letter gives no explicit information about its place or places of origin. If the two-letter hypothesis is correct, chaps. 1–9 were probably written from somewhere in Macedonia after Paul's reunion with Titus (7:5–7). Chapters 10–13 were written either before this reunion (from Ephesus?) or after it (from Macedonia?). This correspondence was probably completed between 55 and 56 C.E.

# Comment

## A Pure Bride or Deceived Eve? (11:2–3)

Paul's obvious concern throughout this letter is that "false" apostles have undermined the Corinthians' loyalty to him and have drawn them away from the gospel that he preached and thus (in Paul's view) from Christ. He expresses his concern here through the familiar metaphor of marriage. Just as the prophets often portrayed Israel as the bride of Yahweh (Isa. 54:4–6; Jer. 2:2; Hos. 2:19–20), so Paul describes the church as betrothed to Christ. He himself is the "father" of the bride, charged to keep her pure and undefiled until the day that the groom returns to claim his bride. (This may have been symbolized in the community by its "virgins"; see the comments on 1 Corinthians 7.) The prophets often denounced Israel's infidelity to God with graphic descriptions of the behavior of the adulterous wife (Hos. 2:2–3; Jer. 3:1–5; 13:25–27; Ezek. 23:1–21). Paul uses somewhat more restraint when he expresses his concerns by introducing the figure of Eve.

In Genesis both Adam and Eve are culpable in the tragic events of the garden, but only Eve admits to having been deceived (Gen. 3:13). It is this idea that Paul uses, leaving the sexual overtones of the word "deceive" undeveloped. Unlike the author of the pastoral epistles, who equates only women with Eve's deception (1 Tim. 2:11–15), Paul sees the issue in broader terms. The whole church is being exposed to "deceitful workers" (11:13), and Paul fears that the church, like Eve, may succumb. When Paul focuses in other letters on Adam's role, the emphasis is quite different: the universal consequences of the fall are described, not the moral flaw that permitted it (Rom. 5:12–21; 1 Cor. 15:42–49). In using the figures of Adam and Eve in these different ways, Paul follows—and perpetuates—sexual stereotypes. Clearly the whole church, comprising both men and women, is in danger of being deceived, but it is Eve who is for Paul the paradigm of susceptibility.

## "Content with Weakness": Paul's Theology of the Cross

Paul counters the charges of weakness and inadequacy that his rivals have raised against him not by refuting them but by embracing them in the name of Christ: "Therefore I am content with weaknesses, insults, hardships, persecutions, and calamities for the sake of Christ; for whenever I am weak, then I am strong" (12:10). Such words are rhetorically powerful, but they must be guarded against misuse. One way to do this is by contextualizing them.

Paul presents his theology of the cross partly to defend himself against charges and partly to undermine the position of his rivals in Corinth, who understand their Christian mission in terms of personal aggressiveness, rhetorical grandeur, and spiritual superiority. His statements about suffering must be heard in this polemical context. The Corinthians are offered a choice, and the way Paul presents this choice—"super" apostles or the apostle of the cross—is determined in large measure by the way his opponents have defined the issue.

Setting Paul's words in this context is helpful, but it is not enough. What can prevent later readers, for whom the context is obscure or irrelevant, from hearing in these words a call to passivity in the face of meaningless suffering or meekness in the face of oppression? Few women would find in this a redemptive message! Paul's argument, however, is infused with irony that transforms the message of the cross into a protest against those who reject him as weak and who find God always and only on the side of strength and power: "You put up with it when someone . . . gives you a slap in the face. To my shame, I must say, we were too weak for that" (11:20–21). Moreover, the cross is inherently paradoxical. It locates God on the side of the weak, the foolish, the have-nots (1 Cor. 1:18–31), but it is at the same time a source of power and a symbol of the God who acts in ways that the world cannot comprehend. When Paul identifies his own sufferings and afflictions as a reflection of the cross, he is claiming for his life all the paradoxes of that symbol. Thus he accepts his rivals' charges of weakness, because they reveal a truth about God. But he accepts these charges with scathing irony and stern severity, and that too reveals a truth about God. The cross may reflect weakness, but not passive weakness. It reflects power in weakness, the power of the God who chooses the weak "to shame the strong" (1 Cor. 1:27).

Paul's letters to Corinth, and especially 2 Corinthians, present us with the challenge of how to claim a suffering Savior, a crucified Messiah. This is an ambiguous symbol. Some will find God powerfully present in it. Others may feel God's absence. It is, in either case, a symbol that claims our attention and demands our reflection.

## BIBLIOGRAPHY

Beker, J. Christiaan. *Suffering and Hope: The Biblical Vision and the Human Predicament.* Philadelphia: Fortress Press, 1987.

Furnish, Victor P. *II Corinthians.* Anchor Bible 32A. Garden City, N.Y.: Doubleday & Co., 1984.

Thrall, Margaret E. *The First and Second Letters of Paul to the Corinthians.* Cambridge Bible Commentary. Cambridge: Cambridge University Press, 1965.

# GALATIANS

*Carolyn Osiek*

## Introduction

No scholars seriously doubt that Paul wrote the letter to the Galatians. It contains some of the ideas considered most central to Paul's theology, namely, salvation through faith in Christ and the Gentile Christian's freedom from the Mosaic law. Galatians differs from the other authentic Pauline letters, though, in being addressed not to the cluster of house-churches in one urban area but to a group of churches in a larger geographical region as a circular letter. Those churches were located either in the Roman province of Galatia (the south Galatian theory) or in the larger, more northerly region that traditionally bore the name (the north Galatian theory). Though there are good arguments on both sides, the south Galatian destination is more likely the correct one because Paul usually uses Roman political names for places. Furthermore, Acts depicts Paul as having been active in the province of Galatia (at Pisidian Antioch, Iconium, Lystra, and Derbe).

The occasion of the letter, probably written in the mid-50s, seems to have been that, after Paul's evangelization of the area, other Christian missionaries threatened to replace Paul's gospel with their own. Their version of the gospel assumed that people's access to Christ required that they obey the Mosaic law, or at least some of its major requirements, including circumcision. Paul wrote in a state of agitation (his usual thanksgiving after the greeting is missing), to reaffirm his own way of preaching the gospel.

Chapters 1 and 2 rehearse events that establish Paul's authority as an apostle and some of the difficulties he encountered. Chapters 3 and 4 set forth the biblical and theological underpinning of the gospel as he preaches it. In chaps. 5 and 6 he develops the ethical and communitarian implications of the life in the Spirit that flows from his gospel of freedom in Christ.

## Comment

### Male-centered Language and Worldview (1:1–3)

The address of the letter provides a good illustration of the male-centered worldview of the New Testament writers, which is often compounded by noninclusive translations. For example, in 1:1, Paul identifies himself as an apostle called by God first and foremost and not by human authorities. The RSV translates the source of Paul's call as "not from men nor through man." In the NRSV the wording has been improved and clarified to "neither by human commission nor from human authorities." The same point is made again in 1:10–12.

In this case, it is a question of translation. The problem is different when Paul includes with himself as senders of the letter "all the brothers with me" (1:2). This terminology is pervasive in the Pauline letters and in Acts (e.g., Gal. 1:11; 4:12, 31; 5:11, 13; 6:1, where it refers to the addressees of the letter). It could be assumed that the masculine language is meant to be generic, as the translators of the NRSV do in using "friends" to translate the plural of the word for "brother." The more astute interpretation, however, is that women are simply marginal to social communication and interaction and therefore need not be specifically addressed. Masculine language can apply to women as well as to men only when women belong to the social group solely as extensions of their male protective figures (fathers or husbands, for example). Including women on such terms was generally the practice in the New Testament world and continues to be so in more traditional societies. Although in other settings Paul demonstrates awareness and even appreciation of individual women (e.g., Phil. 4:2–3; Rom. 16:1–7, 12, 15), this does not change his habitual language, or his habitual social perceptions.

## The Rite of Initiation (2:3–9)

Paul's terms for Jews and Gentiles, generally translated "the circumcised" and "the uncircumcised," are literally "the circumcision" and "the uncircumcision." These categories, which symbolize people's relationship to the whole law of God, express from the Jewish point of view the essential difference between people. In Judaism, however, circumcision is a wholly male ritual, which incorporates the male child (or adult in the case of "proselytes" or converts) into the community of the law. At about the time this letter was written, another rite was also coming into favor for initiation of proselytes—ritual immersion, or baptism—for both sexes. This practice probably grew out of the Jewish custom of purification by periodic ritual washing by immersion in a *miqveh*, or pool. As far as we know, baptism was always a ritual for both women and men.

Probably when it began, baptism symbolized cleansing from the total impurity of being a Gentile. As baptism came to be interpreted in Gentile Christian communities, more attention could be given to the idea of cleansing from the impurity of sin (see Rom. 6:1–8). This was especially true as Paul's version of the gospel, which did not require Gentile Christians to keep the law of Moses, came to represent the dominant theology of the church.

## The Social Meaning of Sonship (3:23–26; 4:4–7)

In chap. 3, Paul has ingeniously used examples from scripture and from life to illustrate his argument that observance of the law of Moses is no longer necessary for Gentile converts to Jesus. He maintains that his argument is valid in spite of the fact that other Christian missionaries have made a good case to the contrary and have presented the practice of Jewish custom in an appealing way (3:1–2; 4:10). In one of those examples, Paul speaks of the law as a "custodian" (RSV) or "disciplinarian" (NRSV). The reference is to a slave assigned as tutor and guardian of the son of a well-to-do Greco-Roman family (3:23–25; 4:1–3). Paul says that we are like that son, heir to the estate but, as a minor, subjected to a mere slave of the household until we attain maturity. The coming of Christ marks that change in status which frees us from the authority of our guardian (the law) in order to enjoy our inheritance as adults.

In this context, Paul proclaims that we are "all sons of God through faith" (3:26, author's translation). Again the question of inclusive language versus social interpretation is important. The easy interpretation would be that the intention of the text is that all are sons and daughters—children—of God. But in the culture in which Paul wrote, a daughter did not have the same status as a son, especially the oldest son and heir referred to here. While daughters could also inherit property, their property was at least nominally always under the control of a male relative or patron who administered it. Even an oldest daughter could never be heir to the authority of the *paterfamilias*, the male head of the household. Though we know of households headed by women (e.g., Lydia in Acts 16:15; Mary in Acts 12:12), such women were probably widows and still operating under the legal fiction of a male authority. Therefore, the best interpretation of 3:26 is most likely that all, both male and female, have the equivalent of the legal status of son before God—that is, all stand with Christ as heirs of eternal life.

Continuing the analogy of our coming to maturity with the coming of Christ, in 4:4–7 Paul speaks of Christ's divine and human origins: God sent the son, who was also "born of woman." The semidivine, semihuman son of a god and a human mother is a familiar motif in Greco-Roman religion: Dionysus, for instance, the god of vegetation, ecstatic sylvan worship, and sometimes of drama, was said to have been born of the human woman Semele, whom the high god Zeus courted and seduced behind his wife Hera's back. The phrase "born of woman" does not, however, witness to the virginal conception of Jesus! The same expression is used in the Gospels of Matthew and Luke to refer to John the Baptist as one among many who are "born of woman" (Matt. 11:11 // Luke 7:28). In fact, it simply emphasizes Jesus' human origins and parallels the following statement about his religious origins, that he was "born under the law." He is fully human and fully Jewish. Christ redeems or ransoms those who, like himself, are under the law (the Jews) and bestows on all believers the status not just of children of the household, in status no better than slaves, but of "sons" and heirs.

### "No Male and Female" (3:28)

Galatians 3:28 has long been a center of controversy, more so in recent years with the rise of feminist readings of the Bible. Two of the three pairs, Jew–Greek and slave–free, occur also in similar statements in 1 Cor. 12:13 and Col. 3:11. The third, male–female, occurs only here, and it will be the focus of comment. Whereas the other two pairs are connected by correlative conjunctions ("There is no . . . or . . ."), the male–female pair is connected by the coordinating conjunction ("there is no male and female"). This difference is seldom noted in translations, though it is in the NRSV. There are at least five possible interpretations of this difficult passage.

1. *Emancipation proclamation ahead of its time.* Some interpreters suggest that the statement endorses an end to sexism and discrimination of every kind. At face value, this may be a bit naïve, since it would seem that elsewhere in Paul's writing (1 Cor. 11:2–16; 14:34–35), he certainly did not understand it that way. Yet, if we believe that biblical texts can be prophetic beyond the vision of author, time, and place, there is some validity to this approach.

2. *A formula used in the baptism of new Christians.* According to this recent interpretation, in the background of Paul's words lies a baptismal ritual of the early church. The language of this ritual echoes the statement from the first creation narrative in Gen. 1:27–28. There God is said to have fashioned humankind after God's own image and likeness, "male and female" God created them. The words in quotation marks are exactly the same in the Greek translation (the Septuagint) of Gen. 1:28 and in Gal. 3:28, where they break the parallel structure, as noted above. In some Hellenistic Jewish exegesis of Genesis, notably that done by the great theologian Philo of Alexandria, a contemporary of Paul, the creation narrative is a metaphor for the makeup of the person. In that metaphor, the division of the original human being into two genders was the beginning of the internal division of the person into rationality (symbolized by the male principle) and sensation (symbolized by the female prin-

ciple). Conflict is soon to follow and indeed does in the story. Against the background of such an understanding of the human condition, the baptismal proclamation quoted by Paul implies that the division and conflict in human nature, the source of sin, can be overcome in the saving grace of baptism.

3. *Reference to the order of creation but not to the order of the Fall.* In this view, the text refers to a fundamental equality of male and female as created by God, alluded to in Gen. 1:27–28. However, with the Fall, that equality was broken, as evidenced in Gen. 3:16: "Your [the woman's] desire will be for your husband, and he will rule over you." Galatians 3:28 therefore has nothing to say about contemporary relationships, but looks back nostalgically to the good old days before equality was lost by sin.

4. *The time of salvation anticipated in the present.* Related to the first interpretation but with a different view of human nature, this view suggests that in God's future the tension between human opposites—Jew and Gentile, slave and free, male and female—will disappear. Because life in the grace of Christ anticipates in part what the future can be like, it is possible to live without these unhealthy tensions even now.

5. *A glimpse of the still-distant future.* Contrary to the previous two interpretations, this reading suggests that Gal. 3:28 speaks of the heavenly realm of relationships in Christ, possible only in a new and transformed creation, like that envisioned in Rev. 21:1–4; 22:1–5. Like the third interpretation, this one would assert that the text has nothing to say to the present time—Paul's or ours.

### God as "Father" (4:4–7)

In addition to bringing about people's transformation from the status of minor children under guardianship of the law to that of mature heirs able to enjoy their inheritance (see above on 3:23–26), the coming of Christ had other consequences as well. One of those consequences is that the Spirit of God, the sign for Paul of the presence of God's action, is sent into our hearts and enables believers to address God as *Abba,* Father (see also Rom. 8:14–17). Surely this characteristically Christian way of calling on and speaking about God goes back to Jesus himself, since it is so well attested of him. Whether or not he was the first or only one to use it in such a personal way is a debated point and is really irrelevant. In memory of Christ,

Christians felt entitled to use this word for God. In its day, this was a groundbreaking move in Jewish and Christian spirituality. Addressing God as Mother today is a contemporary cultural analogy: that is, the feelings it evokes, both positive and negative, are probably quite similar to those evoked by the use of "Abba" for God in the first century.

## Paul as Mother to the Galatian Christians (4:19)

In a very unusual way, Paul here draws upon the metaphor of giving birth to speak of his own relationship to the Galatian communities. Elsewhere he freely uses paternal expressions (1 Cor. 4:14–15; 1 Thess. 2:11; Philemon 10). In 1 Thess. 2:7, he compares his ministry style to the tenderness of a nurse with her children, but here Paul speaks of his own birth pangs in the process of giving birth to Christ in them—a somewhat complicated metaphor. The language of birth pain is a common way to speak about the approaching end time (e.g., Mark 13:8; Matt. 24:8; John 16:21–22; 1 Thess. 5:3; Rom. 8:22; Rev. 12:2). Such language may also imply the mystery of rebirth as spoken of in Hellenistic mysticism and mystery religions. However, the difference here is that it is not the apostle alone who suffers the pain of giving birth, nor the believer alone who is to be reborn through the initiation process, but Christ who is being born and formed within believers. Paul's vivid sense of living in a time when the end of history was near means that this birth process of which he speaks is not limited to the individual apostle and community but is part of the grand scale of suffering and tribulation (see Rom. 8:22). But what does the use of maternal imagery imply about Paul himself? Perhaps a man willing to use such an image is not as alienated from women's experience as Paul is often made out to be.

## The Allegory of Sarah and Hagar (4:21–31)

The great allegory of the two Jerusalems is founded in Jewish imagery in use at the time, but not with such a negative shadow cast on the earthly city. The heavenly Jerusalem and the heavenly Temple were used by other New Testament writers as well (e.g., Rev. 21:2; Hebrews 9) to symbolize eternal transformation. Paul begins his allegory with the story of Abraham's two wives, the first wife, Sarah (never named but clearly intended), and the slave, Hagar, who becomes Abraham's second wife (Genesis 16; 21).

The use of the two women illustrates the importance of the matriarchs in what we call the patriarchal narratives. They are bearers of the lines descending from Abraham, the common ancestor in faith for Jews, Christians, and Muslims. Jews claim both ethnic and spiritual descent through Sarah; Christians, Paul suggests, can trace their spiritual roots back to her; Muslims, in an interpretation attributed to Muhammad himself, claim Hagar and her son, Ishmael, as their spiritual ancestors. There is no denying that for both Genesis and Paul, Hagar is rejected. But precisely because of this interpretation, she becomes the symbol and heroine for all those women who feel rejected or less desired because of personal, economic, ethnic, or racist practices. While Paul's allegory, for his own purposes, ends with Hagar still rejected, the reader of the Bible cannot forget Jesus' outreach to just such oppressed and forgotten ones.

## Freedom in Christ (5:1, 13)

In the last part of the letter, after giving his theological exposition, Paul appeals to the Galatians to live in the true freedom for which they have been freed by Christ. Apparently Paul did not mean by this that they were also to consider themselves free from the restrictions imposed on them by social customs. In this letter, written to people who, Paul thinks, need to be liberated, Paul speaks forcefully about freedom. In 1 Corinthians, on the other hand, where the problem seems to be just the opposite, he does not mention it! It has been suggested that perhaps Paul began preaching freedom in Christ among the Corinthians as well (or that they obtained a copy of the Galatian letter) but that they then went on to take him more literally than he intended. Read in that light, Paul's restrictive measures in 1 Corinthians fall into place. In questions of dress, hairstyles, and public conduct socially appropriate to each gender, for instance (1 Cor. 11:2–16; 14:34–35), Paul sounds quite conservative. Where has his open-mindedness about freedom gone?

Galatians 5:13 gives us a clue: Paul understands freedom not as the opportunity to pursue one's own interests but to be even more at the service of others. That this is costly service can be seen in the fact that in this charter of Christian freedom he also refers frequently to the cross (2:19–20; 3:1; 5:11, 24; 6:12, 14, and perhaps 17). This ideal of service and even self-sacrifice poses definite problems for women of all generations and nearly all cultures, who are socially educated to expect that their true happiness lies in service to others, while men are brought up to pursue their own goals.

But Paul may be doing something quite radical here: he is holding up traditionally feminine values as ideals for everyone, male and female, and perhaps especially for the Christian men who are his principal addressees (see above on 1:1–5). Women too need to appropriate these values, but they need also to balance this ideal carefully against their legitimate psychological needs. Bearing the cross in freedom does not mean enduring abuse and victimhood, but living genuinely for others out of one's own inner freedom by claiming the inheritance of the "sons of God."

## BIBLIOGRAPHY

Betz, Hans Dieter. *Galatians.* Hermeneia. Philadelphia: Fortress Press, 1979.

Boucher, Madeleine. "Some Unexplored Parallels to 1 Cor 11:11–12 and Gal 3:28–The New Testament on the Role of Women." *Catholic Biblical Quarterly* 31 (1969), 50–58.

Bruce, F. F. *The Epistle to the Galatians.* Grand Rapids: Wm. B. Eerdmans Publishing Co., 1982.

Gaventa, Beverly R. "The Maternity of Paul: An Exegetical Study of Galatians 4:19." In *The Conversation Continues: Studies in Paul and John in Honor of J. Louis Martyn,* edited by Robert Fortna and Beverly Gaventa, pp. 189–201. Nashville: Abingdon Press, 1990.

Osiek, Carolyn. *Galatians.* New Testament Message 12. Wilmington, Del.: Michael Glazier, 1980.

# EPHESIANS

### E. Elizabeth Johnson

## Introduction

### The Problem of Pseudonymity

Ephesians and Colossians are both said to have been written by Paul, but a number of literary and theological characteristics lead scholars to think that they were written by a later author. At best, the identity of their author is disputed. It is better to talk about "disputed" and "undisputed" letters rather than "authentic" and "inauthentic" letters, because at issue is authorship, not authority. Whether or not Paul wrote Ephesians and Colossians (or 2 Thessalonians or the pastoral letters) determines whether or not we can legitimately use the undisputed letters (Romans, 1 and 2 Corinthians, Galatians, Philippians, 1 Thessalonians, and Philemon) to interpret them and vice versa. If Paul did not write them, they do not cease to be the church's scripture, but they must be understood in a historical context different from Paul's.

The practice of a later author's writing under a pseudonym, and in fact using the name of an honored predecessor, was common in the first century. It reflected a desire to interpret the predecessor's thought in a later context. A characteristic of Ephesians and Colossians that has led a majority of interpreters to suspect that they are indeed pseudonymous is that they treat very differently themes and issues found also in the undisputed letters of Paul. An important difference concerns these authors' attitudes toward marriage (see the discussion of 5:21–6:9 below). Both letters also make distinctive use of baptismal traditions that are quite different from Paul's. They speak about the "principalities and powers" and the "wisdom of God" in ways that seem to represent a development from Paul's letters. These two letters express greatly reduced expectation of the imminent return of the risen Christ, and they employ vocabulary and stylistic features different from Paul's. Finally, both letters seem to presuppose church situations that are more understandable in congregations one or two generations after Paul's ministry. In general, Ephesians and Colossians appear to come from a time in the last third of the first century, when Gentile Christianity needed to define itself as a religious phenomenon over against both Greco-Roman culture and Jewish Christianity. The marked similarities between the two letters suggest that the author of Ephesians relies heavily on the letter to the Colossians and, to a lesser degree, on the undisputed letters of Paul. Colossians itself is greatly influenced by Paul's letters, particularly 1 Corinthians.

### The Situation of Ephesians

The letter's very general quality, the remarkable lack of reference to individuals or circumstances in the church, and the lack of a specific addressee (the best manuscripts of 1:1 do not name any location) lead many interpreters to conclude that Ephesians is not really a letter at all but a theological treatise addressed "to whom it may concern." According to this interpretation, the document is written to serve as an encyclical or a cover letter for a collection of Paul's epistles, attempting to summarize his thought. Although there may be an element of truth to this notion, Ephesians appears also to be a real letter written to a Christian community (or group of communities) in Asia Minor near the end of the first century. These communities would formerly have been part of the Pauline mission but are now jeopardized by outside teachings of unknown origin and content (see "tossed to and fro and blown about by every wind of doctrine," 4:14). Whatever these outside teachings are, they apparently threaten to divide the community or distance it from its heritage, because the author's greatest concern seems to be to maintain the unity of the church (see particularly the exhortations in 4:1–6). The nature of the danger is by no means clear, but the church's enemies include not only the devil (2:2; 4:27; 6:11, 16) and cosmic "principalities and powers" (6:12–17) but deceitful teachers as well (4:14; 5:6). The language of hostility and reconciliation (e.g., 2:14, 17) and of continuing conflict (see the divine armor in 6:10–17) imply that, from the author's perspective, all is not well with the congregation and that some threat from outside the church demands the protection afforded by an apostolic letter.

## Contents of the Letter

After a familiar "Pauline" greeting and an extended thanksgiving (1:1–22; cf. Rom. 1:1–15; 1 Cor. 1:1–9) that sets the tone and agenda for what follows in the letter, the author embarks on an exalted description of the new life in Christ (Eph. 2:1–22). He employs what sound very much like Pauline slogans (e.g., 2:5b, 8–9) to ground both his authority and his vision of Christian life in Paul's teaching. Relying heavily on Hellenistic Jewish traditions about the accessibility of God's wisdom, the author describes Christian life as sharing through baptism Christ's heavenly status with God.

References to heaven and "the heavenly places" dominate the letter to the Ephesians (1:3, 10, 20; 2:6; 3:10, 15; 4:6, 8, 10; 6:9, 12), which means that the temporal dualism between this age and the age to come so prominent in Paul's letters has given way to a spatial dualism between earth and heaven. Christians no longer live in the tension between Jesus' death and his coming in glory, as Paul envisioned them, but somehow between their own earthly (pre-Christian) and heavenly (Christian) identities.

This contrast between earth and heaven is reflected in the baptismal language which the author borrows from Paul to make a distinctively new point. In Rom. 6:1–12 Paul speaks of Christian baptism as death and resurrection with Christ. Although he is careful to locate Christian resurrection with Christ in the future (6:5), the author of Ephesians (here relying on Col. 2:20–3:4) says that believers have already been raised with Christ and therefore currently share his heavenly status (Eph. 2:1–10). The Pauline slogan in 2:5, 8 ("by grace you have been saved") is thus clearly a development beyond Paul, for whom salvation is always a future, eschatological reality that confirms what has been inaugurated in the justification of sinners and the gift of the Spirit to the church (see Rom. 5:9; 1 Thess. 1:10).

This description of Christian life leads the author into a discussion of God's bringing together of Jew and Gentile in the church, what he calls the "mystery" of God's plan (2:11–3:21). Paul too speaks of God's dealings with Jews and Gentiles as a "mystery" (Rom. 11:25). Ephesians, however, merges the two ethnic groups into "one new humanity" (2:15), whereas Paul steadfastly maintains their separate identities before God and God's abiding faithfulness to ethnic Israel (see Rom. 11:25). The author of Ephesians employs Paul's concept of the "body of Christ" (see Romans 12 and 1 Corinthians 12) to describe not the individual congregations to which Paul refers but the universal—even cosmic—reality of the church (2:16). This universalizing of the concept of the church is yet another result of the author's earthly/heavenly dichotomy. If all believers share the same heavenly identity, then there should be no discernible distinction between individual Christian communities. Whereas Paul describes the church as the body of Christ, the author of Ephesians further specifies Christ as the head of that body (1:22; 4:15; 5:23).

This picture of the church universal as a reflection of God's "fullness" (3:19), harmonious in all its parts and heavenly in its identity, gives way to the second half of the letter, which consists of a series of ethical admonitions (4:1–6:20). The author grounds his call for church unity in the universal confession and baptism of all Christians and the common teaching of church leaders whose authority goes back to the apostles (4:1–16). The bad behavior characteristic of the old, pre-Christian, earthly life is no longer appropriate to the new, Christian, heavenly life (4:17–5:20), and here again the image of baptism surfaces in the language of "putting off" and "putting on" in 4:22, 24 (cf. "put away" in 4:25). Whereas Paul calls for Christians to imitate him even as he imitates Christ (1 Cor. 4:16; 11:1; 1 Thess. 1:6; cf. 2:14), the author of Ephesians exhorts the church to become imitators of God (Eph. 5:1), dissociating themselves from non-Christians (5:3–14) and making their Christian fellowship distinctive in the world (5:15–20).

# Comment

## The Household Code (5:21–6:9)

*Household duties in Greco-Roman culture and early Judaism.* As long ago as the fourth century B.C.E., philosophers considered the household a microcosm, the basic social unit whose structure ought to reflect the pyramidal structure of the whole society and even the universe. Aristotle said "the smallest and primary parts of the household are master and slave, husband and wife, father and children" (*Politics* I.1253b). By the first century, many ethicists, both Greco-Roman and Jewish, discussed this domestic structure by including prescribed duties for each member of the household. The head of the household was expected to hold all three superior roles— husband, father, and master—and the performance of each role was detailed by recommended responsibilities. His wife, children, and slaves also had conventional duties expected of them. If the father/husband/master ruled appropriately in his household, and if governmental authorities similarly performed their duties, human life would consequently reflect the harmony intended by God/the gods as they ruled the universe. The subject was of such concern in the first century that scarcely a pagan philosopher worth reading neglects to discuss it. So also, several important Jewish writers of the period consider family relationships and obligations, particularly in the context of interpreting the Fifth Commandment (to honor father and mother), and their reflections are clearly influenced by Greco-Roman moralism.

*Christian household codes.* The concern for the traditional hierarchy of household order was apparently absent from the first generation of the church, and it is denied rather dramatically in the Pauline baptismal formula of Gal. 3:28 (compare also the prominence of women in the Pauline mission and Paul's preference for celibacy over marriage). Several Christian writers from the second and later generations, however, pick up this cultural value and interpret the hierarchical duties of household members from their own Christian perspectives. It is curious to note that the Christian household codes we have (in Ephesians, Colossians, 1 Peter, and the Pastorals) all come from the Pauline circle. This is probably because Paul's own proclamation of freedom to women and slaves, combined with his emphatic concern for individual Christian communities (that is, house-churches), created significant friction for succeeding generations. Paul himself apparently found the gospel's release of women from social conventions problematic at Corinth, because 1 Cor. 11:2–16 contains the only assertion of gender hierarchy found in the Pauline letters. Furthermore, in 1 Cor. 12:13, when the apostle alludes to the traditional baptismal formula (see Gal. 3:28), he omits reference to the reunification of women and men in Christ.

The household code in Ephesians, although addressing all three traditional pairs of relationships, dwells at greatest length on the marriage relationship, comparing it to the relationship between Christ and the church. That comparison is one of the most remarkable features of this table of domestic responsibilities. The familiar prophetic image of Israel as God's wife (e.g., in Hosea) is here transformed from a metaphor into a description of reality. The prophetic metaphor uses human marriage to illustrate or explain God's faithful relationship to Israel despite Israel's faithlessness. The writer of Ephesians, however, reverses the direction of the comparison by using Christ's relationship to the church to illustrate how men ought to relate to their wives and women to their husbands. The issue of faithfulness so prominent in the prophetic image is left behind, and instead issues of love, nurture, submission, and respect predominate. These issues are far more familiar from pagan and Jewish philosophical reflections on good household management than they are from Israel's religious experience of God. And because the metaphor has been changed into a description of reality, it has become subject to enormous abuse.

To use human marriage as an image of God's faithfulness assumes that God behaves *more* faithfully than human beings do. Even Hosea's much-lauded patience with Gomer is only a human reflection of divine love, which is even more long-suffering and ultimately transforming than is Hosea's. Conversely, to use Christ's relationship with the church as an image of human marriage presents a problem. It holds up a divine standard for human behavior and thus sets up an unavoidable contradiction when human beings cannot live up to the divine standard.

Even the writer of Ephesians seems to recognize the limitations of his language when he says "as Christ loved the church and gave himself up for her ... so husbands should love their wives as they do their own bodies" (5:25, 28). The logic of the analogy collapses because husbands do not die for their wives as Christ died for the church, and Christ did not love his own body, as husbands are urged to do, but rather gave himself up for the church. Men are given an alarmingly self-serving motivation to love their wives (5:28), even though the author says clearly that Christ's love for the church is self-*giving* rather than self-*loving* (5:25). The parallel between Christ's being head of the church and a husband's being head of his wife is disrupted in the very same sentence, when Christ is identified as the "savior" of the body, that is, the body of Christ, a role human husbands can scarcely assume on their wives' behalf.

In 5:32, the author introduces another comparison whose logic falters, although for different reasons. He calls marriage a "mystery," which elsewhere in Ephesians refers to the inclusion of Gentiles into the church (see 3:4). This might suggest that he thinks the relationship between husband and wife ought somehow to mirror the relationship between Jews and Gentiles in the Christian community. Once again, the intended analogy breaks down in practice. In Ephesians the Jew/Gentile distinction is obliterated in the "new humanity" of the church (2:11–22), over which Christ is head (1:22; 4:15). In marriage, however, although a man and woman become "one flesh" (5:31), the distinction between them regarding roles is strictly maintained. Several interpreters have attempted to take the patriarchal sting out of the Ephesian household code by pointing to the generic exhortation that stands over the whole passage: "Be subject to one another out of reverence for Christ" (5:21). They therefore argue that the mutuality the author urges between Jews and Gentiles is similarly envisioned between men and women. However, the emphatic "in everything" that is added to the charge that women be subject to their husbands (5:24) scarcely allows such a possibility. The comparison of the unity of the church to the unity of a human marriage is yet another image that collapses under the weight of social inequality. Although the religious vision of equality between Jew and Gentile finds concrete expression in the Christian community with the author's blessing, any parallel equality between men and women remains a

religious vision rather than a mark of everyday life in the home.

The writer of Ephesians finds in the conventional, patriarchal household structure a reflection of the unity and harmony of the universe effected by God in Christ and calls his church to live appropriately in light of this redeemed cosmic reality. This can be seen most clearly in the fact that, by quoting Gen. 2:24 in Eph. 5:31, the author grounds the institution of marriage not in social order but in creation. Ephesians is concerned that the church faithfully mirror the creation and that the household mirror the church. The result for women is thus a retreat from the initial freedom promised them in Paul's preaching and a reassertion of conventional patriarchal morality.

The reason the author's own images of unity in creation and the church are distorted by the imposition of hierarchy in marriage is itself a mystery. Although in other early Christian household codes, particularly that in 1 Peter, the motivation for imposing patriarchal structure is apparently anxiety for the church's reputation among nonbelievers, there is no similar mention of concern for ecclesiastical public relations in Ephesians. The author's concern to "make the most of the time" in "evil days" (5:15), though, may hint at a similar situation (see Col. 4:5, where a nearly identical phrase occurs). If this is the case, then the author's willingness to contradict—not simply reinterpret—Paul's understanding of relations between women and men must derive from a sense of great peril. The awkwardness of the comparison of Christ to human husbands betrays a deliberate alteration of the received tradition. By subordinating the interests of the women in the congregation to the interests of the church's public image, the author apparently operates more from fear than from faith. By relinquishing Paul's expectation that God will soon complete the salvation begun in Christ and, at the same time, judge human social structures, and instead perceiving the church as an institution within human society, the author of Ephesians has moved a significant step away from Paul's theology.

The challenge to contemporary Christians, for whom the letter to the Ephesians continues to be scripture, is (1) to understand the historical circumstances that seem to have driven the author to move beyond Paul in this respect, (2) to recognize the tension within the letter itself between the author's sense of the gospel's liberating power and the community's social conservatism, and (3) to appreciate the letter's many significant contributions to Christian theology aside from its rather unfortunate view of human marriage.

## BIBLIOGRAPHY

Balch, David L. "Household Codes." In *Greco-Roman Literature and the New Testament: Selected Forms and Genres,* edited by David E. Aune, pp. 25–50. Atlanta: Scholars Press, 1988.

Dahl, Nils A. "Ephesians." In *Harper's Bible Commentary,* edited by James L. Mays, pp. 1212–1219. San Francisco: Harper & Row, 1988.

de Boer, Martinus C. "Images of Paul in the Post-Apostolic Period." *Catholic Biblical Quarterly* 42 (1980), 359–380.

Fiorenza, Elizabeth Schüssler. *In Memory of Her: A Feminist Theological Reconstruction of Christian Origins.* New York: Crossroad, 1983.

Getty, Mary Ann. *Ephesians, Philippians, Colossians.* Read and Pray Series. Chicago: Franciscan Herald Press, 1980.

Sampley, J. Paul, et al. *Ephesians, Colossians, 2 Thessalonians, The Pastoral Epistles.* Proclamation Commentaries. Philadelphia: Fortress Press, 1978.

Stockhausen, Carol L. *Letters in the Pauline Tradition.* Message of Biblical Spirituality. Wilmington, Del.: Michael Glazier, 1989.

# PHILIPPIANS

*Pheme Perkins*

## Introduction

Philippians was written to Christians in Philippi while Paul was in prison. The location of that prison is the first problem that must be addressed. References to the "praetorium" (1:13) and "Caesar's household" (4:22) suggest a locale where imperial officials were stationed. Since information has been exchanged easily between Paul and the community (1:26; 2:19; 2:23–30; 4:18), it was probably not Rome. Ephesus, which is referred to in 1 Cor. 15:32 and 2 Cor. 1:8–10, could have been the location.

In this letter Paul focuses on three issues: conflicts among those preaching the gospel that have resulted from his imprisonment (1:14–18; 4:2–4); thanks for assistance sent to him by the Philippians (4:10–20) and for the recovery of Epaphroditus, the bearer of the assistance (2:25–30); and warnings against those who seek to adopt Jewish customs and insist on circumcising male converts (3:2–4:1). Originally, the thank-you note and the warnings may have been separate letters. In combining them, the Philippian community has preserved a legacy of Paul's teaching to guide the church in the persecutions it will face (1:27–30).

The letter stresses the necessity for unity. Christians are engaged in an athletic contest (1:27; 3:13–14) and a military struggle (2:25) on behalf of the gospel. The famous hymn in 2:6–11, which proclaims that Christ surrendered divinity to accept slave status and death followed by glorious exaltation to divine dignity as Lord over all things, is employed to emphasize the need to subordinate one's own interests to those of the group (2:1, 5, 12).

Philippians (4:2–3) and Acts (16:14–15) indicate that women played important roles in founding the community and in its preaching mission. The letter, however, is ambiguous in the way it portrays their involvement. For example, the dominant images of athletic contest and military service do not reflect their experience. Neither does the exchange of authorized, male representatives: Epaphroditus, for the Philippians, and Timothy, for Paul (1:1; 2:19–24). Women's flesh cannot be marked by circumcision (3:2, 5). Lydia, who hosted the community in her household, might be called a servant (=deacon, like Phoebe in Rom. 16:1) and so be included among the leaders referred to in the greeting, but much of the imagery in Philippians speaks only of male experience. One must ask, therefore, in what sense women might be considered "brothers" called to imitate the example of the apostle (3:17). The role of Lydia and the fact that a generic translation like "brothers and sisters" (NRSV) might be possible here suggest that women might be included, but such a conclusion or translation disguises the masculine imagery that permeates this letter.

## Comment

### Partnership in the Gospel (1:1–30)

Paul's letters usually open with a thanksgiving for the faith of the recipients, assurances of his concern for them, and reference to the judgment (1:3–11). Each thanksgiving also mentions concerns addressed in the letter. Here Paul notes that the Philippians have entered into a partnership with him to spread the gospel (1:5). No other church has done so (4:15). In the commercial world, partnerships were established by groups for a specific purpose. Though individuals might contribute differently to the enterprise, all would share any profits. A partnership could be dissolved because the members no longer agreed about its goals; that is, they had ceased to be "of one mind" (see Phil. 1:27; 2:2). The death of a member also brought the arrangement to an end. Paul assures the Philippians that they will share the fruits of his imprisonment (1:7) and even of his death (2:17). Some Philippians were engaged in preaching (1:15); others provided financial support for Paul (4:16–18). Women involved in business or in running their own households, like Lydia, were a source of material support in the Pauline mission. They were also among those who preached the gospel. Paul refers to Euodia and Syntyche as part of a group of fellow workers who have labored with him in the gospel (4:2–3). Therefore, it seems reasonable to conclude that women were members of this partnership.

Since Paul fears that he may be executed rather than released, the rivalry that has broken out among those who preach the gospel (1:14–17) could reflect the expectation of some that the partnership is about to end. Paul is careful to temper any reference to his death with a reassurance that he will remain among the Philippians (1:24–26; 2:24). If he were to die, the Philippians could continue the original partnership on their own. They might also break up into a number of rival groups. Paul's reminders that all their activities are oriented toward the day of judgment (1:10–11; 2:16) provide a framework for his instruction that regardless of what happens to him, the Philippians should remain united in the effort they have already undertaken.

Just as members have shared financial resources and missionary activity with Paul, they also will experience sufferings like his (1:29–30). Could women members be imprisoned as the apostle was? In the second century C.E., women like Perpetua and Felicitas would be commemorated as martyrs. Romans 16:7 refers to a certain Andronicus and Junia, possibly a husband and wife, as "relatives who were in prison with me; they are prominent among the apostles." There a woman is numbered among those imprisoned for the gospel.

## Having the Mind of Christ (2:1–18)

Though it was customary that persons in a partnership demonstrate dedication to the common

effort, Paul's case for unity does not rest on merely human concerns. Love requires that they always put other persons ahead of themselves. In order to make this point, Paul cites an early Christian hymn (Phil. 2:6–11). The first section (2:6–8) describes Christ's self-emptying. Whether as preexistent divine wisdom or as the obedient "spiritual Adam," he deserves equality with God. Instead, Christ adopts the existence of a slave. Paul emphasizes Christ's degradation by reminding readers that Christ suffered the death reserved for the worst criminals and slaves, crucifixion. The second section (2:9–11) describes the exaltation of the risen Christ. Christ has been given the divine name "Lord" and is the ruler of all the powers. Of course, this victory is invisible to all except believers, who are "lights" in an evil and distorted generation (2:15–16).

How does Paul apply this hymn to Christian experience? He refers to himself and Timothy as "slaves of Christ" (1:1). His own imprisonment honors Christ. He anticipates a future with Christ (1:20–23). He also considers his pre-Christian life as one in which he could claim a position of honor in the Jewish community (3:4–6). In order to "know Christ," Paul had to give up those standards of value. He suffered the "loss of all things," and considered them "rubbish" (3:8). As a Christian, suffering like Christ now, he anticipates a glorious resurrection (3:10–11).

The exhortation to suffer like Christ in expectation of future salvation was frequently used to admonish Christian women and slaves to submit to abusive husbands or masters (e.g., 1 Peter 2:18–3:6). Christians who believe that the present world will soon end often find the idea of a reward for suffering like Christ to be an excuse for failing to struggle against injustice in this world. They forget that the hymn starts not with the suffering Christ but with the Christ who is equal to God. The poor in Latin America who are told to suffer like Christ rather than struggle for freedom, or abused women whose ministers tell them to submit to husbands, are not in the position to copy the Christ of this hymn. Its challenge is addressed to persons of some status and power, just as Christ had the status of God. In order to preach a gospel that centers on a crucified person and that brings persecution in its wake, such people must empty themselves.

## Epaphroditus and Timothy (2:19–30)

Although some women participated in the Philippian partnership, its imagery is taken from the masculine world. The rivalry between preachers of the gospel is a male form of rhetorical contest (1:15). Paul and Epaphroditus are referred to as soldiers (2:25). Paul's imprisonment is an opportunity to make Christ known in the world of Roman soldiers and imperial officials. Paul also describes himself as an athlete seeking a prize (3:14). In addition, those primary representatives of both the community and the apostle are male. Since Paul cannot come to Philippi, he will send Timothy, whose proven devotion to the gospel makes him Paul's "son" (2:21–22). We learn of two women associates only because Paul finds it necessary to ask someone to intervene in a dispute between them (4:2–3). Even there they are absorbed into a larger group of male fellow workers.

## True Circumcision (3:1–21)

The polemical tone of 3:2 and the sudden shift in topic suggest that this section was taken from another letter. The problem (see Galatians) is caused by missionaries who insist that non-Jewish converts ought to adopt Jewish practices. The debate focuses on the mark of male Jewish identity, circumcision. Paul rejects this attempt to establish one's religious identity in the flesh. He had abandoned all the special privileges of a faithful Jew when he recognized that salvation comes to all people in Jesus. Paul accuses this opposition of being concerned with material things, which can lead only to destruction. In this context, Paul refers to Christians as persons whose commonwealth is in heaven. The word "commonwealth" refers to the political organization of a minority community within the larger city-state. The Jewish community in a city was often organized as a "commonwealth."

Paul directs Christians to look to a commonwealth in heaven, when they will be transformed into the bodily likeness of the risen Christ. They should not attempt to establish themselves through the fleshly sign of Jewish identity, circumcision, or to institute a separate, minority community as though Christians were a particular race among the peoples of the earth. Paul makes circumcision appear unthinkable by invoking the male anxieties that link it with castration. He makes an earthly "commonwealth" appear impossible because the risen Christ, its founder, is in heaven. As in the Christ hymn, this advice

might suggest that Christians divorce themselves from political struggles. However, it was just such a gospel of salvation for all peoples, without regard to ethnic identity or gender, that had led to Paul's imprisonment. The social challenge of the gospel was felt in Paul's world.

## Paul's Thanks (4:1–23)

The final section of the letter includes a note, apparently written before Epaphroditus became ill (4:10–20), thanking the Philippians for their assistance. Paul introduces a peculiar distance into this acknowledgment by claiming a philosophic detachment from his own material circumstances. He attributes this indifference to God's power. After acknowledging the extensive aid that the Philippians have given to his mission, Paul again denies seeking such gifts (4:17). This reserve might reflect a concern to distinguish himself from those popular preachers who sought to enrich themselves by their activities. Yet the special relationship between Paul and the Philippians would make it appropriate for others in the partnership to contribute material resources to his effort. Their "gain" is the spiritual reward that comes from bringing people to salvation. Some interpreters suggest that Paul's reserve stems from a desire to avoid the normal forms of patron and client obligation. Normally, Paul would become dependent on those who gave him assistance. Here he will not owe the Philippians anything for their generosity: God is the one who repays such gifts (4:19).

How can this strategy be applied to women's experience? Women are commonly the subordinate members of relationships that permit others to make extensive demands as return for assistance or benefits, as is the case in the traditionally structured roles of wife and mother. Paul's example suggests that Christian forms of mutual aid need not carry the weight of subjection and obligation that can constitute a steep hidden price for the recipient.

## BIBLIOGRAPHY

Craddock, Fred B. *Philippians*. Interpretation. Atlanta: John Knox Press, 1987.

Sampley, J. Paul. *Pauline Partnership in Christ: Christian Community and Commitment in Light of Roman Law.* Philadelphia: Fortress Press, 1980.

# COLOSSIANS

*E. Elizabeth Johnson*

## Introduction

### Authorship

The author is aware that the Colossian church was neither founded nor visited by Paul ("you . . . and all who have not seen me face to face," 2:1) but has no reticence about writing in Paul's name, even though the apostle was himself quite clear about his own policy of noninter-vention in churches he did not establish (see Rom. 1:11–13; 15:20; 1 Cor. 3:10; 2 Cor. 10:15–16). The author of Colossians is a second- or third-generation leader of a Pauline community seeking to interpret Paul's preaching for the new day and situation in which the church finds itself. (See also "Ephesians," Introduction.)

### The Situation of Colossians

The Colossian Christians, originally part of the Pauline circle, have since come under the influence of Jewish mystical Christians who believe that a system or hierarchy of angels, powers, and spiritual rulers stands between them and God. They understand the work of Christ to be the guidance of individual believers through that cosmic hierarchy (back) to God. Christian life for these teachers therefore includes winning the approval of the cosmic powers by worship practices and ascetic disci-plines, probably specifically including circum-cision and Sabbath observance. In response, the author writes in Paul's name and invokes his authority to restore the community to tradi-tional Pauline doctrine and life.

### Contents of the Letter

After a traditional Pauline greeting (1:1–2), the author engages in a long thanksgiving (1:3–2:7) that, as in Paul's letters, alerts the reader to much of what is to follow. Support for the min-istry of a local church leader named Epaphras (1:7; cf. 4:12) is paramount as the author seeks to ground both his own authority and that of Epaphras in the apostle's (see the reminder about Paul's ministry in 1:24–2:7). The purpose of the thanksgiving is to assert the *completed* act of redemption by God in Christ, so as to undercut the claims of the rival teachers who say that the Colossians must yet perform pre-scribed religious rituals in order to be saved.

This competing theology is refuted in 2:8–3:4. Since the death and resurrection of Christ have defeated those cosmic powers about which the Colossians are so anxious, they who share Christ's death and resurrection by baptism have similarly triumphed. The concrete result of this victory is that such practices as ascetic disci-plines, observance of festivals, or the worship of angels are unnecessary. As is true in the letter to the Ephesians, dying and rising with Christ in Christian baptism locate believers' identity in the heavenly rather than the earthly sphere, and the author assures his readers that their lives are "hidden with Christ in God" (3:3). This spatial dualism (contrast between earth and heaven) is different from the temporal dualism (contrast between this age and the age to come) evidenced in Paul's sense that believers already participate in Christ's death but still await their own resurrections (Romans 6).

In 3:5 the argument shifts from a description of Christian reality to exhortations regarding Christian behavior. The meaning of baptism is not only spiritual but decidedly social. Just as early Christians who were baptized removed their clothing before entering the water and were subsequently reclothed in new garments, so the Colossians are urged to "put on" (3:12; cf.

3:10) the behavior appropriate to their new life and identity. In 3:11 the author describes the new, universal human condition in Christ: "In that renewal there is no longer Greek and Jew, circumcised and uncircumcised, barbarian, Scythian, slave and free; but Christ is all and in all!" Paul makes a very similar assertion in Gal. 3:28, also in the context of a discussion of the effects of baptism: "There is no longer Jew or Greek . . . slave or free . . . male and female; for all of you are one in Christ Jesus." Similarly, in 1 Cor. 12:13, baptism unites Jews and Greeks, slaves and free. This has suggested to many that

a traditional baptismal formula (perhaps one used by Paul) stands behind all three texts. The fact that the reuniting of women and men, or the dissolution of distinctions between them, is not mentioned in 1 Corinthians 12 may be because of Paul's concern about some Corinthian worship practices (see 1 Cor. 11:2–16). Why this pair of opposites is left out of Col. 3:11 and replaced by an expansion of the Jew/Greek dichotomy with the mention of circumcised/uncircumcised and barbarian/Scythian apparently has to do with the household code presented in 3:18–4:1.

## Comment

### The Household Code (3:18–4:1)

The author believes that behavior appropriate to the new life is communal in nature (3:12–15), constituted by Christian worship (3:16–17) and marked by the peace and harmony of the reconciled creation (3:14). (For a discussion of the social and philosophical background of the household codes, see the commentary on Eph. 5:21–6:9.) The household code in Colossians moves attention from congregational life to the household, maintaining the same emphasis on harmony. The household is to reflect the church. In many respects this is a traditional form of the household code—each pair of related persons is addressed in order, the subordinate member first. Wives are told to be subject to their husbands for the simple reason that such behavior "is fitting in the Lord" (3:18). In Philemon 8, Paul calls Philemon's responsibility to take the runaway slave Onesimus back "fitting," and in Eph. 5:4, coarse or frivolous talk is said to be not "fitting" for Christian conversation. Fittingness is thus apparently determined not merely by social convention (the "silly talk" mentioned in Eph. 5:4 is perfectly acceptable among pagan ethicists) but by proper reflection of *Christian* community standards.

The alleged appropriateness of the submissive behavior of women in Colossians seems to be a function of the author's concern that believers "conduct [themselves] wisely toward outsiders, making the most of the time" (4:5; cf. Eph. 5:16). If non-Christians are already watching the church with suspicion about its confession of faith, the reasoning goes, then believers ought not to provoke further hostility toward themselves by disrupting traditional social structures. They will already encounter

sufficient trouble on account of their Christian faith (as seen in the reference to Paul's imprisonment, 4:3) without further incurring the culture's wrath on account of nontraditional household relationships. The social as well as spiritual equality in the earlier church between women and men, slaves and free persons, is now a cultural liability, as a later generation learns to live as one of several competing religious groups in society rather than as the beachhead of the advancing reign of God. As expectation of the end time wanes in Colossians and Ephesians, so do the challenges to social structures that marked the earliest Pauline communities.

The greatest attention in the Colossians household code is devoted to slaves, who are told to obey their masters "in everything" (3:22), despite the preceding assurance that "there is no longer . . . slave and free" (3:11) and the following reminder that with God "there is no partiality" (3:25). The net effect of the exhortations to women and slaves is a vision of the household, and therefore of the church, as harmonious and in keeping with the order of the creation as redeemed by Christ (1:15–20). Such household order, however, is indistinguishable from the prevailing values of the culture in which the letter was written. Although these Colossian Christians have heard Paul's word of freedom to women and slaves, and despite their "heavenly" status as participants in Christ's victory over the cosmic powers, they must nevertheless live in a world where outsiders are watching (4:5–6). In this respect, perhaps the author of Colossians is in a situation similar to that of 1 Peter: Christian slaves are owned by non-Christians. Because both wives and husbands are addressed proportionally in Colossians, it is difficult to know whether Christian women are also married to non-Christian men, as seems to be the case in 1 Peter. But in either case, under the pressure of public opinion, the author of Colossians has retreated from the concrete freedom of the gospel once offered to women and slaves in order to insulate the church from its neighbors' charges that it is socially disruptive.

## BIBLIOGRAPHY

Beker, J. Christiaan. "Colossians." In *Harper's Bible Commentary*, edited by James L. Mays, pp. 1226–1229. San Francisco: Harper & Row, 1988.
See also "Ephesians."

# 1 THESSALONIANS

*Pheme Perkins*

## Introduction

First Thessalonians is a letter of encouragement to a church Paul had founded after his expulsion from Philippi (2:2; Phil. 4:16). The turmoil that led to Paul's departure from Thessalonica (Acts 17:1–9) apparently continued in episodes of persecution suffered by the community. Paul praises them for imitating him, the churches in Judea, and the Lord by enduring tribulation (1:6–7; 2:14). Unable to return himself, Paul had sent Timothy to visit Thessalonica. After receiving Timothy's favorable report, Paul wrote 1 Thessalonians to encourage the community (2:17–3:10) and console them over the death of some members of the church, perhaps victims of persecution (4:13–18).

## Comment

### Imitating Paul and the Lord (1:2–10)

Paul praises the Thessalonians for the example they have set for other churches by accepting the gospel despite persecution. The imitation theme appears frequently in Paul. The motifs of thanksgiving (1:2; 2:13; 3:9; 5:17–18) and rejoicing in affliction (1:6; 3:9–10; 5:16–18) recur throughout the letter. References to the coming of the Lord also punctuate the letter (1:10; 2:19–20; 3:13; 4:15–17; 5:2). Christians are to endure persecution because they know that the Lord will reward them. The socially conservative character of this orientation is evident in Paul's later exhortation to live quietly as independent artisans, minding their own affairs (4:11–12). In a society where everyone depended on persons who were better connected, richer, or more powerful to negotiate personal, legal, and business transactions, the command to be independent seems unrealistic. Presumably Paul hopes to lessen the social tensions generated by conversion to Christianity from traditional cults and civic pieties by minimizing situations in which a powerful patron might demand some show of loyalty from a Christian client.

### Paul's Example in the Community (2:1–12)

Paul depicts himself as the true philosopher-guide, concerned for the welfare of his charges. He is not a marketplace flatterer who uses rhetorical ability and the appearance of wisdom for personal gain. These images are taken from the competitive, male world of rhetoricians and popular philosophers. Paul's pursuit of what most people considered slavish trades—leather work and tent making—apparently made the workshops of artisans the center of his missionary effort. In some trades, like garment making, we have evidence that women worked along with men. Paul adopts the striking image of himself as "nurse" to the fledgling congregation (2:7). As examples from other male philosophers demonstrate, this image refers to the type of teacher who tries to adapt his words to the circumstances of his hearers. Evidence from later periods shows that males often identify with female saints or feminine characteristics when a religious conversion leads them to abandon the honors or distinctions they might have gained by competing with other males in the larger society.

## Persecution and Hostility Inevitable (2:13–3:13)

The judgment oracle against those who persecute Christians (2:14–16) offends many today because of its anti-Semitic tone. However, Paul does not think that the Jews as a race are responsible for opposition to the gospel. Throughout 1 Thessalonians Paul envisages his mission as part of a cosmic struggle between the gospel and Satan (2:18; 3:5). God is responsible for the destruction of such opposition. The enemy is not the human person but a more powerful resistance to God's word. Christians can only endure the inevitable persecutions (3:4). In that context of struggle and suffering, Paul is anxious about the congregations he has founded: Satan will make every effort to destroy the work to which Paul has given his life! This anxiety often leads to authoritarian intervention in the local communities by Paul's emissaries like Timothy. Since the legal codes of the time recognized only males as formal emissaries, we find only males in this role. Their mission would become the basis for later excluding women from teaching or leadership in local churches (see 1 Tim. 2:11–12).

## Holiness on the Day of the Lord (4:1–5:28)

The expectation of the coming end of this age governs Paul's ethical exhortation as well. The Christians who have died—possibly victims of persecution—will come with the Lord and be reunited with the community (4:13–18). The admonitions to holiness in 4:2–8 are formulated with males in view. They are to discipline unruly sexual urges by an honorable marriage. They are not to defraud their brothers "in this matter," an ambiguous expression that could refer either to sexual or to business affairs (4:6). It may be the sudden death of male members of the community that has led to the questions about the dead. Women were too constantly victims of early death in childbirth for their fate to cause much comment. First Thessalonians 5:12–22 speaks in more general terms of relationships within the community, respect for its officials, encouragement and mutual support, prayer, prophesying, and "doing good." There are no clues to indicate the extent to which women participated in these activities in Thessalonica. Since no women are mentioned anywhere, the community's leaders may have been all male. The poverty and largely artisan population of Thessalonica would make it less likely to have had women of sufficient wealth or education to act as patrons such as we find in other Pauline churches (despite Acts 17:4, which assumes their presence).

## BIBLIOGRAPHY

Best, Ernest. *The First and Second Epistles to the Thessalonians.* Harper New Testament Commentaries. New York: Harper & Row, 1972.

Jewett, Robert. *The Thessalonian Correspondence: Pauline Rhetoric and Millenarian Piety.* Philadelphia: Fortress Press, 1986.

# 2 THESSALONIANS

*E. Elizabeth Johnson*

## Introduction

Although 2 Thessalonians is said to be from Paul (1:1), the identity of its author is somewhat of a mystery. Many themes and stylistic features found in 2 Thessalonians are found nowhere else in Paul's letters. Despite those unique traits, many phrases and even longer sections of 2 Thessalonians are quotations from 1 Thessalonians—an unusual occurrence, since elsewhere Paul is not found quoting himself from one letter to another. For these reasons, many scholars conclude that someone other than the apostle Paul has written in his name and invoked his authority to correct misunderstandings in the Thessalonian congregation. The specific mention of pseudonymous letters circulating in the community (2:2), repeated references to Paul's original preaching in Thessalonica (1:10; 2:5, 14–15; 3:6–7, 10), reference to Paul's previous letter(s) to the church (2:15), and emphatic claims about the present letter (3:14, 17) combine to deepen the suspicion that the author is anxious to be taken for the apostle and concerned that the letter be taken as a reliable interpretation of Pauline tradition.

The misunderstandings in the church concern Paul's teachings about the end time and the daily conduct of believers. Some in the church are interpreting Paul's teaching (either in 1 Thessalonians or in other "letters purporting to be from" him, 2 Thess. 2:2) to mean that the Day of the Lord has already arrived (2:1–12) and that Christians are therefore absolved of their responsibility to live quietly and support themselves (3:6–12). The author responds by affirming what he considers traditional Pauline positions.

## Comment

A standard Pauline greeting (1:1–2, almost identical to 1 Thess. 1:1) and thanksgiving (1:3–12) set the agenda for the letter by promising God's vindication of the faithful elect and punishment of unbelievers—and perhaps also of believers whom the author considers heretical because they "do not obey the gospel" or "do not know God" (1:8). The Day of the Lord has not come, contrary to reports alleged to be from Paul (2:1–12). The reason for its delay is presented in traditional Jewish apocalyptic terms: God has postponed the return of the risen Christ and the last judgment until some unknown "man of lawlessness" (2:3) shall have fully performed his assigned function in God's plan of salvation, including the delusion of sinners. While the "man of lawlessness" in 2 Thessalonians is not identified, other contemporary descriptions of the last days frequently portray some human or angelic figure in similar satanic terms. This figure becomes the final opponent of God, who attempts to snatch away God's elect before the ultimate destruction of evil and establishment of God's salvation.

The author then urges that the elect take comfort in the fact that the traditions they were given by Paul, both personally and by letter (2:15), will assure their vindication. God will preserve both the apostolic mission (3:1–2) and the Thessalonian church (3:3–5) from evil, if the Thessalonians remain faithful to Pauline tradition. Those who refuse to work for a living should be shunned and the community should not support them (3:6–15). Paul's support of himself while in Thessalonica (1 Thess. 2:9; cf. 1 Cor. 9:6) is instead the model that Christians should imitate. This temporary exclusion from community for the purpose of discipline ("not as enemies . . . but as believers," 3:15) is similar to Paul's judgment in 1 Corinthians 5 on the man living with his stepmother.

Although the author of 2 Thessalonians does not specifically address the roles or concerns of women, the experience of urgent expectation of the end time in first-century Christianity could sometimes touch women's lives quite directly. The anticipation of Jesus' imminent return to gather his elect and restore the creation frequently evoked among early Christians a radical reassessment of traditional relationships between men and women. Both Jesus and Paul, for example, preferred celibacy to marriage in view of their convictions that human history was rushing to a swift conclusion. The option of celibacy, combined with the solidarity and mutual support of Christian communities, sometimes gave women the option of freedom from patriarchal marriage that was previously unavailable to them. This conviction that, in Paul's words, "the present form of this world is passing away" (1 Cor. 7:31) often caused Christians to see mundane social structures as also "passing away," and they therefore devalued conventional social roles.

Although there is no evidence of this in 2 Thessalonians, it is conceivable that the exhortation that members "do their work quietly and . . . earn their own living" (3:12) is an attempt to hold back revolutionary social forces within the church that were unleashed by apocalyptic expectation, in which case women and slaves—for whom those changes were often greatest—might have felt the impact more keenly than freemen.

## BIBLIOGRAPHY

Bailey, John A. "Who Wrote II Thessalonians?" *New Testament Studies* 25 (1978–79), 131–145.

Bassler, Jouette M. "I and II Thessalonians." In *The Books of the Bible*, vol. 2, *The New Testament*, edited by Bernhard W. Anderson, pp. 311–318. New York: Charles Scribner's Sons, 1989.

Jewett, Robert. *The Thessalonian Correspondence: Pauline Rhetoric and Millenarian Piety.* Philadelphia: Fortress Press, 1986.

Krodel, Gerhard. "2 Thessalonians." In *Ephesians, Colossians, 2 Thessalonians, The Pastoral Epistles*, by J. Paul Sampley et al., pp. 73–96. Proclamation Commentaries. Philadelphia: Fortress Press, 1978.

Perkins, Pheme. "2 Thessalonians." In *Harper's Bible Commentary*, edited by James L. Mays, pp. 1234–1236. San Francisco: Harper & Row, 1988.

# 1 TIMOTHY

*Joanna Dewey*

## Introduction

### Author and Audience

First and Second Timothy and Titus, which are very similar in style and content, are called the Pastorals because they contain instructions for pastors of congregations. They claim to be letters from Paul to two of his colleagues, Timothy and Titus; however, they are neither true letters nor from Paul. They appear instead to be handbooks for church administration written in the early second century, decades after Paul's death, by an unknown author. Since a major concern of the writings was to limit the role of women in the church, the author was probably a man.

Pseudonymity, writing in the name of someone else (usually dead), was relatively common in antiquity among both pagans and Christians, as a way to claim the authority of the supposed writer for the contents of the document. Sometimes that practice was considered a legitimate way to extend the thought of the supposed author into a new time and place. At other times it was rejected as deceptive. Ancient evaluation of the Pastorals would probably have hinged on whether or not the evaluator agreed with the author's representation and interpretation of Paul's point of view.

The evidence that Paul did not write the Pastorals is overwhelming. There are no references to these "letters" in any other documents until the late second century, considerably later than references to the other Pauline writings. The writing style is not typical of Paul but rather of a more general Hellenistic literary Greek. The theological concerns and vocabulary differ substantially from Paul's and are similar to vocabulary found in such other early-second-century Christian writings as *1 Clement* and the letters of Ignatius. For example, the Pastorals use the term "savior" frequently, but

Paul uses it only once. The Pastorals speak of Christ "appearing," but Paul never does. The Pastorals are concerned with church offices that had not developed in Paul's time. Finally, it is exceedingly difficult to fit these letters into any biography of Paul. The evidence for pseudonymity suggests a date in the first decades of the second century, perhaps around 125 C.E.

Since the writings are not by Paul, neither are they to the Timothy and Titus of Paul's letters. It is doubtful that they are written to specific church leaders at all. Their late date, their similarity of style and content, and their reference to "books" (2 Tim. 4:13) suggest that they were originally written on a codex (or booklike manuscript), along with other texts, in order to supplement or correct the earlier Pauline letters. The Pastorals are an attempt to use the authority of Paul to influence the understanding of Paul in the second-century churches.

### Major Concerns of These Letters

***The church as hierarchical household.***
The Pastorals are concerned with regulating the conduct of the congregation, specifying the qualifications and duties for congregational leaders (bishops, deacons, elders) and the duties for congregational members (young men, all women, and slaves). Unlike Paul's letters, these writings separate the congregation into groups according to age, gender, and free or slave status, prescribing different behaviors for each. The leaders (older freemen) should be upstanding citizens and heads of households; the members should be obedient, submissive, and silent. The author seems particularly concerned to control the behavior of women. The author is socially

conservative, wanting obedience to the state and conformity to an ideal of a hierarchical household that mirrors the public hierarchy established by the Roman imperial authorities. His ideal is for slaves to obey masters; children, parents; and wives, husbands.

***The church as guardian of doctrine.*** The Pastorals are also concerned with preserving the faith against what the author considers false teachings. Christians are to hold to "sound teaching" (1:10; cf. Titus 1:9), to "guard what has been entrusted to you" (6:20; cf. 2 Tim. 1:14), and to do good works. It is not clear who the author's opponents are, since the author does not debate them but simply labels them as wrong and exhorts people to avoid them. The author is against "myths and endless genealogies that promote speculations" (1:4), "profane chatter and contradictions of what is falsely called knowledge" (6:20), "godless tales of old women" (4:7, author's translation), "liars . . . [who] forbid marriage and demand abstinence from foods" (4:2–3). The references to genealogies, speculation, and knowledge suggest Gnostic Christian groups. The references to stories told by old women and to the asceticism of celibacy and abstinence from foods suggest Christian ascetic groups that might be Gnostic or might be quite orthodox, as in the groups represented in the apocryphal *Acts*. Those groups the author is speaking against often included women as prominent members.

***Prescription, not description, of the behavior of Christians.*** The Pastorals consist of instructions to particular groups of people that reflect the author's ideal for Christians instead of describing their actual practice. In fact, they provide evidence for groups of Christians who did not believe or act in ways the author thought appropriate, for prescriptive material is often historical evidence that the opposite is happening. Commands that women should keep silent in church occur precisely when women are acting as equals within the church. That is why those who disapprove issue such commands. So the Pastorals provide historical information (1) that there were Christian groups who did not define appropriate behavior according to the age, sex, and status of the person and (2) that Christian groups held a wide variety of beliefs and practices to be acceptable. The author is presenting what he believes a Christian congregation should be like, not what they actually were like.

Indeed, the author's ideal of the congregation as a well-regulated hierarchical household was probably not typical of congregations at that time. Other groups advocating different social relations, patterns of leadership, and belief also traced their authority back to Paul. It is likely that the author was countering other traditions about Paul, especially the traditions and legends found in the apocryphal *Acts of Paul*. (See "Early Extracanonical Writings.") In them, Paul appears as a wandering charismatic preacher and miracle worker who is always in conflict with political authorities. He is an ascetic who teaches chastity as a Christian requirement. Often women who hear his preaching leave their husbands and households to follow Paul in a life of celibacy. Some, such as Thecla, become wandering teachers and miracle workers themselves. The use of Paul's name as the author of the pastoral epistles seems to have been an attempt to use the authority of Paul against the ascetic socially and politically radical Christian groups who claimed Paul as their hero.

The Pastorals represent one voice in the debate among Christians about the legacy of Paul. Paul's own letters present a more radical and diverse message, affirming the equality in the church of all regardless of race, class, or gender (Gal. 3:28). Paul recognized women leaders, established no set leadership patterns, and preferred celibacy to marriage for Christians. The apocryphal *Acts* continue the tradition of women's leadership, celibacy, and greater social equality among Christians. On the other hand, the Pastorals continue Paul's concern for unity and order. In the ancient and medieval church, both traditions were known and influential, but the Pastorals eventually became part of the canon whereas the apocryphal *Acts* did not (although they were never considered heretical). These voices from Paul himself and from others in the debate about the legacy of Paul present viable alternatives to the hierarchical household model of the church and of Christian social relationships advocated in the Pastorals.

## Contents

After a typical letter opening, the author (speaking as "Paul") instructs "Timothy" to remain in Ephesus to command persons not to teach false doctrine (1:1–11). The author then recalls his appointment by Christ, and commits this charge to the addressee (1:12–20). Men in the church are instructed to pray and women to keep silent

(2:1–15), and the qualifications for bishops and deacons are specified (3:1–13). "Paul" then reminds Timothy that these are instructions in case their projected meeting is delayed (3:14–16). Heresy is identified as a sign of the end, and there are warnings against asceticism and exhortations to follow the author's commands (4:1–16). The document continues with separate instructions for the behavior of older and younger women and men, and slaves, drastically limiting the role and function of women of all ages and classes (5:1–6:2). Then there are further warnings against false teachers and exhortations to good behavior (6:3–21). The document contains no development of teaching about Christian faith or beliefs, but it does quote several short creedal statements (1:15; 2:5–6; 3:16; 6:14–16).

## Comment

### Instructions on Public Prayer

*Prayers for a quiet life (2:1–7).* There are two Greek words for "man": *anthropos*, which is an inclusive term, referring to both males and females, and *aner*, which refers only to males. *Anthropos* is the term used throughout these verses, as the translation of the NRSV reflects, but most older translations do not. Thus, prayers are to be made for everyone (2:1), and God desires everyone to be saved (2:4). There is only one mediator between God and humankind, the human Jesus (2:5). The stress is on Jesus' humanity, not his maleness.

Prayer is to be offered for the Roman emperor and other non-Christians in authority in order that Christians may lead a quiet, peaceful, pious, and respectful life (see also Titus 3:1–2). These words are common in the Pastorals and rare elsewhere in the New Testament. In Paul's letters, becoming a Christian brings one into tension or conflict with society (see 2 Cor. 11:23–33). In the Pastorals the author advocates good Christian citizenship, that is, accommodation to the dominant values of the culture and avoidance of behavior that would create tension with the larger culture (see Titus 3:1–2). The very need to instruct "Timothy" in these matters suggests that congregations at that time were frequently in conflict with society.

### Instructions on Christian behavior for women and men (2:8–15).

Instructions concerning public prayer are given separately for men and women. The word used for "men" here is *aner*, the term restricted to males. The passage focuses on the women's behavior. Only one of the eight verses refers to men. Furthermore, 2:13–15 presents a theological argument justifying the author's instructions, one of the very few theological discussions about anything in the Pastorals. The fact that the author spends so much time and effort to enjoin silence on Christian women suggests that the actual and accepted practice of women was active and vocal and that the author was attempting to change this behavior.

Since the instructions for women directly follow those for men, they should apply to women praying publicly during worship (see 1 Cor. 11:2–16). Verses 8–10, however, prescribe general rules for women's behavior. Women are exhorted to be modest and decent, that is, chaste. They are to dress simply, without fancy hairstyles and jewels. Such descriptions of the ideal woman are a common part of Greco-Roman men's rhetoric describing their ideal of a virtuous woman (see 1 Peter 3:3–5). Thus the author is asking women to behave in such a way as to give no offense to men in power, to conform to the values of the dominant pagan culture. That the issue is not dress but behavior can be seen in the command to do "good deeds."

In 2:11–12 the author prohibits women from leading public prayer and teaching. Women are to be subordinate to men, not have authority over them, and they are to remain silent, voiceless. The author's injunction is evidence that women were publicly praying and teaching. By claiming to speak as Paul and saying "I permit no woman . . . ," the author is attempting to bring Paul's authority to bear to change the women's behavior. These verses are similar in vocabulary and content to 1 Cor. 14:34–35, which may be a later addition (an interpolation) into 1 Corinthians. Quite possibly the interpolation was made by the author of the Pastorals, to strengthen his case for restricting women's leadership. Thus the command for silence in church is not a command from Paul valid for all time; rather, it is the view of one author (not Paul) or one Christian group on how they would like to see women behave. The historical practice of early Christian women, confirmed by other New Testament passages, suggests different and more active roles for women (see 1 Corinthians 11 and Romans 16).

The author appeals to the creation stories (Genesis 1–3) as justification for women's subordination (2:13–14). Adam was created first, then Eve; furthermore, it was Eve, not Adam, who "was deceived and became a transgressor." The Greek wording suggests that the author may be appealing to a Jewish tradition in which the serpent seduces (not simply "deceives") Eve. If so, her sin is sexual. Paul also uses Adam's prior creation to argue for women's subordination (1 Cor. 11:8–9). However, according to Paul, Adam, the first human, committed the first sin—disobedience (Rom. 5:12–21). Furthermore, Christians are a new creation in which sin is overcome and there is no "male and female" (Gal. 3:28). For Paul, the subordination of woman to man was part of the old order of creation but not part of the new creation in Christ. Thus, the author of the Pastorals contradicts Paul and other early Christian understandings.

According to 2:15, women are to achieve salvation by childbearing, by being mothers. Some have interpreted this passage as a reference to Mary (the mother of Jesus) as the new Eve, similar to the way Christ is interpreted as the new Adam. Thus Mary undoes the sin of Eve. Yet the verse continues "provided they continue in faith . . . ," which suggests that the author is referring to all women. This passage is unique in suggesting that salvation for women is different from that of men. The rest of the New Testament is unanimous in making no distinction by gender, for men and women "are also heirs of the gracious gift of life" (1 Peter 3:7). Furthermore, Paul advocates celibacy rather than marriage and motherhood for women, although he also considers marriage fully legitimate (1 Cor. 7:1–40).

This passage has been used in churches through the centuries to forbid women's religious leadership and to insist that the only permissible role for women is that of wife and mother. Yet the New Testament witnesses to a wide variety of life-styles for women and to their prominent leadership positions in the churches (see 1 Corinthians 7; 11; Romans 16). This passage is only one of several New Testament views on women. There is no reason its prescriptions should be binding and other New Testament views not. Indeed, alternatives to this passage perhaps have a greater claim on Christians. The author of the Pastorals is urging conformity to the dominant pagan culture of the first and second centuries, while alternatives showing women's leadership go against those cultural norms and may arise more directly from Christian experience.

## Qualifications for Bishops and Deacons (3:1–16)

The very existence of bishops and deacons as specific church offices indicates a second-century date. The same virtues are listed as qualifications for bishops, deacons, and widows, and the author urges virtues typically prescribed for pagan leaders (especially public servants) as well. The ideal of the hierarchical Greco-Roman household is applied to the church. Bishops and deacons are to manage their households well, "keeping [their] children submissive and respectful in every way" (3:4). They are to be married, but only once. The women referred to in 3:11 most likely are women deacons but may be wives of male deacons. Being male is not listed as a qualification for either bishop or deacon, though it may perhaps be inferred from the author's previous demand for women's silence and from his stating the requirement for marriage only in terms of the male.

## Against Asceticism and "Old Wives' Tales" (4:1–7)

In 4:3 the author speaks against those "who forbid marriage." In 4:7, he admonishes "Timothy" to "have nothing to do with godless tales of old women" (author's translation), and to value godliness over bodily training. In the social context in which the Pastorals were written, these injunctions all fit together. Women's teaching was generally oral, since they had less access to education and thus to writing. The author is warning against independent ascetic women who preach and work miracles, such as those whose stories are found in the apocryphal *Acts*. Celibacy for women was an ascetic practice, but even more it was a way out of the patriarchal household in which a wife was to submit to her husband. In the ideal hierarchical household, wives, children, and slaves were considered the property of the male head of household. As the apocryphal *Acts* make abundantly clear, the women understood celibacy as freedom from male control. Such a life was another option for Christian women in the first centuries of the church.

## Widows: An Early Christian Office (5:1–16)

In the first decades of Christianity, women and men held leadership roles irrespective of age or sex. By the second century, this had begun to change in some segments of Christianity. In 5:1–2 the author of the Pastorals recommends different behavior toward older and younger men and women, in conformity with the hierarchical ideal of the pagan society. In 5:3–16 the author discusses a separate role for women, one with its own title—"widow." "Widow" is an early title for a woman devoted to Christian ministry who was not dependent on a man (her husband, her father, or another male relative). Since women in that culture were married in their early teens to older men, most of those who were called widows were women whose husbands had died. But some were virgins or women separated from still-living husbands. These widows, including women of all ages, were celibate Christians who lived in communities of women and engaged in teaching, prayer, and ministry. They were supported by the church. The role of widow provided for Christian women an alternative life-style to the patriarchal household.

The author of the Pastorals apparently wishes to reduce the office of widow from its significant beginnings to a system of charity for older destitute women. According to 5:3–8, families should support their older relatives, and if they do not, they are no longer Christian. Besides saving the church money, this would return to the control of the hierarchical household women claiming to be widows on the basis of their Christian ministry. For the author, a real widow is a woman who has no family, who prays constantly, and who is not self-indulgent. Thus, her ministry is secondary to her lack of family in earning her the title of widow.

The fact that the role of widow as a form of ministry for women could not be suppressed altogether, however, led the author of 1 Timothy to propose further controls in the form of additional requirements (5:9–11). Widows were to be women over sixty who had been married only once. There is thus confusion in the Pastorals between "widow" as a Christian minister and "widow" as a welfare recipient. Many women in antiquity were married more than once; indeed, in the verses that follow, the author commands younger widows to remarry. These women too may need financial support in their old age. Yet he restricts the group of widows to those who have married once, just as he restricts bishops and deacons. Insofar as "widow" is a church office, the author considers a single marriage a requirement.

The author provides additional instructions concerning widows under sixty (5:11–15). In principle he disapproves of designating young women as widows because they may later want to remarry and thus break their pledge of celibacy and incur God's judgment. He disapproves also because the women travel about to other Christian households talking. According to the author, they are idle busybodies, speaking what they should not. From these widows' point of view, they are probably going about teaching and proclaiming the faith, carrying out their Christian ministry (see 4:1–7 above). Instead, the author wants these women to marry again and fulfill their role of bearing children.

Nor did the author of the Pastorals want the church to support communities of women. Literally, 5:16 reads, "If a believing woman has widows, let her. . . ." It refers to wealthy women who maintain households for other Christian women, providing communal homes apart from patriarchal households. In this case, the author wants this woman to support her widows as members of her own family and not take money from the church.

The instructions for widows are prescriptive texts. They are historical evidence that, in the churches the author knew, there were groups of celibate women living together and engaged in ministry. The author wishes to limit these groups of women, reincorporating them into patriarchal households under the authority of men. The general culture of antiquity envisioned women either as independent and celibate (usually widows) or as submissive members of the hierarchical household. Neither pagans nor Jews nor Christians conceived of women as independent equals in relationship to men. (An exception may be the early Christian missionary couples; see Rom. 16:3, 7.) The author of the Pastorals supported only the option of submission to male authority. However, the reality of celibate women living in community and doing ministry has flourished throughout Christian history.

## Obligations of Slaves (6:1–2)

The author commands obedience of slaves (male and female) to their pagan or Christian owners, so that the church will appear respectable to the world. Unlike most lists of household duties (e.g., Col. 3:22–4:1; Eph. 5:22–6:9), this section omits any corresponding command to Christian masters. The emphasis throughout the Pastorals is on the duties of the subordinate members of the household—slaves both male and female, and women whether they are slaves or free.

## BIBLIOGRAPHY

Dibelius, Martin, and Hans Conzelmann. *The Pastoral Epistles.* Translated by Philip Bottolph and Adela Yarbro. Hermeneia. Philadelphia: Fortress Press, 1972.

Fiorenza, Elisabeth Schüssler. *In Memory of Her: A Feminist Theological Reconstruction of Christian Origins.* New York: Crossroad, 1983.

MacDonald, Dennis Ronald. *The Legend and the Apostle: The Battle for Paul in Story and Canon.* Philadelphia: Westminster Press, 1983.

Thurston, Bonnie Bowman. *The Widows: A Women's Ministry in the Early Church.* Minneapolis: Fortress Press, 1989.

# 2 TIMOTHY

*Joanna Dewey*

## Introduction

The same unknown author of 1 Timothy and Titus wrote 2 Timothy also around 125 C.E. (see "1 Timothy," Introduction). While those "letters" consist of admonitions to manage a congregation as the hierarchical household of God, 2 Timothy is in the form of a last "testament," or collection of final words, claiming to be from Paul. As commonly occurred in testaments, 2 Timothy warns against false teachers in the last days and exhorts steadfastness during persecution. It makes repeated references to Paul as a martyr facing death. It is possible but not likely that some of the personal comments in chaps. 2 and 4 are from fragments of authentic Pauline letters. The use of the testament form by the unknown author was probably an attempt to enhance the authority of all three Pastorals as the final word of "Paul" to the church.

The typical letter opening and thanksgiving (1:1–7) are followed by instructions to guard the faith, even enduring persecution (1:8–14); details about "Paul's" situation (1:15–18); more instructions to guard the faith (2:1–10); and a hymn (2:11–13). Next are exhortations to avoid controversy, to understand that false teachers are a sign of the end, to expect persecution, and to use scripture (2:14–3:17). Then the addressee is given a formal charge to preach, as the author's death is at hand (4:1–8). The document concludes with comments claiming to refer to Paul's situation and with final greetings (4:9–22).

## Comment

### Lois and Eunice (1:5)

Lois and Eunice are named as "Timothy's" grandmother and mother, who were Christians before him. No male forebears are mentioned, which may imply that probably these men were not Christian. Whether or not the women's names are historically accurate, they do attest to the important role women played in the early spread of Christianity.

### False Teachers and "Silly Women" (3:6–7)

In his warning against false teachers of the last days, the author mentions specifically those "who make their way into households and captivate silly women." This corresponds to the portrayal of Paul in the apocryphal *Acts of Paul:* he preaches to women who abandon their households, follow him, and become heroes among early Christian groups opposed by this author (see "1 Timothy," Introduction). It is also likely that there were women among those the author considers "false teachers" who go into households (1 Tim. 5:13), although the author does not raise that issue here.

### Women Leaders (4:19–21)

The writing closes with greetings to Prisca and Aquila, the missionary couple known from Paul and Acts (1 Cor. 16:19; Rom. 16:3; Acts 18:2, 18, 26). Prisca is mentioned first, which perhaps indicates her greater importance among Christians, since normally in antiquity the person with greater status—the man, for example, or the person from a higher social class—would be named first. Also a woman named Claudia is said to send greetings. We know nothing else about her, but the inclusion of her name here again indicates the importance of women in early Christianity.

## BIBLIOGRAPHY

See "1 Timothy."

# TITUS

*Joanna Dewey*

## Introduction

Titus is by the same unknown author who wrote 1 and 2 Timothy (see "1 Timothy," Introduction). The writing is very similar to 1 Timothy in its concern for church officers, hierarchical household structure, and warnings about those the author considers false teachers.

The letter opening is followed by an exhortation to appoint elders in the towns of Crete, a list of qualifications for elders and bishops, and a warning against those the author considers false teachers who upset households (1:1–16). Then follow duties for various members in the household of the church (2:1–10). After summaries of the history of salvation (2:11–3:8), there are further warnings, personal instructions, and a closing greeting (3:9–15).

## Comment

### Household Duties (2:1–10)

The author spells out his idea of desirable behavior for older and younger women. Older women are to behave respectably and teach young women to love their husbands and children, fulfill their household duties, and submit to their husbands (2:3–5). That is, older women are to teach young women their subordinate status in the household. The author wants to use women to teach other women to internalize their inferior status and their proper function as limited to the household. He does not want widows empowering younger women to live their own lives in the direct service of God (see "1 Timothy," Widows [5:3–16]). Duties for older and younger men are stated (2:2–6), but their duties are not connected to the household.

Their behavior to their wives and children is not mentioned. Slaves are exhorted to be obedient to their masters, but no duties are specified for masters (2:9–10). The author is concerned to control the behavior of the subordinate party in the various relationships in the household, so that the church "may not be discredited" in the public eye (2:5). These are prescriptive texts, indicating that women and slaves were not always submitting, and so the author has to command them to do so. The author is quite willing to sacrifice the fuller life the women and slaves have found in Christ for respectability among pagans.

### BIBLIOGRAPHY

See "1 Timothy."

# PHILEMON

*Pheme Perkins*

## Introduction

Philemon, written during the same imprisonment as that referred to in Philippians, treats a delicate social issue, the return of a runaway slave who has become a Christian and thus "brother" to his master. Not only is Onesimus liable to severe punishment for running away, but Paul's promise to repay anything Onesimus owes (v. 18) is not likely to refer to a loan, since Onesimus is Philemon's property. Paul is hinting that Onesimus may have stolen from his master. By returning the slave and assuming responsibility for any losses, Paul restores the social and legal relationship between Philemon and Onesimus. Other examples of runaway slaves returned to their owners indicate that the writer may include a plea for mercy toward the slave who will prove faithful in the future and appeal to the friendship between the author and the slave's owner. However, Philemon does not follow this pattern. Paul insists that Philemon receive Onesimus as Paul's own son and as his own beloved brother (vv. 10, 16). Further, Paul hints that Philemon should make this new relationship a reality by granting Onesimus freedom so that he can continue serving the apostle (vv. 11–14). Since former slaves were legally bound to provide various services for their ex-owners, Paul can make this proposal and claim that Philemon will now find Onesimus truly profitable.

## Comment

### To the Church (vv. 1–3)

Though Philemon appears to deal with a private matter, the return of human property, Paul makes the issue public. Both the opening (vv. 1–3) and the final greetings (vv. 23–24) address the Christian community that meets in Philemon's house, and Paul singles out two prominent members, Apphia and Archippus. The designations "our sister" and "fellow soldier" suggest that, like Philemon, they may have been patrons of the community and involved in the Pauline mission (see Col. 4:17). Since early Christian communities depended upon patrons, prominent women like Apphia could play a role in the life of the early church. Patrons, whether male or female, expected those who benefited from their generosity to follow their example or preferences in other matters. If Apphia and Archippus are independent of Philemon, then Paul's strategy is to use persons who are Philemon's equals as well as the larger community as an audience who will judge whether or not Philemon has taken the apostle's advice. Paul concludes the letter with the promise that if Philemon acts in a way that goes beyond what he has explicitly demanded, then he will come to his house as a guest upon being released from prison (vv. 20–22). If he rejects Paul's appeal and so breaks off the association between them (vv. 9, 17), Paul can go elsewhere.

### Thanksgiving (vv. 4–7)

The thanksgiving establishes Philemon's public reputation in the Christian community. His faith and love set an example for others. His practical expression of love has been comforting others (literally, "giving rest to the heart," v. 7).

362

Paul himself has received such comfort. He asks Philemon to repeat this action in the matter at hand (v. 20).

## Appeal for Onesimus (vv. 8–22)

Paul opens the body of the letter by claiming the authority to command Philemon (v. 8). Paul grounds this authority in his own public status. He is an ambassador (literally, "old man") and now a prisoner for Christ (v. 9). Instead of commanding, he appeals to Philemon. Paul offers Philemon an opportunity to demonstrate the love for which he is renowned (v. 14).

Paul makes Philemon's compliance more socially acceptable by changing the way in which his action is described. Paul does not ask Philemon to free a runaway slave. Instead, Paul provides a series of new names for what Onesimus now is: "my child"; "once useless, now useful to us both"; "my own heart"; "beloved brother . . . both in the flesh and in the Lord"; "a 'stand-in' for Paul himself" (vv. 10–11, 16–17, author's translation). Though he promises to repay anything that Onesimus owes his master, Paul reminds Philemon that Philemon is indebted to him for much more than any material gain or loss. Just as Onesimus became Paul's "son" when he was converted (v. 10), so Philemon owes the apostle his "self," that is, his Christian faith and life (v. 19).

This appeal demonstrates the significance of publicly shared language. The renaming of the relationships among Onesimus, Paul, and Philemon that takes place opens up the possibility of a response to Onesimus different from that anticipated on the basis of common social practice. Philemon is not asked to "free a bad slave." He is asked to confirm his own reputation for love, for comforting fellow Christians, and to show both his gratitude toward Paul and his own participation in Paul's mission. This example demonstrates the need for new patterns of naming as the basis for changing deeply ingrained patterns of domination. Women struggle with this problem today as sexist and racist stereotypes make it difficult to see "the other" as a "beloved sister or brother."

Unhappily, the renaming of Onesimus did not lead Paul or his early interpreters to conclude that Christians should seek whenever possible to liberate other Christians who were slaves. First Corinthians 7:22–24 tells people not to worry about changing the status in which they became Christians. Ignatius, bishop of Antioch (ca. 110 C.E.), holds that while Christians must not despise slave members of the church, the slaves should not demand that the church buy their freedom (To Polycarp 4.3). Some interpreters think that this advice stems from a cultural stereotype of the ex-slave as one who became involved with various lowly trades including those which pandered to the lusts of others. Augustine thought that slavery is a manifestation of the sinfulness into which humans have fallen, but he concluded that a sinful humanity deserves such forms of subordination (City of God 19.15). These examples make the conflicts between the social and legal institution of slavery and a Christian consciousness of mutual love and equality in Christ barely visible (cf. Gal. 3:26–28). The tensions between the Christian reality and a demeaning and false naming of women are similar, but they hardly surface at all in this letter.

## BIBLIOGRAPHY

Lohse, Eduard. Colossians and Philemon. Translated by W. R. Poehlmann and R. J. Karris. Hermeneia. Philadelphia: Fortress Press, 1971.

Petersen, Norman R. Rediscovering Paul: Philemon and the Sociology of Paul's Narrative World. Philadelphia: Fortress Press, 1985.

# HEBREWS

*Mary Rose D'Angelo*

## Introduction

The work traditionally entitled the Epistle of St. Paul to the Hebrews presents the reader, and especially the feminist reader, with many problems. Most scholars now recognize that Hebrews was not written by Paul. The community to which it was written was not Hebrew-speaking but Greek-speaking, and it is far from certain that they were Hebrews (that is, Jews) by birth. Nor is the work primarily a letter; it is more like a homily, a "word of exhortation" sent as a letter (13:22). The style and thought of the work are among the most difficult in the New Testament. It is sometimes seen as the beginning of Christian philosophy. Its imagery and language are nearly exclusively masculine; its major metaphor for salvation, drawn from the temple liturgy, presents Christ as high priest.

### Form and Content

As a "word of exhortation," Hebrews' main purpose is to encourage its readers. It is organized into three parts by two exhortations, which invite the readers, "let us approach" or "draw near" (4:16; 10:22). The first part, 1:1–4:16, focuses on Jesus as Son of God and apostle, speaker from God to human beings. It uses scripture to compare Jesus to both the angels and Moses and introduces the images of Christ as high priest and pioneer of salvation. The exhortation (4:14–16) both closes this section and opens the second part, which focuses on Jesus as the high priest who speaks to God on behalf of believers.

The second section (4:14–10:39) consists in large part of a series of technically sophisticated arguments from scripture that attempt to show that Jesus is a suitable and effective high priest, indeed the great high priest of "the true tent

that the Lord, and not any mortal, has set up"(8:2). Even more, they claim that the whole liturgical law in Exodus, Leviticus, and Numbers was really written as an allegory of Jesus' ascension to God through "the curtain" that is his flesh (see 10:20). When Hebrews exhorts the reader to "press on" from "the beginning of the word of Christ . . . toward its perfection" (6:1, author's translation), it is this allegorical reading of the scripture that seems to be the "main point" (8:1) of that perfection of the word.

The lengthy and complex exhortation in 10:19–39 makes clear the implications of the invitation "let us draw near": to draw near means not only to go forward in understanding the scripture and the message of Christ but also to endure and resist the persecution that the author foresees, so as to enter into God's presence with Christ. This exhortation not only brings the preceding section to its climax but also begins the third section (10:19–13:25), which focuses on Jesus as pioneer of salvation. Beginning with a series of examples of those whose faith is attested by scripture, it is almost entirely an exhortation to go forward on "the new and living way opened" up by Christ.

### Author and Destination

Because Hebrews lacks the signature and address that normally open a Greek letter, there have been many attempts to identify its author. In 1900, Adolf von Harnack proposed the hypothesis that Hebrews was written by Prisca, in conjunction with her husband Aquila (Rom. 16:3–5; 1 Cor. 16:19; Acts 18:2–4, 18, 26; 2 Tim. 4:19). Suggesting that Hebrews was written to a house-church in Rome after the death of Paul, he concluded that the writer was a member of that house-church and was closely associated with Timothy. Harnack also deduced that the author had to be closely enough associated with another member of the group to be able to speak as "I" or "we" interchangeably. This writer was learned and a teacher but was apologetic about using this authority to exhort others. Assuming that the name of such an author had to be found in Acts or the Pauline corpus, Harnack concluded that this description best suits Prisca. She worked with her husband as a missionary partner and so was likely to speak as both "I" and "we" without a break. In Harnack's view the best explanation for the loss of the author's name was that the author was a woman. There is evidence that women's names were suppressed in the text of the New Testament, and Prisca herself was significantly demoted in some manuscripts of Acts.

In an attempt to defend and extend the suggestion that Prisca wrote Hebrews, Ruth Hoppin created an elaborate biography for Prisca based on the New Testament material, on tradition, and on archaeological deductions. She argued that Prisca was a Roman from a patrician family

who became a proselyte and married Aquila, a Jewish freedman. In her view Prisca wrote Hebrews to Ephesus, using works of interpretation of scripture from an Essene community like the covenanters at Qumran. In part her study is a laudable attempt to refute assertions that only a "masculine mind" could have produced Hebrews. Hoppin's work is of interest as a relatively early attempt (1969) to argue for an enlarged role for women in the twentieth-century church on the basis of the participation of women in the early Christian mission. But neither her case nor Harnack's is convincing. Neither can explain Heb. 11:32, which shows that the author either is, or claims to be, a man, since it refers to the author with the masculine form of a Greek participle.

Any hypothesis that the letter was written by a woman must also acknowledge that most of the women writing in a patriarchal setting share or adopt its perspective. The author of Hebrews does so little to encourage women to "draw near" that the question arises whether the community includes women, though the reference to marriage in 13:4 suggests that it does.

## Comment

### Women in Hebrews

Women are included in Hebrews, but only marginally. Hebrews 11:1–40 remembers a series of elders attested by the scriptures as examples. Only two women, Sarah (11:11–12) and Rahab the harlot (11:31) are remembered by name. Commentators and translators have found 11:11 problematic, because the text appears to claim that Sarah "received the power of begetting seed" (author's translation). This phrase is normally reserved for the male part in procreation. The NRSV has resolved this problem by relegating this version of the verse to a footnote and translating the reference to Sarah as an aside. Abraham then becomes the subject of 11:11–12. But this solution is not necessary. The Greek translation (Septuagint) of Num. 5:28 uses language that seems to describe the emission of sperm (literally, "give out seed") to refer to a woman's part in procreation. The author of Hebrews could have understood this language in either of two ways. First, some ancient medical theories held that women as well as men produced seed. Second, male language used about a woman had spiritual significance in antiquity. Drawing on that tradition, Philo, a Jewish philosopher and allegorist of

first-century Alexandria, regards Sarah as the type of one "who has ceased from the ways of women" (Gen. 18:11), so as to become virgin and male (On the Posterity and Exile of Cain 134; Questions and Answers on Genesis 4.15, 66). The author and audience of Hebrews may have shared with Philo, as well as with 4 Maccabees and some early Christian authors, a spiritual tradition that holds out to women the spiritual ambition of "becoming male," so that Sarah is offered as an example of this "greater perfection."

Rahab is particularly popular in Christian example lists (1 Clement 12.1–8; James 2:25; see also Matt. 1:5); she seems to represent proselytes (Gentile converts to Judaism), who "drew near," and had "to believe that [God] is, and is the rewarder of those who seek [God]" (11:6, author's translation). Sarah, like her husband/kin Abraham (see Gen. 11:27–29; 12:10–19; 20:1–17), could also have been seen as a proselyte.

Some women seem to have been erased from the scriptural traditions Hebrews uses. The Hebrew text of Ex. 2:2 reports that the mother of Moses hid him for three months, and the Septuagint uses "they," referring to both parents. But for Hebrews it was "his fathers" (11:23) who preserved him by faith; the NRSV translation "parents," while it responds to pastoral concerns, is deceptive. The daughter of Pharaoh is named only in reference to Moses' refusal to be called her son (11:24). Miriam appears neither as a participant in the birth and salvation of Moses nor at the crossing of the sea (11:24–26, 29). In the summary lists of 11:32–40, Barak is memorialized among the judges with Gideon, Sampson, and the infamous Jephthah, but Deborah and Jael are forgotten. The author refers to unnamed women who received back their dead through resurrection but finds a still better example in "others" (masculine plural in Greek) who "were tortured, refusing to accept release, in order to obtain a better resurrection" (11:35). The reference here is almost certainly to 2 Macc. 6:12–7:42; "others" must include the mother of the martyrs, praised by 4 Macc. 15:30 as "more noble than males in steadfastness and more manly than men in endurance" (author's translation). But she is not explicitly mentioned by Hebrews.

Thus Hebrews seems not merely to neglect to provide women examples but almost to avoid them. Both Rahab and Sarah appear to represent Gentiles rather than women. Rahab's dubious sexual status renders her problematic as an example to women who also hear, "Let marriage be held in honor by all and let the marriage bed be kept undefiled, for God will judge fornicators and adulterers" (13:4). Does the author then seek to exclude women, to discourage the women of the community from "drawing near"? If Sarah is presented as a woman who has attained the perfection of maleness, then perhaps the women of the community are included but invited to look only to the "manly" heroes of the past.

## Hebrews and Feminist Critique

Not only does Hebrews make little effort to edify the first-century woman reader; it also raises acute problems for the feminist reader of today. One of these is the problem of inclusivity in theological language. "Son" is one of the most important of christological titles in Hebrews. It functions as an image for Jesus' relation not only to God but also to the congregation, who are addressed as sons (as well as children and brothers). This imagery requires women to read ourselves into the male relationship of father and son. The author may know and assume the baptismal tradition in Gal. 3:26–28, which makes women, slaves, and foreigners adult "sons of God" (NRSV: "children of God") and heirs, but Hebrews gives no indication of it.

Perhaps the most acute christological problem for women is the image of Christ as the son and pioneer perfected by suffering. This image is extended into the author's explanation of the persecution in the community's past and future. They are to encounter persecution as God's discipline (upbringing or education) for them, distinguishing them as "sons" from bastards who get no upbringing (12:4–11). The comparison reinforces the patriarchal valuing of "legitimate" over "illegitimate" children that helps to define women's sexuality as a commodity. Here too the NRSV uses language that is falsely inclusive; the Greek text uses "father" and "son," not "child" and "parent," and it evokes the father's concern for his sons' education and discipline, which may be, but need not be, extended to a daughter. The abusive connection of punishment and love has endured as a commonplace of patriarchal education and child rearing from antiquity to this day. Hebrews' counsel puts a divine sanction behind the abuse of women and abusive child rearing. Unchallenged, it collaborates with the images of a father who "perfects" his son "by sufferings" (2:10) and a "son [who] learns obedience through what he suffered" (5:8). Rita Nakashima Brock has analyzed this pattern as the theology of the abused child.

Hebrews' use of the temple liturgy as the metaphor for salvation is also problematic. The allegory focuses on the deed of the high priest on the Day of Atonement, a deed reserved not only to men but to a single man. The metaphor of sacrifice and priesthood, especially high priesthood, has long been used to bar women from Christian ministry. Not only is the content of this allegory a problem; the method of allegory itself involves dangers, because it can be used to eradicate the historical reality of those who are defined as "other." Hebrews' arguments for the superiority of the deed of Christ to the liturgy of the sanctuary provided much material for later anti-Judaism. Allegory has been used not only to appropriate the Bible and the status of "chosen people" from the Jews but also against women and indigenous peoples.

When Hebrews poses so many problems to feminist reading, can it provide any resources for feminist theology?

## Hebrews as a Resource for Feminist Theology

As long as the patriarchal context of the work is not ignored, Hebrews can provide resources for feminist theology and especially for the feminist critique of later Christian theology. The example list in chap. 11 extends beyond the praise of famous men (Sir. 44:1). For Hebrews, the saints are not exemplary for what they have done but for what they have not done. Despite their great faith and the testimony they receive from God, "they are not perfected *without us*" (11:40, author's translation). They function not as models but as a "cloud of witnesses" encouraging the readers to "run the race allotted to us, looking to the pioneer [i.e., beginner or leader] and perfecter [i.e., completer] of our salvation, Jesus, who instead of the joy allotted to him, endured the cross, despising the shame" (12:1–3, author's translation). Jesus is partially treated as a model, but even more as a prototype (see Fiorenza, pp. 33–35). As the first to have finished the race, he has opened for believers "a new and living way" (10:20).

It is also significant for feminists that Hebrews stresses Jesus' humanity (2:11–18), insisting that he "offered pleas and prayers to the one who could save him from death, with a loud cry and tears, and was heard for his piety" (5:7, author's translation).

Hebrews 1:3 explains "son" in philosophical terms that originated as descriptions of Wisdom/Sophia, identifying her as a philosophical creator goddess (Wisd. Sol. 7:22–27). Although in Hebrews the female imagery associated with wisdom disappears behind the language of sonship, the priestly Christology may draw on the image of Wisdom/Sophia as priest in Sir. 24:9.

The liturgical imagery offers other grounds for critique of the tradition. First, Melchizedek is the pattern of Jesus' priesthood precisely because Jesus does *not* fit the criteria for legitimate priesthood in the line of Levi and Aaron (7:11–19; 8:3–5). Hebrews' understanding of Christ's priesthood precludes attempts to "image" that priesthood in the Christian ministry that are based on criteria of flesh and blood like race, gender, and class.

Second, the "main point" of Hebrews' comparison between Christ and the high priest (8:1) is that Christ has ended priesthood and sacrifice. For Hebrews, this involves both reassurance and warning: there is no more sacrifice for sin (10:18, 26–31; 6:4–8). For the feminist reader, the metaphor's emphasis on the once-for-all character of Christ's deed should raise profound questions about the churches' reinstitution of priestly castes.

Third, the death of Jesus is not the sacrifice or offering itself but the *means* by which he entered into the presence of God. For Hebrews,

as for antiquity in general, sacrifice consists not in blood and death (which can be, but need not be, its means) but in *communion* with God, access to God's presence. This is why the author chooses the high priest's once-yearly entry into the sanctuary as the center of the liturgy. By his passage beyond the curtain, Jesus sat down at God's right hand forever (1:3; 8:1; 9:23–28; 10:12; 12:2), "living always to intercede for those who draw near" (7:25, author's translation) on the new and living way he has opened for them (10:19–20). Hebrews dwells on the cleansing and ratifying blood only to explain Christ's death (9:11–28).

Hebrews' vision of Christian life as journey of transformation toward communion offers a starting point for rethinking its message. A feminist reading must reject the demand for submission to suffering, but can look to Jesus' pioneering passage and the "cloud of witnesses" (12:1) as an invitation to revere and remember the suffering of the oppressed who died without having received the promise and as a call to open for all the oppressed a new and living way.

## BIBLIOGRAPHY

Attridge, Harold W. *The Epistle to the Hebrews.* Hermeneia. Philadelphia: Fortress Press, 1989.

Brock, Rita Nakashima. *Journeys by Heart: A Christology of Erotic Power.* New York: Crossroad, 1988.

D'Angelo, Mary R. *Moses in the Letter to the Hebrews.* Society of Biblical Literature Dissertation Series 42. Missoula, Mont.: Scholars Press, 1979.

Fiorenza, Elisabeth Schüssler. *In Memory of Her: A Feminist Theological Reconstruction of Christian Origins.* New York: Crossroad, 1983.

Harnack, Adolf von, "Probabilia über die Addresse und den Verfasser der Hebräerbriefs." *Zeitschrift für die neutestamentliche Wissenschaft* 1 (1900), 16–41.

Hoppin, Ruth. *Priscilla, Author of the Epistle to the Hebrews and Other Essays.* New York: Exposition Press, 1969.

van der Horst, Pieter Willem. "Sarah's Seminal Emission: Hebrews 11:11 in the Light of Ancient Embryology." In *Greeks, Romans and Christians: Essays in Honor of Abraham J. Malherbe,* edited by David L. Balch, Everett Ferguson, and Wayne A. Meeks, pp. 287–302. Minneapolis: Fortress Press, 1990.

# JAMES

*Sharyn Dowd*

## Introduction

James is the first of the documents often classified as the "general" or "catholic" epistles. The two terms are synonymous and refer to the fact that most of these documents seem to be addressed to Christians in general rather than to a particular church. Thus, these letters are known by the names of the persons believed to have written them (James, Peter, John, Jude) rather than by the names of the churches that received them (e.g., Romans, Philippians).

James lacks most of the standard features of a letter, but it does have a greeting. The author claims to be named James, but this tells us little. There are at least five different men in the New Testament named James, but this author does not claim to be any one of them. The author's role in the church is that of a "teacher" (3:1), a person who instructs converts. The recipients are Greek-speaking Christians who understand themselves as the heirs of the traditions of Israel (1:1b). The content of James is traditional ethical instruction of the type often found in Hellenistic Jewish and Gentile circles. Neither the date of the document nor the locations of the author and recipients can be determined.

The emphasis of James is on the Christian life as a life of wholeness or integrity—a life of single-minded devotion to God. All "double-mindedness," attempting to live by the standards of "the world" while claiming to be a Christian, is out of the question (1:8; 4:4). Belief must cohere with life-style. James applies this principle ruthlessly to economics, to language, and to the response to difficulty. Even suffering is understood as serving the interest of wholeness in the Christian life (1:4).

## Comment

### Against Partiality (2:1–13; cf. 5:1–6)

This section addresses the tendency to accord special honor and consideration to the wealthy and powerful. Such partiality is forbidden in the Christian community in the strongest terms. In fact, it is the powerless who are most likely to demonstrate total dependence on God (2:5). Partiality is such a serious fault that those who commit it stand under "judgment without mercy" (2:13), no matter how scrupulously "law-abiding" they may be (2:10). This is a strong word to churches whose criteria for influence and leadership positions show partiality to any one group.

### Living Faith Versus Dead Faith (2:14–26)

The author insists that Christian faith issues in acts of mercy (e.g., to those who lack adequate clothing and food, 2:14–17). Merely having the correct beliefs is not enough; even demons are orthodox (2:19). Two examples support the argument, one male and one female. Abraham's faith was not an abstract idea but a relationship of obedience (2:21–24). Beside Abraham the patriarch the author places Rahab the prostitute, the Gentile woman who was granted a place in Israel because of her faith in the God of Israel, demonstrated by her hospitality to Joshua's spies (2:25; see Joshua 2; 6:17).

368

Rahab comes into the New Testament through Jewish traditions that had grown up around her. Legend had it that she was exceptionally beautiful, that she was a prophet, that she married Joshua, and that among her descendants were Jeremiah and Ezekiel. She was regarded as the archetypal convert to Yahwism. This may have been one of the reasons she was linked to Abraham; Philo the Jewish philosopher emphasized Abraham's conversion from paganism. Her confession of faith in Josh. 2:11 echoes that of Moses in Deut. 4:39. She appears in Matt. 1:5 in the genealogy of Jesus, along with Tamar, Ruth, and Bathsheba, and in Heb. 11:31 in the example list of the faithful. Clement of Alexandria pairs her with Abraham as an example of "faith and hospitality." The idea of hospitality is present in James 2:25, recalling the dilemma of those in 2:15 who lack food and clothing. James concludes that faith without works of mercy is lifeless.

Although James has sometimes been contrasted with Paul on this point, Paul would have agreed wholeheartedly that Christian faith results in ethical behavior (e.g., Gal. 5:16–26; Romans 12). Paul never assumed that faith could be separated from acts of faithfulness.

## BIBLIOGRAPHY

Davids, Peter H. *The Epistle of James: A Commentary on the Greek Text.* New International Greek Testament Commentary. Grand Rapids: Wm. B. Eerdmans Publishing Co., 1982.

Laws, Sophie. *A Commentary on the Epistle of James.* Harper's New Testament Commentaries. San Francisco: Harper & Row, 1980.

Perkins, Pheme. "James 3:16–4:3." *Interpretation* 36 (1982), 283–287.

Tamez, Elsa. *The Scandalous Message of James: Faith Without Works Is Dead.* Translated by J. Eagleson. New York: Crossroad, 1990.

# 1 PETER

*Sharyn Dowd*

## Introduction

First Peter is a letter of exhortation written to be circulated among Christians in a number of provinces of Asia Minor (modern Turkey; see 1:1). Although the letter bears the name of the apostle Peter, its language is more sophisticated than would be expected from a Galilean fisherman for whom Greek was a second language. It is possible that the letter was written by a secretary, but the reference to Silvanus in 5:12 probably means that Silvanus delivered the letter, not that he wrote it. The author was an early Christian leader, probably in Rome (indicated by the common Christian code name "Babylon" in 5:13). The content suggests a date in the last third of the first century, after the death of the apostle.

The Christians to whom 1 Peter is addressed are suffering for their faith (2:12; 4:12–16; 5:9). This is not an empirewide persecution of Christians for refusing to worship the emperor; the recipients of 1 Peter are suffering rejection and harassment from members of the society in which they live as strangers in a strange land (1:1–2, 17; 2:11) because their Christian identity makes them suspect. They had once been pagans, participating in traditional religious and social practices (1:14, 18). Now that they are Christians, they have become new people (1:23–25) and they no longer practice the old religion or join in pagan celebrations (4:3–4). Their community includes women and slaves who defy custom by worshiping a God different from the one worshiped by their husbands and masters (2:18–3:7). Their neighbors would have understood this behavior as subversive of the very foundations of the social order, because worship of the gods of the head of the household was thought to guarantee stability in home and society. To their neighbors, the Christians of Asia Minor looked like a countercultural fringe group with values that tended to undermine those of society. In some respects, the neighbors were right.

In this environment of suspicion and hostility, the Christians need two things to survive, and these two things stand in tension with each other. First, since the Christians are alienated and rejected, they need a strong sense of identity. Second, they need as much as possible to live in such a way as to reassure the society around them that they are not a threat. To support their need for a strong sense of identity, after a traditional letter introduction (1:1–2), the first part of the letter (1:3–2:10) emphasizes how different the Christian community is. Thus, Christians are called a chosen race, a royal priesthood, a holy nation, God's own people (2:9). They have been born anew to hope and joy (1:3, 6, 8, 21). The focus on suffering at the hands of outsiders also reinforces their need to stick together.

To reassure the surrounding society, the author urges the readers to conform to societal conventions (2:11–5:11). They should obey governmental officials (2:13–17), live in stable, well-ordered households (2:18–3:7), and in general maintain a good reputation among their associates. The letter closes with greetings and a blessing (5:12–14). The recipients of 1 Peter are encouraged to walk the tightrope of being radically different from the surrounding culture because of their Christian identity but at the same time affirming the best values of that culture for the sake of acceptance and witness.

## Comment

### The Lord as Source of Nourishment for Growth (2:2–3)

One of the images used for the Christian life is that of the newborn baby who has to be nursed on pure, spiritual milk in order to grow. Alluding to Ps. 34:8, the author encourages the readers to drink deeply from the nourishment that leads to spiritual growth, "since [perhaps a better translation than "if indeed," as in the NRSV] you have tasted that the Lord is good." The author of 1 Peter has worked the psalmist's metaphor into one drawn specifically from the universal experience of children's dependence on the nurse who provides the nourishment necessary for growth.

### Domestic Stability (2:18–3:7)

This passage is a "household code," a form of instruction used by pagans, Jews, and Christians to instruct the members of the household in their various duties. In similar passages in Colossians and Ephesians, the presumption is that a household is composed of the same three sets of relationships that were outlined centuries earlier by Aristotle in his *Politics:* husband and wife, father and child, master and slave. The code in 1 Peter does not address slave owners, which may mean that there were none in the congregations to which it was addressed. On the other hand, considerable space is devoted to advice to women married to non-Christians (3:6), which may suggest that such mixed marriages were common.

According to the conventional wisdom of the time, this way of ordering a household, with the husband having authority over his wife, children, and slaves, was thought to be the natural order of things. The author of 1 Peter advocated this system not because God had revealed it as the divine will for Christian homes but because it was the only stable and respectable system anyone knew about. It was the best the culture had to offer. The author did not adopt the system uncritically. If he had, he would have reminded women and slaves that they were obliged to follow the religion of the head of the household. Instead, he encourages women and slaves to hold fast to their Christian faith even when they are part of a non-Christian household.

The author gives two reasons why women and slaves should be submissive. First, in 3:1–2, the women are told to obey their husbands in order to evangelize them. Second, in 2:11–12, the author explains that the counsel contained in the code is designed to disprove the accusations being made against the church. To that end, Christian homes are to demonstrate stability and support for both public order and cultural values.

The household code in 1 Peter raises two major issues for the contemporary reader. The first is the relationship between Christian behavior and cultural values. On the one hand, one must decide how to interpret the values of the alien culture assumed by the text. Just as slavery is no longer an accepted social institution, so the other patterns of domination and subordination cannot be considered sacrosanct. On the other hand, such texts suggest a positive relationship between cultural values and Christian practice and have led modern readers to affirm not relationships of subordination but an emphasis on the equality of women and men and on mutuality and shared responsibility in the home.

A second issue emerges in what is said in the code about the positive value of bearing unmerited suffering, following the example of Christ (2:19–25). Those words were used to encourage passivity on the part of slaves, even in the face of unspeakable brutality. They are still quoted to women of all ages, children, and elderly men who are being abused in their homes. Such advice is a misappropriation of the message of 1 Peter, which was written at a time when the victims of abuse had no options. In that situation, the author counseled nonviolence (which was a way of demonstrating one's moral superiority over the oppressor) and alluded to the ultimate justice of God, who vindicates the abused (2:23). Today many congregations understand the provision of options for healing for the abused to be part of their mission. Rather than encouraging victims to suffer passively, they support shelters and counseling services to encourage movement toward wholeness.

### BIBLIOGRAPHY

Balch, David L. "Early Christian Criticism of Patriarchal Authority: 1 Peter 2:11–3:12." *Union Seminary Quarterly Review* 39 (1984), 161–173.

———. *Let Wives Be Submissive: The Domestic Code in 1 Peter.* Society of Biblical Literature Monograph Series 26. Chico, Calif.: Scholars Press, 1981.

Best, Ernest. *1 Peter.* New Century Bible. London: Oliphants, 1971.

Brown, Joanne Carlson, and Carole R. Bohn, eds. *Christianity, Patriarchy, and Abuse: A Feminist Critique.* New York: Pilgrim Press, 1989.

Fiorenza, Elisabeth Schüssler. *In Memory of Her: A Feminist Theological Reconstruction of Christian Origins.* New York: Crossroad, 1983.

Martin, Clarice J. "The Haustafeln (Household Codes) in African American Biblical Interpretation: 'Free Slaves' and 'Subordinate Women.'" In *Stony the Road We Trod: African American Biblical Interpretation,* edited by Cain Hope Felder, pp. 206–231. Minneapolis: Fortress Press, 1991.

Mollenkott, Virginia Ramey. *The Divine Feminine: The Biblical Imagery of God as Female.* New York: Crossroad, 1983.

Talbert, Charles H., ed. *Perspectives on First Peter.* Macon, Ga.: Mercer University Press, 1986.

# 2 PETER

## Sharyn Dowd

Second Peter is a letter of exhortation that also has some characteristics of a farewell speech. This blended literary form is used by an anonymous author who claims to be Peter, a well-known authoritative leader of the past (1:1, 16–18). That leader is portrayed as predicting his imminent death (1:14), warning the community about problems that will arise after his death, and giving advice on how to deal with them. That the author's use of Peter's name is a literary device and not an attempt to deceive is clear from his openness about the fact that he is writing long after the death of the apostles. From that perspective he refers to them in reverent terms as "your apostles" (3:2). He also knows that Paul's letters have been collected, are regarded as "scripture," and have been in circulation long enough to have acquired a body of interpretation that in some cases changed their original intent (3:15–16). This anonymous work, therefore, cannot have been written earlier than the first years of the second century.

Like Jude, on which its author relies as a source, 2 Peter is written to counteract the influence of false teachers in the church or churches that received it. Some are denying that God judges human behavior and saying that therefore people are free to live as they please. Since Christ has not returned in judgment as expected, the author's opponents conclude that God is powerless to judge humanity (3:4). Against this position, the author argues

that (1) God has judged the wicked in the past (2:4–16) and (2) the delay in God's judgment is a sign of divine patience and kindness, not of weakness (3:8–10).

Both 2 Peter and Jude were viewed with some suspicion in the early church, and they do not appear in some of the early lists of authoritative writings. The two letters themselves contain polemical language against groups within the church that held different opinions. Thus, both the contents of the letters and their own history testify to the fact that from its earliest days, the church has struggled over issues of correct theology and teaching and over the very sources of authority to which one might appeal to resolve the differences.

## BIBLIOGRAPHY

Johnson, Luke T. "2 Peter and Jude." In his *The Writings of the New Testament: An Interpretation*, pp. 442–452. Philadelphia: Fortress Press, 1986.

Perkins, Pheme. *Reading the New Testament: An Introduction*, chap. 19. 2nd, rev. ed. Mahwah, N.J.: Paulist Press, 1988.

Watson, Duane F. *Invention, Arrangement, and Style: Rhetorical Criticism of Jude and 2 Peter*. Society of Biblical Literature Dissertation Series 104. Atlanta: Scholars Press, 1988.

# 1, 2, AND 3 JOHN

*Gail R. O'Day*

## Introduction

It was not until the end of the fourth century C.E. that 1 John, 2 John, and 3 John were fixed as a group and identified with the name of John, the traditional author of the Gospel of John; however, there is no external or textual evidence to support this traditional designation of authorship. First John identifies no author at all, and 2 and 3 John identify the author only as "the elder." The three epistles do share some theological language and concepts with the Gospel, but they address a quite different situation. The Gospel of John addresses the conflict between the emerging church and the synagogue (see "John," Introduction), but the epistles address an intrachurch conflict. The opponents with whom the epistles debate are members of the Johannine Christian community, and the theological conflict seems to be over the correct interpretation of the Gospel of John. The Johannine epistles, then, are best understood as later writings from the same community that produced the Gospel.

The conflict receives its clearest expression in 1 John. The opponents did not believe that Jesus was fully human (4:2–3), nor were they practicing love toward one another (2:9–11). In 2 John the opponents also deny the full humanity of Jesus (v. 7). In 3 John the conflict focuses on one disruptive church leader (vv. 9–10) rather than purely on questions of theology, but this conflict can be understood as the practical side of the theological dispute of 1 and 2 John. The similarity of the situations that all three epistles address suggests that the epistles were written by persons who lived in the same community and shared the same theological traditions. It is possible that all three epistles were written by the same person, but that cannot be shown conclusively.

The intrachurch nature of the conflict and the relationship between the Gospel and the epistles argue for a late-first-century date. The organized church structure suggested by the role of the elder in 2 and 3 John also argues for a late date.

## Comment: 1 John

Family language is prevalent in 1 John and is used in three distinct ways. First, family language is used to speak of the relationship between God and Jesus (e.g., 2:22–24; 4:14). Second, the author frequently addresses the community as "little children" (e.g., 2:1; 3:7) or "beloved" (2:7), which are terms of endearment and intimacy. Even though the author is in a position of authority with respect to the community, he emphasizes his closeness with them rather than distancing himself. Third, the author describes the community to which he writes as "children of God" (e.g., 3:1; 5:19) and as those who "have been born of God" (5:1). Other members of the community are one's brothers and sisters (e.g., 4:20). The central image for this community is family.

The centrality of family is expressed also in the central ethical demand of the epistle: "that we should love one another" (3:11). The community of 1 John is disrupted by two events: some members deny the full humanity of Jesus (4:3), and some are not loving one another as they should (2:9). Belief in the full humanity of Jesus is tied to the community's emphasis on love, because for Jesus and the community, the

374

sharing of love is the mark of full humanity. Theological doctrine and human experience are thus inseparable: "Those who love God must love their brothers and sisters also" (4:21; see also 2:9–11; 4:11–12, 20). Those who deny the humanity of Jesus show signs of nascent Gnosticism because they subscribe to a dualism between spirit and body, good and evil. Such dualisms were part of the worldview of Gnosticism, which found many followers in the early church, including parts of the Johannine community. The rise of Gnosticism was particularly detrimental for women, because as the spirit/body dualism was refined, women were identified with the inferior, and even evil, body. First John fights against this dualism by affirming the corporeality of Christian faith.

## Comment: 2 John

The author of 2 John, who identifies himself as the "elder" (v. 1), uses feminine imagery to speak of the church. The community to which he writes is addressed as "elect lady" (vv. 1, 5), and the community from which the elder writes is identified as "your elect sister" (v. 13). Lady and sister are thus metaphors for the church.

Two aspects of this feminine imagery deserve mention. First, it continues the family language already noted in the Gospel of John and 1 John. In 2 John members of the Christian community are referred to as "children" of the lady/sister church (vv. 1, 4, 13). Whereas in the Gospel and 1 John believers are described as "children" of God, in 2 John the family of God is becoming the family of the church.

Second, the noun "lady" (kyria) is the feminine form of the noun "lord" (kyrios). The choice of vocabulary thus stresses the relationship between the church (lady) and its Lord. This language links 2 John with other New Testament writings that use feminine images for the church (e.g., Rev. 12:1–2; Eph. 5:22–31). These images may show the value the early church placed on female experience, or they may indicate the beginning of patriarchal structures of governance in which the elder becomes "lord" over lady church.

## Comment: 3 John

The letter known as 3 John differs from 2 John in two important ways. First, whereas 2 John is addressed to the whole community (v. 1), 3 John is addressed to an individual, Gaius (v. 1). Second, the controversy in 2 John (and 1 John) is primarily doctrinal, but in 3 John the controversy focuses on behavior and action, and particularly on the disruptive behavior of Diotrephes (vv. 9–10).

The central ethical issue in 3 John is hospitality. Offering one's table and home to the stranger was an ethical imperative for Christian communities (cf. Heb. 13:2). In vv. 5–8 the author of 3 John commends Gaius for giving hospitality and fellowship to missionaries who have passed through his town. Diotrephes, by contrast, does not show hospitality to the missionaries, prohibits others from doing so, and even expels from the church those who did offer hospitality (v. 10). Gaius is urged not to imitate Diotrephes' behavior (v. 11).

A second ethical concern of 3 John is the problem that unchecked personal ambition can cause in the life of the Christian community. Diotrephes disregards the canons of hospitality because he "likes to put himself first" (v. 9). Diotrephes acts out of his own self-centered ambition to the exclusion of the needs of others. By putting himself first, he clearly violates the spirit of the Johannine vine metaphor (John 15), in which all branches are intertwined.

### BIBLIOGRAPHY

Brown, Raymond E. *The Community of the Beloved Disciple.* New York: Paulist Press, 1979.

——. *The Epistles of John.* Anchor Bible 30. Garden City, N.Y.: Doubleday & Co., 1982.

Kysar, Robert. *I, II, III John.* Augsburg Commentary on the New Testament. Minneapolis: Augsburg Publishing House, 1986.

Perkins, Pheme. *The Johannine Epistles.* New Testament Message. Rev. ed. Wilmington, Del.: Michael Glazier, 1984.

# JUDE

*Sharyn Dowd*

Jude is a letter of exhortation written to a community disturbed by false teachers (v. 4). The precise identity of the author is unknown; there may be an attempt to claim the authority of a brother of Jesus (v. 1). Authorship by a first-generation Christian is unlikely, however, since the writer speaks of the apostles in the past tense (vv. 17–18), perhaps referring to 2 Tim. 2:3–5.

The identity of the false teachers and the content of their teaching are likewise elusive. The author does not specify what they teach or try to refute them but instead accuses them of immorality and threatens them with judgment.

Two issues raised in this brief letter give evidence of the transitional period in the church's history when it was written. The first relates to the meaning of "faith." For Paul, who wrote a generation earlier, "faith" meant a dynamic response to God's offer of covenant relationship. This author, however, thinks of "faith" as a body of doctrine to be transferred from one generation of Christians to another virtually unchanged: "once for all entrusted to the saints" (v. 3).

The second issue has to do with what comprises authoritative scripture. Jude is an interesting testimony to the fluidity of that concept in early Christianity. In addition to the Hebrew Scriptures (the Old Testament), the author appeals to *1 Enoch* and the *Assumption of Moses*, two Jewish documents not generally regarded as scripture today.

## BIBLIOGRAPHY

See "2 Peter."

# REVELATION

## Susan R. Garrett

---

### Introduction

Cast in the form of a vision of things that must "soon take place," the book of Revelation is full of bizarre, psychedelic imagery that allows many interpretations. The imagery would have been slightly more understandable to first-century readers, but even the ancients regarded the book as highly ambiguous and difficult. In part because of its obscure character, several branches of the ancient church were slow to accept the work as authoritative scripture.

Some of the book's most important symbols use feminine imagery. The new Jerusalem is envisioned as "coming down out of heaven from God, prepared as a bride adorned for her husband" (21:2). At the opposite extreme, the city "Babylon" (a symbolic name for Rome) is portrayed as a whore, "holding in her hand a golden cup full of abominations and the impurities of her fornication" (17:4). As a third example, a woman who is "clothed with the sun" and who gives birth to the Messiah plays a role in the pivotal twelfth chapter of the work. Each of these symbols reflects the male-centered culture of the first century: women are caricatured as virgins, whores, or mothers. The author's narrow view of women has also shaped the other uses of feminine imagery in Revelation. In 2:20–23, John labels a rival prophet "Jezebel," claiming that she "refuses to repent of her fornication"; and in 14:4 the seer envisions 144,000 men "who have not defiled themselves with women, for they are virgins." The stereotyped feminine images in the book do not represent the full spectrum of authentic womanhood, either in John's day or in our own. The images grow out of the patriarchal culture of the first century, which valued the *control* or *management* of women's sexuality by men. In such a culture, the virgin (who remains subject to male control) and the whore (who does not) can come to represent diametrically opposite realities: purity and obedience versus corruption and evil. Exploring the cultural roots of John's metaphoric language about women will enable us to understand what he was trying to say at those points, but the dehumanizing way in which he phrased his message will remain deeply troubling.

### Contents

The book of Revelation, or the Apocalypse (Greek for "revelation"), belongs to an ancient type of literature in which a seer describes symbolic visions of the heavens and secrets about the end of the age. This particular revelation came to the seer "John" while he was on the island of Patmos, and it is set in the framework of a letter from the exalted Christ to seven churches in western Asia Minor (modern Turkey; 1:11; 22:16). Each of the churches is either encouraged for its obedience or rebuked for its disobedience to the gospel in the face of persecutions and temptations (2:1–3:22). In the following panoramic vision, those who faithfully confess allegiance to Christ are vindicated (7:13–17). Meanwhile those who persecute the righteous or who practice idolatry and lawlessness are judged (9:20–21; 14:9–11). God's acts of judgment are described in cycles of seven (seven seals, 6:1–8:1; seven trumpets, 8:6–11:19; seven bowls, 15:1–16:21), though these cycles are broken by long and important digressions (7:1–17; 10:1–11; 11:1–14; 11:19–12:17; 13:1–18; 14:1–20). The visions climax in an account of the binding of the devil (20:1–3), resurrection and judgment (20:11–15), and inauguration of a "new heaven and new earth" (21:1–22:5). The book concludes with admonitions, greetings, and Jesus' final assurance that he is coming soon (22:20).

## Authorship

From an early date it was believed that the John who wrote Revelation was the apostle John, but the author himself does not make that claim. His reference in 21:14 to the "twelve apostles" suggests that he viewed them as figures of the past. Though some scholars have suggested that the author was a certain elder from Asia Minor named John, he is probably a figure unmentioned elsewhere in the extant early Christian literature. He appears to have known the Hebrew, not the Greek, version of the Jewish Scriptures. Moreover, he is quite hostile toward Rome ("Babylon"). These traits indicate that the author may have been a Palestinian Jew who had come to Asia Minor in the aftermath of Jewish defeat in the first revolt against Rome (66–73 C.E.).

## Social Setting and Function

For centuries it was assumed that John and his readers were being persecuted by the emperor Domitian (who reigned from 81 to 96 C.E.) for failure to worship him in the imperial cult. More recently it has been shown that the historical evidence for that persecution itself depends on the book of Revelation. Thus, the argument is circular and the conclusions are unreliable. Excluding the reference in 2:13 to the recent execution of Antipas, the book's descriptions of martyrdom probably reflect not the reality of John's day but rather past persecutions (especially under Nero in 64 C.E.) together with the author's vision of what "must soon take place."

If there was no systematic persecution, then what was the reason for the terrifying scenario? John feared for the salvation of the churches, whose members were becoming morally lax and conforming too readily to the standards of the larger culture (see 2:14–15, 20–23; 3:1–3, 15–17). Believers were giving in to the temptations of idolatry, perhaps even worshiping the emperor. By describing the rewards of the faithful and the punishment of the wicked, John may have been trying to encourage the faithful to persevere (14:12) and also to persuade more complacent Christians that even trivial ways of going along with their society's idolatry would be judged by God.

## Use of Sexual Imagery

Several of the feminine images in Revelation presuppose a traditional symbolic use of the image of "adultery" or "fornication" to represent idolatry. The eighth-century prophet Hosea was among the earliest to use the word "fornication" (in Hebrew the meaning of the word is broader than but inclusive of "adultery") as such a metaphor. Hosea depicted God's relationship to Israel as that of a faithful husband to a "fornicating" wife, with the wife's "lovers" corresponding to gods other than Yahweh. "To fornicate" or "to play the whore," then, became virtually synonymous with engagement in idolatry (see, e.g., Hos. 1:2; 2:1–13; 3:1; 4:12–14; Ex. 34:16; Lev. 17:7; 20:5; Deut. 31:16; Judg. 8:27; 2 Kings 9:22; Isa. 57:7–13; Jer. 3:1–10; Ezek. 16:15–58; 23:1–49). John is borrowing this scriptural pattern when he portrays Jezebel and the city of Rome ("Babylon") as "whores" (symbolizing their alleged involvement in idolatrous activities) and also when he depicts the "heavenly Jerusalem" as a pure virgin (suggesting abstinence from any form of idolatry as well as total commitment to God; cf. 2 Cor. 11:2).

## Comment

### Jezebel (2:20–23)

In 2:18–29 John opposes a prophetic figure active in the church at Thyatira—the woman he calls "Jezebel" (most likely not her real name). John's references to his book as "prophecy" (1:3; 22:7, 10, 18, 19; cf. 22:9) imply that he regarded himself as a prophet; probably the woman was a rival. John uses two devices to discredit her as a *false* prophet. First, he calls her "Jezebel" and thus associates her with the notorious woman who opposed Elijah and supported the prophets of Baal (1 Kings 16:31; 19:1–3). Second, John has the exalted Christ use traditional language for a charge of false prophecy when Christ accuses Jezebel of "teaching and beguiling my servants to practice fornication and to eat food sacrificed to idols" (2:20).

In earliest Christianity, there was a fierce debate about whether or not Christians could eat the meat that was left over when sacrifices were made to idols. Much of the meat available for consumption (in the marketplace, at public festivals, and at private gatherings) would have been such "sacrificial" meat. The book of Acts reports that the Christian authorities in Jerusalem had decided that Gentile converts must follow rules designed to ensure that they avoid several very serious sins, including idolatry and illicit sexual activity. The rules, which corresponded to those placed by Torah on "aliens residing in the house of Israel" (Lev. 17:8, 10, 13; 18:26), forbade the eating of meat sacrificed to idols (Acts 15:29; 21:25). By contrast, in Paul's opinion Christians *could* eat sacrificial meat, provided that neither the conscience of the one eating the meat nor that of any Christian observer was offended by the action (1 Cor. 8:1–13; 10:25–30). The seer John adhered to the stricter view, attacking those churches from among the seven that tolerated a group known as "the Nicolaitans" (with whom "Jezebel" may have been connected). The Nicolaitans were said to advocate eating sacrificial meat and practicing "fornication." On the subject of sacrificial meat, they may merely have been following the more tolerant policy of Paul, who founded many of the churches in that region.

It is hard to know how to interpret the accusations of fornication and adultery made against the Nicolaitans. Some scholars take them literally, arguing that the Nicolaitans were a libertine Gnostic sect. But it is just as likely that these charges were unfounded, designed to vilify "Jezebel" and the Nicolaitans by underscoring their "promiscuous" attitude toward idol worship. So also the first Jezebel's idolatry was referred to as her "many whoredoms and sorceries" (2 Kings 9:22). In any case, John's use of the sexual imagery undermines "Jezebel's" authority and incriminates any who follow her teachings: they are not passive victims, but "adulterers" (2:22).

## The Woman Clothed with the Sun (12:1–6, 13–17)

The vision of the "woman clothed with the sun" in chap. 12 is very difficult to interpret. John's symbolism fuses images from the Hebrew Scriptures together with images from ancient myths about the births of certain gods and about divine combat with monsters of chaos. Moreover, in composing the vision, John probably employed literary sources, whose original significance may have been different from John's use of them.

The woman's celestial garb (the sun, moon, and stars) associates her with a high goddess, a "queen of heaven." Several pagan goddesses, including the Ephesian Artemis, the Syrian Atargatis, and the Egyptian Isis, could have laid claim to this title. All three were linked with stars and planets in ancient art. John has combined this pagan imagery with allusions to Jewish traditions. The notice that the woman's child "is to rule all the nations with a rod of iron" echoes Ps. 2:9, understood as a prophecy about the Messiah. Some readers argue that, as mother of the Messiah, the woman should be identified with Mary, the mother of Jesus. On the other hand, because it is said that the dragon will "make war on the rest of her children, those who keep the commandments of God and the testimony of Jesus" (Rev. 12:17), some interpreters argue that she stands symbolically for the church. Neither theory quite fits the scenario: How could the church be regarded as the mother of the Messiah? Or what would it mean to say that Mary was persecuted? A third theory seems most plausible: the woman represents the people of Israel, which gave birth to the Messiah *and* to the church (compare the portrait of Zion as a mother who gives birth to a nation in Isa. 66:7–13; of Zion as a grieving mother in 2 Esd. 9:38–10:60; and of Sarah/Jerusalem as "our mother" in Gal. 4:26). John's use of goddess imagery serves to portray Israel in the most exalted terms possible: the twelve stars of the zodiac (Rev. 12:1) have become, as it were, the twelve tribes of Israel (cf. Gen. 37:9).

In antiquity various stories were told about a divine mother whose child was attacked by a monster of chaos. John's depiction of such events in 12:4–6 resembles both the Egyptian myth of the birth to Isis of Horus (who is then threatened by Seth-Typhon) and the Greek myth of Leto's delivery of Apollo (who is then pursued by the dragon Python). In both myths, the motive for the attack seems to have been to prevent the child from gaining authority over the attacker; and in both, mother and child were given divine assistance in escaping from the adversary. Moreover, both Horus and Apollo were said to have gone on to conquer their erstwhile assailants. These stories would have been well known to a first-century audience in Asia Minor. John seems to have taken over the basic plot of the myths, reinterpreting the woman as the people of Israel and the newborn child as the Messiah. The description of the woman's flight to the "wilderness" on "two wings of the great eagle" (12:14) recalls not only the miraculous rescue of Leto by the north wind but also (and more pointedly) God's rescue of the Hebrew children from Egypt and Pharaoh on "eagles' wings" (Ex. 19:4; Deut. 32:11; cf. Isa. 40:31).

The depiction of war in heaven (12:7–9) has its roots in the so-called holy war traditions of the Hebrew Scriptures. In these traditions, Yahweh the "divine warrior" waged battles on behalf of the Israelites. The holy war traditions sometimes portrayed Israel's enemies symbolically as dragonlike monsters (see, e.g., Isa. 27:1; 51:9). The "dragon" in Revelation 12 represents both political and cosmic enemies of the church. On the one hand, it symbolizes the powers of the Roman Empire, which promoted idolatry through social and political means (Revelation 13). On the other hand, the dragon symbolizes Satan, who is the spiritual force behind *all* worship of idols (see esp. 13:2, 4). John's symbolism suggests that God will defeat the church's earthly adversaries, just as God's servant Michael had defeated the heavenly adversary.

Revelation 12 must have helped first-century believers to interpret their own social and historical situation: they would have perceived that *they* were the rest of the woman's "offspring," and so still under siege by the dragon. They would have realized that the dragon had been defeated in heaven but also that a period of suffering still separated those on earth from final victory (12:17). Perhaps John further intended for his vision to instill a new sense of urgency in those Christians who were, in his opinion, too willing to compromise with pagan culture. The children of "Jezebel" might fare better in the short run, but it was the heavenly woman's children who would eventually triumph!

### The 144,000 Who "Have Not Defiled Themselves with Women" (14:1–5)

In chap. 14, John depicts 144,000 followers of the Lamb, "who had his name and his Father's name written on their foreheads" (14:1). These persons are meant to contrast with those who worship the diabolical beast from the land and who were earlier described as "marked on the right hand or on the forehead" (13:16). John depicts the 144,000 as engaged not in the polluted worship of the beast but in the pure worship of God. Probably John regards the 144,000 as a special, exclusive group of the elect, who die rather than worship the beast or receive its mark (cf. 7:4–17; 14:1; 20:4). These willing martyrs for Christ are the "first fruits for God and the Lamb" (14:4) and as such will participate in the privilege of the first resurrection (20:4), with the "whole harvest" to follow at the second resurrection (20:13). John's portrayal of the 144,000 as ones who "have not defiled themselves with women" may have been influenced by the notion that those who fight alongside Yahweh in holy war must temporarily refrain from sexual intercourse (as well as certain other actions) so as to be ritually pure (see, e.g., Deut. 23:9–14; Josh. 3:5; 7:13; 1 Sam. 21:5; 2 Sam. 11:11). Likewise, the Essenes at Qumran appear to have kept themselves ritually pure in preparation for the eschatological battle. By describing the 144,000 as not merely *refraining* from sexual intercourse but as *virgins*, John implies that the men not only meet but exceed the standard of purity necessary for participation in holy war.

### The Whore, "Babylon" (14:8; 16:19; 17:1–19:5)

After the third cycle of numbered visions, that of the "seven bowls" (15:1–16:21), John reports that one of the seven angels of the bowls showed him "the judgment of the great whore who is seated on many waters, with whom the kings of the earth have committed fornication" (17:1–2a). She is decked out with purple, scarlet, and jewels, and wears her name, "a mystery," on her forehead: "Babylon the great, mother of whores and of earth's abominations" (17:5). The woman is seated on "a scarlet beast that was full of blasphemous names," with seven heads and ten horns (17:3) — in other words, on the beast from the land, introduced already in 13:1–10. The heads of the beast are now identified as "seven mountains on which the woman is seated" and also as "seven kings" (17:10). The details of John's description indicate that the beast symbolizes the Roman Empire as a whole, while the woman represents the city of Rome (17:18). John's portrayal of the woman recalls the depiction of the goddess Roma on some ancient coins: she is seated on Rome's seven hills, with the river Tiber running below. Any Jew or Christian living in the last decades of the first century would have recognized that her "mysterious name" was a symbolic designation for Rome, which — like ancient Babylon, centuries before—had conquered Jerusalem and destroyed the Temple.

As seen above, the Hebrew Scriptures frequently used the image of an adulterous woman or a prostitute to represent idolatrous peoples. Typically, Yahweh was portrayed as the loyal husband, and the people of Israel were equated with the adulterous wife (see especially Hosea; Ezek. 16:8–58). Sometimes, however, the metaphor was extended even to peoples that did not have a covenant relationship with Yahweh. In Isa. 23:15–18 the city of Tyre is described as a prostitute because of its corruption by commerce, and in Nahum 3:4 Nineveh is called a prostitute because of its "debaucheries" and its "sorcery" (regularly linked to idolatry in the Hebrew Scriptures). In John's earlier depiction of the beasts from the land and sea, symbolizing the Roman Empire and the imperial cult, he had made it clear that the idolatrous worship of the emperor was really worship of Satan (Revelation 13). Now, in 17:1–19:4, John portrays Rome as a "whore" so as to elaborate on the idolatry and other sins associated with the empire's leading city. The metaphor also serves as a foil for John's portrayal of the new Jerusalem as the pure bride of Christ (19:6–8; 21:2; 22:17).

John brings at least three types of charges against the city of Rome. First, it is associated with idolatry and sorcery. This association is made explicit in 18:23 and is implicitly suggested both by depiction of the city as a whore and by this figure's proximity to the beast with "blasphemous names" (17:3; cf. 13:1, 5–6 [probably an allusion to the titles of honor given to emperors]). Second, the city is charged with violence: Babylon is "drunk with the blood of the saints and the blood of the witnesses to Jesus" (17:6; cf. 18:24). If John was a refugee from Palestine, then he had experienced firsthand the violent wrath of Rome as unleashed against the Jews in 66–73 C.E. He seems to have been deeply affected also by Nero's persecution of the Christians in Rome (64 C.E.): he alludes to a myth that the deceased Nero would return to life and rule again (13:3; 17:8, 11). John proclaims that, in exchange for her making all nations drink "the wine of the wrath of her fornication" (14:8; 18:3, with "wrath" possibly referring to the empire's violent aggression), Babylon will be made to drink "the wine-cup of the fury" of God's wrath (16:19; cf. 17:16; 18:6; Jer. 51:6, 49). Third, Babylon is condemned for excessive wealth (18:3, 7, 9, 11–19, 23). This wealth is tainted by the city's "fornication" (idolatry), and

its acquisition has led to an arrogance that verges on blasphemy (18:7; cf. Isa. 47:8).

The rehearsal of Babylon's destruction in chap. 18 stands as an important reminder that God is not infinitely tolerant and will indeed judge against the perpetrators of evil: individuals, cities, and entire nations will one day be called to account for their deeds. It is a message that all persons need to hear! And yet one can only regret the misogynist imagery that the author has used to convey this important message. To be sure, the book's imagery is violent from beginning to end; both the people of God and the enemies of God suffer harsh fates. But the author seems especially to delight in describing the gory destruction of the woman Babylon (see, e.g., 17:16). The objection that "Babylon" is only a metaphor, a symbol, does not eliminate the problem that the text creates for women readers. The author's exultation over the mutilation, burning, and eating of a woman—even a figurative one—tragically implies that women are sometimes deserving of such violence.

## The New Jerusalem (19:7; 21:1–22:5; 22:17)

The announcement of Babylon's fall and of the vindication of the saints causes rejoicing in heaven (19:1–5); this heavenly song quickly moves into one of celebration for the imminent marriage of the Lamb and "the bride" (19:6–8). Babylon was the "mother of whores and of earth's abominations" (17:5), but the bride of the Lamb is clothed "with fine linen, bright and pure" (19:8). After this brief anticipation of the appearance of the "bride" follow successive visions of the warrior messiah, the capture of the beasts, the resurrection and millennial reign of those martyred for Jesus, the release and the defeat of Satan, the second resurrection, and the judgment (19:9–20:15). Then, at last, the new Jerusalem appears, "coming down out of heaven from God, prepared as a bride adorned for her husband" (21:2; cf. v 9). Here John has blended the conventional motif of a new Jerusalem, kept in heaven until the last days (cf. 2 Esd. 7:26; 8:52; 9:38–10:60; 13:36), with the metaphor of the church—the people of God—as the bride of Christ (cf. 2 Cor. 11:2; Eph. 5:23–24). Indeed, the "new Jerusalem" envisioned by John is itself a metaphor for the people of God: the bride's "fine linen, bright and pure" is said to be "the righteous deeds of the saints" (19:8).

The bride metaphor (like its opposite, the

prostitute metaphor) functioned especially well in the patriarchal culture of the first century, which placed a high premium on the strict management of women's sexuality. In this culture, the ideal bride was a "pure" virgin who had no interests or liaisons that would compromise her loyalty to her husband (see 2 Cor. 11:2!). In Revelation, "purity" is the central point of the metaphor of the "bride of the Lamb," as is clear from John's continuing focus on this theme even after he drops the metaphor in 21:9 (see especially 21:27; cf. 22:15). Christ had promised that those who remain faithful "will walk with me, dressed in white, for they are worthy" (3:4–5). Such persons, indeed, are to fill the city of God (17:8).

## Conclusion

The author of the book of Revelation mentions only one flesh-and-blood woman, who is hidden behind the incriminating name "Jezebel." All other references to females are in the context of metaphoric or symbolic speech. Studying the cultural background of this symbolism enables one to understand that John uses such language to represent certain basic concepts or realities: the worship of idols versus singleminded devotion to God; the people of Israel, "mother" of the Messiah and of the church; the pollution and sin of the Roman Empire versus the purity of the heavenly city of God. But even when one understands the "point" of Revelation's various references to women, John's language remains disturbing and dangerous. He categorizes women into the wholly good (the woman clothed with the sun and the new Jerusalem) and the wholly bad ("Jezebel" and "Babylon"). The wholly good are those whose sexuality is effectively controlled; the wholly bad are those whose sexuality escapes male management and manipulation. The woman reader is thus divided: she wants to identify with the good but is reluctant to do so because the images deny female self-determination; she hesitates to identify with the bad but may endorse the defiance of the "whores" against those who would control or destroy them. John's feminine imagery is dangerous because (whether intentionally or not) it promotes an ethos in which women are not allowed to control their own bodies and

their own destinies and in which violence against women is—at least in some cases—condoned.

John sought to convince readers of the need for their unswerving commitment to God in the face of omnipresent temptations to apostasy, idolatry, and arrogance. He hoped to inspire them to hold fast to their beliefs, even if such singlemindedness meant that they, like soldiers, should have to die for their loyalty to Jesus. It was a message designed to sustain those undergoing temptation and affliction and to stir the apathetic to repentance and reform. This central message of the book is an urgent one for Christians to hear today, especially where they have become complacent toward the pervasive idolatry of our culture. Revelation conveys a radical message for desperate times, but this radical message calls for radical critique. Revelation's approval of violence and implicit disparagement of women threaten to undermine the book's central truth. Modern readers must boldly decry those aspects of Revelation that celebrate bloody retribution rather than mercy and justice and that compromise the full humanity of women. One may protest in this way even while acknowledging the truth of John's claim that one day God will call all persons to account for their deeds on earth.

## BIBLIOGRAPHY

Aune, David E. "Revelation." In *Harper's Bible Commentary*, edited by James L. Mays, pp. 1300–1319. San Francisco: Harper & Row, 1988.

Bird, Phyllis. "'To Play the Harlot': An Inquiry Into an Old Testament Metaphor." In *Gender and Difference in Ancient Israel*, edited by Peggy L. Day, pp. 75–94. Minneapolis: Fortress Press, 1989.

Collins, Adela Yarbro. *Crisis and Catharsis: The Power of the Apocalypse*. Philadelphia: Westminster Press, 1984.

Fiorenza, Elisabeth Schüssler. *The Book of Revelation: Justice and Judgment*. Philadelphia: Fortress Press, 1984.

———. *Revelation: Vision of a Just World*. Proclamation Commentaries. Minneapolis: Fortress Press, 1991.

# EARLY EXTRACANONICAL WRITINGS

*Deirdre J. Good*

Is there anything of interest to be learned about women in nonbiblical writings of the early church? Why would a collection of texts not part of the New Testament be relevant for contemporary Christian women? Within the New Testament there are few stories about women. Those that do exist, amplified by a careful process of reconstruction of the history and experiences to which they point, give some suggestions about the situation and concerns of female ancestors in the faith. There is little evidence, though, that women wrote any books of the Bible, and there is equally little evidence that women's concerns were of much interest to male biblical authors.

Outside the New Testament canon—the twenty-seven books that comprise the New Testament—on the other hand, for the first time in Christian tradition one can find indisputably female voices articulating religious visions, prophecies, and experiences of martyrdom, and women who baptize and carry out ministries of healing. There is even one story of a woman who raises someone from the dead! These accounts were written about women and in some cases by women themselves. Valued for their own sake, these accounts were known to women in the early church, who were drawn to them for help in expressing and interpreting their own experiences of Christian life and ministry.

The very popularity of these works was often used by church authorities as a reason to discredit them, and for centuries they languished unread and in many cases unknown. Now that these resources have been recovered, they give a much broader picture of women's activities in the early Christian communities. That broader picture in turn helps to counteract a reading of Christian history that gives the oversimplified picture of early days when women and men shared equally in the church's ministry and later periods when women's roles were increasingly limited.

The extracanonical writings, like all texts, reflect the communities in which they were written. To understand those writings, one must work to recover the questions, conflicts, needs, and affirmations that lie behind them. In order to recover as fully as possible the varied strands of the Christian past, that historical study has to precede theological judgments about whether the documents present correct ("orthodox") or incorrect ("heretical") statements about the Christian faith. Labels of orthodoxy or heresy reflect the judgments of a later age, when the earlier diversity had been resolved into clear categories of winners and losers, insiders and outsiders. The chorus of outsiders' voices is often the only place to hear women's stories. That chorus of voices makes it clear that in the early years of the church—at least until 150 C.E. in Rome and for a much longer time in other areas—diverse forms of Christian communities flourished.

A number of extracanonical writings were discovered at the beginning of the twentieth century in Egypt. Called the Nag Hammadi library (from the town near the discovery), these books were a collection of texts translated from

Greek originals into Coptic, the language of Christian North Africa, some time in the latter part of the third century C.E. Many of these texts reflect a religious movement called Gnosticism (from the Greek word *gnosis*, "knowledge"), which seems to have originated from forms of Judaism in the Greek-speaking world. Most Gnostic texts present revelations about the creation of this world and about the divine beings that inhabit the heavenly worlds. These texts represent an ambivalent attitude toward material existence; several describe the creation of this world as the mistake of a god who thinks of himself as the only god, while others describe the way in which secret "knowledge" or sacraments provide a way to salvation.

Valentinus was a Gnostic Christian who came from North Africa to Rome in the middle of the second century. There he founded the form of Christianity known as Valentinian Gnosticism, a movement that existed within Christianity in Rome for several decades, and elsewhere for several centuries. Some women seem to have been attracted to Valentinianism. Ptolemy, a follower of Valentinus, wrote what was intended to be the first of several letters to Flora (a woman probably from Rome) explaining Valentinian beliefs in some detail. It is a straightforward account showing three kinds of laws in Hebrew Scriptures, behind each of which lie three divine principles—a perfect and good god, a just god, and an evil devil. From the letter it appears that Flora was a Christian and, since Ptolemy does not regard her inquiry as exceptional, that she was not alone in her interest. Unfortunately, no copy of her reply has been found. She seems to confirm the diversity of Christianity in Rome in the mid-second century—a Christianity that tolerated the presence of Jewish Christians; of Valentinus, Ptolemy, and other Valentinians; and of Marcion, a man who saw little value in the Old Testament. These Christians worshiped in different places (such as house-churches and synagogues) under the leadership of presbyters (elders). Shortly after this, Marcion was expelled, and Christianity in Rome became gradually consolidated under a single bishop, whose ecclesiastical authority extended even into the civic realm.

In Syria and Asia Minor, however, the Christian communities seem to have been organized differently. Here a variety of leadership roles for both men and women flourished side by side. Some of these are described in the apocryphal *Acts* of apostles such as Thomas, John, Philip, and Andrew. Among the most important of those roles were prophet, ascetic, martyr, widow, and deacon. Before exploring those particular roles, it is important to begin by looking at what is said about women as witnesses to the resurrection of Jesus.

## Women Witnesses to the Resurrection

After the death of Jesus, resurrection appearances were reported in several places, including Galilee, Jerusalem, and Syria. Such appearances to individuals or groups were often interpreted as granting authority, particularly as apostles or other leaders, to those who witnessed the appearance. At least three of the Gospels, Matthew, Luke, and John, include stories of such appearances to particular followers (for example, Thomas, Cleopas, and Mary Magdalene). Paul uses his vision of the risen Jesus to explain his mission to the Gentiles. The account he gives in 1 Corinthians 15 of the appearance to him of the resurrected Christ reports other appearances as well. Similarly, extracanonical writings such as the *Gospel of Mary*, the *Secret Book of John*, and *The Sophia of Jesus Christ* also report Jesus' appearance to Mary, to John, to some called simply "women disciples," and to men and women prophets. Thus, from the time immediately following the death of Jesus, the authority of women in leadership positions was established on the basis of resurrection appearances.

The *Gospel of Mary* relates the encounter of the risen Jesus with Mary Magdalene (though in a form different from the account in John 20). After a dialogue between them, Mary recounts her experience to the other disciples, including Peter and Levi. Peter questions the truth of Mary's encounter with Jesus: "Why would he speak to you?" he asks rhetorically. Mary denies that she has made up any of the story, and her part is taken by Levi, who accuses Peter of attacking Mary "just like the adversaries." The gospel text concludes with the exhortation of Levi to all the disciples to get on with the work of preaching the gospel.

This text mirrors a debate about the religious authority of women that took place in some early Christian communities. The legitimacy of Mary's experience of the risen Christ is challenged by Peter, who may well represent the "orthodox" position. Besides, he can claim his own experience as reported in Matthew 16. Mary may well stand for the experiences of communities in conflict with Peter and his heirs in what had become the dominant church.

If resurrection appearances gave legitimacy to those who were granted them, that legitimacy was seen also to extend to those taught by the one who saw the risen Christ, and to those taught by them, and so on. One can see that principle of derived authority operating in the writings of Paul, in Revelation, and in the Gospel of John, as well as in noncanonical writings. Ptolemy promised Flora that she was a recipient of the apostolic tradition that Valentinians believed was traced back through Valentinus, who received it from Theudas, who, in turn, received it from Paul.

Resurrection appearances, of course, are not subject to verification. Quite early in the history of the church there were struggles over the relative value of the experiences that granted authority to various communities through their apostolic founders. For example, against competing claims, the Christian community in Rome after 150 C.E. attempted to consolidate its dominance over other Christian communities, primarily by the establishment of the rule of a single bishop. That process seems effectively to have excluded women from most leadership roles and reserved for them the offices of deacon, widow, and virgin. These formal "offices" held by women had as forerunners the greater diversity of women's leadership roles in the earlier years of the church. That the same office could imply different functions and authority in different places is probably explained by the relative freedom or restriction of social roles in different places.

## Women Prophets

The role of prophet in Christianity was widely recognized from the earliest times. A prophet spoke with the voice of God—in direct communication with divinity. In the books of Luke, Acts, and the *Didache* (the *Teachings of the Twelve Apostles*, written at the end of the first century), one encounters references to women prophets in Syria and Asia Minor throughout the first century. According to Tertullian and Epiphanius, church "fathers" who wrote in the third and fourth centuries respectively, such activity seems to have continued until an even later date in the Montanist churches of Asia, Phrygia, and North Africa. The hallmarks of these churches were spiritual gifts, such as prophecies and visions. Founded by Montanus, together with the female prophets Maximilla and Prisca, the churches seem to have valued the roles of both women and men.

Although Epiphanius was hostile to the Montanist churches and quoted material he thought would discredit the movement, even his hostile reports give testimony to the intensity of the prophets' charismatic speech. Maximilla, for example, tells of her vision of the resurrected Christ. "In the form of a woman, clothed in a shining robe, Christ came to me and put wisdom in me and revealed to me that this place is sacred and that it is here that Jerusalem will descend from heaven" (Epiphanius *Panarion* 49.1, author's translation). In this extraordinary vision reported in her own words, Maximilla connects the appearance of Christ in a female form with wisdom granted to a woman. The personification of Wisdom (Sophia in Greek) as female is described in Hellenistic Jewish writings. In the Wisdom of Jesus ben Sirach (Ecclesiasticus), Wisdom searches for a place on earth to dwell, and descends to Jerusalem. In the Wisdom of Solomon, Sophia protects the righteous (children of God) from the wicked. It is quite likely that early Christian writers drew on these ideas in shaping their understanding of Jesus' life and death. Both John 1 and Philippians 2 describe the descent of a figure to earth and later identify Jesus as this figure in the person of "Lord" or "Word."

The complicated history of the relationship of the Montanist churches to their more orthodox counterparts finally resulted in a schism. One of the consequences of that split was that any prophetic activity by a woman was regarded as especially suspicious. In fact, female prophetic activity was not officially recognized in the church after the fourth century, and the office of prophet itself was regarded with suspicion by church historians of that century. This distancing of the church from prophetic styles of leadership and authority reflects a concern to consolidate ecclesiastical power and authority within institutional structures. By the third century, this suspicion may have led to the institutional transformation of women's prophetic roles into the more defined office of widow discussed below.

## Women Ascetics

In the fourth century, asceticism, the practice of heightening spiritual awareness through renunciation of physical desires, became widespread in the Christian church. To be sure, several early Christian communities seem to have held asceticism in high esteem, but it does not characterize all early Christian behavior, nor is the ascetic life-style understood as exemplary in the literature of the first two centuries. By the fourth century, however, such practices were regarded as a way for people to advance their spiritual lives, and even to regain the innocence of paradise.

Accounts of women and men ascetics are strange to modern readers, for they not only describe but also praise life-styles contemporary judgment would regard as disturbed. To sympathize with such accounts is not just an exercise in historical imagination. It is also a matter of understanding how controlling the body can be an expression of freedom, especially freedom from social expectations. A woman ascetic who does not choose motherhood, for example, not only circumvents social expectations, but *through her body* experiences visions and revelations that show she is connected to the realm of the sacred. If her autonomy is supported by a community that in turn is supported by society (as in the case of religious orders), so much the better for her. In the early period of the church's history, however, female monastic orders were rare. One such community within Judaism, the Therapeutrides (corresponding to the male community of Therapeutae), is described by Philo of Alexandria, the first-century Jewish writer, in his book *On the Contemplative Life*.

The *Acts of Paul and Thecla*, probably written in the late second century, tells the adventures of Thecla, a woman who followed Paul. By the fourth century the fame of Thecla was so widespread that a shrine to her was found by the pilgrim Egeria (see below) in Seleucia, the ancient port city of Antioch in Syria. In the story, Thecla is captivated by Paul's teaching, and leaves the embrace of her fiancé to follow the apostle. At a dramatic point in their travels, she is thrown to the lions, miraculously baptizes herself, and escapes being eaten alive when the sympathetic women onlookers throw perfumes into the arena, causing the wild animals to become drowsy. In order to travel freely, she cuts off her hair and wears men's clothing. We know that Thecla's act of baptism and her teaching were emulated by other women, for Tertullian criticizes such actions as if they were authorized by Paul. Obviously, for those women they were! Since Thecla renounced the courtship of various suitors to follow Paul, she also became a model of asceticism. According to the *Acts of Paul*, the larger document of which Thecla's story is a part, Paul enthusiastically endorses the ascetic life of the wandering missionary for both women and men.

A similar story is told of Drusiana in the *Acts of John*. Although she is imprisoned by her fiancé in an attempt to coerce her into marriage, he is finally converted to asceticism. In another episode, Drusiana and a different suitor, Callimachus, are both resurrected by the apostle John. Drusiana in turn brings about the resurrection of the pagan Fortunatus—the only known account in the early church in which a woman is said to have raised someone from the dead. The text, however, does not imply that this miracle was in any way exceptional. Rather, such accounts of miracles suggest a certain equality of women and men alike engaged in activities of healing and exorcism. The stories were told to encourage conversion to the celibate Christian life, and their intention was to entertain as well as to edify.

Women who chose an ascetic life-style were called "virgins." Jerome, a fourth-century Christian from Rome, appears to have held a high regard for virginity, as did many people in the period. Adam and Eve, he argues in *Against Jovinian* I, 16 (393 C.E.), "were virgins in Paradise before the sin; however, after the sin and outside of Paradise, immediately they were married.... Marriage fills the earth (but) virginity fills Paradise." In his *Letter to Eustochium*, the daughter of his aristocratic friend Paula, Jerome congratulates her on choosing a life of virginity in early adolescence. This life-style, he argues, is especially suited to women because of their sex. "Death came through Eve, life through Mary. And for that reason, too, the gift of virginity pours forth more richly upon women, because it began with a woman." Here, Jerome is using biblical figures (Adam, Eve, and Mary) as types or examples. He associates "the fall" with sexual knowledge. Although the human condition is understood as "fallen," paradise can be regained by choosing an ascetic life-style. This life-style is modeled by the virgin Mary who, although a mother, "perfects" the sin of Eve by conceiving a child virginally. From the number of women to whom Jerome wrote and from the high regard in which Paula was held, one can conclude that this reasoning was both appealing and successful, however strange it sounds to modern ears.

## Women Martyrs

As is seen in the stories about Thecla, women and men ascetics were often persecuted as

Christians. Thus, toward the end of the second and during the third century, accounts were handed down about women and men martyred for their Christian faith. Recent scholarship has suggested that at least some of these accounts were written by women themselves, and this is almost certainly the case with the *Martyrdom of Perpetua.*

Perpetua was probably martyred in North Africa in 203 C.E. The account of her martyrdom is an important text for several reasons. First, its presentation of martyrdom as a powerful symbol of human liberation and self-fulfillment became the standard way of understanding martyrdom in Christianity. Reflecting the outlook of a persecuted minority, it attests their ultimate hope—eternal life. It is thus quite remarkable that the account is about, and even by, a woman. Second, the account is introduced by an editor, but it then continues in the first person—in the voice of the martyr herself. This is probably the authentic voice of an early Christian woman, and it shows the ways in which she transcends contemporary gender-role expectations both by her rejection of her father and young child and by the courageous way she faces death. Yet she suffers greatly when she cannot help either her father or her baby from her prison cell: she still feels the human pangs of remorse at leaving her physical blood ties. Her son remains with her for a brief while, but then his father takes him away. When that happens, Perpetua says, "God saw to it that my child no longer needed my nursing, nor were my breasts inflamed. After that I was no longer tortured with anxiety about my child."

In martyrdom Perpetua voluntarily dies for her faith and so brings about her own salvation. She asks for and is granted visions, and she intercedes for others (including a priest and a bishop). The real focus of the text, however, is her martyrdom, which is called "a second baptism." Obviously this "baptism" is independent of ecclesiastical power! All this is said to be possible because of her devotion to Christ, whose presence replaces earthly with heavenly reality, and present life with eternal life. On her way to be martyred she is called "a true spouse of Christ" and "the darling of God." The early popularity of the story of her martyrdom is shown by the existence of several Latin and Greek copies of the text, by the dedication to her of a basilica in Carthage, and by the commemoration of the date of her martyrdom in the official calendar of the church in Rome.

## Widows

The term "widow" means "a person without." In the usage of the early church this usually designated a woman whose husband had died, leaving her without financial support. As can be seen in the pastoral epistles, by the middle of the second century the ministry of widows was recognized as a special category of leadership and service in the church. It remained a significant category until the fourth century, when it seems to have declined in popularity and importance. It is quite likely that during the first four centuries, the ministry of widows overlapped with that of virgins, and both of those ministries were related to those of deacons (see below).

In the *Apostolic Constitutions* of the fourth century, there is evidence that qualifications for the order of widows were similar to those listed in the pastoral epistles. Such women were to be over sixty, married once, mature, economically dependent, and with the pastoral duties of counsel and comfort. Their teaching function was to train younger women. They were not permitted to teach in the church, "but only to pray, and to hear those that teach." This coincided with the example of Jesus, who did not send out women to preach although there were women he could have sent (his mother, Mary Magdalene, Martha and Mary, or Salome). Similarly, widows were not permitted to baptize men, "for the man is the head of the woman" (1 Cor. 11:3), and, besides, Jesus was not baptized by his own mother. Widows were, however, permitted to anoint women in the ceremony of baptism. In third-century Syria, according to the *Didascalia Apostolorum,* widows' duties were expanded to include care of the sick (visiting and laying hands on them) in addition to fasting and prayer on their behalf. It was the bishop alone who gave permission for them to visit homes or to engage in other forms of religious activity. Questions about matters of doctrine were outside the widows' domain, and such questions were referred to (male) ecclesiastical authorities. The strange image in the text of a widow as an altar of God is interpreted to mean that she should stay in one place and not run around. This image may reflect a tendency to restrict the order's influence. At least by the fourth century in Syria, and perhaps elsewhere, it appears that the roles of widows passed to the deacons.

## Women Deacons

The office of deacon was held in the early church by men and women designated to care for the underprivileged, such as widows and orphans. Evidence of that office is found in a letter written at the end of the first century by the Roman administrator Pliny to the emperor Trajan. In that letter Pliny speaks of questioning two women "deacons" about Christian practices. By the third century, admission to the office of deacon was by ordination, and its functions lay in the care of men by male deacons and of women by female deacons. Those functions probably included bringing the Eucharist or "Lord's Supper" to the sick. In Syria women deacons also anointed with oil the female candidates for baptism, and they may well have given these women their prebaptismal instruction. In the West, however, the role of the women deacons seems to have been more restricted. According to the *Apostolic Constitutions*, the women deacons stand at the women's entrance to the church and, at the appropriate point in the service, give the women the Lord's kiss, as the male deacons do to the men.

## Women Scholars

The activity of women scholars and scribes is attested in Christian tradition of the fourth and fifth centuries, when Christianity had spread to the aristocracy. For example, Jerome describes Paula, a woman who belongs to a wealthy Roman family and whom he admires for her zeal in learning biblical languages. Melania the Elder is portrayed in Palladius's *Lausiac History* (written about 419 or 420) as being extremely well versed in commentaries on scripture. From similar circles in Rome comes the poem of Faltonia Betitia Proba in the form of a cento, a poem composed of verses of Virgil's poetry. This poem, whose subject matter spans creation and the ascension of Christ, remained popular until the Middle Ages in spite of a decree by Gelasius, bishop of Rome, in 496 C.E., relegating it to the apocryphal writings.

Among the writings of women ascetics who retreated to the desert to live in celibate communities under female leadership are the sayings of the Desert Mothers. The sayings of Syncletica, a fourth-century Egyptian woman, and those of her contemporaries Sara and Theodora are preserved in the *Sayings of the Fathers*! They contain interesting maxims about monastic life and give general advice in anecdotal form. Apart from these sayings, we know nothing else of the lives of these women ascetics, who clearly were valued for their wisdom. A sampling of sayings attributed to them (presented in the author's translation) makes clear the nature of their teachings. Sara said, "It is good to give alms for humanity's sake, for even if it is done for the sake of pleasing others, it begins to effect pleasing God." She also said, "Even if I prayed to God that everyone would think well of me, I should be found at the door of each, repenting. I shall pray rather that my heart be pure toward all." A number of sayings are attributed to Syncletica, including the following comments on an ascetic life-style: "Just as poisonous beasts are driven out by the bitterest of medicines, so evil thoughts are driven out by prayer with fasting." "If you should happen to be in a monastery, do not go elsewhere, for you will be greatly harmed; just as a bird abandoning the eggs makes them sterile and useless, so also a monk or a nun [virgin] grows cold and their faith dies when they go from place to place." She has some sound advice about the inner life:

> It is dangerous for anyone to teach not having been trained in the practical life, for if a person who owns a ruined house makes strangers welcome there, he or she harms [them] on account of the poverty of the house. So it is also with those not having first built up themselves: those coming to them are destroyed. By words they may be called to salvation, but by a wicked manner of life, they are injured.

Also from this period, although difficult to date exactly, comes *Egeria's Diary* (a text discovered in 1884), the account of the pilgrimage of Egeria through Egypt, the holy land, and Syria. Egeria seems to have been well educated (particularly in scripture) and of high social status, for she is welcomed at famous sites by local clergy anxious to show her people and places of interest. She writes of her experiences for a group of women interested in the liturgical observances she encounters. She addresses these women as "sisters." In the course of her travels she visits the shrine of St. Thecla, where she hears a reading from the *Acts of Paul and Thecla*.

Doubtless made possible by economic independence, Egeria's life is that of a laywoman. She shows that not all early Christian women were drawn to asceticism or monastic life, although she admires such a life-style. Some historians have suggested that Egeria was herself a Spanish nun, but that argument is a good example of the way in which the few women who emerge in Christian history are immediately identified with the official church hierarchy. To address female recipients of a letter as "sisters" does not necessarily imply that they are part of a religious order. Indeed, her stated admiration for the ascetic life-style speaks against her membership in such a community! It is quite likely that as a laywoman she belonged to a group of pious women interested in the monastic life, who knew of liturgical matters since they performed the daily office. Such groups of women "canons" emerge in subsequent Christian history associated with cathedrals. It may be that Egeria and her sisters are foremothers of these uncloistered women.

On the other hand, the learned Paula (referred to above) went on a pilgrimage to Jerusalem and settled near Bethlehem, where she established monasteries for men and women. Perhaps she followed the example of her predecessor Melania the Elder. Both Paula and Melania in turn served as models for other women in their families and spheres of influence. Melania the Elder, for example, appears to have been such a role model for Melania the Younger and Olympias, a wealthy widow from Constantinople who was a virgin and an ordained deacon. Many Christian women also found encouragement in the influential role model of Thecla.

## Conclusion

The extracanonical literature of the early church provides evidence of a much fuller participation of women in the life and ministry of the church than such "fathers" as Jerome or Tertullian suggest. In many of their activities, women and men served together or in parallel ministries with equal authority. Reading all the available evidence from Christian tradition uncovers this variety and richness and corrects the distorted picture of women's roles that comes from seeing the canon as descriptive of the first two centuries of Christian history.

## BIBLIOGRAPHY

### Texts

Clark, Elizabeth A. *Women in the Early Church.* Wilmington, Del.: Michael Glazier, 1983.

Heine, R. *The Montanist Oracles and Testimonia.* Macon, Ga.: Mercer University Press, 1989.

Hennecke, E., and W. Schneemelcher, eds. *New Testament Apocrypha.* 2 vols. Translated by R. McL. Wilson. Philadelphia: Westminster Press, 1963 (revised 1990), 1965 (revision forthcoming, 1992).

Kraemer, Ross S., ed. *Maenads, Martyrs, Matrons, Monastics: A Sourcebook on Women's Religions in the Greco-Roman World.* Philadelphia: Fortress Press, 1988.

Robinson, James M., ed. *The Nag Hammadi Library in English.* New York: Harper & Row, 1987.

Ward, Benedicta, trans. *The Desert Christian: Sayings of the Desert Fathers.* New York: Macmillan Publishing Co., 1980.

Wilson-Kastner, Patricia, et al., eds. *A Lost Tradition: Women Writers of the Early Church.* Washington: University Press of America, 1981.

### Studies

Bauer, Walter. *Orthodoxy and Heresy in Earliest Christianity.* Edited by Robert Kraft and Gerhard Krodel. Philadelphia: Westminster Press, 1971.

Brooten, Bernadette. "Early Christian Women and Their Cultural Context." In *Feminist Perspectives on Biblical Scholarship,* edited by Adela Yarbro Collins, pp. 65–91. Decatur, Ga.: Scholars Press, 1985.

Brown, Peter. *The Body and Society: Men, Women and Sexual Renunciation in Early Christianity.* New York: Columbia University Press, 1988.

Davies, Stephen. *The Revolt of the Widows: The Social World of the Apocryphal Acts.* Carbondale, Ill.: Southern Illinois University Press, 1980.

King, Karen, ed. *Images of the Feminine in Gnosticism.* Philadelphia: Fortress Press, 1988.

Thurston, Bonnie Bowman. *The Widows: A Women's Ministry in the Early Church.* Minneapolis: Fortress Press, 1989.

# EVERYDAY LIFE
# Women in the Period
# of the New Testament

*Amy L. Wordelman*

The New Testament contains many images of women but reveals very little about the larger fabric of their everyday lives. Images of women drawing water, grinding grain, anointing bodies, traveling, conversing, and praying hint at widely diverse worlds of women's activity. But these individual images do not provide a social context from which to make sense of them as pieces of a larger whole. Fortunately, other forms of literature, along with archaeological research, make possible a more complete picture of women's lives. This picture will never be as detailed as one might wish because few ancient Mediterranean women had the opportunity to write personally about their lives, and many of their material possessions, tools, and dwellings have been lost or misidentified over time. Nevertheless, modern historians are uncovering some aspects of ancient women's lives. Remnants of women's writing, writings by men about women, inscriptions by or about women, ancient works of art, and archaeological excavations of private and public buildings have become sources revealing women's lost or hidden worlds.

The New Testament itself suggests great diversity among women's lives, and these other sources confirm the impression. Geographic and ethnic variety in the huge Roman Empire accounted for some differences among women; however, economic status figured even more prominently in shaping the conditions and choices a woman encountered in her work, family, social relations, and religious life. Economics affected the amount of time required

to provide necessities like food, clothing, and shelter and also affected the extent to which a woman's life was determined by the requirements of people in authority over her. For early Christian women, economic status shaped significantly the ways in which they could participate in Christian communities and the ways in which they could live out their faith in everyday life.

## Women's Context: The Roman Empire

Early Christian women lived under the Roman Empire. Through military and economic conquests during the prior three centuries, Rome had expanded its domain to encompass parts of Asia, Europe, and Africa that surround the Mediterranean Sea. A male emperor, along with a senate of wealthy Roman males, governed the empire with a heavy hand. They appointed male governors for the outlying provinces and administered the taxes and military forces through which Rome exercised its power over the vast empire. Many local communities handled their own affairs through a council consisting of men from the wealthiest strata of the community. A view of women as mentally and physically inferior beings, irrational and superstitious, supported the norm of male political power and authority.

On the periphery of the empire and just beyond its borders a few exceptional women held political power, demonstrating that the Roman model was neither universal nor inevitable. In a Roman-controlled region southeast of the Black Sea, a woman named Pythodoris ruled in the late first century B.C.E. Pythodoris inherited her power from her husband, but retained it even after her remarriage to a nearby king and in spite of having two grown sons. In Egypt, Cleopatra VII ruled from 50 to 30 B.C.E. Cleopatra served as an able administrator of Egyptian economic and military matters, in spite of her fame as consort of Caesar and Marc Antony. Acts 8:27 refers to one strong and persistent line of female rulers, the queens of Ethiopia in northeast Africa, called "Candace" by Greek speakers. In the late first century B.C.E., the army of Candace turned back a Roman effort to invade her territory and exact tribute from its inhabitants.

Rome established its rule under the rubric of creating peace and order throughout the empire. New roads and campaigns to control pirates who plagued sea travel enabled greater freedom of movement and communication for those who had the economic means to take advantage of them. However, behind these signs of peace and order lay conflicts deeply rooted in Rome's methods of domination and policy of granting privilege on the basis of wealth and culture.

Rome favored its own political and economic interests, along with Greek culture expressed through language, education, literature, art, and religion. For Jews, Egyptians, Syrians, Anatolians, and countless other people of the provinces—whether they lived in their homelands or in settlements far away—this dominance of Roman power and Greco-Roman culture created tensions and conflicts in everyday life. Privilege and prejudice based solely on race were relatively rare. Brown-, black-, and white-skinned peoples intermingled and intermarried throughout all regions and social strata of the empire. However, full participation in Greco-Roman culture, economics, and politics required wealth. Citizenship, which gave the right to own property and transmit that property to heirs, was granted on the basis of wealth, adoption of Greco-Roman culture, and sympathy with the interests of those already holding economic and political power. One could become a local citizen and/or a citizen of Rome itself. Rome granted citizenship to the aristocracies of conquered territories in exchange for their cooperation. Poorer people of all ethnic groups could not fulfill the prerequisites for citizenship, and the policies of Rome worked to perpetuate their exclusion from the empire's riches.

Rome's official policy allowed Jews and other ethnic groups to live according to their own laws and customs without government interference. Various regions, families, and individuals developed different strategies for managing tensions with Greco-Roman society. In some communities, particularly in Asia Minor, Jewish families enjoyed a relatively peaceful existence and played prominent roles in local politics and social life. In other communities, Jews also lived a stable existence, but with more independence from Greco-Roman society. Violence stemming from ethnic and related religious conflicts occurred occasionally, usually triggered by local circumstances. In Alexandria, Egypt, in the early first century C.E., years of uneventful coexistence between Jews and local Greco-Egyptian inhabitants erupted into a series of bloody riots. At stake were conflicts over support for Rome, taxation, access to citizenship, and the right to live by Jewish law and custom. Sporadic violence over similar issues also occurred in other places.

In outlying provinces and rural areas, Rome kept "order" by using military occupation, colonization, taxes, and favors granted to cooperative local aristocracies. The lives of the predominantly rural populations in Palestine showed the ill effects of this kind of "peace." For these women and men, the worries of everyday life included the threat of losing land and livelihood because of high taxes owed to Rome, a mandate (on threat of punishment) to give a Roman soldier anything he wanted, and intermittent guerrilla warfare. Local revolts against Rome broke into full-scale war by 66 C.E. Everyday life then came to include fleeing destroyed villages and homes, famine, and constant threats to life itself. Roman military might finally prevailed over the local people, and the resulting destruction of the religious and political capital Jerusalem altered irrevocably the structures and focus of the region.

## Women's Class and Women's Work

The class structure of the Roman world resembled a pyramid with the small, wealthy or "citizen" class occupying the upper tip of the structure and controlling most of the empire's wealth and political power. A huge gap in resources and life-style existed between wealthy citizens and the wide and densely populated base of the pyramid. This base consisted of slaves, former slaves, urban working people, and rural farmers and laborers, none of whom held citizenship. A small middle class of merchants, soldiers, civil servants, traders, and other entrepreneurs also existed, often dependent on the state or citizen patrons for capital and employment. Although typically noncitizens, some of these people managed an upwardly mobile path to citizenship, while others merged into the working-class base.

The fundamental unit of social organization was the household, a structure very different from the modern family. Household structure mirrored the pyramidal shape of the empire's economic structure. The head of the household and immediate family occupied the upper tip and controlled slave members of the household, who could range from one to five hundred in number. According to the Greco-Roman ideal, a citizen male acted as household head and his wife oversaw the running of the household according to his orders. In actuality, widows of citizen men and a few independently wealthy women also served as household heads with authority over other members. Household dependents included merchants and other clients or employees for whom the household head acted as patron and as a source of capital. Former slaves often remained dependents under obligation to work for and obey the household head.

Just as male power and authority dominated political life, men also controlled many aspects of economic and household life. Law and tradition strictly regulated, according to a woman's class, her property and inheritance rights, her occupational choices, and her reproduction. The standards differed for each class but worked together as an interlocking system of law and custom that served to maintain both male power and authority and the economic and political privilege of the citizen class.

Citizen women enjoyed the economic security and social privileges of property ownership and inherited wealth. In most cases, actual ownership and control lay in the hands of fathers, husbands, or other male relatives. Some women, however, owned and controlled property which they obtained through widowhood, inheritance, and even some lucrative business deals. Although most cases required a legal male guardian, these guardians did not always exercise control over the estate. However, even if a woman had only limited control, she still enjoyed the material benefits and social privileges that accompanied the possession of wealth.

Citizen women had one primary responsibility: to marry and produce an heir. Virtually every citizen woman had to marry, and she had to marry a citizen man. Fathers and potential husbands arranged a marriage contract in what was first of all an economic venture designed to produce heirs and to cement family alliances. Some marriages included concerns of love or companionship, but these were not prerequisites. In the interest of assuring a legitimately conceived heir, a citizen woman could not consort with any man apart from her husband without risking severe punishment, even death. Her husband, however, only risked this punishment if he consorted with the wife of another citizen. Otherwise he could, and often did, make unions with noncitizen women, slave or free. These unions were regarded as "legitimate," but they did not convey to the woman (or to any children) the man's citizenship or property rights. In this context, the term "adultery" did not refer to breaches of mutual fidelity between any two marriage partners but rather to any behavior that threatened a pure line of blood succession for the property of a citizen household. Once a citizen woman produced an heir, she completed the part of her work deemed most crucial by her society.

In large and wealthy households, household management could be delegated to high-ranking slaves. In less-affluent households, citizen women participated more directly in the work. Greco-Roman descriptions of an ideal wife often refer to her care for her children, her diligence in overseeing the work of household slaves, and her skill in spinning and weaving. Wool working was the one household task that occupied the time of all but the wealthiest women. Both literary and artistic portrayals of women of all ranks often show them with spindle in hand or walking back and forth before the loom.

In contrast to citizen women, slave women were legally classified as "property." Slave women, in fact, constituted part of the "property" that citizens owned and transmitted through inheritance. The Roman economic system fed itself on the involuntary labor of slaves. Slave labor and reproduction served to maintain and expand the property base of wealthy citizens, which in turn allowed them to purchase more human "property" and begin the cycle over again. Slaves became slaves by being born to a slave mother, by capture in war, through kidnapping by pirates or land brigands, and (especially in the case of females) by the exposure of infants at birth. Because property rights and social conventions favored males, citizen households sometimes chose not to rear female babies. They would place them outside where anyone who wanted could take them. Some infants died, but many ended up as slaves or prostitutes.

Slave women did work assigned to them by their masters. Inscriptions on tombstones of slave women usually identify them by their occupation: wool worker, weaver, seamstress, midwife, nurse, caretaker for children, handservant, laundry woman, hairdresser, secretary, stenographer. Many of these occupations required apprenticeships arranged by the household head. Legally, Roman society recognized marriage only between free citizen partners, but tombstones set up by slaves for lifelong companions attest to the strength and endurance of informal slave unions. These informal marriages by slaves had to be approved by the household head. A slave woman could most easily form a union with a slave of the same household, although some formed unions with slaves of other households or noncitizen freemen.

Any child born to a slave woman became the "property" of her owner's household. Thus the fate of the whole slave family lay in the hands of the household head, who could sell any member at any time. A slave woman had little or no protection against sexual abuse and rape. In the eyes of society, she was typically regarded as "available" for any male, free or slave, who wanted to use her. In some cases, household heads controlled a slave woman's reproduction by preventing her union with her chosen partner or by forcing reproduction in order to increase the household's slave holdings.

Other working women were either free, noncitizen women of the lower classes or women who had been freed from slavery. By Roman law, a woman could be freed from slavery after age thirty, either by her owner's decree or by buying her own freedom—often with the help of relatives or friends. Release agreements often still obligated the woman to work for her master by doing the same work she had done in slavery. Many poor freewomen and former slave women worked as vendors of various types of goods such as salt, sesame seeds, fish, grains, vegetables, spices, perfume, honey, and clothing. A few women developed quite lucrative businesses. Women also earned money by hiring themselves out as wet nurses for citizen-class infants.

Some working women earned their livelihood by professions deemed less respectable by their society: entertainers and prostitutes.

Entertainers, such as actresses, dancers, harpists, and flutists, were not necessarily prostitutes; and prostitutes were not necessarily skilled artists or entertainers. But they all shared a common status because they lived and worked in settings that "respectable" women did not frequent. Some entertainers and prostitutes were slaves working for their masters; others were former slaves and poor freewomen working their trade in order to feed themselves and their families.

A large number of women, perhaps even a majority, lived and worked in rural areas on which urban centers like Rome depended for food. The agricultural economies of Palestine, Egypt, and Asia Minor survived by the work of both women and men. Chief crops included wheat, barley, millet, and legumes. Sheep farming provided wool for women's constant work of spinning and weaving. Some rural working women were slaves on large agricultural estates, organized on the same household principles as in the cities. In some areas poor families worked land as serfs or tenant farmers producing crops for a landowner. Some families owned their own small piece of land, and women's work on that land contributed directly to the survival of the family. These small family farms often operated at subsistence level, producing just enough to support the family. Losses from bad weather and high taxes imposed by Rome made them vulnerable to takeover by large landowners.

The differences among women's lives stemming from class status had one fundamental element at their core: a difference in power. Citizen women had rights similar to citizen men in exercising control over slaves and even over former slaves. A first-century Greek inscription from the temple of Apollo at Delphi records the release from slavery of a woman named Onasiphoron. Onasiphoron paid her own purchase price to her owner, a woman named Sophrona, and the inscription shows how Sophrona arranged the terms of Onasiphoron's release. While Sophrona clearly had the legal standing necessary to make such an agreement, it did take seven different men to carry it out correctly. A man wrote it on her behalf. Her son, presumably the heir to her property, gave his consent. Further, a man served as the required guarantor of the sale, along with four other men who served as witnesses. Sophrona thus exercised legal rights but only with the aid and consent of male authorities.

However, with the help of these male authorities, Sophrona maintained control over

Onasiphoron, even after her release from slavery. Onasiphoron had to remain with Sophrona as long as Sophrona lived, do everything that Sophrona wished (or accept whatever punishment she inflicted), and finally give one of her children to Sophrona's son to serve as a slave in her place. Sophrona could maintain this control through the mechanism that held the Roman slavery system in place, legally sanctioned punishment for any slave or freed slave who challenged the control of the owners. Thus, one of the ways the social structure maintained class privilege was by giving one woman power over another. The effects of these power relations permeated relations among women of different classes, not just in economic life but in social and religious life as well.

## Stages of Life

Several Greco-Roman sources provide more intimate and detailed glimpses into the stages of women's lives. Few fragments of women's writing have survived, but the poetry of Erinna reveals the rare voice of a young girl describing her childhood in her own words. Erinna wrote while mourning the death of her girlfriend Baucis. She spoke fondly of their playing games of tag along the sea and in the garden, playing with dolls and pretending they were newly married wives, and of their fear of the female monster called Mormo. Erinna's memories turned to sorrow at her separation from her friend, first because Baucis married, and almost immediately after, because Baucis died. Erinna wrote before the New Testament period, but her poetry still reflects the centrality of marriage dreams and sorrows for the daughters of citizens — a centrality that endured well beyond the founding of Christianity.

In contrast to Erinna's poetry, no surviving literature passes on the thoughts and feelings of young slave girls. Images of their lives come primarily from people who measured their value according to their work capacity. For instance, one list of purchase prices for slaves shows a girl under the age of eight costing one third the purchase price of an adult male, and a girl between eight and sixteen costing two thirds. Another source shows the apprenticeship of a young slave girl named Thermuthion to a master weaver. The agreement stated that the girl must work from sunrise to sunset for four full years, with only eighteen days off a year for festivals. If she did no work or was ill on other days, she had to make up that work at the end of her term. For Thermuthion, childhood meant day-long and year-long work, a sharp contrast to Erinna's poetry and play.

Regardless of a girl's class, early motherhood often signaled the end of childhood or adolescence. Throughout the empire, marriage often took place in the mid-teens (sometimes as early as age twelve), in spite of physicians' warnings about the dangers of early pregnancy. For lower-class females, slave or free, who could not make formal marriages, early pregnancy still took place, both because of informal marriages and because of their vulnerability to the sexual whims of slave owners and other more powerful males. Women used some forms of questionably effective birth control, such as resins used to block the cervix or herbal concoctions that caused infertility. Soranus, a first-century Roman physician, advised a woman desiring to prevent pregnancy to hold her breath and draw back at the exact moment of ejaculation; and then to get up immediately, squat down, start sneezing, wipe herself, and drink something cold. Concoctions to induce abortion, and shaking or jumping to induce expulsion were also used. On the whole, pregnancy was almost inevitable unless a woman was physically unable to conceive or in a rare situation that either made possible or required abstinence.

Births were women's domain, attended by a midwife and several female helpers. Soranus wrote detailed instructions for midwives, but he and other male physicians rarely attended births and received much of their information from the midwives themselves. The midwife brought with her a birthing stool that had bars for handgrips on each side, a back to lean against, and a crescent-shaped hole cut into the seat through which the infant could pass. In the absence of a stool, the woman was to sit on the lap of another woman who was strong enough to hold on to her during contractions. The midwife knelt on the floor in front so that she could see both the mother's face and the emerging child. Before cutting the umbilical cord, the midwife had to make a medical decision whether the child was sufficiently healthy and well formed to raise. Extremely premature, weak, or deformed babies were not allowed to live beyond this point. Even after an infant was declared healthy, the father or household head had the right to determine whether the child would be raised in the household or left outside for someone else to claim. After tying the umbilical cord, the midwife would swaddle the child from head to toe with wool bandages, so that the child would develop into a desirable shape. Citizen women often employed wet nurses for their infants, rather than nursing them themselves.

Women often died from either childbirth or disease. High infant and high maternal mortality rates made childbirth a constant arena of danger and grief in women's lives. Diseases, plagues, widespread malnutrition, and generally poor health and safety conditions meant that many women were dead by age forty. The epitaph of Arsinoe, an Egyptian-Jewish woman, says that she died giving birth to her first child and that her mother had died when she was a little girl. Athenodora of Athens died while her children still needed her milk. Socratea is described as being taken from happy life to death by the cruel and implacable birth of her third child. A freed slave Aurelia Philematio lived to age forty before violent death took her. On a less tragic note, Claudia of Rome is remembered by her family for loving her husband, bearing two sons, making pleasant conversation, walking gracefully, keeping house, and working with wool. Finally, Epicydilla of Thasos, who was married at fifteen, lived a full fifty years of "unbroken agreement" with her husband, making her at least sixty-five before her death.

## Women and Religion

The slave girl Thermuthion's apprenticeship agreement, which gave her eighteen days off a year for festivals, points to the mainstay of Greco-Roman religious life. Each city or region celebrated public festivals in honor of its favored deity or deities. Many cities honored one particular god or goddess as primary, such as the worship of Artemis at Ephesus (Acts 19), but also honored other deities as well. Judaism acknowledged only one deity, Yahweh, the God of Israel. Festivals varied in type from solemn prayers and fasting to jubilant processions and banquets, and from serious ritual dramas to ecstatic dancing frenzies. Some regions reserved certain festivals for women, such as the Greek Thesmophoria, a festival to Demeter, goddess of grain, celebrated at spring planting time. Citizen women sometimes served as festival priestesses, an honor bestowed on a woman who could contribute the financial resources needed for the celebration. An inscription from Asia Minor shows a woman named Tata, called priestess, who at her own expense provided oil for athletes, many sacrifices, public banquets, dances, and plays. As her cultic duty, she

presided over the animal sacrifices that played a primary role in most festivals. Meat from sacrificed animals provided a banquet for everyone, and, for many people of the lower classes, these festivals were the only times they ate meat.

In addition to public festivals, women also participated in private religious associations of many different sizes and types. Jewish synagogues, groups of initiates to deities such as Isis or Demeter, and the earliest groups of Christians all formed voluntary associations, which brought together people with shared beliefs, practices, and interests. Most of these groups had in common a concept of membership that required formal initiations, moral and ritual obligations, and obedience to the group's authority structures. Some of these groups were small enough to meet in homes of members; others expanded into large buildings. Some groups mixed together women and men of various classes; others confined themselves to certain classes, one sex, or one occupational group. In a world that barred women from direct political power, these religious associations provided an arena in which women could and did exercise leadership roles. For example, inscriptions show women exercising various types of teaching and administrative roles in Jewish synagogues. Rufina and Theopempte are described as heads of synagogues; Sophia of Gortyn as a head of a synagogue and an elder; and Sara Ura, Beronike, Mannine, Faustina, Rebeka, and Mazauzala as elders. Jewish and Greek women who converted to Christianity, such as Prisca (Rom. 16:3–5; 1 Cor. 16:19; Acts 18:2–3, 18–20, 26), Phoebe (Rom. 16:1–2), and Junia (Rom. 16:7), exercised similar roles in Christian congregations. Leadership roles in religious associations tended to follow the class hierarchies of the Greco-Roman world, and many of these women may also have had significant financial resources to use in behalf of the congregation.

Throughout the Greco-Roman world, purity rules related to gender shaped participation in religious rituals. Some temples made their rites all female or all male. Others restricted certain cultic functions to either females or males, such as requiring a female high priestess or a male high priest. Sexual intercourse, menstruation, childbirth, and death were often regarded as imparting cultic impurity, which necessitated purifying rituals. Accounts of the temple of Artemis at Ephesus suggest that male eunuchs and young unmarried women performed the rites, while married women were excluded from the temple altogether. The Artemis temple at Cyrene required new brides and pregnant women to make ceremonial visits, but women could not enter if they had any flow of blood or had recently had sexual relations. Childbirth and miscarriages required purification rites, including sacrifice of an animal victim. According to the first-century Jewish historian Josephus, the Jerusalem Temple had similar purity rules. Women with a flow of blood were excluded from the Temple altogether, and Jewish men entering the inner courts of the Temple had to observe a variety of purity rules, including abstention from sexual relations with a menstruating woman. The priesthood was restricted to males of the hereditary priestly class. For both Judaism and other Greco-Roman religious traditions, specific purity rules and rituals varied considerably from place to place, among various centers of worship, and among classes of people, but the general idea that worship required purity restrictions and abstentions was part and parcel of religious life.

The effects of Roman rule, class and household hierarchies, and natural life cycles intertwined themselves with women's religious life as well. For both public festivals and private associations, crucial decisions about which women could participate, in what way, and at what time depended on economic, political, and personal circumstances. Leadership roles for women often depended on possession of wealth; slave women depended on an owner's discretion to allow time to participate.

In a few unusual cases, women lived apart from the direct effects of these circumstances. A Jewish monastic community in Egypt, a precursor of Christian monasticism, contained both women and men. The women, called Therapeutrides, lived lives of contemplative prayer, fasting, communal worship, and celibacy. At weekly feasts, they sang hymns of thanksgiving in the tradition of Miriam at the parting of the Reed Sea (Ex. 15:20–21). Some temples, such as Rome's temple of Vesta, goddess of the hearth, required virgin priestesses who lived most of their lives within the temple

precincts. Groups of priestesses in Asia Minor and Italy are said to have practiced such spiritual discipline that they could walk on hot embers with their bare feet. Other women, regarded as divinely inspired or as possessed by a deity, lived at temples and sanctuaries providing oracles and prophetic utterances. The lives of these women had a different pattern from other women, because they lived apart from the usual structures of property, household authority, and sexual relations. Their removal from these structures in order to focus on ritual or spiritual life, however, points solidly to the everyday circumstances within which most women of the New Testament world lived out their religious lives: the alternating blessings and violence of the Roman Empire; the privileges of property and the exploitations of slavery; and the mixed joys, sorrows, dangers, and benefits of every stage of a woman's life.

## BIBLIOGRAPHY

Bradley, Keith. *Slaves and Masters in the Roman Empire: A Study in Social Control.* New York: Oxford University Press, 1987.

Brooten, Bernadette J. *Women Leaders in the Ancient Synagogue.* Chico, Calif.: Scholars Press, 1982.

Kraemer, Ross S., ed. *Maenads, Martyrs, Matrons, Monastics: A Sourcebook on Women's Religions in the Greco-Roman World.* Philadelphia: Fortress Press, 1988.

Lefkowitz, Mary R., and Maureen B. Fant. *Women's Life in Greece and Rome.* Baltimore: Johns Hopkins University Press, 1982.

Pomeroy, Sarah B. *Goddesses, Whores, Wives, and Slaves: Women in Classical Antiquity.* New York: Schocken Books, 1975.

Rousselle, Aline. *Porneia: On Desire and the Body in Antiquity.* Oxford: Basil Blackwell Publisher, 1988.

Van Sertima, Ivan, ed. *Black Women in Antiquity.* Journal of African Civilizations 6. New Brunswick, N.J.: Transaction Books, 1984.